THE SCROLL OF THE WAR
OF THE SONS OF LIGHT
AGAINST THE SONS OF DARKNESS

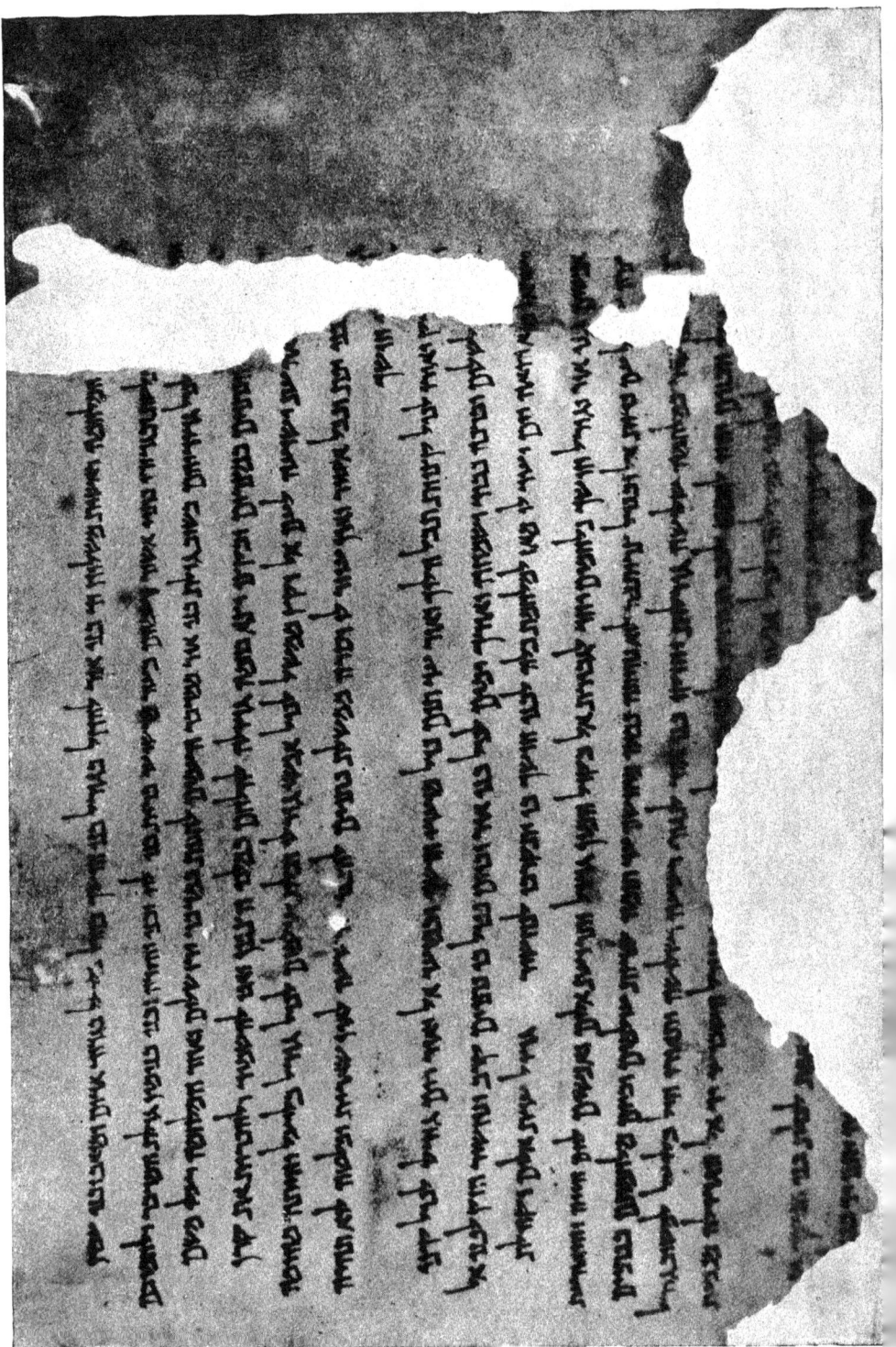

(Frontispicce

THE SCROLL OF THE WAR OF
THE SONS OF LIGHT
AGAINST
THE SONS OF DARKNESS

EDITED WITH COMMENTARY
AND INTRODUCTION BY

YIGAEL YADIN

Associate Professor of Archaeology
The Hebrew University, Jerusalem

TRANSLATED FROM THE HEBREW BY
BATYA AND CHAIM RABIN

WIPF & STOCK · Eugene, Oregon

Wipf and Stock Publishers
199 W 8th Ave, Suite 3
Eugene, OR 97401

The Scroll of the War of the Sons of Light Against the Sons of Darkness
By Yadin, Yigael and Rabin, Batya
Copyright©1962 Oxford University Press
Paperback ISBN: 978-1-5326-9760-9
Hardcover ISBN: 978-1-5326-9761-6
Publication date 7/24/2019
Previously published by Oxford University Press, 1962

In Memory of my Father and Teacher
PROFESSOR E. L. SUKENIK,
who planted, but did not live to reap

‎ת·נ·צ·ב·ה·

PREFACE TO THE ENGLISH EDITION

This English edition is a comprehensive version of my Hebrew book which was published in 1955 in Israel by Mossad Bialik. Professor and Mrs. Chaim Rabin started translating from the original Hebrew manuscript submitted to the Clarendon Press early in 1955. But several circumstances including the Rabins' move from Oxford to Jerusalem following Professor Rabin's appointment at the Hebrew University, and the inevitable technical problems involved in preparing a work of this kind for the press, delayed its appearance until now.

However, this time lapse has been—as much as was technically permissible, exploited for the introduction of some changes which are the result of further reflection on some of the conclusions I had reached earlier. I have also been enabled to include in this edition *all* the new textual material of Qumran relating to our subject which has been published since the publication of the Hebrew edition. Of special importance are the fragments of another copy of DSW which were published by Hunzinger. (C.H. Hunzinger: Fragmente einer älteren Fassung des Buches Milḥamā aus Höhle 4 von Qumrān, *ZAW* 1957, pp. 131–51.) With the help of these, it has been possible to improve the interpretation and restoration of Column XIV (see p. 326, notes to lines 5–16 in the present book).

We have found it advisable to make some changes in the structure of the English version, notably in the Commentary to the text, for the translation of the Scroll itself into English naturally involved a certain interpretation of the text, which required no repetition in the Commentary. The Commentary has accordingly been shortened. On the other hand, it was thought helpful to add several observations which, in the Hebrew version, were self-understood and required no elaboration. Moreover, since the Hebrew edition was the first complete study on this Scroll, certain necessary aids to an understanding of the text were included in that publication which may be dispensed with in the English edition. For example, I included in the Hebrew edition the partial comparative-concordance which I had prepared for myself while studying the Scroll. Today, the reader can refer to the recently published complete concordance to this Scroll. (J. Carmignac: Concordance hébraïque de la *Régle de la Guerre*, *Revue de Qumran*, 1, 1958, pp. 7–49).

The reader unfamiliar with the modern Hebrew language, who has not, therefore, had access to the Hebrew edition, may be surprised by the occasional lengthy discussion in this translation of several ideas and terms which are now apparently accepted in the translations of and commentaries on the Scroll which have appeared since the publication of my original work. It may, therefore, be appropriate to recall that when the original study was made, many problems required clarification and several of the conclusions were likely to give occasion to controversy. This made necessary the support of the theses by detailed argument and discussion. Some of this has found acknowledgement in the works of later scholars. But I have thought it well to retain in the English edition, most of the original passages so that the reader can gain an indication of the arguments and reasoning which led to these conclusions.

Those interested in discovering the measure in which the views presented in this book are accepted or rejected by later scholars may be referred to the following principal publications devoted to DSW which have appeared since the publication of the Hebrew edition :—

P. Boccaccio & G. Berardi : *Bellum filiorum lucis contra filios tenebrarum*, Transcriptio et versio latina, Fani, 1956.

Jean Carmignac : *La Régle de la Guerre des Fils de lumière contre les Fils de ténèbre*, Paris, 1958.

J. van der Ploeg : *Le Rouleau de la Guerre*, Leiden, 1959.

Also the translations and brief commentaries in the following books :—

Th.H. Gaster : *The Dead Sea Scriptures*, New York, 1956, pp. 281, 306, 315–21.

A. Dupont-Sommer : *Les écrits Esséniens découverts près de la Mer Morte*, Paris, 1959, pp. 179–211.

In addition, it may be found very useful to study the following publications, which disagree, wholly or partially, with some of my basic views on the dating of the Scroll and its literary composition, though they do not agree among themselves on an alternative conclusion :—

R. North : ' Kittim ' War or ' Sectaries ' Liturgy ? *Biblica*, 1958, pp. 84–93.

M. H. Segal : The Qumran War Scroll and the Date of its Composition (in *Scripta Hierosolymitana*, IV, Aspects of the Dead Sea Scrolls, ed. by C. Rabin and Y. Yadin, Jerusalem, 1958).

J. M. Grintz : The War Scroll—its Time and Authors (in *Essays on the Dead Sea Scrolls* (Hebrew) in Memory of E. L. Sukenik, ed. by C. Rabin and Y. Yadin, Hekhal Ha-Sefer, Jerusalem, 1961, pp. 19–30.

C. Rabin : The Literary Structure of the War Scroll (*Ib.* pp. 31–47).

These and other studies on DSW were known to me while I was engaged in the various stages of proof reading of the present edition, but to have introduced new discussions on the controversial points they raised would have led to endless delays in our publication date. Moreover, I consider that it is as yet too early to be definite about several of these points at issue. It may be possible to be more positive after the publication of some of the fragments of texts of DSW and other scrolls found in Jordan. At all events, no persuasive evidence, to my mind, has so far been furnished which prompts me to change my original conclusions that the Scroll was written *after* the Roman conquest of Syria and Palestine and *not* in the second century B.C.—it was apparently written in the second half of the first century B.C.; that the Scroll is basically the work of a single literary hand—drawing of course from other sources for the various subjects dealt with ; and that its main purpose was to provide a kind of manual of warfare for the eschatological war which the author believed to be imminent—the war between the Sons of Light and the Sons of Darkness.

I take this opportunity of expressing my sincere thanks to my friends Professor and Mrs. Chaim Rabin, for their painstaking translation and for the skill with which they met the demands of clothing the Hebrew text with an English garb. In the course of this work, Professor Rabin was kind enough to draw my attention to several errors in the Hebrew text which I was able to correct, and to make a number of useful suggestions which I have incorporated in this edition, acknowledging them in parentheses. I am particularly appreciative of his conscientious efforts to present a faithful translation of my views, even though I know that he disagrees with some of them.

In rendering the text of the Scroll itself into English, we have sought to avoid the epigrammatic style, so that the literal meaning of the original Hebrew text can emerge with more clarity.

I know that I speak also for Professor Rabin when I express sincere thanks to Professor G. R. Driver, who was kind enough to review the translation and make valuable suggestions. I am deeply indebted to the staff of the Clarendon Press for their assistance and their patience during a six-years' correspondence and to Mr. Freundlich for having prepared the detailed indices.

It is my hope that the collective effort which produced this English edition will have resulted in a modest contribution to the body of research on this extraordinary Scroll, which holds so unique a place in the literature of the 'Sect of the Wilderness', a literature which, since its discovery in 1947, has shed such important light on the history of Judaism in the twilight period of the Second Temple and on the history of Christianity at its dawn.

Y. Y.

Jerusalem, July, 1961.

EXTRACTS FROM THE PREFACE TO THE HEBREW EDITION

In 1948, shortly after my father, Professor E. L. Sukenik, had acquired the scrolls containing DSW, DSH, and DSIb and made a first study of these texts, he asked me to examine the photographs of several columns of the scroll here edited. I was at the time, immediately before the War of Independence, collecting material on the methods of warfare in Biblical times, and my father thought I would find interest in several passages, the purely military character of which was obvious at first glance. However, my years of service in the Israel Defence Forces during the War of Independence and afterwards allowed me little time to devote myself to the study of these matters in an ancient scroll, and all I could do was to make some notes and preliminary observations.

As the War Scroll was in a much better state of preservation than the other two scrolls in his keeping, my father was forced to expend most of his time and energy in the period following the acquisition of the scrolls on the delicate problems involved in opening, photographing, and deciphering the latter two. On account of the shortage of photographic materials in Israel at the time he had to go abroad in order to acquire some and to make provision for the complete publication of the scrolls. In spite of all these difficulties he succeeded in including in his first publication in this field, *Megilloth Genuzoth I* (1948), not only a general account of the appearance and contents of DSW, but also a transliteration and detailed commentary of two columns. In his second publication, *Megilloth Genuzoth II* (1950)—published, like the first, by Mossad Bialik—he added a further fragment, the part of the 'Prayer for the Appointed Time of War' which opens with the words 'Rise, O Hero', with a photograph and comments.

Although he dedicated a large part of the time at his disposal to research on DSH—selected chapters from which he published with commentary in the two books mentioned—and to DSIb, he did in fact achieve, before his death, the decipherment of DSW almost completely, and among his papers was found the transliteration of most of the scroll. In this labour he was faithfully assisted by Dr. N. Avigad of the Department of Archaeology of the Hebrew University and by Mr. J. Licht.

After my father's untimely death in 1953, a committee appointed by the Hebrew University and consisting of the University's President, Prof. B. Mazar (Chairman), Dr. N. Avigad, Mr. S. Ginossar, Prof. L. A.

Mayer, Prof. M. Schwabe and myself, resolved to publish the facsimile plates of all three scrolls with transliteration and an introduction which consisted of the introductory chapters previously published by my father in *Megilloth Genuzoth I–II*. Dr. Avigad, Mr. Licht, and I prepared the book for the press, and it was published in 1956 by Mossad Bialik and the Hebrew University under the title *Oẓar ha-Megilloth ha-Genuzoth*. The same committee decided to entrust me with the task of editing the War Scroll with an introduction, restoration of damaged portions, and commentary. Only after I had begun the task did I realize its difficulty and complexity. Before I could even start on the investigation of detailed points, I had to restore the transliterated text where it had been damaged in course of time—by no means an easy or short matter. The main difficulty, however, was in the contents of this curious scroll, which deals with such a rich variety of subjects far removed from each other, at any rate from a technical point of view: matters of warfare and armament, liturgy, angelology, rules on the purity of the camp, tasks of priests and levites, the organization of the community, etc.

. . . Owing to the peculiarity of the scroll in dealing with all kinds of subjects in combination and without continuity, I had to divide the discussion into two distinct parts, viz. a general Introduction and a Commentary following the order of the scroll. Subjects which required detailed discussion, full analysis, and comparison with other sources, were concentrated in separate chapters of the Introduction. In this way the Commentary could deal principally with questions concerning the text, suggested restorations, lexicographical matters, and linguistic parallels.

Hence the reader who is mainly interested in the *subjects* dealt with by the scroll, will find these fully discussed in the Introduction, while any reader whose main concern is the *text* and *language* of the scroll will find these discussed in the Commentary. In order to ease the way of those interested in both aspects, and also because it is practically impossible to understand the text without some acquaintance with the subjects it deals with, I have in the appropriate places in the Commentary summed up the conclusions of the discussions in the Introduction and provided detailed references to the relevant chapters of the latter.

I have given as many references as possible to parallels to the subject-matter and language of the scrolls which I have been able to trace in the Bible, in Talmudic literature, and in the writings of the sect, for only in this way is it possible to establish with any degree of confidence the inter-relation of the various sources and to arrive at a correct understanding of the words and subject-matter of the scroll. On the other hand, since this, the same as the other DSS, throws much light on much-debated problems in Biblical and post-Biblical literature, I have permitted myself to go at times beyond the strict needs of the interpretation of my text, and to turn my attention to more general problems . . .

. . . The great privilege which fell to my lot of being the first to comment on this scroll, has also meant that I was the first to err. No one knows better than the author in how many points he did not arrive at a full understanding or exhaustive treatment of this strange scroll, and yet he thinks it his duty to dare and offer his findings, hoping that the readers will judge him with indulgence.

YIGAEL YADIN.

Jerusalem, 12th November, 1955.

CONTENTS

LIST OF ILLUSTRATIONS xvi
LIST OF ABBREVIATIONS xvii

PART ONE: INTRODUCTION

1. CONTENTS AND PURPOSE OF THE SCROLL 1
    1. General Remarks 3
    2. Principal Contents and Purpose. 4
    3. Contents of the Scroll 7
    4. Summary of the Sections of the Scroll 14
    5. Notes on the Introduction 14
    6. Summary (Sources, Content and Structure) . . . 14
2. THE PLAN OF THE WAR 18
    1. General Remarks: The Phases of the War and the Division of the Enemies 18
    2. The Method of Reckoning the Years of Fighting . . 20
    3. The First Phase 21
    4. The Second Phase 26
    5. The Third Phase 26
    6. The Plan of the War and its Background . . . 33
    7. Summary Table 35
3. THE BANNERS OF THE CONGREGATION AND ITS ORGANIZATION 38
    1. General 38
    2. The Banners and their Inscriptions (List 1) . . . 40
    3. The 'Banner of the Whole Congregation'. . . . 42
    4. The Banners of the Heads of the Camps of the Three Tribes 46
    5. The Banner of the Tribe 48
    6. The Family, the Myriad, the Thousand, the Hundred, and the Battalion 49
    7. The 'Banners' of the Families of Levi (Lists 2 and 3) . 53
    8. Summary of the System of the Banners . . . 57
    9. The Organization into 'Thousands, Hundreds, Fifties and Tens' and the Sect 59
    10. The Banners in other Armies 61

CONTENTS

4. THE LAW OF CONSCRIPTION 65
   1. General Remarks 65
   2. Conscription for the War of the Entire Congregation . 65
   3. The Laws of Exemption for Reasons of the Purity of the Camp 70
   4. Age of Conscription and Exemption and the Division of Combatants according to Age 75
   5. The Organization and Conscription of the Divisions . 79

5. THE TRUMPETS 87
   1. General Remarks 87
   2. The Trumpets in the O.T. 87
   3. The Trumpets in the Scroll 88
   4. The Ceremonial Trumpets 90
   5. The Trumpets of Battle 92
   6. The Sounds and Signals of the Trumpets . . . 99
   7. The Inscriptions on the Trumpets 104
   8. The Horns and their Purpose 107
   9. The Trumpets and Horns in the O.T. 109
   10. The Trumpets in the Maccabaean and Roman Period . 110
   11. Summary 113

6. THE WEAPONS 114
   1. General Remarks 114
   2. The Shield 115
   3. The Greaves 122
   4. The Helmet 123
   5. The Cuirass 124
   6. The Sword 124
   7. The Darts 131
   8. The Staff 133
   9. The Inscriptions on the Darts 134
   10. The Lance 135
   11. The Spear 135
   12. The Sling 139
   13. The Bow 140

7. TACTICS AND ORGANIZATION 141
   1. General Remarks 141
   2. General Terminology in Forming up for Battle . . 142
   3. Service Units 150
   4. Combatant Troops: The Skirmishers 156

5. Combatant Troops: The 'Front Formations'	162
6. Combatant Troops: The Cavalry	176
7. Regrouping the Army for Pursuit and the Decisive Battle	183

8. THE RITES OF THE CONGREGATION 198
    1. General Remarks 198
    2. The Sect's Attitude to Sacrifices 198
    3. The Organization of the Temple Service . . . 202
    4. The Prayers and Thanksgivings in Battle, I . . . 208
    5. The Prayers and Thanksgivings in Battle, II . . . 210

9. THE ANGELOLOGY OF THE SCROLL 229
    1. General Remarks 229
    2. Terminology 230
    3. Belial 232
    4. 'The God of Israel and the Angel of His Truth' . . 234
    5. 'The Prince of Light' 235
    6. The War of the Angels 237
    7. 'The Elect of the Holy People' and the Angels . . 240
    8. The Lot of Light and the Lot of Darkness . . . 242

10. THE DATE OF THE SCROLL AND THE IDENTITY OF THE SECT . 243
    1. General Remarks 243
    2. The Contents of the Scroll and the Time of its Composition 244
    3. The Sect 246

11. THE SCROLL 247
    1. General Remarks 247
    2. Measurements 247
    3. The Writing 248
    4. Irregularities and Corrections 249
    5. The Spelling 251
    6. The Present Edition 252

PART TWO

TEXT, TRANSLATION AND COMMENTARY 253
INDEX OF AUTHORS 355
INDEX OF REFERENCES TO ANCIENT LITERATURE . . . 357
INDEX OF FOREIGN WORDS AND PHRASES 372
GENERAL INDEX 376

LIST OF ILLUSTRATIONS

Frontispiece. The First Column of the Scroll

FIG.
1. Ornaments on the Dura Europos *scutum*. (The Excavations of Dura-Europos, Preliminary Report, VI, New Haven, 1936, Pl. XXV, A.)   119
2. Suggested reconstruction of the Shield of the 'Front Formations' .   120
3. Method of attaching the *gladius* (detail of fig. 5, no. 10) .   .   127
4. Suggested reconstruction of the Sword and the Scabbard .   .   128
5. Roman soldiers of the second and first centuries B.C. (Couissin, pl. II)   129
6. Roman soldiers of the end of the first century B.C. and of the first century A.D. (Couissin, pl. II)   130
7. Suggested reconstruction of the Spear   136
8. The advance of the skirmishing battalions from the 'battle intervals'   159
9. Deploying the columns into 'arrays'   160
10. Front formation deployed and 'arrayed'   168
11. The seven front formations: 'formation behind formation' .   .   171
12. The front formations, forming up in face of the enemy .   .   .   172
13. The method of opening the 'battle intervals'   172
14. Schematic plan of the 'tower'   188
15. The Roman *testudo* (Kromayer-Veith, Taf. 51, Abb. 144) .   .   189
16. The battle of Cannae (Spaulding, p. 127, pl. 7)   195
17. The battle forms and the 'towers'   197
18. Scribal errors, groups A–C .   .   .   .   } *between pp.* 252–3
19. Scribal errors, groups D–G .   .   .   .
20. The script of the Scroll   254

LIST OF ABBREVIATIONS
(apart from the usual abbreviations for books of the Bible and Apocrypha)

Aalen	S. Aalen, *Die Begriffe 'Licht' und 'Finsternis'*, etc., Oslo 1951
AJSL	*American Journal of Semitic Languages and Literatures.*
Ant.	Josephus' *Antiquities.*
Aperçus	A. Dupont-Sommer, *Aperçus préliminaires sur les manuscrits de la mer morte*, Paris 1950 = L'Orient illustré 4.
Apocr.	R. H. Charles, *The Apocrypha and Pseudepigrapha of the Old Testament*, Oxford 1913.
Aspects of the Dead Sea Scrolls	*Aspects of the Dead Sea Scrolls*, ed. C. Rabin and Y. Yadin, Jerus. 1958 = Scripta Hierosolymitana 4.
Ass. Mos.	Assumptio Mosis.
A.V.	Authorized Version (King James Version).
Avigad and Yadin	N. Avigad and Y. Yadin, *A Genesis Apocryphon*, Jerus. 1956.
A. Zar.	Abodah Zarah.
BA	*Biblical Archaeologist.*
Barrois	A. G. Barrois, *Manuel d'archéologie biblique,*
BASOR	*Bulletin of the American Schools of Oriental Research.*
B.B.	Baba Bathra.
B.C.	Bellum Civile.
BDB	F. Brown, S. R. Driver, C. A. Briggs, *A Hebrew and English Lexicon of the O.T.*, Oxford 1907, etc.
Bekh.	Bekhoroth.
Ben Jehudah	see *Thesaurus*.
Ber.	Berakhoth.
B.G.	Bellum Gallicum
Bibl.	Biblical.
BH	Biblical Hebrew.
BH³	*Biblia Hebraica*, 3rd and 4th edition.
BHM	A. Jellinek, *Beth ha-Midrasch, Sammlung kleiner Midraschim*, etc., 6 parts, Leipzig and Vienna 1853–77.
Bikk.	Bikkurim.
BJ	Bellum Judaicum.
BJRL	*Bulletin of John Rylands Library.*
B.M.	Baba Meṣiʿa.
Brownlee, *Manual*	W. H. Brownlee, *The Dead Sea Manual of Discipline*, BASOR, suppl. Studies 10–12, 1951.
BT	Babylonian Talmud.
BO	*Bibliotheca Orientalis.*
B.Q.	Baba Qamma.
CDC	Damascus Covenant (Zadokite Fragments).
ch.	chapter of the Introduction.
Couissin	P. Couissin, *Les armes romaines*, Paris 1926.
Daremberg Saglio	Ch. Daremberg and E. Saglio, *Dictionnaire des antiquités Grecques et romaines*, etc., Paris, 1877–1919.
D.B.	Hasting's *Dictionary of the Bible.*
DSD	Discipline Scroll.
DSH	Habakkuk Pesher.
DSS	Dead Sea Scrolls.
DST	Thanksgiving Hymns.
DSW	War of the Sons of Light etc.
Eduy.	ʿEduyoth.
E.I.	*Encyclopaedia ʿIvrith*, Jerusalem.
E.M.	*Encyclopaedia Miqra'ith*, Jerusalem 1955, etc.
En.	Enoch.
Enc. Miqr.	*Encyclopaedia Miqra'ith*
Enc. Talm.	*Encyclopaedia Talmudith*, Jerus.
Erub.	ʿErubin.
Eth.	Ethiopic.
Galling	K. Galling, *Bibl. Reallexikon*, Tuebingen 1937.

B

LIST OF ABBREVIATIONS

GK	*Gesenius' Hebrew Grammar*, 2nd. Engl. edn., Oxford 1910, etc.
H.	Hilkhoth.
Ḥag.	Ḥagigah.
HDB	Hasting's *Dictionary of the Bible*.
Hil.	Hilkhoth.
Hor.	Horayoth.
HUCA	*Hebrew Union College Annual*.
Ḥull.	Ḥullin.
IEJ	*Israel Exploration Journal*.
Intr.	Introduction.
JBL	*Journal of Biblical Literature*.
JEA	*Journal of Egyptian Archaeology*.
JJS	*Journal of Jewish Studies*.
JNES	*Journal of Near Eastern Studies*.
JPOS	*Journal of the Palestine Oriental Society*.
JQR	*Jewish Quarterly Review*.
JRomSt	*Journal of Roman Studies*.
JSS	*Journal of Semitic Studies*.
Jub.	Jubilees.
Junge	E. Junge, *Der Wiederaufbau des Heerwesens des Reiches Juda unter Josia*, Stuttgart 1937.
Krauss	S. Krauss, *Paras we-Romi ba-Talmud uva-Midrashim*, Jerus. 1948.
KS	*Kiriath Sefer*
K.-V.	J. Kromayer and G. Veith, *Heerwesen und Kriegsführung der Griechen und Römer*, München 1928.
Licht Hodayoth	Jacob Licht, *The Thanksgiving Scroll*, Jerusalem, 1957 (Hebrew).
M.	Mishnah.
Maimonides	Maimonides, *Code* (*Yadh Ḥazaqah*).
Manual	W. H. Brownlee, *The Dead Sea Manual of Discipline*, New Haven 1951 = BASOR Suppl. Studies 10–12.
Marquardt	J. Marquardt, *L'Organisation militaire chez les Romains*, tr. M. Brissaud, Paris 1891.
Meg.	Megillah
Men.	Menaḥoth.
MG I, MG II	E. L. Sukenik, *Megilloth Genuzoth* I, Jerus. 1948, II, Jerus. 1950.
MH	Mishnaic Hebrew.
Mid.	Middoth.
Midr.	Midrash.
Naz.	Nazir.
Ned.	Nedarim.
Nid.	Niddah.
Nouveaux Aperçus	A. Dupont-Sommer, *Nouveaux Aperçus sur les manuscrits de la mer morte*, Paris 1953.
O.C.D.	*Oxford Classical Dictionary*.
Oẓar	*Oẓar ha-Megilloth ha-Genuzoth*, Jerus. 1956.
Pent.	Pentateuch.
Pes.	Pesaḥin.
Pesh.	Peshitta.
PRE	Pirqe Rabbi Eliezer.
PT	Palestinian Talmud.
P.-W.	Pauly-Wissowa, *Realencyclopaedie d. klass. Altertumswissenschaft*.
QC I, Qumran I	D. Barthélemy and J. Milik, *Qumran Cave I*, Oxford 1955.
1Q, etc.	Terminology of QC I.
R.	Rabbi.
Rabb.	Rabbinic.
RB	*Revue Biblique*.
RÉJ	*Revue des Études Juives*.
Rost.	L. Rost, *Die Damaskusschrift*, Berlin 1933 = Kleine Texte 167.
RSh	Rosh ha-Shanah.
Sam. Heb.	Samaritan Hebrew Version of the Pentateuch.

Sanh.	Sanhedrin.
Shab.	Shabbath.
Shek.	Sheqalim.
Sukk.	Sukkah.
T.	Tosephta.
Taan.	Taʿanith.
Tam.	Tamid.
Tanḥ.	Tanḥuma.
Targ.	Targum.
Targumim	J. Levy, *Chaldäisches Wörterbuch über die Targumim*, etc., Leipz. 1867.
Test.	Testament.
Tg.J.	Targum Jonathan (Ps.-Jonathan) on the Pentateuch.
Tg.O.	Targum Onqelos.
Thesaurus	E. Ben-Jehudah, *Thesaurus Totius Hebraitatis*, Berlin & Jerus., 1908, etc.
ThLZ	*Theologische Literaturzeitung.*
Toh.	Ṭohoroth.
Tos.	Tosephta.
trsl.	translated by.
vs., vss.	verse, verses.
Vulg.	Vulgata.
VT	*Vetus Testamentum.*
Yedioth, YHLE	*Yediʿoth ha-Ḥevrah le-Ḥeqer Ereṣ Yisra'el.*
ZATW	*Zeitschrift für Alttestamentliche Wissenschaft.*
ZD	C. Rabin, *The Zadokite Documents*, Oxford 1954.

PART ONE

INTRODUCTION

Chapter 1

CONTENTS AND PURPOSE OF THE SCROLL

'The God of Israel has called a sword upon all the nations,
   and through the saints of His people He will do mightily.'
                                                     DSW xvi, 1.
'Let the high praises of God be in their mouth, and a two-
   edged sword in their hand
   To execute vengeance upon the nations and chastisements
   upon the peoples.'
                                                     Ps. cxlix, 6–7.

§ 1. GENERAL REMARKS

The late Professor E. L. Sukenik named the scroll 'The War of the Sons of Light against the Sons of Darkness', on account of its contents and by way of summarizing the first line of col. i: 'The first engagement of the Sons of Light shall be to attack the lot of the Sons of Darkness'.[1]

We do not know the name of the author of this scroll, or what its readers called it. One may assume that its title comprised its opening word or words, as was the custom. Unfortunately, the words which originally preceded the first extant words, 'the war,' have been eaten away. Taking into account other passages in the scroll, a tentative restoration is: '[and this is the book of the disposition] of the war'.[2] Since we cannot propose a definitive restoration, we shall continue in the present study to use the name given by Sukenik, which sums up its contents.

Our scroll forms an organic part of the literature of the Qumran Sect. This is proved by its style, its language, and the views expressed in it. Many of its expressions, and even whole sentences, recur in other sectarian writings.[3] Similar parallels between our scroll and several Pseudepigrapha, e.g. Enoch, Jubilees, and the Testaments of the Twelve Patriarchs, provide a *terminus post quem* for the scroll, and confirm the view that the literature of the 'scrolls sect' belongs to the same religio-social stream that produced those works, parts of which have now been found in their original languages amongst the fragments in the Qumran caves.[4]

The influence of some Pseudepigrapha on DSW is so considerable

---

[1] Cf. *M.G. I*, 18.
[2] See § 6 and cf. comm. i, 1; xv, 5–6.
[3] See ch. 8, § 5–6.
[4] E.g. *Qumran* I, p. 82 sq.; RB 63 (1956) 49 sq.

that at times we can understand the contents of the scroll only with the help of these books; this is most noticeable, of course, in cases where a matter is mentioned by the author only incidentally, without full explanation, on the assumption that it is known to the reader from that literature.

§ 2. Principal Contents and Purpose

The main subject of the scroll [1] is the war which will take place 'when the exiles of the Sons of Light return from the wilderness of the nations to encamp in the wilderness of Jerusalem', between 'the Sons of Light and the Sons of Darkness'. This war will be fought between 'the sons of Levi, Judah, and Benjamin' and the rest of the tribes of Israel, assisted by the powers of light and justice and the angels appointed over them, against the enemies of Israel, at whose head stands a nation called 'Kittim', assisted by Belial and the powers of darkness and evil under his authority. This war, which will last six years and in which the entire congregation will participate, will end, after the Sons of Light and the Sons of Darkness have each been victorious three times, with the victory of the Sons of Light, to be achieved in the seventh Lot through the intervention of 'the mighty hand of God'. At the completion of this war the fight will be carried on in separate divisions by the tribes of Israel for twenty-nine years against the rest of the nations.

The main purpose of the scroll seems to consist in supplying the members of the sect with a detailed set of regulations and plans in accordance with which they were to act on the day of destiny appointed 'from of old for a battle of annihilation of the Sons of Darkness' (i, 10).

Even though the result of this war is preordained—for God Himself will intervene on the side of the Sons of Light who are 'the Lot of God' on the day appointed as 'His time to conquer and bring low the lord of the rule of wickedness' (xvii, 5-6)—yet this intervention will take place only after a series of real battles in which the Sons of Darkness will alternately be defeated and victorious. This war will have to be fought not only according to all the general rules of war practised by the nations against whom they will fight, but also in accordance with all the laws and statutes of warfare specified in the Law of Moses. The exact fulfilment of the Law is an essential condition, since the war will be fought not only between the Sons of

---

[1] Cf. *M.G. I*, 19; *Oẓar* p. 31.

Light and Darkness on this earth but also by the cosmic powers of light and darkness. The fact that the angels fight on their side obliges the Sons of Light to conduct themselves in accordance with all the Biblical laws of purity of the camp, and 'any man who is not pure with regard to his sexual organs on the day of the battle shall not join them in battle, for holy angels are in communion with their hosts' (vii, 6).

This basic conception passes through the scroll like a purple thread. It determines its content, structure, and sequence. The regulations or *serekh* must specify in detail the Laws of the Torah and the laws of tactics and strategy and the interrelation between them.

The ideological conflict which results from the difficulties created by the exact fulfilment both of the Laws of the Torah and of warfare during the period of the Second Temple is expressed in Agrippa's famous speech in which he attempted to restrain the uprising against the Romans. Most skilfully he tries to weaken the hands of the people by insisting on the two conditions which form the basic conception of warfare as expressed also in the scroll:

'What remains, therefore, is this, that you have recourse to divine assistance; but this is already on the side of the Romans; for it is impossible that so vast an empire should be settled without God's providence. Reflect upon it, how impossible it is for your zealous observation of your religious customs to be here preserved, which are hard to be observed, even when you fight with those whom you are able to conquer; and how can you then most of all hope for God's assistance, when, by being forced to transgress His law, you will make Him turn His face from you? And if you do observe the custom of the Sabbath-days, and will not be prevailed on to do any thing thereon, you will easily be taken, as were your forefathers by Pompey, ... but if in time of war you transgress the law of your country, I cannot tell on whose account you will afterwards go to war; for your concern is but one, that you do nothing against any law of your forefathers; and how will you call upon God to assist you, when you are voluntarily transgressing against His religion? Now, all men that go to war do it either as depending on divine or human assistance; but since your going to war will cut off both those assistances, those that are for going to war choose evident destruction.'[1]

The scroll emphasizes that this apparent contradiction does not exist in the ultimate war conducted by the Sons of Light at the time ordained for it by God.

[1] Jos. BJ II, xvi, 4.

The author of the scroll aims to provide answers to four questions :
(1) When is the 'appointed time of retribution' and against whom will the war be waged ?
(2) What, according to the Law of Moses, are the laws and commandments of warfare ?
(3) What are the laws and tactics of warfare practised by the nations of the world and how do they interlink with the Laws of the Torah ?
(4) How will the war be conducted in practice on 'the appointed day' ?

This purpose obliges him to offer his readers an expert discussion, not only on questions 1 and 2 but more particularly on questions 3 and 4, that is the military 'dispositions' (סרכים).

The first part of the scroll sets out to answer question 1. In this part the author defines the time appointed for the war and the enemies to be fought, in order of their importance. The date was determined from all eternity by God and was in fact revealed by the prophets : 'And by the hand of thine anointed, the seers of things ordained, Thou has told us the epochs of the wars of Thine hands, so as to glory over our enemies by bringing to fall the troops of Belial, the seven nations of vanity' (xi, 7–9).[1] Against the principal enemies, the 'Kittim', and their allies, the whole congregation will fight for six years, but against the other and more remote enemies selected units will fight for twenty-nine years. The series of sections dealing with this subject I have called, for convenience, the War Series. The middle part of the scroll sets out to explain, in detail and in a factual and legal style, the matters indicated above under 2 and 3. These chapters are for the most part marked by the title *serekh* so as to show that they deal with regulations. This section I call the Serekh Series. It is divided into two parts : one describes the *serakhim* of fighting, the other the method of the fulfilment of the Laws of the Torah and the prayers. I have accordingly named them the Battle Serekh and the Ritual Serekh. The last part of the scroll is devoted to a description of the actual war against the Sons of Darkness on the 'appointed day' (question 4). More precisely, this part describes the engagements taking place on the last day of battle against the Kittim and their allies. On this day, seven engagements will be fought in which the Sons of Light and the Sons of Darkness will each be victorious three times. The decision will come with the seventh Lot in which the mighty hand of

---

[1] See comm. ad loc.

God will subdue the Sons of Darkness; this section I have called the Kittim Series.

The last page of the scroll in our possession describes the victory and the prayers on the following day. Since it is not known how many columns of the scroll are missing, it is difficult to decide whether this description constitutes the end of the scroll or if, after it, the author devoted additional chapters to the battles of the twenty-nine years. In order to answer this question and likewise to consider the exact structure and division into sections of the scroll as indicated above, we shall briefly explain its contents in accordance with the order of the sections marked by the scribe.[1]

§ 3. CONTENTS OF THE SCROLL

War Series

Section 1 (i, 1–7). General introduction, defining the opposing forces in the various phases of the war and the final result: victory of the Sons of Light over the Sons of Darkness in general and over the Kittim in particular.

The Sons of Light include the sons of Levi, Judah, and Benjamin, called 'exiles of the wilderness'. Their enemies are named collectively the 'Lot of the Sons of Darkness'. The war will be in three phases. In the first it will be conducted against the alliance of Edom, Moab, Ammon, and Philistia, led by the Kittim of Asshur. Joined to these will be a group of 'offenders against the Covenant' from amongst the Jews. This phase of the war will take place 'on the return of the exiles of the Sons of Light from the wilderness of the nations to encamp in the wilderness of Jerusalem'. In the second phase they will fight the 'Kittim who dwell in Egypt'. In the third and last phase the war will be waged against 'the kings of the north' in general.

Victory will bring 'deliverance for the people of God', i.e. the Sons of Light, and 'eternal annihilation for all the Lot of Belial, which consists principally of the chief enemies of the Sons of Light, i.e. the Kittim, and 'thus the dominion of the Kittim shall depart'.

The author mentions neither himself nor the circumstances in which were revealed to him the things which he tells his readers; nor does he attribute the revelation to righteous men of the past, as we so often find in the apocalyptic works. His style is matter-of-fact and summary, describing the occurrences as facts, self-evident and known to his readers.[2]

---

[1] The scribe has marked the beginning of a new section by leaving a line blank if the preceding line ended close to the left margin, otherwise by starting a new line. Cf. *Oẓar* p. 23.

[2] Cf. chs. 2 and 9.

Section 2 (i, 8-15). Description of the last day of the war with the Kittim. This day, 'the day on which the Kittim fall', is 'the day appointed by Him from of old for the battle of annihilation of the Sons of Darkness' (line 10). This day, on which the forces of darkness will be subdued, will be for the Sons of Light (as explained in several of the eschatological chapters of the Bible and Pseudepigrapha), the beginning of the period of 'peace and blessing, glory, joy, and long life' (line 9), in contrast to the period which preceded it, which is 'a time of mighty trouble for the people to be redeemed by God. In all their troubles there was none like it' (lines 11-12).

The decisive battle will be fought simultaneously by 'angels and men' representing the forces of light and darkness on earth and in heaven. The battle will be hard and cruel and will end, after three alternate defeats each of the Sons of Light and the Sons of Darkness, in the seventh engagement in which the Sons of Light will be victorious with the aid of 'the mighty hand of God' which will subdue Belial and all the people of his Lot.

The style and contents of this Section greatly resemble the eschatological chapters of the Pseudepigrapha. Its main purpose is to give courage to the Sons of Light—liable to despair because of their defeats—by telling them that this sequence of defeats and victories has been determined from time immemorial.

Section 3 (i, 16-ii, 14). Analysis of the period of the forty years of war from three points of view :

(1) The years of fighting and the sabbatical years, and the conduct of the Temple service during those years.
(2) The general division of the fighting into the six-year campaign of the entire congregation against the principal enemies (phases 1-2) and the twenty-nine year campaign against the more distant enemies (phase 3).
(3) Detailed descriptions of the twenty-nine year campaigns.[1]

This completes the War Series.

Battle Serekh Series

Section 4 (ii, 15-iii, 11). Description of the trumpets to be used by the congregation in different ceremonies in peace-time and in battle. The style, like that of the rest of the Serekh Series, is legislative and descriptive.[2]

Section 5 (iii, 12-iv, 5). The banners of the congregation according

---

[1] Cf. ch. 2 ; ch. 8, § 2-3 ; ch. 4, § 5.   [2] Cf. ch. 5.

CONTENTS AND PURPOSE OF THE SCROLL

to its different units and the permanent inscriptions on each one. The description differentiates between the banners of the general congregation and those of the families of the tribe of Levi.[1]

Section 6 (iv, 6–14). The inscriptions on the banners at different phases of the battle: Going out to war; advance into battle; and return from the war.[1]

Section 7 (iv, 15–v, 2). Measurements of the banners, starting with the 'banner of all the congregation' and ending with the banner of the unit of ten.[1]

Section 8 (v, 3–14). The 'front formations', i.e. units equipped with heavy arms. This *serekh* briefly explains the structure of the formation[2] and the arms of its soldiers: the shield, the spear, and the sword, their shape, measurements, and ornaments.[3]

Section 9 (v, 15–vi, 6). Deployment of the skirmishing battalions,[4] their armour (with its inscriptions),[5] and their method of fighting.

Section 10 (vi, 7–16). Cavalry units, their number, duties, weapons, the age of the riders, the quality of the horses, and the attachment of the different cavalry units to the skirmishing units and front formations.[6]

Section 11 (vi, 17–vii, 7) deals with three subjects:

(1) Division of the men into age groups (with special emphasis on non-combatant troops).
(2) Disqualifications from army service.
(3) Laws of the 'purity of the camp' in battle.[7]

Section 12 (vii, 8 ix, 9), one of the longest of the scroll. Operational matters of the skirmishing units and their tactical signals. This section in fact represents a combination of sections 4, 9, and 10. It enlarges upon several subjects only briefly mentioned in former *serakhim*:

(1) The duties of the priests, their dress and trumpets.
(2) The levites and the function of the horns used by them in the course of battle.[8]
(3) 'Sounds' and 'signals' made by the different trumpets and their significance.[9]
(4) Regrouping for pursuit.[10]

Section 13 (ix, 10–16). Reforming the various formations and units

---

[1] Cf. ch. 3, § 5.
[2] Cf. ch. 7.
[3] Cf. ch. 6, §§ 2, 6, 11.
[4] Cf. ch. 7, §§ 4 (1), 5, 14.
[5] Cf. ch. 6, §§ 7, 10, 12.
[6] Cf. ch. 7, § 6, and cf. 6, § 2–4, 7, 11, 13.
[7] Cf. on the non-combatant troops ch. 7, § 3; on other matters ch. 4.
[8] Cf. on these priests ch. 8, § 3 (2–3); on the trumpets and horns, ch. 5, § 6.
[9] Cf. ch. 5, § 8.
[10] Cf. ch. 7, § 7.

for the phase of pursuit and decision. Shields of the 'towers' and their inscriptions (i.e. the names of the four archangels).[1] End of the Battle Serekh Series.

Ritual Serekh Series

Sections 14–21 (ix, 17–xiv, 15). Forms of prayer for the various phases of the war.[2] To these must be added several passages found in the Kittim Series: xv, 7–xvi, 1; xvi, 13–xvii, 3; xvii, 4–9).

Kittim Series

Section 22 (xiv, 16–xv, 3). Transition from the Serekh Series to the Kittim Series. This section returns to the consideration of the principal subject of the scroll (cf. Section 2). After praying to God that He should rise to the aid of Israel, the author again notes that the period is 'a time of trouble for Israel' (xv, 1) and the appointed time has arrived for the war 'against all the nations'. This section concludes with a sentence which connects it with the Kittim Series: 'And all those [prepared] for battle shall go and encamp over against the king of the Kittim and all who are gathered unto him for a day of [vengeance] by the sword-of-God' (xv, 2–3).

This passage is most important, for in this section the author again mentions the Kittim as the principal object of the war, while in the whole Serekh Series (excepting xv, 11) he uses general terms for the enemy: 'the enemy' or 'Belial', 'darkness', etc. From here onwards the Kittim are mentioned very frequently.[3]

It seems that this interpretation of the structure of the scroll explains the system adopted by its author. When describing the battles against the Kittim, he is not compelled to enter into minute details of the system of fighting—a discussion which would have interrupted the description of the course of the battles—and contents himself with a short formulation based on the detailed descriptions in the Serekh Series. At times he merely gives 'references', e.g. xv, 5–6.

The most important problem is to understand the structure of the Kittim Series itself. The key appears to me to be found in two passages:

(1) Section 2: 'On the day of their battle against the Kittim they shall go forth for a carnage in battle: in three lots shall the

---

[1] Cf. ch. 7, § 7; 9, § 6.
[2] Cf. ch. 8, § 4 j.
[3] The Kittim are mentioned 14 times in the Scroll: 5 times in the War Series, once in the Serekh Series, and 8 times in the Kittim Series.

Sons of Light prove strong so as to smite the wicked and in three the army of Belial shall recover to repel the lot [of light. The] skirmishing battalions—their hearts shall be melted, while the might of God strengthens [the heart of the Sons of Darkness], but in the seventh lot shall the great hand of God subdue . . .' (i, 12–14).

(2) The fragment at the end of column xvii (line 16), fortunately preserved, which contains the remnants of the words ' in the th[ird] lot '.[1] From this fragment it can be concluded that the Series actually dealt with the six engagements ' on the day the Kittim fall ' on which the Sons of Light will in turn be victorious and defeated, and it ended with a description of the victory attained with the seventh lot.

Section 23 (xv, 4–xvi, 1) describes the preparations for the first engagement or Lot. After noting the fact that the High Priest reads the ' prayer for the appointed day of battle ' in front of all the combatants, ' [as is written in the boo]k *Serekh 'Itto* ' (xv, 5) and deploys formations ' as is writ[ten in the book of the wa]r ' (xv, 6),[2] the Section gives the address of ' the priest destined for the appointed time of vengeance ' (ibid.).[3]

Section 24 (xvi, 2–8) apparently describes the first engagement. In order clearly to set it apart from the preceding accounts and to emphasize that it begins the description of the engagements themselves, the author opens with the sentence : ' All this disposition they shall carry out on that day in the place where they stand facing the camp of the Kittim. Afterwards the priests shall give them a signal,' etc. (xvi, 2). The description of the fighting is short and constitutes an extract from the detailed *serekh* dealing with the subject (sec. 12). This engagement ends in the victory of the Sons of Light : ' And the battle is waged victoriously against the Kittim ' (line 8).

Section 25 (xvi, 9–12) describes the defeat of the Sons of Light (= second Lot) briefly—for self-evident reasons—and contents itself with the heading : ' And when [Belial] girds himself for assistance to the Sons of Darkness, and the slain among the skirmishers begin to fall through God's mysteries to test thereby those destined for battle ' (line 9), and a description of the process of relieving the formation beaten in battle by a reserve formation.[4]

---

[1] See commentary ad loc.

[2] As the prayer is given in full in the Ritual Serekh Series and the order of formations in the Battle Serekh Series, the author contents himself with a mere reference in each case.

[3] For this priest and his oration, see ch. 8, § 4 (3), 5 (2).

[4] For the last term, see ch. 7, § 7 (10).

Before the renewal of battle the High Priest once more addresses the warriors. His words are given in the following sections.

Sections 26 (xvi, 13–xvii, 3) and 27 (xvii, 4–9). The address of the High Priest after the defeat of the Sons of Light (in the second Lot). Its principal content is that war serves as a crucible in which God tests the members of the sect and causes Himself to be hallowed through their judgment, as happened with Nadab and Abihu, the sons of Aaron. The Sons of Light must take courage and not be afraid, for the fate of the Kittim was decided since eternity and this day is the appointed time of God ' to subdue and bring low the Prince of the Kingdom of Evil '. On this day God will raise the station of the archangel Michael over Belial [1] and through this will bring about for the Sons of Light the period of light and joy, peace and blessing in which the ' authority of Michael ' is raised over all angels and the ' dominion of Israel over all flesh '.

Section 28 (xvii, 10–xvii, 8). Detailed description of the third Lot, in which the Sons of Light are victorious, followed apparently [2] by a very brief description of the fourth Lot (the recovery of the Sons of Darkness), the fifth (the recovery of the Sons of Light), the sixth (the recovery of the Sons of Darkness), and ending with a description of the seventh Lot : ' When the great hand of God shall be raised up against Belial and all the army of his dominion for eternal defeat ' and ' the Kittim shall be smashed without [remnant] ' (xviii, 1–3).

Since the Battle Series explains that all six battles will take place on the last day of the war with the Kittim, it is obvious that the last and decisive battle starts towards evening. Immediately after the commencement of the pursuit, the High Priest is obliged to turn to God with a prayer : ' When the sun hastens to set on that day, the chief priest and the priests and [levites] that are with him, and the chiefs and the elders of the Serekh shall stand up and bless in that place the God of Israel ' (xviii, 5, etc.). After giving thanks for the commencement of victory and recalling the miracles and deliverances which God wrought in the past for His name's sake, the High Priest passes on to the main purpose of his prayer, the continuation of which is given in section 29.

Section 29 (xviii, 9, etc.). This section, the end of which is lost, contains the prayer of the High Priest to God that ' He shall appear ' on that day and make possible the destruction of the Kittim, ' Now the day is hastening for us [to] pursue their multitude '. The assump-

---

[1] Cf. ch. 9, § 4–5.   [2] I.e. in the lost portion of col. xvii.

tion that the purpose of the prayer is the request that God should perform a miracle as He did for Joshua, is supported by its style, which is markedly influenced by the Book of Joshua, chapter x.[1]

Section 30 (xix, 1–8). Only the end of this section is extant on an isolated fragment, which clearly belongs to a different sheet from that containing the preceding sections (24–29). The exact place of the column in the sheet cannot be known since no margins either on its right or left side are preserved. For the reason that the second part of the column (Section 31 and onwards) continues with a description of the actions of the combatants after final victory, and since that fragment of Section 30 which is preserved contains in fact an almost exact repetition[2] of the end of the prayer for the appointed time of the war which is found in Section 16 ('Rise O Hero', etc.), it is not unreasonable to assume that column xix was the first of the sheet and continued the prayer begun in Section 28 (xviii, 6 and onwards) before the final pursuit. The request 'rise O Hero', which ends the prayer before the battle, fits also the conclusion of the prayer before the general pursuit. In both cases the Sections following deal with new subjects.[3]

Section 31 (xix, 9–13). Of this section only the middle of five lines (9–13) is preserved. In spite of this it can be shown that it is the part of the Kittim Series paralleling the descriptions of rituals and prayers in the Ritual Serekh Series, Section 21. It seems that the other pages of this sheet dealt with the prayers upon the return from the battlefield to Jerusalem and probably also with the thanksgiving in the Temple itself.

As was noted earlier, we cannot know if the scroll dealt with the twenty-nine year war against the rest of the nations, the outline plan of which is given in Section 3 within the War Series. Since the principal content of the scroll is the war with the Kittim, who are Israel's main enemies in the period concerned, it may be assumed that the scroll ended with the description of the final victory over them. On the other hand, the possibility cannot be excluded that at its end were several sections which described, though briefly, the conquest of the other nations mentioned in the plan of war.[4]

---

[1] Cf. further ch. 8, § 5 (5), and p. 222, nn. 1, 3.

[2] For the differences, see commentary.

[3] In our case the activities on the morning after the victory. Section 16 is followed by the prayers, etc., after the fall of the Kittim. Cf. ch. 8, § 5 (6).

[4] A fragment published in *Qumran* I, Pl. xxxi, 33, 2, belongs to the left part of col. xix. The letters visible on the left side of this fragment indicate that the sheet contained at least one further column. Cf. comm. ad loc.

§ 4. SUMMARY OF THE SECTIONS OF THE SCROLL [1]

Sections	Columns	
1– 3	i–ii	War Series
4–13	ii–ix	Battle Serekh Series
14–21	ix–xiv	Ritual Serekh Series
22–31	xv–xix	Kittim Series

§ 5. NOTES ON THE INTRODUCTION

The close interrelation in any army organization between structure, armaments, and tactics makes it impossible to treat each one separately. For this reason the author had to add numerous details touching on different questions, as he did also to the sections mainly dealing with other subjects, and this in spite of the basic division into three sections. Our introduction therefore does not follow the division of the scroll but deals with each subject as a whole.[2]

§ 6. SUMMARY (SOURCES, CONTENT, AND STRUCTURE)

The structure and aim of the scroll, as defined above, did of course also determine the sources on which the author relied. It is natural that the War Series and the Kittim Series, which determine the time and plan of the apocalyptic war, are mainly based on the apocalyptic and eschatological parts of the Bible and of pseudepigraphic literature. This is apparent not only from the content but also to a large extent from the style and terminology. This is not the place [3] to enumerate all the sources which influenced our author. Suffice it to note the influence of the eschatological chapters of the Prophets in general and of Isaiah in particular, not only in ideas but even in direct quotation. The enormous influence of Daniel is expressed in the style of sections 1–2 of the scroll, in the terms connected with the doctrine of the angels and in the extensive use of apocalyptic and eschatological terminology typical of this book. Equally great is the influence of the apocalyptic books of the Pseudepigrapha in such matters as the determination of the time appointed for the war with the enemies at whose head stands Belial,[4] the doctrine of the angels, their names and the position of

---

[1] Sections 14 and 22 form transitions between the respective series. Sections 23, 26, and 28–30 in the Kittim Series contain additional prayers.

[2] For the relation of the sections of the scroll and the parts of the Introduction, see par. 3 above.

[3] Cf. chs. 2, 9, and 11, and commentary on sections 1–2, 14, 21, and 27.

[4] Cf. ch. 9 and end of ch. 2. Among the references given there, note particularly Test. Dan v, 8.

Michael, Light and Darkness, the connexion between the angels and the ancient worthies of Israel, the annihilation of the angels of destruction on the appointed day, the description of the Day of God,[1] the place of 'knowledge', 'justice', and 'truth', and finally the calendar of fifty-two weeks.[2]

One can also discern the connection with other scrolls found in the same cave. There are many parallels of style and content between DSW and the Thanksgiving Scroll and especially between DSW and the Discipline Scroll. The Lot of Light and the Lot of Darkness are mentioned in DSW as facts, and practically without explanations, while this subject is explained at length in DSD.[3] Similarly, the parallelism between the Blessings and the Curses in these two scrolls is most interesting.[4]

The revelations and visions which are in apocalyptic literature ascribed to righteous men of the past and whose aim is to confirm the apocalyptic, deterministic doctrine,[5] appear in this scroll solely as a background and starting point for explaining the course of the war and for determining the methods of administration and warfare.

DSW, like other scrolls which aim to provide the sect with a set of rules for its conduct in everyday life (i.e. DSD and CDC), was not essentially written for the purpose of consolation and description of the splendid future at the End of Days. *Its purpose was to supply an urgent and immediate need*, a guide for the problems of the long-predicted war, which according to the sect would take place in the near future.

The return of the 'exiles of the wilderness' to the 'Wilderness of Jerusalem' is very near, for the period of the composition of the scroll was 'a time of mighty trouble for the people to be redeemed by God. In all their troubles there was none like it, from its hastening until its completion for an eternal redemption' (i, 11–12).[6]

The members of the sect must prepare for this war not only by perfect conduct but also in their organization, which must befit the 'hosts of God'.[7] That is why a *serekh* is needed; this is given in the scroll.

Naturally the sources on which the author of the scroll based himself

---

[1] Cf. commentary on i, 8–9.
[2] Cf. ch. 8, § 3 (4).
[3] Cf. ch. 9, § 8.
[4] Cf. ch. 8, § 5 (6).
[5] Cf. M. Weiss, 'Apocalypse,' *Enc. Miqr.* I, 497; H. Z. Hirschberg, 'End of Days,' ib. 230; Th. C. Vriezen 'Prophecy and Eschatology,' *Suppl. to V.T.* I (1953), 199–229.
[6] On this typical, phrase, cf. commentary ad loc.
[7] Cf. ch. 3, § 1–2.

in the Serekh Section and especially in the Battle Serekh were different from the ones which served him as the background for the War Section. The three subjects which occupy the author in the Serekh Section are: The laws of war and of military organization as set out in the Torah, tactics of the armies of the world, and the prayers; these obliged him to base himself on different sources. For the first subject he of course relies mainly on Numbers and Deuteronomy.[1] His use of those sources is instructive. Not only are there interesting variations in the text of some of his direct quotations,[2] but it appears he possessed additional sources, in accordance with which he was able to describe in great detail the organization and banners of the congregation. These need not necessarily have been written sources, but may have been oral tradition and the customs of his sect and his period.[3]

On the other hand, when he came to write on the second subject—the tactics of war, arms, the trumpet signals, etc.—he had to turn to different sources. The number of accounts of battles in the Bible is not large and they could not serve him as a source for a detailed and professional description such as he wished to present to his readers. Also, the descriptions of wars in the Apocrypha and Pseudepigrapha[4] are very general and could not supply him with the material needed.

An analysis of the chapters in question[5] and of the terminology employed proves that he used contemporary military sources. Unfortunately the only sentence in which he mentions the sources from which he drew his knowledge has mostly been eaten away. In Section 23 (xv, 6, etc.) we find: ' he shall array all the formations, as writ[ten in the   ],' Hebrew:]ה[ככת]וב.

That this sentence gave the name of the source on which he relied can be concluded from the preceding sentence, which is preserved almost completely. In it he names the book containing the prayer for the appointed time of the war: ' [as it is written in the Bo]ok *Serekh 'Itto*'. If we complete the missing words ' as is written in the *serekh* of the war' ככתו]ב בסרך המלחמ[ה, he might, of course, have meant the *serakhim* set out in the scroll itself (sections 8, 9, etc.); If we complete ' as is written in the book of the war ' ככתו]ב בספר המלחמ[ה, this would be a reference to a book of general military rules[6]

---

[1] Cf. ch. 3; ch. 8, § 4–5, and ch. 4.
[2] Cf. commentary on xi, 6–7; x, 1–8; vii, 5–7, and ch. 8, § 4–5, also 4, § 3.
[3] Cf. n. 1.
[4] E.g. Test. Judah III–vii, ix, Jub. ch. xxxiv, xxxvii–xxxviii, and the corresponding Midrash passages. Cf. p. 33, n. 3.
[5] Cf. chs. 5–7.
[6] See also M. Kasher, *Talpiyoth* iv, 606 sq. To his references, add B. T. Moed Qatan 25b.

CONTENTS AND PURPOSE OF THE SCROLL

or perhaps to a kind of handbook on military matters for the use of priests.

The fact that for writing the Battle Serekh Series the author had to rely on contemporary military sources is of the utmost importance, not only for the dating of the scroll but for an understanding of the structure of the Jewish army at the end of the period of the Second Temple and indirectly also in the period of the First Temple. The 'military' sources which describe the composition of the Jewish army in the days of the Hasmoneans are very few. The only important ones are the books of the Maccabees, which, however, leave wide gaps with regard to problems of military organization, methods of fighting, weapons, and methods of giving and transmitting commands. The works of Josephus—which are so important for an understanding of the structure of the Roman army in his period—prove in fact that the Jewish army of the time was organized on the whole on the pattern of the Roman army and particularly of its auxiliary units.[1] However, his writings can neither supply us with the vital details found in the scroll; nor, being in Greek, can they compete with its rich store of Hebrew military terminology.

In the Ritual Serekh two sources are in evidence:

(1) The Bible. The beginning of the 'prayer for the appointed time of the war' relies on Deuteronomy with slight and interesting variants. The insertion of passages from Numbers (xxiv, 17), Samuel, and Isaiah completes its dependence on the Bible.[2]

(2) A sectarian source. The content and style of the remaining parts of the prayers and thanksgivings definitely prove the existence of a sectarian source on which the author of the scroll based himself. This source he names as 'The Book *Serekh 'Itto*' (xv, 5). This book, as its name shows, was a kind of 'prayer book' for the various festivals and occasions which the sect observed. The contents of its prayers certainly differed from those accepted at that period by the Jewish community as a whole.[3] As with the 'Book of the Hagi' which is mentioned a number of times in the other writings of the sect,[4] we do not as yet know anything about the 'Book *Serekh 'Itto*', but it is not impossible that it may be found amongst the scrolls and fragments still being uncovered in the caves at Khirbet Qumrân.

---

[1] See further chs. 3 and 5–7.
[2] Cf. ch. 8, § 4–5.
[3] See further ch. 8, § 2–3 (4). Cf. *Qumran I*, plates xxv–xxix.
[4] Cf. commentary on xv, 5.

Chapter 2

THE PLAN OF THE WAR [1]

§ 1. GENERAL REMARKS : THE PHASES OF THE WAR AND THE DIVISION OF THE ENEMIES

Sections 1, 3–6, and to some extent also Section 2, deal with the plan of the war of the Sons of Light against all their enemies on earth. A certain difficulty in understanding the plan arises at first glance from the fact that the beginning of Section 3 (end of col. ii) is eaten away, and also because the author interspersed with the description of the phases of the war an explanation of the administration of the Temple service in the sabbatical years in which the congregation does not fight. The insertion of this description is not accidental, since according to the conception of the sect the entire congregation constitutes the 'hosts of God': both those in the 'host of service' and those in the 'host of war'. Therefore the description cannot omit the duties of any part of the 'host' during the various periods of the war. In the description of the general plan of the war the author adopts a logical, military arrangement comparable with that customary in 'strategic directives' of our own day. This kind of 'directive' does not deal with methods of fighting (tactics) but must clearly indicate the following points :

(1) A general definition of the fighting forces, those of the enemy and 'our forces'.

(2) Definition of the aims of the war (destruction of the enemy, conquest of his territory, etc.).

(3) Definition of the principal phases of the war (taking into consideration factors of terrain, the time element and the importance of the enemy) and its general plan.

(4) The assignment of the forces and the time-table for the fighting during the various phases.

This order expresses the logical thought process of the military commander and is still the practice in almost all armies. It enables the 'recipient of the directive' appointed to carry it out to realize the intention of the Supreme Commander and to understand his own duties in the framework of the general plan.

The description of the plan of war in the scroll contains something

---

[1] This chapter deals with sections 1 and 3 of the scroll.

of all those elements and their arrangement closely resembles that noted above. Section 1, which is in the nature of a general introduction, comprises a definition of the first three sections, i.e. the general fighting forces :

(1) The Enemy and Our Forces

(*a*) Enumeration of the principal enemies of the Sons of Light : the Lot of the Sons of Darkness, the armies of Belial, Edom, Moab, Philistia, the Kittim of Asshur, and the Offenders against the Covenant.

(*b*) Definition of ' our forces ' : the ' sons of Levi, Judah, and Benjamin—the exiles of the wilderness '.

(2) War Aims

The Sons of Light will fight their enemies aiming to ' destroy and to exterminate '.

(3) The Principal Phases of the War

(*a*) The first and main phase against the enemies mentioned above will take place on the return of the Sons of Light from the ' wilderness of the nations ' to ' encamp in the wilderness of Jerusalem '.

(*b*) The second phase, against the ' Kittim in Egypt ', will be after the battle in the ' wilderness of Jerusalem '.

(*c*) The third phase, against the kings of the north.

Section 2 briefly describes the happenings on the day ending in the seventh and decisive battle against the Kittim, after six battles, three of which ended in victory for the Sons of Light and three in victory for the Lot of Darkness. Section 3 deals with an enumeration of the principal section of the plan of the war, namely, the assignment of the forces and the time-tables for the various phases (with an explanation of the method used in reckoning the time-table).

Against the principal enemies mentioned in the first and second phases, the entire congregation will fight for six years. Against the remote enemies, included in the third phase, the war will last for twenty-nine years, a year or two against each enemy. During this phase not all the congregation will fight as a whole but in ' separate divisions ', called up every year in their turn. These thirty-five years constitute the actual years of fighting out of a period of forty years of which five are sabbatical years during which the Sons of Light will not fight.

In clearing up the problems arising from this plan of war, the enumeration of the enemies and the reckoning of the time-table, we shall follow the order adopted by the author, except that we must first explain the method of reckoning the years of fighting.

20 INTRODUCTION

§ 2. The Method of Reckoning the Years of Fighting

The apparent lack of clearness in reckoning the years of fighting described in Section 3 derives from the fact that this reckoning is done twice, from two points of departure:

(1) The general division of the war period (which includes the sabbatical years) into two main periods: the war of the entire congregation and the war of the separate divisions.

(2) The division of the actual years of fighting (after deducting the sabbatical years) according to the various enemies.

The description of the Temple service in the first sabbatical year, after six years of fighting by the whole congregation (the first part of which is missing at end of col. i) closes with the words (ii, 6): 'All these they shall dispose at the time of the sabbatical year. In the remaining thirty-three years of the war shall the men of renown summoned to assembly and all the chiefs of the clans of the congregation choose from time to time for them warriors for all the lands of the gentiles: from all tribes of Israel they shall mobilize for them men of valour to go forth to serve according to the pre-ordained periods of the war.'

It results that the inclusive period devoted to the war by separate divisions (including its four sabbatical years) after the seven years' war of the whole congregation (including the first sabbatical year) will be thirty-three years.

However, in enumerating the years of actual fighting (including the period of the war of the entire congregation) the scroll deducts, in addition to the first sabbatical year at the end of the war of the whole congregation, the four sabbatical years during the war of the separate divisions: 'But in the sabbatical years they shall not mobilize men to go forth to serve, for a sabbath of rest it is for Israel' [1] (8–9), and

---

[1] Fighting during sabbatical years is not expressly forbidden by the Pent., but the language of the scroll points to the prohibition having been derived from 'sabbath of rest', Lev. xxv, 4; cf. also Ant. XII, vi, 2. The passage appears to be influenced by Jub. L, especially vss. 3 seq., 12–13. Cf. also *Qumran* I, p. 94. 1 Macc. vi, 49, explains the fall of Bethsura as due to the 'sabbath to the land', and ib. 53 the famine in Jerusalem 'because it was the seventh year'. Jos., DJ I, ii, 4, and Ant. XIII, viii, 1, says Hyrcanus abandoned the siege of Dagon because the sabbatical year had arrived on which the Jews rest as on sabbath. In contrast to the former case, this detail shows that fighting in the sabbatical year was avoided not merely for lack of food, though, of course, the interruption of regular food supplies would have gravely hampered an attacking army. Cf. further R. North, 'Maccabean Sabbath Years,' *Biblica* 34 (1953), 501 ff.; M. Z. Neriyah, *Sabbath Wars* (Hebrew), Jerus., 1959.

arrives at thirty-five years of Temple service and fighting: 'In the thirty-five years of service the war shall be carried on: for six years the whole congregation shall carry it on together and the war of separate divisions shall be waged in the remaining twenty-nine' (9–10).

The following schematic table will make clear the method of reckoning according to both points of departure:

Division of the Congregation		Total	Division of the Years		Total
whole congregation	separate divisions		years of service (war)	sabbatical years	
6	–	6	6		6
				1	1
–	6	6	6		6
				1	1
–	6	6	6		6
				1	1
–	6	6	6		6
				1	1
–	6	6	6		6
				1	1
–	5	5	5		5
6	29	35	35	5	40

Years of fighting	.	35	Or: War of whole congregation	.	6
Sabbatical years	.	5	War of separate divisions	.	29
		—	Sabbatical years	. .	5
Total	.	40			—
			Total	. .	40

§ 3. The First Phase

The first and principal phase of the war will be fought against 'the troop of Edom and Moab and the sons of Ammon and the army [of the dwellers of] Philistia and the troops of the Kittim of Asshur, and in league with them the offenders against the covenant' (i, 1–2). This group of enemies is therefore divided into three groups:

(1) Israel's neighbours and traditional enemies.
(2) The Kittim of Asshur.
(3) The Offenders against the Covenant.

(1) *The Traditional Enemies.*—The names of the enemies of the Sons

of Light who dwell within the Biblical boundaries of Palestine are all mentioned many times in the Bible, in various periods and in much the same order.[1] The early and later Maccabees also fought against them,[2] and in the descriptions of the war in Jubilees they are mentioned a number of times in a similar form.[3]

(2) *The Kittim of Asshur*, or the Kittim, stand at the head of the enemies of the Sons of Light (xv, 2, 3; xix, 10), and the scroll is mainly devoted to the description of the decisive battle in which the rule of the Kittim will cease (i, 6) and they 'shall be smashed without [remnant and survivor]' (xviii, 2-3).[4]

Their identification—essential for determining the period of the composition of the scroll—served as an important point of discussion for different scholars. Further on we shall sum up what is known about the Kittim from the scrolls and from outside sources. Amongst the scrolls published so far the Kittim are mentioned only in DSW, DSH, and the Pesharim.[5] Even though in DSW the word is spelt כתיים and in DSH כתיאים, the meaning is the same.[6]

DSW.—These enemies are mentioned simply as Kittim or in various combinations, e.g. 'the troops of the Kittim', 'the rule of the Kittim', 'the camps (or armies) of the Kittim', 'the formations of the Kittim', 'the slain of the Kittim', 'the army of the Kittim', 'the mighty men of the Kittim'. At their head stands a king ('the king of the Kittim', xv, 2.).

The Kittim are also called the Kittim of Asshur (i, 2), or Asshur is mentioned as a synonym. They belong to the sons of Japheth, in contrast to Asshur the son of Shem mentioned in the war of the separate divisions (ii, 12 and further on, see also ch. 8, § 15 and p. 215, n. 1): 'There shall be [great] panic [amongst] the sons of Japheth. Asshur shall fall, and none shall help him, and the dominion of the Kittim shall depart' (i, 5-6) or '... in pursuit of Asshur, then the sons of Japheth shall fall, never to rise again, and the Kittim shall be smashed without [remnant and survivor]' (xviii, 2-3, cf. xi, 11).

---

[1] Cf. Isa. xi, 14; 2 Kings xxiv, 2 (Pesh. 'Edom' for MT 'Aram'); Dn. xi, 41; 2 Sam. viii, 12; 1 Chr. xviii, 11, and the fuller list Ps. lxxxiii, 7-9.

[2] Cf. 1 Macc. v, 3 (Idumaea), ib. 6 (Ammon), etc., and M. Avi-Yonah, 'The War of the Sons of Light, etc.', IEJ 2 (1952) 3.

[3] Jub. xxxvii, 6 ff., the sons of Esau call for help on Aram (!), Philistia, Moab, Ammon, Edom, the Horites, and the Kittim. On the 'Kittim' here see below, p. 24, n. 8.

[4] The K. occur 14 times in DSW and 9 times in DSH.

[5] 4QpNah (JBL 75 (1956), 90); 4QpIsaª (ib. p. 177 ff.); cf. Qumran I, p. 82.

[6] Cf. the spellings גוים and גואים.

The Kittim are also found in Egypt and they, like the Kittim of Asshur, are the enemies of the Sons of Light (i, 4).

DSH.—The Chaldees mentioned in Hab. i, 6, are explained by the author of the scroll as the Kittim [1]; here too the 'rule of the Kittim' is mentioned (ii, 13, 14) and the 'army of the Kittim' (ix, 6). Instead of the 'king of the Kittim', the 'rulers of the Kittim' are mentioned (iv, 5; iv, 10) as in PNahum. The author of DSH adds details about the character and customs of the Kittim. 'They are quick and mighty in war,' 'And they come from afar, from the islands of the sea' with their horses and their beasts like an eagle. Their fear has fallen upon all nations and all their thought is to do evil; they despise the fortresses of the nations, which they conquer and destroy; they gather much booty and are cruel, having no pity on boys and old men, women, and infants; their 'rulers' come and go but each in his turn shall come to destroy the land. 'They sacrifice to their *signa* and their weapons are their object of worship' (vi, 3-5). And finally, the property and gain of 'the last priests of Jerusalem' will be given 'into the hands of the army of the Kittim' (ix, 4-7).

Pesher Nahum (4*QpNah*).—The relevant passages are: '[Its interpretation refers to Deme]trius, king of Greece, who sought to enter Jerusalem by the counsel of the Seekers after smooth things' (line 2), and 'the kings of Greece from Antiochus until there arose the rulers of the Kittim' (line 3). The latter passage [2] is the most decisive evidence so far found in the DSS for the identity of the Kittim with the Romans.[3]

Pesher Isaiah (4*QpIsa*^{a}).[4]—The Kittim are mentioned several times in terms reminiscent of DSW : 'the war of the Kittim' (frg. B, line 6); 'the mighty men of the Kittim' (frg. C, line 5).

In the Bible and Versions.—According to Gen. x, 4, Kittim is the son of Javan the son of Japheth [5] and the author of DSW therefore write ' and the sons of Japheth shall fall ' (see above). In Num. xxiv, 24 (the Song of Balaam), the Kittim are mentioned in a very difficult verse : ' But ships shall come from the coast of Kittim, and they shall afflict Asshur, and shall afflict Eber, and he also shall come to destruction.' To this verse, which strongly influenced the author of the scroll, we shall return later.[6] Here we may only mention that 'Kittim' is here understood by Targum Onkelos and the Vulgate as

---

[1] For 'the troops of the Chaldees' of 2 Kings xxiv, 2, DSW has 'the troops of the Kittim of Asshur'.
[2] See p. 25, n. 1.
[3] Cf. Allegro, JBL 75 (1956), 93.
[4] 4QpIsa^a (JBL 75 (1956), 177 ff.
[5] See ib. vs. 2 and 1, Chr. i, 7.
[6] Cf. end of this par. and par. 5 (3).

referring to the Romans.[1] With the Kittim in Isaiah xxiii, 1, 12, and Ezekiel xxvii, 6,[2] we shall deal further on. The phrase in Daniel xi 30,[3] 'For ships of Kittim shall come against him,' is understood as referring to the Romans both by Septuagint and Vulgate, and this is accepted by most contemporary scholars.[4]

In the Apocrypha and Pseudepigrapha.—1 Macc. indicates that Alexander came from the Land of Χεττιείμ [5] and calls Perseus, the king of Macedonia, 'King of the Kittim.'[6] In Jub. xxiv, 28–9, Isaac, in cursing the Philistines, threatens them with falling into the hands of the Kittim.[7]

The Kittim are mentioned once more in Jub. xxxvii, 10, in the description of the war of the sons of Esau with Jacob, as allies of the sons of Esau together with Aram, Moab, Ammon, Philistia, Edom, and the Horites. This description, as it has reached us in its latest form,[8] is of special interest as it describes also the war of the Sons of Jacob (= Light) against Esau (= Darkness)[9] and the enemies described in DSW. Possibly the Kittim are also mentioned (Test. Simeon vi, 3), 'Then shall perish the seed of Canaan, and a remnant shall not be unto Amalek, and all the Cappadocians shall perish, and all the Kittim [10] shall be utterly destroyed.'

Josephus (Ant. I, vi, 1) mentions the name Χεθίμ, given by the Hebrews to all islands and to most maritime countries.[11]

---

[1] *mē-Rōmā'ē*; *de Italia*; the T.J. also has *mē-ăra' Iṭalyā*.

[2] Vulg. has again *de insulis Italiae*.

[3] The style of this chapter deeply influenced our scroll. Cf. further H. L. Ginsberg, *Studies in Daniel*, N.Y., 1948, and R. J. Tournay, RB 56 (1949), 211, n. 2.

[4] Dupont-Sommer, *Jewish Sect*, p. 15.

[5] i, 1. For the various spellings of 'Kittim' and 'Hittites' in the Versions and the Apocr. and Pseudep., see Abel, *Les Livres des Maccabees*, p. 1; and cf. Charles, *The Book of Jubilees*, 1902, p. xxxi and p. 155 note.

[6] Κιτιέων, viii, 5.

[7] So in Charles, *Apocr. and Pseudep*. II, 50. The Ethiopic texts read *Kiṭi'im*, *Kiṭ'ēm*, the Latin *Cettin*. The word 'Kittim' in this passage gives the impression of being a later addition.

[8] On the reading 'Kittim' see Charles, *The Book of Jubilees*, p. 216, n. 10. Again it appears that the name 'Kittim' has been added by a later hand, since they are missing in xxxvii, 6, and while of every other group one thousand chosen men come, no number is specified for the 'mighty men of war' from the Kittim. The four thousand warriors of vs. 14, 15, do not allow for the Kittim, nor are any slain of the Kittim mentioned in the enumeration xxviii, 8. It thus appears that the 'Kittim' were added in these passages at a period when they had become the chief enemies of Israel.

[9] Cf. Gen. Rabba ii, 3: 'And God called the light Day—that is Jacob; and the darkness He called Night—that is Esau.' Cf. also ch. 9, § 8.

[10] See the note by Charles, *Apoc.* II, 303. The chapter shows similarities with DSW xviii, 2–3.

[11] 'Chethimos held the island of Chethima—the modern Cyprus—whence the name *Chethim* given by the Hebrews, etc.'

The result of the above consideration of the sources agrees with Josephus that the name Kittim could have applied both to the Greeks and the Romans, depending on the period and the context.[1] We must still ascertain the meaning of the name 'the Kittim of Asshur'. The combination of Asshur and all the nations mentioned in the first group might have been influenced by the Psalms, especially as it appears at the end of the list.[2] However, it seems that the expression 'the Kittim of Asshur' is due to the fact that in at least three places in the Bible in which the Kittim are mentioned, Asshur also is mentioned and in close proximity.[3] Let us note that apparently the addition of Asshur to the name Kittim also indicates that these Kittim, a coast-dwelling nation, had their dwelling place or centre to the north of Palestine. In this way they complete the list of the enemies of the Sons of Light belonging to the first group from the geographical point of view also; Edom (south), Moab and Ammon (east), Philistia (west or south-west), the Kittim of Asshur (north).[4]

The ultimate defeat of the Kittim is in DSW xix compared to the destruction of Sennacherib's troops near Jerusalem, and the very verse from Isaiah referring to this event is quoted with application to the Kittim in xi, 11. This proves that the author's identification of the Kittim as 'Kittim of Asshur' was made in order to enable him to

---

[1] For 'Kittim' as designation of Romans in later periods, see p. 24, n. 4. Note, however, also CDC viii, 11 (= xix, 23): 'and the Head of the Asps is the chief of the kings of *Yāwān*, who comes to wreak vengeance upon them,' all the more interesting as the Kittim are not mentioned elsewhere in CDC. Cf. now also 4QpNah.

[2] Cf. p. 22, end of n. 1.

[3] Nu. xxiv, 24 (many variant readings exist; perhaps the author had before him one in which *Kittim* appeared next to *Asshur*), Onkelos reads for *Eber*: 'beyond the Euphrates' (cf. DSW ii, 11); Is. xxiii, 12–13 (for *Chaldaeans* = Kittim, cf. DSH ii, 12); Ez. xxvii, 6.

[4] It will be seen below, § 5, that these 'Kittim' fill the space between the Euphrates and Palestine. As shown by J. M. Grinz (*Sinai* 16 (5713), 26, n. 34), 'Asshur' denotes also in Jub. xiii, 1, the same country, between Haran and Shechem (Charles emends *Asshur* to *Canaan*).

Zeitlin (JQR 40 (1949–50), 60 ff.) adduces this usage as an argument for late dating. He quotes in support Gen. Rabba xvi, 4: 'R. Huna says in the name of R. Aḥa, All heathen kingdoms are called after Nineveh, because they beautify themselves (*mithnā'ōth*) from Israel's spoil. R. Jose b. Halaphta says, All heathen kingdoms are called after Egypt (*Miẓrayim*) because they oppress (*mĕẓēroth*) Israel.' This midrash only proves that these combinations of early and late enemies were elastic, and influenced, inter alia, by the desire to interpret Biblical prophecies about Asshur, Egypt, Edom, etc., as referring to the enemy of the day (cf. DSW xi, 11–12). Perhaps one should not ignore the problem of censorship (in spite of the objections by D. Flusser, *Yedioth* 17 (5713), 44). Against Zeitlin, see Burrows, JQR 42 (1951–2), 108. On the Kittim see also J. Carmignac, NRTh 77 (1955), 737, whose conclusions, however, do not seem convincing.

'interpret', in the manner of the Pesharim, passages about the Assyrian defeat as applying to the Kittim.

(3) *Offenders against the Covenant.*—The third group in the first phase of the war are the 'offenders against the Covenant'. The phrase is taken from Daniel xi, 32,[1] 'And such as do wickedly against the covenant shall corrupt by blandishments,' and doubtlessly referred to those amongst the Jews whom the sect considered to be traitors and persecutors of the righteous. This is almost the only indication in DSW of a subject which occupied the author of DSH to an extent almost equal with the Kittim and fills most pages of DST.[2]

§ 4. The Second Phase

In this phase, which comes immediately after the crushing of the enemy in Palestine and its immediate surroundings, only the Kittim in Egypt are mentioned. This fact to my mind only indicates that the Kittim living in Egypt—even though they are not within the Biblical boundaries of Palestine (and are therefore not included in the first group)—belong from an ethnographical point of view to the Kittim mentioned earlier, and must be liquidated before the beginning of the third phase against the kings of the remote north.

§ 5. The Third Phase

Out of the total war of forty years, thirty-three years will be devoted to the war with the nations enumerated in Gen. x. After deducting the four sabbatical years, twenty-nine years remain for the actual fighting. The first nine years are devoted to the war with the sons of Shem. The author enumerates the exact number of years to be devoted to the war with every one of the descendants of Shem, some a year and some two years. To the war with the sons of Ham the following ten years will be devoted. No details are given, but it is said that the war will be against 'all the sons of Ham [according to their families in their dw]elling places'. The same applies to the sons of Japheth to whom the last ten years of the war are devoted, after a part of them—the Kittim—have been fought in the first phase.

The names of the nations, the order of fighting against them, and their geographical position, and also the additions and omissions as compared with the Biblical list of nations, are most instructive and enable us to determine the extra-Biblical sources on which the author relied. Before embarking on this question we shall in the following

---

[1] See also CDC xx, 25–7.   [2] See ch. 10.

table present a list of the nations mentioned in the third phase, the war of separate divisions, and the numbers of years of fighting against each one : [1]

Years	Nations
1	Aram Naharaim
1	Sons of Lud
1	Rest of the sons of Aram : Uz, Hul, Togar, and Masha—that are beyond the Euphrates
2	Sons of Arpakhshad
2	All sons of Asshur, Persia, and the Kadmonite—until the great wilderness
1	Sons of Elam
1	Sons of Ishmael and Keturah
10	All sons of Ham [to their families in their dw]elling places
10	All [sons of Japheth] to their dwelling places

The assignment of the years does not seem to be accidental. Even though it was necessary to condense all the sons of Shem to a nine-year period, the enumeration is based, so it seems, on military and geographical considerations. The nations to be fought for two years do not appear at the end of the list, i.e. in the distribution of the remainder left to the author after having assigned a year to each of the earlier ones. The nature of these nations, too, must have been taken into consideration.[2] In analysing the list of the nations mentioned (and those not mentioned) we must on the one hand compare it with the parallel lists in the Bible (the tables of the nations found in Gen. x and xxv and 1 Chron. i) and on the other hand with the views held by the author's contemporaries or sect. The sources closest to it and its period are Jub. viii and ix and Jos. Ant. I, iv–vi.

Two conclusions may be anticipated :

(1) The List comprises the nations living outside the territory promised to Abraham in the Covenant of Pieces (Gen. xv, 18) : 'From the river of Egypt unto the great river, the river Euphrates.'[3]

(2) The order in which the sons of Shem are mentioned is from 'the nearer to the farther' in accordance with the geographical conception of the author as is made clear by the following table :[4]

---

[1] See the *Summary Table*, § 7.

[2] Cf. Agrippa's words in BJ II, xvi, 4 : 'Do you think you are going to fight the Egyptians or the Arabs ? '

[3] See subsection 3 below and the Rabbinic sources quoted in § 6.

[4] The enumeration of the later descendants of Noah in our scroll follows their order of seniority of his sons (Shem, Ham, Japheth), while other sources change the order so as to give prominence to the descendants of one son (Japheth, Ham, Shem in Gen., 1 Chr., Ant. ; Ham, Shem, Japheth in Jub.).

Gen.	Elam	Assyria		Arpakhshad	Lud	Aram	Sons of Aram *	
Chron.	Elam	Assyria		Arpakhshad	Lud	Aram	Sons of Aram *	Ishmael Keturah
Jub.	Elam	Assyria		Arpakhshad	Aram	Lud †		
Ant.	Elam	Assyria		Arpakhshad	Aram	Lud	Sons of Aram *	
DSW	Aram Naharaim	Lud	Rest of Sons of Aram beyond Euphrates *	Arpakhshad	Assyria Persia Kadmonite	Elam		Ishmael Keturah

* For details of the Sons of Aram, see below.
† Thus according to Charles; M. Goldmann (apud Kahana, *Ha-sefarim ha-ḥiẓonim*, I, p. 242) reads ' for his son ' instead of ' for Lud '. No such reading is recorded in the apparatus to Charles' edition of the Ethiopic text

The above table shows that the enumeration of the sons of Shem in the Bible is along a line from south-east to north-west. Aram and his sons are mentioned at the end of the list, apparently, because of their proximity to Palestine.[1] Jub. and Ant. adopt the same order except for putting Aram before Lud in accordance with their geographical position; while Jub. in the text available to us does not enumerate the sons of Aram; they are mentioned in Ant. at the end of the list after Lud.

The author of DSW on the whole adopted the reverse order from that of the Bible: a line from the nearer to the farther and from the north-west to the south-east. Moreover he did not copy the list mechanically from the Bible but tried to adapt it to military and geographical logic. He therefore inserted the sons of Aram, who in his opinion dwelt in the area between the sons of Lud and the sons of Arpakhshad, between the two, adding, so as to avoid misunderstanding, ' who are beyond the Euphrates '.

(1) *Aram Naharaim*.—While elsewhere the peoples are mentioned, here it is the country. This is significant for it implies that he wished to emphasize that he meant the area north of the Euphrates (since the other areas, between the Euphrates and the River of Egypt had been conquered in the first phases—see below in the summary). This area, in which the city of Nahor, the brother of Abraham, is situated,[2] will be conquered first because of its position between the two rivers in north-western Mesopotamia. This is also the conception of Jub., which defines the main part of Aram thus: ' And for Aram . . . between the

[1] Cf. the map in *Westminster Hist. Atlas to the Bible*, pl. II Inset, and p. 26 ib., and Albright's articles enumerated by Maisler, ' The Genealogy of the Sons of Nahor and the Historical Setting of Job,' *Zion* 11 (5706), 1 ff.

[2] Gen. xxiv, 10. On Aram Naharaim, cf. R. T. O'Callaghan, *Aram Naharaim*, Rome 1948; S. A. Loewenstamm in *Enc. Miqr*. I, 581.

Tigris and the Euphrates to the north of the Chaldees to the border of the mountains of Asshur and the land of Arârâ ' (ix, 5).[1] See further under 3.

(2) *Lud.*—From Aram Naharaim he passes to the north to the land of the sons of Lud, the mountainous region of Asia Minor,[2] as if to cover the flank before turning from Aram Naharaim to the rest of the sons of Aram and to Arpakhshad

(3) *Rest of the Sons of Aram.*—' With the rest of the sons of Aram [3] with Uz and Hul and Togar and Masha beyond the Euphrates '; this sentence, which contains details additional to the Biblical sources, is most instructive in three respects :

(*a*) The insertion of the sons of Aram between Lud and Arpakhshad (see table).
(*b*) The words ' which are beyond the Euphrates '.
(*c*) The variants for Togar, Masha, Purath, and the way they are spelt.

(*a*) I have already indicated that the difference in the order of the sons of Shem between the scroll and the Bible shows that the author did not mechanically copy from the sources but adapted them to the plan of the war and his geographical ideas. It is significant that he placed the rest of the sons of Aram after Lud and before Arpakhshad.

(*b*) The significance of this becomes obvious as soon as we consider the addition with which he defines the sons of Aram, viz. ' who are beyond the Euphrates '. This shows that he wished to rule out any possibility of confusion between these sons of Aram with any other Aram not beyond the Euphrates. Perhaps he also wished to stress their geographical position in opposition to other conceptions, accepted perhaps in his time, that the sons of Aram did not dwell beyond the Euphrates. What, however, is the meaning of ' beyond the Euphrates ? '[4]

---

[1] On the Land of Ararat, see A. J. Gelb and M.D. Cassuto in *Enc. Miqr.* I, 743–6. Cf., however, Ant. I, vi, 4 : ' Aramus ruled the Aramaeans, whom the Greeks term Syrians,' and see subsection 3 below. On the ' mountains of Asshur ', see now Avigad and Yadin, p. [30].

[2] The definition of the territory of Lud in the versions of Jub. ix, 6, is unclear in some respects, though it is fairly clear that the mountain region from the Great Sea in the west to the mountains of Assyria in the east or the ' mount of the Ox ' is meant. Ant. I, vi, 4 : ' those whom they now call Lydians were then Ludians, founded by Ludas.'

[3] The author uses the version of Gen., not that of 1 Chr., where ' and the sons of Aram ' is missing. The addition ' the rest of ' is influenced by Is. xvii, 3. Our present text of Jub. has no enumeration of sons of Aram, though remnants of such a list seem to be discernible (M. Goldmann in Kahana's *Ha-sefarim ha-ḥiẓonim*).

[4] On the spelling פורת, see commentary ad loc.; Avigad and Yadin, p. [29].

In the Bible we have instead 'beyond the river'. Since the rule of Asshurbanipal, this denotes the area included in the Assyrian realm south-west of the Euphrates [1] (*ebir nāri*) on the one hand, and on the other the place of origin of the Patriarchs,[2] which is to the north-east of it. One must in every instance refer to the context so as to establish its identity.[3] Josephus uses the expression 'beyond the Euphrates' several times to indicate the areas east of the Euphrates.[4]

Taking into account that the Sons of Light had fought in the area west of the Euphrates during the first phase, and also the lack of military and geographical logic in fighting against Aram Naharaim and Lud and then returning to Northern Syria, one must conclude that by 'beyond the Euphrates' our author means the far, i.e. left side of the Euphrates. Moreover it seems that it was this ambiguity which caused him to use the expression 'beyond the Euphrates' instead of 'beyond the river' as in 2 Sam.[2]

This is an important conclusion, for it shows that the author thought that the sons of Aram dwelt on the far side of the Euphrates.[5] This assumption is confirmed by the discussion of the identity of each of the sons of Aram separately.[6] We have already noted that according to Jub. the territory of Aram lay between the two rivers and Jub. did not therefore further specify the territory of the sons of Aram. We must conclude that in the opinion of the author of Jub. all the sons of Aram mentioned in the Table of Nations dwelt in this area.

Uz. The location of this people presents a difficulty to modern scholars, too, especially since Uz is also mentioned as the native country of Job. It is interesting that Maisler [6] expressed the opinion, for quite different reasons, that Uz (and in fact also the other sons of Aram mentioned above) must be located in Aram Naharaim, exactly as in the scroll. Josephus locates them in Trachonitis and Damascus 'which is between Palestine and Coelesyria' [7] even though he locates the rest of

---

[1] Ezr. viii, 36; Neh. ii, 7; also 1 Kings v, 4. Cf. M. Avi-Yonah, *Geographia historith shel Ereṣ Yisrael*, p. 9.

[2] Josh. xxiv 15, and cf. vs. 14. Interesting is 2 Sam. x, 16: after the defeat of the Aramaeans hired by the Ammonites 'Hadadezer sent and brought out the Aramaeans that were beyond the river', i.e. no doubt those beyond the Euphrates. The language of our scroll is certainly influenced by this verse.

[3] Cf. O'Callaghan, op. cit., p. 116, and B. Gemser, 'Be'ēber Hajjardēn,' VT 2 (1952), 349 ff.

[4] BJ I, Prooem. 2; ib. II, xvi, 4.

[5] Cf. *Enc. Miqr.* I, 572, and bibliogr. there.

[6] See the article mentioned in p. 28, n. 1.

[7] Ant. I, vi, 4. Maisler (op. cit., p. 5, n. 18) shows that this information is based on the popular tradition locating Job's dwelling at Karnaim (Sheikh Sa'd) in Baṣan, which is known from sources dating from the Roman period onwards.

THE PLAN OF THE WAR

the sons of Aram (as will be shown later) in the neighbourhood of Asia Minor.

Hul. Josephus identifies Hul with Armenia.[1]

Togar. This is a very interesting name and (in this form) has no parallel in the sources, where only *Gether* appears. This is unlikely to be a scribal error. It is with some hesitation that I suggest connecting this name with the Τόχαροι who, according to Strabo among others, together with the Scythians took Bactria from the Greeks.[2] In my opinion the suggestion for this identification gains force from the fact that Josephus connects *Getheres* with the Bactrians.[3]

Masha. The fourth in the list of the sons of Aram is *Mash* (Gen.) and *Meshekh* (1 Chron.). The Septuagint reads Μόσοχ in both places. The form *Masha* as used in the scroll is also the reading of the Samaritan text and of Josephus (Μῆσας).[4]

In the light of all this it may be assumed that according to the author of the scroll (and likewise Jub. ; see p. 29, n. 1) the sons of Aram mentioned above dwelt between the Euphrates and Tigris near the sources of these rivers, to the east of the sons of Lud.

(4) *Arpakhshad.*—After the successful war on the left flank and before the expedition to the mountainous region of Assyria and Elam and from there towards the great wilderness, they will turn to the rest of the low country between the rivers. According to the Bible, Arpakhshad was one of the ancestors of Abraham.[5] According to Jub. the main habitat of Arpakhshad is Chaldaea : ' And for Arpakhshad came forth the third portion, all the land of the region of the Chaldees to the east of the Euphrates.'[6] Josephus too connects Arpakhshad with the Chaldees.[7] With the conquest of Arpakhshad begins the expedition to the mountains of Asshur and Elam.

---

[1] Ant. I, vi, 4 (var. ῎Οτρος).

[2] Strabo XI, viii, 2. In some sources the name appears in forms closer to *Togar* : Geogr. Ptolem. VI, 16, 8, Θογάρα πόλις ; Trogus Pompeius XLI *reges Thogarorum* ; cf. A. Hermann in Pauly-Wissowa, pp. 1633–37, and E. Sieg and W. Siegling, *Tocharische Sprachreste* (1921) p. III.

[3] Ant. I, vi, 4 : καὶ Γεθέρης (κτίζει) Βακτριανούς.

[4] Ant. I, vi, 4, here identified with Spasinou Charax, but Ant. XX, ii, 2, 3, with Adiabene. Cf. further B. Maisler, ' Palestine at the Time of the Middle Kingdom in Egypt,' *Bull. des Ét. Hist. Juives*, Cairo, I (1946), 53.

[5] This may be the reason why the scroll does not enumerate the sons of A., though this is done in Gen. x, 11.

[6] ix, 4, though later in the same vs. their territory is extended to ' the tongue of the sea which looketh towards Egypt and all the land of Lebanon and Sanir and Amana to the border of the Euphrates' .

[7] Ant. I, vi, 4. The identification may be due to the similarity of כשד(ארפ) and כשד(ים) ; cf. S. A. Loewenstamm, *Enc. Miqr.* I, 602 ; Thackeray's note ad loc. in the Loeb edn.

(5) *Asshur, Persia, the Kadmonite until the Great Wilderness.*—Jub. defines the territory of Asshur as ' all the land of Asshur and Nineveh and Shinear unto India '.[1] Persia, which is mentioned in combination with Asshur, is here introduced (in the territory of Shem) for its geographical position [2] and its political importance in the period of the composition of the scroll, similar to the definition of the territory of Shem in Jub. The second and most interesting addition is the ' Kadmonite '. The mention of the Kadmonite in Gen. xv, 19, and the special meaning which the Rabbis attached to this passage,[3] caused the Kadmonite to be introduced here amongst the nations of the third phase (see below).[4] However, its location can be understood only from a description of the territory of the sons of Shem as defined in Jub. viii, 21 : ' . . . and the whole land of the east, and India . . . ' (cf. also ibid. 16).[5]

(6) *Elam.*—According to Jub. ix, 2, its territory is ' East of the Tigris, until it approacheth the east, all the land of India '.[6] Here, in the mountains of Elam which border on the Persian Gulf, ends the expedition against the sons of Shem who dwell between the two rivers and to the east of them.

(7) *The Sons of Ishmael and Keturah.*—The inclusion of the sons of Ishmael and Keturah at the end of the list, even though they are not mentioned in the table of the nations with the sons of Shem, seems to be for the purpose of closing the major flank on the eastern border of Palestine (according to Gen. xv, 18). There seems to be in addition to the geographical reason a political one. It is interesting that in Gen. xxv the sons of Keturah and Ishmael are described as separate groups and their territories mentioned separately,[7] yet here they are mentioned as one group. The following passage from Jub. (xx, 12–13) will solve our difficulty : ' And Ishmael and his sons, and the sons of Keturah and their sons, went together and dwelt from Paran to the entering in of Babylon in all the land which is towards the East

---

[1] ix, 3 ; for the continuation cf. Charles, *The Book of Jubilees* p. 76, and *Westminster Atlas* pl. II Inset. Ant. I, vi, 4, does not mention Shinear and India.

[2] Josephus, Ant. I, vi, 4, derives the Persians from Elam. Cf. also En. vi, 5, and *Westminster Atlas* p. 27.

[3] See below, end of § 6.

[4] No doubt Joel ii, 20, ' into a land barren and desolate,' led to the inclusion of ' the great desert ' here.

[5] Possibly ' the east ' (*sĕbāḥ*) translates an original *ha-Qadhmōnī*. The Great Desert is the Salt Desert of Persia. In Gen. xv, 19, the Eth. Bible has *Qēmēnēlōs*. Cf. Avigad and Yadin, p. 29.

[6] See Charles's note on ' the east ' in *The Book of Jubilees* p. 75.

[7] Keturah vss. 2–7, Ishmael vss. 12–18, ' from Havilah unto Shur, that is before Egypt, as thou goest toward Asshur '.

(*qedem*)¹ facing the desert. And these mingled with each other, and their name was called Arabs, and Ishmaelites.'

(8) *Ham and Japheth*.—The remaining twenty years of the war in separate divisions are devoted to the sons of Ham and Japheth. The author does not, however, enumerate them and contents himself with emphasizing that he means all of them, according to their families and their settlements.²

§ 6. THE PLAN OF THE WAR AND ITS BACKGROUND

Even though the scroll has no parallel in the Bible, the Apocrypha, the Pseudepigrapha, or the Midrash, yet descriptions of the war of the end of days and detailed descriptions of war in general are not lacking.³

It is interesting to note that in describing the war of the Sons of Levi, Judah, and Benjamin as taking place ' on the return of the exiles of the Sons of Light from the wilderness of the nations to encamp in the wilderness of Jerusalem ', and as a war against Belial and all gentiles, our scroll strongly resembles the description in Test. Dan v. After noting that the Sons of Dan will sin together with Levi and Judah (verse 7), its author goes on to say (verse 10) : ' And there shall arise unto you from the tribe of [Judah and of] Levi the salvation of the Lord ; and he shall make war against Belial. And execute an everlasting vengeance on your enemies.' ⁴

The names of the various enemies are given in greater detail in Test. Simeon vi, 3–4 : ' Then shall perish the seed of Canaan, and a remnant shall not be unto Amalek, and all the Cappadocians shall perish,⁵ and all the Kittim ⁶ shall be utterly destroyed. Then shall fail the land of Ham, and all the people shall perish.'

There is little doubt that the plan of the war on their return from exile, in these sources and even more so in DSW, is influenced by Isa. xi. The author of the scroll, who was definitely influenced by its content, thought, and style, was at the same time independent in elaborating the details which he wished to adapt to his period. Verse 11

---

¹ Cf. Gen. xxv, 6, and Maisler's article cited note 1, p. 28.

² For the ideas of the period about the territories of Ham and Japheth, see Jub. viii, 9, and Ant. I, vi. For the general principle of world domination, see Jub. xxxii, 18–19.

³ For the O.T., see especially Ez. xxxviii-xxxix, and cf. H. Z. Hirschberg, *Enc. Miqr.* I, 230–4 ; for the Pseudep. cf. Jub. xxxiv, 1–8, xxxvii–xxxviii ; Test. Judah iii–vii, ix ; for Midrash the *Midrash Wayyissa'u* and *Sefer ha-Yashar*. Cf. ch. 6, §§ 3, 6, ch. 7, § 5.

⁴ For Levi and Judah and the Messiah problem, see Y. Yadin, ' The DSS and the Epistle to the Hebrews,' *Aspects of the Dead Sea Scrolls* p. 49.

⁵ Om. Armen.

⁶ See note p. 24, n. 8.

onwards: 'And it shall come to pass in that day, that the Lord will set His hand again the second time to recover the remnant of His people, that shall remain from *Assyria*, and from *Egypt*, and from Pathros, and from Cush, and from *Elam*, and from Shinar, and from Hamath, and from the islands of the sea. And He will set up an ensign for the nations, and will assemble the dispersed of Israel, and gather together the scattered of Judah from the four corners of the earth. The envy also of Ephraim shall depart, and they that harass Judah shall be cut off . . . And they shall fly down upon the shoulder of the *Philistines* on the west; Together shall they spoil the *children of the east*; they shall *put forth their hand* upon *Edom* and *Moab*; and the children of Ammon shall obey them. And the Lord will utterly destroy the tongue of the Egyptian sea; and with His scorching wind will He shake His hand over the River, and will smite it into *seven streams*, and cause men to walk over dryshod. And there shall be a highway for the remnant of His people, that shall *remain from Assyria*; like as there was for Israel in the day that he came up out of the land of Egypt.'

The problem of the future war is discussed also in rabbinic literature which deals, though for different reasons, with the frontiers of Palestine according to the different sources, trying to define the areas which will be allotted to Israel with the coming of the Messiah. These discussions also shed light on the plan of the war and its various phases as mentioned in the scroll.[1] They start by discussing the frontiers as defined in the Covenant Between the Pieces (Gen. xv, 18–21) (cf. also Jub. xiv, 18). From the fact that Israel was only given the land of the seven nations while in this list ten are mentioned, the Rabbis conclude that 'the three, Kenite, Kenizzite, and Kadmonite were not given to them now . . . and their land will be inherited in times to come' (Gen. Rabba xliv end). Another statement runs: ' " When the Lord thy God shall enlarge thy border, as He hath promised thee " (Dt. xii, 20)—What is it He has promised thee ? These are the Kenite, the Kenizzite, and the Kadmonite' (Sifre Dt. lxxv, ed. Finkelstein, p. 139); 'Your fathers inherited a land of seven nations, but you will inherit a land of ten nations' (P.T. Qidd. i, 8, 61d, commenting on Dt. xxx, 5). These additional conquests belong to the Messianic Age (Gen. Rabba, loc. cit.).

These conquests must be undertaken only after the conquest of Palestine within the above frontiers, ' for it is written : " and ye shall dispossess nations greater and mightier than yourselves " (Dt. xi, 23)

---

[1] These matters are dealt with at length in *Enc. Talm.* II, 205 ff., in the framework of the article *Ereṣ Yisra'el*.

and afterwards, " Every place whereon the sole of your foot shall tread " (ib. 24), so that the Land of Israel be not defiled with their idols while you return and conquer outside Palestine, but when you have conquered Palestine you will be permitted to conquer outside Palestine ' (Sifre Dt. li, p. 116).[1]

Most interesting also in the light of DSW is the discussion as to the meaning of the *Kenite*, the *Kenizzite*, and the *Kadmonite* ; Rabbi Judah says : ' The Arabs, the Shalmaites, and the Nabataeans ' (P.T. Shebi. vi, 1 ; Qidd. i, 8, etc.). Rabbi Simeon says : ' Asia and Spain and Damascus ' (ib.). Rabbi Eliezer b. Jacob says : ' Asia, Carthage, and the Turks ' (ib.) ; Rabbi Judah the Prince says : ' Edom and Moab and the beginnings of the sons of Ammon ' (ib.) (based on Isa. xi, 14, see note to i, 1).

This discussion, indicating the tradition known to the Rabbis from an early period, to some extent explains the conception of the scroll. First of all Palestine must be conquered according to its frontiers, including the seven nations (this is a ' war of duty ' [2]) and in it the entire congregation will take part (cf. ' the seven nations of Vanity ', DSW xi, 8–9), and only afterwards, in the war of separate divisions, will they turn to the rest of the nations (of which the Kadmonite is one). The statements of the Rabbis confirm our earlier conclusion that all the nations mentioned in the third phase (including the sons of Aram) are outside the frontiers as defined in Gen. xv and the war against them is a ' war of free choice ' to extend the frontiers.[2]

§ 7. SUMMARY TABLE

The following table sums up the entire plan of the war ; the division of the forty years into sabbatical years and the years of

---

[1] It is interesting to note that R. Judah found no acceptance for his thesis that ' every place whereon the sole of your foot shall tread ' is a general statement, the meaning of which is defined by the particular statement ' from the wilderness . . . unto the hinder sea ', according to the fourth hermeneutical rule. Cf. P. T. Ḥallah 2, 1, and Maimonides, Code, Hilkhoth Melakhim v, 6.

[2] Maimonides, loc. cit. 5, 1 : ' A war of duty is that against the seven nations (of Canaan), that against Amalek, and that to save Israel from an aggressor. Afterwards he (the king) fights the war of free choice, i.e. a war with the remainder of the people in order to enlarge the frontiers of Israel and to increase its might and glory.' Cf. B. T. Sotah 44b : ' Raba said, All consider that Joshua's war of conquest was a war of duty and the wars of the house of David for extending their domain were wars of free choice.' For the direction of the war of separate divisions (which corresponds to the war of free choice) by ' the men of renown . . . and all the chiefs of the clans of the congregation ' (ii, 6–7) cf. Mishnah Sanhedrin ii, 4 : ' He (the king) leads the people to a war of free choice by the decision of the court of seventy-one ' ; cf. ib. i, 6. See further ch. 4, § 2.

fighting; the division into the war of the entire congregation and of the separate divisions; indication of the strategy of the separate divisions, and years assigned to each enemy:

Years	Sabbatical Years	Years of Fighting	War of entire Congr.	War of Separate Divisons	Phase One	Phase Two	Phase Three		
							Shem	Ham	Japheth
1–6		X	X		Lot of Darkness. Belial. Edom. Moab. Sons of Ammon. Pelesheth. Kittim of Asshur	Kittim in Egypt			
7	(1)X								
8		X		1			Aram Naharaim		
9		X		2			Sons of Lud		
10		X		3			Rest of Sons of Aram: Uz, Hul, Togar and Masha beyond Euphrates		
11–12		X		4–5			Sons of Arpakhshad		
13		X		6			Assyria, Persia, and the Kadmonite until the Great Wilderness		
14	(2)X								
15		X		7			,, ,,		
16		X		8			Sons of Elam		
17		X		9			Sons of Ishmael and Keturah		
18		X		10				X	
19		X		11				X	
20		X		12				X	
21	(3)X								
22		X		13				X	
23		X		14				X	
24		X		15				X	
25		X		16				X	
26		X		17				X	
27		X		18				X	
28	(4)X								
29		X		19				X	
30		X		20					X
31		X		21					X
32		X		22					X
33		X		23					X
34		X		24					X
35	(5)X								
36		X		25					X

Years	Sabbatical Years	Years of Fighting	War of entire Congr.	War of Separate Divisions	Phase One	Phase Two	Phase Three		
							Shem	Ham	Japheth
37		X		26					X
38		X		27					X
39		X		28					X
40		X		29					X
40	5	35	6	29	6	6	9	10	10

$$\begin{aligned}
\text{Total period of the war} &. \quad . \quad 40 = 40 \\
\text{Sabbatical years} &. \quad . \quad \left.\begin{array}{r}5\\35\end{array}\right\} = 40 \\
\text{Years of fighting} & \\
\text{War of entire congregation} &. \quad \left.\begin{array}{r}6\\29\end{array}\right\} = 35 + 5 = 40 \\
\text{War of separate divisions} & \\
\text{War of entire congregation} & \\
\text{(incl. sabbatical year)} &. \quad \left.\begin{array}{r}7\\33\end{array}\right\} = 40 \\
\text{War of separate divisions} & \\
\text{(incl. sabbatical years)} &
\end{aligned}$$

The Forty Years and the Seven Years.—In summing up this chapter some remarks are necessary on the two decisive numbers in the plan of war : (1) The duration of the war as a whole—forty years. (2) The war of the entire congregation against the principal enemies—seven years (including a sabbatical year).

The first number apparently derives from two conceptions which are in fact one. The sect compares the period of its sojourn in the wilderness with the forty years the Israelites wandered in the wilderness. This is the period before ' their return ' and their ' re-entry ' into the Land of Israel. This has considerable influence on their conduct and organization (cf. ch. 3, § 1).

The Children of Israel's forty years' wandering in the wilderness also served as the foundation for the various calculations attached to the statements of the Rabbis about the time of the Messiah.[1] The author's reasoning, that the war against the Sons of Darkness will last forty years, is influenced by the above two conceptions. The fixing of the seven years (including the sabbatical year) for the war of the entire congregation against the principal enemies, which does not mean the end of the war altogether, is partly influenced by Ezekiel's words [2] in reference to the war of Gog and Magog and partly by various traditions in which the number seven is mentioned in connexion with ' Messianic ' wars, and these are echoed in a number of statements of the Rabbis.[3]

---

[1] B. T. Sanh. 99a ; Midr. Shoḥar Ṭob p. 393 ; Pesiqta Rabbathi iv, 1 ; N. Wieder, JJS 4 (1953), 172, n. 6–7. This meaning of the number is perhaps hinted at CDC xx, 15. Also pPs xxxvii, frg. 1, l. 8.

[2] xxxix, 9.

[3] The conquest of Joshua lasted, according to Rabbinic tradition, seven years (cf. *Enc. Talm.* II, 202), and cf. B. T. Meg. 17b.

Chapter 3

THE BANNERS OF THE CONGREGATION AND ITS ORGANIZATION

§ 1. General

The author devotes Sections 5, 6, and 7 to the description of the congregation's banners (*signa*, אותות). The mass of information on this subject emphasizes the fact that the author not only draws his knowledge from the Bible, but is explaining a whole complicated system which was still employed or at least known at his time from written sources or oral tradition. This system does not of course contradict the Bible but is adapted to the practical needs of the congregation. Indirectly it sheds light on the organizational structure of the people as described in the Bible, or at least as the Bible was understood at the time of the scrolls.

It will be shown below that the military structure reflects that of the congregation as a sect which for various reasons strove to adapt its own organization to that of the tribes during their wandering in the wilderness. The conditions in which the sect lived while sojourning in the desert obliged it to adopt a military organization which enabled it to conduct its affairs with discipline. Moreover, the reintroduction of tribal organization clearly defined the tasks of the priests, the levites, and the lay leaders.

An additional reason for considering this structure suitable for its purposes was that the sect saw in its sojourn in the wilderness a time of transition corresponding to the forty years' sojourn of the Israelites in the desert, and, like the latter, preparatory to its own return which would follow the pattern of the first Conquest.[1]

This seems to me most important for understanding the nature of the organization; and while mainly expressing the aspiration to organize the entire Congregation of Israel in the future, it also reflects the organization of the sect at the time of the composition of the scroll.[2]

---

[1] See also N. Wieder, JJS 4 (1953), 171–2, 174.

[2] The main difference between the organization of the sect and that of the future congregation of Israel is that the use of the titles as given in Num. is as far as possible reserved for the future, restored, congregation. The exact replica of the organization described in Num. would be possible only at the End of Days, when the Two Anointed Ones will again be in the midst of Israel, and re-establish the organization of Num. Cf. Yadin, JBL 78 (1959), 238 ff.

Even though the military organization of Israel until its settlement in Canaan is described several times in the Bible, the description of the 'banners' and their inscriptions in the scroll are in fact based on two places in Num. :

(1) Num. ii, 2, the only place where the banners are mentioned in connexion with the organization of the congregation: 'The children of Israel shall pitch by their fathers' houses; every man with his own standard,[1] according to the banners; a good way off shall they pitch round about the tent of meeting.' This description recurs several times in various forms in Num., though without mention of the 'banners'.

(2) The description of the system of the inscriptions on the 'rods' of the princes of the tribes: 'Speak unto the children of Israel, and take of them rods, one for each fathers' house, of all their princes according to their fathers' houses, twelve rods; thou shalt write every man's name upon his rod. And thou shalt write Aaron's name upon the rod of Levi, for there shall be one rod for the head of their fathers' houses' (Num. xvii, 17–18 [A.V. 2–3]). 'And the Lord said unto Moses: Put back the rod of Aaron before the testimony, to be kept there, for a token against the rebellious children; that there may be made an end of their murmurings against Me, that they die not' (ib. 25 [10]).

These two descriptions form the basis of the system of the banners and their inscriptions in the scroll. Before analysing the scroll sections under discussion one further point must be elucidated. Corresponding with the description of the 'plan of the war' (see ch. 1) and the numerous descriptions in Num., in the scroll also the military structure of the congregation as a whole is divided into two basic parts: (a) 'The host of service' (Num. viii, 25), which mainly consists of the families of the tribe of Levi also organized on military lines for their tasks: (b) The 'host of battle' (cf. Num. xxxi, 21), consisting of the rest of the congregation—in its militia organization—in accordance with their duties in war. Since the host of service accompanies the congregation to the war in order to fulfil its special tasks (see ch. 5), its organization (and the system of its banners and inscriptions) is founded on the same principles which characterize the structure of the congregation. The author divides his exposition into three parts.

(1) Section 5 describes the basic inscriptions on the banners, the banners of the congregation (list 1) and of the tribe of Levi (list 2) separately.

[1] In the O.T. and in DSW *degel*, as also in Rabb. literature, always denotes a unit, not a flag. See further p. 62, n. 2, below. For 'banner' (*oth*) in various sources, see end of this chapter.

(2) Section 6 describes the additional and changing inscriptions on the banners of the Levites (list 3) and of the general congregation (list 4) in accordance with the phases of the war: going out, advance, and return.

(3) Section 7. The measurements of the different banners (list 5); this chapter ends with the inscriptions on the shield of the Prince (list 6).

Only lists 3 and 4 are complete, the bottom pages of the others having been destroyed. However, by minute analysis and comparison of the lists (helped by some fragments of words and letters at the margins of the missing parts) they can be acceptably restored and a complete picture of the system obtained.

§ 2. THE BANNERS AND THEIR INSCRIPTIONS (LIST 1)

The heading of this list is: 'Disposition of the banners of the whole congregation according to their groupings' (iii, 12). The term 'according to their groupings' must, I think, be understood to mean 'their hosts', Num. i, 52,[1] that is to say, the banners of the congregation in accordance with the 'grouping' of the units and their military duty.

The military organization of a congregation consisting of tribes and families, and founded on a militia basis, must fulfil the following demands: (1) Full identity of 'conscription units' and 'tribal units'. This identity is especially vital in the higher ranks, for the heads of tribes and 'fathers of the congregation' are responsible for the primary selection of combatants from their tribes (see ch. 4, §§ 2 and 5). (2) The permanent organization, within the tribal conscription units, of sub-units whose structure and number must agree more or less with the structure of the combat units. (3) A flexible structure of combat units enabling the sub-units mentioned to merge into them if need arises.[2]

As will be seen, the list of units described in this *serekh* deals not only with the tribal or combat structure but also with the units as such in accordance with their tribal and military composition and answers all these demands. The term מסורות is also mentioned in the list of trumpets (iii, 3, and see ch. 5, § 4 (2)). Here also the inscription proves

---

[1] Parallel ii, 17 (for *yadh* = banner, cf. ch. 5, note 3, p. 100); ibid. 34.

[2] As we shall see, countries which base their army on a militia principle and endeavour to preserve regional or tribal traditions in it, such as Switzerland or the British Territorial Army, are still faced by similar problems.

BANNERS OF THE CONGREGATION AND ITS ORGANIZATION 41

that the *serekh*[1] consists of the מְסוּרוֹת, i.e. the militia formations of the congregation. In my opinion this assumption is strengthened in the light of the various uses of the term, the fundamental meaning of which is the act of 'tying' and 'joining', which both in Hebrew and other languages serves as the basis for many terms denoting military units.[2] This fact stands out also in list 4, which speaks of the 'banner of the first one', the 'banner of the second one', etc., and not the 'first banner', etc., i.e. the 'banner of the first grouping', the 'banner of the second grouping', etc.

Table 1 makes clear the system of the banners and the division of the congregation into groupings. This table consists of lists 1, 2, and 5, which complement each other in the destroyed parts of the pages.[3] Fortunately, at the end of list 5 the name of the banner of the smallest grouping, the 'banner of a ten', is preserved (iv, 17). This enables us to complete with certainty lists 1 and 5, which follow the list of groupings of the families of Levi, which is fully preserved. This completion is confirmed by the fragments of the inscriptions on the 'banner of the thousand' in list 1.[3]

List 4 supplies additional terms for the various groupings. List 5 deals with the basic inscriptions of the banners of the congregation, which change in accordance with the three principal phases of action. In the list under discussion I included apart from the inscriptions of the first phase (on going out to war) which also denotes the kind of unit,[4] the inscriptions of the two other phases showing the *phase*: 'inscriptions of battle' 'inscriptions of thanksgiving and prayer'.

It seems to me that for various reasons list 4 (in contrast to list 3 [5])

---

[1] On *serekh* as a general term and as designation of a comprehensive unit, see ch. 7, § 2 (5).

[2] With regard to DSD x, 4, Burrows, *apud* Brownlee, *Manual*, has already noted the connexion of the word with the action of tying together. Its use in DSW is perhaps influenced by Nu. xxxi, 3–5, and may even contribute to the interpretation of that difficult passage. In connexion with the mobilization of selected units for the war against Midian, v. 5 states: '*way-yimmāsĕrū* (A.V. so there were delivered) out of the thousands of Israel, a thousand of every tribe, etc.' The verb is in LXX ἐξηρίθμησαν, in Vulg. *dederunt*, in Tg. O. 'there were chosen'. In the light of DSW it appears that it denotes the process of 'grouping' the warriors of each tribe into units of one thousand. Cant. Rabba 20a makes it denote the conscripted soldiers as opposed to the volunteers: possibly it knew of *msr* as a term for forming military units in conscription. Cf. also Midr. Tanḥuma, Maṭṭoth iv (cp. p. 168, n. 4). See Z. Ben-Ḥayyim in *Aspects of the Dead Sea Scrolls* p. 211.

[3] For detailed justification of the restorations, see commentary.

[4] Note that on leaving home the units march in order of their militia formation, not in battle formations, i.e. battalions and formations. These are formed up only in the vicinity of the battlefield, after their establishment is 'filled' (v, 3), cf. ch. 7, § 5.

[5] See below, on the families of Levi.

must be understood as denoting the changing inscriptions on the banners of the groupings mentioned in lists 1 and 5, i.e. of the *congregation* (and not of the families of Levi or of 'one camp' or of 'formations', etc.). The following are the main reasons :

(1) The heading of this list reads : 'The disposition of the banners of the *congregation on going out to war*' (or 'on advancing' or 'on returning'); compare the heading of lists 1 and 2, 'All the congregation', which includes both the families of Levi and the rest of the congregation.

(2) The total number of inscriptions (and groupings) mentioned in each phase is eight—this number is in exact accordance with the number of the types of units in lists 1 and 5.

(3) The inscriptions for the phase of 'going out to war' are parallel in their *content* with the list of the units mentioned in lists 1 and 5 (congregation, camp, tribe, etc.), i.e. they denote the various ranks of units and not the number of units of equal rank (e.g. eight battalions or eight families, etc.) as in the list of the changing inscriptions of the families of Levi.

(4) The list of the inscriptions in Table 5 ends with the sentence : 'And they shall write their names in full according to their whole disposition.' This sentence shows that, in contrast to the short changing inscription, no change occurs in that part of the inscription which enumerates the names of the people belonging to each grouping. These inscriptions have been enumerated in list 1 and the author does not therefore repeat them here but contents himself with the sentence mentioned above.[1]

§ 3. The 'Banner of the Whole Congregation'

The use of the word *'edhah* for the community of the tribes of Israel is very frequent in the Pent. (esp. in Num.), Joshua, and Judges and bears this meaning—as in similar compounds frequently mentioned in the Bible—in DSW in the sections under discussion and in sections 3 and 4.[2]

---

[1] This sentence recurs several times in varying forms : iv, 6 ; iv, 7 ; iv, 8 ; iv, 12–13. Its meaning clearly is : the inscription with detailed and explicit enumeration of names, e.g. 'Nethaneel the son of Zuar, prince of Issachar' (Nu. vii, 18), with the subordinate officers or the men of the unit of ten in order of precedence, etc. This sense of *pērūsh*, e.g. CDC ii, 9, 13 (see commentary on xi. 7–8) ; iv, 5–6, and cf. ib. iv, 8 ; xiv, 17–18 ; xvi, 2 ; and Charles, Apoc. II, 804 ; Rabin, *ZD*. p. 8. Same use also Tg.J. Num. ii, 3.

[2] 'Fathers of the congregation,' ii, 1, 3, 7 ; iii, 4 ; 'Prince of all the c.', v. 1 ; and see ii, 9 ; iii, 2, 11, and ch. 2, ch. 5, § 4; ch. 8, § 3.

THE BANNERS AND UNITS OF THE WHOLE CONGREGATION

List 1.	The Source. List 5.	List 4.*	Ordinal number of the unit acc. to List 4.	Name of the 'banner' and the grouping acc. to List 1.	The basic inscription acc. to List 1.	Name of the banner acc. to List 5.	The changing inscriptions on the banners of the groupings† of the congregation in the various phases of the war (List 4).			Length of banners in cubits (List 5).
							When they go to battle	When they close in for battle	When they return from battle	
iii 12–13	iv 15	iv 9	First	'The large banner at the head of all the people'	'People of God'; 'and the names Israel and Aaron as well as the names of the twelve t[ribes of Israel], acc. to their order of birth'	'Banner of the whole congregation'	'Congregation of God'	'Battle of God'	'Deliverance of God'	'Fourteen'
iii 13–14	iv 15	iv 9	Second	'Banners of the heads of the camps of the three tribes'	[?]	'Banner of the th[ree tribes]'	'Camps of God'	'Vengeance of God'	'Victory of God'	'[thir]teen'
ii 14–15	iv 16	iv 9	Third	'Banner of the tribe'	'Ensign of God'; 'and the name of the prince of the tr[ibe and the names of the princes]' of its fa[milies]'	'[Banner of the tribe]'	'Tribes of God'	'Struggle of God'	'Help of God'	'twelve'
iii 15	iv 16	iv 10	Fourth	[Banner of the myriad]	'[ ] [and th]e name of the prince of the myriad and the names of the commanders of [his thousands]'	'Banner of the myriad'	'Families of God'	'Retribution of God'	'Support of God'	'ele[ven]'
iii 15–16	iv 16	iv 10	Fifth	[Banner of the thousand]	'[ ] [and the name of the commander of the thousand and the names of the commanders] of his hundreds'	'[Banner of the thousand]'	'Battalions of God'	'Strength of God'	'Joy of God'	[ten]
iii 16–17	iv 16	iv 10	Sixth	[Banner of the hundred]	'[ ] [and the name of the commander of the hundred and the names of the commanders of his tens]'	'[Banner of the hundred]'	'Assembly of God'	'Retaliation of God'	'Thanksgivings to God'	[nine]
iii 17–18	iv 17	iv 10–11	Seventh	[Banner of the fifty]	'[ ] [and the name of the commander of the fifty and the names of the commanders of his tens]'	'[Banner of the fifty]'	'Those summoned by God'	'Might of God'	'Praise of God'	[eight]
iii 18	iv 17	iv 11	Eighth	[Banner of the ten]	'[ ] [and the name of the commander of the ten and the names of the nine men in his charge]'	'Banner of the ten'	'Hosts of God'	'Annihilation by God upon all nations of vanity'	'Peace of God'	[seven]

* Only for the phase of going to battle.

† At the end of the list is written: 'And they shall write their names in full according to their whole disposition' i.e. the inscription repeats that of list 1.

The inscription 'congregation of God' on the banner of the congregation on going out to war is of the same structure as all other inscriptions [1] and corresponds to the Biblical 'congregation of Yahweh'.[2] It is, however, obvious that the terms 'congregation' and 'congregation of God' served to denote the sect itself along with its other names.[3] In stressing that this banner is 'the large one which is at the head of the whole people' (its length is 14 cubits), or 'the banner of the whole congregation' (iv, 15), similarly by its inscription 'people of God', the author means that this is the banner of the *whole* congregation both of the host of service and the host of war, in contrast to the rest of the banners of the congregation and of the families of Levi.[4] Here the term *'am* (as also in the descriptions of the battle, viii, 9; see ch. 5, § 8, and in i, 5), marks, as in the O.T., the military character of the congregation organized for war.[5]

Some scholars have already noted that the term 'people of God' also occurs in the official title of Simeon the Maccabee.[6]

The fixed inscription on the 'banner of the congregation' is 'Israel', 'Aaron', and the 'names of the twelve tribes of Israel in the order of their birth'.[7] The names of the twelve tribes compose the fixed inscription which does not change in all the phases as proved by the sentence which ends the inscriptions in list 4.

The text of this inscription is directly influenced by the account of the inscriptions on the shoulder pieces of the ephod in Ex. xxviii, 9-10: 'And thou shalt take two onyx stones, and grave on them the

---

[1] Cf. § 8 below.

[2] Num. xxvii, 17; xxxi, 16; Josh. xxii, 16-17. On the other hand, *'ădhath ēl*, Ps. lxxxii, 1, differs in meaning, and has been correctly adapted by our author in i, 11; cf. p. 230, n. 1.

[3] E.g. DSD v, 20; CDC vii, 20; x, 4. Cf. Barthelemy, RB 59 (1952), 204–5. For the various designations of the community, see ch. 7, § 2 (5).

[4] Similarly Lev. x, 6; Num. i, 18 (see, however, ibid. 47), etc. The Prince is of 'all the congregation' (v.l). In iv, 9, where the tribe of Levi is excluded, it is 'the congregation' without 'all'.

[5] Cf. C. Umhau Wolf, 'Terminology of Israel Tribal Organizations,' JBL 65 (1946), 45, and ibid. for Acc. *ummānu* and Ar. *'amm*. Similar use in Ju. as, a (for which cf. 2 Sam. xiv, 13). The *'am ēl* of DSW corresponds to the O.T. *'am Yahweh*. Num. xi, 29; xvii, 6; Ju. v, 11; 1 Sam. ii, 24; 2 Sam. i, 12, etc.

[6] Ἐπὶ Σίμωνος τοῦ ἀρχιερέως ενασαραμελ (א V; ἐν Σαραμελ A), 1 Macc. xiv, 27–8. Abel, *Livres Macc.* p. 256, note, maintains the rendering 'high priest in the court of the people of God' (*ḥăṣar 'am ēl*). Flusser, *Yedi'oth* 17 (5713), 32, n. 12, interprets it as *śar 'am ēl*, equivalent to ἐθνάρχης, ib. 47. However, of the three titles mentioned there, *śar 'am ēl* fits rather the military title στρατηγός, while 'ethnarch' would be *nĕśi' hā-'ām*. Perhaps the title should be read ενα(σι)σαραμελ = *nāśi', śar 'am ēl*, so that the title in 27 corresponds to all *three* titles in 47.

[7] For 'Israel and Aaron', and 'Israel, Levi, and Aaron' v. 1, see ch. 10.

names of the children of Israel : six of their names on the one stone, and the names of the six that remain on the other stone, *according to their birth*'[1] and also by the description of the stones on the breastplate (ib. 21) : '. . . everyone according to his name, they shall be for the twelve tribes.' The inscription on the banner of the congregation : ' Israel,' ' Aaron ' and underneath the names of the twelve tribes also brings to mind the continuation of the description of the shoulder pieces of the ephod (verse 12) : ' And thou shalt put the two stones upon the shoulder-pieces of the ephod, to be stones of memorial for the children of Israel ; and Aaron shall bear their names before the Lord upon his two shoulders for a memorial.'

A certain difficulty arises in determining which twelve tribes are written on the ' banner of the whole congregation '. For several reasons it seems that here is meant the list of tribes as enumerated in Num., ' The whole of the congregation of the children of Israel ', including Ephraim and Manasseh and excluding Levi, and not the list of the sons of Jacob[2] nor the list of the names of the tribes in Ezek. xlviii, 31, etc. The main arguments for this are :

(1) If the author had meant the sons of Jacob, he would hardly have used the rather ambiguous phrase ' Tribes of Israel '.[3]

(2) The description of the structure of the congregation and their banners in the scroll is based upon Num., which excludes Levi from the twelve tribes and at the same time stresses the identity of and difference between Levi and Aaron. Not only is the description of the banners of the congregation divided into two : the banners of the tribes and the banners of the families of Levi, and amongst those the priesthood and the rest of the families of Levi are kept apart, but also Levi's name is mentioned *outside* the list of the twelve tribes.[4]

(3) The banners of the heads of the camps of the three tribes are based on the organization of the camps of the three tribes in Num. ii.

All this shows that the organization of the tribes of Israel according to their banners and their hosts which the author has in mind, is the

---

[1] Cf. also Ant. III, vii, 5.

[2] For list of tribes in Apocr. and Pseudep., see Charles, *Book of Jubilees* p. 170, note ; for the O.T., Noth, *Das System der Zwölf Stämme Israels* (1930), and the excellent comparative table by Bennet in Hastings, *D.B.* iv, 811.

[3] Where the city-gates are called after the tribes, including Levi and Joseph, but excluding Ephraim and Manasseh.

[4] On the banner of the whole congregation, the name Aaron covers also Levi, in keeping with Nu. xvii, 18, while on the shield (?) of the Prince of the Whole Congregation both names appear, followed by ' the twelve tribes of Israel ' (cf. also Ant. IV, iv, 2). The difference is no doubt intentional, cf. p. 44, n. 7.

organization enumerated in its essentials in Num., i.e. the twelve tribes (including Ephraim and Manasseh), the tribe of Levi being outside the count. With regard to the order of the tribes, except for stressing 'in the order of their birth' (which excludes a geographical arrangement) the author does not indicate their exact order.[1]

§ 4. The Banners of the Heads of the Camps of the Three Tribes

In this formula the author alludes to the organization of the tribes in camp and on the march as described in Num. ii,[2] to distinguish it from the meaning of the word 'camp' as used by the sect in referring to their settlements. His desire to avoid ambiguity is shown also in the name of the banner in list 5 in which the word 'camp' is omitted; 'banner of the th[ree tribes]' and similarly in the plural 'banners', 'camps', and not 'banner of the camp' corresponding to 'banner of the tribe', etc.

According to Num. the tribes are divided into camps as follows:[3]

Camp of Judah.	Camp of Reuben.	Camp of Ephraim.	Camp of Dan.
Judah	Reuben	Ephraim	Dan
Issachar	Simeon	Manasseh	Asher
Zebulun	Gad	Benjamin	Naphtali

According to Num. the camps had no separate leaders, the prince of the tribe after whom the camp was called serving, apparently, in both functions. Unfortunately the basic inscription in list 1 is not preserved and we cannot therefore know exactly the 'whole list of their names in full' of the banner of the camp. However, the fact that every camp possessed its own banner, the inscription as well as the measure of which differed from that of the tribe, enables us to assume that the author considered the 'chief of the camp'[4] to be different from the prince of any tribe. Also it must be noted that while the banners in

---

[1] For the different orders, see literature quoted p. 45, n. 2.

[2] At first glance it might be thought that 'of the three tribes' refers to 'the sons of Levi, Judah, and Benjamin' mentioned i, 2. However, the whole system of banners etc., as well as the separate mention of Levi, shows that four camps of three tribes each are meant, as in Num.

[3] On the habit of the sons of Jacob to go to war three at a time, see Jub. xxxviii and the corresponding passages in the Midrashim. In Pseudo-Philo (ed. L. Cohn, p. 288) we find a division into three groups of four sons each. Cohn draws attention, ad loc., to the four groups of three each in the parallel passage in the book of Jasher.

[4] In the letter to Joshua b. Galgola from Wadi Murabbaʿat, he is styled רוש המחניה, cf. de Vaux, RB 60 (1953), 270; M. Habermann, Haareṣ 18, ix, 1953 (who reads rēsh, the Aram. form); Ginsberg, BASOR 131 (Oct. 1953), 26.

BANNERS OF THE CONGREGATION AND ITS ORGANIZATION 47

lists 1 and 5 are always related to the unit itself (even though the name of its leader is written at the top) yet in this case he expressly mentions the ' banners of the chiefs of the camps '.

The division into four camps at the head of which stand four chiefs each of whom rules over three tribes (which in their turn are divided into thousands, etc.), corresponds exactly to the description of the stars and of the heavenly host, and the chiefs who *rule over the four seasons* and the months, in Enoch.[1]

In DSW as in the Bible the term ' camp ' serves to denote the military grouping as a description of the whole fighting force in the field, as well as the place of encampment in the field.[2] Since this usage of the term ' camp ' came to be the most suitable for the *settlements of the sect* [3]—who lived under military discipline and at times in field conditions—it seems that the term ' *chiefs of the camps* ' was used by the sect along with the names for other officials in the camps.[4]

The basic inscription on the banners of the heads of the camps can be completed : ' [and his name and the names of the princes of his tribes] '. As in the rest of the ' basic ' inscriptions (and according to the size of the gap) it may be assumed that it was short—consisting of two words—and the same on the banners of all four chiefs of the camps.

It is most interesting to compare the system of the scroll with that described in Tg.J. (e.g. for the banner of the camp of Judah) : ' And its banner was of fine wool in three colours as against the three precious stones on the *ḥoshen* : red and green and emerald colour, and on it were in full (מפרש) engraved the names of the three tribes Judah, Issachar, and Zebulun and in the middle was written : let God rise and may thy enemies be scattered and thy opponents flee from before thee, and on it was depicted a young lion.' [5] This description has only two points

---

[1] In particular lxxxii, 9–15, a chapter which in its original form seems to have contained many terms typical for the scrolls ; cf. Aalen, *Licht und Finsternis* p. 160 ff., and see ch. 8, § 3 (1).

[2] iii, 4 ; vii, 1 (cf. ch. 7, § 3 (1)) ; vii, 7 (cf. ch. 4, § 3) ; xiv, 2 ; vi, 9 (cf. ch. 7, § 6). In the O.T. : Gen. xxxi, 7–8 ; Ex. xxxii, 26 ; Num. i, 52 ; Dt. xxiii, 10–15 ; Ju. vii, 19 ; 1 Sam. xvii, 1 ; Ps. xxvii, 3, etc. Cf. Ahiram inscr. line 3. Also in the Zkr inscr., e.g. line 5. Cf. παρεμβολή in Macc. and LXX in both meanings, and see Abel, *Maccabees* p. 52, note.

[3] CDC vii, 6 ; xii, 22 ; xiii, 4, 7 ; xiv, 3, 8–9 ; xix, 2–3 ; xiii, 20, 13. *Qumran I*, p. 110, ii, 15.

[4] Cf. ' the camp prefects ', vii, 1.

[5] The banners of the other camps differ in colour, names, emblem, and text. The latter are, for Reuben, ' Hear O Israel, the Lord our God is one God ' ; for Ephraim, ' The cloud of the Lord is above them by day to shield the camp ' ; for Dan, ' Dwell again, O Lord, in thy glory amidst the myriads of thousands of Israel '. Cf. also p. 105, n. 3, and M. M. Kasher in *Talpioth* 4 (1949–50), 690

in common with the system of the scroll: the writing of the names of the three tribes and the writing of a 'slogan' on the banner. On the other hand the differences are great:

    (1) No banner for the *head of the camp*.
    (2) The *basic* inscription differs for every camp.
    (3) The inscription is very long.[1]
    (4) The inscriptions do not change.
    (5) Addition of the colours and the emblem.
    (6) Omission of indication of measurements.

§ 5. THE BANNER OF THE TRIBE

The banner of the third grouping is the 'banner of the tribe'; it is twelve cubits long.[2] Its inscription is based upon the same principles: 'slogan' (for the religious ceremonies) and a permanent inscription indicating the nature of the grouping with its sub-groupings, the name of its leader and the names of the subordinate officers. The head of the tribe is called prince (נשיא).[3] The term in this meaning is again taken from the organization in Num.[4] and is identical with the titles of the head of the entire congregation and the heads of the families. For the purpose of summoning the *princes* there are special trumpets on which the inscription is 'Princes of God'.[5] The basic 'slogan' on the banner of the tribe is 'ensign (נס) of God'. This usage is most interesting since this inscription, like the inscriptions of the other groupings, must also denote the character of the grouping in question; since they already used the term 'tribe' on the inscription of this grouping, on going out to war (list 4), therefore—except for repeating the same term—they had the choice of writing '*maṭṭeh*', this being the term most frequently found in Num. to denote the tribe. The reason for not doing so seems to be that the phrase 'מטה אל' would in fact have had a different meaning, since it meant the 'rod of God' used by Moses.[6] The use of the word 'ensign' (*nes*) admirably

---

[1] It is interesting that part of these inscriptions appears in our scroll upon the trumpets.

[2] Is it accidental that the 12 cubits correspond to the 12 tribes?

[3] For the spelling of the word, see commentary.

[4] ii; vii, 2, 18; xxxiv, 18, 25. In their present form, these verses might create the impression that the princes of the congregation were the same as the commanders of thousands. In the light of the scroll, however, this identification must be rejected. For Nu. x, 4, see ch. 5, § 4 (2, 3); for the other passages § 6 below. For the 'princes', cf. Noth, *System etc.*, pp. 151, 156, 162, and V.d. Ploeg, 'Les chefs du peuple d'Israel et leurs titres,' RB 57 (1950), 47 ff.

[5] Cf. ch. 5, § 4 (2, 3).

[6] Dt. iv, 20, xvii, 9.

BANNERS OF THE CONGREGATION AND ITS ORGANIZATION   49

solved the difficulty. It is parallel to the two terms for 'tribe' and synonymous with the word *oth*, which has like it the two meanings of 'banner' and 'omen'.[1]

As with the 'banners of the chiefs of the camps', the tradition in the Midrash about the banners of the princes of the tribes is completely different from the scroll.[2]

§ 6. The Family, the Myriad, the Thousand, and the Battalion

The definition of the banners of these groupings constitutes in the scroll, as we shall see, the most important contribution towards an understanding of the complicated problem of the connexion between the tribal structure and its division into 'families' and 'clans' and the conscription units which every tribe must organize. The difficulty in understanding the connexion between the different units arises from the treble terminology existing with every nation whose army is based on a system of militia organization. This terminology at times uses the names for the tribes and its subdivisions as terms for the units conscribed from it and vice versa. Likewise the above terms may be used (especially in a poetical style) to denote the actual combat units.

A comparison of the names of the groupings, their banners and the inscriptions on the latter (Table 1) clearly shows that the conscription unit which was formed from the 'family' (the main subdivision of the tribe) is the 'myriad'. The myriad is composed of 'thousands' formed by the subdivisions of the family. The myriad is not mentioned at all amongst the names of the combat units in the descriptions of battle in the scroll, a fact which confirms that the myriad is a conscription unit and not identical with a corresponding tactical unit bearing a similar name. On the other hand, the inscription '*degalim* of God' (list 4) on the banner of the thousands denotes that the point of intersection in the military organization between the conscription units and the combat units was just at this level. The *degel* served as a common denominator for both a conscription and a combat unit. This assumption is fully confirmed also by an analysis of the names of the combat

---

[1] Cf. Tur-Sinai, JQR 39 (1948–9), 367, and Num. xxi, 8; Ex. xvii, 15.

[2] Cf. Num. Rabba ii, 6 : 'With banners —each prince had a sign consisting of a cloth, the colour of each cloth corresponding to the precious stones on Aaron's breastplate. From these the heathen kingdoms have learnt to make cloth banners with special colours to each banner. The colour of the cloth of each tribal prince corresponded to that of its stone : Reuben had a sardius ; his cloth was red and its emblem mandrakes . . . hence it is said of the banners that they were signs for each prince.'

units and the ways of making up the combat 'formations' in the battle descriptions in the scroll.[1] In other words, if the '*degel*' constitutes the largest *permanent* tactical-organizational unit, then the 'myriad' cannot be considered a tactical permanent unit, but a formation or grouping uniting all combatants of a family. It has to supply the soldiers needed for replacing the losses of the *degel*. This method, which results from organizational and tactical considerations and the desire to create *esprit de corps*, was almost the only current system in all armies (including the Roman army), until the present day.[2]

A re-examination of the O.T. sources in the light of the conclusions derived from the description in the scroll shows that this conception is not artificial, but was derived from that of the Biblical texts. On the other hand, the value of the scroll lies in the fact that it clearly shows the connexion between the treble terminology, while the Bible sometimes has to describe the basic organizational structure of the congregation, sometimes the military structure, and at times the battle-formation, very often doing so in a metaphorical and picturesque style.

This may account for the fact that most contemporary scholars came to a conclusion different from that of the scroll. A survey of the principal researches on this subject from the beginning of this century shows that the identification of the 'family' with the 'thousand' passes through them like a purple thread and is the one most widely accepted.

B. Luther in his study on the structure of the tribes of Israel was first amongst the scholars of this century to arrive at this conclusion, though he added that decisive proof for it was lacking.[3] Similarly, Ed. Meyer took the thousand to be the unit identical with the family, and the myriad with the tribe.[4] Lods,[5] Wolf,[6] Barrois,[7] Van der

---

[1] Cf. v, 3. See further ch. 7, § 4-5, also ch. 4, § 2-3, and p. 62, n. 2.

[2] In the Roman army the cohort was the largest tactical and administrative unit which was as far as possible left intact, while legions were made up by varying combinations of cohorts. In accounts of battles the participating cohorts are enumerated as well as the legions. In today's armies—especially in militia armies—the battalion is the permanent unit, while higher groupings, though their names are fixed, often change their constituent battalions. In this way the fighting morale of the unit is preserved and the administrative basis of the army safeguarded.

[3] 'Die israel. Stämme,' ZATW 21 (1901), 6: 'Es liegt nahe zu glauben dass beide identisch sind, aber strikt beweisen lässt es sich nicht.'

[4] *Die Israeliten und ihre Nachbarstämme* (1906), p. 503.

[5] *Israel* (1930), p. 223.

[6] 'Terminology of Israel Tribal Organization,' JBL 65 (1946).

[7] *Manuel d'archéologie biblique*, II, 37 (1953).

Ploeg,[1] Albright, and others [2] followed them. Now, the clear distinction which the scroll establishes between the various groupings necessitates a re-examination of the Biblical texts on which these scholars based their views.

The book of Joshua clearly shows the system of the division of the congregation for mustering into tribes, families, and 'clans'.[3] In such a muster there is no place for the myriad and the thousand. The system does not deal with conscription and therefore only gives the division into families, etc. There are numerous references to this in the O.T.[4] Yet in the war between Israel and Benjamin described in Judges xx, which also throws interesting light on the organization of supplies in battle and the percentage of soldiers who were engaged in this service, we find the description of a parallel system, i.e. the military conscriptional organization most similar to the system of the scroll. The tribes of Israel are facing the problem that the engagement is likely to be drawn out, making it necessary to organize supplies. 'And all the people arose as one man, saying: We will not *any of us turn into his house*. But now this is the thing which we will do to Gibeah: we will go up against it by lot; and we will take *ten* men of a *hundred* throughout all the tribes of Israel, and a *hundred* of a *thousand*, and a *thousand* out of *ten thousand*, to fetch victuals for the people' (Ju. xx, 8–10). This description makes no mention of the clans and families, for the army was already mobilized for battle and organized in military groupings. A comparison of the three sources gives the following result:[5]

	Joshua	Judges		Scroll
The permanent tribal organization and the military conscription units	Tribe	Tribe	Tribe	Tribe (ensign of God)
	Family	Ten thousand	Family	Myriad
	Clan	Thousand		degel/thousand
The sub-division of the thousand	Men by men	Hundred Ten	Congreg. of God Those summoned by God Hosts of God	Hundred Fifty Ten

[1] 'Les chefs, etc.' RB 67 (1950), 48, on Nu. x, 4.

[2] Petrie, *Egypt and Israel* (1923), proposes a rather different scheme, designed to account for the large numbers in the Pent., but which does not fit the O.T. terminology, cf. also Albright, 'The Administrative Divisions of Israel and Judah,' JPOS 5 (1925), 20, n. 10; and J. Guttmann, *Enc. Miqr.* I, 141. For the

The identity of the myriad with the family (and not with the tribe) is also brought out by the analysis of the lists of the musterings of the children of Israel during their wanderings in the wilderness.¹ These lists contain two important pieces of information bearing on the examination of this problem: the number of combatants, and the families in accordance with their tribal affinities.

The following Table proves that in most cases the numbers of families in each tribe is identical with the number of the myriads.²

	Numbers 'able to go forth to War'		Number of Families	
	Num. i	Num. xxvi	Num. xxvi	Various Sources
Reuben	46,500	43,730	4	4 (Exod. vi) 4 (1 Chr. v)
Simeon	59,300	22,200 (!)	5	6 (Exod. vi) 5 (1 Chr. iv)
Gad	45,650	40,500	7	4 (1 Chr. v)
Judah	74,600	76,500	2 + 3 + 2 = 7	Cf. 1 Chr. ii, iv
Issachar	54,400	64,300	4	4 (1 Chr. vii)
Zebulun	57,400	60,500	3	
Ephraim	40,500	32,500	1 + 3	
Manasseh	32,200	52,700 (!)	6 (+ 2)	Cf. also Josh. vii
Benjamin	35,400	45,600	5 + 2	3 (1 Chr. vii) 5 (ib. viii)
Dan	62,700	64,400	List incomplete	
Asher	41,500	53,400	3 + 2	4/5 (1 Chr. vii)
Naphtali	53,400	45,400	4	4 (1 Chr. vii)

In fact we see that the conception of the scroll, which identifies the family with the myriad and the clan with the thousand and the *degel*, and fixes the point of intersection between the tribal, conscriptional,

---

alluf in relation to the *elef*, see Cassuto and Torczyner, *Enc. Miqr.* I, 332–3.

³ Josh. vii, 14.

⁴ E.g. Ju. xviii, 19; 1 Sam. ix, 21; x, 21; Gen. xxiv, 38; Nu. ii, 34.

⁵ For the subdivisions of the 'thousand', see below.

¹ We are not concerned here with the correctness or date of these figures. Cf. J. Guttmann in *Enc. Miqr.* I, 139.

² The number of combatants in each tribe is clear (though varying with the lists), which cannot be said of the numbers of families. I have used only passages where the number of families is clearly marked. If my suggestion is accepted, it may be feasible to get the right numbers of families also in places where it is not clear. The 'myriad' was the conscription unit to be provided by the family, hence the 'strength' of the family might well be larger, since a certain number would always fall away for the various causes of exemption (cf. ch. 4, § 5, and Ant. VII, xiii, 1).

and tactical units at the level of the thousand, derives from the author's understanding of the scriptural data.

This is not the place to review all the O.T. information on the subject; however, it seems to me that it not only confirms the picture given above, but that with the aid of the clear and detailed arrangement in the scroll we can explain a number of apparently unintelligible passages.[1]

§ 7. The 'Banners' of the Families of Levi (Lists 2 and 3)

Before passing on to an examination of the division into thousands,

---

[1] In particular 1 Chron. v, 23–6; vii; xii. These lists enumerate the tribes and families according to households, and include the census lists for mobilization purposes. In them the title 'mighty men of valour' is given to the chiefs of the households, the highest rank in the tribal division, who often served *ex officio* as commanders of the thousands. Instructive are v, 24; vii, 4, 7, 11. In vii, 40, the words 'chiefs of the princes' must be excised. For the connexion between banners and households, Nu. ii, 2, 34, are of interest. Most scholars who identify the Thousand with the Family rely, *inter alia*, on Ju. vi, 15 : 'Behold my thousand (A.V. 'family') is the poorest in Manasseh and I am the least in my household,' as proof that the 'Household' (our 'clan') is a part of the Thousand, and since the Household is also part of the Family, the latter = the Thousand. I would suggest that just this verse proves that the Household = the Thousand. Gideon's argument is twofold : (1) that it would be absurd for the weakest Thousand to go to war ; (2) that it would be impossible for Gideon, the least of the Household, to command it, this being the prerogative of the chief of the Household. Thus the two clauses are parallel and stress the connexion between the Thousand, as the military unit drawn from the Household, and the Chief of the Household, its commander. For the connexion between Household and Thousand, see also 1 Sam. xvii, 17–18, which shows that David's three brothers served under one chief of thousand, as well as 2 Chr. xvii, 14; xxv, 5 : the latter especially demonstrates that the Household = Thousand was the point at which tribal and military organization interlocked. Cf. also E. Junge, *Der Wiederaufbau des Heerwesens des Reiches Juda unter Josia* (1937) p. 54 ff., and ch. 4 below. The plural, 'thousands,' figuratively denotes the totality of the army, as in 1 Sam. x, 19 ; xxiii, 23. This figurative use seems to apply in some passages in Nu. and Josh. where the 'Princes of the Tribes' appear to be identical with the Chiefs of Thousands, e.g. Nu. i, 15. In other cases, e.g. Nu. x, 4, a comma must be inserted between 'Princes' and 'Chiefs of Thousands', cf. ch. 5, § 4 (2, 3). Instructive in this respect is Josh. xxii, 14, a difficult verse on either view : 'And with him ten princes, of each household (A.V. 'chief house') a prince for all the tribes of Israel ; and each one *was* an head of their household for the thousands of Israel.' The 'princes' were, according to context, heads of tribes, and the double designation is illogical. In vs. 30, 'and the princes of the congregation and the heads of the thousands of Israel,' the distinction corresponds to that in the Scroll. It shows that Phineas's mission included not only chiefs of tribes, but the latter had taken with them the commanders of the principal military units, the Thousands, which thus corresponded to the Households. Perhaps we ought to read vs. 14 as follows : 'And with him ten princes ⟨of each household⟩, a prince to each of the tribes of Israel, and each one [with] the heads of their households for the thousands of Israel.'

hundreds, fifties, and tens and its relation to the structure of the sect, we have to consider the organization of the families of Levi and their banners [1] and to sum up the system of inscriptions on the banners of the congregation.

After the author has enumerated the banners of the congregation, he goes on to enumerate the banners of the families of Levi and their sub-units in accordance with the military organization of the host of service and of war.

The end of this list is complete; it describes the banners and inscriptions of the sub-units (thousands, hundreds, fifties, and tens); its beginning is defective. Had not the inscription on the banner of Merari (iv, 1) been preserved we would have been in the dark with regard to all matters concerning the banners of the tribe of Levi.

The inscription runs as follows: ' Upon the banner of Merari they shall write: " Heave-offering of God " and the name of the prince of Merari and the names of the commanders of his thousands.' This proves that the formula of the inscriptions on the banners of the families of Levi exactly resembles that of the banners of the congregation:

(1) A slogan indicating the character of the grouping.
(2) The name of the leader of the grouping.
(3) The names of the heads of the sub-groupings under his command.

The text on the inscription on the banner of Merari, as well as the custom of enumerating the families of Levi separately after the other tribes, come from Num. ii–iv. For Merari in particular, see Num. iii, 35. With the help of verses 23 and 30 the list of the banners of the families of Levi can be completed by adding the Gershonites and the Kohathites, though their basic inscriptions cannot be known.[2] Nor is it possible to know whether the order of their banners followed the geneological order: Gershon, Kohath, and Merari,[3] or the order of their importance (which puts Kohath before Gershon).[4]

---

[1] For the *degel*, cf. ch. 7, § 4; for the form רבוא, see comm. on iii, 15.

[2] I do not know why Nu. xviii, 6, 8, 24 (said of all Levites), is here applied specially to Merari; cf., however, Test. Levi xi, 2–7.

[3] Gen. xlvi, 11; Ex. vi, 16; Nu. iii, 17; xxvi, 57; 1 Chr. v, 27; xxiii, 6, etc. Cf. also Test. Levi iii, 2, 4, 7.

[4] Nu. iv, 2, 22, 29; Josh. xxi, 1–8, 10, 20, 27; 1 Chr. vi, 42 ff. (we are not concerned with the arrangement in 1 Chr. xv, 5–7; 2 Chr. xxix, 12, which puts Merari before Gershon, since in DSW Merari comes last, anyway). Cf. Num. Rabba iv, 11: ' of all Levites none are as important as the sons of Kohath, who include both priests and Levites . . . hence they are counted first.'

The list of the sub-units: 'And on the banner of the thousand' (iv, 1), etc., follows immediately on the 'banners of Merari' and does not, I think, refer only to Merari, but constitutes the list of the sub-division of every family, whose inscriptions were uniform (except for different lists of names). This assumption is based on the fact that the enumeration of these inscriptions takes up four complete lines. Thus we would have required c. eight lines for the two other families, while in the missing part of page iii there appears to be room for four lines at the most.[1]

The principal problem which arises with regard to the banners of the families of Levi is whether there was a special banner for the tribe of Levi and three other banners, one for each family (i.e. the priests, the sons of Aaron being included in the family of Kohath together with the 'sons of Kohath the Levites') or were these *four* banners: the sons of Aaron (priests), Kohath, Gershon, and Merari (Levites)? In my opinion it can be assumed almost with certainty that the latter was the system described in the scroll. The following are the main reasons:

(*a*) The division of the tribe of Levi into priests and levites serves as the basis of the whole organization of the tribe as explained in Num.

(*b*) The Dead Sea Sect lays great stress on this division in ceremonial matters.[2]

(*c*) The fourfold division of the tribe of Levi is the one described in Num. iii in connexion with the camps of the families of Levi round the tabernacle. Gershon to the west, Kohath to the south, Merari to the north, Aaron and his sons to the east.[3] This fourfold division is also used in several other places.[4]

(*d*) The list of the inscriptions which change according to the phases of the war (list 3) which appears immediately after the enumeration of the banners of the families of Levi and which must be referred to the banners of Levi,[5] demands a fourfold division of the families of the

---

[1] See commentary ad loc., and below.

[2] iii, 1-2; vii, 9, 13; xiii, 1; xv, 4; xviii, 5; DSD i, 21; ii, 1, 4, and in particular ii, 19-21; CDC x, 5; xiii, 2-6, and particularly xiv, 3-7. Cf. also *Qumran I*, p. 110, i, 22-3.

[3] Cf. Num. Rabba iii, 12: 'Kohath was granted that his sons should flank the sanctuary on two sides; thus the tribe of Levi was divided into four sections so as to surround the sanctuary on four sides, corresponding to the four standards, etc.' Cf. ib. iv, 7.

[4] Cf., e.g., Josh. xxi, 4-7; CDC x, 5: 'four of the tribe of Levi and Aaron.'

[5] While list 4 has a special heading, list 3 carries on without break.

tribe of Levi for the following reasons: there are four changing inscriptions; in contrast to list 4 which mentions the 'first banner', the 'second banner', etc., and corresponds to the groupings of the congregation proceeding from the larger to the smaller (see above), List 3 does not mention the 'first banner', etc., and applies to a horizontal division into four units of equal rank and not to a vertical graded division. This assumption is confirmed by the fact that a vertical division of the families of Levi would have required at least five or six inscriptions (tribe, family, thousand, hundred, fifty, ten). Similarly the character of the inscriptions of the *phase of going out to war*, 'Truth of God,' 'Justice of God,' 'Glory of God,' 'Judgment of God,' which does not differentiate between the kinds of units—as do the banners for the corresponding phase in the disposition of the banners of the congregation—points to groupings of equal rank. These inscriptions can be substituted for the short inscription 'Heave-offering of God', etc., which is on the banner of the family, but not for the long inscriptions on the banners of the thousand, the hundred, etc. These long inscriptions, as well as their clearly war-like character, prove that the inscriptions on the banner of the sub-groupings of the families of Levi, enumerated in list 2, do not change during the phases of the war.

The above reasons seem to me to indicate that the author describes four banners of the families of Levi: the sons of Aaron, Kohath, Gershon, Merari. The division of the above inscriptions, which does not differentiate the four banners according to rank, rules out a special banner for the tribe of Levi as a whole; the banner of the sons of Aaron served at the same time also as the banner of the tribe of Levi.

We have already mentioned (see n. 4, p. 45) Num. xvii, 18. Here it must be added that the list of the princes of the families of Levi in Num. iii (which influenced the system of inscriptions on the banners of the families of the levites under discussion) ends with the sentence (verse 32): 'Eleazar the son of Aaron the priest being prince of the princes of the Levites.'[1]

The above conclusions and the system of the structure of the banners of the tribe of Levi and their inscriptions can be summarized as follows:[2]

---

[1] Cf. Büchler, *Die Priester und der Cultus* (1895), p. 90.

[2] The list of the names of the commander and his subordinates recurs, of course, on the banners of each unit in the various phases.

Group-ing	Basic inscriptions	On going out to war	On going into battle	On return from battle
Sons of Aaron (Priests)	—	'Truth of God'	'Right hand of God'	'Exalt God'
Kohath	[...¹of God and the name of the prince of Kohath and the names of the commanders of his thousands]	'Justice of God'	'Appointed time of God'	'Magnify God'
Gershon	[...¹of God and the name of the prince of Gershon and the names of the commanders of his thousands]	'Glory of God'	'Panic sent by God'	'Praise of God'
Merari	'"Heave-offering of God" and the name of the prince of Merari and the names of the commanders of his thousands'	'Judgment of God'	'The slain by the hand of God'	'Glory of God'

Thousand	.	'Anger of God in wrath against Belial and all men of his lot without remnant.' 'And the name of the commander of the thousand and the names of the commanders of his hundreds.'
Hundred	.	'Hundred of God, a hand of battle against all unjust flesh.' 'And the name of the commander of the hundred and the names of the commanders of his tens.'
Fifty	.	'Ceased is the existence of the wicked by the might of God.' 'And the name of the commander of the fifty and the names of the commanders of his tens.'
Ten	.	'Rejoicings of God upon the ten-stringed lyre.' 'And the name of the commander of ten and the names of the nine men in his charge.'

§ 8. SUMMARY OF THE SYSTEM OF THE BANNERS

1. *The Congregation*

(a) The groupings of the entire congregation, the families of the tribe of Levi, and their subordinate units possess banners.

(b) The banners of the congregation are of eight types (omitting the families of Levi): congregation, camp, tribe, family/myriad, thousand/battalion, hundred, fifty, ten.

(c) The length of the banners varies, the largest, that of the entire congregation, being 14 cubits, down to the banner of the ten, which

---

¹ A lacuna sufficient for one word.

is 7 cubits. Their width is not mentioned so it must be assumed that they were all equally wide.

(d) The inscription on every banner consists of a short slogan denoting the kind of grouping, the name of its leader and those of his subordinates.

(e) The banner of each type (the banners of the twelve tribes, four camps, etc.) resembles its companions in all features except the difference in the names.

(f) The *slogan inscription* changes with the three phases of war (going to war; going into battle; return) to denote the character of the phase. On going to war: indication of the division of the groupings according to their military tribal affinity, which was necessary for maintaining the order of the units on the march. During the fighting: hortatory inscription, noting that it is a War of God and that with His help they will be victorious. On the return: thanksgiving for the victory.[1]

2. *The Families of Levi*

The system of the banners of the families of Levi differs from the above in a number of details due to the special features, duties, and organization of the levites.

(a) Every family has its own banner, apparently all of equal size, with a different basic inscription.

(b) The system of the inscription ' the disposition of the enumeration of the names of the commanders ' resembles that of the congregation.

(c) The corresponding sub-units in each family have the same inscriptions. They are rather lengthy inscriptions, of a clearly war-like character, resembling several of the inscriptions on the trumpets and the javelins, and indirectly indicate the kind of unit.[2] These inscriptions do not change during the different phases of the war.

(d) The slogan inscription on the banners of the families change

---

[1] Cf. further comm. ad loc. Perhaps the system of short legends changing with phases of the war derives from the custom of giving out passwords to units in battle (e.g. Ju. vii, 18, 20). Several scholars have pointed out the resemblance between our slogans and the συνθήματα which Judas Maccabaeus gave out, e.g. θεοῦ βοηθείαι (2 Macc. viii, 23), cf. אל ישועות iv, 13; or θεοῦ νίκη (xiii, 15), cf. אל נצח ibid. Cf. Dupont-Sommer, *Aperçus* p. 102; M. Ari Yonah, IEJ 2 (1952), 3. 2 Macc., of course, does not mention banners. Cf.

perhaps also the short songs of the Levites on each day of the week, Tamid vii, 4.

[2] E.g. אף for the אלף; מאת אל for the מאה; נבל עשור on the banner of ten. The connexion between חדל מעמד רשעים בגבורת אל and the unit of fifty is explained rather unconvincingly by P. R. Weis, JQR 41 (1950–1), 149, n. 79, as acrostic or *gematria*; see also Brownlee, BA 14 (1951), 70. For the relation between the banner legends to those of the trumpets and javelins, cf. ch. 5, § 7, and ch. 6, § 9.

with the phases, like the banners of the congregation but with one basic difference: the inscriptions of the phase of going to war do not indicate the nature of the grouping (superfluous since the number of the families is limited) but the justification of the war aim. The character of the inscriptions of the phases of fighting and return resemble those of the congregation except for different wording.[1]

(e) The part dealing with the measurements of the banners of the families of Levi is not preserved (bottom of col. iv), though it seems that their measurements resembled those of the corresponding grouping of the congregation.[2]

(f) The banner of the ten has the names of the nine subordinates of its commander. The corresponding part of list 1 (the banners of the congregation) is not preserved, but it may be assumed that the same principle applied also to the banner of the non-levite ten.

According to this system the names of all the members of the congregation were written on the various banners. This is an important conclusion in the light of the descriptions of the ceremonies of the sect enumerated in other scrolls (see below).

§ 9. The Organization into 'Thousands, Hundreds, Fifties, and Tens' and the Sect

This division set out in the scroll for military and administrative purposes within the tribal units is interesting because of the light it sheds on the customs of the sect, though it makes no special contribution to the problem of dating. This division corresponds perfectly to the 'reorganization' attributed in Ex. xviii to Jethro,[3] for the needs of administration and justice, which is repeated (though at times in a shortened form) in texts belonging to all periods of the Bible whether for the purpose of administration or military organization.[4]

When Judas Maccabaeus put his army on a regular footing, he divided it into thousands, hundreds, fifties, and tens.[5] Josephus in describing the organization of his own army, on the Roman pattern, actually uses those very terms.[6]

---

[1] See note 1, page 58.

[2] It is, however, unlikely that the Levite banner of ten was longer than 14 cubits or their banner of the family smaller than 7.

[3] Ex. xviii, 21; cf. ib. 25, and Ant. III, iv, 1 (where the ten is excised by some).

[4] Shortened versions in Dt. i, 15; Nu. xxxi, 14, 48, 52; 1 Sam. viii, 12 (see, however, the versions); 2 Sam. xviii, 1, 4. Cf. also 1 Sam. xxix, 2; 1 Chr. xxvi, 26; xxvii, 1; xxix, 6; 2 Chr. i, 2; xxv, 5.

[5] 1 Macc. 3, 55. Josephus, Ant. XII, vii, 3, stresses that Judas' armies were organized τὸν ἀρχαῖον τρόπον καὶ πάτριον.

[6] Wars II, xx, 7.

On the other hand there is much of interest in the description of the organization of the Scrolls Sect and its ceremonies as described in the other scrolls. A comparison of these sources with the detailed description of the banners of the congregation (including the priests and levites), their inscriptions, and especially the custom of writing the names of all the congregation on the banners, proves that this system was in fact customary in the everyday life of the sect. Hence we know that the descriptions in DSW are based on the practice of the sect on the one hand and on its interpretation of the O.T. descriptions on the other.

CDC (xii, 22–23 ; xiii, 1–2) : ' And this is the order of the meeting of [the camps]. They that walk [1] in these during the epoch of wickedness until there shall arise the [Messiah] of Aaron and Israel,[2] shall be groups of ten men as the minimum, by thousands and hundreds [3] and fifties and tens.' That is to say the sect is organized during the Epoch of Wickedness exactly like those military units whose banners are described in DSW.[4]

Furthermore, the holding of musterings of the members of the sect and the writing of their names according to their divisions are expressly noted in CDC (xiv, 3 ff.) : ' And the order of the meeting of all camps. *They shall be mustered all of them by names*, the [priests] first, the Levites second, the children of Israel third and the proselyte fourth ; and they shall be written down [by name] each man after his brother : the priests first, the Levites second, the children of Israel third, and the proselyte fourth. And *so they shall sit*, and so they shall be asked about everything.' Similarly in DSD (v, 23 ff.) : ' And he shall write them in order each man before his fellow, according to his intellect and his deeds, each one to obey his fellow, the lower to the higher, and that they should muster their spirit and their deeds year by year, to advance each man according to his intellect and the perfection of his way, or to demote him according to his sinfulness.'

The above descriptions, though they establish that the organization of the sect in its settlements closely resembled the military organization of the congregation in DSW, still do not prove that the sect also used the banners described above. This we may perhaps conclude from a passage of DSD which shows that in the different ceremonies and musterings of the sect its members were grouped and marched

---

[1] A re-examination of the photographs has convinced me that חמתחלכים is the right reading ; cf. Rabin ad loc.

[2] Cf. ch. 10.

[3] מאיות, cf. commentary.

[4] Cf. Dupont-Sommer, *Aperçus* p. 76.

BANNERS OF THE CONGREGATION AND ITS ORGANIZATION

according to the above groupings (DSD ii, 19 ff.) [1] ' Thus it shall be done every year all the days of the dominion of Belial : the priests shall pass first in order [2] according to their spirits one after the other, and the Levites shall pass after them, and the whole people shall pass third in order one after the other in thousands and hundreds and fifties and tens so that each man of Israel shall know [3] his place of standing [4] in the community of God for eternal council. And let no man be lowered from his place of standing nor rise from the place allotted to him,[5] for all shall be in a community of truth.'

In this kind of mustering and marching past, in which the members of the sect are arranged and march according to groupings whose banners are described in DSW, there is much occasion for using such banners. Parallel to the military usage of the banners in parades and in battle (e.g. the Roman army) it may be assumed that the banners were set up on the parade-ground before the start of the parade according to a fixed order. The inscriptions on them, which showed the type of grouping,[6] the names of its commanders, and the names of the members of the sect belonging to it, enabled everyone to find his exact place when called to muster. The names of the members of the sect on the banners also enabled everyone to discover the place and position of his fellow in the ' community of God '. It is also easy to imagine the role of the various trumpets in this kind of parade, and especially the non-combat trumpets.[7]

§ 10. THE BANNERS IN OTHER ARMIES

In concluding this chapter we must compare the description of the banners in the scroll with their use in war in the various armies during

---

[1] Cf. Brownlee, *Manual* p. 11 and Appendix G, p. 53.

[2] DSW v, 4, shows clearly that military order is meant, not 'spiritual rank' (Brownlee, l.c., n. 20). Cf. ch. 7, § 2 (5).

[3] So v.d. Ploeg, *Le manuel etc.*; not, as Brownlee has it, ' according to the knowledge of every man . . .'

[4] For this term, cf. ch. 8, § 3 ; ch. 7, § 2 (3).

[5] Cf. ch. 4, § 4 (3). For the yearly assembly, see also Brownlee, ' Light on the Manual of Discipline from the Book of Jubilees,' BASOR 123 (Oct. 1951), 30.

[6] V.d. Ploeg, ' *Quelques traductions*, etc.,' BO 9 (1952), 122 ff., considers all this mere figurative speech to indicate the totality of the sect, but gives no further evidence than that it must have been unpractical to organize on this basis.

[7] Cf. ch. 5, § 4. Their part in the mustering may account for the order in which they are enumerated in iii, 2-4. It may be assumed that ' calling the congregation ' was the ' attention ' signal ; ' calling the commanders ' the signal for the various officers to take up position next to their respective banners ; while the ' trumpets of the formations ' gave the signal for each man to take his prescribed position behind his banner and his officer. This is the present-day practice in all armies, by whatever means the signals are given.

the period of the scrolls. In spite of the fact that the custom of carrying banners in battle (though not necessarily with a clearly military organizational aim) is very old and was widespread amongst all the peoples of the orient,[1] it must be noted that apart from Num. ii, 2 : ' Every man with his own standard according to the ensigns,' there is in the O.T. no mention of the use of ' banners ' in the armies of Israel [2] for organizational and military purposes. Neither do the Books of the Maccabees mention banners in the Hasmonean armies, nor do we possess much information about their use in the armies of Alexander and his successors.[3]

The facts do not of course force one to conclude that in those armies

---

[1] For Egypt, cf. R. O. Faulkner, ' Egyptian Military Standards,' JEA 27 (1941), 12 ff. Here, from early times, banners served both for identification and as means of maintaining *esprit de corps*. Perhaps the custom of inscribing on them names of gods indicates that their first use was to symbolize the presence of the god with the army in battle. For Assyria, see Meissner, *Assyrien und Babylonien* I (1920), p. 93 ; Galling, *Bibl. Reallexikon* p. 160 s.v. *Feldzeichen*.

[2] On *nes* cf. § 5 above, and the article by Tur-Sinai cited on p. 49, n. 1. Cf. also Bea, *Biblica* 21 (1940), 196, n. 1. Already the ancient versions (LXX, Vulg.) understood the *othoth* in Num. as *signa*, cf. also p. 49, n. 2 for the Midrash. Some scholars still mantained that *degel* in the O.T. is ' flag ', e.g. Galling, loc. cit. ; Delcor, *Midrash d'Habacuc* (1951), p. 31 ; Rowley, *Ephem. Theol. Lovanienses* 28 (1952), 273. Yet both the ancient versions and the Rabbis always took the *degel* to be a military unit ; in LXX it is mostly τάγμα ' unit drawn up in military order' (cf. ch. 7 § 2 (5) and p. 150 n. 4) in the Vulg. various terms of this general meaning, in the Targums *ṭēqas* or *ṭiqsā* (cf. ch. 7, § 2 (5), p. 149, n. 2).

In Num. Rabba xv ' *dega'im* is nothing but armies ' ; Midr. Tehillim xx end ' each one recognizes his *degel* through its *signum* ', i.e. his unit through its banner (cf. ch. 5 § 6, and p. 100, n. 3 there) ; Num. R. ii, 2, ' when they saw that they (the angels) were arrayed in *degalim*, they began to long for the *degalim* and said,

would that we were arrayed in *degalim* like them.' Cf. further, p. 168, n. 4.

This meaning of *degel* is absolutely clear in the Elephantine Papyri, where these units are named after their commanders, just as in DSW.

The word cannot be taken in this sense in Cant. ii, 4 : ודגלו עלי אהבה, nor has any convincing interpretation with the meaning ' flag ' been found. The renderings in the ancient versions are mere guesses. Ben-Yehudah (II, 889) rightly rejects ' flag ', but his ' admiration ', based on Acc. *diglu* ' cynosure ' (Bezold : *Augenziel*) equally fails to convince. The Midrashic interpretations take resort to transpositions or *gematria*.

I would suggest reading רגלו ' his leg ', corresponding to ' his left hand ' and ' his right hand ' in vs. 6, and to transpose the clauses :

' He brought me to the banqueting house
　He stayed me with flagons (rd. סמכני)
　He comforted me with apples (rd. רפדני)
　For I *was* sick of love.
His left hand *was* under my head,
　While his right hand embraced me,
　And his leg was over me *in* love.'

Confusion of *resh* and *daleth* is common in both the ancient Hebrew script and the square script (see commentary on v. 13). The Sam. Heb. reads Gen. xlix, 10, *dĕgālāw* for *raglāw* ; for the same confusion see also p. 167, n. 1. cf. Yadin, IEJ 7 (1957), 66 ff.

[3] Cf. Kromayer-Veith, p. 132, who point out that in an army fighting in a close phalanx there was little need for signa. Cf. ib. p. 133, n. 1 ; and see p. 63, n. 6 below.

BANNERS OF THE CONGREGATION AND ITS ORGANIZATION 63

or in the Hasmonean armies banners were not used, but they do at any rate prove that they did not occupy such an important place in the systems of military organization and fighting. The position is totally different with regard to the Roman army. The banners (*signa*) occupied a most important position in the whole system of signals and arrangement of units in battle,[1] and since every unit possessed its own banner, their numbers in these armies were very large.[2] Even though their primary purpose was for signalling, and during the marshalling of the forces and in the thick of battle they also served as means of identification and rallying points for the soldiers of the different units,[3] they became in course of time an object of worship.[4] It is therefore natural that a member of the sect, where the system of the banners played such an important role, when remarking on the negative qualities of the Kittim condemned them not for *employing* banners, but for *sacrificing* to them.[5]

Dupont-Sommer was the first who saw in this detail a clear pointer to the Romans, and in fact this has remained, in spite of several attempts to disprove it,[6] one of the most important points of support for his identification of the Kittim with the Romans. In spite of what has been said above it cannot be assumed that the Israelite army in the time of the Second Temple (and certainly not the sect) borrowed the use of banners as such from the Roman army. It appears that the development of the use of banners in Israel and in Rome went along different and opposite lines: in the Roman army the use of banners at the outset was mainly for military and tactical purposes and in the end it changed into an object of worship and religious adoration,[7] while in Israel (and similarly in several other eastern nations) the process was probably reversed. From the general use of the word *oth* in the O.T. one learns that in ancient times the banner was clearly connected

---

[1] See p. 98, n. 4 and p. 100, n. 3. Cf. Marquardt, Index, under *signum, signifier*; Kromayer-Veith, pp. 277, 323, 402 ff., 518. Note that Roman *signa* bore both the name of the Emperor and of the unit.

[2] Pompeius, whose army numbered c. 117 cohorts, lost at Pharsalus 180 *signa*. Antonius lost 60 *signa* on an occasion when he had only 22 cohorts. Cf. Kromayer-Veith, p. 404.

[3] Cf. note 1 above, and see Midr. Tehillim xx at end: 'each one recognizes his unit (*degel*) through its *signum*'; P. T. Sotah viii, 3: 'And troubled the host of the Egyptians (Ex. xiv, 24), he stunned them and confused them, and caused their *signa* to fall down.'

[4] Cf. Kromayer-Veith, p. 404, and see note 6 below.

[5] DSH vi, 3–5. N. Wieder, JJS 4 (1953), 14 ff., suggests this is a corrupt borrowing from the Targum ad loc.

[6] Cf. Dupont-Sommer's reply to his critics in *The Jewish Sect* p. 20 ff.

[7] Cf. also Wars III, vii, 2, and especially VI, vi, 1.

with religious and magical concepts [1] while the system described in the scroll denotes the end of this development and the point when the banners actually changed into instruments of military and organizational technique.[2] The strong disgust felt by the members of the sect for the custom of adoration of the banners and weapons amongst the Kittim [3] clearly shows that it must not be concluded from the character of the inscriptions on the banners of the congregation (the repeated use of 'God' in all the inscriptions) that the actual banners served as hallowed objects. They were (in addition to their regular tasks in battle and in organization) a means of encouraging the combatants by keeping before the eyes of the warriors the fighting slogans whose principal aim was (in the instance under discussion) to show that the war of the Sons of Light was a 'war of God' and that the soldiers of the congregation are the 'chosen ones of God' and His hosts.

On the other hand one must face the fact that this system of banners in the final development described in the scroll—a banner for every single unit according to the needs of battle—closely resembles the system of the military banners in the Roman army.[4] It is likely that the influence of this system on the banners of the army of Israel was not in the use of banners in itself but in the increase in their number and their adaptation to the needs of battle which arose from the multiplication of independent and tactical units. The Roman system of warfare, i.e. the employment of units with tactical intervals, as against the Hellenistic phalanx which acted as one, caused the Romans to develop and extend the system of banners and to allot a banner to every sub-unit. The transition in Israel's army from the earlier systems of warfare required an extension of the system of banners.[5]

It is unlikely that the system of banners described in the scroll is an entirely artificial creation of the author or the sect. As in other military fields, it appears that the system of banners represents in principle the practice of the Judean army of the time as adapted to the special needs of the sect and its organization.

---

[1] Cf. Tur-Sinai's article cited, p. 49, n. 1, and see next note.

[2] See on all this the instructive article by Rostovtzeff, 'Vexillum and Victory,' JRom.St. 32 (1942), 92–106.

[3] DSH vi, 3–5. N. Wieder, JJS 4 (1953), 14 ff., suggests this is a corrupt borrowing from the Targum ad loc.

[4] See p. 98, n. 4, and p. 100, note 3. Cf. Marquardt, Index under *signum*, *signifier*; Kromayer-Veith, pp. 277, 323, 402 ff., 518. Note that Roman *signa* bore both the name of the Emperor and of the unit.

[5] Cf. ch. 7, § 2 (4), and p. 62, note 3.

Chapter 4

THE LAW OF CONSCRIPTION

§ 1. General Remarks

Having dealt with the relation between the normal (tribal) organization of the congregation and its military structure we now come to the rules and system of conscription as applied in the war of the entire congregation and the war of the divisions.

Though the descriptions of the scroll are in partial agreement with Biblical and Rabbinic sources, it is especially interesting to note the difference in several important aspects, due perhaps to the sect's structure and ideology.

§ 2. Conscription for the War of the Entire Congregation

It has been shown in the first chapter that the descriptions of battles in those parts of the scroll which are preserved do not deal with the war of the divisions against the remote enemies but describe the war of the whole congregation against the principal enemies led by the 'Kittim', the 'seven nations of vanity' (xi, 8–9) who dwell within the boundaries of the Land of Israel as defined in Gen. xv, 18.[1]

It is evident that the war of the entire congregation against its principal enemies is a 'war of commandment'[2] (or duty)[3] according to Rabbinic definition, while the war of the divisions for the purpose of extending the frontiers is a 'war of free choice'.[4] This distinction must be kept in mind while analysing the laws of conscription in the scroll.

The conscription of an army organized on a militia structure in an emergency and disbanded at its end is a complicated matter, requiring even in our day a territorial or tribal organization which can speedily set up complete units ready for battle and not just mobilize combatants. This problem was dealt with in ch. 3, §§ 1, 6. This system has always required organizational decentralization and devolution of the burden of conscription in its early stages, and before assembling the military formations, on the tribal and local authorities. On the other hand, in order to prevent discontent arising from inequality in local conscription

---

[1] See also ch. 2.
[2] M. Sotah viii, 7.
[3] Ib. and T. Sotah 7, 24, and cf. P. T. Sotah viii, end.
[4] Cf. ch. 2, § 6, and n. 2, p. 35.

laws and in order to ensure complete agreement for tactical purposes [1] between the age composition and the classes of soldiers mobilized, this system requires a strong central legislative authority with means to supervise impartially all phases of the mobilization. This system must also apportion the authority for exemption from service between the local and central authorities, having regard to the various causes of exemption : [2]

(*a*) Some of these causes can be discovered only *before* battle (e.g. faint-heartedness).[3]

(*b*) Some are not permanent, being liable to change at the very last moment.

(*c*) Some of those exempted from active service must serve behind the lines.[4]

Hence also the places for exemption : the home-town, frontier, or battlefield. Accordingly the men going out to war were divided into three groups (M. Sot. viii, 2–4) : ' Of them some go out and return, some go out and do not return, and some do not go out at all ' (Tos. Sot. vii, 23). These Rabbinic rules are of course based on the laws of conscription and exemption in Dt. xx, 2–9 ; xxiv, 5.

The scroll subdivides the laws of conscription and exemption into :

(*a*) Those derived from Deut. xx.

(*b*) Those connected with the ' purity of the camp '.

Already in examining the various laws contained in the first group we come across an interesting phenomenon. The beginning of the ' prayer for the appointed time of war ', which is a survey of the laws of warfare in the Bible, points out that the congregation ' in going out to war ' observes those laws (x, 1–8)—mentions their main points : (1) the purity of the camp ; (2) the speech of the Priest before battle ; (3) the words of the officers ; (4) the law of sounding the trumpets.

Though the words of the Priest are given in full (' Hear O Israel ', etc., lines 3 ff., cf. ch. 8, § 5) the scroll leaves out the important first part of the officers' speech : ' What man is there that hath built a new house, and hath not dedicated it ? ', etc. (vs. 5–7), and only supplies

---

[1] With reference to the cavalry (vi, 11) the Scroll specifies ' five hundred from each tribe ', thus extending the militia and quota system also to that branch ; this further strengthens the impression that we have here a war of the whole congregation.

[2] On the procedure of applying for exemption, cf. P. T. Sotah viii, 9, 23a.

[3] ' He cannot endure the joinings in battle (see note p. 167, n. 6, below) or bear to see a drawn sword ' (R. Akiba, M. Sotah viii, 5) ; cf. also ch. 7, § 5, and p. 168, n. 4.

[4] Cf. M. Sotah viii, 4, and Tos. Sotah vii, 23.

an abridged form of the officers' speech relating to the 'fearful and faint-hearted'.

Dt. xx	DSW x
(8) And the officers shall speak further unto the people, and they shall say: What man is there that is fearful and faint-hearted? let him go, and return unto his house, lest his brethren's heart melt as his heart.	(5) 'And our provosts shall speak to all those prepared for battle, the willing-hearted, to hold fast through the might of God and to turn back all the faint-hearted, and to hold fast together with mighty men of valour.'

This omission is hardly accidental. It seems capable of three explanations :

(a) *The Character of the Sect*

It may be assumed that the law concerning exemption on account of having ' built a new house or planted a vineyard ' had no practical application to the sect since its members lived together in camps without private property. The same applies to the law exempting one ' that hath betrothed a wife ' since members of the sect did not marry.

Yet there are two reasons which should make us hesitate to accept this explanation. (1) At least some members of the sect married, as we know from CDC (vii, 6–7 = xix, 2–3) and from the exploration of the cemetery at Khirbet Qumran ; this would have required mention of him ' that hath betrothed a wife '. Similarly, for ' him who hath built a house ' or ' planted a vineyard ', cp. CDC xii, 8–11. (2) The description deals with the laws of the war of all the tribes of Israel and not with the members of the sect alone. The laws according to which the Sons of Light are to fight must be in agreement with those of the Bible and it is therefore unlikely that a law specifically set out—applying to the general congregation—be omitted in the literature of a sect which is so particular in the fulfilment of the commandments of the Pentateuch as they stand. An additional argument may be found in the fact that the scroll deals subsequently with laws forbidding women to be present in the military camps. Thus we know that the laws of conscription recognize the ' existence ' of women of the sect or of Israel in general.

(b) *War of Duty*

The war of the entire congregation can be defined as a ' War of Duty ' (מלחמת מצוה, מלחמת חובה), if we assume that the author followed the existing custom which finds its expression in the Rabbinic tradition : ' In a war of duty all go out, even a bridegroom from his chamber and a bride from her bridal canopy,'[1] i.e. there was no exemption for him who has built a house, or planted a vineyard or betrothed a wife. However, this explanation also presents several difficulties: (1) The speech of the officers about the return of the 'faint-hearted'; according to the Rabbis every one must go forth in a War of Duty, including the faint-hearted. (2) The scroll exempts women even from non-combatant service and forbids the disabled to go to war. If we explain the omission of the laws of exemption of him who builds a house, etc., as due to their obligation to serve in a War of Duty, we are forced to conclude that these laws did not apply to the faint-hearted, women, and disabled even in a War of Duty, contrary to Rabbinic rulings.

On the other hand, if we disregard for the moment the problem of the women and disabled, it may be that the scroll differentiates between two types of exemption, for economic and social reasons on the one hand (which do not exempt from fighting), and for the faint-hearted on the other (who are at least exempted from active service). The Rabbis, even though they include the faint-hearted amongst those obliged to fight in a War of Duty, clearly distinguish between the two types and stress that the reason for exempting the faint-hearted is purely military (as defined in the Pentateuch: 'Lest his brethren's heart melt as his heart') since the flight of the faint-hearted is likely to cause the flight of all the combatants.[2] Moreover, so as to prevent such a flight even after the acknowledged faint-hearted have returned, they took special measures at the actual time of battle.[3] Some support for this can be found in the system of exemption employed by Gideon, who in fact exempted both the faint-hearted and the inexperienced.[4]

On the other hand this interpretation contradicts 1 Macc. iii, 56, in connexion with the organization of the army by Judas before the battle of Emmaus: 'And he said to them that were building houses, and were betrothing wives, and were planting vineyards, and were fearful,

---

[1] M. Sotah viii, 7; and cf. p. 65, n. 2, 3, 4.

[2] 'For with a beginning in flight comes defeat' (M. Sotah viii, 6); cf. also B. T. Sotah 44b and R. Simeon Tos. Sotah vii, 22.

[3] Cf. Mishnah l.c.

[4] Ju. vii, 3–6. Field-marshal Wavell, *The Good Soldier* (1948) p. 164, ingeniously suggests that Gideon selected those who knelt down and drank from one hand, leaving the other free to hold on to his weapons (so also A. Malamat, PEFQS 1953, p. 61 ff.). The text, however, bears to my mind only the explanation that 'lapped with their tongue' were the ones selected; the words 'their hand to their mouth' in vs. 6 are out of place, cf. Biblia Hebraica 3rd ed. ad loc. I would suggest that Gideon selected those warlike enough to give up their good manners in the face of the enemy and to drink 'as a dog lappeth' in order to escape observation.

that they should return, each man to his own house, according to the Law.'[1] The War of Judas Maccabaeus certainly was a War of Duty, if ever there was one, yet he exempted all these types of person.[2] All this shows that in applying to the scroll the distinction between the laws of a War of Duty and a War of Choice we are faced with contradictions. The Pentateuch does not specifically distinguish between the two kinds of wars and demands exemption for all the types mentioned in Deut.; Judas Maccabaeus acts in agreement with this. The Rabbis distinguish between the two kinds of war, exempting all the types in a War of Choice and conscripting all of them in a War of Duty. The scroll apparently conscripts the builders of houses, etc., and exempts the faint-hearted.

Since the sect interprets the Pentateuch literally,[3] and taking into consideration the antiquity of Macc., it can hardly be assumed that the customs of the sect differed in this respect from the Pentateuch. We must therefore consider a third explanation :

(c) The Phases and Places of Exemption

It has been noted above that those going out to war fall into three types : those who do not move at all ; those who go out and return, and those who go out and do not return. It seems superfluous to bring those exempted for economic and social reasons to the actual battle-field in order to exempt them. This can be done in the place of authorized conscription or near the frontier before leaving for battle. On the other hand the sorting out of the faint-hearted, a trait liable to alteration and depending on the feeling of the soldier in the face of the enemy, can and must be done as near to the enemy as possible.[4] The Rabbis possessed a distinct tradition that the sorting out of those exempted was done twice, although they differed in details. Those exempted for objective reasons are set apart before the departure, and the exemption from actual fighting of the faint-hearted takes place close to the battle-field.[5] Since the prayer for the appointed time of the war

---

[1] Cf. Charles, *Apocr. and Pseudep.* I, 79.

[2] The ' man who hath taken a new wife ' (Dt. xxiv, 5) is omitted because such men did not leave home at all, cf. M. Sotah viii, 4.

[3] Cf. § 3 below.

[4] Cf. note p. 66, n. 3.

[5] Tos. Sotah vii, 18 ; B. T. Sotah 42ab ; Maimonides, H. Melakhim vii, 2, preserve the tradition that there were two such occasions, ' one at the frontier and one on the battle-field.' The Rabbis believed, however, that those who had built houses, etc., were obliged, even after the first ceremony, to proceed to the battle-field, and dismissed only there. It seems more probable to me that those exempted for objective causes were dismissed ' at the frontier ', the ' faint-hearted ' on the battle-field.

mentioned in the scroll is recited close to the battle-field (see ch. 8, §§ 4, 5), this is not the place for the words of the officers concerning the exemption of the builders of houses, etc., which must have been pronounced before departure. In fact, in Gideon's war, too, the final sorting out of the 'fearful and trembling' took place in the very presence of the enemy. Also with Judas Maccabaeus we see that those exempted were released at Mizpah, and only on the completion of this act did he move to Emmaus.[1] Summing up, it appears that the problem must be explained in one of the following ways :

(1) The sect distinguished between a War of Duty and a War of Free Choice but it applied the exemption of the faint-hearted also in a War of Duty.

(2) It interpreted the text literally that all the above types must be exempted in a War of Duty too, except that the exemption for social and economic reasons took place before the departure (and was therefore not mentioned in the prayer for the appointed time of the war), while that of the faint-hearted took place on the battle-field. For the reasons adduced above, I incline to the latter view.

§ 3. THE LAWS OF EXEMPTION FOR REASONS OF THE PURITY OF THE CAMP

The scroll emphasizes that the warriors shall 'all of them be volunteers for battle and sound in mind and spirit, and ready for the day of Vengeance' (viii, 5),[2] 'for the holy angels are in communion with their hosts' (ib. 6). This forces them to exempt the social and economic cases and the faint-hearted who were likely to fight without much enthusiasm and also to stress the observance of the laws of the purity of the camp and the warriors, and to prevent women and young boys from taking part in the battle, for their presence is likely to divert the warriors and cause them to sin.

It is thus obvious why the scroll united in one passage the three prohibitions connected with women and young boys, the disabled, and those who are not pure 'with regard to their sexual organs'.

After defining the types of warriors and their ages (vii, 1–3), the

---

[1] 1 Macc. iii, 46, 57. According to the same source, however, the faint-hearted, too, were dismissed at Mizpah, perhaps owing to special circumstances; the hortatory oration was delivered at Emmaus (cf. ch. 8, § 5 (2)). Cf., however, Sifre, Dt. cxcii, p. 233 : 'See how careful God is not to put men to shame : when the faint-hearted man returns home, people will say, maybe he hath built a new house or taken a new wife.'

[2] Cf. also x, 5, and the commentary.

author passes on to a definition of the three groups who for reasons of the purity of the camp do not go to war or take part in battle.

(*a*) ' No young boy [1] or woman shall enter their encampment when they go forth from Jersualem [2] to go to war and until they return ' (vii, 2–4).

(*b*) ' And anyone halt or blind or lame or a man in whose body there is a permanent defect, or a man affected by an impurity of his flesh, all these shall not go to war with them ' (ib. 4–5).

(*c*) ' Any man who is not pure with regard to his sexual organs on the day of the battle shall not leave camp with them ' (ib. 6).

The first formula, which is the most comprehensive, states that they shall not move away from their *place of abode* and shall not be *found* in the encampments of the warriors *from the time they go to war* [3] until they *return*. The second formula is less emphatic. The possibility cannot be ruled out that they were employed behind the lines, outside the camps of the combatants. The third formula deals of course with the combatants themselves who for only a limited time shall not *go down* to battle (here in the sense of ' engagement ') in spite of being present in the camps.

(*a*) *The Young Boys and the Women*

Even though we find no specific prohibition in the Pentateuch for these two classes to go out to war, yet it is due to the literal interpretation of certain passages by the sect, e.g. ' Take ye the sum of all the congregation of the children of Israel . . . according to the number of names, every *male*, by their polls ; from twenty years old and *upward*, all that are able to go forth to war in Israel ', Num. i, 2–3, and see Rashi *ad. loc.*

Though this text excludes them from the duty to fight, not from being present on the field of battle, their mention in the scroll together with the third group indicates that the sect aimed at ruling out any possibility of soldiers temporarily becoming unfit for reasons of common impurity (Lev. xv, 18, etc.) and for preventing homosexuality (ib. xviii, 22 ; xx, 13).[4] It has a special significance, which points to the existence of divergent opinions on this subject as we also learn from the Rabbinic injunctions mentioned above in connexion with the War of Duty. It is,

---

[1] i.e. under 25 years old, and cf. § 4 below. For the whole list cp. M Hag. i, 1.

[2] Cf. CDC xii, 1, and Rabin's remarks ib.

[3] For these three phases, see also ch. 3, § 2.

[4] It may be for these same reasons that ' male horses ' were specified as mounts (vi, 11), cf. Lev. xviii, 23 ; xx, 15—unless the sole cause was their suitability for battle.

on the other hand, natural that a sect, a considerable part of whose members abstain from women altogether, should be extremists in this matter.[1]

(b) Those Suffering from Physical Defects and Blemishes

This group includes two types: those affected permanently [2] and sufferers from various blemishes. The list of the former group, taken from Lev. xxi, 17–20, in connexion with the sons of Aaron, 'in whose body there is a permanent defect,' is to cover all the further cases enumerated there. The above list applied of course only to the sons of Aaron and not to wars. Since the scroll mentions the probability of those with a defect going to war amongst the prohibitions connected with matters of the purity of the camp, it may be assumed that the reason arose not from military causes but from regard for the purity of the camp.

The exemption of those with a defect from military duty is not mentioned in the O.T., but echoes of a tradition connected with this subject are preserved in Sifre *Shofĕṭim*: 'R. Jose the Galilean says: How do we know that a man does not go to war unless he has hands and feet and teeth? from what is said in Dt. xx' (cf. ib. Rashi).[3] The phrase 'affected by an impurity on his flesh', which does not occur in the O.T., indicates the intention to include all defects

---

[1] Perhaps one should also connect with this BJ II, vii, 10, on the Essenes: 'So far are the juniors ($\mu\epsilon\tau\alpha\gamma\epsilon\nu\acute{\epsilon}\sigma\tau\epsilon\rho\text{o}\iota$) inferior to the seniors ($\pi\rho\text{o}\gamma\epsilon\nu\acute{\epsilon}\sigma\tau\epsilon\rho\text{o}\iota$), that if the seniors should be touched by the juniors, they must wash themselves, as if they had intermixed with company of a foreigner.' In view of the Scroll's rules about ages, it should be reconsidered whether this does not apply to physical age rather than to seniority in membership. Cf. also *Qumran* I, p. 110, ii, 19–22. The fact that most members of the sect were celibate and lived (at least for a while) in the wilderness, enables us to interpret DSH xii, 4–5, 'for the Lebanon is the council of the community and the BEHEMOTH are the simple ones of Judah, who observe the Law,' based on Hab. ii, 17. Light on this is thrown by En. lx, 7–8: 'two monsters parted (*tabdfalu*; 4 Ezra vi, 49 *conservasti*) on that day, a female ... but the male is named Behemoth, who occupied with his breast a waste wilderness, etc.' With this compare Gen. Rabba vii, 4: '" And God created monsters " (A.V. " great whales ") R. Phineas in the name of R. Aha said: the monsters mentioned here are Behemoth and Leviathan, who have no mates. R. Simeon b. Laqish said, Behemoth has a mate but no sexual desire, as is said (Job xl, 17) "The sinews of his thighs are wrapped together ".' Cf. further p. 180, n. 1.

[2] i.e. those affected with a 'lasting blemish', as opposed to a 'passing blemish', cf. M. Bekh. ii, 2; Zeb. xii, 1, etc.

[3] Here, again, R. Judah denies that the reference is to a war of duty. On the halt and blind, see also Yadin, 'The Blind and the Halt and David's Conquest of Jerusalem' (Hebrew), in *Ha-Kinnus ha-'Olami le-Madda'ē ha-Yahaduth* (1947), I, 222 ff.

THE LAW OF CONSCRIPTION

enumerated in Lv. xiii ;[1] and even though the Pentateuch does not expressly prohibit this group from going to war, it is obvious that they cannot be present in the *camps* of the combatants since they must be set apart until their impurities have passed, cf. Lv. xiii, 46.

(c) *A Temporary Disqualification in Battle*

Those ' not pure with regard to their sexual organs ' on the day of the battle are yet present on the battle-field, not being completely disqualified of course, but they do not take part in the battle until they have become pure. It can be concluded from the following parallelism that this was the author's intention.

Dt. xxiii, 11–12	DSW vii, 5–6
' If there be among you any man, that is not clean by reason of that which chanceth him by night, then shall he go abroad out of the camp, he shall not come within the camp. But it shall be, when evening cometh on, he shall bathe himself in water ; and when the sun is down, he may come within the camp.'	' Any man who is not pure with regard to his sexual organs[2] on the day of the battle shall not join them in battle, for holy angels are in communion with their hosts.'

The ' Hand '

Though the matter of the ' hand ' is not directly connected with the laws of conscription and exemption, we may consider here its meaning in the scroll, since the author, like the Pentateuch, mentions it at the end of that group of laws dealing with exemption for reasons of the purity of the camp.

Again the scroll does not give the exact wording of the Pentateuch but adds several interesting details :

Dt. xxiii, 13	DSW vii, 6–7
' Thou shalt have a "hand" also without the camp, whither thou shalt go forth abroad.'	' There shall be a space between all their camps and the place of the " hand ", about 2,000 cubits.'

The text in the scroll shows that it did not intend simply to mention the duty of setting up the ' hand ', which was known and accepted, but to establish a rule as to the distance between the place of the ' hand '[3] and the camps. The distance ' about 2,000 cubits ' is not mentioned

---

[1] ' Blemish,' ' uncleanness,' and ' flesh ' frequently recur in this chapter.

[2] For the distinction between nocturnal pollution and uncleanness ' from his source ', and the meaning of ' to go down ', cf. the commentary.

[3] At first, no doubt, the ' hand ' was a sign erected at the place of easement (perhaps originally in the form of a hand) ; then ' hand ' became a euphemism for the place itself. For ' hand ' = sign, cf. ch. 5, § 6, and p. 100 n. 2, ib.

in the Pentateuch in connexion with the hand, but the author's terminology shows that he apparently borrowed it from Josh. iii, 4.[1] That is to say that he regarded the distance mentioned in Joshua, which separates the Sanctuary and the community of Israel, as a principal rule for determining the minimum distance between the holy camps and the place of the 'hand'. On the other hand, it is only right to ask whether the 2,000 cubits mentioned here are not connected with the 'Sabbath boundary', that is, they placed the 'hand' at the maximum distance which still enabled it to be used on the Sabbath too.[2] According to Rabbinic Judaism this was 2,000 cubits,[2] but it is not certain that this also was the custom of the sect; on the contrary, according to CDC it seems that they distinguished between the Sabbath boundary for the purpose of walking, which was 1,000 cubits (x, 21), and that for 'going after a beast', which was 2,000 cubits (xi, 5–6).[3] In spite of the fact that a great many scholars, beginning with Schechter, regarded the '1,000 cubits' of the first passage as a scribal error, this does not appear to be so.[4] It seems that we have here two different rulings which determine the 2,000 cubits as a maximum boundary only for 'going after a beast', but the 1,000 cubits as a boundary for 'walking about'.[5] In the light of the above either going to relieve oneself was included in the boundary of 2,000 cubits, or if the hand was placed at a distance of 2,000 cubits, members of the sect were unable to go out and perform their needs on the Sabbath.

The second possibility gains special significance in the light of the customs of the Essenes as explained by Josephus. He notes that they behaved in strict accordance with the words of the Pentateuch in having a paddle among their tools for these needs (Deut. xxiii, 14, following on the matter of the hand) and furthermore states that *they refrained from relieving themselves on the Sabbath*.[6] We can establish two points from Josephus: (1) That they chose desolate and remote

---

[1] The Scroll reads רוח for MT *rāḥōq*, and כאלפים באמה for MT *kĕ-alpayim ammāh bĕ-middāh*. The word *middāh* is om. by Vulg., ʿimdū in LXX. The Joshua passage served as a secondary source for fixing the Sabbath limit at 2,000 cubits, cf. Midr. Tanḥuma *Bamidbar* ix, and Num. Rabba ii, 9.

[2] Cf. M. Erub. iv, 3; v, 7; Sotah v, 3; and refs. in Rabin at CDC x, xi. See also Num. Rabba ii: 'When God commanded Moses to let the Israelites encamp in banner-sections, He said: cause them to encamp at distances of 2,000 cubits in each direction (*ruaḥ*).'

[3] Cf. the apparatus of Rost and of Rabin.

[4] The MS excludes the possibility of a scribal error: the three words are written with a broader pen, as if the scribe wished to stress them.

[5] Rabin suggests that this fixation of the limit is based on Num. xxxv, 4 sqq., about the levite cities. See ib. for further refs. and a discussion of the Sabbath limit.

[6] BJ II, viii, 9.

places for relieving themselves. (2) Since relieving their needs was bound up with digging they refrained from going out to relieve themselves on the Sabbath.¹ These two facts both fit the description in the scroll and the conclusion we have reached. This serves as strong supporting evidence for the identification of the sect with the Essenes, or at least for their having identical customs.²

§ 4. Age of Conscription and Exemption and the Division of Combatants According to Age

(1) Division According to Age

DSW vi, 6-11 ; vii provide interesting details on the division of the warriors according to age. Section 10 deals with the cavalry, their numbers, their qualities, and horses, including age groups. The beginning of section 11 is destroyed ; it may, however, be assumed to have contained corresponding descriptions of infantry. From the top of col. vii (being the continuation of Section 11), which starts : ' The men of the Serekh shall be from 40 to 50 years old,' it may be assumed that the last line of col. vi contained the ages of the skirmishers.³ The table below shows the division of the soldiers according to age and duties.⁴

	Cavalry		The Infantry and the Service Troops	
Service troops			'Those that despoil the slain', 'collect the booty', 'cleanse the land', 'guard the arms', 'prepare the provisions'	25–30
Warriors	'Those who go to war with the skirmishers'	30–45	[skirmishers]	[30–45]
	'The cavalry of the Serekh'	40–50	The men of the Serekh, provosts	40–50
Special duties			'The camp prefects'	50–60

¹ CDC x–xi prove how strict the sect was in matters of Sabbath observance, DSD vii, 13, their punctiliousness with regard to bodily functions ; for the latter cf. also Jub. iii, 7 sqq.

² For comparison with the MT, see commentary.

³ For ease of reference, I give here a summary of the organization of the army, as elaborated in ch. 7 :

(a) Infantry.

(1) Skirmishers (light infantry) armed with long-range weapons, organized in seven battalions, operate between the lines in the first stage of the battle.

(2) Front Formations (heavy infantry, also called ' men of the Serekh '), organized in seven formations, operate at a later stage of the battle.

(b) Cavalry.

(1) 'Those that go forth with the Skirmishers,' and those stationed ' all

In addition, the author notes in the description of the service in the Sanctuary in the sabbatical year that the representatives of the congregation witnessing the service shall be 'from the age of fifty years upwards'.[1]

With the above division of age for military purposes one may compare the details given in CDC (x, 6) in connexion with the ages of those holding civil posts in the sect at a certain period in its history:

(1) 'The judges of the congregation.'[2]   25–60
(2) 'The priest that is appointed at the Head of the Many.'[3]   30–60
(3) 'The overseer over all the camps.'[4]   30–50

The two sources are based on common principles:
(1) The minimum age for any duty is 25.
(2) The maximum age is 60.[5]

Additional details in DSW are: (a) The age of conscription is 25. (b) The age of the actual fighters is from 30 to 50 and they are divided into two groups according to their military duties: 30–45 and 40–50, but these overlap in the age group 40–45. (c) The service troops consist of the youngest age group (25–30) and those fulfilling special duties, these being the oldest men (50–60).

The division of the types of soldiers into age-groups was and is still practised by all armies and especially those based on the militia system.[6] Details differ and are influenced by various factors, e.g. the differing ages at which men mature and are mentally developed in the different countries, systems of fighting, the nature of the terrain, etc.[7]

---

around the camp', armed with light long-range weapons, fight in conjunction with the Skirmishers and at the flanks of the Front Formations.
(2) 'The horsemen of the Serekh' (heavy cavalry) operating in conjunction with the heavy infantry.
(c) Service Troops (cf. ch. 7, § 3).
[4] The ages of the cavalry are given vi, 13; those of the others at the end of vi (as restored) and vii, 1–3.
[1] ii, 4–5; cf. ch. 8, § 3.
[2] x, 6 sqq.
[3] xiv, 6–7. For the אש הרבים of the MS (sic, not אשר as in Rost), read ⟨בר⟩שא, with Rabin.
[4] xiv, 8–9.
[5] CDC x, 7–8, explains the reason for the upper limit of 60 years in a manner based on two recurring themes of pseudepi-graphal literature and the Scrolls: (1) After the Coming, men will live longer; (2) until then man's life has been cut short on account of his sins. See comm. on i, 9.
[6] I am unable to agree with M. Avi-Yonah's judgment: 'The distribution of military duties by ages as described above is entirely unpractical' 'DSW and Maccabean Warfare', IEJ 2 (1952), 2.
[7] Compare the age-grouping of the Roman militia:
   Juniores (field army)   17–46
   Seniores (garrison army) 47–60
Cf. Marquardt pp. 9–10 and p. 10, notes 1–3. Comparison with a modern militia is instructive: according to the law of 12.iv.1907, the Swiss army is divided into
   Auszug   20–36
   Landwehr 37–48
   Landsturm 49–60

The system described in the scroll, which is also based on specific factors which will be discussed below, was suited to mental conditions and physical development at the time of the Second Temple as we know them also from other sources.[1] The youngest group was directed to the services mainly demanding agility. The middle group is employed in assault tasks requiring both physical and spiritual strength, while the next oldest is employed in static fighting requiring spiritual strength and discernment rather than physical strength. The senior group is used for performing special additional duties which do not demand physical stamina and ease of movement.[2]

Before going into the details of every one of these groups, two general problems must be cleared up, i.e. the ages of conscription and demobilization:

The Pentateuch clearly lays down the age of 20 as the general age of conscription.[3] On the other hand it appears that the sect, in determining 25 years as the actual age of conscription—which was done by them for special reasons, as will be shown further on, took the Biblical statement as meaning that no one is mustered below the age of 20,[4] but that men are not necessarily conscripted at this age.

On account of the special character of the sect, since its membership was composed of priests, levites, and Israelites, and on account of its aspiration to equalize the tasks and rights of its members (see, e.g. DSD vi, 2–3), it determined the age of 25 (this being the age of service of levites, see below) as the minimum service age for the entire congregation. However, it seems that this decision was influenced also by their desire to rule out as far as possible the presence of young people in their camps, for the reasons explained above. This assumption is strengthened in view of the fact that the prohibition of 'every young boy' going out to the camps comes at the end of the list of the ages (vii, 3) and as a transition to matters concerning the purity of the camp.

Their decision, too, that the age group 25–30 was not to take part in active service but was to serve in auxiliary duties, and only on reaching the age of thirty entered active service, seems to be influenced

---

[1] Cf., e.g. Aboth v, 21, and the saying, quoted in several midrash works, 'a man of forty is not like one of sixty, and one of sixty not like one of seventy,' cp. S. Krauss, *Paras we-Romi, etc.* (1948), p. 219.

[2] The present Israel Defence Army is on broad lines organized by age-groups: the youngest groups (including the pre-military *Gadna'* units) for auxiliary services, the middle ones for field units, and the older age groups for static defence duties; many older soldiers are set aside for special service tasks.

[3] e.g. Num. i, 3, and fr.; xiv, 29; xxvi, 2, 4; 2 Chr. xxv, 5.

[4] Cf. also 1 Chr. xxvii, 23.

by the levitic practice. On the one hand we find in Num. viii, 24:
'This is that which pertaineth unto the Levites; from twenty and
five years old and upward they shall go in to perform the service in
the work in the tent of the meeting,' but in iv (2, 23, 30, 35, 39, 47):
'Take the sum of the sons of Kohath ... from thirty years old and
upward ... all that enter upon the service to do work in the tent of
meeting' [1] The scroll and CDC [2] apparently confirm the text in Num.
viii, 24, and the LXX in iv which always reads 'twenty-five'.

One hesitates to accept this assumption since according to DSW
the 25–30 age group only does service duty. It rather appears to have
taken the differences between Num. iv and viii to mean that only at 30
one reaches responsibility for fulfilling all the commandments while
between 25 and 30 one is regarded as a kind of novice. The same
explanation is found also in Num. Rabba iv, 11 : ' " From thirty years
and upwards " and another verse reads : " From twenty-five onwards," how can these two verses be harmonized ? The answer is :
from twenty-five for study, from thirty for service.'

(2) *The Age of Demobilization*

As the table of ages shows, the combatants served in the fighting
force until the age of 50. On the other hand some of those holding
offices were chosen from amongst those above this age group, for special
duties which they performed until the age of 60. Though the age of
demobilization is not expressly given in the Pentateuch, it must be
assumed that the above practice (which indeed suited military needs) [3]
was based on two different passages : according to Num. viii, 25–26,
the levites at the age of 50 retired from active service in the 'host of
service' but continued in subsidiary duties.[4] The sect ruled in this
manner also with regard to lay soldiers on reaching this age : they did
not go out with the host of war but served in the Sanctuary [5] except
for a few who continued in their special duties until 60; this term for
old age,[6,7] at which they were obliged to cease any military service, was
apparently based on Lev. xxvii, 3 : 'Then thy valuation shall be for
the male from twenty years old even unto sixty years old.' [8]

---

[1] The terminology varies somewhat from verse to verse. Cf. also Ezra iii, 8 ; 1 Chr. xxiii, 24, 27.

[2] The Judges in CDC x, 5, aged 25–60, include four priests and levites.

[3] See p. 76, n. 7.

[4] The LXX reads 'and his brother shall serve',

[5] ii, 4–5 ; cf. ch. 8, § 3.

[6] See p. 76, n. 5.

[7] See p. 77, n. 1.

[8] Though CDC fixes 60 as ultimate age of retirement from all duties, DSW seems to have had a different tradition. In vii, 1, the scribe first wrote 'the camp prefects shall be from 40 to 50 years old', then he or someone else changed this into '50–60 years', without, however, emending the

(3) Age Division and the Sect

As far as I know we possess no other sources from this period likely to help us in deciding whether the division into *four* age groups described in the scroll was common in the Israelite armies. It must, however, be mentioned that this division into four age groups is in partial agreement with Josephus' statement about the Essenes: 'Now after the time of their preparatory trial is over, they are parted into four classes' (Wars II, viii, 10).[1]

§ 5. THE ORGANIZATION AND CONSCRIPTION OF THE DIVISIONS

(1) *The Problem*

The problem of conscription is not confined to laying down the laws for the individual to be conscripted. Only in times of general emergency, or for fulfilment of a commandment requiring the participation of the entire people, is the whole congregation mobilized. Obviously a state of general mobilization cannot endure for a long period since it is likely to destroy the economic foundation on which the people exists.

Therefore, besides the system of general conscription, a parallel system of partial conscription has to be established, making possible long-term fighting side by side with the continued existence of economic life. This is one of the most difficult problems even in countries possessing a regular army. It is incomparably more difficult in countries whose armies are organized on a militia, territorial, or tribal basis. There are two extremist solutions which, however, do not solve the problem :

(a) *The Conscription of Each Tribe in Turn.*—This is not a practical proposition for it is apt to wipe out whole tribes and also stir up quarrels and complaints of favouritism ; should the battle end in defeat, the complaint will be made that the tribe in question was specially chosen to fight this difficult opponent, and vice versa. An additional

---

next phrase, 'the provosts, *too*, shall be 40–50 years old.' We cannot say whether he forgot to strike out the word 'too', or to change the age of the provosts (whose duties were similar to those of the prefects, cf. ch. 7, § 3 (1–2)). I doubt whether we can assume an older and a later usage. On the age of 60 years, cf. Rabin on CDC x, who also quotes Ps.-Hieronymus, ' ab anno sexagesimo et levitae ministrare et milites pugnare desinebant' (Migne, *Patr. Lat.* XXIII, p. 1433).

[1] BJ II, viii, 10. The term μοῖρα, usually translated 'class', seems to correspond to the *goral* so frequent in the Scrolls as designation of the 'lots' of Light and Darkness, etc. Μοῖρα, too, denotes on the one hand the effect of higher forces on human life, on the other military, etc., divisions. In the latter sense it is frequently used by Josephus (e.g. Ant. VII, xiv, 8, where it corresponds to *maḥlaqoth* of 1 Chr. xxvii). Cf., however, J. M. Grinz, *Sinai* 32 (5713), 20 sq., 26.

difficulty arises from the fact that the tribes vary in number. This, the worst possible way, typical for a period when a central authority was lacking, was in fact used, though without planning and system, in the period of the Judges.¹ With the faults of this system, even for needs of defence, we shall deal below.

(b) *Conscription of Individuals According to Age.*—This system, too, has numerous faults. Beside the need to establish a complicated skeleton staff, it will also cause serious complaints of favouritism since the composition of fighting units from different age groups according to their duties (see above) involves mobilization of only part of every age group from each tribe. Moreover, the process of forming fighting units is a lengthy process. Most armies organized on a militia or territorial basis have therefore adopted a solution which aims not only at distributing the burden of conscription evenly over the whole community but also to conscript organic fighting units. The general principles of the solution (its details vary of course) might be as follows :

Every tribe (which is organized according to conscription and military units, see beginning of this chapter) without exception mobilizes at every conscription parts of several complete units according to a predetermined quota and plan. The units mobilized according to their turn (determined in every tribe by the chief of that tribe), constitute the conscripted army for a set period. This army, constituting only part of the army conscripted at a time of general mobilization, is sometimes designated differently from the terms denoting the regular conscription and fighting units.

(2) *The Solution According to the Scroll*

We saw in chapter 2 that the war against all the lands of the nations by the separate divisions lasts thirty-three years (including four sabbatical years). On the subject of the conscription of these divisions the scroll reads : ' In the remaining thirty-three years of the war shall the men of renown summoned to assembly and all the chiefs of the clans of the congregation be choosing for them warriors for all the lands of the gentiles : from all tribes of Israel they shall mobilize for them men of valour to go forth to serve according to the pre-ordained periods of the war year after year ' (ii, 6–8). This period comprises the ' war of the divisions ' (ib. 10). From this description we can deduce the following principles :

---

¹ Op. the war of **Barak and Deborah** (Ju. v), and the complaints in Ju. viii, 1. See also F. Junge, op. cit., p. 4 sq., and my review (*Yedi'oth* 15 (5710), 88).

THE LAW OF CONSCRIPTION

(1) The selection of the soldiers was done by the civil officials according to their tribal organization.

(2) Mobilization was by a selective process.

(3) Mobilization affected all tribes.

(4) The divisions change annually.

(5) Those mobilized go out according to 'the pre-ordained periods of the war'.

(1) 'The Men of Renown summoned to Assembly and all the Chiefs of the Clans of the Congregation': These terms are mentioned in the scroll a number of times in connexion with the Temple service: '... the fathers of the congregation fifty-two' (ii, 1) and similarly: 'The chiefs of the tribes and the fathers of the congregation' (ib. 3); in another passage they are mentioned in connexion with the trumpets (iii, 3-4). The problem of their identity and number is dealt with elsewhere.[1] The stylistic similarity between the description of their activity connected with conscription, and their trumpets, might suggest also the possibility that the above-mentioned assemblies of the men of renown and the heads of the clans of the congregation constitute a kind of council for planning the war and the conscription of the soldiers (cf. ch. 2, § 6).

(2) Mobilization and selection: The phrase 'be choosing for them' proves that in contrast to the act of general mobilization in which exemptions are made according to fixed laws (see above) and the tribe as a whole is mobilized, the problem of organizing the divisions imposed upon the chiefs of tribes the selection of men from their tribes according to the 'pre-ordained periods of the war'. We may have to explain in a similar way the term 'choose', which occurs so very frequently in the O.T. and especially in connexion with the organization of a part of the warriors, composed of representatives of all the tribes. The following examples are instructive:

(a) In the description of Israel's war with Benjamin (Judges xx and see also chapter 3, § 6) it is written that in the beginning the number of all the warriors in Israel was: 'Four hundred thousand men that drew sword; all these were men of war' (ib. 17), but in the 'ambush' were 'ten thousand chosen men out of all Israel' (ib. 34).

(b) Similarly in connexion with the ambush at Ai (Josh. viii, 3).

(c) About Saul's army during his pursuit of David: 'Then Saul took three thousand chosen men out of all Israel' (1 Sam. xxiv, 3) and

---

[1] Cf. ch. 8, § 3; ch. 5, § 4 (3); ch. 3, § 6.

similarly 'Having three thousand chosen men of Israel with him' (ib. xxvi, 2).

(d) In connexion with the division which Saul set up: 'And Saul chose him three thousand men of Israel' (ib. xiii, 2).

(e) A twofold process appears in the description of Joab's war against Ammon (2 Sam. x, 4) in connexion with the crisis in the battle: 'Now when Joab saw that the battle was set against him before and behind, he chose of all the choice men of Israel,[1] and put them in an array against the Arameans.' This passage does certainly not refer to a personal choice just in the thick of battle but to a choice of units and their grouping into a 'task force' from amongst the general selected army.

The above passages bear witness to the close connexion between the act of selection and the term 'chosen' as denoting the soldier selected to go to war from amongst all those liable to conscription.[2]

(3) 'Out of all tribes of Israel': The scroll, in common with the O.T. passages mentioned above, stresses that the act of selection is not accomplished for every tribe separately but comprises all the tribes. Moreover, it appears that it wished to emphasize that every division should contain selected soldiers from amongst all the tribes. This assumption gains ground from the fact that the war of the divisions lasts twenty-nine years and the divisions are exchanged every year. This shows that the scroll saw no connexion between the number of tribes and divisions. It has been pointed out above that a system of 'divisions' identical with the territorial or tribal system, i.e. every tribe or area providing a complete division, has numerous faults.[3]

(4) 'Year after year': For the purposes of defending and manning fortresses the militia divisions can be relieved monthly. Quite clearly, this is impractical for warfare outside the boundaries of the country, as in the case of the divisions described in the scroll. Indeed, though we

---

[1] Read with Qere and many MSS. מכל בחורי ישראל; cf., however, 1 Chr. xix, 10 מכל בחור בישראל. Cp. Ex. xvii, 9; 2 Sam. xvii, 1.

[2] It is easy to see the semantic development of the term to mean *all* men of military age (esp. 2 Chr. xxv, 5 sq.) and finally any strong young man.

[3] It is interesting to compare this with the description by the medieval adventurer Eldad ha-Dani of his own 'Camp of Dan'. 'Each month a different tribe goes out to war and stays abroad for three months ... thus they do until the end of the three months, then they return and bring all booty before King Uzziel, who then shares it with all Israel ... for three months Naphtali goes out, for three other months Gad, and so on, until the twelve months are completed, and then they start again.' This interesting story, which no doubt preserves some tradition of 'wars of separate divisions', seems to me to be influenced by an erroneous interpretation of 1 Chr. xxvii and 1 Kings v, 28.

might explain the system described in 1 Chr. xxvii as relating to defence or a state of alert (see above), we learn from the scroll of the existence of another system (at least at the later period of the Second Temple) for the needs of an offensive war, based on annual replacement.[1]

To sum up :

(1) The ' division ' is the highest military framework at the time of partial mobilization.

(2) In the division, tribal units mobilized according to a fixed plan and according to selection by the heads of the congregation are grouped together.

(3) The units change annually.

(4) Every single division is composed of units from all the tribes.

(3) *Old Testament*

In the light of these conclusions we must re-examine the description of the ' courses ', i.e. divisions in the Davidic period, as set out in 1 Chr. xxvii, 1–5 : ' Now the children of Israel after their number, to wit, the heads of father's houses and the captains of thousands and of hundreds, and their officers that served the king, in any matter of the courses which came in and went out month by month throughout all the months of the year, of every course were twenty and four thousand. [2]Over the first course for the first month was Jashobeam the son of Zabdiel ; and in his course were twenty and four thousand. [3]Of the children of Perez was he, and the chief of all the captains of the hosts for the first month. . . . [5]The third captain of the host for the third month was Benaiah the son of Jehoiada, the priest, chief ; and in his course were twenty and four thousand.' A considerable number of scholars saw in this passage a theoretical description lacking any practical military foundation. From amongst the reasons put forward by scholars the following might be mentioned : the monthly changing, the number ' 12 ' and its apparent connexion with the tribal organization, the names of the commanders of the divisions which do not agree with any tribal or territorial division, and the fixed number 24,000 for every division (which imposes, so to say, an equal quota on tribes and districts varying in size).[2] Junge makes an important contribution towards an explanation of the description as based on the principle of a militia army by noting that the above twelve divisions cannot be identical with the

---

[1] This also fits the law in Dt. xxiv, 5.

[2] Cf. Junge, op. cit., p. 60 sqq., and my review, *Yediʿoth* 15 (5710), 97 ; also p. 80, n. 1. S. Yeivin, ' Families and Political Parties in the Kingdom of Judah ' (Hebrew), *Tarbiz* 12 (5711), n. 106, brands these as ' theoretical divisions '.

twelve tribal districts, since it is illogical and impracticable to conscript every month the inhabitants of a complete district and to scatter them over the whole country; moreover, the number of inhabitants in the different districts varies. Junge thinks that those liable for general military service served in fortresses in the neighbourhood of their homes and took turns in the fortress districts month by month so that in actual fact every month one-twelfth of the general militia army served in the entire country.[1] Since the scroll expressly states that the system of the militia divisions served also for the needs of agressive war and the organization of 'expeditionary units', a new light is thrown on the passage in 1 Chr. The following are the outstanding facts:

(1) A 'captain of the host' stood at the head of every division.[2]

(2) Every division contained the same number of men (24,000).

(3) The division into twelve was not according to tribal or territorial zones, as may be learned from the birth places of the captains of the host.

(4) The division was relieved monthly.

The explanation which to my mind best fits the above facts—taking into account the information now provided by the scrolls—is based on

[1] Junge dates this and similar accounts in the time of Josiah; see, however, my review (above, note 1). His main argument, that David and Solomon had regular armies, not militias, is not borne out by the accounts of David's wars. Cf. Yadin, *Biblica* 36 (1955), 332 sq.; *Ma'arakhoth* 101 (1956), 9 sq. We may assume that during David's expansionist wars the army was mainly professional, but in his latter days, and in Solomon's, its purpose was defensive and nothing prevented the creation of a militia. I would suggest that the transition from the professional to the militia system forms the real background of the quarrel between David and Joab about the census. The census clearly was for military purposes, since its execution was entrusted to the chiefs of the army, and its results were 'eight hundred thousand valiant men that drew the sword', etc., cf. also 1 Chr. xxi, 5. If this census marked the preparations for creating a regular army to replace the militia existing from before the monarchy, it is strange that of all people Joab, 'the captain of the king's host' (1 Chr. xxvii, 34) should be against it: 'but why does my lord the king delight in this thing?' The professional soldier must have objected not to the census, but to its purpose (which I take to be the creation of a militia), in which he saw a danger to efficiency and the end of regular soldiering. Many parallels can be found in history to such an attitude (generally unjustified) of regular soldiers to a citizen army. In our particular case the accompanying circumstances make it probable that after accomplishing his military aims the king inclined towards the creation of a militia, against Joab's advice. In the light of all this, I see no reason—*pace* Junge—for not dating the census in the end of David's reign. Its results presumably provided the basis for the army as described in 1 Chr. xxvii, which is clearly a militia.

[2] Cf., however, Yeivin's article quoted p. 83, n. 2. The double use of *zava*: 'total armed forces' and 'largest independent formation', is easily understood. In our case the 'division' in fact constitutes at the time of its mobilization the total armed forces.

the systems customary to this day in countries whose army is organized mainly on the militia principle. This solution requires the existence of two separate frameworks, one based on the division of the country into independent territorial areas and another based on the distribution of the warriors into central fighting formations.

All soldiers dwelling in a certain area are grouped according to their domicile (or tribal affinity) in basic combat units, e.g. every unit consisting of 1,000 men. Every such unit belongs to one unit of the central framework. As long as a certain area needs to be defended, all units of that area according to their turn are mobilized for its defence, as needed, under the command of the officers appointed over that district. If reinforcements are needed, units from outside are moved in. On the other hand, in an offensive war, the different units from various zones are combined into their national units. This combination, too, can be general, if the whole army is conscripted, or partial, if according to the needs of the war in question only part of the army is mobilized.

The description in 1 Chr. deals solely with the organization of the militia army in its central formations called 'courses' or 'divisions'. The area or tribe with a large number of soldiers supplies a large number of units and the small ones supply less units. The central command divides up the general number of units into the various divisions and thus ensures that the number of soldiers is equal in every division. Moreover, this system makes it possible to extend to every area or tribe the training suitable to its character [1] without impairing the balance of the types of weapons in the different divisions, since a certain area supplies the archers to the general divisions and another area supplies those carrying shields and spears, etc.

In peacetime the division on duty need not be gathered at one central point, since its sub-units can be concentrated in their district for training purposes or the manning of fortresses as need arises. Since the obligation of regular service is one month per year,[2] the number of soldiers in every area or tribe must also be divided into twelve sub-units, every one of which belongs to a different division. This system necessitates the existence at the head of every division of a commandant and a group of regular officers who have to deal with all problems of registration and organization even when their division is not on duty. This system, to my mind, fits the description in 1 Chr. xxvii, which

---

[1] E.g. in 1 Chr. xii the soldiers hailing from different tribes are differently equipped: 'And from Naphtali . . . with shield and spear,' etc.

[2] The monthly changes and the existence of 12 divisions show that periods of service recurred annually, as in DSW.

deals solely with the organization of the divisions. On the other hand, we know of the existence of a parallel system organized by districts, 1 Kings iv, 7. We learn from the definition of the districts given there that this system, in contrast to that of the divisions, was clearly territorial.

For organizational purposes, as described above, it was obligatory for the number of the sub-units in every area to be identical with the number of the divisions, but this does not apply to the number of districts. The fact that the districts too were twelve in number may perhaps be due to the other duties incumbent on the districts in the field of economic and civil administration, including provision for the king's household, which also was on a monthly basis as described in 1 Kings.[1]

According to this explanation the two systems need not necessarily coincide in number or area of districts, though one must not ignore the connexion existing between them as explained above.[2]

At the first glance this appears to be an involved system requiring a high level of organization, but all references in the O.T. to the organization of the state at the end of the Davidic period and in that of Solomon bear witness to the high level of economic and political organization, which has been surpassed by few states even in our day.[3]

The description of the activities and organization of the divisions in the scroll which in its details is independent of the O.T., shows that this system in different forms continued until the end of the Second Temple period. The Israel Defence Army, re-established after an interval of 2,000 years, is organized on a similar pattern.

---

[1] This does not mean that each month one district provided for all needs of the royal household, since the agricultural produce of each district varied both in kind and in season. More probably the system resembled the military one, being both territorial and centralized: each 'officer' was responsible for apportioning the total quota of his district among the inhabitants and to collect it at the proper times (1 Kings v, 18), the total district quota being reckoned as equal to one month's provision for the royal household. There were other officers at the centre who apportioned the quota of each article among the districts which produced it; such were the officers enumerated ib. xxvii, 25 sqq. Cf. Yadin (p. 83, n. 2, supra).

[2] Junge, op. cit. p. 68, who thought that the system in 1 Chr. xxvii applied only to the manning of fortresses, was compelled by this erroneous assumption to deny all connexion between it and the districts of 1 Kings.

[3] We may imagine the complicated planning and administrative effort involved in the dispatch of corvee workers to the Lebanon (1 Kings v, 27-8). On the related problems of the Temple service, cf. ch. 8, § 3.

Chapter 5

THE TRUMPETS

§ 1. General Remarks

The large space which the author allots to the description of the trumpets, to their names, duties, and inscriptions throws much light also on the problems of the organization of the army and the congregation, tactics, and the duties of the priests in battle, with which I deal in the relevant chapters. In the present chapter I intend to discuss the descriptions and duties of the trumpets themselves.

The relation between the scroll's descriptions of the trumpets compared with those of the O.T., especially their duties at religious ceremonies on the one hand, and its independence of the O.T. with regard to everything connected with their use in battle on the other, makes imperative a thorough examination of the points of identity and difference. Such an examination will help us to understand the description given in the scroll, and also to throw light on the problem of the period of the scroll's composition.

§ 2. The Trumpets in the O.T.

The principal and most important passage is Num. x, 1–10.[1] Two other passages, Num. xxxi, 6, and 2 Chr. xiii, 12–14, occur in contexts which also influenced the author in other respects.[2]

These passages stress the main features of the trumpets:

(1) Their purely religious character is stressed in a number of ways: (*a*) Their use is commanded to Moses. (*b*) In battle, too, they are to be 'remembered' before the Lord. (*c*) The use of trumpets at the festivals as an integral part of the order of sacrifices. (*d*) The priests are in charge of the trumpets in battle also.

(2) None of the above nor any other descriptions mention the use of trumpets in battle for giving tactical signals (except for the 'alarm'[3] or 'war-cry' (תרועה) whose principal purposes are to be 'remembered' before the Lord, to bring fear upon the enemy, and to strengthen the hearts of the warriors). In contrast, Num. tells us of the existence of a complete system of signals for the journeys of the camps and for

---

[1] In vs. 6 LXX adds a third and fourth alarm for the western and northern camps.

[2] For further passages and for the conquest of Jericho, see §§ 8, 9.

[3] E.g. Hos. v, 8.

calling the congregation and its chiefs. This system warrants special attention for its points of similarity and difference from that described in the scroll. It is based on the three possible distinctive features of the signals: (*a*) The number of trumpets. (*b*) The types of sound. (*c*) The sequence of the signals.

(*a*) Continuous sound on two trumpets: signal for the congregation to assemble at the tabernacle. A continuous sound on one trumpet for the gathering of the princes and chiefs of the thousand.

(*b*) *Těqi'ah* for the gathering of the congregation; *těru'ah* for moving the camps and in battle.

(*c*) First alarm—for the camps lying to the east, the second alarm—for the camps lying to the south, etc.

§ 3. THE TRUMPETS IN THE SCROLL

The 'dispositions' of the trumpets occur in Sections 4 and 12.[1] The names of the different trumpets are twice mentioned in Section 4: (1) in the list enumerating their duties; (2) in connexion with their inscriptions. Every list is subdivided: the list of trumpets for calling the congregation, its chiefs, and units for the various ceremonies (cf. Num.), and the list of the trumpets for battle purposes. The list of the trumpets according to their duties (hereafter called list A) beginning at the end of ii (mostly destroyed) and ending with iii, 2, can be restored with the help of the complete [2] second list (hereafter called list B) (iii, 2–11). In col. vii the list of trumpets is mentioned once more (hereafter called list C). This list contains only the names of the battle trumpets of the six priests of the sons of Aaron [3] (vii, 11–12). In addition the scroll enumerates their different sounds and the meanings of their signals in battle (viii). The three lists are similar in general but differ in several details relating to terminology or in the order of mention. It is therefore difficult to identify exactly the various trumpets in the different lists; the synoptic table on page 89 brings out their similarities.

List B is the fullest and most detailed. In the corresponding part of list A, which is preserved (the battle trumpets), only the 'trumpets of withdrawal' without further details are mentioned (cf. list C); while list B mentions two types of trumpets for this purpose. From this one may assume that the missing part of list A contained a shorter list than

---

[1] Condensed accounts also in sections 14, 24, 28.

[2] See commentary.

[3] As in Numbers. For the connexion of the priests with the trumpets, see §§ 8–9.

THE TRUMPETS

LIST A		LIST B			LIST C
Name of Trumpet	Task	Name of Trumpet	Task	Inscription	
[Summoning the congregation]		'Trumpets for summoning the congregation'		'Those called by God'	
[Summoning the commanders]		'Trumpets for summoning the commanders'		'Princes of God'	
'[and hundreds and fifties and] tens'		'Trumpets of the formations'		'Serekh of God'	
[Men of renown, the chiefs of the clans]		'Trumpets of the men of renown, chiefs of the clans of the congregation'	'When they assemble at the house of convention'	'Convoked by God for a council of holiness'	
[Trumpets of the camps]		'Trumpets of the camps'		'Peace of God in the encampments of His Saints'	
[Trumpets of the expeditions of the camps]		'Trumpets for their expeditions' [trumpets for the expeditions of the camps)		'God's mighty deeds to scatter the enemy and to put to flight all opponents of justice and disgraceful retribution to the opponents of God'	
'[Trumpets] of the battle arrays'		'Trumpets of the battle arrays'		'Arrays of God's battalions for His wrathful vengeance upon all Sons of Darkness'	'Trumpets of summoning'
'Trumpets for their calling' (of the skirmishers)	'When the battle intervals open for the skirmishers to go forth'	'Trumpets for calling the skirmishers'	'When the battle intervals open for them to go forth against the line of the enemy'	'Vengeful remembrance at the appointed time of God'	'Trumpets of remembrance'
'Trumpets for the fanfare of the slain'		'Trumpets of the slain'		'The hand of God's might in battle to strike down all sinful slain'	'Trumpets of the fanfare'
'Trumpets of ambush'		'Trumpets of ambush'		'Mysteries of God for the perdition of the wicked'	
'Trumpets of pursuit'	'When the enemy is smitten'	'Trumpets of pursuit'		'God hath smitten all Sons of Darkness, His wrath shall not cease until they are annihilated'	'Trumpets of pursuit'
'Trumpets of withdrawal'	'When the battle returns'	'Trumpets of withdrawal'	When they disengage from battle to re-enter the line'	'God hath gathered'	'Trumpets of withdrawal'
		'Trumpets for the way of return'	'From battle with the enemy to come back to the congregation to Jerusalem'	'Rejoicings of God in peaceful return'	

the one I have restored, i.e. 'the trumpets of the camps' only, without the 'trumpets of their journeys'. On account of the almost complete parallelism between list A and B, the latter will serve us as the principal basis for clarifying the names and tasks of the trumpets. List C, the shortest, is important for containing several types of trumpets under one name, thus facilitating a clear understanding of the general terms, e.g. 'war-cry', 'remembrance', 'calling'. List C also raises the problem of the number of trumpets.

List C mentions five types of trumpets used by six priests; the fact that list A mentions six types does not make the solution any easier. In vii, 14, we read: 'The priests shall blow the two trumpets of summoning,' which is similar to the passage in Numbers. On the other hand, in viii, 8–9: 'Then the priests shall blow on the six trumpets of assault'; hence the number of priests corresponds to the greatest number of trumpets of one type, 'trumpets of the slain.' This large number of trumpets is due to their being used at the peak of the battle when the tumult and noise are at their greatest.[1]

§ 4. THE CEREMONIAL TRUMPETS

The first group (list A) is markedly influenced by Num. x. Trumpets of this type are not meant for military purposes but for those connected with the various ceremonies of the congregation, as is also borne out by their inscriptions. The scroll mentions this group of trumpets for the self-same twofold reason for which its author devotes much space to a description of the standards of the 'host of the war' and 'host of the service'; the organization of the congregation in general and the rites of the Temple service during the sabbatical years, etc.[2] It is, therefore, natural that the names and tasks and inscriptions of these trumpets should be specially close to the O.T.

With this type of trumpet, and its bearing upon the structure and ceremonies of the congregation, I have dealt in chapter 3 (cf. ib. n. 7, p. 61). For the moment some general remarks regarding the problem of the trumpets are needed.

(1) *The Trumpets for Summoning the Congregation.*—Their tasks are defined in Num. x, 2, 3: 'And they shall be unto thee for the calling of the congregation. . . . And when they shall blow with them, all the congregation shall gather themselves unto thee at the door of the tent of meeting.' The different procedures for calling the congregation are

---

[1] See further, p. 107, n. 1. An interesting parallel for the use of six trumpets is in the Crusade chronicle of Geoffrey de Vinsauf: 'It had been resolved by common consent that the sounding of six trumpets in three different parts of the army should be a signal for a charge,' cf. H. B. Farmer, *Rise and Development of Military Music* (London, 1912). Farmer adds: 'it appears that no distinct calls were sounded but were dependent for their significance on orders previously issued.' The system was thus more primitive than that described in the Scroll.

[2] As indicated, ch. 3, § 1–2, and in ch. 2, these regulations stem (*a*) from the author's desire to base the war of the Sons of Light as closely as possible on Biblical legislation, (*b*) from established practices in the sect's annual gatherings (cf. ch. 3, § 9).

also defined in Num. x, 7 : ' But when the assembly is to be gathered together, ye shall blow, but ye shall not sound an alarm.' Apparently for this reason the trumpets had an additional name (or at least an additional epithet) as we learn from CDC xi, 21–23 : ' And everyone who enters the house of meeting in order to pray, let him not come in a state of uncleanness requiring washing. And when the trumpets for assembly sound, let him go earlier or go later, and let him not make void the whole service.' [1]

(2) *The Trumpets for Summoning the Commanders*.—Cf. Num. x, 4 : ' And if they blow but with one, then the princes, the heads of the thousands of Israel, shall gather themselves unto thee.' Since the inscription on these trumpets is ' Princes of God ', we must conclude that when their call was heard, only those chiefs assembled who belonged to the group of the ' princes '. This group, as the inscriptions of the banners and the O.T. testify, was composed solely of the heads of tribes and families. These princes do not of course serve in a purely military capacity but are the civil leaders of the congregation (cf. ch. 3, § 6).

(3) *The Trumpets of the Formations*.—Corresponding to the formations in this list, which to my mind are the units formed according to the militia structure,[2] we find, I think, the fragments of the enumeration of list A : [   ] and tens.' This word doubtlessly stood, as the list of banners testifies, at the end of the usual formula ' [in myriads and hundreds and fifties] and tens '. Hence we must conclude that when the sound of the trumpets of the formations was heard, the units (or their chiefs) assembled according to their militia structure. This distinction of the trumpets for calling the princes and the rest of the chiefs indicates perhaps that the sect interpreted Num. x, 4, similarly to several of the ancient versions : ' Then the princes and the heads of the thousands of Israel shall gather themselves unto thee.' [3]

Also the inscription on these trumpets, ' Serekh of God,' shows that the reference is to the sum of the units making up the Serekh, which word also denotes the congregation as organized in a militia fashion.[4]

(4) ' *The trumpets of the men of renown—the chiefs of the clans of the congregation, when they assemble at the house of convention.*' [5]—These

---

[1] Cf. also DSW ii, 15, which is a heading to the chapter describing the use of trumpets both in peace and war.

[2] For this term (also iii, 12) see ch. 3, § 2, and p. 41, n. 2. For the use of trumpets in ceremonies, see ib., note 7, p. 61.

[3] Cf. ch. 3, note 4, p. 48, and § 6 and notes, particularly note 1, p. 53.

[4] Cf. ch. 7, § 2 (5).

[5] Cf. ii, 6–7, and comm. there and on iii, 3–4. See also ch. 4, § 5 (2), and ch. 8, § 3. Cf. Yadin, JBL 78 (1959), 238 ff.

trumpets, which are not mentioned in Num., were apparently introduced to fulfil a need in the eschatological ceremonies of the congregation. This assumption is borne out by the fact that only they, from amongst the trumpets mentioned in this group in list B, get explanatory additions by the author of the scroll to indicate their purpose, viz.: ' when they assemble at the house of convention.' [1]

(5) ' *Trumpets of the camps,*' and ' *trumpets of their journeys.*'—Num. mentions only one kind: for causing the camp to set forward ' (verse 2) and: ' And when ye blow an alarm, the camps . . . shall take their journey ' (5). The difference between the two kinds of trumpets is explained by their inscriptions; that on the first type, which is non-military, denotes that they are used in the camps in peace time, while that on the trumpets of the journey, which bears a clearly military character (see below), stresses their connexion with military marches. These two types of trumpets are not again mentioned in the scroll, since its description starts at the battle, after the march.

§ 5. THE TRUMPETS OF BATTLE [2]

This group of trumpets, whose name occurs in all three lists, is mentioned every now and again in descriptions of the various phases of the battle. An examination of the comparative table (above) shows that several corresponding names were given to a number of these trumpets; or to be more precise: list C, the shortest, includes under one name a number of trumpets serving different purposes. An additional difficulty in identifying them lies in the fact that the order of the trumpets in list C fits the battle order of the skirmishing units, but lists B and C deal with an enumeration of the trumpets of all the units and at all phases of the war. Hence, in my opinion, the best way of comparing the lists is to start at the end, which is the clearest part.

(1) ' *The trumpets of withdrawal.*'—Lists A and C end with the trumpets of withdrawal. List B also has the trumpets of withdrawal, i.e. ' when they disengage from battle to return to the line '; their inscription is: ' God hath gathered.' The additional type of trumpet, mentioned only in list B, is: ' the trumpets for the way of return from battle with the enemy to come back to the congregation to Jerusalem.'

In the description of the activities of the various skirmishing units in section 12, it is twice mentioned that on completion of the throwing

---

[1] Cf. Nu. xi, 30, and Neh. viii, 13, etc. In Num. x, 3, the whole congregation assembles ' to thee (om. LXX) at the door of the tabernacle of the congregation ', but in vs. 4 the princes only ' unto thee '.

[2] For the tactical details, cf. ch. 7.

of slings and ' darts ' the skirmishers are called to return to the position of the formations which are not fighting at that moment and are drawn up facing the enemy. ' Then the priests shall give them (the men of the slings when they have finished throwing) a signal on the trumpets of withdrawal, and they shall come to take up position by the side of the first formation to fall in at their proper position ' (viii, 2–3). Similarly : ' Then the priests shall give them (the skirmishers who are armed with darts) a signal on the trumpets of withdrawal.' Similarly xvi, 11, in the description of the replacement of the formations after the defeat of the Sons of Light : ' While to those already engaged they shall give the signal to withdraw.' All these passages clearly define their tasks : they are trumpets for giving the signal for the rearward movement of the fighters on the completion of their task, without enemy pressure, or for actual retreat under enemy pressure. The scroll took care to define exactly also the second type : ' Trumpets for the way of return,' i.e. the return of the army from the battlefield to its bases. This fits the three principal phases in the movement of the army : ' On their going to battle,' ' on their advance into battle,' and ' on their return from the war ' (iv, 6–8).

The names of these trumpets, ' withdrawal ' and ' return ', must be regarded then like ' ambush ' and ' pursuit ' and in contrast to ' remembrance ' and ' calling ' as tactical terms, not connected solely with the names of the trumpets and denoting the various phases of the war and the systems of fighting. Hence the word for withdrawal must be pointed *ma'ăsaf* and not *mĕ'assef*. The latter form in the O.T. always denotes the rearguard.[1] The O.T. frequently uses the root אסף in the meaning ' to return '.[2] For that reason one has to read *ha-mashov* and not *ha-meshiv*.[3]

(2) ' *The trumpets of pursuit.*'—In the lists they come between the ' ambush ' and the ' withdrawal ', i.e. at the final stage of the actual fighting. This phase, as defined in list A, is ' when the enemy is smitten '. The inscription bears this out : ' God has smitten all sons of darkness, His wrath shall not cease until they are annihilated ' ;

---

[1] Eg. Num. x, 25 ; Josh. vi, 9, where the ' rereward ' is opposed to the advance guard (*ḥaluẓ*, A.V. ' armed men '). It is possible, however, that Num. x, 25, which has some connexion with the passage on the trumpets, influenced the inventors of the term.

[2] See comm.

[3] Cf. also Sukenik, *M.G. I*, 25. J. Ratz-havi (*Sinai* 12 (5709), 173 sq.) connects the word with *heshiv yadh*, i.e. a signal for ceasing from throwing ; however, as we have seen, the signal was only given after the throwing was finished. Cf. further comm. on viii, 15. Palaeographic considerations, too, favour the reading משוב, cf. comm. at iii, 10

ix, 6, in the description of pursuit: 'The priest shall give them a signal on the trumpets of pursuit,[1] and they shall spread out against the whole of the enemy for a pursuit of annihilation.' Here also it appears that one must point *mirdaf* to indicate the tactical phase.

(3) '*The trumpets of ambush.*'—These trumpets are mentioned in lists A and B only. List C mentions the 'trumpets of the fanfare' which includes both the 'ambush' and the 'slain'. The explanation for this seems to be that those waiting in ambush are treated like any other unit once they commence fighting and are given the signals on the trumpets of 'assault' (see below). On the other hand, since the real success of an ambush depends on the surprise factor, it is of special importance to have a clear and unmistakable signal for action. As a matter of fact, the description of the conquest of Ai by Joshua deals mainly with the problem of timing the action of the ambush and with the signals for bringing it into action.[2] Also the word *ma'ărav* indicates the form of fighting or its place in the terrain, and not the unit itself, which was called *orev*.[3]

(4) '*The trumpets for the fanfare of the slain.*'—This is their name in list A. In list B they are called the 'trumpets of the slain'; in list C, however, they are included among the 'trumpets of the fanfare'. Hence list A gives their full name, which contains an indication of their purpose and their sound. List B abbreviates but retains an indication of their duties, while list C links them together with the 'ambush' and contents itself with a description of their tone. The trumpets of the fanfare have the same name as those which Phineas took to the war with Midian and those used in Jeroboam's and Abijah's war. In the O.T. these trumpets are not used for actual signalling but for encouraging the warriors and for 'melting the heart of the enemy'. In blowing them, the soldiers, as it were, turn to God and ask for His help: 'And when ye go to war ... then ye shall sound a fanfare with the trumpets; and ye shall be remembered before the Lord your God,

---

[1] Only here מרודף, apparently influenced by *yirdofu* in the preceding line; elsewhere always מרדף. For the tactical role and the inscription of these, see § 7 and ch. 7, § 7.

[2] As does DSW ix, 17. Cf. also 'and they ran as soon as he had stretched out his hand', Josh. viii, 19. It is possible, of course, to argue that the signal was given by hand in order to achieve complete surprise. Moreover, admittedly we have no proof that Joshua used trumpets for signalling purposes at all, cf. § 9.

[3] Josh. viii, 19, as opposed to *ma'ărav* in vs. 9. For *orev* in vs. 7 read *ma'ărav*, cf. BH³. In Ju. xx the unit is always called *orev*. Cf. also Ezra viii, 31. In Ju. ix, 35, and 2 Chr. xiii, 13, *ma'ărav* must be taken as denoting the place or action of the ambushing unit (though in the latter place it could be taken as the unit itself). For the tactical concept, see ch. 7, p. 196, n. 1

and ye shall be saved from your enemies ' (Num. x, 9). Here, too, in spite of the fact that they are used as a signal to begin throwing missiles, the sounding of the fanfare on the trumpets of the slain—during the first phase—together with the fanfare of the horns constitutes ' a great battle fanfare to melt the heart of the enemy ' (viii, 10). With the problem of the fanfare in relation to the horns I shall deal below in § 8. Outside the three lists, the trumpets are mentioned several times in the scroll: while the slings are used ' the trumpets shall keep blowing to direct [1] the sling men until they have finished throwing seven times ' (viii, 1–2). The beginning of this description, which was on page vii, is missing, but from the parallels and the use of *mĕri'oth* [2] it is clear that these trumpets are meant. The scroll supplies a detailed description of the action of the darts (viii, 8–12) : ' then the priests shall blow on the six trumpets of the slain a high-pitched intermittent note to direct the fighting . . . the priests shall keep on blowing . . . until they have thrown into the line of the enemy seven times.' [3] The six trumpets blow in unison to make themselves heard above the clamour of battle (see p. 90, n. 1). The ceaseless blowing until the soldiers have thrown their missiles also ensures that they are thrown in volleys. The description recurs in connexion with the defeat of the enemy before the beginning of pursuit (ix, 1–2) : ' the priests keep on blowing a fanfare upon the trumpets of the slain to direct the fighting, until the enemy are discomfited and turn their backs.' Similarly cf. xvii, 12–15. The above passages show that the fanfares on the trumpets of the slain were given as a signal for throwing the missiles. This continuous noise goes on as a ' fanfare ' until the defeat of the enemy or until the soldiers have finished throwing their missiles.

The ' trumpets of remembrance ' and the ' trumpets of summoning '. The trumpets of remembrance mentioned in list C, and also in several other places describing the battles, do not occur in lists A and B under this name. In order to establish their nature and the corresponding term in the two lists, we must first of all clarify the purposes of the ' trumpets for summoning the skirmishers ' and the ' trumpets of the battle arrays '.[4]

---

[1] For *nzḥ* see comm. on viii, 1. Dupont-Sommer's ' sans arrêt ' (*Aperçus*, pp. 100–1), ' without ceasing,' ' ceaselessly ' (*Dead Sea Scrolls* p. 81), seems to me impossible.

[2] The scroll practically always uses the root *rw'* for battle signals (but cf. § 4 (1) on CDC xi, 21–2), but also employs *tq'*. Note, however, Num. x, 7 : ' But when the congregation is to be gathered together, ye shall blow (*tq'*) but not sound an alarm (*rw'*).' Cf. further, p. 104, n. 1.

[3] I have omitted the passage dealing with the horns and the various sounds of the trumpets, for which see below.

[4] For the terms, see ch. 7, §§ 2–5.

(5) '*The trumpets for summoning the skirmishers.*'—List B clearly defines their purpose : ' when the battle intervals open for them to go forth against the line of the enemy.' In list A the trumpets which are required ' when the battle intervals open for the skirmishers to go forth ' are called for short the ' trumpets for summoning them '.[1] This definition of their duty is especially suited to the use of the trumpets of summoning in the various descriptions of battle : ' The priests shall blow the trumpets of summoning, and three skirmishing battalions shall go forth from the intervals and take up position between the lines ' (viii, 3, 4). This description contains in fact all the data mentioned in list B. On hearing the sound of the trumpets of summoning, the skirmishing battalions go forth towards the line of the enemy from the open intervals. Their task is similarly explained in other passages.[2]

(6) '*The trumpets of the battle arrays.*'—These trumpets, mentioned in lists A and B (but not under this name in list C), not only serve for bringing into action the skirmishers but also for the ' arraying ' of ' all the battalions of battle ', including the skirmishers. This results not only from the other descriptions in the scroll but also from their inscription, ' battalions of God '.[3]

These trumpets served, in the different phases of the war, for ' forming up ' both the battalions in general and the skirmishing units. The ' forming into lines ' in general is described in v, 15–17, which unfortunately is only partially extant ; however, in various places in the scroll this phase is mentioned again. It does not specifically concern the author, who is interested in describing the actual battle, beginning after the battalions were formed into ' lines ' in the various formations [4] and all is ready for the battle being started by the skirmishing units. In the descriptions of the action of the skirmishing units we find a detailed description of the use of the ' trumpets of the arrays ' :

' The priests shall blow on their trumpets a level note, signals [5] to array for battle, and the columns shall (deploy into) their proper arrays, each man to his place ' (viii, 5–6), or ' and the skirmishers shall go

---

[1] ii, 1, is either ' The battle arrays and the trumpets for calling them ', or ' ⟨The trumpets of⟩ the battle arrays and the trumpets of summoning them ' : the second reading corresponds to List B and is preferable. Thus here, too, the first two trumpets in the list are those of the battle arrays and those for summoning ⟨the skirmishers⟩.

[2] ix, 3 ; xvi, 10 ; cf. also vii, 14.

[3] Cf. p. 166, n. 2, and p. 62, n. 2.

[4] vii, 8 ; v, 3 ; xiv, 3 ; xv, 5–6 ; xvii, 10. In most of these passages ' to array ' is used for forming up any kind of unit in frontal arrays (resembling those of the skirmishing units) with the help of trumpet signals.

[5] For this term, and for the notes used, see below.

forth and take up position in columns between the lines. The priests shall blow a fanfare for them for the array, and the columns shall keep [fanning out] at the sound of the trumpets until they have fallen in, each man in his position' (xvi, 3–4). From these and other descriptions [1] it is quite clear that the trumpets of arrays serve for signalling the deployment of columns into arrays. However, their purpose does not end with this, for the same trumpets (of course on another note) send the arrays in mass towards the fighting position: 'When they are drawn in three arrays the priests shall blow for them a second fanfare and a low legato note, signals to advance until they approach the enemy,' etc. (viii, 6–8).

(7) '*The calling*' *and the* '*remembrance*'.—From what has been stated above it appears that the 'trumpets of calling the skirmishers' and the 'trumpets of their calling', are one and the same. Hence, the item corresponding to the 'trumpets of the battle arrays' in list C is the trumpets of remembrance. This conclusion, which to my mind it is difficult to reject, raises some problems. The language in Num. 'and ye shall be remembered before the Lord' in connexion with the fanfares in battle, on the one hand, and 'and they shall be to you for a memorial before your God' in connexion with the trumpet-sounds on the festivals on the other, do not seem to reinforce this identification; also the description of the use of the trumpets of remembrance in the scroll itself is vague: 'then (after arraying the formations and reciting the prayer for the "appointed time of the war") the priests shall blow for them a signal on the trumpets of remembrance. They shall open the [battle] intervals, and the skirmishers shall go forth and take up position in columns between the lines. The priests shall blow for them a fanfare for the array, and the columns shall keep [fanning out] [2] at the sound of the trumpets' (xvi, 2–4). In the description of the formation for pursuit it says: 'At that time the priests shall sound a fanfare [on the six trumpets] of remembrance and all battle formations shall follow their call and spread out,' etc. (xviii, 3–4). Similarly list C begins with the trumpets of summoning followed by the trumpets of remembrance, while in lists A and B the order is reversed. However, since the identification of the 'trumpets of their calling' with the 'trumpets of calling the skirmishers' seems quite certain, the difference in order in the various lists can be explained quite easily. Their order in lists A and B is due to the fact that these lists give the trumpets for all phases of the

---

[1] E.g. xvii, 10. [2] For the terms, see ch. 7, §§ 2–5.

war, clearly the arraying of the formations must precede the summoning of the skirmishers, therefore the trumpets of the arrays were put at the head of the list, even though they were used again for the deployment of the columns of skirmishers after being called and the grouping into arrays.[1] List C enumerates the trumpets according to the sequence of their appearance *after* the formations in general have been arrayed.[2] The first trumpets then to be used by the priests are the trumpets of calling the skirmishers.

As regards the two passages in which mention is made of the trumpets in the context of the battle descriptions, we must remember that the battle descriptions in this series are much condensed, since the detailed descriptions were already given in the Serekh Series, Section 12. In the first description (xvi, 2–4) the author omits the trumpets of calling and this creates the impression that the columns of skirmishers go forth to the sound of the trumpets of remembrance (which is in contradiction to list C and the rest of the descriptions quoted). This may be explained by assuming that the author intended to indicate the first action carried out at the signal given by these trumpets : 'and the battle intervals are opened.' The opening of these intervals as explained in chapter 7, § 2 (4) and § 5, was accomplished by narrowing the spaces between the soldiers of the front formation drawn up in arrays. Only after the intervals are opened do the skirmishing units go out to the sound of the trumpets of calling.[3] This second signal is left out in the brief description, which quickly passes on to a description of the second task of the 'trumpets of the arrays' in connexion with the deployment of the columns of skirmishing units and the forming of their arrays. These two actions, while given in detail in the Serekh Series, are also left out in the description here and it appears as though they are accomplished by one signal.

The second passage describes the bringing into action of all battle formations for pursuit [4] *after* being formed into the requisite arrays.

---

[1] Cf. xvi, 4–5 ; xvii, 11.

[2] This emerges clearly from the order in vii, 8–12. Cf. ch. 8, § 5 (2).

[3] This is confirmed by the order of trumpets in lists A and B : (1) Trumpets of arrays, (2) Trumpets of summoning 'when the battle intervals are opened', i.e. the opening of the intervals was brought about by the Trumpets of Arrays.

[4] xviii, 4, literally reads : 'all battle formations shall gather unto them (the priests)' (a technical impossibility) and means, no doubt, that all units, including the reserve, are drawn up ready for pursuit. Cf. Kromayer-Veith on *signa conferre* (p. 438) and *signis in unum locum collatis* (Bellum Gall. II, xxv, 1 ; Bellum Civ. lxxi, 3), which, according to K.-V. 'nichts anderes bedeuten kann, als dass alle Reserven eingesetzt waren und daher alle *signa* in einer Front standen'. On the formation for pursuit, see ch. 7, § 7.

THE TRUMPETS

To sum up : the trumpets of their calling are also named trumpets of calling the skirmishers ; the trumpets of the battle arrays are also called the trumpets of remembrance. At the sound of these trumpets the army passes from its marching formation to its fighting formation. Their function is, therefore, that of ' signalling trumpets ' (for remembrance in the sense of ' sign ' see next paragraph and note 2, p. 100).

§ 6. The Sounds and Signals of the Trumpets

(1) *Battle Signals*

The battle signals vary by the different sounds produced on the trumpets, every signal having its own special sound. In order to clarify the nature of the sounds described in the scroll we must first consider the important term *yĕdhē*, which occurs several times in the description of the sounds. It appears in the following passages :

(*a*) ' The priests shall blow on their trumpets a level note, signals (*yĕdhē*) to array for battle and the columns shall deploy into their proper arrays,' etc. (viii, 5, 6).

(*b*) ' When they are drawn up in three arrays the priests shall blow for them a second fanfare, and a low legato note, signals (*yĕdhē*) to advance, until they approach the enemy line ' (ib. 6–8).

(*c*) ' Then the priests shall sound another fanfare on the trumpets, signals (*yĕdhē*) for engaging. When the skirmishers have reached the line of the Kittim within throwing range,' etc. (xvii, 11, 12).

(*c*ᵃ) ' The priests shall blow for them another fanfare [signals for engaging]. When they are in position near the line of the Kittim within throwing range,' etc. (xvi, 4, 5).

(*d*) ' While on the trumpets the priests shall keep on blowing a high-pitched intermittent note to direct, signals (*yĕdhē*) for fighting, until they have thrown,' etc. (viii, 11, 12).

Sukenik explained the phrase in (*a*) : ' for the battle order,' cf. Mishnaic Hebrew ידי חובה, ידי שמים. In this he has been followed by most scholars.[1] On the other hand, H. Yalon suggested that *yĕdhē* means ' soldiers ',[2] a suggestion which it was difficult to accept even at the time when only col. viii was published,[3] and it

---

[1] *M.G. I*, 25 ; cf. also R. J. Tournay, RB 56 (1949), 214, n. 4.

[2] Sinai 26 (5710), 287. *y. mifsaʿ* = marching soldiers ; *y. sedher milḥamah* = men of the line ; *y. milḥamah* = fighting men. One of his arguments is that ' hand ' was used as *pars pro toto*, especially as it denotes in Hebrew also ' strength '.

[3] Yalon's theory led him to understand the musical terms *mĕruddadh*, etc., as terms of military action. His explanation of *yedhē sedher milḥamah* as ' men of the line ' is impossible as this signal is given while the men are still formed in columns, before they fan out into ' arrays '.

must in my opinion now be ruled out in the light of the other examples. מִפְשָׁע in (*b*) corresponds to הִתְקָרֵב in (*c*); hence it cannot—as Yalon thought—denote a type of warrior, but in both cases the word following *yĕdhē* expresses the action achieved by the signal. To my mind, *yĕdhē* means signals, i.e. the scroll indicates that a level note constitutes a signal to advance or to engage. The others constitute signals to deploy into arrays, etc.[1] This use of the word 'hand' can be understood quite easily if we remember that the simplest way of giving signals in battle (and in fact in all everyday activities), always has been by means of the hand of the commander: raising, inclining, lowering, turning, or any other agreed movement. In the O.T., too, we find the hand mentioned for signalling in battle, e.g. in the description of the conquest of Ai Joshua uses the javelin stretched out in his hand as a signal for the ambush, as shown by the verse 'And the ambush arose quickly out of their place, and they ran as soon as he had stretched out his hand' (Josh. viii, 19); similarly in Ecclus. (cf. chapter 6, p. 130, n. 1). The beginning of the Burden of Babylon is also instructive. (Isa. xiii, 2): 'Set ye up an ensign upon the high mountain, lift up the voice unto them, wave the hand, that they may go into the gates of the nobles.' This waving of the hand corresponds to the other methods of signalling.[2] From what I have said so far we may conclude that the above terms in the scroll are technical expressions for signals derived from the actions resulting from those signals.[3]

The difference between the various signals must have been clear

---

[1] Cf. ch 7, § 2

[2] For 'hand' = signal, sign, cf., e.g., 2 Sam. xviii, 18; 1 Chr. xviii, 3; Isa. lvi, 5, and see ch. 4, § 3, about 'hand' in vii, 7.

[3] There is a striking similarity with the semantic development of *signum* and *manipulus*. The latter—which at one period denoted the basic unit of the army, cf. ch. 7, § 4—was at first a staff with a figure of a hand at the top (hence its name) with which the commander gave directions to his unit. Later it came to mean the unit thus directed. For a long time the m. was the only *signum* in the Roman army, marking in itself a step forward from the system of signalling by the commander's hand, since it was visible to a larger number (Veith in K.-V. p. 277, cf. n. 2 ib.) but the hand attached to it symbolized its derivation. K.-V. (p. 438) further stress that *signum* practically meant 'tactical signal' (e.g. *signa inferre; s. referre*). They conclude that for the individual soldier the *signa* were the tactical directives, while the trumpet signals served more for direction of commanders and to direct attention to commands about to be given, cf. ib. p. 520, and below with regard to Josephus's descriptions. Yalon shows that in some O.T. passages 'hand' denotes a military unit, suggesting that this use developed via the meaning 'strength'; it may, however, also have been originally the unit directed by one 'hand' or signal. For a possible occurrence of 'hand' = unit in DSW, see ch. 7, p. 175, n. 5. Note that 'every man upon his hand by their standards', Num. ii, 17, corresponds to 'each man by his standard (*dighlo*) with ensigns', ib. 2, while in i, 52, we have 'each man by his own camp and each man by his own

THE TRUMPETS

enough to rule out any possibility of error. Therefore every signal differed not only in sequence but principally in the differing make-up of its tone.

(2) *The Tones*

The terms which the scroll uses for the tonal differences between the signals are most interesting. Though all the terms are easily explained etymologically, they have no parallel equivalent in any of the known sources. This shows the author's independence of the above sources and strengthens the assumption that he drew on a special military source.[1] The following summary containing all the information on this subject in the scroll may be found helpful.

There are two possible approaches towards an understanding of the

Reference	Sound	Name of Signal	Manœuvre	Trumpets [6]
12, viii, 5–6 [2]	מרודד	'Signal to array for battle'	'The columns shall deploy into their proper arrays, each man to his place'	'Trumpets of calling the battle arrays' First fanfare
12, viii, 6–8	נוח וסמוך	'Signal to advance' or 'Signal to approach'[3]	'Until they (the arrays) approach the enemy line'	(As above) Second fanfare
12, viii, 11–13 [4]	חד טרוד	(To direct) 'a signal for fighting'	e.g. 'The battle darts shall go forth to slay', 'Until they have thrown into the line of the enemy seven times'	'Trumpets of Assault'
12, viii, 13–14 [5]	נוח מרודד סמוך		See above, § 5 (1)	'Trumpets of Return'

standard (Samar.: by his own hand)'. Since the 'standard' is a military unit, and the 'ensign' a flag, etc., 'hand' serves here in the same meaning as 'ensign'; cf. further ch. 3, § 10. On the 'hand' in the Roman army, cf. Daremberg-Saglio, iv, 2, p. 1313, and fig. 6417 ib.

[1] This has been shown by M. M. Kasher, *Talpiyot* 4 (5710), 682-3—though it is hardly necessary to search for such a source in the pre-exilic period or even earlier, as K. does.

[2] In the descriptions xvi, 4; xvii, 11, the tones are not specified.

[3] The signals are mentioned without specifying the tones in xvi, 5; xvii, 11.

[4] Cf. also viii, 8–9; xvi, 6, and without specification of the tone: viii, 15–16; xvii, 13–15; viii, 1.

[5] Without specification of the tone viii, 2; incomplete viii, 17; without specification of tone xvi, 11.

[6] The name in brackets is not mentioned in connexion with the description of the tone.

nature of these tones. (1) Their names hint at the kind of action they bring about; (2) their names indicate the quality of the sound. Yalon (ib., p. 287) who suggests in his article using the first approach about קוֹל נוּחַ וְסָמוּךְ : '"*samukh*" means proximity and seems to be a military term.' He explains that קוֹל מְרוּדָד served as a command for deployment, its basic meaning being 'flattening' and here 'scattering'. As for קוֹל חַד טָרוּד, since *ṭrd* in Mishnaic Hebrew means also to banish and drive away, e.g. Gen. Rabba xi, its meaning here is: 'after they put their hand to their weapons the priests blew a high-pitched note to startle the enemy's line and to put them to flight and again they blew to melt the heart of the enemy '.[1] To my mind, this ingenuous suggestion does not fit all the facts. It was clearly desirable for the nature of the *sound* to symbolize the type of action so that the soldiers might remember the signal, and the tone help them in carrying out their action.[2] But from this assumption one cannot conclude that the technical musical terms need necessarily refer to the action. Even assuming that *samukh* as a term for the signal for advance symbolizes proximity to the enemy, its second appearance, with the trumpets for the return of all places, contradicts this. Moreover, Yalon's suggestion is partly based on the assumption that *yĕdhē* means soldiers.[3] If these terms had the meanings he attributes to them, we would expect active not passive participles. Similarly, the meaning of קוֹל נוּחַ cannot be understood according to this system. It seems to me that we must follow the second approach and try to understand the meaning of the terms as having a bearing only on the sound.[4] Consultations with military musical experts[5] have shown that the system for indicating the differences between the various sounds of trumpet signals (without having recourse to musical notes of course) consists in defining them from two acoustic viewpoints simultaneously:

(*a*) Volume and quality, i.e. low or high; full or thin and high-pitched.

(*b*) The sound form, i.e. staccato or legato.

In analysing the terms mentioned in the scroll we must ask if perhaps they used the same system.[6]

---

[1] This refers specifically to the great fanfare sounded by trumpets and horns together.

[2] e.g. by a rhythmical pattern fitting the action to be performed.

[3] See p. 99, n. 2.

[4] Following Sukenik, Kasher, and others.

[5] I take this opportunity of thanking the Director of the School for Military Music of H.M. War Office for his kind assistance in discussing these terms with me.

[6] The importance of the mass of material collected by Kasher, op. cit., p. 684 sqq., from halakhic discussions on trumpet and

THE TRUMPETS 103

(a) חד וטרוד—נוח וסמוך. I have chosen these two as a starting-point since they both indicate actions carried out close to the enemy, though they completely differ from each other, and one must assume the tones of their signals to have differed as much as possible so as to rule out any possibility of error. This maximal differentiation can be expressed by the pitch and form of the tone simultaneously.

חד—נוח. The general meaning of these two words is clear;[1] they indicate the difference in pitch; נוח means mainly quiet, low, soft, and חד noisy, high, strong and loud.

סמוך. It seems to mean here: connected, close, and is thus well suited to indicate legato.[2]

According to this טרוד indicates staccato; and the different uses of this verb point to division, removal, etc. *Ṭoredh* (Prov. xix, 13) in describing the raindrops falling close to each other but yet separately suits the description of the intermittent trumpet sounds coming close on each other without being joined.[3]

To sum up: the pitch of the signal to advance is low and its sound rises and falls continuously (legato). The pitch for the signal for fighting is high and their sound is interrupted at short intervals (staccato). These sounds differ diametrically and suit their purpose, particularly the signal for fighting which has to continue throughout the whole period of fighting and must be audible in the tumult and shouting of the battle.

(b) מרודד. This is the only tone defined by only one term. Hence it can be either high or low pitched. The principal meaning of the root *rdd* is flat, even, spread out, straight. I suggest that it is a sound which neither rises nor falls and continues without changes in strength

---

shofar blowing lies in the proof that no terminological connexion exists, though it also shows that, in spite of the paucity of parallel terms, the Rabbis adopted similar methods in describing the sounds of wind-instruments. Their descriptions are far from being clear or consistent, and already Maimonides states that 'owing to the passage of time and our exile we have no clear conception of the nature of the *tĕruʿah* prescribed in the Law' (Code, Bk. III, Hilkhoth Shofar, iii, 2).

[1] For philological treatment, see comm.

[2] So Sukenik and with reservations Kasher (op. cit. p. 681). The latter suggests either 'sounds closely joined' or 'a thick sound'; the second explanation seems out of place as the quality has already been indicated. However, *samikh* 'thick' is no doubt closely related to our terms. Cf. further for this and the following terms Tournay, RB 56 (1949), 214.

[3] B.D.B., Ben-Yehudah, etc., translate 'continuous dripping', which led Sukenik and Kasher to render here 'without interruption'. Cf., however, Tos. Maksh. i, 8: 'At first it drips slowly, but now *ṭoredh*, drop following drop,' i.e. the drops are still separate. Possibly *ẓarudh* in the B.T. R.Sh. = *ṭarudh*. [Cf. also Arab. *ṭarrada* 'to prolong (a note)'—Driver.]

or interruptions, in fact a simple blow.¹ This signal is given at a distance from the place of fighting and denotes the change in the formation from columns to arrays. Since the signal for the return is a low note alternately level and legato (see below) it seems to me that the level note here is not low pitched.

(c) נוח מרודד סמוך. This is the signal for the arrays to return from the fighting position to the line, i.e. on hearing this signal two actions must be performed: turning the arrays into columns and causing the columns to move back. Thus this signal is actually made up of the two above sounds (following on each other): a level note which signifies change of formation—and a legato one which signifies march. It is interesting that the word low appears before level; we would have expected level—low legato. The purpose of this change is to rule out any misunderstanding: the low note signifies the transition from arrays to columns while the high level note signifies transition from columns to arrays (see the graph).²

Level	מרודד	───────────
Low legato	נוח וסמוך	∼∼∼∼∼∼∼∼∼∼
High-pitched intermittent	חד טרוד	─ ─ ─ ─ ─ ─ ─
Low alternately level and legato	נוח מרודד סמוך	∼∼∼∼─────

§ 7. The Inscriptions on the Trumpets

The inscriptions on the trumpets have the same features as the other inscriptions on the banners and darts.³

The word 'God' is mentioned in each inscription and indicates the connexion between the Lord and the congregation and its war. The

---

¹ So Zeitlin (JQR 39 (1948/9), 350), who adduces B.T. Rosh Hashanah 34a where těqiʿah is identified as a simple (pěshuṭah) sound; so also Sifre Zuṭa (ed. Horovitz, 1910) p. 71; Naḥmanides on Num. x, 7. Sukenik has 'thin and drawn-out', apparently to distinguish it from the 'return' signal; so also Kasher. Cf. Dupont-Sommer, Aperçus p. 100. For Yalon's view see above.

² Quality:
   thin, high-pitched ───────
   thick, low-pitched ───────
Form:
   level   ───────
   legato   ∼∼∼∼∼∼∼
   intermittent ─ ─ ─ ─ ─
   (staccato)

³ Cf. ch. 6, § 9.

inscriptions fit the difference between the two major groups: in the first group (the ceremonial trumpets for peace-time) the inscription supplements the name of the trumpet and defines the groups which it directs like the basic inscriptions on the banners of the congregation (iii, 12–16), or the inscriptions of the banners on the expeditions of the congregation ('on going out to war') and before reaching the battlefield (iv, 9–11).[1] The inscription on the trumpets of the expeditions of the camps is of special interest, as it constitutes the transition from the first to the second group, closely resembling the passage in Num. x, 35 (this chapter exerted the greatest influence on the subjects of the banners and trumpets; cf. also Ps. lxviii, 2): 'And it came to pass, when the ark set forward, that Moses said: Rise up, O Lord, and let Thine enemies be scattered; and let them that hate Thee flee before Thee.' The inscription on the trumpet says: 'God's mighty deeds to scatter the enemy to put to flight all opponents of justice and disgraceful retribution to the opponents of God.'[2] It is interesting that according to a different tradition this text appeared in one of the inscriptions of the tribal encampments. According to Tg.J. (in the list of inscriptions of the camps) the inscription of Judah's camp was 'Rise O Lord and let Thine enemies be scattered and let Thine adversaries flee from before Thee'.[3]

The inscription on the trumpets of the battle arrays, being the first inscription of the battle trumpets, is divided into two parts. The first, as in the first grouping, indicates that these trumpets activate the arrays of the battalions of God (not merely the skirmishing unit), like the inscription on the banner of Thousand amongst the banners of the whole congregation on going out to war (see ch. 3, § 2). The second part expressly calls the enemies 'Sons of Darkness' as does the inscription on the trumpets of pursuit (which bears some resemblance to it).

The word 'vengeance' mentioned here and in the following inscription as well as in the inscriptions of the banners of the congregation in the hour of battle ('vengeance of God', iv, 12), is typical of war slogans. One might attribute the double mention of this word to the words of Moses in connexion with the war of Midian: '... to execute

---

[1] The phrase 'summoned by God' recurs on the standard of the seventh grouping.

[2] For *ḥesed* = 'disgrace', see comm. One wonders why the words 'and ... God' (parallels Ps. lxxvii, 12; Dn. xi, 18.; Neh. iii, 36) were added to the long sentence from Numbers x, 35. Perhaps

רבבות in vs. 36 was understood by the sect as 'quarrels' or read דבבות 'enmities' (Levy, *Targ.* s.v.). The commentators and versions differ on the sense of the passage. In Tg.J. this verse is quoted as inscription on the standard of Dan.

[3] Cf. ch. 7, p. 196, n. 1.

the Lord's vengeance of Midian' (Num. xxxi, 3), which occurs close to the incident of the trumpets of the war-cry which Phineas took to war. These words of Moses are most suitable for inscribing on trumpets. So also Tanh. Mattoth 2 : 'And when they went to war with Midian, they wrought vengeance on them with trumpets, as it is said, " and the holy vessels and the trumpets of the war-cry were in his hand ".'

'*Vengeful remembrance at the appointed time of God*' ('*the trumpets for calling the skirmishers*'). This short inscription (based on Num. x, 9) actually combines two different inscriptions : the one on the banner of hundred of one of the families of Levi on closing in for battle : 'Appointed day of God' (iv, 7), and the inscription of the entire congregation on closing in for battle : 'Vengeance of God' (iv, 12). A similar combination (not on the inscriptions) is : 'The appointed time of vengeance' (xv, 6).

The inscription on the 'trumpets of assault' marks the phase of fighting. It resembles the inscription of the 'banner of the hundred'. With the wording 'The hand of God's might in battle to strike down all sinful slain' compare the inscriptions of the darts of the three battalions : 'Flash of a lance to the might of God' ; 'Sparks of blood to slay by the anger of God' ; 'Glitter of a sword devouring the sinful slain by the judgment of God.' This is hardly incidental since these inscriptions on the trumpets and darts appear in the stage of actual fighting.

The inscription on the trumpets of ambush indicates the character of the ambush : a hidden stratagem.[1]

The trumpets of pursuit (cf. above, the trumpets of battle array). The whole inscription is influenced by Jer. xxiii, 20, and other verses but its main feature lies in the insistence on pursuit unto annihilation. Similarly in ix, 5, 6 : 'All these shall take up the pursuit to destroy the enemy in the battle of God for eternal annihilation.' This emphasis agrees with a principle stressed in military literature : pursuit must exploit victory to the full.

The inscription on the 'trumpets for the way of return' ('Rejoicings of God in peaceful return'), i.e. the return from the battlefield to Jerusalem speaks of the joy in safe return, and closely resembles the inscriptions on the banners of the congregation at this stage. In fact it combines two of these inscriptions, 'Joy of God' and 'Peace of God' (iv, 14).

---

[1] Cf. ch. 7, p. 196, n. 1.

§ 8. The Horns and Their Purpose

Along with the detailed description of the different trumpets and their purpose, the author mentions a number of times the role of horns in the fanfares. In addition to the six priests blowing on the trumpets seven levites are mentioned as carrying seven rams' horns (vii, 12–13).[1] This designation as 'rams' horns' as well as their number is based on the description of Joshua's conquest of Jericho,[2] except that in the scroll the levites and not the priests blow on them (see below). The purpose of the horns is first defined in viii, 8–13, after the dart throwers take position near the enemy line and put their hands to their weapons: the sound of the fanfare on the trumpets represents a signal for the levites and the band of horn-blowers [3] to commence blowing and also for the dart throwers to commence throwing darts. A certain difficulty arises with regard to the further action of the trumpets (after the beginning of dart throwing): 'The sound of the horns shall cease, while on the trumpets the priests shall keep on blowing a high-pitched intermittent note,' etc. (viii, 11–12). The scholars who have dealt with this page have taken the verb 'shall cease' (יחושו) as meaning 'shall hurry', i.e. after the dart throwers have gone forth, the sound of the horns shall be 'speeded up'. But although the word can be understood in this sense, the purpose of the speeding-up is not clear, especially since the author immediately repeats that the trumpets shall keep on blowing until the end of the dart throwing. It is difficult to assume that during the great fanfare the trumpet signals could possibly be heard. It therefore (in the light of the later parallels) appears that the opposite is meant: in the beginning, when the signal of the trumpets of assault is given, the horns and all the people shall blow simultaneously and at that moment, at the sound of this signal the

---

[1] The distinction between *six* priests with trumpets and *seven* levites with horns is interesting; actually seven priests come forward, but one addresses the ranks (cf. ch. 8, § 4–5). Cf. 1 Chr. xv, 24, which enumerates *seven* priests with trumpets; so also Neh. xii, 41, and cf. Büchler, ZATW 1899, p. 329.

[2] Josh. vi, 4, where they are called *shofĕroth ha-yovĕlim*, 'rams' horns' (in DSW *yovel*, cf. Josh. vi, 5; Ex. xix, 13), cf. F.-M. Abel, 'Les stratagèmes dans le livre de Josué,' RB 56 (1949), especially pp. 325–9, describing the combination of war-cry and horns. In the light of DSW, I doubt whether we need follow Abel in emending vs. 16. See further S. B. Finesinger, 'Musical Instruments in O.T.', HUCA 3 (1926), 56.

[3] This means that also other levites or even non-levites blew horns (cf. the Gideon episode). I cannot accept Dupont-Sommer's rendering 'and the levites and all (*kullam*) at the same time as (*'im*) the horns' (*Dead Sea Scrolls* p. 81; *Aperçus* p. 100), nor Tournay's 'les levites et tout le monde feront retenir avec les trompes' (RB 56 (1949), 214). The phrase is influenced by Josh vi, 5, 9, 20.

dart throwers begin throwing their darts. The principal aim of this great fanfare is 'to melt the heart of the enemy', but immediately afterwards they shall all cease (*yeḥĕshu*),[1] except for the trumpets which shall keep on blowing to direct, by battle signals, the dart throwing until the end. Thus two aims are achieved: the great battle fanfare on the one hand and directing the rhythm of the throwing on the other. The precise timing of the fanfare and the silence represents a most important element for achieving the psychological effect as described in the conquest of Jericho.[2] This conclusion, which it was difficult to reach at the time when only col. viii was published, is confirmed by the parallel descriptions given further on in the scroll:

(1) (ix, 1, 2.) 'As the sound goes forth, they shall attack to slay. *All* the band shall cease *the fanfare*, while the priests keep on blowing a fanfare upon the trumpets of the slain to direct the fighting, until the enemy are discomfited and turn their backs, while the *priests sound the fanfare to direct the fighting*.'

(2) (xvi, 6–8.) 'Then the six [priests shall blow on] the trumpets of assault a high-pitched intermittent note to direct the fighting, and the levites and the whole band of horn blowers shall sound [a battle fanfare], a great noise. As soon as the sound goes forth, they shall attack to slay the Kittim, and all the people shall cease from the sound of the fanfare, [while the priests] keep on *blowing on the trumpets of assault*.'

(3) (xvii, 12–15.) 'While the priests sound a fanfare on the trumpets of the slain [and the levites and the whole] band of horn-blowers sound a battle fanfare, the skirmishers shall attack the army of the Kittim [and as soon as there goes forth the sound] of the fanfare, they shall assault them. All the people shall cease [3] from the fanfare, while the priests keep on sounding a fanfare [on the trumpets of the slain.]'

The language of these passages [4] confirms that the author intended

---

[1] Prof. G. R. Driver suggests 'shall decrease' (*yaḥishu*), cf. Arab. *khāsa* (med. *y*) 'decrease (value)'.

[2] Cf. on all this Abel, op. cit. (p. 107, n. 2). For phraseology, see commentary.

[3] For the restoration see commentary.

[4] For parallels see commentary. Cf. also Neh. viii, 11 (which is likely to have influenced our passage, since all the operative words occur there). The recognition that *ḥashah* and *nuaḥ* are synonyms enables us to propose a solution for the difficult verse Ecclus. xxxv, 18, 20:

הלא דמעה על לחי תרד
ואנחה על מרודיה
תמרורי רצון הנחה
וצעקה ענן חשתה

It clearly recalls Lam. iii, 44. If we take both הנחה and חשתה as expressions meaning 'to silence, to restrain', we can translate: 'As the tear remains upon the cheek and the sigh upon him that causeth them to fall, so the bitter plaints of good-will have been silenced and the cloud has

the cessation of the general fanfare while the fanfare of the trumpets of the slain continues to direct the fighting. To sum up : the trumpets and horns were co-ordinated in four stages :

(a) Sounding a fanfare on the trumpets of the slain as a sign for commencing the battle.

(b) At the same time the levites and the band of horn-blowers sound a great fanfare to melt the heart of the enemy.

(c) The fanfare of the horns ceases.

(d) The sounding of the trumpets of the slain continues.

§ 9. THE TRUMPETS AND HORNS IN THE O.T.

The trumpets as well as the horns play a part in the battles described in the scroll (the trumpets mainly for signalling and the horns for the great fanfare whose principal purpose is psychological and magical : to melt the heart of the enemy). In the light of this we must examine what is known to us on this subject in the O.T., and especially the description of the conquest of Jericho, in which trumpets are not mentioned at all, but it is the priests who sound the horns. In descriptions of the battles in the O.T. which mention the blowing, for signalling as well as for religious and psychological purposes, almost without exception horns only are mentioned. The description of the conquest of Jericho and the war of Gideon against Midian on the one hand and the defence plan of Nehemiah on the other are obvious examples. The same is true of other passages, including those in which the blowing is mentioned only incidentally (which makes the information all the more reliable).[1] On the other hand trumpets, not horns, are mentioned in the description of the battle between Jeroboam and Abijah.[2] The Rabbis who gave the fact careful consideration (and especially the contradiction between Num. and the conquest of Jericho) tried to explain it mainly by connecting the account in Num. with the person of Moses. In this explanation they were already influenced by

---

retained the sigh,' i.e. restrained it from reaching God. To this argument, Ben Sira immediately replies : ' The appeal of the lowly traverses the clouds (so M), and is not silenced until it arrives ; it does not depart (*tamush*, or read *tahush* ' is not restrained ' ?) till God pay heed *to it*, and the righteous judge executes judgment.'

[1] Most important passages : 1 Sam. xiii, 3 (signal for mobilizing the tribes) ; 2 Sam. xv, 10 (call to rebellion) ; ib. xviii 16 (signal to stop pursuit) ; xx, 1 ; xx, 22 ; 1 Kings i, 39 (crowning) ; Isa. xviii, 3 ; Jer. iv, 5, 21 ; vi, 1, 17 ; Ezek. xxxiii, 3 ; Neh. iv, 12.

[2] 1 Chr. xiii, 12–14, which is strongly influenced by Num. Trumpets are frequently mentioned in contexts other than warfare, in 2 Kings, Ezra, Neh., Ps. (xcviii, 6, by the side of horns), and particularly Chr. It is remarkable that in Ex. and Lev. only the horn appears. Cf. further HDB iv, 815, and Galling p. 394.

110   INTRODUCTION

the post-Biblical situation when the place of the trumpets and horns which were used in the Temple and in war was taken by the horns alone, and the words 'trumpet' and 'horn' both indicated rams' horns.¹ The Romans, in fact, forbade the Jews to use horns at certain periods and in various places.²

The use of both trumpets and horns as described in the scroll on the one hand and the description of the use of horns in the O.T. on the other, compels us to assume that until the time of the Second Temple mainly horns were used for signalling in battle and for frightening the enemy. When the trumpets were brought into use, being more adaptable and able to produce signals of differing nuances, as described in the scroll, the ancient form was kept for the fanfare intended to encourage the soldiers and to terrify the enemy. The purpose of the horns, which had not changed since the conquest of Jericho, was given over to the levites while the priests from now on sounded the trumpets, as described in Num.³

§ 10. THE TRUMPETS IN THE MACCABEAN AND ROMAN PERIOD

We possess much information about the use of wind instruments in battle from passages in Macc., from the writings of Josephus, and of course from Roman literature.⁴

---

[1] Cf. the article by Finesinger quoted p. 107, n. 2, on the use of trumpets and horns in the temple. F. quotes Rabbinic passages in which horns and trumpets are confused; e.g. B. T. Sot. 43a: 'The trumpets of the fanfare are the horns'; B. T. Shabb. 36a: 'R. Ḥisda said, Three things have changed their names since the Temple was destroyed: the trumpet became a horn and the horn a trumpet . . .' See also Kasher (op. cit. p. 680, especially n. 2), who has collected much material on this, though some of his conclusions are hardly acceptable. Sifre, Behaʿalothĕkha lxxv; B. T. Men. 28; Tanḥuma Behaʿ-alothĕkha x, imply that the trumpets disappeared after the time of Moses.

[2] Cf. J. Mann, 'Changes in the Divine Service,' HUCA 4 (1927), 299, who quotes P.T. R.Sh.: 'Because it once happened that they sounded them and their enemies thought they were preparing to attack them, rose against them and killed them.'

[3] This theory forces us, of course, to take much of the terminology in Num. x for a description of the practice in the Second Temple period.

[4] To enable the reader to assess the evidence for the meaning of the instruments in the sources, in relation to the scroll, I quote Finesinger's summary (op. cit. p. 56 sq.). The numbers in brackets show the frequency of each translation.

Hebrew.	LXX.	Vulgate.
shofar	σάλπιγξ (42) / κερατίνη (25)	bucina (38) / tuba (29) / tuba cornea (1)
ḥăẓoẓĕrah	σάλπιγξ (27)	tuba (27)

While ḥăẓoẓĕrah is always σάλπιγξ or tuba, shofar may also be translated by κερατίνη (in a minority of cases) and bucina (in a slight majority of cases). From this it has been concluded that the ḥăẓoẓĕrah was straight and the shofar curved; and in fact the ḥăẓoẓĕrah (ασωσρα) is described by Jos. Ant. III, xii, 10, as a narrow tube, in length little short of a cubit, and compared with the σάλπιγξ. This is its shape on the Arch of Titus.

It is difficult to compare the information from Macc. with the contemporaneous practice in the Hellenistic armies since we possess next to no information on their use by these armies. Perhaps, as in the case of the banners, which were also little used by them, this derives from the fact that they fought in closed formation (in contrast to the Roman army) and therefore did not need a complicated signalling system either by means of banners or trumpets.[1] In 1 Macc. vii, 45, it is stated that the Judean army, while pursuing the remnant of Nicanor's army, sounded an alarm after them ταῖς σάλπιγξιν τῶν σημασιῶν.[2] On hearing the trumpet the rest of the population from the surrounding villages would join in the pursuit. In the battle against Gorgias (1 Macc. iv, 13) Judas's soldiers sound the trumpets or horns [3] on going to battle after Judas's prayer. On the other hand, the same trumpets of the war-cry are once more mentioned (ib. 40) at the time of prayer at the desecrated Temple and not in battle. Also in the great battle at Elasa in which Judas fell, it is stated (1 Macc. ix, 12) that the Greek army as well as the soldiers of Judas went forth to battle to the sound of trumpets or horns.[4]

As against this, 2 Macc. xv, 25, 26, states in the description of the battle against Nicanor that the Greek army advanced to the sound of trumpets and paeans. But 'Judas and his men joined battle with the enemy, calling upon God and praying'. Josephus also mentions the use of trumpets in the battles of the Maccabees.[5]

We may conclude that it was customary in the Maccabean armies to sound the trumpets at the beginning of battle as well as during pursuit. This information unfortunately is not enough to establish with certainty the names and role of the various trumpets. In other words, though the above information does not rule out the possibility of the use of trumpets by the Maccabean army for definite signals at different stages of the battle, it does not expressly confirm it. The above passage in 2 Macc. represents a tradition according to which the use of trumpets was typical of the Greek but not of the Judean armies.

Parallels to the system of military signalling described in the scroll multiply when we come to deal with the Roman period. Josephus in describing the Roman army (Wars, III, v, 4) deals at length with the

---

[1] Cf. Kromayer-Veith pp. 132–3, and n. 1 on p. 133.

[2] This is the LXX rendering of ḥăẓoẓ-roth ha-tĕru'ah. Though the use of trumpets is probable, it is not certain that they, and not horns, are meant in 1 Macc.,

and see Abel, *Maccabees* p. 82, n. 40.

[3] ἐσάλπισαν.

[4] ταῖς σάλπιγξι.

[5] Ant. XII, vii, 5 ; viii, 3 (τὸν σαλπιγκτὴν σημᾶναι), for tactical signals.

trumpet signals and mentions that the Roman army got ready for departure to the sound of three trumpet signals. At the first fanfare they take down their tents, at the second one they load the beasts of burden, and only the third fanfare gives the order to commence the expedition. Before setting out, the crier asks the soldiers three times whether they are ready to go out to war, and the soldiers confirm their readiness with three shouts; similarly Josephus writes: 'They do this as filled with a kind of martial fury, and at the time that they so cry out, they lift up their right hands also.'[1]

In his description of the precision and discipline of the units acting on command, Josephus mentions that even in battle the principal military movements (including advance and retreat) were accomplished with precision at the sound of orders.[2] A description closely resembling that of the scroll with regard to the link between the trumpets and the throwing of missiles is given by Josephus in connexion with Vespasian's siege of Jotapata. The description stresses the general blowing of trumpets, the great war-cry of the army, and the throwing of the darts to the sound of the signal.[3] Amongst the information which Josephus supplies, the most interesting is the passage in which he describes how he organized his army on the pattern of the Roman army. Among the many 'innovations' he introduced, he notes that he taught the army ways of passing on orders and the use of trumpets for signalling advance and return.[4]

It is interesting to compare the types of trumpets used by the Roman army with those in the scroll. The following is a division of the tasks of the three principal types (*cornu, bucina, tuba*):[5] the *tuba* signals the assembly, advance, and return and other military signals; the *bucina* and *cornu* serve for secondary signals of an administrative and ceremonial nature,[6] i.e. for signalling in battle the *tuba* (= trumpet) is used while the rest (which correspond more or less to the horns) are used for secondary or ceremonial activities. On the other hand Vegetius notes that during the actual fighting the *tuba* and *cornu* were blown simultaneously[7] (cf. above the combination of the fanfare with the

---

[1] Cf. p. 100, n. 3, for signals by hand. Here σάλπιγγες certainly denotes trumpets. For the language used to describe the third blast, cf. DSW viii, 7.
[2] Wars III, v, 4.
[3] Wars III, vii, 27.
[4] Wars II, xx, 7. Here πρόσκλησις = מפסע and ἀνάκλησις = משוב; Thackeray: 'advance' and 'retreat'.

[5] According to Vegetius iii, 5, the *tuba* is straight, the *bucina*, and especially the *cornu*, curved like the *shofar*.
[6] Vegetius ii, 22: 'Tubicen ad bellum vocat milites et rursum receptui canit'; cf. Marquardt p. 295, Kromayer-Veith p. 323.
[7] Ibid.: 'quotiens autem pugnatur, et tubicines et cornicines pariter canunt.'

horns). Vegetius in summing up the section under discussion numbers the battle phases effected by the various signals as 'halt', 'assembly and advance', 'return', and 'pursuit'.[1]

It must be noted that the number of trumpets and horns at the disposal of the 'central command' of the legion did not exceed seven of each type.[2]

§ 11. SUMMARY

The principal difference between the practice in Israel and other nations concerning the use of trumpets in battle may be summarized as follows. While with the others they were mainly for tactical purposes, to encourage the warriors and frighten the enemy with their terrifying sound,[3] their principal function in Israel was to stress the religious character of the war—to be remembered before the Lord—and only secondarily for actual signalling. The scroll emphasizes this not only by allotting the task of blowing them to the priests, in conformity with the Pentateuch, but also by the inscriptions engraved upon the trumpets. The Midrash indicates this difference succinctly (Lev. Rabba xxix, 4) : ' " Happy is the people that know the fanfare " (תרועה, A.V. "joyful shout", Ps. lxxxix, 16). But do not the nations of the world know how to sound the fanfare ? How many *bucinae* do they possess ! how many σάλπιγγες ![4] And yet you say " happy is the people that know the fanfare " ? They [Israel] know how to win the favour of their Creator with the fanfare !'

---

[1] Ib. iii, 5 : 'Nam indubitatis per haec sonis agnoscit exercitus utrum stare vel progredi an certe regredi oporteat utrum longe persequi fugientes an receptui canere.' So also ii, 22, referring to training, and cf. Kromayer-Veith p. 438.

[2] Cf. Kromayer-Veith p. 519, where E. v. Nischer works out, from inscriptions of the reign of Caracalla, that each legion had 37 trumpet-blowers, including their officers, and 35 horn-blowers, including officers. Since each *manipulus* had one of each, he concludes that the legion headquarters (including that of the legion's cavalry) had only 5–7 trumpets and 4–5 horns at its disposal.

[3] Cf. Caesar, B.C. III, 92.

[4] In the original the Latin and the Greek words are written in Hebrew characters.

Chapter 6

THE WEAPONS

§ 1. General Remarks

The scroll devotes much space to the weapons of the Sons of Light.[1] It does not merely specify their names and use but gives their measurements, ornaments, the material from which they are fashioned, the inscriptions some of them bear, as well as the types of warriors that use each one.

To my knowledge, so far no Hebrew or Jewish source has been found from either before or after A.D. 70 which contains so much important and detailed material on this subject. In some details it excels even parts of the relevant sources in classical literature.

The pedantry of the author in giving even the exact measurements of the weapons may be explained in two ways. Since part of the measurements mentioned (e.g. the shield) exactly correspond to the measurements of several of the holy vessels mentioned in the Pentateuch, their specification may be due to faith in the magical properties of these figures. But this interpretation cannot account for the many other measurements which show no connexion with the O.T. sources. Hence one may conclude that they were perhaps taken from a source which dealt with measurements of the different weapons and the material from which they were made for the purpose of determining the rules of levitical purity similar to those in the Mishnah, tractate Kelim, for various vessels including some weapons.

The language describing the various ornaments adorning the shields, spears, and swords follows the descriptions of the ornaments of the holy vessels in the Bible, which proves that they were considered to have prophylactic force. On the other hand, the additions to the Biblical descriptions and especially the many new terms in which these descriptions abound bear witness to the independence of the source. This also applies to the fact that for only part of the names of the weapons mentioned can parallels be found in the O.T. and in Rabbinic literature.

Moreover, some Biblical weapons are here called by different names. Similarly it must be stressed that the author employed no Greek or

---

[1] See the discussion of Sections 8-9, 12-13, in ch. 1.

Latin terms, unlike Rabbinic literature.[1] On the contrary, even in those instances when it seems that the weapon described is not typically local, the scroll gives it a Hebrew name.[2]

The scroll does not treat the different weapons as a separate subject, each type according to its various uses, but as part of the description of the units : front formation, skirmishers, according to their battalions.

In this chapter I shall deal with the weapons and the different equipment of each type of combat unit ; the tactical use of the weapons will be dealt with in chapter 7. A precise examination of the descriptions of weapons and especially of those details not mentioned in the O.T. is most important for deciding the period of the scroll, since here more than elsewhere the author used military sources or at least described what he saw in his period.

The inclusive term for weapons is : *kĕlē milḥamah* (viii, 8).[3] Amongst the combat units appear those who 'guard the arms' whose age is 25–30 years as that of some other service units.[4] The soldiers 'carry' (*maḥăziqim*) their arms and the various units are distinguished as ' those who carry . . . '.[5]

§ 2. THE SHIELD

The scroll uses *maghen* to denote all types of shields, rectangular or round.[6] The different types are indicated by specifying the measurements or describing the shape. The shields are carried by the front formation, some of the skirmishers (those with short range weapons) and the heavy cavalry.[7]

(1) *The Shield of the Front Formation.*

A. *The Shape and Measurements.*—The description of this shield (v, 4–6) is most detailed, including particulars relating to the material, ornaments and measurements : ' The length of the shield shall be two

---

[1] See S. Krauss, *Persia and Rome in Talmud and Midrash* (Hebrew), Jerus. 1948. P. T. Meg. i, 11, states : ' Four tongues are fit for the world to use, Greek for song, Latin for war, Aramaic for dirges, and Hebrew for conversation.'

[2] See below, § 6–7, and ch. 7, § 7.

[3] viii, 8, and cf. xvi, 5–6 ; xvii, 2 ; Dt. i, 41 ; Ju. xviii, 11 ; 2 Sam. i, 27, etc.

[4] vii, 2 ; see ch. 7, § 3 (5).

[5] v, 4 ; vi, 5, 14 ; cf. Ps. xxxv, 2 ; Neh. iv, 11, 16 ; Jer. vi, 23. The scroll avoids the more common O.T. expressions with *nś*', as well as those with *shlp* and *nshq*.

[6] Though the O.T. also knows *ẓinnah*, yet *maghen* is the more comprehensive term, cf. Ju. v, 8 ; Neh. iv, 10 ; 2 Chr. xxvi, 14, etc.

[7] The shield does not appear among the equipment of the sling and darts men, but may have been mentioned in the missing part of v ; also part of the equipment of the cavalry may have been discussed in the destroyed line vi, 15. See comm. ad loc. and to v, 1.

cubits and a half and its breadth one cubit and a half '. This description makes it certain that it was rectangular. This is also borne out by the words 'length' and 'breadth' without additional indications (cf. 'round shields', below, (3)) as well as by the rectangular shape of those weapons described also in the O.T.[1] In modern terms [2] the measurements would be (the cubit = 45·8 cm.).

> Length :   114·5 cm.
> Width :   68·7 cm.
> in round numbers :   115 × 69 cm.

This shape of the shield of the front formation has no parallel in the Hellenistic army in any period : its typical shield was round and varied in size.[3] We know nothing about the shields of the Maccabean army[4] but one may assume the weapons to have resembled those of the Hellenistic army of their time, at any rate in the early period, since they had taken the greater part of their equipment as booty from the enemy.[5] On the other hand, the shape and measurements of the shield agree exactly with the rectangular *scutum* of the Roman army. Until the discovery of the wonderful *scutum* at Dura Europos a few years ago,[6] the shape and measurements of this important weapon could only be guessed from short descriptions in Roman literature and from its representations on reliefs and tombstones.[7] Now we can compare the measurements of the shield in the scroll with those given by Polybius

---

[1] e.g. Ex. xxv, 10 ; see further in comm.

[2] The cubit here is the medium one of 6 handbreadths. The measures—as shown by their interplay in the scroll—are :
cubit = 6 handbreadths   . 45·72 cm.
handbreadth = 4 thumbs or 5
  fingers . . . . 7·62 ,,
(B.T. Men. 41b, but cf. B.T. Bekh. 39b)
thumb . . . . 1·905 ,,
finger . . . . 1·52 ,,
For convenience we shall reckon the cubit at 45·8 cm. See S. Krauss, *Talm. Archaeol.* ii, 388–90 ; Galling p. 367 ; Barrois, *Manuel d'Arch. Bibl.* ii, 243 sq. I have been able, to my surprise, to confirm these figures from the scroll itself, assuming that it was written according to the rules for Torah scrolls recorded in B.T. Men. 30a :
Upper margin : B.T. 'two fingers'. Scroll 3·0 cm. Hence finger = 1·5 cm.
Between columns : B.T. 'one thumb'. Scroll *c.* 1·9 cm. Hence thumb = 1·9 cm.

[3] K.-V. p. 108, and cf. the 'round shields' of the Serekh cavalry.

[4] Ant. XIII, xii, 5, states that Jannaeus' προμαχόμενοι (see ch. 7, § 4) had θυρεοί covered with bronze, while those of Ptolemy had ἀσπίδες.. In BJ III, v, 5, the general's bodyguard carry the ἀσπίς, the legionaries the θυρεός. Domaszewski (apud Marqu. p. 11, n. 7) thought Josephus had confused the terms, but as Couissin, p. 58, n. 2, shows, the θυρεός—where both terms are used—merely designates a more elongated form, be it oval, hexagonal (as were the Roman cavalry shields then), or rectangular.

[5] See M. Avi-Yonah, IEJ 2 (1952), 4.

[6] *Excavations at Dura Europos*, Preliminary Report VI, 1936, pp. 456–66 (by F. E. Brown), and Pl. xxv A and frontispiece. Cf. fig. 1.

[7] On the *scutum*, see Couissin s.v. and Brown, op. cit. p. 461.

THE WEAPONS 117

(vi. 23) and with the *scutum* from Dura,[1] in spite of the fact that 350 years separate them.

        Polybius :   120 × 75 cm.
        Scroll :   115 × 69 cm.
        Dura Europus : 102 × 83 cm.

This comparison proves that the measurements of the shield in the scroll represent the average of the two others.

The rectangular and convex *scutum*,[2] i.e. the typical shield of the Roman legion, was not generally used by the legions before Caesar.[3] This shield continued to be used by the legions along with differently shaped shields in the period of Augustus,[4] until it disappeared by degrees and in the beginning of the second century gave way to the oval and hexagonal *scutum*.[5] We know from several sources that during the first century A.D. the quadrangular scutum was rather small.[6]

B. *The Material*.—These shields were made of 'burnished copper, like a face mirror' (v, 4–5).[7] The O.T. mentions copper shields which, like the golden shields, were for ceremonial use.[8] On the other hand, much information exists proving the use of polished metal shields (including copper) in the armies of the Hellenistic and Roman periods. In the armies of Alexander the Great the types of soldiers were named according to the type of metal covering their shields : silver shields, copper shields, white shields etc.[9] In 1 Macc. vi, 39 in the famous description of the battle near Beth-Zacharias the author mentions the sun shining on the gold and copper shields of the Greeks.[10] I already mentioned the description by Josephus (Ant. XIII, xii, 5) of the copper shields of the soldiers of Alexander Jannaeus and the Greeks. The shields of part of the Spanish auxiliaries of Pompey were made of metal.[11] The purpose of shields being covered with shining metal 'like a face mirror' (to the extent that they were used by common soldiers) was amongst others to blind the eyes of their opponents.[12]

---

[1] Ibid.

[2] The 'bent shield' of M. Kelim xxiv, 1 ; cf. Krauss, op. cit. (note 2, p. 209.)

[3] Cf. Couissin, pp. 248, 314, 316, especially p. 318, and p. 320, n. 2.

[4] Ib. p. 390.

[5] Ib. p. 393 ; cf. *Dura-Europos* VII–VIII, 330, and see fig. 5.

[6] Contemporary reliefs show its height to have been up to 85 cm., cf. Brown, op. cit. p. 462, n. 75. Though the Dura *scutum* is rectangular, we know from contemporary representations and from *scuta* actually found (*Dura-Europos* VII–VIII, 327 sq.) that they were normally oval, measuring 92–97 cm. by 107–118 cm.

[7] On these terms, see comm.

[8] They were made by Rehoboam (1 Kings xiv, 27–8).

[9] Cf. K -V p. 133, particularly n. 10.

[10] Cf. Abel, *Livres Maccabées* pp. 120-1 and n. 39.

[11] Caesar, Bell. Civ. i. In general, see Brown, op. cit. p. 461.

[12] Cf. Abel, *Livres Maccabées* p. 120-1 and n. 39.

C. *The Ornamentation*.—The description of the ornaments on the shield is interesting : ' The shield shall be bordered with a rim of cable work and a pattern of running spiral, work of an artificer, in gold, silver and copper welded together and precious stones in ajour work, work of a smith, artificer's technique '(v, 5–6). והמגן) מוסב מעשי גדיל שפה וצורת מחברת מעשה חושב זהב וכסף ונחושת ממוזזים ואבני חפץ אבדני ריקמה מעשה חרש מחשבת) This description appears at first sight purely imaginative, but comparison with the shield from Dura Europos proves great similarity between them. Before doing so we must establish the meaning of the terms.[1]

A Rim of Cable Work.—Since *gĕdil* = several cords twisted together and *śafah* = rim, I propose to see in the ' rim of cable work ' the most typical and widely used pattern for adorning the rims of mosaic floors and other objects in Hellenistic, Roman, and Jewish art, the guilloche.

A Pattern of Running Spiral.—The *maḥbereth* frequently mentioned in the description of joints of the edges of the curtains in the Tabernacle,[2] by means of loops and clasps, also points to a border pattern whose general form must resemble a curling rounded line with entwined loops. To my mind this description suits the second border pattern which like the former was in common use, namely a scroll pattern.

Welded together.—This term apparently indicates the technique of joining the silver and gold to the copper shield. It hardly means simple joining and beating but melting the precious metals into grooves forming the pattern.

The description of the socket of the spear and the blades of the spear and sword mentions an additional linear pattern, the ' ear of corn ', i.e., a continuous ear-of-corn pattern. On comparing these patterns with the Dura shield (fig. 1, 2), the surprising resemblance becomes apparent. The ornaments of that shield are composed of three border patterns. The first one corresponds to the running spiral of the scroll, the middle one to the ear of corn, and the innermost one to the rim of cable work. The scroll has only the ' rim of cable work and the running spiral ' and in inverse order. In fig. 2., I have tried to reconstruct the shape of the shield as described in the scroll, based on the resemblance between them. It is of interest that the drawing of the ornaments on the shield from Dura leaves no doubt that the painter tried to imitate inlay work or relief work.[3] Similarly, one must consider some of the ornaments, especially the ones filling the empty space in the Dura shield, as an attempt to

---

[1] For these terms, see comm.
[2] Cf. in particular Ex. xxxvi, 11–13.
[3] Cf. Brown op. cit., p. 466.

Fig. 1. Ornaments on the Dura Europos Scutum.

represent precious stones inlaid in the metal.¹ Couissin in his description of the ornaments on the Roman shields notes that it was customary to draw on them, in addition to the geometric patterns, scrolls and circles, figures of ornaments and jewels also, which they regarded as talismans against the ' evil eye '.²

(2) *The Shields of the Skirmishers.*

These shields are not described in detail. The scroll merely states that one battalion carries ' lance and shield ' and the second ' shield and

---

[1] Note (apart from the similarities pointed out in the comm.) the parallels with the description of the table (Ex. xxv, 23 sq.) as given in the Letter of Aristeas, 57 onwards. The *zer* (A.V. ' crown ') is here rendered as κυμάτια στρεπτά, which ' suggests a cable moulding ' (H. T. Andrews in Charles, *Apoc.* ii, 101)—it is attractive to identify this with the ' rim of cable work and a pattern of running spiral ', v. 5 ; Josephus (Ant. III, vi, 6) renders *zer* by ἕλιξ ' a spiral '. Note the further correspondences : ' layers of precious stones (" precious stones in ajour work ", v. 6) on it in the midst of the embossed cord-work (= cable work), and they were interwoven with one another by an inimitable artistic device (" in ajour work ", *riqmah* = embroidery) '.

[2] pp. 396, 401.

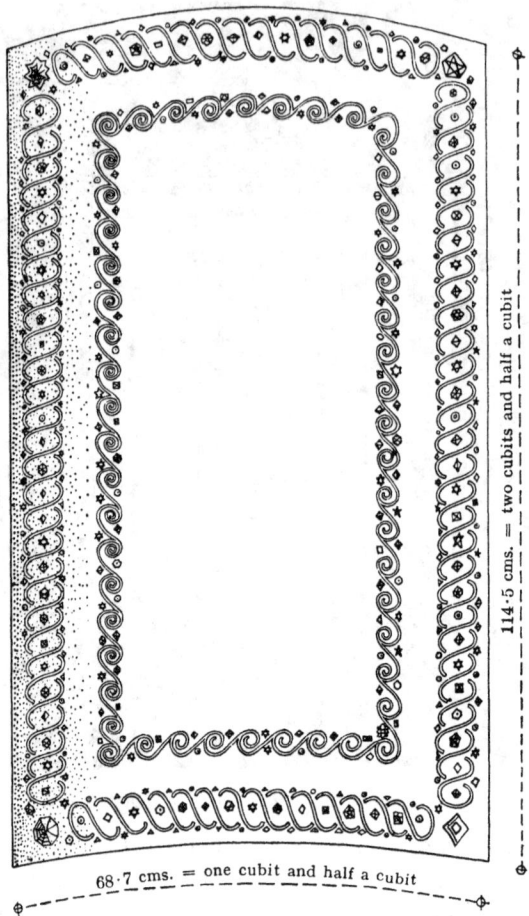

Fig. 2. Suggested reconstruction of the Shield of the 'Front Formations'.

sword'. The description of the weapons of the first standard puts the lance before the shield [1] because it constitutes the principal weapon, but with the second battalion, armed with the sword, the shield serves as the main weapon, which may be the reason for its precedence.[2]

(3) *The Shields of the Heavy Cavalry.*

The horsemen of the *serekh*, i.e. the heavy cavalry who fight with the infantry,[3] are 'armed with round shields' (vi, 15).

---

[1] Cf. 2 Chr. xxiii, 9; perhaps also 2 Kings xi, 10. See, however, 1 Chr. xii, 35.

[2] So in 1 Chr. v, 18; Ezek. xxxviii, 4; cf. Jer. xlvi, 9. The corresponding units in the Roman army, too, were called *cohors scutata* or *caetrata*, cf. ch. 7, § 4.

[3] Cf. ch. 7, § 6.

THE WEAPONS

This term is most interesting since מגני עגלה corresponds to the Aramaic term for the round shield (the *parma* or the *clipeus*) and with the Hebrew shield *soḥerah* (Ps. cxci, 4) which the Targum translates עגילא.[1] The translation of this verse emphasizes the use of this term for the round shield (as is also suggested by the etymology).[2] The form עגלה (not עגלים) shows it to be a technical term for this type of shield.[3] The insistence of the author that the shields of the horsemen were round in contrast to those of the infantry, etc. (unfortunately vi, 15 which might have described the shields of the light cavalry is destroyed), proves that he was well versed in military practice. This information is very important for dating the scroll. The *parma* or the *clipeus* (the round shield) was the typical shield of the Roman cavalry.[4] It is very interesting that these shields, which were still used by the cavalry at the time of Julius Caesar, completely disappeared immediately afterwards, and during the days of Josephus, for instance, the cavalry carried hexagonal or oval shields.[5] Couissin, who claims that the round shield went out of general use in the cavalry at the time of Julius Caesar, admits the value of the literary and archaeological descriptions which prove the existence of round shields at that period, but he assigns them, as does the scroll, to the mounted infantry and not to the real cavalry.[6]

(4) *The Shields of the 'Towers'*.

The shape of the shields of the 'towers' resembles that of the infantry except that they were longer: 'The shields of the towers shall be three cubits long' (ix, 12); since their width is not specified we may

---

[1] On the *tĕris* see p. 116, n. 4, and p. 117, n. 2, and Levy, *Targumim* s.v. On *soḥerah* Zimmern, *Akkad. Fremdwörter* p. 14. This meaning of *soḥerah* is doubted by many scholars.

[2] The Tgs. frequently use this word also for *ẓinnah* (cf. also comm. on vi, 14). May we conclude that the latter was round or oval? Such a shape would fit the description of Goliath's shield, many of the large shields of this and later periods being made of convex plaited work like a flat basket.

[3] The reading *'ăghaloth*, 'carriages,' makes little sense. Cf. however, Ps. xlvi, 10, 'He breaketh the bow and cutteth the spear in sunder; He burneth the *'ăghaloth* in the fire,' where only Pesh. has 'chariots', but LXX, Vulg., and Tg. 'shields'. LXX, by the way, has here θυρεούς.

[4] See above, p. 116, n. 4, and K.-V. p. 410.

[5] BJ III, v, 5 (cf. p. 116, n. 4), says that the cavalry shields were elongated; cf. K.-V. p. 522 and ib. pl. 37.

[6] pp. 143, 238, 315, and particularly 248 sq. In his detailed discussion, Couissin distinguishes between *chevaliers* and *la véritable cavalerie* (p. 143). All data about the round shield both before and after Caesar refer, in his view, to the first group only, including the mention of the *parma equestris* in the *Hist. Fragm.* of Sallust, who served in Caesar's army (p. 250, n. 4). This affects our argument very little, as the 'cavalry of the Serekh' are in fact mere *chevaliers*, in contrast to the regular cavalry serving with the skirmishers and on the army's flanks (ch. 7, § 6).

assume that it was the same as the shields of the infantry, a cubit and a half. Hence the measurements of these shields were :

Length : 137·4 cm.
Width : 68·7 cm.

For these shields, which served a special tactical purpose, cf. the discussion of the towers, chapter 7, §7 (2). For the inscriptions on these shields cf. chapter 9, §6 (2) ; and §§7 and 9 below.

It must be noted that the author used the width of the shield for indicating various frontal widths. Thus ' (when the battle intervals shall open) to a width of fifty shields ' (vii, 14), i.e. to a width of $75 \times 0·458 = 34·35$ metres, or ' The towers shall protrude from the formation by a hundred shields, hundred being the face of the tower ' (ix, 12, 13), i.e. a frontal width of $150 \times 0·458 = 68·7$ m.[1]

Body Armour [2] : Armour of the body, head and shins are mentioned only in connexion with the heavy cavalry.[3] The first part of the description of the armour of the cavalry who go out with the skirmishers is missing and we cannot know whether body armour was mentioned, too.[4] From the *argumentum e silentio* in the detailed description of the weapons of the front formation, it must be assumed as a certainty that these soldiers, according to the scroll, did not wear body armour.

The following passage describes the body armour of the heavy cavalry : ' (garbed in) cuirasses, helmets and greaves ' (vi, 14).[5] The order is the same as in the Mishnah (Shab. vi, 2) ' A man may not go out . . . not with a cuirass or helmet and greaves.'

§ 3. Greaves

The O.T. mentions the term *miẓhoth* once in the description of the armour of Goliath : ' And he had *miẓhoth* of brass upon his legs ' (1 Sam. xvii, 6), LXX, rendered κνημῖδες ' greaves '. This term does not appear any more in Mishnaic Hebrew, which uses *maggafayim*.[6] Obadiah of Bertinoro explains them ' as a kind of iron shin-guard (*batté shoqayim*) worn in battle '. The language of the Mishnah shows that during the Second Temple period the word *miẓhoth* (which can

---

[1] Cf. ch. 7, §§ 2 (4), 5.

[2] One might almost use L. A. Mayer's term ' wardrobe of metal ' (*Mamluk Costumes*, Geneva 1952, p. 36), except that the scroll gives no indication of its material, and parts may have been of leather.

[3] Horse armour was perhaps mentioned in a missing passage, see comm. to vi, 14 ; cf. the excellent treatment *Dura-Europos* VI, 144 sq., and pl. xxi–xxiii.

[4] I consider it improbable, cf. comm. on vi, 15.

[5] For the restoration, see comm.

[6] Cf. also M. Kelim xi, 8, and S. Krauss, op. cit. (n. 2), p. 210.

also be explained as a head-shield) was not in use any more. The term *battē shoqayim*, like the Greek word, is derived from the part where the armour is worn. However, in comparatively late examples adduced by Ben-Yehudah, the shin-guards are mentioned with other terms from the Mishnah, e.g. finger-stall (*beth eẓbaʻoth*, M. Kelim, xxvi, 3) or hand-guard (*beth yadh*, B. T. Shab. 65a).[1] This points to an early tradition which these sources possessed : it may be that they had a source containing this very term בָּתֵּי־שׁוֹקַיִם.[2] The use of *bayith* for anything having a receptacle, which is so extensively used in Mishnaic Hebrew and apparently also at times in the O.T.,[3] suits the concave shin-guard (see next section). The use of greaves was common in the Greek as well as in the Roman army in the second century B.C. In the first century B.C., they disappeared as part of the infantry's equipment [4] so that at the time of Julius Caesar they had completely gone out of use in the infantry.[5] On the other hand, greaves continued to be used by certain ranks in the cavalry of select units [6] until in the end they disappeared completely.

The reason is that while the round shield which covered only part of the body was in use, it was essential to use greaves. On the other hand, the appearance of the oblong shield at that very period made the heavy and constricting greaves superfluous except for those horsemen whose shields were round and whose legs formed the main weak spot when fighting against infantry.[7] This fact is clearly brought out by the scroll. The armour of the front formation, i.e. the bearers of the long shields, does not include greaves, while the horsemen who hold round shields in their hand use them.

§ 4. The Helmet

These same horsemen also wear a ' head-guard ', *beth rosh*, equivalent to the Biblical *qovaʻ*.[8] The Biblical word, like that for greave, was

---

[1] Ben-Yehudah, *Thesaurus* xiv, 6989.

[2] Test. Judah iii, 1, says in some versions that Judah struck the Amorite king on his ' shin-guards ', in others on his ' shins ', and Charles (*Test. of Twelve Patriarchs*, 1908, p. 70) emended κνημῖδας to κνήμας. An original *beth shoqayim* could have given rise to both versions. The midrashic versions of the story have ' ankles ', e.g. *Yalkuṭ Shimʻoni*, Wayyishlaḥ 33. On these versions see ch. 7, p. 167, n. 1.

[3] e.g. Ex. xxxvii, 14 ; 2 Kings xxiii, 7 ; Isa. iii, 20.

[4] K.-V. pp. 108, 324 ; Couissin p. 347 sq.

[5] Couissin pp. 350, 468.

[6] Ib. p. 467.

[7] K.-V. p. 410 explains why shin-guards ceased to be used. I cannot agree with his view that the shin-guards of officers served merely as badge of rank : since many officers were mounted, they needed them, though of course the fact that only officers wore them made them also a sign of rank. For the different view of Holmes and Conquest, see ibid. n. 9.

[8] Particularly Jer. xlvi, 4.

given up in Mishnaic Hebrew [1] and in its place appear terms borrowed from the Roman army.[2] The occurrence of ' head-guard ', בית־הראש, in the scroll shows that this term, which appears in later literature,[3] was old like ' shin-guard '. This tendency towards the end of the Second Temple period to change Biblical terms for compounds with *beth-* finds expression in the passage : ' A sling the hollow of which is woven ' (M. Edu. iii, 5) with *beth qibbul* instead of the Biblical *kaf ha-qelaʻ*.

§ 5. THE CUIRASS

I have restored this in a missing passage (vi, 14) and therefore deal with it in the commentary.

Offensive Weapons.—I shall deal with these in the following order : Sword, dart, lance, spear, sling, bow. I have chosen this sequence, which differs from that of the scroll (spear, sword, sling, dart, lance, bow, in the order of the units using them), so as to facilitate the exposition of the problems related to them. This order more or less corresponds to the length of the weapons (in ascending length) and not to their range (in ascending order : sword, spear, lance, dart, bow, sling).

§ 6. THE SWORD (כידן)

The front formations carry a sword in addition to the shield and spear. Also the men of the skirmishing battalions are armed with this weapon. The description of the sword is very detailed, giving its measurements, how it was carried, its ornaments and an enumeration of its parts. This description raises a number of difficult problems since the author uses several terms hitherto unknown to us.

It is perfectly clear that *kidhon*, as employed by the author, means a sword, and not a lance or similar weapon. With the implications of this fact and its connexion with the Biblical *kidhon* I shall deal later. It is invariably spelt כידן in DSW.[4]

(1) *Measurements and Shape.*

' The length of the sword shall be a cubit and a half and its breadth four fingers '[5] (v, 12, 13) ; that is to say (cubit = 45·8 cm.) :

$$\text{Length}: \quad 68\cdot 7 \text{ cm.}$$
$$\text{Width}: \quad 6 \quad \text{ cm.}$$

---

[1] See, however, in Levy, *Talmud* s.v. כובע.

[2] Cf. Krauss, op. cit. n. 2, p. 209, and M. Shab. vi, 2.

[3] Cf. Ben-Jehudah, *Thesaurus* II, 536b.

[4] In O.T. כידון, except Jer. l, 42 : כידן.

[5] Cf. p. 116. n. 2. The measures, of course, apply to the blade, as does also the description of the material.

These measurements show that the *kidhon* is a long sword. Its shape is defined as follows : ' And lips straight up to the point, two on either side ' (ib. 12). To understand this description we must clarify the terms used.

(2) *Lips*.

In various utensils, and particularly those having a ' mouth ', the word שפה (more commonly spelt שׂפה) denotes not just the rim or edge, but the sloping part near and including the edge or rim. Thus the rounded rims at the ' mouth ' of earthen vessels are called שפיות, ספיות.[1] The sword has ' two lips on each side ' : this means that each of the two edges of the sword has two ' lips ' (see fig. 4), the edge being the ' mouth ' (Ju. iii, 16 ; Ps. cxlix, 6 ; Pr. v, 4) and the ' lip ' being the curving slope from the full thickness to the cutting edge.

On the other hand, in contrast to the Biblical passages, which speak of the sword having ' two mouths ' (= sharp edges) only—as opposed to a curved sword for striking, which had a single ' mouth '—the scroll specifies further, and describes each ' mouth ' as having two ' lips '.[2]

(3) *The Point*.

The edges of the sword extended straight up to the point (literally ' head ', cf. Tos. Sanh. xiv, 6 and cf. n. 2 below, and n. 2, p. 128). This meaning becomes obvious on comparing this description with the blade of the spear, which is defined as ' tapering towards the point ' (v, 10, 11) (cf. below, § 11).

It thus appears that the *kidhon* of the scroll was a straight double-edged sword, not a ' sickle sword '.

(4) *The Material and the Ornaments*.

The sword is made of ' iron refined and purified in the furnace and tempered like a face mirror, work of a smith, artificer's technique '. From the parallels which appear in the commentary it becomes probable that steel [3] is meant. Certainly the quality of the iron of the spear is inferior to that of the sword, since it is only ' iron tempered in fire, work of a smith, artificer's technique '.[4] The fact that the iron of the

---

[1] Cf. Ex. xxviii, 32 ; M. Kelim iv, 3, and see comm.

[2] This finally settles the meaning of the Biblical *lĕ-fi ḥerev* as meaning ' by the *edge* of the sword ', also borne out by Tos. Sanh. xiv, 6, where the ' head of the sword ' is opposed to its ' edge ', and disposes of Meek's proposal (BASOR 122, p. 31 sq.) that the *peh* is the animal head with open mouth (sometimes two) at the lower end of the hilt of some Canaanite swords. This would make nonsense of the specification of *ḥerev pifiyoth* in the Ehud story, while ' two-edged ', of course, explains why it could also be used for piercing.

[3] Cf. Lieberman, *Greek in Jewish Palestine* 1942, pp. 51–2.

[4] Cf. Mayer, op. cit. (n. 42), p. 43, n. 6.

sword is harder than that of the spear is brought out by the explanation of the ornaments : the spear has an 'ear of corn in pure gold in the midst of the blade' (v, 10) but the sword has 'ear of corn figures of pure gold appliqué on it on both sides' (v, 11, 12). This description suggests a different technique for the gold appliqué on the blade. For the ear of corn cf. fig. 4, and below, § 11.

(5) *The 'Belly'.*

After the description of the sword, its measurements, the material and ornaments (but before the description of the 'handle') we read : 'the belly shall be 4 thumbs, and 4 handbreadths up to the belly, the belly being tied on both sides with thongs of 5 handbreadths' (v, 13, 14). The width of the 'belly' (4 cm. $\times$ 1·9 = 7·6 cm.) exceeds that of the blade by 1·9 cm.

It is not easy to identify the 'belly'. The fact that the edges extend straight up to the point excludes the possibility of identifying the 'belly' with the middle part of the blade of the sword (i.e. a bi-convex or 'sickle' sword). This identification is impossible also for the following reasons :

(*a*). If the distance to the 'belly' is 4 handbreadths (i.e. *c.* 4/9 of the length of the sword) and its width is 7·6 cm. then this width can only be reached gradually. Similarly the blade must narrow gradually towards the point. In the light of this there is no sense in saying that the width of the sword is 6 cm.

(*b*). If the 'belly' forms the middle part of the sword, how can one explain the phrase : 'tied [1] on both sides with thongs of 5 handbreadths'?

Thus, in my opinion, in the word 'belly' we find the name for a very important part of the sword, namely the scabbard.

(6) *The Scabbard.*

Though I find no parallel supporting this identification,[2] the various uses of 'belly' (especially in Aramaic) may explain how this word came to be borrowed for describing the scabbard, which contains the sword like an embryo in the womb.[3] Various conclusions can be drawn from the system of girding on the sword, which varies at different periods

---

[1] See comm. for the reasons for reading with *r*, not *d*.

[2] *nĕdhan* occurs only 1 Chr. xxi, 27 ; the normal BH word is *ta'ar* (also DST v, 15) ; in MH also *tiq* (e.g. M. Kelim xvi, 5).

[3] As here 'belly' for the sword, so scabbard' has been borrowed for the human body B.T. Sanh. 108a, 'that their soul will not return to its scabbard' (play on *nĕdhan* and *yadhon*, Gn. vi, 3). Cf. Latin *vagina* (so also Ezek. xvi, 33 ?), and for a similar semantic development in Hebrew, Lieberman, *Tosefeth Rishonim* iii, 267.

according to the type of soldier, since it greatly influences the comfort of the wearer and the speed with which the sword is drawn.[1] I think that the sentence ' the scabbard being tied (*mĕruggeleth*) on both sides with thongs of 5 handbreadths ' indicates the method of girding on the sword. The use of the root *rgl* in Mishnaic Hebrew [2] allows us to assume that this term describes the system of girding on the sword without attaching it directly to the belt,[3] but joined by means of two straps and thus suspended over the leg (see fig. 3). Hence by saying ' on both sides

Fig. 3. Method of attaching the gladius *(detail of fig. 5, no. 10).*

5 handbreadths ' the author means that the length of the straps for tying, one to the left and the other to the right, was *c.* 38 cm. The phrase ' four handbreadths up to the scabbard ' (v, 13) denotes the distance between the belt and the scabbard, or more probably, to the place where the scabbard is joined to the straps, since the subject of the description is the method of attachment.[4] For reconstruction, see fig. 4.

---

[1] Cf. the Accadian curse ' may his sword-belt become undone when he faces his enemy ', Oppenheim, *Orientalia* 14 (1945), 239.

[2] M. Shab. v, 3, uses *raghul* of a camel, explained in Tos. Shab. iv (v), 3, as ' tying one foreleg to one hindleg'.

[3] As stated 2 Sam. xx, 8, of Joab's sword.

[4] If the 4 handbreadths referred to the distance between the belt and the top of the scabbard, the sword would dangle around the knees. If we are to take it as the length of the hilt above the scabbard, we would have a hilt over a foot long.

(7) *The 'Hand of the Sword'*.

The description of the sword ends with a description of its 'hand': 'The hand of the sword shall be of smooth horn, artificer's work, inlaid in ajour with gold and silver and precious stones'. This evidently means the handle, which is once mentioned in the O.T. under the name *niṣṣav*,[1] in agreement with Mishnaic usage.[2] The use of horn for the handle of the sword as well as the ornaments is common in many

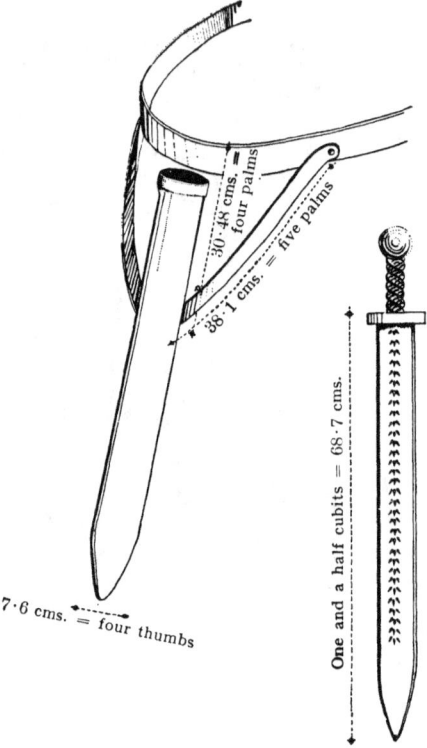

Fig. 4. Suggested reconstruction of the sword and the scabbard.

periods. For a reconstruction of the handle, based upon the descriptions of the ornaments and on Roman examples (cf., e.g., the sword of soldier no. 14 in fig. 6) see fig. 4.

(8) *Dating of the Sword*.

From the above discussion we learn that the sword of the front formation was 68·7 cm. long, *c*. 6 cm. wide, straight, and two-edged with bevelled edges. It was in a scabbard (*c*. 7·6 cm. wide) tied to the

---

[1] Ju. iii, 22.   [2] e.g. M. Kelim xiii, 1; xxix, 6.

hips by means of two straps *c.* 38 cm. long. This description, which is completely different from that of the short sword, meant only for thrusting, of the men of the phalanx at the time of the Diadochs,[1] fits the *gladius* of the Roman army whose shape (see fig. 3) and measurements (60–70 cm.)[2] exactly correspond to the sword here described.

Couissin[3] devotes a long discussion to the method of attaching the sword, mentioning that in the first century B.C., until the time of

Fig. 5. *Roman soldiers of the second and first centuries* B.C.

Augustus, it was customary to carry the sword solely by means of straps, as described in the scroll (cf. fig. 5, soldiers nos. 10 and 11). The method of attaching the sword to the belt and to the shoulder strap, which is typical from the first half of the first century A.D. onwards, started only in the time of Augustus[4] (cf. fig. 6).

(9) *The 'Kidhon' in the Scroll and in the O.T.*

The obvious fact that in the scroll the *kidhon* is a sword and not a lance demands a re-examination of this word in the O.T. and other sources. The *kidhon* appears nine times in the O.T., three times in connexion with the conquest of Ai (Josh. viii, 18, 26), twice in connexion with Goliath (1 Sam. xvii, 6, 45), once in connexion with the 'people

---

[1] K.-V. p. 134 remarks on effectiveness of the long Roman cutting-sword against this. The absence of the dagger is due to its use in the first century B.C. being restricted to officers: in Josephus it plays a great role. Cf. K.-V. p. 410. See figs. 5–6.
[2] ib. p. 325.
[3] Especially p. 309 sq.
[4] ib. p. 313.

from the north country' riding upon horses (Jer. vi, 23; l, 42) and twice in Job (xxxix, 23; xli, 21).

In every one of these passages *kidhon* may well mean 'sword'. Joshua stretched out his hand holding the *kidhon* to give the signal for the ambush, a description which fits also the sword held by the commander-in-chief and not necessarily a lance.[1] Jeremiah mentions the

Fig. 6. Roman soldiers of the end of the first century B.C. and of the first century A.D.

kidhon in connexion with the mounted bowmen ('*bow and kidhon*') who would surely carry a sword rather than a lance. In the description of the courage of the horse (Job xxxix, 23) which does not take fright, it is written: 'The quiver rattleth upon him, the glittering spear and the *kidhon*', from which we may assume that the *kidhon* is not identical with the lance, and there is no reason for not taking it to be a sword. Ib. xli, 21 has: 'He laugheth at the rattling of the *kidhon*'. The use of rattling for describing the sound of a weapon is only mentioned this once in the O.T. and it can no doubt be used to describe the sound of a sword when swung through the air.[2]

The most difficult passage and one which has been explained in various ways is the description of the *kidhon* amongst Goliath's weapons:

---

[1] Gressmann's theory (*apud* Galling p. 161) that Joshua's *kidhon* was some kind of standard, is improbable. Ecclus. xlvi, 4 (2), paraphrases this 'when he stretched out (*ba-hănifo*) a *kidhon* (LXX ῥομφαίαν) against the city'. The O.T. uses *henif* of a sword (Ex. xx, 25), a saw (Isa. x, 15), a sickle (Dt. xxiii, 26), i.e. things not normally thrown.

[2] See, however, Tur-Sinai in his Job comm. ad loc. and xl, 18, as well as comms. on Job xxix, 20; 2 Sam. xxi, 16.

'And a *kidhon* of brass between his shoulders.'[1] A short time ago O'Callaghan suggested various reasons for taking the *kidhon* of Goliath to be a sword.[2] In addition to his interesting arguments (which however do not entirely exclude ' lance ') I believe that from an analysis of the chapter [3] it is possible to understand the *kidhon* here as being a sword, because its being worn on the shoulder [4] is explained by the soldierly habit of supporting the long sword on the shoulder.[5] Whether this conclusion is accepted or not, it seems clear that this is how the scroll and the sect used the word.[6]

§ 7. The Darts (זרקות).

Three of the skirmishing units (vi, 1–4) and the light cavalry (vi, 15) were armed with darts.[7] The principal passage describing the darts is: ' After these three skirmishing battalions shall go forth and take up a position between the lines. The first battalion shall throw into the enemy line seven battle darts. On the blade of the dart they shall write " Flash of a lance to the might of God ". On the second weapon they shall write " Sparks of blood to slay by the anger of God " ; on the third dart they shall write " Glitter of a sword devouring the sinful slain by the judgment of God ". Each of these shall throw seven times and then return to their position ' (vi, 1–4).[8]

This passage brings out the main features of the darts : the dart is thrown ; it has a blade ; the soldiers of each battalion hold seven darts ; the darts bear inscriptions, a special inscription for every battalion.

Before dealing with the nature of the dart we must prove two of the above conclusions : (1) That every soldier holds seven darts. (2) That

---

[1] LXX ' shield '. Rashi : ' a kind of bronze spear protruding from the helmet to protect his neck from blows ' ; Kimchi thinks it might be a spare lance carried on the back.

[2] O'Callaghan, *Orientalia* 21 (1952), 48, suggests, on the basis of Ugaritic and a Canaanite loan word in Egyptian, that *bên kĕthefaw* here may mean ' among his weapons '.

[3] 1 Sam. xvii, 6–7, show Goliath to be armed only with spear and *kidhon*. Vs. 51 says David drew G.'s *ḥerev* ' from its scabbard ' (om. LXX^B), and xxi, 10, that the *ḥerev* was kept as a memorial. Only xvii, 45, lists ' with *ḥerev*, spear, and *kidhon* ' : I would suggest that the last is a gloss by a harmonizing editor.

[4] Cf. Y. Kutscher, *Leshonenu* 7 (1945–6), 266.

[5] O'Callaghan cites pictures of Šardanu and ' Sea People ' men carrying their weapons on their shoulders.

[6] Midrash *Wayyissaʿu* (BHM iii, 1) mentions *kidhon* as a weapon which is drawn, and which cuts limbs and splits a shield. The swords of Jub. xxxvii, 15, appear in corresponding Midrash passages as *kidhonim*. In M. Kelim xi, 8, ' the *kidhon* and the νίκων,' nothing in the list prevents *k.* from being taken as ' sword '.

[7] See comm.

[8] See § 9 below.

the inscriptions on the darts differ with each battalion but are uniform within the battalion itself.

Concerning the first problem, one might assume that each soldier holds only one dart and that the number seven is due to the fact that the battalion is arranged in seven arrays like the front formation (v, 3–4 and chapter 7, §§ 4–5), i.e. that the seven arrays of the battalion throw their darts—array by array—there being thus seven darts. However, we learn from the detailed description of the fighting of the darts battalions (viii, 6) that these skirmishing units, in contrast to the front formation, were arrayed in three arrays and yet they threw seven darts (ib., 13). Hence every soldier held seven darts, this fact being confirmed also by a comparison with other armies, as we shall see.

Now to the second problem. Though the author writes : ' On the third dart they shall write ', he mentions altogether three incriptions, corresponding to the number of darts battalions and not to the number of darts. Hence we must take it as though he had written ' On the dart of the third battalion ', etc. This is confirmed by : ' The first battalion shall throw into the enemy line seven battle darts. On the blade of the dart they shall write . . .', i.e. a single inscription for all the seven darts of the first battalion, and so for the other two.

While the root *zrq* and the fact that it is ' thrown '[1] prove that the זרקות are missiles, the expressions ' to hurl ' (ib. line 4 ; and cf. viii, 15) ' The blade of the dart ', ' Flash of a lance ' indicate that they are weapons resembling the lance, with a wooden body and a metal blade.[2] The term ' battle darts ' vi, 2, 15 ; viii, 11 was apparently to prevent any ambiguity which might arise from the resemblance between the name of the weapon we are discussing and other, non-military, instruments having similar names.

Neither in Biblical nor in Mishnaic Hebrew is there a weapon called *zrq* though the use of the verb *zrq* occurs frequently to indicate the ' throwing ' of various weapons.[3]

As against the silence of our sources it may be noted that a considerable number of short types of lances which were in use amongst the pre-Islamic Arabs [4] were called by names derived from *zrq*.[5]

---

[1] BH *hishlikh* of throwing missiles corresponds to MH *zaraq* (only Ezek. x, 2, of coals), cf. also the *Midrash of Goliath* (BHM iv, 140) where David kills 800 enemies with one *zĕriqah*.

[2] The use of *naṭah yadh* in connexion with the darts, viii, 8, is not specific to missiles, but is the action preparatory to the use of any weapon, cf. e.g 1 Chr. xxi, 16.

[3] See n. 1.

[4] The Arabic *mizraq* is listed in the *Kitāb al-Mukhaṣṣaṣ* amongst lances, and said to be lighter than the *'anazah*. The latter is

The dart closely resembles both in name and in use (and most interesting, also in the number held by each soldier) the Roman *iaculum*. It was also called *hasta velitaris* since it was used by the light and skirmishing units (the *velites*) in the second century B.C. and later on passed to the auxiliary battalions which fulfilled similar duties. This weapon and its measurements are described in an interesting chapter in Livy in connexion with the battle of Capua. Livy tells us that the Romans had adopted new tactics; they chose the young, strong and fleet soldiers from all the legions and trained them to fight alongside the cavalry. Every one of these youngsters was armed with seven *iacula*; the length of the *iaculum* was 4 feet, it had an iron blade like the *hasta*. They also carried round shields, smaller than those of the cavalry.[1] From this description it follows that the *iaculum* was a missile about 1·17 m. long (of this 15–22 cm. for the blade)[2] and was used by the light skirmishing units. Every soldier held seven darts. As noted above, the light cavalry also had darts (vi, 15), though no number is mentioned. One may assume that it did not exceed four, following the descriptions of Josephus.[3]

§ 8. The Weapon (שלט)

The phrase ' On the second *sheleṭ* ', instead of an expected ' on the second dart ' is difficult. Even assuming a scribal error, its appearance here suggests that the *sheleṭ* resembled the dart or was another missile or served as a collective term for a weapon. Indeed there is none amongst the terms for weapons in the O.T. which the LXX translated in such different ways as *sheleṭ*. This fact necessitates a re-examination of the seven passages in the O.T. mentioning the *sheleṭ*:

1–2: 2 Kings xi, 10: ' And the priest delivered to the captains over hundreds the spear and the *shĕlaṭim* that had been King David's '. In the parallel, 2 Chr. xxiii, 9: ' And Jehoiada the priest delivered to the

---

about half the length of the spear (*rumḥ*), stated to be on the average 11 cubits (cf. Schwarzlose, *Waffen der alten Araber* p. 243); this makes the ʿ*anazah* 5–6 cubits, the *mizraq* c. 3–4 cubits.

[5] *mizraq, mizrāq, mizraqah* (Lane: a short javelin; Dozy: javelot); cf. perhaps also Tg. Isa. xxxiii, 4, *zirqĕthā*.

[1] Marquardt p. 13, n. 6; p. 33, n. 5; p. 40, n. 5; K.-V. pp. 326–7; Couissin pp. 214, 217.

[2] Livy xxvi, 4, 4: ' Ex omnibus legionibus electi sunt iuvenes maxime vigore ac levitate corporum veloces: eis parmae breviores quam equestres et *septena iacula quaternos longa pedes* data praefixa ferro, quale hastis velitaribus inest.' For the rest of this important passage, see ch. 7, § 6.

[3] BJ III, v, 5: τρεῖς ἢ πλείους ἄκοντες, πλατεῖς μὲν αἰχμάς, οὐκ ἀποδέοντες δὲ δοράτων μέγεθος, in the horsemen's quivers. These seem to correspond to the *iacula*.

captains of hundreds the spears, bucklers, and *shĕlaṭim* that had been King David's '.[1]

3 : Jer. li, 11 : ' Make bright the armours, fill the *shĕlaṭim* '. On account of the ' armours ' and the verb ' fill ', the LXX and others (including the A.V.) understood *sh.* as ' quivers '[2] but מלאו may mean here ' prepare '.[3]

4–5 : 2 Sam. viii, 7 : ' And David took the golden *shĕlaṭim* that were on the servants of Hadadezer ' (= 1 Chr. xviii, 7) ; here the LXX took the *shĕlaṭim* to mean ornaments (κλοιούς).[4]

6 : Ezek. xxvii, 11 : ' They hanged their *shĕlaṭim* upon thy walls round about ', just here, where to all appearances shields are meant,[5] the LXX translates ' quivers '.

7 : Ct. iv, 4 : ' Whereon there hang a thousand shields, all the *shĕlaṭim* of the mighty men '; just here the LXX translates ' darts ' or ' javelins '.[6]

The above analysis shows either that this term included several types of weapons or that there were various opinions as to its meaning.[7] On the other hand, the influence of Aramaic on the author makes it advisable to compare the use of שולטן as a translation for מטה and שבט.[8] On Gen. Rabba xciii, 7 (' and what are the signs of Judah ? the House of Shilo say, two שולטונין dripping with blood '), the commentary ascribed to Rashi has the remark : ' That is two staffs (שלטין) dripping blood from its (*sic*) ends ; בשבט is translated as בשולטן.'

The use of שבט in a number of places in the O.T. as a synonym for a ' javelin ' might explain the use in the scroll, e.g. 2 Sam. xviii, 4 : ' And he took three staffs (A.V. ' darts ') in his hands, and thrust them through the heart of Absalom '.[9]

§ 9. The Inscriptions on the Darts

Here we shall indicate only the connexion between the inscriptions and the character of the weapon.[10]

---

[1] LXX translate here *shĕlaṭim* as τὰ ὅπλα, probably because ' shields ' were already mentioned in the verse.

[2] τὰς φαρέτρας.

[3] See comm. on v. 3. Cf. the crux 2 Sam. xxiii, 7, and G. R. Driver, JQR 28 (1937–8), 127.

[4] 2 Sam. χλιδῶνας ; 1 Chr. κλοιούς.

[5] Cf. *Yediʿoth* 13 (1946–7), 23, n. 24.

[6] πᾶσαι βολίδες.

[7] Tur-Sinai, in Ben-Jehudah, *Thesaurus* xiv, 7154, n. 2, says that probably *sheleṭ* basically means ' prowess ', in keeping with the root-meaning, and came to be used of ' tools of prowess ', be these shields or other arms.

[8] e.g. Ex. xxi, 20 ; Isa. ix, 3 ; x, 5 ; also for *mishʿeneth*, Ju. vi, 21, and *maṭṭeh*, Mic. vi, 9, derivatives of *shlṭ* are used. See also Dozy, *Supplément* s.v. سلطة ; Syr. *shĕlāṭā* ' missile ' (Brockelmann, *Lex. Syr.* 2nd edn.).

[9] Cf. 2 Sam. xxiii, 21.

[10] For the relation between the inscriptions on darts and standards and trumpets, see ch. 3, § 2 ; ch. 5, § 7.

First Dart	Second Dart	Third Dart
Flash of a lance to the might of God.'	'Sparks of blood to slay by the anger of God.'	'Glitter of a sword devouring the sinful slain by the judgment of God.'

The inscriptions (except for the first) are made up of three parts :
1. The appearance of the dart at the time of throwing.
2. The object to be achieved by throwing it.
3. The war of God.

Two and three resemble some other inscriptions [1] and only (1) is an inscription typical for darts, which in flight resemble flashes of lightning,[2] like the Biblical descriptions of lances and arrows [3] (for the inscriptions cf. also below, § 12).

§ 10. THE LANCE (חנית)

The author does not describe the lance, but its mention in the inscription of the dart and the description of the spear (see below) prove that the lance, according to the scroll and also to the O.T.,[4] is a missile. The lance was apparently longer than the dart and in consequence its range was shorter. This may be assumed since a battalion 'armed with lance and shield'[5] (vi, 5) is mentioned between the darts battalions and the battalion armed with the sword. The skirmishing units fight in the following order : the long range weapons first (slings, darts) and the short range (sword) last. Cf. chapter 7, § 4.

§ 11. THE SPEAR (רומח)

As with the shield and sword, the author describes at length the spear, its measurements, shape, material and ornaments. The spear was the principal weapon of the front formation (v, 6–7), of the 'heavy' cavalry (vi, 14), and of the soldiers of the 'towers' (ix, 12) in contrast to the dart and lance used by a part of the skirmishing units and the light cavalry.

(1) *Shape and measurements.*

Only the spears of the front formation are described in detail. Of

---

[1] See page 134, note 10.
[2] Cant. viii, 6 ; Ezek. xxi, 3. In Ezek. x, 2, glowing coals are thrown (*zrq*) on the city.
[3] Reference probably to the burning sword, Gn. iii, 24. For 'devour', see comm. The possibility should not be excluded that here *ḥerev* = Ar. *ḥarbah* 'lance'.
[4] e.g. I Sam. xviii, 11.
[5] Cf. 1 Chr. xii, 35 ; 2 Chr. xxiii, 9.

the spears of the heavy cavalry and the men of the 'towers' it is only said that they were longer (8 cubits). The spear of the front formation was: 'seven cubits, of which the socket and the blade *take up* half a cubit' (v, 7), i.e. its general length was $c.\ 45 \cdot 8 \times 7 = 3 \cdot 206$ m.[1] of which the blade and socket were 22·9 cm. For possible alternative measurements, see the comm. ad. loc.

The blade.[2]—The shape of the blade is defined as 'shaped like a spit (שפוד) towards the point' (lines 10–11) in contrast to the shape of the sword whose 'lips' go 'straight up to the point' (see above, § 5 (3)). The spear is thus rhomboid in shape, tapering towards the point.[3]

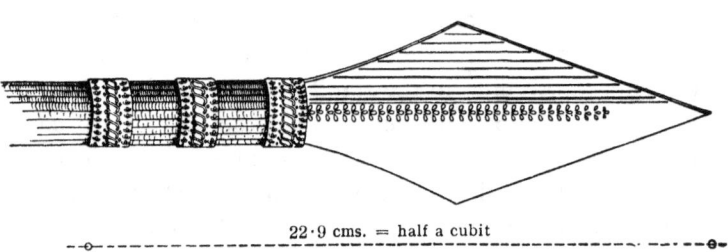

Fig. 7. *Suggested reconstruction of the spear.*

In fig. 7 I have tried to reconstruct its shape, being guided by the shapes of spears customary in the Roman period (cf. figs. 5, 6).

(2) *Material and Ornament.*

'The blade shall be iron tempered in fire, work of a smith, artificer's technique' (line 10). The sword is made of 'iron refined and purified in the furnace and tempered like a face mirror, work of a smith, artificer's technique'. I have already mentioned that the difference between the two descriptions proves that the iron for the spear was of a lower quality. This difference obtained at all periods, since the strength of the spear lies in its sharp point and tapering shape while the sword, whose edges are sharp and thin and which is used for striking sideways, must be of harder material.

The blade is adorned with 'ear of corn in pure gold' (line 10). The same motif forms part of the ornaments of the blade of the sword.

---

[1] See p. 116, note 4.
[2] Spelt להב; cf. comm.
[3] For 'head' = point see p. 125, n. 2. and p. 128, n. 2.

THE WEAPONS

The scroll uses different terms in describing the attachment of the ' ears of corn ' to the blades of the spear and sword respectively ; this permits us to assume that it intended to indicate two different techniques of metal work. With the spear the ' ear of corn ' is placed in the ' midst of the blade ' (line 10) while in the blade of the sword the ' ear of corn ' is of pure gold ' appliqué on it on both sides ' (lines 11–12). This difference can probably be ascribed to the fact that the metal of the spear was softer and the ear of corn could be worked into the blade, while that of the sword was very hard, requiring the gold to be *attached to the surface* of the blade.[1] Both the author's style and terminology can be traced back to the description in Ex. xxxix, 3, 4 of the holy garments of Aaron : ' And they did beat the gold into thin plates, and cut it into threads, to work it *in* the blue, and *in* the purple, and *in* the scarlet, and *in* the fine linen, the *work of a skilful workman*. They made shoulder-pieces for it, *joined together ; at the two ends was it joined together* '.

For the ear-of-corn pattern cf. Zech. iv, 12 describing the candelabra : ' And I answered the second time, and said unto him : What are these two *olive ears* (A.V. ' branches '), which are beside the two golden spouts that empty the golden oil out of themselves ? ' The reconstruction of this pattern amongst the ornaments of the blades of the spear and sword (figs. 4, 7) follows the middle rim of the shield from Dura Europos (fig. 1) which I have chosen from amongst several other examples so as to preserve some unity of style in the reconstruction of the ornaments on the various weapons.

(3) *The Socket or Clasp of the Blade.*

The scroll calls the metal part which joins the blade to the wooden staff סגר. Though we know of no passage in the sources using the word in this meaning,[2] the root meaning and the location of the part and its ornaments leave no room for doubt as to its identity. The detailed description of its ornaments points to the importance of this piece, which had to enclose and strengthen the weakest part of the spear. The construction of the clasp or socket presented one of the most difficult technical problems in the manufacture of the spear, and it was solved in different ways in the different periods.[3]

---

[1] Cf. Galling p. 381. For the Arabic terminology of the methods of applying precious metals to steel, cf. Mayer, op. cit. p. 122, n. 2.

[2] See comm. for the terminology.

[3] Cf. Galling p. 353 sq. See below, p. 138, n. 4, for Roman lances. Read perhaps *segher* for *sĕghor* in Ps. xxxv, 3 : by assuming that this important part of the spear was mentioned next to the spear itself, we avoid the need for dragging in the Scythian *sagaris* or emending to *sĕghodh* = Acc. *šukūdu*.

Shape and Ornaments.—' On the socket there shall be three rings engraved like a rim of cable work, of gold, silver and copper welded together like a pattern cunningly wrought, and running spiral, the pattern being on both sides of the ring all around, precious stones in ajour work, work of a smith, cunningly wrought, and ear of corn.' (v, 7-9).

With some of the above terms (' rim of cable work ', ' welded ', ' precious stones in ajour work ') we have already dealt in connexion with the ornaments of the shield. The principal subject in the above passage are the three rings forming the socket.[1] Whether the words ' The pattern being on both sides of the ring all around, precious stones ',[2] etc., describe the method of attachment of the cable work pattern to the ring to the socket (cf. the reconstruction, fig. 7), or not, we can recognize the similarity between this ornament and that mentioned in the Letter of Aristeas, 58-9.

The spears of the Roman soldiers (fig. 5, soldier no. 12, and cf. Kromayer-Veith, table 41, illus. 127) actually show the three rings in the socket.

The space between the rings was also ornamented : ' The socket shall be fluted between the rings like the working of a column, cunningly wrought ' (lines 9-10). The word ' fluted ' (מחורץ), which suggests parallel incisions like furrows,[3] and the definition ' like a column, cunningly wrought ' must, I think, be understood as likening the shape of the ' column of the socket ' to the fluted body of the classical column (for the reconstruction cf. fig. 7*b*).

(4) *Affinities of the Spear.*

The overall length of the front formation spear was *c.* 3 m., the combined length of blade (tapering in shape) and socket (fluted between the three rings) *c.* 22 cm. The spear of the ' towers ' and of the heavy cavalry was somewhat longer (3·6 m.). These measurements exclude any possibility of identifying the spear with the *pilum* of the Roman legion, which was a throwing weapon not exceeding 2 m. in length, and whose blade and socket were quite different.[4] The *pilum* must, to my mind, be compared with the ' lance ' (*hănith*). Nor can we compare the spear with the σάρισα of the Hellenistic phalanx. The length of the *sarissa*

---

[1] See comm. for terminology.

[2] To take the first two words as part of the preceding phrase would leave the sentence unfinished. For the whole description, cf. Ex. xxxvi, 11-13 (p. 118, n. 2).

[3] e.g. M. Kil'ayim, v. 3, ' a ditch (*hariz*) that passes through a vineyard.'

[4] For the *pilum*, see Couissin, p. 181 sq., 207, fig. 57 ; Marquardt, p. 28 sq. ; K.-V., p. 278.

at the time of Alexander, whether it differed in the various ranks or not,[1] was very large; the sources vie with each other in exaggerating it. At the time of Polybius (i.e. mid-second century B.C.) the length of the *sarissa* reached 14–16 cubits (nearly 6 m.),[1] i.e. double the length of the spear of the scroll. However, the spear as described in the scroll bears some resemblance to the Roman *hasta*. This was not a throwing weapon and was also heavier and larger than the *pilum* (figs. 5, 6). According to some of the literary sources, the *hasta* came to be used by part of the auxiliary forces from the period of Marius onwards, while the *pilum* became the weapon of the ordinary legionaries. But Couissin, who studied this subject extensively, reached the conclusion that the *hasta* continued in use also by the legionaries when fighting in phalanx order.[2] However, it should be noted that the spear of the scroll, though smaller than the *sarissa*, exceeded the length of the *hasta* by about 2 cubits. This fact proves perhaps the existence of a transitional stage during which the spear became quite distinct from the long *sarissa*, but had not yet been shortened to the dimensions of the *hasta*.[3] It is of interest that the blade of the *hasta*, like that of our spear, was very short.[4]

The cavalry spear was longer, since a soldier on horseback needs a longer spear.

§ 12. THE SLING.

The sling, though not described,[5] was the weapon of part of the skirmishing units, whose activities are set out in detail.[6] I shall restrict myself to a few remarks concerning the terminology, and concerning the number of sling-stones.

The soldiers carrying slings are called 'sling-men' (viii, 1).[7] The throwing is denoted by the verb *hishlikh*. As with other skirmishing units, at the time of action the 'trumpets shall keep blowing to direct...' (viii, 1 and cf. § 5 (4)). The sling-men are the first to open battle on

---

[1] K.-V. p. 134.

[2] ib. p. 279.

[3] The skirmishers have here *pila*, the heavy infantry *hastae*, cf. ch. 7, § 4 (6).

[4] The blade of the *hasta* is 15–22 cm. long, just like the spear here. Couissin, p. 217, suggests that the *iaculum* was called *hasta velitaris* because its short blade resembled that of the *hasta*.

[5] Cf. H. Bonnet, *Waffen der Völker des alten Orients* 1926, p. 144 sq.; O. R. Sellers, *Bibl. Archeologist* 2 (1939), 41–4; Yadin, BASOR 107, p. 12; *Yediʿoth* 13 (1946–7), 19 sq.

[6] vi, 1; viii, 1–2; and comm. On the *funditores*, especially in Pompey's army, see Marquardt p. 34, and below, ch. 7, § 4 (5–6).

[7] Cf. similar terms with 'men' in DSW. They are not called *qallaʿim*, as in 2 Kings iii, 25.

account of the long range of their weapon (cf. chapter 7, § 4). Like the darts, each sling-man throws seven times (viii, 1–2). The number seven, much beloved by the author of the scroll, may be more or less exact here: on the Assyrian reliefs of sling-men (e.g. in the siege of Lachish) we see in most cases five to seven sling-stones near each sling. 1 Sam. xvii, 40 states that David chose 'Five smooth stones'. Midrash Sam.[1] informs us that David chose five smooth stones from out of the brook, ' one for the name of the Almighty, one for the name of Aaron and three for the three Patriarchs'. On the other hand it is interesting that Pseudo-Philo states that David selected *seven* sling-stones and *wrote*[2] on them the names of Abraham, Isaac, Jacob, Moses, Aaron, his own name and the name of God.[3]

§ 13. THE BOW

The scroll mentions the bow only among the weapons of the light cavalry (vi, 15) ' And bow and arrows and battle darts '.[4]

---

[1] Ed. Buber, xxi, p. 108.

[2] See L. Cohn, JQR 10 (1898), 305, and below, ch. 9, p. 270, n. 2. The destroyed part of col. v may have given the inscriptions on the sling-stones. Such was the practice in the Roman army, cf. Marquardt p. 34, and n. 12 ib.

[3] For the difference between these and the inscriptions in DSW see ch. 3, § 8, and ch. 5, § 7; see, however, comm. on v. 1.

[4] Possibly one of the skirmishing battalions was armed with bows, cf. comm. on viii, 1; vi, 1, and ch. 7, § 4.

Chapter 7

TACTICS AND ORGANIZATION

§ 1. GENERAL REMARKS

This chapter deals with the fighting units [1] and their tactical employment as described in the scroll. Owing to the peculiar structure of the scroll,[2] the descriptions of battle are repeated a number of times in the Serekh Series as well as in the Battle Series. This repetition clears up a number of points of detail left vague in each series. Some chapters, though not devoted primarily to methods of fighting (e.g. the chapters dealing with the banners, weapons, trumpets, and customs of the congregation [3]) form an important supplementary source, since the author has to add from time to time some notes touching on methods of fighting, in his endeavour to explain things clearly.

A detailed analysis of the tactics and organization of the fighting units is of special importance also for determining the date of the scroll, since with this subject, more than with any other, the author had to make use of sources not peculiar to the sect. It is not impossible that he used some contemporary military manual.[4]

However, while using the tactical yardstick for fixing the period we must remember the extensive similarity in basic principles between military action in all periods and beware of far-reaching conclusions drawn from such similarities.

Thus the use of cavalry, the practice of placing it at the flanks of the infantry, the employment of light units before the decisive phase of the battle to soften up the enemy lines, ambushes [5] and so on, are common property of all armies at all times, though carried out with certain variations. Such obvious expedients, sometimes unimportant in themselves, can neither be used to characterize an army nor do they ever provide the whole picture. We must also remember that every army, however strongly influenced by contemporary methods, still maintains some independent characteristics deriving from its structure and tradition. In our analysis of the tactics described in the scroll, we must consider several possibilities : (*a*) the tactics described are peculiar to the Judaean army in the period under discussion ; (*b*) they are an

---

[1] For the organization of the congregation and its fighting units, see ch. 3 and 4.
[2] See ch. 1.
[3] See ch. 3, 5, 6, 8.
[4] See ch. 1, § 6.
[5] See p. 196, n. 1.

imitation of Hellenistic tactics; (*c*) they are an imitation of Roman tactics; (*d*) they are a combination of some or all of these factors.

It will of course be our aim to search for the latest influences, since only they alone are relevant for establishing the period of the scroll.[1] We shall concentrate on three main subjects:

The general terminology employed in forming up for battle (§ 2).

The different types of troops (§§ 3–6).

The organization and nomenclature of the various units, and the tactics (§ 7).[2]

§ 2. GENERAL TERMINOLOGY IN FORMING UP FOR BATTLE

We shall commence with the elucidation of some terms—array, column, deployment, advance, position, interval, disposition—which will serve as a key for the understanding of actual tactics.

(1) '*Array*'.

This word occurs both as a noun and as a verb.

As a noun: the *sedher* (pl. *sĕdharim*) denotes a clearly defined formation of soldiers who stand in one line next to each other, shoulder to shoulder. The array is not identical with a definite battle unit (but cf. below under 'cavalry'); every unit can be organized into one or more arrays (three or seven) depending upon the tactics employed and the frontal width it has to cover. This structure, in contrast to the columns (see below), is a purely technical arrangement, enabling each soldier, fighting as a member of a team, to engage the enemy soldier opposite him. The distance between each soldier and the next in the arrays also differs according to circumstances (see below).

(*a*) '*Battle Arrays*'.—The term 'battle arrays' or 'arrays of the battalions' is used for indicating the arrays of all units without distinction as we learn from iii, 6 'upon the trumpets of the battle arrays they shall write " arrays of God's battalions " '.[3]

(*b*) '*Frontal Arrays*'.—The scroll also mentions 'frontal arrays', an abbreviation of 'arrays of the front (formation)' (in contrast to the

---

[1] Cp. the discussion in ch. 6. Future historians will no doubt use the inventions of gunpowder, machine-gun, aeroplanes, tanks, or atomic bombs to date military documents, since all these profoundly affected tactics.

[2] We must keep in mind that new units are often called by old names. A good example in our own time is the transfer of cavalry terminology to tank units.

[3] For these trumpets, see ch. 5, § 5 (6). M. Avi-Yonah, IEJ 2 (1952), 1, who identified the skirmishing battalions with the phalanx, thought that *sedher* denoted the three sections of the front, viz. the phalanx and the two cavalry flanks. This is—apart from the reasons against identifying the skirmishers with the phalanx—untenable in the light of those parts of DSW published since.

skirmishers, cf. below) : '... battle line ... seven frontal arrays to one line, arrayed in disposition of posting one man behind the other'[1] (v, 3-4).

(c) *Cavalry arrays.*—The cavalry units are also organized in this manner when lined up for battle : ' Seven arrays of horsemen shall also be posted at the right and at the left of the line : these arrays shall take up position on either side ' (vi, 7). In this context, ' array ' may also denote the unit,[2] since the author employs no other term (e.g. battalion or formation) in his description of the cavalry for naming the units.

(d) *Arrays of skirmishing battalions.*—This term was apparently also used—though it does not actually appear in this form—for the skirmishing battalions : ' And the columns (of the skirmishing battalions) shall deploy into their proper arrays, each man to his position. When they are drawn up in three arrays ...' (viii, 6).

As a verb : For the process of forming units into arrays, a special signal by the ' trumpets of the battle arrays ' is used.[3] These signals are called ' signals [4] to array for battle ' (viii, 5) or collectively : ' a fanfare for them for the array ' (xvi, 4). At hearing the fanfare, they ' arrayed ' the battalions (xvii, 10) : ' The priests shall blow for them *a signal* to array the battalions of the formation '.

In a wider sense, this verb denotes the whole process of deploying troops for battle, which resulted in the formation of ' arrays '. ' In that place he shall array all the formations ' (xv, 5-6) ; ' They shall form themselves into seven formations, one behind the other ' (v, 15) ; ' When the battle formations are arrayed over against the enemy ' (vii, 8) ; ' To the place where they had stood, where they had arrayed the formation ' (xiv, 3).[5]

Other sources.—The term *sedher* does not occur in the O.T. [6] which mainly uses the root *'rk* to express the same idea. This is instructive, especially since our author almost never uses the verb *'arakh* (except vii, 3 ; ix, 10). This may be due to the fact that at his time the earlier word (*ma'ărakhah*) served both for a military grouping drawn up for battle in ' array ' form and for a part of the army deployed in a number of arrays.[7] On the other hand, *sedher* is frequent in Mishnaic Hebrew, occasionally in connexion with ' laying out ' the altar : ' He set in order

---

[1] i.e. each man of the second *sedher* stood behind a man of the first *sedher*, etc., cf. § 5 below.

[2] Similar to the double use of *ordo* in Roman military parlance, cf. K.-V. p. 319.

[3] See page 142, note 3.

[4] For this word, see ch. 5, § 6.

[5] Cf. also v, 3 ; ix, 10, and § 5 below.

[6] Except Jb. x, 22, where LXX apparently read *sĕharim*. Cf. Tur-Sinai's comm. ad loc.

[7] Like the *acies*, cf. § 5 below.

(*sidder*) the greater of the altar fires to the east side '.[1] The root *sdr* is frequently used as a military term by the Targums to render *'arakh* and *ma'ărekheth*.[2]

To sum up: It must be emphasized that the scroll takes care to distinguish between the 'arrays' and the 'formation' which is made up of several 'arrays'.

It also very carefully distinguishes between 'array' and its near-synonym 'disposition' (*serekh*) (cf. v, 5, where the scribe originally wrote סרוכים but later corrected סדורים): while *serekh* indicates (*inter alia*, cf. below) in a general way anything arrayed in a definite order, *sedher* is confined to the formation as described above.

(2) 'Columns', 'Deployment', 'Advance'.
   a. 'Column' (ראש), 'to deploy' (פשט).
   1. (viii, 6): 'And the columns shall deploy into their proper arrays'.
   2. (ix, 11): 'With protruding columns'.
   3. (xvi, 3): 'And the skirmishers shall go forth and take up position in columns between the lines. The priests shall blow a fanfare for them for the array, and the column shall keep [fanning out] at the sound of the trumpets until they have fallen in, each man in his position'.
   4. (xvii, 10–11): 'The priests shall sound for them a signal to array the battalions of the formation. The columns shall fan out at the sound of the trumpets', etc.

The first example forms part of a passage published in *Megilloth Genuzoth* I.[3] At the time the *rashim* mentioned there were understood as 'commanders'.[4] The above examples, as well as our explanation of *sedher*, show this to be impossible. This is clearly brought out by example 3 which proves that by *rashim* the scroll indicates the formation of the unit before fanning out (see above) and arraying itself into 'arrays', i.e. the formation of the unit on the march or at the moment of its completion. The skirmishing battalions set out in column formation to the sound of the 'fanfare of summoning',[5] marching towards the enemy until they halt at a certain distance from the latter. On hearing the fanfare signalling the 'arraying for battle', they deploy into array formation. Thus in column formation the soldiers stand in a line behind each

---

[1] M. Tamid ii, 4; B. T. Yoma 24b; cf. also Ecclus. L.19(14). For *sĕdharim* with numerals, cf. M. Men. iii, 6; Tamid iii, 5; Mid. iii, 5; Kelim xiv, 2; etc.

[2] Gn. xiv, 2; 1 Sam. xvii, 35; 1 Chr. xii, 38; 2 Chr. xi, 1, etc.

[3] Pl. viii and p. 25.

[4] Sukenik: the officers shall disperse to their units and stand by them; Tournay, RB 56 (1949), 214: les chefs; Dupont-Sommer, *Aperçus* p. 100: les chefs (de file); similarly Avi-Yonah, op. cit. (n. 8).

[5] See ch. 5, § 5 (5).

TACTICS AND ORGANIZATION   145

other, the head of each soldier (except for the last one) being in front of the face of his neighbour, who stands or marches behind him.[1] A unit marching in column formation can of course be made up of several parallel files according to circumstances and the nature of the terrain.[2] This term (and the verb 'deploy', *psht*, connected with it) occurs frequently in the O.T. Its use in the scroll makes it possible to establish the meaning of some O.T. passages more precisely.

For instance Ju. ix, 43 sq. : 'And he took the people and divided them into three columns (' companies ' A.V.) and lay in wait in the field . . . and Abimelech and the columns that were with him deployed ('rushed forward' A.V.), and stood in the entrance of the gate of the city ; and the two columns deployed against all that were in the field, and smote them.'

Here clearly *psht* denotes the transition of the unit from the close column formation, intended principally for marching, to battle formation. Similarly : 'The Chaldeans set themselves in three columns (' bands ' A.V.) and fanned out ('fell' A.V.) against the camels, and have taken them away, yea, and slain the servants with the edge of the sword ' Job, i, 17, sq.). This verb, indicating the change of formation necessary for combat, thus also acquires the meaning of actual combat.[3]

From other O.T. passages it can be clearly established that *rashim* was used of units on the march, whether from the rear base to the field or in the field from their initial position towards the area of fighting. e.g. : 'And the spoilers came out of the camp of the Philistines in three columns (' companies ' A.V.) : one column turned unto the way that leadeth to Ophrah', etc., (1 Sam. xiii, 17). Similarly in the description of the battle of Gideon : 'And he divided the three hundred men into three columns ' (Ju. vii, 16). Gideon organized the columns at a short distance from the enemy (after having first reconnoitred with his servant) and in this formation they marched towards the enemy line.[4] Again : 'And it was on the morrow, that Saul put the people in three columns (' companies ' A.V.) ; and they came into the midst of the camp in the morning watch ' (1 Sam. xi, 11).[5]

b. The Advance (מפשע).—The columns are deployed into arrays

---

[1] Theoretically only the head of the first man in each file should be visible from the front.

[2] For the fanning out of the three dart-throwers' battalions, see § 4 below.

[3] For the meanings of *pashat*, cf. Hos. vii, 1 ; 1 Sam. xxiii, 27 ; xxvii, 8. See now also Tur-Sinai, *Sefer Iyyov* 1954, p. 9 sq.

[4] In the darkness this was the only practicable formation.

[5] In 1 Macc. v, 33, ἐν τρισὶν ἀρχαῖς translates 'in three *rashim* ', cf. Abel's comm., p. 99, n. 33.

outside the range of the enemy's weapons. Only after deployment into arrays do they commence marching towards the actual fighting area, entering in battle formation within effective range of their own and the enemy's weapons; the scroll calls this movement *mifsaʿ*: 'When they are drawn up in three arrays the priests shall blow for them a second fanfare, a low legato note, signals to advance, until they approach the enemy line' (viii, 6–8).[1]

(3) *Position.*

The term *maʿămadh* occurs frequently in the writings of the sect and particularly in our scroll.[2] In chapter 8 we shall deal with its special meaning relating to the organization and structure of the sect.

This term applies specially to the organizational units of the sect and their place in the 'disposition' (see below), containing priests, levites and Israelites. We shall see [3] that the author used this word to describe the position of the soldiers when they stand arrayed for combat. The following instances will establish this usage:

(1) 'Each of these shall throw seven times and then return to their position' (vi, 4).

(2) 'And they shall come to take up position by the side of the first formation to fall in at their proper position' (viii, 2, 3).

(3) '[And take up positi]on at their proper places in the formation' (viii, 17).

(4) 'Disposition to change the array of the battle battalions so as to arrange their position (= form up) . . .' (ix, 10);

(5) 'Arrayed in disposition of placing (*maʿămadh*) one man behind another' (v, 4);

(6) 'To take up position with the host of holy ones' (DST iii, 21–22);

(7) 'And to take up position before Thee with the eternal host' (DST, xi, 13).[4]

(4) *The Battle Intervals* (שערי המלחמה).

Great importance for the dating as well as for understanding the method of warfare attaches to the exact meaning of these 'gates', mentioned several times in descriptions of battles, which serve as starting points for the skirmishing battalions:

---

[1] For this signal see ch. 5, § 6. For *pasaʿ*, see comm. on viii, 7; *mifsaʿ* corresponds to *concursus*.

[2] ii, 3; iv, 4; v, 4; vi, 1; viii, 3, 17; ix, 10; xiii, 16; xiv, 6, 8; xvii, 9; xviii, 12.

[3] Ch. 8, § 3 (5), p. 206, n. 8, p. 207, n. 4.

[4] Cf. also Isa. xxii, 19; Ps. lxix, 3. In *Yalkut Shimʿoni*, Wayyishlaḥ 33: 'they took up position (ועמדו על מעמדם) to wage battle against them.'

(1) 'And the trumpets for summoning them when the battle intervals are opened for the advance of the skirmishers' (iii, 1);

(2) 'Upon the trumpets for summoning the skirmishers when the battle intervals open for them to go forth against the line of the enemy' (iii, 7);

(3) 'When the battle formations are deployed opposite the enemy, formation opposite formation, there shall go forth from the central interval into the space between the lines seven priests' (vii, 8–9);

(4) 'And fifty skirmishers come forth from the one interval' (ib. 15);

(5) '[And two skirmishing formations shall go forth] from the intervals and take up position between the two lines' (ib. 16–17);

(6) 'The priests shall blow the trumpets of summoning, and three skirmishing battalions shall go forth from the intervals and take up position between the lines' (viii, 3–4);

(7) 'All this disposition they shall carry out on that [day] in the place where they stand over against the camp of the Kittim. Then the priests shall blow for them the trumpets of remembrance. They shall open the [battle] intervals, and the skirmishers shall go forth and take up position in columns between the lines' (xvi, 2–3);

(8) 'Each tower shall have two intervals, one on [the right and] one on the left' (ix, 14).

The explanations which were given for these 'openings' when example no. 6 only was published ('gates of the city' or 'gates of the camp'),[1] cannot be maintained in face of the other examples, which deal with events on the battlefield and close to the enemy position (3, 4, 6, and especially 7). Also the full form, 'battle intervals' (which does not appear in example no. 6) proves that we have here a term connected with battle technique. An examination of the above examples enables us to discover the nature of these 'gates': they were openings or intervals in the front line, which were opened at the sound of a certain trumpet signal to let the skirmishers go forth in columns into the space between the two lines.[2] The use of the word *sha'ar* (originally a breach or cleft in a wall) for these spaces derives from the fact that the soldiers standing in close formation were currently compared to a wall and in fact such a formation was called a 'wall'.[3] Also in ix, 10 sq. (cf. above, example no. 8) 'towers' are mentioned, which were special units who took up

---

[1] Sukenik, *M.G.* i, 25: the gates of Jerusalem; Tournay, RB 56 (1949), 214: the gates of the camp; similarly Dupont-Sommer, *Aperçus* p. 100.

[2] The 'gates' were 'opened' by closing up the ranks, cf. below, § 5 (9).

[3] K.-V. p. 141.

position in front of the line in a quadrangular formation; they were so named on account of their resemblance to the towers of a city wall.[1]

This conclusion is of far-reaching importance, since this formation of the lines, with spaces between and inside them, was typical for the Roman system of warfare, in contrast to the solid Hellenistic phalanx.[2] If this conclusion is accepted, then ' gates ' correspond to the famous *intervalla* of the battle order of the Roman legions.[3]

(5) *Disposition* (סרך).

This word occurs frequently in all DSS.[4] DSW uses it as meaning disciplinary rule, custom, order,[5] especially at the beginning of chapters dealing with the rules on any subject,[6] as do the other scrolls, but extends its uses further: in addition to the nominal form,[7] it appears as a verb to indicate the action to be accomplished in a certain sequence or according to rule[8] and those responsible for carrying it out.[9] Special interest attaches, however, to the numerous instances in which the word *serekh* occurs in this scroll to indicate the actual body or unit as arrayed into a formation or acting according to a prescribed order, as in these examples:[10]

(1) ' Upon the trumpets of the formations[11] they shall write " Serekh of God " ' (iii, 3);

(2) ' The horsemen of the Serekh ' (vi, 13);

(3) ' The men of the Serekh ' (vii, 1);

(4) ' And his brother priests and the Levites and all the elders of the Serekh ' (xiii, 1).

Thus *serekh* also served as a military term (though, like other military

---

[1] Cf. § 7 (2) below.

[2] K.-V. p. 357 : ' Den Kernpunkt des ganzen Fragenkomplexes bildet das für Rom grundlegend charakteristische System der Treffen und Intervalle.' For its influence on the development of trumpet signals and banners, see ch. 3, § 10 ; ch. 5, § 10.

[3] On *intervallum*—likewise borrowed from fortification technique—see Marquardt p. 42, n. 2 ; p. 45, n. 1 ; p. 138, n. 3. The use of ' gate ' here may have been influenced by O.T. verses where ' gate ' occurs in connexion with ' betwixt the two walls ' : 2 Kings xxv, 4 = Jer. xxxix, 4, ib. lii, 7. Krauss, *Paras* p. 186, thinks that *petḥaḥ* was used in this sense in MH.

[4] There are 34 occurrences in the DSS.

[5] On this word, which is frequent in MH (B. T. Ḥul. 106a ; Nid. 67b, etc.), see Sukenik, *M.G.* ii, 27, n. 4 ; Brownlee, *Manual* p. 7, n. 4 ; Yalon, KS 28 (1951–2), 68. For *serekh* in CDC Ms. A = ḥuqqim in Ms. B, see Rabin on CDC vii, 6a.

[6] iii, 12 ; v, 3 ; viii, 14, etc. ; DSD v, 1, etc. ; CDC x, 4 ; xii, 19, etc.

[7] Which he uses, so far alone among the DSS, also with possessive suffixes in iv, 11 : parallel phrases in DSD (v, 23 ; vi, 22) appear to avoid this consciously.

[8] *yisrokhu* ii, 1 ; 6.

[9] *sorěkhē*, vii, 1 ; cf. § 3 (1) below.

[10] See also vi, 9, 10 ; xv, 4 ; xviii, 6.

[11] For מסורות see ch. 3, § 1–2 ; ch. 4, § 5 (2). The two roots *srk* and *msr* have cognate meanings, see below, § 5 (4).

terms, it was also used in connexion with the community's organization), denoting both the whole congregation with all units arrayed and organized (examples nos. 1, 4),[1] and the front formations as a body as opposed to the skirmishing battalions (example no. 3).

This two-fold use, as well as the fact that in the scroll *serekh* does not denote any definite tactical unit (e.g. battalion or formation) shows that it essentially indicated a body of undefined size but comprised of a considerable number of tactical units in military formation.

The meaning of this word and its affinity with Greek and Roman terminology is clarified to some extent in the light of the obvious connexion between it and the Greek τάξις, as seen in the Greek text which corresponds to one of the Aramaic fragments of Test. Levi.[2] An examination of the various meanings of the Greek τάξις throws light upon the subtle differences in the uses of *serekh*.[3]

Similarly, an exact parallel to the above meaning of *serekh* (both the congregation in general and the body of troops including the front formation) is found in the various uses of Greek τάξις which represents not only a tactical, numerically defined sub-unit in the Hellenistic phalanx,[4] but also a formation of indeterminate size of soldiers drawn up,[5] and a congregation or group of people making up a religious or political body.[6] Since—according to DSW—the members called their sect *serekh*, it seems that also DSD i, 16 must be interpreted: 'All who enter the *serekh* of the Community [7] shall enter into the Covenant in God's presence': '*serekh* of the Community' means approximately

---

[1] So in vi, 10, as will be shown below, § 6.

[2] וכל דתהוי עביד בסרך הוי עביד, in the Greek (ix, 1) ἐν τάξει ; cf. Charles, *Apocr.* ii, 815 ; Sukenik, *M.G.* ii, 27, n. 1. For the connexion of τάξις with 'law', see Aalen, p. 158 sq., who thinks it translates *ḥoq* of the Hebrew Pseudepigrapha ; see also Mowinckel, VT Suppl. i, 1953, p. 88 sq. Of course, τάξις may in some cases represent original *serekh*, or even טכסיס (Ex. Rabba viii). An original *serekh* would also go far towards accounting for the meanings of *ordo* (in Syr. 'way') in 4 Ezra v, 88 sq.: (1) 'way, law,' (2) 'military ranks'.

[3] The following table, classifying some uses of *serekh*/τάξις (according to Liddell-Scott) will help to bring out some of the finer distinctions.

1. Drawing up in rank and file, order, or disposition	DSD ii, 20–2.
2. A single rank or line	DSW ii, 1 ; v, 4.
3. Post or place in the line of battle	
4. Register, list	DSD v, 23 ; vi, 22, DSW vi, 6. 11.

[4] K.-V. pp. 49, 99, 102. In DSW *serekh* never means a tactical subdivision (as do *deghel* and *maʿărakhah*), but only the complete body.

[5] Liddell-Scott : body of soldiers generally.

[6] Liddell-Scott : class of men, political order.

[7] = *ha-yaḥadh* (and so in the following lines).

'the sect of the community'.¹ This was then, at least amongst its members, one of the official names of the sect. The compound ' *serekh* of God ' (iii, 3)—corresponds to ' God's counsel' (DSD, i, 8, 10) and 'God's lot' (xv, 1, etc.)—and appears to have had a special meaning among the sect, denoting not only the military structure which comprises all the military groupings, but principally the actual sect as being the ' *serekh* of the community '. No doubt the frequent military term ' men of the Serekh ' (or ' elders of the Serekh ') ² aroused associations with ' *serekh* of the community ' ‖ ' *serekh* of God ' as names of the sect.

This double meaning of *serekh* recalls the language of Josephus when dealing with the Essene groups. They are frequently called τάγμα,³ a term which closely resembles τάξις in its several meanings and denoted at one and the same time organizational groups and military formations, and is in particular applied to the Roman legions by Greek writers, including Josephus.⁴

It was imperative to devote this lengthy discussion to the term *serekh* in its military use so as to discover the exact meaning of the divisions described in the scroll. If we have arrived at the correct meaning of the term, then ' men of the Serekh '—as opposed to ' skirmishers '— means the soldiers constituting the body of the front formations (i.e. all formations except the skirmishers) ; on the other hand when the scroll uses *serekh* in a general sense ('*serekh* of God', 'elders of the Serekh ') it indicates the members of the congregation in general as being organized in a military structure. With this double meaning we shall deal below, when explaining the terms ' front formation ' and ' cavalry disposition ' (§§ 5, 6).

§ 3. SERVICE UNITS

On the battle field the army was divided into three main bodies : (*a*) combatants, (*b*) service troops, (*c*) priests and levites.⁵ We have

---

¹ i.e. the same as ʻăzath ha-yahadh (DSD vii, 22, etc.). Cf. Segal JBL 70 (1951), 131, n. 3 ; Barthélemy, RB 60 (1953), 456 ; and Marcus' article quoted in n. 3.

² Cf. anshē ha-yaḥadh DSD v, 1. Similarly cp. with DSW v, 4, the description DSD ii, 21 sq., cf. ch. 3, § 9 ; ch. 8, § 3, and p. 206, n. 8, p. 207, n. 4.

³ BJ II, viii passim. He also calls so the marrying section of the Essenes (II, viii, 13). This in itself, of course, is no evidence for the identity of the Qumran Sect with the Essenes, all the more so as Jos. himself uses the word also for other sects (ib. 14), and cf. Marcus, JBL 72 (1953), 209.

⁴ For the Greek name of the legion see Daremberg-Saglio iii, 1047 sq. ; P.-W. xiv, s.v. τάγμα.. BJ III, vi, 2, τοῦ τάγματος ἱππικόν ' the legionary cavalry ' is exactly parallel to *parashē ha-serekh* (vi, 13).

⁵ Midr. Tanḥuma, Maṭṭoth 4 (on Nu. xxxi) : ' 12,000 fighting men (ḥăluzē ẓava') and 12,000 who were guarding their equipment and 12,000 for praying.'

already dealt with the tasks and organization of the latter.¹ In order to place the discussion of the types of fighting units and their organization next to that of the system of fighting connected with them, we shall first deal with the service units described in the scroll.

The relevant passage occurs in connexion with the age groupings :² 'The camp prefects shall be from 50 to 60 years old. The provosts, ⟨too⟩, shall be from 40 to 50 years old. All those that despoil the slain and collect the booty and cleanse the land and guard the arms and he who prepares the provisions, all these shall be from 25 to 30 years old' (vii, 1–3).

This list can be subdivided into two main groups :

(1) The camp prefects and the provosts ;

(2) Those that despoil the slain, collect the booty, cleanse the land, guard the arms and prepare the provisions.

The author treats the second group as one since they form one age group. In connexion with the first group, it is interesting to note that at first the scribe fixed the age of the camp prefects at the same figure as that of the provosts (40–50) but later this was changed (by some scribe ?) to 50–60, without, however, erasing the ' too '.³

(1) *The Camp Prefects.* (*sorĕkhē ha-maḥănoth*).

Possibly this indicates that the camp prefects and provosts belonged to the same group, but their ages differed according to their place of service, with the combatants or at the rear. We saw above that the root *srk* has different uses, its basic meaning being similar to *shṭr*. Also the language of the Targums, who use *sārĕkhayyā* to translate *ha-shoṭĕrim* ⁴ shows the connexion between these roots.

The name ' camp prefects ' as well as their age, which is higher than that of the combatants, prove that they were not counted with the provosts, who went out to battle (see below) but that they accomplished their task inside the camps close to the battlefield. It is difficult to decide what exactly was their task, but it is probable that they were appointed to keep law and order and supervise the execution of orders while the soldiers were in camp and perhaps also to guard the camps when the soldiers had left for the battlefield. On account of the need for exact planning due to the rules for setting up the camps on the battlefield, the possibility cannot be ruled out that the camp prefects were also responsible for marking out the camp and assigning places to the different units. They were thus administrative officials.

¹ Cf. ch. 5 ; ch. 3, § 7 ; ch. 8, § 3–4.
² For details of age groups, see ch. 4, § 4 (1).
³ Cf. n. 2 and ch. 11.
⁴ Dt. i, 15 ; xx, 5 ; Pr. vi, 7, etc.

The advanced age of the camp prefects proves that they were not amongst those liable for conscription ; [1] possibly their position was semi-civilian.[2] Equally, the possibility exists that they fulfilled these same tasks also in the settlements or 'camps' (CDC, vii, 6) of the sect in peace time.

(2) *The Provosts (shoṭĕrim).*

Their age (40–50), equal to that of the front formation and its cavalry, shows that their various tasks associated them with the fighting force.

The scroll mentions the provosts a number of times : At the ' prayer of the appointed time of the war ' in connexion with their duty to turn back the 'faint-hearted ' ; [3] in the description of the seven priests and levites who go forth before the line (including the priest ' set aside for the day of vengeance ') the ' three provosts from among the levites ' going before them [4] are also mentioned ; the third time they occur in the same chapter, apparently in connexion with the skirmishing battalions.[5]

In the first two instances the text clearly intends the task of the provosts as set out in the Pent.,[6] namely the weeding out of the faint-hearted. The third instance might possibly hint at their task of preventing the flight of the faint-hearted soldiers at the actual time of battle.[7]

A review of the provosts' duties in the O.T. proves that they were equivalent to the adjutant general's branch and the adjutancy [8] in today's armies, dealing with conscription problems,[9] matters of law and order,[10] transmission of orders, [11] and supervising their execution.[12]

Quartermaster Services.—The service troops aged 25–30 all belong to those services which in our days are included in the domain of the

---

[1] For details of age groups, see ch. 4, § 4 (1).

[2] Cf. the *accensi velati*, who according to Delbrück and his school were the administrative camp staff. K.-V., p. 268, concludes that they were from an early date a civilian rather than a military group.

[3] x, 5 ; cf. ch. 4, § 1 ; ch. 8, § 5 (1) and p. 211, n. 2.

[4] vii, 13. For the significance of the number, see below, § 5 ; for the ' levite provosts ', see 1 Chr. xxiii, 4 ; 2 Chr. xxxiv, 13.

[5] For the restitution of that much-destroyed passage, see comm.

[6] x, 5 ; cf. ch. 4, § 1 ; ch. 8, § 5 (1) and p. 211, n. 2.

[7] Cf. ch. 4, p. 68, n. 2, and n. 12 below.

[8] i.e. dealing with all manpower problems in the army.

[9] Dt. xx, 5 sq. ; cf. Junge p. 45 sq.

[10] Dt. i, 15 ; xvi, 18 ; Josh. viii, 33 ; xxiii, 2 ; 1 Chr. xxiii, 4 ; xxvi, 29.

[11] Josh. i, 10 ; iii, 2.

[12] Ex. v, 6 sq., 19 ; 1 Macc. v, 42. Cf. Avi-Yonah, IEJ 2 (1952), 3. Macc. shows that they not only supervised tasks, but also prevented desertion.

quartermaster general (American S-4).[1] As far as I know, this is the only list of its kind preserved in Hebrew and Jewish sources.

(3) '*Those that despoil the slain and collect the booty*'.

The etymological elements of these terms are taken from the O.T., where the verb *pshṭ* is used in this sense (both in the Piel [2] and in the Hif'il as in the scroll),[3] as is also *shll* 'to take booty'.[4] The assignment of special men to the above tasks was important in two respects. The natural inclination of soldiers to despoil the slain during the course of the battle is a very real source of danger, since it may deflect them from their principal duty, to pursue the enemy to their final destruction. In many instances in the past and in our days the course of battle actually changed as a result of lack of control by the staff in this matter and carelessness in organizing a suitable service to take charge of the booty. The second problem concerns the just division of the booty between the fighting troops and those serving behind the lines. Only soldiers appointed for despoiling the slain and collecting the booty, as well as laws specially devised for this purpose, made the solution of this important problem possible. A decisive solution of this problem was so important that the O.T. devotes to it several detailed descriptions which stress that these laws go back to Moses. A considerable part of Num. xxxi is devoted to this subject. The chaos following the war with Midian serves as an occasion for detailed legislation concerning this subject. For the matter in hand the following decision is of special interest: ' And divide the prey into two parts : between the men skilled in war, that went out to battle, and all the congregation ' (ib. 27 and cf. below), as is also the description of the mustering after the battle for collecting the spoil ' for the men of war had taken booty, every man for himself ' (ib. 53).[5] The aim of collecting the booty is indicated ib. 50–51. The second time the O.T. deals extensively with this subject is in connexion with the deceit of Achan, who in spite of Joshua's decision that ' all the silver, and gold, and vessels of brass and iron, are holy unto the Lord ; they shall come into the treasury of the Lord ' (Josh. vi, 19), admitted to violating the ban : ' When I saw among the spoil a goodly Babylonish mantle, and two hundred shekels of silver, and a wedge of gold of fifty shekels weight, then I coveted them, and took them ' (ib. vii, 21). The

---

[1] i.e. dealing with material problems of the army.

[2] 1 Sam. xxxi, 8 ; 2 Sam. xxiii, 10 ; 1 Chr. x, 8.

[3] 1 Sam. xxxi, 9 ; 1 Chr. x, 9.

[4] Cf. xii, 9–10 ; and cf. Isa. x, 6 ; Ezek. xxxviii, 12–13.

[5] Verse 27 apparently stood originally before vs. 53 and explained the reason for the review.

third time concerns the war against Ziklag. The details of this description and the laws laid down on that occasion are most instructive and prove the existence of a special body amongst whose duties was the inspection and division of booty : ' Then answered all the wicked men and base fellows, of those that went with David, and said : " Because they went not with us, we will not give them aught of the spoil that we have recovered, save to every man his wife and his children, that they may lead them away, and depart " ' (1 Sam. xxx, 22). David answered this objection with the important military and moral principle : ' For as in the share of him that goeth down to the battle, so shall be the share of him that tarrieth by the baggage ; they shall share alike ' (ib. 24). The author of the Book of Samuel adds : ' And it was from that day forward, that he made it a statute and an ordinance for Israel unto this day ' (ib. 25).[1] The despoilers of the slain constitute only part of the general body of non-combatant troops, and their existence cannot be used as proof that the scroll belongs to the Hasmonean period, as has been suggested.[2]

(4) *'Those that cleanse the land'*.

The name for these men who were appointed to bury the fallen, is taken from Ezek. xxxix, 12, 14.

(5) *The guardians of the arms*.

We know of the existence of such officials also from Biblical sources. ' Guardians of the arms ' accompanied the fighting force but their place was at the rear, close to the front line.[3] One may assume that it fell to their lot to look after the depots which were concentrated near the front line and represented the reserves of ammunition (darts, sling-stones) and arms. Keeping the weapons in repair, counting, arranging and cleaning them were their tasks,[4] which included also guarding them from thieves

---

[1] Contra Apionem ii, 29, states : ἀλλὰ καὶ σκυλεύειν ἀπείρηκε τοὺς ἐν μάχῃ πεσόντας. Taken literally, we may well ask from where Jos. derived this ' law ' (contrary to Hasmonean practice, cf. n. 2 below); perhaps he did so from the general tenor of Num. xxxi and Josh. vi. We may conclude, at any rate, that in his time the fighting soldier was not allowed to take spoil, this task presumably being that of specially appointed men.

[2] Avi-Yonah, IEJ 2 (1952), 4, comments on ' the peculiar prominence given to the " spoilers " etc.', and points out that the Maccabee army equipped itself at first largely by despoiling the enemy dead. The sources cited by him, however, show that there was at the time no special body of men for this task, as Judas before the battle of Emmaus had to warn his men in general not to delay for booty, but to wait till after the battle (1 Macc. iv, 17–18).

[3] 1 Sam. xvii, 22, where the ' keeper of the baggage ' is within the ' circle ' (vs. 20) i.e. the temporary camp at the front. Cf. also ib. xxx 24 ; xxv, 13.

[4] A similar task with regard to holy implements Num. iii, 8 ; 1 Chr. ix, xxix.

and raiders. Except for noting the existence of this service and defining the age of the officials, the scroll throws no further light on their function or numbers.[1]

(6) *He who prepares the provisions* (*'orekh ha-ẓedhah*).

This compound occurs in none of the sources known to me, but it is not difficult to establish its meaning. The root *'rk* does not occur in the O.T. in connexion with duties in battle except to indicate the combatants themselves.[2] On the other hand, the frequent use of *'rk* in connexion with sacrifices and food in general [3] is well suited to describe those appointed to prepare and distribute the provisions. I have not been able to discover why this term appears in the singular, in contrast to the others. Perhaps this is simply an accident.

Procuring and distributing food during action is one of the most difficult problems facing an army fighting at some distance from its base and for a long period. It has troubled the armies of all periods, and the O.T., too, indicates a number of times how concerned they were to solve it. In general the militia men looked after their own provisioning.[4] In the event of the battlefield being close to the bases and action proceeding for some time, the soldiers would be looked after by their families.[5]

We find an ad hoc organization for supplying provisions in the description of the war against Benjamin : ' And we will take ten men of a hundred throughout all the tribes of Israel, and a hundred of a thousand, and a thousand out of ten thousand, to fetch victuals for the people ' (Ju. xx, 10).

Apart from this exceptional case, we do not seem to possess any information about the development of this service during the periods of the First and Second Temple. Hence the importance of the mention here of the ' preparers of provisions ' as a body appointed for the purpose, whose age was the same as that of other non-combatant units.[6]

The importance of this list lies in its contribution to our knowledge of military terminology in the Second Temple period (and perhaps during part of the First Temple period).

---

[1] We may compare the *custodes armorum*, of which there was one in each *centuria* and in each auxiliary unit, at times as many as 62 per legion, K.-V. pp. 516–7.

[2] 1 Chr. xii, 8 ; xxxiv, 35 ; Jer. xlvi, 3.

[3] e.g. Ex. xl, 23 ; Pr. ix, 2, a. fr.

[4] Josh. i, 11 ; Ju. vii, 8.

[5] 1 Sam. xvii, 17.

[6] Tos. Soṭah vii, 23 : ' those who are sent back from the campaign care for the fortifications of the city, provide water and food for the campaign, and mend the roads.' Those freed from military service (cf. ch. 4) would of course be of all ages, but the reference here may be to tasks in the rear, not with the army.

§ 4. COMBATANT TROOPS: THE SKIRMISHERS (אנשי הבינים)

(1) *General Remarks.*

The general fighting force was divided into infantry and cavalry. Each one of these was once more divided into two main types : light and heavy. In our investigation we shall proceed from the light to the heavy, since for reasons to be explained below, the scroll deals mainly with the tactics of the light infantry or ' skirmishers '.

Considering the focal role which the skirmishers play in the battles and the large space which the scroll devotes to their organization, arms, and tactics in the *Serekh* Series, it is of importance to establish their nature clearly and in detail so as to facilitate the understanding and dating of the scroll.

(2) *The name.*

The soldiers belonging to this force are called ' skirmishers ',[1] literally ' men of the [space] between [the lines]', *anshē benayim*. Their units are called ' skirmishing battalions,' *dighlē benayim*.[2] Four out of the fourteen mentions of the word בנ(י)ם [3] are spelt *defective* [4] as in the O.T.,[5] and ten *plene*.[6]

Many opinions exist concerning the term as applied to Goliath. Some see in it a characteristic of Goliath himself, meaning strength, might or greatness or other qualities attributed to him.[7]

The unambiguous use which the scroll makes of this term to indicate the units fighting between the lines,[8] as well as the *plene* writing connecting it with בין ' between ', prove that this biblical term was understood at that period (as it was by many of the early and modern commentators) [9] as referring to soldiers fighting between the lines, to which category Goliath was thought to belong, whatever other notable characteristics he may have possessed.[10]

The largest permanent organizational and tactical unit for the skirmishers is the ' battalion ' (דגל). Whenever the scroll mentions skirmishers as a whole, their units are named ' skirmishing battalions '[11];

---

[1] iii, 1, 7 ; vi, 8, 11 ; vii, 15 ; ix, 3 ; xvi, 3 ; xvii, 13. ' The slain of the skirmishers,' xvi, 9.

[2] See below.

[3] i.e. those listed in note 2 and below in the discussion on *deghel*.

[4] i, 14 ; iii, 1, 7 ; vi, 11.

[5] 1 Sam. xvii, 4, 23.

[6] Such variations in spelling occur also in other terms, as in the DSS in general. The *defective* spelling occurs only once in *dighlē benayim*, three times in *anshē b.*, perhaps due to the fact that in the O.T. *benayim* occurs only twice, both times in *ish ha-benayim*, and both *defective*

[7] See now *Enc. Miqr.* i, 274.

[8] Cf. vi, 1 ; viii, 4 ; xvi, 3.

[9] So also Josephus, *Ant.* vi, 9, 1.

[10] For the skirmishers in the period of the Judges and the early Monarchy, see Yadin, *JPOS* 21 (1948), 110.

[11] i, 14.

detailed battle descriptions (especially in the *Serekh* Series) mention a single battalion, two battalions, three battalions, and six battalions.[1] We may infer that for the skirmishers no permanent tactical framework existed above the battalion.

(3) *The number of skirmishing battalions.*

They were seven in number, as can be concluded from the preparations for the general pursuit, for which all the skirmishing battalions moved forward from amongst the front formation and stood at the head of the army ready for pursuit.[2] This number, supported also by the number of cavalry skirmishers,[3] fits the general system of the scroll (seven front formations, seven arrays in every formation, seven 'lots', seven cavalry 'arrays', etc). This makes it possible to restore the two chapters in the Serekh Series which deal with the fighting system and weapons of the skirmishing battalions as describing the fighting of the seven battalions.[4]

(4) *Number of skirmishers in every battalion and their age.*

Though the number of skirmishers belonging to each one of the battalions is not definitely stated in the part of the scroll preserved, we are able to calculate it indirectly as not exceeding one thousand, similar to the battalion of the front formations. In giving the number of 'cavalry going forth with the skirmishers' as 1,400, the scroll states: '200 horsemen shall go forth with each thousand of the formation of the skirmishers' (vi, 8, cf. also p. 159, n. 4). Hence the inclusive number of the skirmishers was 7,000, who were grouped, as we saw, into seven battalions, and each battalion contained a thousand soldiers.[5] The conclusion is confirmed by the inscriptions on the 'banners of the congregation on going forth to war', as the inscription on the banner of the 'thousand' reads: 'battalions of God'.[6]

Since the number of soldiers (excluding cavalry) was 28,000 (ix, 4–5, and cf. below), the skirmishers comprised about 25 per cent of the total infantry.

The age of the skirmishers was probably given in the missing part

---

[1] ix, 4; vi, 4; viii, 3–4, 14; ix, 4. See also p. 159, n. 4.

[2] ix, 3–4, i.e. the 7th battalion, which had been engaged just before the other six are thrown into battle.

[3] vi, 7–8: the 1,400 cavalry with the skirmishers are divided into seven units of 200, see below, under (4), and § 6.

[4] vi, 1–6; viii, 1 sq.; see subsections 5–6.

[5] On this problem see below, § 5–6.

[6] Cf. in detail ch. 3, § 6, where we have shown that the *deghel* is the same as the 'thousand'. Eldad the Danite, the medieval pseudepigrapher, tells us that in the army of Uzziel, prince of Asher, 'each deghel had 1,000 men' (BHM ii, 103).

of the beginning of Section 11, (vi, 17 seq.). As the cavalry which fought with the front formation were aged 40–50 years, the same as the front formations (vi, 13; vii, 1), and the 'cavalry who went forth with the skirmishers' were aged 30–40 (vi, 13), we may conclude with certainty that the age of the skirmishers was also from 30–40, i.e. lay between the age of the non-combatant units (25–30) and that of the front formations.[1]

(5) *The weapons of the skirmishing units.*

vi, 1–6 discusses these in detail, viii, 1 ff. more briefly. The description begins with long-range weapons and ends with the battalions armed with weapons for close combat. This order fits the sequence of fighting. The skirmishing units were divided into the following groups according to their equipment:[2]

(a) Two battalions of slingers;[3]
(b) Three battalions of 'battle darts';
(c) One battalion armed with 'lance and shield';
(d) One battalion armed with 'shield and sword'.

Translated into numbers this means: 2,000 slingers;[3] 3,000 dart throwers (carrying a total of *c*. 21,000 darts);[4] 1,000 lance-bearers; 1,000 sword-bearers.[5]

(6) *The skirmishers in fighting.*

Here we shall deal with them as independent fighting units, their relation to the front formation to be explained below (§§ 5, 7). As compared with the front formation, whose weapons were uniform and mainly for close combat, the skirmishers' distinctive armament, consisting of weapons of different range, points to their principal tasks:

(1) Opening the battle from a comparatively long range so as to disarrange the enemy lines.

(2) Engaging and destroying the enemy's skirmishing units.

(3) Exploitation of any local success for breaching the enemy lines.

(4) Keeping in contact with the defeated and fleeing enemy and pinning him down so as to enable the heavy front formations to destroy him in close combat.

In these tasks they were assisted by special cavalry units[6] (the 'cavalry that go forth to battle with the skirmishers', vi, 10–11), also

---

[1] Cf. ch. 4, § 4 (1), with table of age-groups.
[2] These types of weapon are discussed in the relevant sections of ch. 6.
[3] Or one battalion of bowmen and one of slingmen. In both passages (vi, 1; viii, 1) the operative words are destroyed.
[4] See under 6 below and ch. 6, § 7.
[5] For *kidhon* = 'sword', see ch. 6, § 6.
[6] For fuller details, see § 6 below.

TACTICS AND ORGANIZATION 159

equipped for long-range fighting (bows and darts, vi, 15).[1] These horsemen, 1,400 in number, were organized into fourteen 'arrays', each of 100 horsemen; their position was on the two flanks of the battle line, seven arrays on each. Two 'arrays' were attached to each one of the skirmishing battalions, accompanying it on both flanks (vi, 7-8; viii, 4-5; cf. fig. 8).

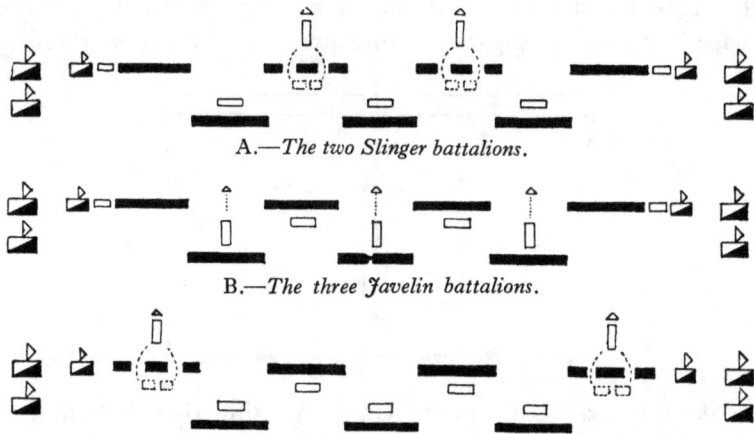

A.—*The two Slinger battalions.*

B.—*The three Javelin battalions.*

C.—*The 'Sword and Shield' and 'Javelin and Shield' battalions.*

Fig. 8. *The advance of the skirmishing battalions from the 'battle intervals'.*

The skirmishing battalions went into action in groups: the first contained two slingers' battalions [2] who opened battle at long range (vi, 1; viii, 1-2). The second group, which went into action after the withdrawal of the first, contained three dart-throwers' battalions (vi, 1-4; viii, 3-17) who conducted the battle from a medium range.[3] The third group contained two battalions, one of which bore lances and the other swords. These fought at short range and in close combat (vi, 4-6).[4]

Their tactics are discussed in detail in several passages, mainly

---

[1] Cf. ch. 6, § 7 and § 13.

[2] Or one battalion of bowmen and one of sling-men. In both passages (vi, 1; viii, 1) the operative words are destroyed.

[3] All this invalidates, of course, the view of Avi-Yonah (cf. p. 152, n. 12), that these three battalions were the Phalanx. It also disposes of the translation 'flags of the middle'—i.e. between the two cavalry wings—and the comparison (ib. note 31, p. 3) with the division of Judas' army.

[4] This was, of course, not a fixed division.

The battalions going into action simultaneously made up a 'formation' (of two sling units, three darts units, etc.); this may explain the expression, used vi, 8, of the skirmishers' cavalry, 'shall go forth with each thousand of the formation of the skirmishers.' Since, in contrast to the front-formations, these 'formations' were not of fixed size, this clumsy way of indicating the numbers of cavalry had to be adopted; see further note p. 161, n. 1, and § 5.

in v, 15–vi, 6 and vii, 8–ix, 9. Before the opening of the ' intervals,' the skirmishing battalions were drawn up behind the front formations.¹ At the sound of the trumpets of remembrance,² the intervals (cf. § 2 (4)) within the front formations opened ³ and the battalions advanced through them, the first being the slingers. On completion of their action these took up position next to the first formation (vii, 3). Then came the turn of the three battalions of dart throwers (who could advance through the gaps between the separate formations). Every one of these threw

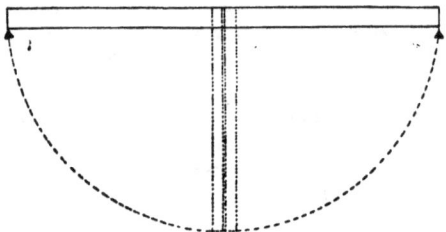

Fig. 9.—*Deploying the columns into ' arrays '.*

seven darts (vi, 2 ; viii, 13).⁴ On completing their action the two battalions belonging to the last group (vi, 4–5) went out. The method of deploying the battalions from columns into ' arrays ' and their advance towards the enemy are quite clear. The battalion halts between the lines in the formation in which it marched out, i.e. in columns. At the trumpet signal (' signal of battle array ') they deploy into array formation. They thus form up into fighting order while still outside the range of the enemy's weapons (cf. fig. 9). At the third trumpet signal (' signal to advance ' or ' signal to engage ') they advanced all together until they came within effective range (viii, 7–8 ; xvi, 11–12), and reached for their weapons (ib.). Simultaneously with the priests sounding the ' trumpets of the slain ' and the Levites and the band of horn-blowers sounding the great fanfare, the skirmishers began to use their weapons. Then this first general fanfare subsided, so that the soldiers could hear the continuing sound of the ' trumpets of the slain ' directing their action.⁵

---

¹ For their exact position see below, § 5, and the drawings in fig. 8.

² See further, ch. 5.

³ For the method of opening the ' gates ', see below, § 5.

⁴ The reasons for taking the text in this way are discussed, ch. 6, § 7.

⁵ Cf. ch. 5, § 8. In connexion with the columns fanning out before entering the range of enemy weapons, we may recall the difficulties scholars experienced in determining the stages by which the legion passed from marching to battle order when suddenly attacked, cf. K.-V. pp. 358–70, and see below, § 5.

Since the author speaks of the three battalions as 'drawn up in three arrays' (viii, 6), we assume that each battalion formed one 'array', in contrast to the battalions of the front formations, which were drawn up in seven 'arrays' (see below). This seems logical, since in this formation all the skirmishers can operate simultaneously and can expose the enemy to rapid 'bursts of fire' of any quantity desired. It must moreover be assumed that the three arrays were not drawn up on the pattern of the frontal arrays 'one man behind another', but 'formation beside formation' in one line, perhaps in echelon.[1] For the general pursuit all seven battalions advanced and were drawn up before the line (ix, 3-4).

The use of light units armed with bows, slings and lances, fighting between the lines or at the flanks with the support of cavalry, was frequent both in the Hellenistic and Roman armies. The structure of the serried phalanx, especially at the period of the Diadochi,[2] ruled out any movement of light units amongst the phalanx, while the structure of the Roman army was especially suited to it, both in the period of the *manipula*—when the *velites* were placed behind the *manipula* and operated through the intervals between them [3]—and in the period of the Cohorts, when light units (now composed of *auxilia*) operated from the spaces between the legions and at their flanks.[4]

The operational cooperation between the light units and the cavalry in the Roman army reached its climax at this period, for both types belonged to the *auxilia* and only a comparatively small number belonged to the legion itself.[5]

The identification of the *deghel* with the Roman *cohors*[6] brings out several additional points of resemblance between the skirmishing battalion in DSW and the organization of the auxiliary cohorts:

(1) Like the skirmishers, the *auxilia* operated only within the framework of single cohorts.[7]

(2) The auxiliary cohorts were organized—like the skirmishing

---

[1] The three 'arrays' are not the *acies triplex*. Each *acies* consisted of several cohorts and was drawn up in several 'arrays'. The nearest to the *acies* seems to be the *ma'ărakhah*. The 'first *ma'ărakhah*' (viii, 2) corresponds to the *prima acies* or *frons prima* (Marquardt p. 48); cf. p. 159, n. 4, and § 5 (2).

[2] K.-V. pp. 134, 136.

[3] Marquardt p. 44 with drawing, and the quot. from Polybius ib. p. 48, n. 5; K.-V. p. 370.

[4] K.-V. pp. 433-4. Their use was elastic at that period, and depended on individual commanders' idiosyncrasies. Pompey in particular used them in large numbers and in close collaboration with the legionaries.

[5] See § 5 for the types of cavalry and its tactical collaboration with the auxiliaries.

[6] Further § 5.

[7] K.-V. p. 393; G. L. Cheesman, *The Auxilia of the Imperial Roman Army*, 1914; Parker, *O.C.D.* p. 127.

battalions—according to the types of their weapons, i.e. each unit had its standardized equipment. The units were named according to their weapon : *sagittarii, scutati, contarii, funditores*, etc.[1]

(3) Some of these cohorts also numbered approximately one thousand men, as is proved by their designation as *cohors milliaria*, divided into ten ' hundreds '.[2]

The author's descriptions deal mainly with the tactics of the skirmishing battalions. This can be explained from the fact that a considerable part of the Eastern Roman army consisted of *auxilia* cohorts. Moreover, the vassal armies in the Roman Empire were mainly organized on the *auxilia* pattern, which on the one hand suited the abilities and national character of each people, and on the other hand made it easy to engage them in aid of the legions, which consisted mainly of Roman citizens.[3]

§ 5. Combatant Troops : The ' Front Formations '

(1) *General remarks.*

Though most of the technical part of the scroll is devoted to the skirmishing units, the author has a complete chapter (v, 3–14) in the *Serekh* Series on the structure and weapons of the heavy infantry disposed in the ' front formation '. Confrontation of the two following passages will enable us to gain an exact idea of the front formations :

v, 3–4, 6–7	ix, 3–5
' Disposition for arraying the battle battalions when their establishment is at full, so as to form a front formation. The formation shall be composed of units of a thousand men, seven frontal arrays to one formation, arrayed according to the disposition of placing one man behind another. All of them shall carry shields of burnished copper . . . they shall hold a spear and a sword.'	' When they are discomfited before them, the priests shall blow the trumpets of summoning and all the skirmishers shall go forth against them from within the front formations and take up position, six battalions as well as the battalion already engaged. The whole army, seven formations, 28,000 warriors and the horsemen, 6,000 in number, all these shall take up the pursuit to destroy the enemy in the battle of God for eternal annihilation.'

These show the following :

(1) The ' front formation ' constitutes a tactical unit distinct from the skirmishers.

---

[1] Marquardt pp. 155, 192 ; K.-V. p. 385. Compare here the battalions of dart-throwers, slingers (archers ?), those armed with spear and shield, and those armed with shield and sword.

[2] K.-V. p. 495. Cf. p. 161, n. 7 and n. 3 below.

[3] Detailed description, BJ III, iv, 2.

(2) Their equipment is heavier and different from that of the skirmishers.

(3) In contrast to the skirmishers, whose arms differ according to their battalion, the armament of the front formations is standardized.

(4) These soldiers, though organized in battalions (called 'battle battalions'), are grouped into front formations of equal complement.

(5) The front formation consists of seven 'frontal arrays'.

(6) The phrase 'seven frontal arrays to one formation' on the one hand and the plural 'front formations' on the other, prove the existence of several front formations.

(7) The skirmishing battalions go into action from a position within the front formations.

(8) The front formations, who are not active in the first contacts, participate in the general pursuit.

(9) Each formation has its own 'chief' (xix, 12). This proves that the formation constitutes a well-defined unit with an independent tactical role.

These general conclusions seem to be certain. Before proceeding to work out the number of formations, the number of men to a formation and its set-up, we must clarify the meaning of the terms 'front formation' (מערכת פנים), 'battle battalions' (דגלי מלחמה), 'to compose' (אסר), 'to form' (השלים).

(2) *The meaning of 'front formation'.*

As long as Israel's hosts fought as a closed primitive military formation, facing the enemy in one or several arrays, i.e. in phalanx order, few terms were needed for describing details of structure. The term *ma'ărakhah* sufficed to indicate the army formed into arrays.[1] Furthermore, since the *ma'ărakhah* in fact represented the general fighting force drawn up for action, this term in the course of time came to stand for a number of different concepts: fighting force, battle field, front,[2] while 'forming the *ma'ărakhah*' denoted also the actual fighting.[3] This practice seems to have continued into the period of the Diadochi, during which the army was essentially organized as an undifferentiated whole, as in the First Temple period.

It is natural that the change in the organizational set-up of the army involved the rise of new terms as well as the use of some old terms in new meanings. I already mentioned that during the scroll's period two

---

[1] 1 Sam. xvii, 8, 10, 26, 36; xxiii, 3, etc. Ch. xxiii influenced the terminology in DSW, cf. comm. on xiv, 3; vii, 8.

[2] 1 Sam. xvii, 20–2; iv, 2, 12, 16.

[3] 1 Sam. xvii, 2; 2 Chr. xiii, 3, a. fr. For MH, see § 2 (1). Cf. B. T. Soṭah 43b as against M. Soṭah viii, 2, מערכי מלחמה; Tos. Soṭah vii, 18.

new military terms were introduced: 'array' (סדר) and 'disposition' (סרך), in order to distinguish between three different concepts which until then had all gone under the name *maʿărakhah*, viz. the single line drawn up to face the enemy, a military body arrayed in any formation, and a secondary grouping in a mainly frontal structure. It is instructive that the LXX, in translating *maʿărakhah* in its various military meanings, almost invariably uses the term παράταξις.[1] The Vulgate, on the other hand, in trying to suit the Biblical formations to the Roman military structure (not always successfully, of course, on account of the differences between the two) uses different terms.[2] In the scroll we are confronted with two interesting phenomena. On the one hand, in general descriptions it uses the term *maʿărakhah* in its various Biblical meanings,[3] on the other—occasionally with the addition of another term—it employs it to denote a definite formation or part thereof. This practice often makes it difficult to decide the exact meaning unless the context is taken into consideration. The new content of the term manifests itself mainly in the fact that the scroll uses it at times to denote groups made up of fixed numbers of soldiers, armed with standard weapons, operating independently, sometimes arrayed one behind the other (v, 15) and at others, next to one another (vi, 8), with special officers at their head (xix, 12) and extremely flexible in its structure (ix, 10).

The compound 'front formations' is peculiar to the scroll, and as far as I know does not occur in Rabbinic sources. It is intended mainly to distinguish them from the skirmishing battalions. The word *panim*, fairly common as a military term in the O.T., is not intended to show that all these formations stand in one forward line without depth, but that they constitute the 'front' between which and that of the enemy the skirmishing units fight. An example for this is the description of the 'towers' (see below): 'Thus there shall be all round the tower in the three "frontal" aspects ...' (ix, 13), i.e. the term *panim* in a military context denotes all those units forming the front and not merely the anterior lines. This usage is clearly brought out in passages like: 'Now when Joab saw that the front (*pĕnē*) of the battle was set against him before and behind',[4] and 'Set ye Uriah in face of the front (*mul pĕne*) of the hottest battle'.[5]

---

[1] In 1 Sam. iv, 16: ἐκ τῆς παρεμβολῆς (many emend to *ha-maḥăneh*).

[2] *acies, proelium, certamen, pugna, agmen* (the first is most frequent), once *phalangas Israël* (1 Sam. xvii, 8).

[3] iii, 7; vi, 1–2, 4, 5–6, 7; vii, 8, 13, 17(?); viii, 4, 8, 12; ix, 11, 13; xiv, 3; xvi, 3, 5, 9, 10; xvii, 12.

[4] 2 Sam. x, 9; 1 Chr. xix, 10.

[5] 2 Sam. xi, 15. From 'front', the meaning of *panim* was extended to 'fight': 2 Kings xiv, 8, etc.

TACTICS AND ORGANIZATION 165

For this reason *all* the ' arrays ' of the front formation are called
' frontal arrays ' (v, 3-4) and not just the first rank in each formation.¹

(3) *The number of ' front formations '.*

It is important to determine the exact number of front formations
in order to know the number of soldiers serving in them, for reasons
given below. In agreement with the author's system, which is based
throughout on the number seven,² it may be supposed that seven front
formations take part in the war. Hence, ' . . . They shall form themselves
into seven formations, one behind the other ' (v, 15),³ can be taken
almost with certainty as referring to the number of front formations.
For reasons explained in the following paragraph, I am inclined also to
take ' the whole army, seven formations ' (ix, 4) as giving the number of
front formations, though the number of warriors mentioned immediately
afterwards includes also the skirmishing battalions.

(4) *The structure of the ' front formation ' and the number of soldiers in it.*

This is one of the most difficult problems in the scroll. The passage
defining its structure (v, 3-4) appears simple enough at first glance :
' Disposition for arraying the battle battalions when their establishment
is complete, so as to form a front formation. The formation shall be tied
at (*te'aser 'al*) a thousand men,⁴ seven frontal arrays to one formation,
arrayed according to the disposition of placing one man behind another.'
Hence each formation contained several battalions and was formed up in
seven ' arrays '. If we understand the term ' tied at ' to refer to arrays,
then each front formation was of equal number i.e. 7,000 (since each
array corresponds to a battalion which numbers 1,000 men), the total
number of soldiers in the front formations being 49,000 ; this interpretation, however, creates serious difficulties. To begin with, it contradicts
the description of the preparations for pursuit : ' And all the skirmishers
shall go forth against them from within the front formations and take up
position, six battalions as well as the battalion already engaged. The whole
army, seven formations, 28,000 warriors and the horsemen, 6,000 in

---

¹ Similarly *acies* originally means the edge of a sword (cf. *panim* Ezek. xxi, 21) ; used of the phalanx, it is extended to denote the whole fighting body in depth ; with the Roman system of fighting it comes to mean a formation of some tactical units, drawn up in one or several ' arrays ' (K.-V. p. 428).

² Seven ' lots ', years, ' arrays ', darts, skirmishing battalions, etc.

³ Though this part of the column is worn away, some traces in line 17 can be read clearly as פנים, and the context makes it probable that we have here the deployment of the front formations and the place of the skirmishers.

⁴ In the Translation : ' shall be com-posed of units of a 1,000 men.'

number, all these shall take up the pursuit to destroy the enemy' (ix, 3–5). These lines give the total number of combatants (as is proved also by the number of horsemen, 6,000, which includes also the cavalry of the front formations, cf. below) as 28,000. That is to say that the number of men in each front formation—including the skirmishing standard which is attached to it—is 4,000. If the skirmishing battalion numbers 1,000 men, then 3,000 only remain for the front formation.

If one takes the 28,000 as referring to the skirmishing battalions only, then each one of these battalions, which according to this corresponds to a 'formation', numbers 4,000 men.[1] This interpretation is not feasible in the light of the clearly established conclusion that the total number of the skirmishers, grouped into seven battalions, is 7,000 men, as we know from the number of horsemen attached to them: 2,000 horsemen with each 1,000 skirmishers, 1,400 in all (see above). Moreover, this will lead us to the conclusion that the front formations did not participate in the fighting even at the initial stage of the collapse of the enemy. This is in contrast to the statement in xviii, 4, (which, in the Kittim Series corresponds to the description of the preparations for pursuit in Section 12) that for the general pursuit 'the priests shall sound a fanfare [on the trumpets] of remembrance, and all battle formations shall follow their call'. This means that in the general pursuit the front formations participated as well as the skirmishing battalions. In addition, ix, 10–16, deals with the re-deployment of the army as a whole, including the heavy infantry (see below).

It is equally, if not more difficult to take 'the formation shall be tied at a thousand men' as referring to the strength of the whole front formation.

In the light of all this, we must look for a different interpretation of the structure of the front formation and in particular account for the technical meaning of the expression 'tied at'. We must try to reconstruct the sequence of operations accomplished in the process of assembling the formation, from the concentration of the soldiers until they stand in line opposite the enemy. The starting point is our earlier conclusion that the 'battle battalions'[2] which make up the front formations are identical with the 'thousand'.[3] The process of drawing up the front

---

[1] As we have shown in ch. 3, the *deghel* is a unit of fixed size corresponding to the 'thousand'. Though there may have been slight fluctuations, it is difficult to assume that there were 'battalions' of 4,000 men. Cf. also note 6, p. 157.

[2] So called in distinction from the 'skirmishing battalions'. Both together are 'the battalions of God', iv, 10; cf. p. 168, n. 3.

[3] See above and ch. 3, § 6, and p. 62, n. 2.

formation and placing its component battalions [1] in their position and 'arraying' them for battle, has to pass through three principal stages:

(1) Forming up the battalion after its soldiers have reported at the appointed place marked by the banner.

(2) The soldiers take up their correct position in the formation, keeping to the required intervals between each other, and form into a tactical unit.

(3) The battalions deploy into their proper 'arrays' within the formation.

The author indicates the first stage with the words: 'Disposition for arraying the battle battalions when their establishment is at full, so as to form a front formation' (v, 3). The phrase 'when their establishment is at full' can be understood as meaning either when their full quota has been reached [2] or, when they have gathered according to their quota,[3] which comes to the same. The use of 'so as to form' (להשלים) at the end of the clause stresses that this action is performed as a preparation towards building up the front formation according to a preconceived plan.[4] The third phase is clearly set out at the end of the description: 'Seven frontal arrays to one formation arrayed in disposition of placing one man behind another'.

Hence, the description of the second phase, i.e. posting the battalions at their correct position in the formation with proper spacing, must be sought in the words: 'The formation shall be tied at a thousand men'.[5] The root 'sr, whose basic meaning is 'to knot, group, join, attach',[6] occurs several times in the O.T. in connexion with organising the ma'ărakhah and its relation to its sub-units. 'Then he (Ahab) said: "Who shall tie the battle?"' (1 Kings, xx, 14); 'And Abijah tied the battle with an army of valiant men' (2 Chr., xiii, 3). This expression

---

[1] In the light of this, we must clearly prefer the text of Lauterbach's edn. of Midrash Wayyissaʻu: ערוכים למלחמה בדגליהם, to that of Yalkuṭ Shimʻoni, Wayyishlaḥ 33, and BHM iii, 4, ברגליהם. We might make the same change in BHM iii, 1, where Judah is said to have jumped into the midst of the מערכת הרגלים, especially in view of דגלי המערכה DSW xvii, 10.

[2] Isa. xl, 2; cf. also Gen. xxix, 21; Jb. vii, 1, and see comm.

[3] Cf. malʼu, Jer. iv, 5, a verse explained by Rashi and Kimchi as a call for mobiliza-tion. Kimchi explains millo' as 'a place near the wall where the people assembled'; cf. also Winton Thomas, JJS 3 (1952). While based on Isa. xl, 2, the addition ẓĕvaʼam shows that Num. i, 52, or ii, 3, were also in the writer's mind.

[4] Isa. xxxviii, 12; xliv, 26; M. RSh. iv, 6; DSD x, 6–7, and cf. comm. Compare aciem constituere, cf. Daremberg-Saglio, s.v. acies.

[5] For ʻal see comm., and cf. ix, 9.

[6] Gen. xlix, 11; 1 Sam. vi, 7; 1 Kings xviii, 44; Jer. xlvi, 4; Neh. iv, 12, etc.

refers mainly to the operation of gathering and grouping soldiers for battle according to their units, as we know also from the Targum, which reads : ' Who will draw up (יִטְקוֹס ⟨τάξις⟩) the battle ? ' The Targums use *tqs* also for tying and joining in other senses [1] as well as to translate the term *deghel* [2] or the activity of gathering into battalions. Thus the verse וּבְשֵׁם אֱלֹהֵינוּ נִדְגֹּל (A.V. : ' And in the name of our Lord we will set up our standards ',[3] Ps. xx, 6) is translated : ' And in the name of our God we shall form up (נִיטְקֵס) '.

Accordingly, the passage under discussion should be understood as if it ran : ' The formation shall-be-set-up-of-battalions-of (תדגל) a thousand men ', i.e. the formation is made up of units of 1,000 men each.[4] If we deduct from the total number of the infantry, which is 28,000, the number of skirmishers (7 × 1,000 = 7,000) we get a total of 21,000 soldiers of the front formations organized into seven formations. Hence, each front formation numbers 3,000, made up of 3 battalions of 1,000 men each, or 7 × (3 × 1,000) + 7 × 1,000 = 28,000.

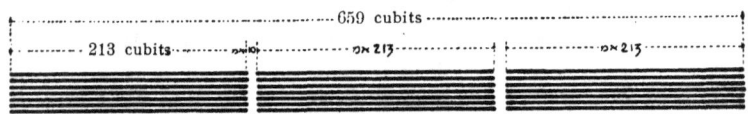

Fig. 10. Front Formation, with three battalions drawn up in seven arrays (numbers represent cubits).

Since each one of the battle battalions thus, ' tied ' in the front formations—one next to the other like horses in a carriage—is arrayed in seven frontal arrays, also the formation as a whole may be said to be ' arrayed in seven arrays ' (cf. fig. 10).

(5) *The age of the ' front formation ' soldiers.*

If we are right in assuming that the ' men of the *Serekh* ' mentioned in the age list (vii, 1) are the men of the ' front formation ',[5] then their age was from 40–50, in contrast to that of the skirmishers which was

---

[1] Jer. xlvi, 4, etc. ; Tg.J. Ex. xxviii, 28.
[2] Cf. p. 62, n. 2.
[3] Cf. Ben-Yehudah, *Thesaurus*, s.v. Also Num. Rabba ii, 2, 5.
[4] Cf. ch. 3, § 2, and p. 41, n. 2. Possibly also our passage is based on Num. xxxi, 5, with its insistence on ' thousand '. Other names for units or groups derived from the idea of ' tying ' are *aghuddah* (2 Sam. ii, 25, and cf. Lv. Rabba xxx : ' they shall all be tied into one *aghuddah*') ; *qesher* (M. Soṭah viii, 5 ; Danby : ' armies joined in battle,' Bertinoro : ' tied together so as to stand in closed ranks ' ; cf. also Neh. iv, 2) ; *ḥăvurah* ; *ḥever* (Hos. vi, 9).
[5] This seems to me practically certain ; cf. ch. 4, § 4 (1).

from 30–45.¹ This is logical since less strenuous movement was required from the men of the front formations.

(6) *Weapons of the front formation.*

Their armament was standardized. Each soldier carried a spear seven cubits (3·20 m.) long: a straight double-edged sword for cut and thrust one and a half cubits (0·68 m.) long; a rectangular shield, two and a half by one and a half cubits (1·14 × 0·68 m.). These weapons ² again prove that the principal task of the front formations lay in close fighting; on coming within a range of five yards they used their spears and immediately afterwards their swords.

The system of forming the front formations differed according to the battle phases.

(7) *The phase of 'forming'* (השלים) *the formations.*

The method of arraying the battle formations in this phase, which took place at some distance from the front line, is, I think, described in v, 15–17.³ Owing to the fact that part of this page has been eaten away, facts important for an understanding of the military structure are lost to us but from the fragmentary words some details may be salved. I give this passage with suggested restorations ⁴ : (15) ' When the [   ] are on the spot, they shall form themselves into seven formations, one behind the other (16) and there shall be a space (between each front-formation and the next . . . th]irty cubits, where the [skirmishers shall take up their position . . . (17) . . .] to the front [   ].'

From this passage we see that at this stage the formations were arrayed 'one behind the other' (cf. below) with a certain distance between them in which stood (if my restoration is correct) the skirmishers. This space was at least 30 cubits (*c.* 14 m.) wide. The gap before the word '[th]irty' may also be restored : '[a hundred and th]irty cubits ' or the like.

If we try to determine the exact space between the formations and the arrays respectively and the width of the front in the closed formation, we come up against one of the subjects of controversy between the two schools of Roman (and Hellenistic) military history, that of Delbrück and that of Kromayer.

Delbrück ⁵ fixes the space taken up by the individual soldier in this formation at 1½ ft. (i.e. 1 cubit) while Kromayer fixes it at 3 ft. (i.e. 2

---

¹ The partial overlapping may mean that some groups amongst the skirmishers had tasks requiring less agility.

² For details of the weapons, see ch. 6.

³ Cf. ch. 1, § 3.

⁴ For the palaeographic reasons, see comm.

⁵ K.-V. p. 358, n. 4.

cubits).¹ Our task is simplified since the scroll, having given the width of the shield as 1½ cubits,² uses this particular measurement also for the width of the front.³ It follows that the minimum space between each soldier and the next (and between each array and the next) in the closed formation in which the soldiers are when their shields touch (συνασπισμός) was 1½ cubits (i.e. 2¼ ft. = c. 66 cm.), i.e. the mean between the above two opinions.⁴ If it is possible to accept Delbrück's opinion with regard to the Macedonian phalanx, since the diameter of the round shield of the phalanx was c. 1 cubit,⁵ the width would hardly have been sufficient for the legionary bearing the *scutum*, whose measurements resembled those given by the scroll for the shield.

The following calculations are based on 1½ cubits as the minimal space in the closed formation. Assuming the skirmishing battalions to be placed at this stage in close arrays, then the space of 'thirty cubits' between the formations would allow a distance of 20 cubits (c. 9 m.) between the skirmishing battalions and the arrays of the formation: 10 cubits in front and 10 cubits behind. This space suffices for the phase with which we are dealing.⁶ If, on the other hand, we assume that at this stage the skirmishing battalions were already drawn up in columns, then we must reconstruct: '[Two hundred and th]irty cubits,' since the minimum depth needed to draw up a battalion of 1,000 men into column formation of seven parallel files is c. 213 cubits $\left(\frac{1000}{7} \times 1 \cdot 5\right)$.

Considering that the order at this phase was meant, *inter alia*, to enable the High Priest to be heard by all combatants,⁷ the first alternative, in which the formations are most closely concentrated, seems the more likely one.

The width of the front, which at this stage corresponded to that of the front formation, was therefore c. 660 cubits (c. 300 m.),⁸ while the depth of the area taken up by all formations was c. 270 cubits (c. 120 m.), cf. fig. 11.

(8) *Second phase: forming up in face of the enemy.*

At this phase, while the main fighting was done by the skirmishing

---

¹ ibid.; Marquardt p. 38. This is mainly founded on Polybius XVIII, xxx, 6, where the space taken up by each legionary is stated to be 3 ft. by 3 ft.
² v, 6; cf. ch. 6, § 2 (1).
³ e.g. vii, 14; ix, 13.
⁴ This may be the true solution.
⁵ K.-V. p. 135.

⁶ There is no contradiction with the column formation in which the skirmishers march out: the transition is achieved by a simple 'right turn' (or 'left').
⁷ Ch. 8, § 5 (1).
⁸ Assuming the distance between the battalions at this stage to have been minimal, say 10 cubits.

battalions and the task of the front formations was to cover their deployment and to open the intervals for them to emerge, they were drawn up in a defensive formation covering the space in front of it.

It is difficult to determine how many formations were placed in front and how many at the rear. The *serekh* which in the present writer's view describes this phase, begins with : ' When the battle formations are deployed over against the enemy, formation opposite formation, (cf.

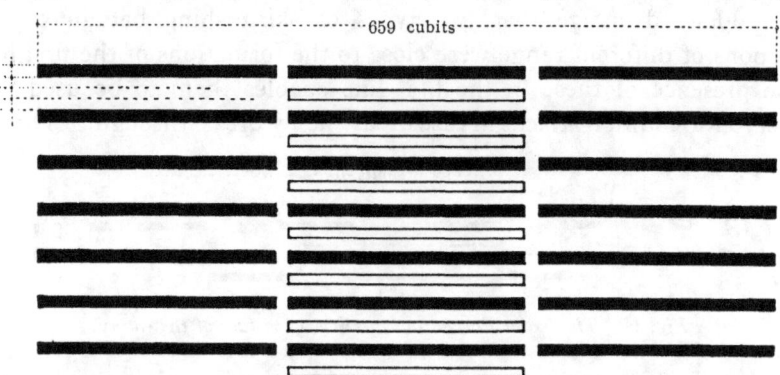

Fig. 11. *The Seven Front Formations : formation behind formation.*

above " formation behind formation ") there shall go forth from the middle interval into the space between the lines [1] seven priests' (vii, 8–9).[2]

The term ' middle interval ' proves that the first line contained an even number of units, with an odd number of intervals between them.[3] If we have correctly assumed that there were three units with each formation, then there are two intervals in each formation and no ' central interval '. We must draw the conclusion that while part of the skirmishing units issue from the intervals within each formation [4] and part from the intervals between the formations, the priests go forth only by way of the intervals between the formations. In the first line there must therefore be an even number of formations : 2, 4, or 6. The third being improbable, we must choose between the first two possibilities—no easy matter. Since the skirmishing battalions go forth in groups of 2, 3, and 2 (cf. above) we might prefer the first alternative, that there were three lines (the *acies triplex*). However, considering that for pursuit all formations were drawn up in one line (*acies simplex*)—as will be seen below—the *acies duplex* seems more probable, i.e. 4 formations in front and 3 in the rear. In such a pattern there would be three spaces in the front line,

---

[1] Here = the battle lines.
[2] Cf. ch. 5 ; ch. 8, § 4 (3), § 5 (3).
[3] That ' middle ' requires at least three

is the basis of the calculation of the number of ' watches ' Tos. Ber. i, 1.
[4] See fig. 8 ; comm. on vii, 14–15.

each one the width of a formation, each protected by one of the rear formations which closed the interval for pursuit.

This assumption, to my mind, is supported by the fact that the 'towers' were four in number (cf. below). There is moreover no contradiction in the skirmishing battalions going out in groups of 2, 3, and 2: the first and the third group were stationed behind the first line and the second behind or in front of the second line. This grouping has the added advantage that two types of skirmishing battalions with weapons of different range were close to the formations of the first line. The presence of these in the first line enables them to be used as a reserve for counter-attacks in case of an enemy break-through. Though

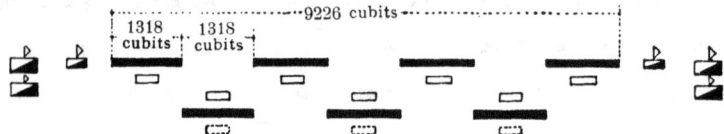

Fig. 12. *The Front Formations forming up in face of the enemy.*

this pattern (fig. 12) is thus more probable, the first alternative cannot be entirely ruled out.

(9) *Opening of the intervals within the formations.*

The description of the advance of the skirmishing battalions showed that the intervals within the front formations were opened after the formations stood facing the enemy. If during the forming-up stage the soldiers stood in closed concentrated ranks ($1\frac{1}{2}$ cubits per man),[1] it may

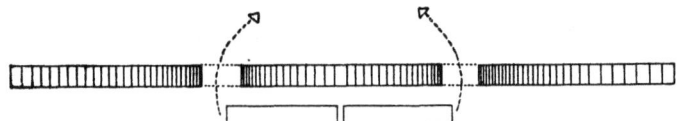

Fig. 13. *The method of opening the battle intervals.*

be assumed that in formation for battle the intervals were increased and the soldiers stood in open ranks.[1] According to classical sources the space per man in open rank was double that taken up in closed rank, i.e. in this instance 3 cubits.[2] The method of opening the intervals was simply by letting the men close up in all three units or only in the central one [3] (cf. fig. 13). As a matter of fact, since the scroll states that

---

[1] Cf. *laxatis ordinibus, confertis ordinibus*, see Marquardt p. 38 and criticism by Veith in K.-V. p. 438, n. 3.

[2] See p. 169, n. 5, p. 170, n. 1. The space is 2 cubits according to Delbrück, 4 cubits according to Kromayer.

[3] Or by a similar manœuvre of the middle and one of the flank units.

TACTICS AND ORGANIZATION

the intervals were opened to a width of 'fifty shields', there was no need to close up fully, but only to some extent.[1]

Fig. 8 shows, schematically, the actions of the different skirmishing battalions according to the scheme proposed here. I have placed the slingers' battalions at the completion of their task next to the first line, since the scroll states: 'And they shall come to take up position by the side of the first formation to fall in at their proper position' (viii, 2–3). The other battalions on the completion of their task are drawn up in their former position, as the text simply says they shall 'fall in at their proper position'. In my opinion this is not accidental, for this arrangement is tactically sound, leaving the two slingers' battalions at the flanks to cover the retreat of the skirmishing battalions in action.

In order to enable the rear units to move up into the front line at the pursuit phase, I did not place the three returning dart-throwers' battalions in the spaces between the formations of the first line.

The total width of the front in this pattern is $7 \times 1,318 = 9,226$ cubits (a little more than 4,000 m.) and its depth is at least 140 cubits [2] (i.e. $c.$ 65 m.)—these measurements suffice for 28,000 infantry men.

The tactics described in the scroll and especially that of opening the intervals of the front formation (if my reconstruction is correct) are very flexible, for they enable the commander to regroup the battalions of the front formations according to the needs of the battle, with intervals completely open, half open or completely closed, depending on the enemy's tactics.[3]

If we compare the tactics and military organization as described above with the methods of warfare customary in the Hellenistic armies after Alexander and those of the Roman army, there is little doubt that it is not identical with the tactics of the phalanx of the Diadochi. This is

---

[1] Passing from open to close formation would produce an interval of over 300 cubits, while only 75 cubits are required.

[2] I have doubled the distance between the front formation and the skirmishers behind it: it may of course have been increased by more than that. I have also assumed the space between 'arrays' to be equal to that between men in each 'array', though we know that at times it was larger (Vegetius iii, 14).

[3] DSW may here contribute to a solution of the thorny question at what stages the intervals between cohorts were closed and the legionaries spread out into an open continuous line for sword-fighting (K.-V. p. 430 sq.). It shows that procedure was much more elastic than hitherto assumed—a feature which fits particularly the period of Caesar. Its description of the skirmishers spreading out outside the range of enemy fire is more logical than the widespread assumption (e.g. Spaulding, *Ancient Warfare* p. 154) that the manœuvre under discussion took place within 15 or 20 yards of the enemy line. One has only to imagine the confusion likely to result from such regrouping under fire.

clearly proved by the division into independent secondary fighting units [1] with intervals, the oblong shields, the short spears as compared with the long *sarissa* and the swords for cut and thrust.[2] In this connexion two further points should be considered: the number of 'arrays' to a formation and the problem of the reserve formation.

According to the scroll there are seven frontal arrays. Even if we assume that this number was influenced by the author's fondness for the number 7, the real number must at any rate have been near it, say 6 or 8. In either case this number clearly differs from the phalanx of the Diadochi, which generally fought in 16 or more ranks.[3] On the other hand, this number fits the Roman army well. The most important piece of evidence on this point is Josephus' famous passage in the description of the Roman legion on the march, which lays down that the body of the army (ἡ φάλαγξ), which includes the legions, marched in 6 files.[4] Other indications confirm that the legion was generally drawn up in 6 ranks, as is accepted by most scholars.[5]

(10) *Reserve formation.*

In section 25, xvi, 10–11, which deals with the defeat of one of the formations of the Sons of Light in the 'Second Lot' we read: 'The priests shall blow the trumpets of summoning for another formation to go forth as a battle reserve, and these shall take up position between the lines, while to those already engaged they shall blow *a signal* to withdraw'.

Whether the description deals with a skirmishing battalion or a front formation [6] we clearly have here the conception of the reserve, which is generally regarded as an innovation of the Roman army and more particularly of the time of Julius Caesar.[7] This is an important point, since the Macedonian phalanx attacked as a whole without leaving behind units stationed in reserve; this system was inherent in its structure and changed with the system of warfare employed by legionaries, one of whose most characteristic features was the detailing of part of the cohorts

---

[1] The phalanx, still fairly elastic under Alexander, was in the Diadochi period 'fast immer als eine grosse Masse aufgestellt' (K.-V. p. 136); cf. Polybius II, lxix, 9; XVIII, xxix, 5), quite differently from the army of DSW.

[2] See in detail ch. 6, §§ 2, 6, 11.

[3] Cf. K.-V. p. 136; Polybius XVIII, xxx, 1, also II, lxvi 9 (32 arrays), etc.

[4] BJ III, vi, 2 : ἡ φάλαγξ τὸ στῖφος εἰς ἓξ πλατύνασα.

[5] Discussed in K.-V. pp. 287, 429.

[6] See comm.

[7] K.-V. p. 119; ib. p. 433 sees the completion of this process in Caesar's famous command at Pharsalus: *tertiae aciei imperavit ne iniussu suo concurreret.*

for reserve duties and bringing them into battle in a crisis or for exploiting a success.[1]

We thus have not only an original Hebrew term for 'reserve unit'—חליפה למלחמה,[2] but also the important military principle that the defeated formation is withdrawn only after the relieving formation is in position facing the enemy.

(11) *The front formation and the Roman army.*

Our analysis makes it highly probable that the front formation—in the military structure described by the scroll—corresponds to the Roman legion. This identity does not cover all structural details. While the legion at this period was still divided into 10 cohorts of 3 maniples each (i.e. 30 maniples to the legion), the front formation is made up of three battalions only. The difference is, however, only apparent. At the time of Julius Caesar the legion, in fact, contained only 3,000–4,000 combatants,[3] the same as the front formation. In this structure—of 10 cohorts = 30 maniples = 60 *centuriae*—no cohort contained more than 300–400 men: the maniples had 100–130 men, and the century 50–60 men.[4] In such a legion there were thus 30 maniples of 100 men[5] or 60 centuries, each containing 50 men. On comparing this with the structure of the front formation, we see that also its 3,000 soldiers are divided into 30 'hundreds' or 60 'fifties'.

That the three battalions of the formation were placed in one line does not contradict the Roman usage. At the time of Julius Caesar it was customary to use also the *acies simplex*.[6] A front formation of 3,000 combatants divided into three units of 1,000 men each, fits in well with the tradition of the Israelite army, as we know it from other sources.[7] This identity between the combat units of 3,000 men, customary in Judaea, and the legion of 3,000 men points particularly to the second

---

[1] Polybius XVIII, xxxii, notes it as one of the chief differences between phalanx and legion tactics that the Romans leave part of their troops in reserve. BJ III, vii, 27, contrasts the Roman reserve tactics with Josephus' own, τοὺς ἑαυτῶν ἀμείβειν οὐκ ἔχοντες.

[2] On this term see comm.

[3] Marquardt p. 151 states their number as 3,000–3,600; in n. 3 he adds that at Pharsalus, for instance, it was even smaller. Caesar's army of 22,000 consisted of 80 cohorts, i.e. 275 per cohort, less than 3,000 per legion. K.-V. gives the establishment in Caesar's time as 3,600–4,200.

[4] K.-V. p. 388.

[5] If the maniple was 100 men, this may explain the inscription on the banner of the 'hundred' (iv, 3) '. . . hand of battle against all unjust flesh': for 'hand' and its relation to *manipula* cf. ch. 5, § 6, and p. 100, n. 3.

[6] K.-V. p. 428.

[7] e.g. Josh vii, 3, 4; Ju. xv, 11; 1 Sam. xiii, 2; xxiv, 3; xxvi, 2; 1 Chr. xii, 30. Cf. § 2 (2) *a–b*. Judas Maccabaeus faces Gorgias with 3,000 men (1 Macc. iv, 6); he sends 3,000 with Jonathan to Galilee (ib. v, 20). Cf. Avi-Yonah, IEJ 2 (1952), 3.

half of the first century B.C., as is proved also by statements of Josephus about the army of Herod.[1]

It may be coincidence that the number of the infantry (21,000) and their organization into seven front formations agrees with the number and composition of Caesar's army in the battle of Dyrrhachium.[2]

§ 6. Combatant Troops: The Cavalry

(1) *General remarks.*

The whole of Section 10, vi, 7–16 describes the cavalry, its organization, number, arms and age-composition. The cavalry is again briefly mentioned in vii, 4–5 ; ix, 5–7.

In spite of the detailed survey of its organization and numbers it is difficult to discover the exact method of its division, since the author uses the terms *maʿărakhah* and *serekh* in various meanings. Notwithstanding this difficulty, the main outline is clear enough and may help us to explain also the more difficult passages.

First and foremost we note the division of the cavalry into two main types, as shown by the age groups :

(*a*) ' All the cavalry that go forth to battle with the skirmishers shall be on male horses fleet of foot, tender of mouth, long of wind, full in the measure of their years, trained for battle and accustomed to hearing noises and to the sight of all spectacles   Their riders shall be men of valour for battle, trained in horsemanship, the measure of their age being from 30 to 45 years '[3] (vi, 10–13) etc.

(*b*) ' The horsemen of the Serekh shall be from 40 to 50 years ' (line 13).

Those fighting with the skirmishers (*a*) have the better mounts and are younger than the Serekh horsemen (*b*). The former are armed like the skirmishers, but the armour of the latter is heavy and resembles, with slight differences, that of the front formations.

---

[1] Herod led 3,000 men against Antigonus (BJ I, xvi, 5). His army, while besieging Jerusalem, numbered 30,000, organized in 11 legions, i.e. an establishment per legion close to that of DSW (Ant. XIV, xvi, 1 ; cf. BJ I, xvii, 9). Note that in addition he had 6,000 cavalry—exactly the number given in DSW. Cf. Abel, *Hist. de la Palest.* i, 389, 427 ; also Caesar, *B.G.* I, xlviii, 5. With skirmishers, each legion would number about 4,000 : this, by the way, is the number of the Essenes, as given by Ant. XVIII, i, 5.

[2] Cf. Veith, *Feldzug von Dyrrhachium* 1920, p. 164 ; Stoffel, *Histoires de Jules César, Guerre Civile* 1887, I, 128, 344 ; Spaulding, *Ancient Warfare* p. 175 ; above, p. 175, n. 3.   For my suggestion to arrange the formations in two rows of four and three, see also Domaszewski, *Die Phalangen Alexanders und Caesars Legionen*, Sitzb. Heidelberger Ak. d. W., Ph.-H. Kl. 1925/6, i, 79.

[3] For the terms see comm.

No less significant is the numerical proportion of the two groups: In the section which describes the general pursuit by all combatants, we read, after the total number of infantry has been given as 28,000: 'And the horsemen 6,000' (ix, 5). This number recurs in vi, 10: 'Thus the horsemen with the cavalry of the men of the Serekh will be 6,000, that is 500 to each tribe'. The author here uses the term Serekh for the congregation as a whole as in 'elders of the Serekh' and 'all the men of the Serekh with him' (xv, 4), '*serekh* of God', etc.,[1] while 'horsemen of the Serekh' in (*b*) refers to the soldiers drawn up in the 'disposition' of the front formations, who are distinct from the cavalry of the skirmishers. Similarly he uses the term in 'the men of the Serekh shall be from 40–50 years old' (vii, 1) when giving the age of the front formation as opposed to that of the skirmishers.[2]

(2) *The light cavalry*.

From these two points of departure we may proceed to the elucidation of details. The chapter opens with a description of the organization of the cavalry who go into action with the skirmishers: 'Seven arrays shall also be posted at the right and the left of the *ma'ărakhah*: these arrays shall take up position on either side, seven hundred horsemen being on one side and seven hundred on the other. Two hundred shall go forth with each thousand of the skirmishing formation'. This is quite clear; *ma'ărakhah* indicates here the front line, as often,[3] in contrast to the 'camp' (cf. below) which indicates, *inter alia*, the whole army, including all formations. Instead of saying: 'Two arrays of horsemen shall go forth with each battalion of the formation of the skirmishers', the author uses a numerical term, in keeping with the context which speaks of numerical divisions and not of units. I have already mentioned, when discussing the skirmishing battalions, that this passage gives a clear account of the fighting methods of the skirmishers and states their number: seven skirmishing battalions flanked right and left by 100 horsemen. The skirmishing battalions fight in 3 *acies*: 2 slingers' battalions; 3 dart-throwers' battalions; 2 battalions with short range weapons. Accordingly, with the first group 400 horsemen went forth, with the second 600 and with the third again 400. At this phase the cavalry is not used for independent fighting aiming at penetration, outflanking, or the like. Split up into small units closely associated with the skirmishing units, their purpose is to cover the immediate flank of the skirmishers and to engage the enemy's light cavalry. This method

---

[1] Cf. § 2 (5).
[2] Cf. ch. 4, § 4 (1).
[3] Cf. § 5, and see below, p. 193, n. 2, for Gellius' account.

of employing the light cavalry, customary also with Hellenistic armies,[1] developed during the Roman period, especially in the first centry B.C., when the light infantry and most of the cavalry belonged to the auxiliary units. The cooperation between light units and cavalry reached its climax at the time of Julius Caesar.[2] The identical armament also fitted these horsemen particularly for fighting alongside the skirmishing units.

The 4,600 horsemen.—After having described the tasks of these 1,400 horsemen, the author goes on : ' And likewise they shall take up position on all sides of the " camp ". In all there shall be 4,600 ' (vi, 8–9). At first glance we might assume that these horsemen belong to the second group, the heavily armed ' cavalry of the Serekh ', an assumption apparently supported by the total number of cavalry, 1,400 + 4,600 being 6,000. Yet it does not fit what follows. The author, in addition to the above 4,600, enumerates : ' 1,400 cavalry attached to the men of the Serekh of the formations,[3] 50 to each formation ' (ib. 9–10). Only after this does he state : ' Thus the horsemen with the cavalry of the men of the Serekh will be 6,000, that is 500 to each tribe ' (vi, 10) ; i.e. the 6,000 cavalry were made up of the first 4,600 cavalry and 1,400 ' cavalry attached to the men of the Serekh of the formations '. It may be concluded that his statement ' in all there shall be 4,600 ' (line 9) was meant to convey that this number includes also the 1,400 cavalry attached to the skirmishers as well as those who ' shall take up position on all sides of the camp '. The latter were thus 4,600 − 1,400 = 3,200. The inclusion of these two classes in one number as distinct from the 1,400 ' cavalry attached to the men of the Serekh of the formations ' shows that they belonged to the same group (aged 30–45, lightly armed), but did not participate in battle with the skirmishers, and were placed on all sides of the ' camp '.

The phrase ' on all sides of the camp ' gives us to understand that these horsemen were placed not only at the flanks but also at the rear of the body of combatants.[4] Since 3,200 is not divisible by three, I have

---

[1] K.-V. p. 137.

[2] Caesar B.C. III, lxxv, 5, tells of his successful experiment in training agile foot-soldiers to fight in combination with cavalry, claiming that 1,000 of each together were able to repel 7,000 horsemen. A similar method was used by the Germans under Ariovistus, the foot-auxiliaries being carried into battle as ' pillion-riders ' (B.G. I, xlviii, 5 ; cf. ib. VII, lxv, 4 ; VIII, xiii, 2), and is recommended by Vegetius (iii, 16) ; cf. Marquardt p. 41, n. 1 ; K.-V. p. 435. Though the method described in DSW does not agree in details, it appears that we have here some form of specialized collaboration, as opposed to the rest of the cavalry, on which see below.

[3] In the translation : ' men drawn up in formations.'

[4] For ' camp ' = army in action, see ch. 3, § 4, and p. 47, n. 2.

TACTICS AND ORGANIZATION 179

in fig. 8 divided them arbitrarily into 4 units of 800 each, placed one at each flank and two at each extremity of the rear. This is not an unusual arrangement : the two rear units, besides defending the rear, also serves as a kind of reserve with whose aid the front can be lengthened and the enemy be harassed at his flanks while the ordinary flank cavalry unit engages his cavalry.[1] We shall once more deal with this formation when discussing the organization for pursuit and annihilation of the enemy.

(3) *The heavy cavalry.*

We must now turn to the complicated problem of the '1,400 cavalry (*rekhev*) attached to the men of the Serekh of the formations' (אנשי סרך המערכות) (vi, 9). Since the term *rekhev* nowhere in the scroll denotes chariots but always horses, or horses and horsemen together,[2] these 1,400 horses constitute the mounts of the cavalry of the Serekh, armed with long spears and round shields, whose age (40–50) resembles that of the soldiers of the front formation.

The principal difficulty in understanding their allocation to the infantry units lies in the words : ' cavalry attached to the men of the Serekh of the formations, 50 to each line (*ma'ărakhah*) ', since the concluding clause implies the existence of 28 such ' lines ' (1,400 ÷ 50 = 28). If we were to identify these ' lines ' with the front formations (*ma'ărkhoth ha-panim*), we would get a contradiction, for the latter number 7 only. On the other hand, the number 28 corresponds to the 28,000 which according to the scroll (ix, 4) constitutes the sum total of the infantry. Thus each 50 horses of this group are attached to 1,000 combatants of the Serekh. Unless ' 50 to each *ma'ărakhah* ' is a scribal

---

[1] Cf. K.-V. p. 296 sq. on Scipio's battle order at Zama, and the order of Antiochus IV's army as analysed by Lt.-Col. E. Galili, *Ma'rakhoth* 81 (Dec. 1953), p. 44. For the placing of cavalry behind the legion see Marquardt, p. 138.

[2] It may be useful to summarize the terminology in DSW :
(*a*) Horsemen :
  (1) *parashim* (vi, 7, 8, 10, 13 ; xii, 8, cf. comm.) ;
  (2) *rokhĕvim* (vi, 12 ; ix, 5) ;
  (3) *anshē ha-rekhev* (viii, 4).
(*b*) Horses : *rekhev* (clearest vi, 10 ; ib. 12 ; viii, 4).
(*c*) Horses with Riders : *rekhev* (ix, 6–7). Where he means ' chariots ', the author uses *markĕvoth-* (xi, 10). We may briefly note that *parash* is used as in MH and Tgs. ; BH uses it for horse + rider. The use of *rekhev* is based on 2 Sam. viii, 4 ; Isa. xxxvi, 8–9 ; cf. also Josh. xi, 9. The absence of any reference to chariots—which can be clearly proved—points definitely to the Roman period. Dr. J. Brand kindly drew my attention to B.T. Soṭah 48b, ' since the first Temple was destroyed, there was no more silk, *pĕranda*-silk, white glass, or iron chariots,' which probably refers to the last part of the second Temple period. Note also that there is no mention of elephants, so typical for Seleucid warfare. Lambert (N.R.Th 1952, p. 272) and Stauffer (Th.L.Z. 76 (1951), 667 sq.) did try to find elephants in DSH, but see Dupont-Sommer, *Nouveaux Aperçus* p. 49 sq., and above, ch. 4, p. 72, n. 1.

error for ' 50 to each thousand of each *ma'ărakhah* ',[1] or ' 50 to each *serekh* of each *ma'ărakhah* ',[2] *ma'ărakhah* must here denote the largest unit drawn up without spaces and intervals, i.e. in the present instance, the ' thousand '.[1] This conclusion forces us to re-examine the phrase אנשי סרך המערכות. Had the author meant the front formations only, he would have written אנשי מערכות הפנים as in other instances.[3] The fact that the phrase immediately follows on the description of the other 4,600 cavalry makes it appear as though he wished to stress that those 1,400 horses form an organic part of the infantry units, being attached 50 to each 1,000 of the infantry, in contrast to the 4,600 horsemen mentioned before who are organized in independent cavalry units partly for covering the skirmishing battalions, partly for the flanks of the whole army.

The author was here compelled to use different terms, since he sometimes wishes to speak of the whole cavalry available to the congregation, as distinct from the infantry—at others of the independent cavalry, as against the one allotted to other troops. If the above analysis is correct, the author names the different groups of the cavalry as follows :

(4) *Terminology.*

   A. The cavalry in general :
1. ' Horsemen with the men of the Serekh ' (vi, 10) indicates the total cavalry of the congregation or militia, namely, 6,000 (comprising both independent and attached cavalry).
2. The ' cavalry ' and ' riders ' indicates the cavalry in general, as against the infantry, namely, 6,000 (ix, 5–6).

   B. *Cavalry attached to the infantry :*
1. ' Cavalry attached to the men of Serekh of the formations ' (vi., 9), namely, 1,400, or
2. ' The horsemen of the Serekh ' (vi, 13) (40–50 years old).

   C. *Independent cavalry :*
1. ' The cavalry that go forth with the skirmishers ' (vi, 10–11)   1,400 ⎫
2. Who take up position ' on all sides of   ⎬ 45–50 years old
    the camp ' (vi, 9)   3,200 ⎭

                                  Total : 4,600

---

[1] Cf. the language in vi, 8 ; v, 3.
[2] Cf. v, 4.
[3] Cf. § 5 (3) and ch. 4, § 4 (1) on the age of the ' men of the Serekh '.

TACTICS AND ORGANIZATION

The cavalry is therefore divided into the tactical units as follows :

1. *Independent cavalry.*
    (*a*) 200 securing the flanks of each of the seven
    skirmishing battalions.   Total : 1,400
    (*b*) Stationed around the army, 1,600 at each flank.
                                                           Total : 3,200
                            Total of independent cavalry : 4,600

2. *Attached cavalry.*
    (*a*) 150 to each of the front formations (3 × 50)
    Seven formations (7 × 150).   Total : 1,050
    (*b*) 50 to each of the 7 skirmishing battalions [1]
                                                           Total :   350
                            Total of allotted cavalry : 1,400
                                          Grand total : 6,000

(5) *Cavalry units of the Roman army.*

This set-up, so strange at first sight, can only be understood in the light of the organization of the cavalry in the Roman army from the beginning of the first century B.C. onwards. The basic change which took place in the structure of the Roman army with the rise of the *auxilia* resulted in the cavalry being almost completely made up of auxiliary units while the legion increasingly was converted into a pure infantry unit, its cavalry being reduced in number and made into a kind of 'mounted infantry', which mainly served for transmission of orders, adjutancy, guard duties, etc.[2] During the period preceding Julius Caesar the 'legionary' cavalry numbered 300 to a legion of 6,000 infantrymen; [3] at the time of Josephus it did not exceed 120.[4] Caesar himself, who fought with legions of 3,000 men (see above), almost completely abolished the 'legionary' cavalry and used a very small number (corresponding to the reduction of the legion by half), viz. 100–200,[5] exactly

---

[1] Since part of the 'cavalry of the Serekh' belong to the skirmishing battalions, this may explain why their age overlaps that of the light cavalry by five years, if the age group 40–45 was the one attached to the skirmishers.

[2] K.-V. pp. 379, 387, 393, 434, 476 ; Marquardt pp. 154, 174.

[3] Cf. especially Marquardt pp. 22, 39 ; K.-V. p. 308.

[4] BJ III, vi, 2, the *locus classicus* for the legionary cavalry. Τὸ ἴδιον τοῦ τάγματος ἱππικόν exactly corresponds to *rekhev anshē ha-serekh*.

[5] Cf. note 2. Caesar left Brundisium with seven legions and 600 cavalry, i.e. nearly 100 per legion. Antonius led to Dyrrhachium four legions with 800 cavalry (200 each). At Pharsalus, Caesar tells us, he had 22,000 infantry in 80 cohorts, but only 1,000 cavalry, cf. Veith, op. cit. (p. 176, n. 2) ; Spaulding, *Ancient Warfare* p. 175 sq. and literature cited there.

as in the scroll where 150 horsemen fight with a front formation of 3,000 soldiers. Moreover, the seemingly odd fact that each skirmishing battalion was accompanied by 50 cavalry of this type is explained in the light of a phenomenon peculiar to auxiliary cohorts up to and during the period of Augustus: these were divided into two types (apart from the independent cavalry units), pure infantry cohorts called *cohors peditata* and infantry cohorts with a small cavalry contingent called *cohors equitata*.[1]

The structure of the Roman army not only closely resembles that described in the scroll, but I submit that only with its help can we account for the division of the cavalry into a very small number which forms part of the infantry (in fact ' a mounted infantry force ') and a large number of horsemen grouped into independent units. This resemblance is most remarkably underlined by the armament of the two types of cavalry.

While the independent cavalry is armed with bows and darts, the cavalry of the infantry is armed with a long spear, a round shield and greaves.[2] In chapter 6 we dealt at length with these different weapons and noted that the round shield was in Caesar's period (it had completely disappeared by the time of Josephus) used only by the cavalry of the infantry, i.e. the mounted infantry which fought as part of the legion.[3] As shown there, the fact that only these horsemen wore greaves proves that not only was the sect's army not built on the pattern of the Hellenistic army (where also the infantry of the phalanx wore greaves) but it is indicative of the special duties these horsemen performed (transmitting orders, adjutancy, guard-duties, etc.), since only those engaged in such duties in the Roman army wore greaves.[4]

(6) *The stallions.*

The author insists that the light cavalry ' shall be male horses,[5] fleet of foot, tender of mouth, long of wind ' (vi, 11). To the reason mentioned in chapter 4, § 3,[6] I should add here that the prevention of bestiality may be only a side-issue. Stallions were normally used by cavalry, as we know from other sources.[7] Their sex is part of the requirement for fitness in battle.

---

[1] Marquardt p. 193–4; K.-V. p. 495.

[2] Their equipment is described vi, 14–15, partly destroyed.

[3] Details in ch. 6, § 2 (3), p. 121, n. 4, 5, 6.

[4] Ch. 6, § 3, p. 123, n. 4, 5, 6, 7.

[5] So literally in Hebrew.

[6] Cf. ch. 4, p. 71, n. 4.

[7] B.T. Pes. 113b; Ex. Rabba xxiii: ' the waves appeared to Pharaoh's horses like mares '; Cant. Rabba on Cant. i, 9, gives special reasons why Pharaoh rode on a mare; Josh. xi, 6, 9; Jer. v, 8; Ezek. xxiii, 20, etc. Cf. also Tos. A. Zar. ii, 3.

§ 7. REGROUPING THE ARMY FOR PURSUIT AND THE DECISIVE BATTLE

(1) *General remarks on battle orders.*

Section 12, vii, 8–ix, 9, describes the fighting of the skirmishing battalions. It ends with the beginning of the enemy's collapse (ix, 3) and the immediate activation of all skirmishing battalions and the cavalry for pursuit and keeping contact with the enemy (ib. 4 ff.). This is immediately followed by a short chapter (ix, 19 ff.) headed: 'Disposition to change the array of the battle battalions', i.e. regrouping for various tactical manoeuvres. The purpose of this chapter, considering its place in the scroll, is, I think, to describe the manner of regrouping the army for the general attack by all units together. This assumption gains ground when we compare the title of this section with that dealing with the structure of the front formation (v, 3):

8, v, 3	13, ix, 10
'Disposition to array the battle battalions when their establishment is at full, so as to form a front formation.'	'Disposition to change the array of the battle battalions.'

Both chapters deal with 'battle battalions' (as distinct from skirmishing battalions). The first explains how to array them in the usual formation for the commencement of battle, convenient both for defence and attack; the second how to change the array of the battle battalions. As we have shown, the 'dispositions' preceding them mainly dealt with the skirmishing battalions, who carry on the fighting until the enemy begins to weaken (the first six 'lots'). Now, with the enemy's collapse in sight, the time has come for the offensive by the whole army.

The passage describing the various formations is short and is apparently copied from the chapter-heading of a military manual which, without doubt, went on to set out in detail how these formations were drawn up. The author of the scroll was not interested in the full enumeration, since he intended to describe one of the formations (the 'towers'), in particular the inscriptions on their shields, with the names of the four archangels. This subject was close to his heart for reasons explained elsewhere.[1] It was for this reason that the author devoted so much space to the 'towers', without regard to the importance of the other formations, which he just mentions by name. The following is the main passage of this chapter with suggested restorations:[2]

'Disposition for changing the array of the battle battalions so as to form up in the shape of a rectan[gle with "tow]ers", enveloping

---

[1] Cf. ch. 9, § 6.   [2] For the restoration see comm.

arms with "towers", and arc with "towers", a flat arc with protruding columns, and wings [issuing] from [bot]h sides of the line [to] disorganize the enemy' (ix, 10–12).

We can see immediately that this passage refers to several battle formations in sequence, not to one single fixed formation. This is underlined by the recurrence of 'towers' after three of the formations. This passage is therefore a list of formations which differ from the order described before but are formed from it as required in different phases of the battle. In separating the individual terms we are helped by the recurring 'towers', as also by the 'and' which appears both before each 'tower' and before each new term.

The following is the most likely division:
(1) 'A rectangle with towers'.
(2) 'Enveloping arms with towers'.
(3) 'An arc with towers'.
(4) 'A flat arc with protruding columns'.
(5) 'Wings issuing from both sides of the line'.

If we break up this list into its basic components, we get the following series: 'A long rectangle'; 'enveloping arms'; 'an arc'; 'a flat arc'; 'columns'; 'towers', which bears an astonishing resemblance to the list of the names of battle formations employed by the Roman army as found in Gellius' *Noctes Atticae*, x, 9:[1] 'Vocabula sunt militaria, quibus instructa certo modo acies appellari solet: frons; subsidia; cuneus; orbis; globus; forfices; serra; alae; turres.'[2] Not only does the general character of this list closely resemble that of the scroll, but some of the terms appearing in both lists literally correspond, especially *alae* = wings; *turres* = 'towers'. Considerable help in understanding the terms in the scroll may be derived from Gellius' remarks that the relation of these terms, as well as of others in military nomenclature, to the objects so named is merely one of external resemblance in form.[3]

In spite of this remark, the military implication of some of the terms mentioned by Gellius is not altogether clear, though their general meaning can be guessed. Basing ourselves on Gellius' statement and on similar practices of modern armies,[4] we may consider the meaning

---

[1] By Aulus Gellius, lived first half of second century A.D., and based on ancient sources, mostly lost.

[2] In the Loeb edn., 1927, ii, 235–7.

[3] 'Haec est quaedam item alia invenire est in libris eorum qui de militari disciplina scripserunt. Tralata autem sunt ab ipsis rebus quae ita proprie nominantur earumque rerum in acie.'

[4] Compare names for formations such as 'arrowhead'.

of the terms mentioned in the scroll. First, however, it will be useful to compare some of the terms adduced by Gellius with the detailed description of battle formations in the Roman army, supplied by another Roman writer, which sheds considerable light on our problem.

Vegetius, in his comprehensive military handbook,[1] enlarges upon the advantages and disadvantages of seven principal forms of battle order. With some of these, recurring in Gellius' list and resembling terms in the scroll, we may occupy ourselves more closely :[2]

1. *Fronte longa, quadro exercitu* (*quadratus exercitus*) — in this formation the army is deployed in a longish rectangular front, the long side facing the enemy. According to Vegetius, military experts do not recommend this formation, especially in uneven terrain, mainly on account of the difficulty, when drawn up in this formation, of meeting an enemy attempt at outflanking. Vegetius goes on to say that an army of trained and courageous soldiers outnumbering the enemy can fight in this formation without risk.[3] This formation corresponds to the *frons* in Gellius' list. This is a transitional formation during battle, and Vegetius, when discussing training,[4] states that the troops must be taught to change quickly from this formation to that of the *cuneus*.

2. Attack on the right flank only } *depugnatio obliqua*.
3. Attack on the left flank only

These formations are mainly used when one's soldiers differ in quality. It enables the commander to concentrate the weak men at the defensive flank and the best forces at the attacking wing. Success depends on the enemy's flank being deployed in the opposite order.

4. A two-pronged attack, enfolding the enemy with two wings which commence their advance from a distance of 400–500 paces. This manoeuvre is likely to bring about a speedy decision and the defeat of the enemy. On the other hand, it is risky, for in the event of the attack being unsuccessful the centre is left exposed. This formation should therefore be used mainly when the commander is certain that the attack will lead to the retreat of the enemy (or after the retreat has already begun).[5]

5. The formation most likely to remedy the defects of the fourth, in which skirmishing and slingers' units are posted in the centre and in

---

[1] *Epitome rei militaris* iii, 20. Like so much in his book, V. seems to have copied this passage literally from Cato's *De re militari*, cf. Marquardt p. 138, n. 6.

[2] Briefly discussed by Marquardt, p. 138 ; in detail by E. v. Nischer (K.-V. p. 598).

[3] ibid. and again in the chapter *Regulae bellorum generales* iii, 26 : qui multitudine et virtute praecedit quadrata dimicet fronte, qui primus est modus.

[4] In his chapter on training, i, 26.

[5] iii, 20 ; also ii, 26.

front of the formation. In the event of success, these units too, will contribute to the enemy's defeat; should the attack fail, they can defend the centre.[1]

The sixth and seventh formations do not concern us; the sixth is for attack while on the march, the seventh pivots on some natural obstacle, such as a river or mountain. Vegetius' description of the first, fourth, and fifth formations is of special interest to us. Before identifying the formations mentioned in the scroll, we must clarify the meanings of the rest of the terms mentioned by Gellius, used already by historians before him:

Subsidia (the formation with a reserve) more or less corresponds to the first-phase order (four formations in front and three at the rear. cf. above § 5 (8)), and does not concern us in this context.

Cuneus ('wedge') denotes any formation resembling a trapezoid, arc, or wedge whose narrow end faces the enemy.[2] It resembles the initial order of Hannibal's army at the battle of Cannae, called by Polybius 'crescent' (cf. below on the 'arc').

Orbis is generally supposed to be a circumference array, the soldiers forming a kind of circle or full square in an encircled defensive position or during a retreat.[3]

Globus is not a formation in the accepted sense, but denotes an independent unit which operates mainly at the enemy flanks.[4]

Forfex (scissors) is a v-shaped formation, according to Roman sources mainly used to counter the *cuneus*. In fact it resembles—if used in an attack—Vegetius' fourth formation [5] as we shall see.

Serra (saw) indicates the action of the units advancing and retreating in a hit-and-run manner so as to disarrange the enemy line or merely to keep contact. In operation, the formation resembles the teeth of a saw. These units were composed of high-quality troops.[6]

---

[1] iii 26; also iii, 20; 'Quinta depugnatio est quartae similis sed hoc unum amplius habet, quod levem armaturam et sagittarios ante primum aciem ponit, ut illis resistentibus non possit inrumpi.'

[2] Cf. p. 185, n. 3; Marquardt p. 139. Cf. also Vegetius iii, 19: 'Cuneus dicitur multitudo peditum quae iuncta cum acie primo angustior deinde latior procedit et adversariorum ordines rumpit, quia a pluribus in unum locum tela mittuntur.' This order was called in soldiers' slang *caput porcinum* 'hog's head'.

[3] Cf. Marquardt p. 135, with literature in n. 1.

[4] This is the original meaning of *peloton*, from which our *platoon*. Cf. K.-V. p. 598; Marquardt p. 135 with n. 2; Vegetius iii, 19.

[5] Vegetius iii, 19: 'Contra quod ordinatio ponitur quam forficem vocant. Nam ex lectissimis militibus confertis in similitudinem V litterae ordo componitur et illum cuneum excipit atque ex utraque parte concludit quo facto aciem non potest rumpere.'

[6] Vegetius, loc. cit.

TACTICS AND ORGANIZATION 187

Alae (wings)—Gellius' exact meaning is not clear. This formation seems to approximate to Vegetius' fourth formation.

Turres (towers). On this formation as well as on *testudo* see below, section 2.

Thus the principal formations employed by the Roman army were: the long rectangle, the wedge or arc, the pincers for effecting a double envelopment; a similar formation, adding light units in the centre in serrated order; wings, resembling the modern envelopment movement; and finally the ' towers '.

(2) *The ' towers '*.

A detailed description appears in ix, 12–15 : ' The shields of the men of the towers shall be three cubits long and their spears eight cubits long. The towers shall protrude from the line by a hundred shields, a hundred shields being the face of the tower. Thus there shall be all round the tower in the three frontal directions 300 shields. Each tower shall have two intervals, one on [the right and] one on the left. On all the shields of the towers they shall write,[1] on the first " Mi[chae]l ", [on the second " Gabriel ", on the third] " Sariel ", on the fourth " Raphael " : " Michael " and " Gabriel " on [the right side and " Sariel " and " Raphael " on the left side] '.

This description permits us to infer that :

1. There were four towers.

2. They protruded from the formation, two being on the right and two on the left.

3. They were distinguished by their long shields which surrounded the tower in three directions.

4. Each tower had two intervals, one on its right and one on its left side.

5. The frontage of the tower was a hundred shields, i.e. 150 cubits (*c.* 68 m.).

These features show that the towers were units [2] arranged in a special formation with suitable weapons, enabling them to advance without fear of missiles (since almost their whole body was covered by their long shields [3]) or of assault by spear and sword, their own spears being extra

---

[1] For the inscriptions on these shields see ch. 9, § 6 (2).

[2] This makes it impossible to think here of mobile siege towers (Marquardt p. 269 ; K.-V. p. 444). Their front was much too narrow for the data given in DSW.

[3] Their shields were half a cubit longer than the hefty ones used by the front formations, cf, ch, 6, § 2 (4).

long[1]. In view of their hollow formation,[2] the intervals on the right and left sides (cf. Fig. 14) and their close ranks, it appears that their main purpose was to enable other combat units to advance behind them and to debouch close to the enemy from their intervals. The name ' towers ' for these units was apt, for they protruded from the line like towers in a wall.[3] This resemblance was still increased by the long shields which suggested real towers with the shields of their defenders hanging over their sides.[4]

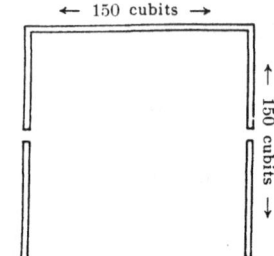

Fig. 14. Schematic plan of a ' tower '.

The fact that the *turres* occur in Gellius' list of battle formations, corresponding in all probability to our towers, supports our assertion that the towers in the scroll denote battle formations [5]—not siege towers etc.—but unfortunately we know nothing about the nature of these *turres*.[6]

From the scroll it seems that the tower must be identified with the famous Roman *testudo* which was used to indicate a formation of combat units for defence as well as attack and assault on fortified positions.

Testudo was a closed formation whose ' faces ' (mostly three) were protected by the shields of the soldiers standing in the outer ranks, sometimes combined to increase their length The rest of the soldiers

---

[1] Eight cubits, one cubit longer than that of the front formations, cf. ch. 6, § 11.

[2] This is already suggested by the 'gates' in their sides. Moreover, a solid ' tower ' with a side of 100 men would contain 10,000; thus the four towers would need 40,000 men, more than the whole army of DSW! Such solid formations were indeed used at one time, but were of little use, as pointed out by Xenophon, *Cyropaedia* VI, iii, 22, and soon ceased to be employed.

[3] Cf. Cant. viii, 10.

[4] Cf. Yadin, *Yediʿoth* 13 (1946–7), 19 sq., especially p. 23, n. 24. The ' tower ' formation is perhaps alluded to in Cant. Rabba on Cant. iv, 4 : ' a turret . . . whereon there hang a thousand shields— all the myriads and thousands that went to war against Midian.'

[5] Already in Homer the πύργοι Ἀχαιῶν (*Ilias* iv, 334, 347) are protruding military formations. Cf. also πυργηδόν ' in massed array '.

[6] Cf. the note by J. C. Rolfe in the Loeb edn., or of M. Mignon in the French translation, ii, 181 : formation en carrés.

TACTICS AND ORGANIZATION

could move behind this 'tortoise shell'. Since their front was secured by the wall of shields, they could raise their own shields above their heads and defend themselves from the sling-stones, darts, etc., which were hurled at them from the wall. This formation was used as a defence from surprise attack,[1] for an attack on a fortified enemy [2] (cf. fig. 15), as well as for camouflaging the activities of units in no man's land.[3]

Fig. 15. *A Roman testudo in operation.*

Identification of the 'tower' with the *testudo* also explains the fact that the 'towers' constitute an indivisible part of each of the formations described. While changing its formation for attack, the army is covered by the towers, able to overcome every obstacle or barricade which the retreating enemy might put up.

---

[1] Most detailed description in Dio Cassius xlix, 31, from which it clearly results that the heavy infantry armed with long rectangular convex shields formed the outer shell of the rectangular formation; they raised them over their heads, so that only the shields were visible, and the soldiers behind them were protected. Cf. also the Josephus quot. in note 3 at end.

[2] Ibid., and cf. note 3.

[3] Cf. Caesar, *B.G.* V, ix, 7, and T. Rice Holmes' note (Oxford edn., 1914, p. 181): 'Probably the work of piling the lumber was performed by men who advanced between the files under the protection of their comrades' uplifted shields.' On the *testudo* see K.-V. p. 446; Marquardt p. 135. Josephus describes a *testudo* in BJ III, vii, 27, without mentioning the name; he names it in II, xix, 5. If we accept the equations 'tower' = *turris* (Gellius) and 'tower' = *testudo*, we can also account for the surprising absence of the *testudo*, that most famous of Roman stratagems, from Gellius' list.

INTRODUCTION

The four towers were organized from amongst the front formations which at the skirmishing stage of the battle stood in the first line.[1] While open at the back, the 'towers' were surrounded on three sides by shields, because their flanks were exposed to the enemy's missiles on account of the large intervals between each tower and the next.[2]

(3) *The rectan[gle]*.

This restoration is based on the first form of battle as defined by Cato :[3] *fronte longa, quadro exercitu*. It fits exactly into the empty space.[4] In this instance the word 'rectangle' (*ribbuaʻ*) denotes any shape with straight sides and four right angles, however elongated, as did the parallel Latin term, noted by Marquardt.[5] The transition from the initial pattern, four formations in front, three at the back, to this one was easy : the rear formations marched forward and filled the intervals (cf. fig. 17a). This pattern served in fact as a transition from the initial one (which was intended mainly for defence in depth) to the various attacking formations developed from it. All the skirmishing battalions are now stationed in front of the seven formations and it may even be that they had begun to pursue the enemy with the aid of the cavalry, intending to pin him down and to keep in contact with him until the whole army could be redeployed for the final attack (ix, 4–6) cf. fig. 17a.

(4) '*Enveloping arms*'.

Before we can decide whether to read *gĕlil kappayim* (verbal noun) or *galol kappayim* (infinitive used as imperative) two remarks must be made :

(1) I take the two words as one term since they are not separated by the *waw conjunctive* as is usual in this list between two different terms.[6]

(2) The word כפים is clearly written and there is no reason to assume it to be a scribal error for כנפים, on which cf. below. Since *kappayim* refers not only to the palms of the hands but also to the arms,[7]

---

[1] In MH 'tower' also denotes a type of chest made in tower shape, and is generally closely associated with *tevah* 'box' (M. Shab. xvi, 5 ; M. Kelim xx, 5, a fr.). This enables us to explain P.T. Soṭah viii, 3, 'they were formed (*ʻaśuyin*) in boxes, and the arrows dispersed them, yet the thunderbolts gathered them again,' as referring to our 'tower' formation. That we have here a military formation was recognized by Krauss, *Paras* p. 241.

[2] Each 'tower' was 70 m. wide ; the front was over 4,000 m., hence the distance between each pair of towers was *c*. 1,300 m.

[3] Apart from Vegetius, cf. also Nonius, quoted Marquardt p. 133, n. 1 : 'Una depugnatio est fronte longa, quadrato exercitu.'

[4] See comm.

[5] pp. 132–3, with further details about the use of this term in military Latin. See also p. 98, n. 4.

[6] If the text had גליל וכפים, we might perhaps compare the *globus*.

[7] See comm.

TACTICS AND ORGANIZATION 191

I suggest identifying this formation with the two-pronged enveloping move mentioned above;[1] most armies, until this day, use for this move terms containing words for 'arms', 'pincers', etc. The meaning of the root *gll* is also suitable, cf. B.T. Sanh. 68b : ' Woe unto ye, my two arms, for they are like two rolled-up scrolls of the Law ' ; Cant. Rabbah on v, 14 : ' His hands were of sapphires and yet could be rolled up ' (i.e. could envelop).

In these two examples, as in the scroll, *gll* is used to denote an enveloping movement of the arms. Though, in my opinion, the Biblical term *galil* used in combination with pillars [2] and similarly the ' two *gulloth* of the capitals '[3] may well indicate capitals with volutes,[4] it appears for syntactical reasons preferable to read here *gillul kappayim* or *galol kappayim*. In any case the phrase proves that in this formation the straight line changes into a concave line with two arms to envelop the enemy [5] (cf. fig. 17*b*), like that which Hannibal adopted in the battle of Cannae in the third phase (cf. below).

(5) ' *Arc* '.

The shape of this formation is the reverse of the preceding one : the outside of the curve is now turned towards the enemy. This formation closely resembles the Roman *cuneus* or ' crescent ' formation which Hannibal adopted at the second phase of the battle of Cannae [6] (cf. fig. 17*c*).

(6) ' *Flat arc* '. (דרוך מעט)

Since this formation follows immediately on the ' arc ', and on account of the common use of the verb *drk* in the action of stretching a bowstring,[7] one must assume that it bears a basic resemblance to the former. In this, the ' bow ' was tightly stretched and consequently narrowly arched, but now, the ' bow ' being stretched only lightly, the line is straightened, though it still remains convex.[8] This formation develops naturally in the battle when the convex centre of the arc—after having made contact with the centre of the enemy front—is checked in its advance, while the flanks of the arc continue to advance, resulting in a partial straightening of the curve. This formation can of course also be

---

[1] See Vegetius' fourth formation, and Gellius' *forfices*, V-shaped.
[2] Cant. v, 14–15 ; Est. i, 6.
[3] 1 Kings vii, 41.
[4] Only this type of capital is possible for Solomon's temple, as we know from the Proto-Aeolic capitals found at Megiddo, see Galling p. 452.
[5] i.e. the prayer-attitude, cf. Ex. ix, 29.
[6] Polybius III, cxiii, 8 : $\mu\eta\nu o\epsilon\iota\delta\grave{\epsilon}s$ $\pi o\iota\hat{\omega}\nu$ $\tau\grave{o}$ $\kappa\acute{\upsilon}\rho\tau\omega\mu\alpha$; cf. Marquardt p. 139, n. 6, and see below.
[7] Properly speaking, pressing with the foot on the bow in order to stretch the string.
[8] We can hardly attempt to define the exact degree of ' bending '.

planned as a transition from the arc to the ' (long) rectangle ' or ' enveloping arms ' (cf. fig. 17*d*).

(7) *Protruding columns.*

The columns, as we saw above, are military units moving in files. As the columns issue from the front line so as to establish additional contact with the enemy, the line assumes a close resemblance to a saw. This term may well correspond to the *serra*, whose name Vegetius explains from its resemblance to that implement.

It can hardly be assumed that the ' protruding columns ' are an independent formation. The words apparently form part of the name of the foregoing formation (' a flat arc with protruding columns ' corresponding to ' an arc with towers '), or possibly of the following one (' wings ... from both sides of the line '). This would accord with Vegetius' recommendation that in the ' wings ' formation it is better to place bowmen and skirmishing units in front of the centre to cover it. However, the structure of the sentence makes it appear preferable to attach the words ' with protruding columns ' to the preceding item.

(8) '*And wings [issuing] from [bo]th sides of the line to disorganize the enemy* '.

At first glance this seems to be the same as the second formation, ' enveloping arms ', a resemblance which gains in likelihood considering the similarity between the words כפים and כנפים ' arms ' and ' wings ', which are synonymous in many idioms.[1] There must be a reason why in this instance ' wings ' and not ' arms ' was used. The continuation shows that the ' wings ' here do not indicate the formation's name (as do ' arc ', ' towers ', ' arms ') since ' they issue from both sides of the *line* to disorganize the enemy '. Moreover, the ' wings ' do not even form part of the actual infantry formation, as is proved by the words ' from both sides of the line '. The definition closely resembles that used in vi, 7–8 concerning the position of the cavalry units : ' At the right and left of the line : these arrays shall take up position on either side, 700 horsemen being on one side and 700 on the other ' (cf. ib. line 9).

Hence one may suppose that the ' wings ' refer to the cavalry units stationed in the wings of the line, an assumption which is strengthened by the fact that the auxiliary units in the Roman army were called *alae*. Though this name originally described the auxiliary force, the cavalry units, as being stationed at the wings of the formation, in course of time *ala* became the name of the tactical and organizational cavalry unit

---

[1] Cf. Liebermann, JBL 71 (1952), 201, n. 25.

corresponding to the cohort of the infantry and also referred to the cavalry in general.[1] If the identification of 'wings' with *alae* is accepted, then the words ' and wings [issuing] from both sides of the line to disorganize the enemy ' simply mean that at this phase the cavalry issued from both sides of the line towards the enemy's flanks or rear so as to disorganize them, and thus decide the battle.[2] This strategy, which threw the cavalry at the decisive stage against the enemy's flanks and rear, was widely accepted and exploited in the two famous battles of Cannae and Zama.

Of course the cavalry, especially that of the Serekh and those who went forth with the skirmishing battalions, entered the battle at its very beginning, operating against the enemy's cavalry and other units during its whole course. But as we saw above, cavalry units were placed not only at the flanks of the skirmishing battalions but also at the flanks and rear of the line ' on all sides of the camp '. The present, decisive stage is well suited for the action of the ' cavalry wings ' which were in reserve at the flanks and rear of the line. These ' wings ', being unengaged, could by a wide outflanking move strike at the rear and flanks of an enemy front engaged along the whole line in holding the infantry and the other cavalry units.

The difference between the layout at this stage and the ' enveloping arms ' at the first stage is quite clear. With the ' enveloping arms ', an attempt was made at encirclement by means of all units of the front line, advancing in two enveloping arms. This attempt does not necessarily lead to an immediate decision, but only to the retreat of the enemy's centre and the exposure of his flanks. On the other hand, in the ' wings ' formation, in which the front line can be straight or bent in an arc or enveloping arms, the enveloping and fighting is accomplished by the cavalry alone.

(9) *The course of battle.*

The one remaining problem is whether the changes of formation describe simply unconnected forms of battle order or the estimated sequence and development of the battle. The latter is, I think, preferable, since the changes in formation fit in well with the logical way a battle would develop under those circumstances.

---

[1] Marquardt p. 104 : ' L'aile, *ala*, etait une division propre à la cavalerie alliée, comme la *cohors* à l'infanterie ; la cavalerie légionnaire n'était pas divisée en *alae* ... Le mot *ala* n'a pas seulement la signification étroite que nous venons de lui donner ; c'est un terme dont on se sert aussi pour désigner tout corps de cavalerie, comme on appelle *cohors* toute division d'infanterie.'

[2] Marquardt p. 103-4. Gellius (XVI, iv, 6) quotes Cincius as saying : ' alae dictae exercitus equitum ordines, quod circum legiones dextra sinistraque tanquam alae in avium corporibus locabantur.' This closely resembles DSW vi, 7.

To throw some light upon this problem, we may compare the scroll's description with what is known, say, of the battle of Cannae, one which in the course of time has come to be regarded as the classic example of the exploitation of the 'enveloping arms' and 'wings' at the final stage. We have detailed descriptions by Polybius and Livy,[1] which leave in doubt only minor details.[2] Fig. 16, representing the stages in the battle, is taken from O. L. Spaulding's *Warfare*, and is based on Delbrück's analysis.[3]

Hannibal's army was composed of 40,000 infantry (8,000 skirmishers; 32,000 front formation) and 10,000 cavalry. The Roman army had 70,000–80,000 infantry (of all types) and 6,000 (!) cavalry. At the first stage the two armies were drawn up opposite each other in a straight, long line (= 'rectangle'[4]), their cavalry being at the flanks. The battle was opened by the skirmishing units (cf. in the sketch, opening stage); immediately afterwards, Hannibal deployed his centre, which was composed of the heavy units, into an echeloned 'arc' (or 'wedge') which resembled a crescent,[5] leaving the lighter units and the cavalry behind at its flanks. Immediately the cavalries of both armies joined battle at the flanks. Hannibal's cavalry succeeded in pinning down the flank of the Roman army, and not only prevented the outflanking of their own army but pressed the Roman army towards its centre. The Roman army actually also advanced in an arc formation which at the first stage was a 'flat arc'[6] (cf. fig. 16, intermediate stage).

Hannibal's 'arc' did not withstand the pressure of the legions—superior to his soldiers in offensive and defensive equipment—and the centre of his army began a hasty retreat. The Roman line, which had begun as a 'flat arc', turned into a full 'arc', while Hannibal's 'arc' became a concave line (cf. fig. 16—final stage). Hannibal's genius immediately proved itself when he turned the passive concave formation into aggressive 'enveloping arms'. Simultaneously with this process the heavy cavalry was brought into action. With this 'enveloping' flank movement they reached the rear of the Roman army. Hemmed in

---

[1] Polybius iii, 113–4; Livy xxii 44–9; fully discussed in Kromayer-Veith, *Antike Schlachtfelder* iii, 278–388, with map no. 8.

[2] A different interpretation in Delbrück, *Geschichte der Kriegskunst* i.

[3] Following Spaulding (pp. 122–6 and fig. 7) and Delbrück, rather than Kromayer-Veith, I shall in the following keep close to Polybius' account.

[4] Polybius iii, 113, on Hannibal: ἐπὶ δὲ πάντι ἐπὶ μίαν εὐθεῖαν ἐξέτεινε.

[5] Described by Polybius as a crescent (see here p. 191, n. 6, and note 6 below) with its convex side facing the enemy, i.e. the 'arc' of DSW.

[6] Note how similar is the language of Polybius (ib. 115): . . . διὰ τὸ τοὺς κελτοὺς (*who were in the centre*) ἐν μηνοειδεῖ σχήματι τεταγμένους πολὺ προπεπτωκέναι τῶν κεράτων ἅτε τοῦ μηνίσκου τὸ κύρτωμα πρὸς τοὺς πολεμίους ἔχοντος.

between the 'arms' of the infantry at its flanks and the cavalry 'wings' at its flanks and rear (cf. fig. 16—final stage), the latter was almost completely annihilated.

The echo of this great victory, the victory of the 'enveloping arms', movement and manoeuvre over superior strength, and the stress on the

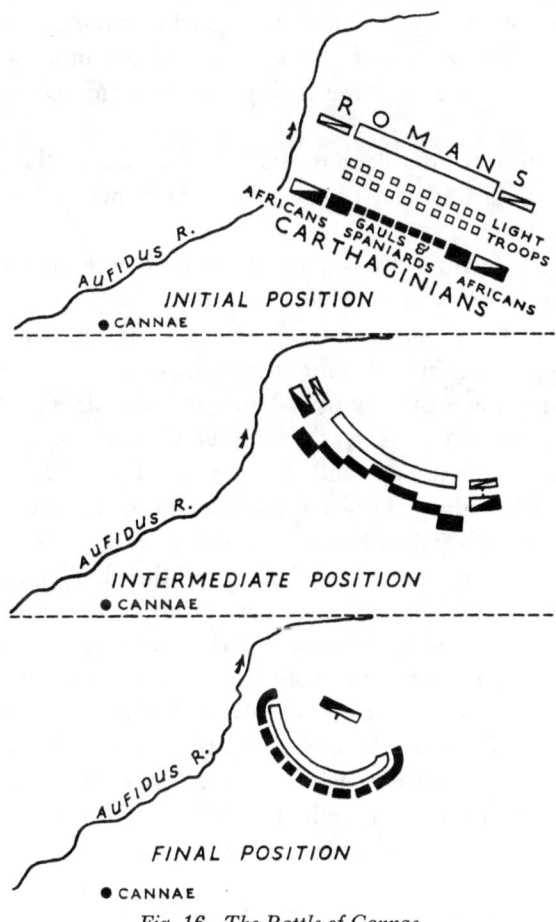

Fig. 16. *The Battle of Cannae.*

importance of cavalry as against infantry, made the battle of Cannae a classic of textbooks until our times. Scipio learned the lesson of this battle when he defeated Hannibal at the battle of Zama: he perfected this strategy by leaving a strong reserve of infantry and cavalry at his rear, which enabled him to accomplish the 'envelopment of arms' and onslaught on the enemy's rear by means of the cavalry unit in a way superior to that of Hannibal at Cannae. Polybius rightly states that the lesson of Cannae shows for all time the importance of the correct balance between infantry and cavalry, the deep and decisive move being possible only by correct use of the cavalry.

The descriptions and numbers in the scroll prove that the lesson had been well digested. The ratio of cavalry and infantry—6,000 : 28,000—is 1 : 4·6, similar to that of Hannibal's army (1 : 4) and unlike that of the Roman army (1 : 13). Also with regard to strategy had this lesson been learned. The stages of attack and pursuit commencing with the first signs of the enemy's weakening can be summed up as follows (cf. fig. 17):

(1) Transition from a deep defensive formation to that of the 'long rectangle', with strong cavalry reserves at the flanks and at the rear and the towers in front;

(2) Pinning down and engaging the enemy with all the skirmishing units and the light cavalry, while the army is deployed into the 'enveloping arms' formation with the intention of immobilizing the enemy flanks and restricting his freedom of movement;

(3) Pinning down the enemy's flanks and assault with the intention of breaking up his centre; retreat of the enemy's centre under the pressure of the skirmishing battalions and the 'towers'; transition to the 'arc' formation which mainly engages the enemy's retreating centre;

(4) The enemy's flanks begin to retreat; pursuit of his flanks by a forward movement of the ends of the arc and the forming of a 'flat arc';

(5) Engaging the whole of the enemy front by means of the advance of the arc's ends beyond the retreating enemy flanks (a re-formation of the enveloping arms) and sending 'columns' of various units to harrass and destroy the enemy lines simultaneously with the rapid advance of the 'cavalry wings' from the flanks beyond the enemy's flanks, who in his retreat comes upon the ambush.[1] The encirclement of the enemy is complete: 'The sons of Japheth shall fall, never to rise again, and the Kittim shall be smashed without [remnant or survivor]' (xviii, 2–3).

---

[1] Of the destroyed beginning of the section following on the 'disposition of the towers', we can just decipher and restore: 'and they shall lay an ambush for the Kittim.' 'Trumpets for the ambush' are listed iii, 2, after the 'trumpets of the slain' (i.e. the general attack) and before the 'trumpets of pursuit'; cf. ch. 5, § 5 (3). Avi-Yonah, IEJ 2 (1952), 4, sees in this an added pointer to the Maccabees. Of course the Maccabees must have used ambushes, though of his quotations only one (1 Macc. ix, 38 sq.) actually mentions an ambush—and that against beduins—possibly also 1 Macc. iii, 12. The others stress the value of surprise and of night attacks. Besides, all armies use ambushes, including the Romans, e.g. at Ashkelon (BJ III, ii, 3), and cf. Frontinus' *Strategemata* I, iv, 2; II, v (*De insidiis*), esp. §§ 20, 33, 35; also Vegetius iii, 19. The use of an ambush is thus hardly a criterion for dating.

TACTICS AND ORGANIZATION

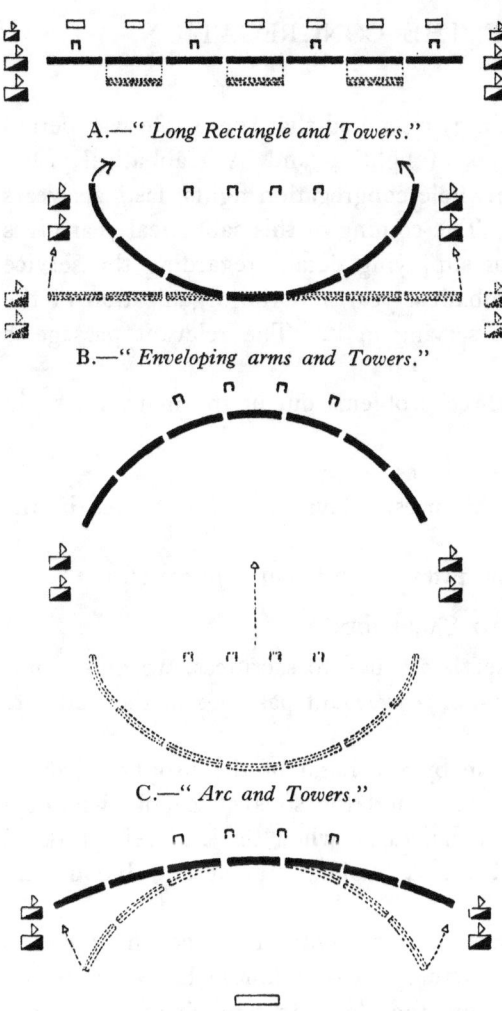

A.—"*Long Rectangle and Towers.*"

B.—"*Enveloping arms and Towers.*"

C.—"*Arc and Towers.*"

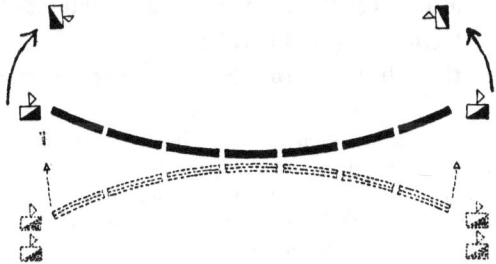

D.—"*Flat Arc and Protruding Columns.*"

E.—"*Attack from the Wings.*"

Fig. 17. *The battle forms and the 'towers'.*

Chapter 8

THE RITES OF THE CONGREGATION

§ 1. GENERAL REMARKS

In the *Plan of the War* (ch. 2) we noted that the whole war period is divided into thirty-five years of fighting and five sabbatical years. The first phase, in which the whole congregation fights, lasts six years until the first sabbatical year. The coming of this sabbatical year gives the author the opportunity of supplying details regarding the service in the Temple during the sabbatical year and the organization of the priests, levites, and Israelites serving in it. The relevant passage is ii, 1–6.

We shall here deal with three problems out of the many raised in this passage.[1]

(1) The sect's attitude to sacrifices;

(2) The terms of service of priests, levites, and Israelites in the sanctuary;

(3) The organization of the priests into twenty-six courses.

§ 2. THE SECT'S ATTITUDE TO SACRIFICES

In order to evaluate the sect's attitude to sacrifices, we must compare the passage under discussion to relevant passages in the Zadokite Documents:[2]

(*A*) 'As God swore to them by the hand of the prophet Ezekiel, saying: the priests and the levites and the sons of Zadok, who kept the charge (*mishmereth*) of My sanctuary when the children of Israel strayed from Me, they shall ⟨ . . . ⟩ offer Me fat and blood' (iii, 20–iv, 2);

(*B*) 'But all those that have been brought into a covenant not to ⟨ . . . ⟩ have come into the sanctuary so as to kindle His altar in vain and have become such as shut the door, forasmuch as God said: who amongst you will shut My door, and ye shall not kindle My altar in vain; unless they take care to do according to the exact statement of the Law for the period of wickedness' (vi, 11–14);

(*C*) 'Let no man offer on the altar on the Sabbath except the

---

[1] For the division of the years and the place of the sabbatical years within it, see ch. 2, §§ 2, 7; for the general military age, ch. 4, § 4 (2); for the connexion of the sacrifices as described here with the O.T., see comm.

[2] For the linguistic interpretation and the O.T. sources, see Rabin, *Zadokite Documents* ad loc.

burnt-offering of the Sabbath; for thus it is written: apart from your Sabbath-offering. Let no man send to the altar a burnt-offering or a grain-offering or frankincense or wood by the hand of any man affected with any of the types of uncleanness, thus empowering him to convey uncleanness to the altar; for it is written: the sacrifice of the wicked is an abomination, but the prayer of the righteous is like an offering of delight' (xi, 17-21).

In comparing these passages with those from DSW, we must remember the basic difference in the purpose of the two books. DSW describes the sanctuary service in the Time to Come; at that time the service will of course be carried out according to all the Pentateuchal rulings as understood by the sect and by the priests recognized by it. We see, at any rate, that the sect, like all Jews, accepted the need for sacrifices as set out in the Pentateuch.

As against this, the passages from CDC give guidance to the members of the sect relating to the sacrifices in the *Period of Wickedness*. They explain to the members of the sect that during that period they are forbidden to bring sacrifices in the Temple for the following reasons:

(*a*) The priests and levites officiating are not legitimate and consequently defile the altar (passages (*A*) and (*C*) above).

(*b*) The whole Temple service (including the methods of offering sacrifices) is not in accordance with the Law as understood by the sect (passage (*B*)).[1]

As long as these two factors prevent the sect from sacrificing in their way in the Sanctuary of Jerusalem [2]—sacrificing in another place being prohibited [3]—they have no choice but to renounce the literal fulfilment of this law for the time being and to seek a substitute for it on the basis of the verse: 'The sacrifice of the wicked is an abomination, but the prayer of the righteous is like an offering of delight' [4] (passage (*C*)).

The provisional substitution has to be effected in such a way as to emphasize its special character.

DSW uses the following terms in its description of the sanctuary

---

[1] Of course there was also the difference in calendar, see below.

[2] We ought probably to read in the same sense Ass. Mos. iv 8, and v, 4 ('some shall pollute the altar with the very gifts which they offer to the Lord, who are not priests but slaves, sons of slaves'). For its connexion with the DSS, see Mowinckel, Suppl. to V.T. i (1953), 88-96; and comm. on i, 12; vii, 5; cf. also ch. 9, § 5.

[3] Cf. Jub. xlix, 15 sq.; l, 11; both chapters are close to CDC and DSW.

[4] In greater detail DSD ix, 3 sq.; cf. ib. iii, 4-11, and B.T. Ber. 32b.

service: 'To set out the incense-offering of sweet savour for the pleasure of God ... and to bring fat sacrifices before Him perpetually on the table of glory' (ii, 5–6). It is impossible not to notice—though the author's (or more correctly, the sect's) use of the word 'table' for the altar has a Biblical basis [1]—the resemblance between this and the description of the sect's meal: 'And it shall be when they arrange the table to eat or arrange the wine to drink, the priest shall first stretch out his hand to invoke a blessing with the first of the bread or the wine to drink' (DSD vi, 4–5).[2] There seems to be some foundation for the assumption that this sect, which calls the altar 'table' as well as sanctifying its dining-table with a special ceremony, including the priestly benediction, regarded this ceremony and prayer as a substitute for the sacrifices. 'As long as the Temple existed, the altar atoned for Israel, now, a man's table atones for him' (B.T. Ber. 55a). Though we are not as yet dealing with the question of the relation of the sect to the Essenes, we note the strong resemblance between the sect and the Essenes in this respect, as described by Josephus: 'And after this purification is over, they every one meet together in an apartment of their own, into which it is not permitted to any of another sect to enter; while they go, after a pure manner, into the dining-room, as into a certain holy temple, and quietly set themselves down; upon which the baker [3] lays the loaves in order; the cook [3] also brings a single plate of one sort of food, and sets it before every one of them; a priest says grace before meat; and it is unlawful for any one to taste of the food before grace be said. The same priest, when he hath dined, says grace again after meat; and when they begin, and when they end, they praise God, as He that bestows their food upon them; after which they lay aside their (white) garments, and betake themselves to their labours again till the evening; then they return home to supper, after the same manner' (Wars II, viii, 5). It has been shown long ago that this ceremony—which is almost identical with the description in DSD—is of a special nature and is intended to serve as a substitute for the sacrifices.[4]

Much research has been devoted to the problem of the relation between the above passages from CDC and the statements of Josephus and Philo on the Essenes' attitude to sacrifices.[5] According to Philo,

---

[1] See comm.
[2] Similar in the DSD material *Qumran I*, p. 111, ii, 17. Cf. also Dupont-Sommer, *Nouveaux Aperçus* p. 134 sq.; Yadin, JBL 78 (1959), 238 ff.
[3] A priest, according to Ant. XVIII, i, 8. Cf. also J. M. Grinz, *Sinai* 32 (1953), 15.
[4] Cf. Delcor, RB 58 (1951), 545.
[5] Cf. note 1 below.

the Essenes refrained from sacrificing animals.[1] Philo's statement must be re-examined in the light of what we now know about the scrolls sect. Philo does not say that they opposed sacrifices in principle, but states the fact, which was well known in his time, that the Essenes did not bring sacrifices and instead served God by holy thoughts and actions. The principal subject of the discussions was the meaning of Josephus' words. Not only is this passage somewhat vague, but in some versions the important word οὐκ [2] is missing which occurs in several later MSS. It seems to me, however, that whether we read with [3] or without [4] the οὐκ, we must take the general meaning of his words to indicate that the Essenes did not sacrifice in the sanctuary on account of differences of opinion concerning matters of purity and that they observed ceremonies substituted for the sacrifices amongst themselves.

To return to the Dead Sea Scrolls, we may say in summing up that a sect which believed in the Pentateuchal laws and desired to observe them in every detail was compelled to prohibit its members from participating in the existing sacrificial service, since the priests who then officiated in the Temple of Jerusalem, the only place where sacrifices may be brought, defiled the altar, and their practice was not according to the Pentateuchal Laws as understood by the sect. With the approach of the time described in DSW, when legitimate priests again officiate and the Temple service is conducted according to the spirit of the sect, the members of the latter will be able once more to offer up lawful sacrifices. Until that time, for the reasons specified in CDC, they must content themselves with prayers and special ceremonies at home. These prayers are such as to prove their sincere will to observe the Law, since 'the prayer of the righteous is like an offering of delight', preferable to the 'sacrifice of the wicked' which is an 'abomination'.

---

[1] *Quod omnis probus* 75; Ant. XVIII, i, 5.

[2] Delcor, op. cit. p. 544

[3] With most scholars, cf. Delcor p. 545.

[4] For an interpretation of the text without the οὐκ, see Flusser, *Zion* 19 (1953-4), 99, n. 29. Amongst the many who discussed this matter, we may cite Dupont-Sommer, *Aperçus* pp. 109-10), Grinz (cf. p. 200, n. 3) and Delcor (cf. ib., n. 4) as representing the extreme views. The first two, for different reasons, deny that Josephus' statement excludes identification of the Qumran sect with the Essenes: D.-S. reads οὐκ, but thinks CDC refers to the Messianic period; Grinz reads no οὐκ (see, however, his note 22, p. 20). Delcor claims that reading οὐκ makes the identification impossible. We may perhaps assume that CDC merely tried to explain to members of the sect why they could not participate in sacrifices, for the time being (see Flusser and Grinz, 11, citt.).

§ 3. The Organization of the Temple Service

(1) *General*

The interest of this description is not confined to the mass of information it contains about the set-up of the service and the interrelation of priests, levites, and Israelites, which in general resembles our information from other sources; of greater importance to us is the numerical information on the chiefs of the fathers of the congregation, the priests, and the levites and especially the definite statement that the priests' courses number twenty-six.

(2) *Officiants of the Sanctuary*

Before dealing with the latter subject, we shall briefly summarize the method of service described. The scroll classifies those serving in the sanctuary from two parallel points of view:

(*a*) A division of offices among priests, levites, and Israelites.

(*b*) Division into those who serve continually and those who serve in courses (ii, 1–4):

Service	Continuous	Changing
Priests	Twelve chief priests to 'serve in the daily burnt offerings before God'	'The chiefs of the courses twenty-six, in their courses they shall serve'
Levites	Twelve chief levites ('one to each tribe') 'to serve perpetually'	The chiefs of the levite courses 'each man in his *ma'ămad*'
Israelites	'The chiefs of the tribes and the fathers of the congregation' 'to stand perpetually in the gates of the sanctuary'	'The chiefs of the courses with their subordinates (from the age of 50 and upwards) shall stand by on their festivals, on their new moons and the sabbaths, and on all the days of the year'

Even though the scroll's terms for describing the Temple service are largely taken from Biblical sources and have many parallels in Rabbinic literature,[1] it is precisely the divergence in details which is instructive, since it reflects the differences of opinion between the sect and other Jewish groups on vital points affecting the Temple service.

(3) '*Course*' and '*Ma'ămad*'

The most outstanding amongst these points is the fact that the priests' courses are twenty-six in number and not twenty-four as is generally accepted. To find the reason for this divergence we will briefly state the principles on which the organization of the services rests, first of all the connexion between the 'course' and the *ma'ămad*.

---

[1] See comm.

As with the 'shift' division of the militia army (cf. ch. 4, § 5) so also the organization of the Temple service was obliged to take two independent factors into consideration:

(1) The need for the constant presence of a group representing the priesthood, levites, and Israelites.

(2) An interior sub-division of each one of these in order to provide the constant quota from each one of them according to a logical and fair system of turns based upon the division of the year into fixed service periods.

Actually there need be no connexion between these two divisions in their interior organization. The first is based on the requirements of the Temple service and sacrifices and on considerations resulting from the tasks placed on each group, while the second is determined solely by the need for replacements, and its main consideration was the length of the period possible or desirable to impose on each one during his annual service period.

The clearest account of this system as practised during the period of the Second Temple is in the Mishnah (Ta'an. iv, 2): 'What are the *Ma'ămads*? In that it is written: Command the children of Israel and say unto them, My food which is presented unto Me for offerings made by fire, of a sweet savour unto Me, in its due season (Num. xxviii, 2). How can a man's offering be offered while he does not stand by it? Therefore the First Prophets ordained twenty-four courses, and for every course there was a *ma'ămad* in Jerusalem, made up of priests, levites, and Israelites. When the time was come for a course to go up, the priests and the levites thereof went up to Jerusalem, and the Israelites that were of the selfsame course came together unto their own cities to read the story of Creation, and the men of the *ma'ămad*, etc.'

The Tosephta, in the corresponding passage (ib. iv, 3) reads: 'When the time was come for a course, the priests and levites went up to Jerusalem, and the Israelites that were of the selfsame course and *were not able to go up to Jerusalem* came together into their own cities to read the story of the Creation.' [1]

Similarly, the scroll ordains that of the Israelites—apart from chiefs of tribes and fathers of the congregation—only those attend the sacrifices

---

[1] Dr. J. Brand kindly drew my attention to P. T. Ta'an. iv, 2: 'If all Israel were to go up to Jerusalem, the Law says only "three times every year"; if they were all to sit idle, does not the Law say "and thou shalt gather in thy grain"? Who then is to gather the grain for them? This is why the first prophets instituted the twenty-four courses, etc.'

who are fifty or older (and thus were in fact exempted from military duty, for details cf. ch. 4, § 2) to represent their tribes.

The scroll does not enumerate the sub-divisions of the courses into their clans ('households') since this division differed for each course. Moreover, in every course also the division of labour between the clans differed, though some general formula seems to have existed.[1] It was the perpetual officiants' duty to see to it that the sacrifices did not suffer from the weekly replacement of the courses.[2] The division into twelve corresponded to the tribal system ('one to a tribe'), and was moreover, so it seems, connected with the allocation of tasks amongst the members of the *maʿămad*, as appears from a number of parallels in the Bible and Mishnah.[3]

On the other hand, it may not be chance that the scroll so insistently stresses this number here, along with the fifty-two fathers of the congregation and twenty-six chiefs of the courses, which numbers, as we shall see, held special significance.

(4) *The Courses* (משמרות)

In coming to deal with the problem of the twenty-six priests' courses we are immediately faced with the obvious difference between the sect's division and that customary in the period of the Second Temple.

According to 1 Chr., Josephus, and Rabbinic sources, there is no doubt that the number of courses both of priests and levites in the Second Temple was twenty-four.[4] However, most Rabbinic sources agree that this number is not of Mosaic origin, but was changed time and again as need arose until its final fixation.[5]

---

[1] Tos. Taʿan. ii, 2 : 'If there are four in a course, three bring the offering on two days and one on one day ... if there are six, five bring the offerings on five days, and one on two days,' followed by rules for those 'who appointed themselves for permanent service'. Cf. A. Büchler, *Die Priester und der Cultus*, 1895, p. 90 sq. With the Tos. passage, cf. DSD ii, 22. See also ch. 3, § 9.

[2] Büchler, op. cit. p. 91.

[3] The influence of Num. vii and vs. 2 in particular (cf. ch. 3, § 5) is unmistakable ; cf. also Büchler p. 103. Ezra viii, 24, mentions twelve 'chiefs of the priests', though not in connexion with the courses. 1 Chr. xxv, 10, shows that the 24 levitical courses were each divided into 12 sub-units. Mishnaic sources : Tamid i ; Shek. v ; Yoma ii, 5 (9–12 priests officiate at Tamid).

[4] 1 Chr. xxiv, 1–18 ; xxv, 9–31 ; M. Taʿan. iv, 1 ; Tos. Taʿan. iv ; Tos. Sukk. iv ; B.T. Taʿan. 27ab ; P.T. Taʿan. iv, 2 ; Num. Rabba iii, etc. ; Ant. VII, xiv, 7. Enc. Miqr. i, 131, s.v. *Běnē Aharon*.

[5] Tos. Taʿan. iv, 2 : Moses established 8 priestly and levite courses, David and Samuel instituted 24 priestly courses, the prophets in Jerusalem 24 levite courses. B.T. Taʿan. 27a says Samuel increased the priestly courses to 16, David to 24. For the precedence see M. Hor. xiii, 1 , for relation between chiefs of courses, chiefs of *Maʿamad* and chiefs of clans, see Büchler p. 92.

Seeing that the courses were replaced weekly [1] and taking into account days on which all courses served together,[2] the system of replacement is seen to be based on semi-annual turn-rounds.[3]

Obviously, a sect which differs from the rest of the Jews in reckoning the length of the year and the number of weeks in it is compelled to change the number of the courses—which change weekly in the semi-annual turn-rounds—according to the number of weeks in a half-year. It thus appears that the solution to the question of the number of courses in DSW is concealed in the divergent calendar of several of the Apocrypha and Pseudepigrapha.

The Book of Jubilees states that the year was divided into four periods, with a Day of Remembrance between each period (vi, 23 ff.) and continues (ib. verse 29 ff.): ' And they placed them on the heavenly tablets, each had thirteen weeks ... from the first to the second, and from the second to the third, and from the third to the fourth. And all the days of the commandment will be two and fifty weeks of days, and (these will make) the entire year complete. ... And command thou the children of Israel that they observe the years according to this reckoning—three hundred and sixty-four days, and (these) will constitute a complete year ... ... and make an abominable (day) the day of testimony, and an unclean day a feast day, and they will confound all the days, the holy with the unclean, and the unclean with the holy; for they will go wrong as to the months and sabbaths and feasts and jubilees,' etc.[4]

We need not enter here into the intricate problem of the dates of the festivals and new moons according to this calendar [5] since the following facts, which are of importance to us, are clearly defined in the above description:

The year consists of fifty-two weeks divided into four seasons, each of which consists of thirteen weeks (i.e. twenty-six weeks to each two

---

[1] M. Sukk. v, 8; Tam. v, 1; Büchler p. 91.

[2] e.g. M. Sukk. v, 5, 7.

[3] On the division of the year into two semi-annual cycles see N. H. Tur-Sinai, BO 8 (1951), 14 sq.; cf. also Jub. xii, 27.

[4] Cf. En. lxxiv, 12; lxxv, 2; lxxxii, 5 sq.

[5] Much has been written on this problem. See Epstein, RÉJ 12 (1891), 10-13; id., *Eldad ha-Dani*, Pressburg 5651, p. 152 sq.; Poznanski, RÉJ 50 (1905), 10 sq.; Charles, *Book of Jubilees* 1902, p. 54 sq.; Morgenstern, HUCA 3 (1926), 87 sq.;

Aalen p. 123 sq.; De Vaux, RB 57 (1950), 426; Talmon, *Biblica* 32 (1951), 549 sq.; Barthélemy, RB 59 (1952), 187 sq.; Dupont-Sommer VT 2 (1952), 229 sq.; id., *Nouveaux Aperçus* p. 147; Brownlee, BASOR 123, p. 30 sq.; Grinz, *Sinai* 32 (1953), 27, n. 36, 40; Jaubert, VT 3 (1953), 250 sq.; and most recently, Talmon, *Aspects of the Dead Sea Scrolls* p. 162 sqq. Cf. also J. T. Milik, *Dix ans de decouvertes*, etc., 1957, p. 70; Jaubert, *La date de la Cène*, 1957.

periods). There are therefore 364 days to the year, divided into twelve months, each one consisting of thirty days with an additional remembrance day to each season.[1] This division is exactly parallel to the numbers given in the scroll: fifty-two fathers of the congregation; twelve chief priests and levites,[2] and most important, twenty-six chiefs of the weekly courses. That is to say, thirteen courses serve in each period, a course each week, and after a turn-round of two periods or twenty-six weeks the first course returns and begins its service.[3] This is an important fact, for it confirms that the sect completely accepted the calendar of Jubilees and Enoch—a fact which has been known for some time.[4] This difference, among others, not only hindered the sect from participating in the bringing of sacrifices with other Jews, but was also an important factor in the continual clashes on matters concerning the observation and times of the festivals.[5] This makes it all the more urgent to interpret the other passages in the scrolls dealing with matters of calendar and festivals [6] according to the data in Jubilees and Enoch, though attempts to do so have not always met with success.

(5) *The Maʿămad in the Usage of the Sect*

In the light of this conclusion we may surmise that at various stages in their ceremonies, which were organized on orderly military lines,[7] the members took their stations according to *maʿămadoth*. The word *maʿămad* occurs frequently in the scrolls; in DSW it often indicates also the soldiers' position in their 'arrays'.[8] However, a strong resemblance exists between the above description of the Temple service and DSD ii, 19-24, which explains one of the congregation's ceremonies whose meaning has been dealt with elsewhere: [7] 'The priests shall enter the covenant first in the order pertaining to their spirits, one after another; and after them the levites shall enter; then thirdly all the people shall enter in order one after another, by thousands and

---

[1] En. lxxv, 1; lxxxii, 4 sq.

[2] As stated, the twelve chiefs of levites correspond to the twelve tribes; these, acc. to Jub. xxv, 16, correspond to the twelve months. Cf. ch. 3, § 4.

[3] On the division of the year into two semi-annual cycles see N. H. Tur-Sinai, BO 8 (1951), 14 sq.; cf. also Jub. xii, 27.

[4] The Jub. calendar is cited CDC xvi, 2 sq. Fragments of Jub. have been found at Qumran, see *Qumran* I, p. 82; RB 63 (1956), 60.

[5] This supports Talmon's view that DSH vi, 11, refers to a difference about the date of the Day of Atonement. The members of the sect are enjoined neither to advance nor to delay the festival dates, DSD i, 13-15; cf. Talmon p. 555. The correct dates have been revealed only to them, CDC vi, 17-19.

[6] See Dupont-Sommer, Barthélemy, and Brownlee, opp. citt.

[7] Ch. 3, § 9 and p. 47, n. 1.

[8] The word occurs in different meanings 13 times in DSW, 6 in DSD, 7 in DST, and once in CDC. Its military meaning is discussed ch. 7 § 2 (3).

hundreds, and fifties, and tens, so that every man of Israel shall know each his *beth ma'ămad* in God's community according to the eternal counsel; and one shall not fall from his *beth ma'ămad*, nor rise from the place of his lot (*goral*); for they all shall be in a true community.'

This passage would lack clarity were we to interpret *ma'ămad* in its usual literal sense.[1] On the other hand, if the word is taken to denote the body containing the priests, levites, and Israelites (each group according to its own subdivision) then the concluding clause, ' for they all shall be in a true community,' makes sense. This sect, made up of three classes of members, desiring on the one hand the preservation of the characteristics, duties, and organization peculiar to each one of them, and on the other hand to unite them on a footing of some equality, could not have chosen a form better suited to its organization and ceremonies then the structure of the *ma'ămadoth* as described above.[2] Also the parallelism between *ma'ămad* and *goral* might be intended to attest to the connexion between this *ma'ămad* and the organization of the courses.[3]

The frequency of *ma'ămad* also in its other meanings (none of which is far removed from the above) may derive from the fact that this word, as employed in the sect's terminology, was well suited to indicate a body of men of such structure as to contain all members of the sect.[4]

(6) *The Chief Priest* (כהן הראש)

In view of the important task assigned to the ' chief priest ' in the ceremonies both in Temple and battle, we may briefly comment on the form of his title. The O.T. mentions it a number of times,[5] especially when dealing with the priesthood of the First Temple.[6] The problem of the use of this title in the scroll has attracted special attention, since it was thought that with its aid the scroll could be dated before the

---

[1] e.g. Brownlee translates ' in the status of his office '.

[2] Cf. Charles *Apocr.* ii, 803 ; V.d. Ploeg, BO 8 (1951), 113–126; ib. 9 (1952), 127 sq., who already connects the word in DSD with its organizational use.

[3] 1 Chr. xxiv, 7 ; xxv, 8 sq. Cf. passages quoted p. 204, n. 4, and ch. 4, § 4 (3) and p. 79, n. 1.

[4] Cf. p. 206, n. 8, and DSD vi, 9–24.

[5] Cf. Morgenstern, AJSL 55 (1938), parts 1, 2, 4, ' A Chapter in the History of the High Priesthood,' also published as offprint (references here are to the latter).

See also *Enc. Miqr.* s.v. *Běnē Aharon*, i, 131 sq.

[6] They had a second in command, as in DSW : 2 Kings xxv, 18 ; Jer. lii, 24. In 2 Kings xxiii, 4, read the singular with Tg., and cf. Büchler, op. cit. (n. 17) p. 105. This official was the chief of all officiating priests. The ' chief priest ' is mentioned : (*a*) 2 Chr. xix, 11 (Jehoshaphat) ; (*b*) ib. xxiv, 11 (in 2 Kings xii, 11, ' the high priest ') ; (*c*) ib. xxvi, 20 (Uzziah) ; (*d*) ib. xxxi, 10 (Hezekiah) ; (*e*) ib. xxiv, 6 (Joash) ; (*f*) Ezra vii, 2–5. Cf. note 9.

Hasmonean period, during which the title 'high priest' (*ha-kohen ha-gadhol*) was more common.¹

I doubt, however, if this usage can serve as proof for the pre-Hasmonean origin of the scroll. All its terms for office holders are drawn from those Biblical sources on which the sect based itself (cf. ch. 3, §§ 5 and 6). That applies with special force to this term, since neither Aaron nor his direct successors, Eleazar and Phineas, are called 'high priest' in the sources.² Moreover, a sect which regarded the sons of Zadok as the legitimate priests³ had good reason to regard 'chief priest' as the legitimate title.⁴

In the light of the above, we may go further and maintain that if the use of the title 'chief priest' can be of any help in dating the scroll, it proves it to have been written during or at the end of the Hasmonean period. By using this title, the sect also in this instance demonstrated its opposition to the rule of the Hasmonean priests, who bore the title of 'high priest'.⁵

§ 4. The Prayers and Thanksgivings in Battle. I

(1) *General Description of Prayers*

The scroll contains much detailed and instructive information about the 'prayer for the appointed time of battle', the thanksgivings and words of encouragement before, during, and after the battle. Not only their content, which forms the strongest link between the scroll and the rest of the sect's writings, is supplied, but we have here the exact division of tasks between the chief priest and the other priests in performing the prayers and addresses and the precise times of the prayers at the different stages of deployment and fighting.

These descriptions are important in that they fill a large gap in our knowledge on this important subject and supplement the information to be obtained from Rabbinic sources. No one would question the importance of the Rabbinic sources on this subject, but we must remember that many important details fell into oblivion between the time when Jewish armies had last fought and the redaction of these sources.

Already the earliest information on this subject, in the Mishnah, though no doubt based on a reliable tradition, contains much midrashic material (e.g. the first part of the prayer of the priest 'appointed for

---

¹ Sukenik, *M.G.* i, 18, n. 6; see, however, Avi-Yonah, IEJ 2 (1952), 5.
² Morgenstern, op. cit. p. 2.
³ CDC iv, 3.
⁴ Cf. note 5, in particular 2 Chr. xxxi, 10; and cf. 2 Sam. xv, 27, צדוק הכהן הרואה, where Wellhausen and many others read הכהן הראש, spelt as in DSW xvi, 11. Cf. Morgenstern p. 12, n. 34.
⁵ Cf. Gottstein, *Molad* 43 (Nov. 1951), 39.

battle', M. Soṭah viii ; see below). The homiletic element continually increased until later Rabbis differed amongst themselves on points of principle on which the scroll sheds much light.

Before analysing what the scroll has to say on this subject, we must briefly review our information from Rabbinic sources :

(2) *' The priest anointed for battle' in the O.T. and in Rabbinic Literature*

The Rabbis' discussions are based on Dt. xx, 2 ff. :[1] ' And it shall be, when ye draw nigh unto the battle, that the priest shall approach and speak unto the people, and shall say unto them : Hear, O Israel, ye draw nigh this day unto battle against your enemies ; let not your heart faint ; fear not, nor be alarmed, neither be ye affrighted at them ; for the Lord your God is He that goeth with you, to fight for you against your enemies, to save you. And the officers shall speak unto the people, saying : " What man is there that hath built " . . . And the officers shall speak further unto the people, and they shall say : " What man is there that is fearful and faint-hearted " . . . And it shall be, when the officers have made an end of speaking unto the people, that captains of hosts shall be appointed at the head of the people.'

The following problems arise : Who is this priest ? How does he say these words ? What is said by the priest and what by the officers ? When were these words spoken ?

The following are some conclusions drawn from Rabbinic literature which have a direct bearing on the subjects discussed in the scroll :

(1) The priest, named ' the one anointed for battle '[2] was specially appointed, for this task,[3] and he ranks higher than the *sĕgan* (deputy), but lower than the high priest.[4]

(2) The ' priest appointed for battle ' speaks twice : once at the frontier and once in battle.[5]

(3) Opinions differed in the later sources as to the method by which the priests' words were transmitted to the soldiers and what was said by the priest and the officers respectively.[6]

(3) *The ' chief priest ', the ' priest destined for the appointed time of vengeance ' and the Appointed Times of the Prayers According to the Scroll*

The scroll returns several times to this subject, both in the Ritual *Serekh* Series and in the Kittim Series. The information in the *Serekh*

---

[1] The speech of the ' officers ' about mobilization rules is discussed ch. 4, § 1–2.

[2] M. Soṭah viii, 1. He speaks in Hebrew.

[3] B. T. Soṭah 42a ; cf. Maimonides, *Code*, Hil. Kĕlē ha-Miqdash iv, 21.

[4] B.T. Hor. 13a ; cf. Naz. 47b ; Yoma 71b, etc.

[5] See also ch. 4, § 2.

[6] B.T. Soṭah 43a.

Series is of importance as it provides us with the full text of the prayers and thanksgivings. The importance of the information lies in the division of tasks between the chief priest and the other priests and the times of the prayers in the different stages of the battle. As shown in chapter 4, the author begins his description at the stage when the army was already in the camp close to the battlefield (but before its final deployment) and does not deal with the earlier stages of organization nor with the speeches of the officers and priests at the frontier.

We shall arrange our discussion according to the stages at which the prayers, thanksgivings, and words of encouragement were recited:

(1) Before the arraying of the formations: x, 1 ff. (*Serekh* Series); xv, 4–5 (Battle Series);

(2) After the arraying of the formations but before the battle: xv, 6–16 (Battle Series); vii, 11 (*Serekh* Series);

(3) After the defeat of the Sons of Light: 25, 27, 27, xvi, 11–xvii, 9 (Battle Series);

(4) After the beginning of the defeat of the Sons of Darkness in the seventh 'lot' during the general pursuit: 28, 29, 30, xviii, 5–xix, 8.

(5) After the defeat of the Sons of Darkness:

(*a*) In close proximity to the slain enemies: 17, 18, 19, 20, xii, 16–xiv, 1 (*Serekh* Series); xix, 9–10 (Battle Series);

(*b*) On their return to camp: xlv, 2 (*Serekh* Series);

(*c*) The day after the victory: xiv, 3–15 (*Serekh* Series; xlx, 11 ff. (Battle Series);

(6) On the return to the congregation in Jerusalem (?).

§ 5. THE PRAYERS AND THANKSGIVINGS IN BATTLE. II

(1) *Before the Arraying of the Formations* (' the prayer for the appointed time of battle ')

The Battle Series begins in section 22, which ends: ' And all those prepared for battle shall go and encamp over against the king of the Kittim,' etc. (xv, 2–3, and cf. ch. 1, § 3). This is immediately followed by the first description (xv, 4 ff.): ' The chief priest and his brother [priests] and the levites shall stand up, and all the men of the *Serekh* with him, and he shall read in their hearing the prayer for the appointed time of battle [as is written in the] book *serekh 'itto*, including all the texts of their thanksgivings. In that very place he shall array all the formations, as written [in the book [?] of the wa]r. Then the priest destined for the appointed time of vengeance by the agreement of all his brethren shall walk along and strengthen [their hands for the battle], and he shall solemnly declare.'

This passage provides us with some important information: the prayers and words of encouragement before the battle are divided into two parts and recited by two different priests. The prayer for the 'appointed time of battle' is recited while the soldiers are in view of the enemy but before the arraying of the formations. The chief priest himself recites this prayer from the book *serekh 'itto* [1] standing in front of the whole people. After this prayer and the thanksgivings, the chief priest arrays the formations for actual battle according to the battle disposition. Immediately afterwards another priest comes forth and walks along the lines of the soldiers to encourage them (cf. below, § 5.2).

Of special interest is the author's insistence that the chief priest's long speech was to be given to the men assembled in a body (cf. ch. 7, § 5) enabling him to give it while remaining at one and the same spot, without an assistant to repeat it more audibly. But after the formations were arrayed for battle and deployed in their arrays, the short speech of encouragement of the 'priest destined for the appointed time of vengeance' was delivered while he 'walked along' in front of them. This is quite a logical arrangement and explains the difficulty experienced by the Rabbis: they possessed a clear tradition of two priests who recited prayers and words of encouragement, but the details of the exact division of tasks between the two priests had been lost. This then was the cause of the differences of opinion between them.[2]

The most important fact which emerges from this description is that the title 'the one anointed for battle' does not occur here at all, and the main tasks which the Mishnah allotted to the 'priest anointed for battle' are according to the scroll carried out by the chief priest himself;[3] at certain stages the 'priest destined for the appointed time of vengeance' assists him (below, § 5. 2) exactly as the 'priest anointed for battle', according to the Rabbis, was assisted by another priest who 'caused his words to be heard'. Note that the definition of the second priest as 'destined for the appointed time of vengeance', contains in other words the elements of the 'priest anointed for battle'.[4]

---

[1] On which see ch. 1, § 6 and comm.

[2] Cf. p. 209, n. 6. This is underlined by comparison with Maimonides' arrangement, *Code*, Hil. Mĕlakhim vii, 3–4; cf. Hershman, JQR 40 (1949–50), 407 sq. For the 'officers', cf. ch. 7, § 3 (2).

[3] See comm. on ix, 7–9, and cf. Zeitlin, JQR 39 (1948–9), 344–5. For the chief priest performing the duties of the 'priest anointed for battle' cp. *Pesiqta Rabbathi* viii (f. 30a): ' " and two olives upon it " (Zech. iv, 3)—these are the two anointed ones, the one anointed for battle and the other anointed as king over Israel,' with the interesting discussion by Ginzberg, *Eine unbekannte jüd. Sekte* i, 346.

[4] For ḥaruẓ see § 5 (2).

The general distinction between the prayer to God and the request for His help—with mention of past deliverances—and the words of encouragement which were spoken separately, brings to mind the description in 2 Chr. xx.[1]

The prayer for the appointed time of battle, recited by the chief priest, does not occur in the Battle Series (xv, 5) but is given in full in the *Serekh* Series, section 14 onwards (x ff.). The following is the content and structure of the prayer:

(1) Recall of certain Pentateuchal laws of warfare:

(a) Purity of the camp (x, 1; Dt. xxiii, 10–15) and the mention of God's presence in the midst of the camp (x, 1–2; Dt. xxiii, 15; xx, 4; and especially vii, 21);

(b) The priestly address before battle (x, 2–5; Dt. xx, 2–4);

(c) The officers' action with regard to the faint-hearted (x, 5–6; Dt. xx, 5 ff.);

(d) The trumpet fanfare (x, 6–8; Num. x, 9)

Most of the prayer in this passage consists of direct quotations from the Pentateuch with small but interesting textual changes.[2]

(2) Praise to the God of Israel ('Who is like Thee, O God of Israel, in heaven and earth', x, 8–9).

(3) Indicating that Israel was chosen by God from amongst all the nations ('And who is like unto Thy people Israel which Thou hast chosen from all the nations of the lands', x, 9).

(4) Praise to Israel and to God and a description of the wonders of Creation (x, 10–16).

(5) Invocation to God that He may answer Israel's call for help ('incline, pray, Thine ears for our deliverance', x, 17 ff.).

(6) Emphasis that this is God's war and that with His help victory will be theirs ('For Thine is the battle', xi, 1, 4, 5).

(7) Recall of past deliverances:

(a) David's victories over Goliath and others (xi, 1–3);[3]

(b) Victories of the kings of Israel (xi, 3–4);

---

[1] The prayer is spoken by Jehoshaphat in vs. 6 sq., the words of encouragement by the levite Jahaziel, vs. 15 sq. For verbal agreements, see comm.

[2] For variant readings see § 5 (2).

[3] The mention of David proves that—contrary to the view of some scholars—the sect was not opposed to the Davidic line, or expected a messiah from elsewhere. Nor, since the 'sons of Judah' form part of the sect (i, 2), can we interpret any other passages as signs of opposition to Judah; at most they were against the 'princes of Judah' (CDC viii, 3). 'Israel' is not opposed to 'Judah' (cf. CDC vii, 12–13), but means at times the whole people, at others the people without Levi and Aaron. Cf. Yadin, *Aspects of the Dead Sea Scrolls* p. 56 sqq. See also the 'Midrash', JBL 77 (1958), 350 sqq.

THE RITES OF THE CONGREGATION

(c) The drowning of Pharaoh and his captains in the Red Sea (xi, 9–10);

(d) The defeat of Sennacherib (xi, 11–12);

(e) The 'testimony' of the verse 'there shall come a star out of Jacob' (xi, 6–7);[1]

(f) Allusion to prophetic testimonia ('By the hand of Thine anointed,[2] the seers of things ordained, Thou hast told us the epochs of the wars of Thy hands', xi, 7–8).

Comparison of this part of the prayer with other sources in which the prayers before the battle are given proves that this evocation of past deliverances and especially of past miracles forms an important element of this prayer.

The Books of the Maccabees several times mention words of encouragement and prayers of Judas before battles in which he invokes God's help as He had helped his forefathers. However, in each case he recalls different precedents:

(1) *Pharaoh at the Red Sea.*—Before the battle with Gorgias at Emmaus.[3]

(2) *David and Goliath, Jonathan and the Philistines.*—Before the battle at Bethsura.[4]

(3) *The Defeat of Sennacherib.*—Before the battle with Nicanor near Bethhoron.[5]

(4) *The Conquest of Jericho by Joshua.*—At the siege of Caspin.[6]

Similar precedents are mentioned in other sources:

(5) *Goliath and Shobach.*—In the concluding part of the speech of the 'priest appointed for battle' as quoted in M. Soṭah viii, 1: 'They come in the strength of the Almighty. The Philistines come in the strength of Goliath. What was his end? In the end he fell by the sword and they fell with him. The children of Ammon came in the strength of Shobach. What was his end? In the end he fell by the sword and they fell with him. But not so are ye, for the Lord your God is He that goeth with you, to fight for you,' etc.

(6) *Sisera and Jabin (Barak); Oreb and Zeeb (Gideon); Zebah and Zalmunna.*—In the Song of Asaph, Psalm lxxxiii, 10–13, a psalm which influenced our author.[7]

---

[1] Often interpreted eschatologically by Rabb.; in DSS it appears CDC vii, 18–21, and in *Qumran* I, p. 128, v. 27, cf. comm. See also 4QTestimonia, JBL 75 (1956), 184.

[2] For the parallel in CDC see comm.

[3] 1 Macc. iv, 8 sq.

[4] Note that the victory over Goliath took place not far from Beth Zur.

[5] Ibid., vii, 40 sq.; 2 Macc. xv, 22 sq.

[6] Jericho is mentioned because of the siege, 2 Macc. xii, 15.

[7] Cf. p. 22, n. 1.

These are obvious passages for this occasion since they relate to miracles in battle, just as other prayers evoked miracles of a non-military nature, though even such prayers often mention the division of the Red Sea and the defeat of Sennacherib.[1]

In the following table, the historical precedents mentioned in the various battles are collected so as to set out the connexion between the scroll and the other sources.[2]

DSW	1 Macc. iv, 9	1 Macc. iv, 30	1 Macc. vii, 41	2 Macc. xii, 15	Soṭah viii
David and Goliath		David and Goliath			David and Goliath
David and the Philistines		Jonathan and the Philistines			Shobach (Sons of Ammon)
Victories of the Israelite kings					
Pharaoh at the Red Sea	Pharaoh at the Red Sea				
Sennacherib's defeat			Sennacherib's defeat		
				Fall of Jericho	

The content of Section 14 can thus be summed up as an 'introductory prayer' which stresses that Israel deserves God's assistance in its present war, since He chose them from all nations and helped them in the past, and as He promised through the true prophets, thus He will also assist them in this war, which is the Lord's war.

Section 15 (xi, 13 ff.) stresses the significance of this fact in the war to come:

(a) As a result of God's intervention, the weak [3] will vanquish the mighty men of all nations and wreak retribution upon the wicked (xi, 13-14);

---

[1] Also the prayer of Simeon the priest (3 Macc. ii, 1-20) bears all the features of the prayer for the appointed time of battle, fitting the occasion. It adduces: the Flood, Sodom, and Pharaoh's death. The prayer of Eleazar (ib. vi, 1-15) adduces: Pharaoh, Sennacherib, the three in the fiery furnace, Daniel in the lions' den, and Jonah. Cf. also M. Ta'an. ii, 4: Abraham on Moriah, the Red Sea, Joshua at Gilgal, Samuel at Mizpah, Elijah on the Carmel, Jonah in the fish, David and Solomon at Jerusalem. Cf. also BJ V, ix, 4.

[2] I have listed only parallels in Soṭah and in the story of the wars of Judas. Cf. further 2 Macc. ii, 15, 8 sq.

[3] In the text *evyonim*; for Teicher's explanation of the word, see comm.

(b) In this battle, the Lord will be sanctified in the presence of all the nations and will fight them from heaven, as predicted by Ezekiel for the war with Gog and Magog ;[1]

(c) The 'elect ones of the holy nation' who are together with the host of angels in the 'habitation of glory' and in the 'holy abode'; all of them together, mustered and arrayed 'by their thousands and myriads' will go forth to battle (xii, 1–5).[2]

Section 16, the last in the series, is the climax of the prayer. A short introduction connects it with the preceding section and explains how the host of angels and the elect ones of the holy people join with a 'people of saints', fighting upon earth, into one unified host under the leadership of the 'King of Glory' (xii, 6–9).

Now the chief priest turns to God 'the mighty one of war and man of glory' and requests Him to go forth at the head of the warriors and to place His hand in the neck of His enemies, etc. The prayer continues with quotations from Isaiah mentioning the victory of Zion and Jerusalem and all the cities of Judah and ends with the sentence : '[And the kingdom shall be God's and] Israel shall be for an eternal dominion.'[3]

This demand for God to intervene in the battle like a mighty man of war and Himself to direct the army brings to mind Judas' call upon the Lord 'to show He was their ally and leader in the fight; then, raising the war-cry and songs of praise in the language of the fathers, he made an unexpected rush against the troops of Gorgias and routed them'.[4]

The last part (section 16) recurs on the solitary column (which belonged to the fifth sheet, cf. ch. 1) with slight changes.[5] Since col. xviii deals with the preparations for the general pursuit after the collapse of the Kittim, while the end of the solitary col. xix (line 9 ff.) deals with the prayers and blessings after the final victory, it must be

---

[1] For the restoration of this largely destroyed passage see comm. Gog appears only here, and it seems that there is no identification of Gog with the 'Sons of Darkness', only a reference to Ezekiel's description. The parallelism between 'sons of Japheth' and 'Kittim' (i, 5–6, and xviii, 2–3, cf. ch. 2, § 2 (2)) is based on Gn. x, 2–3; but Gog, as king of Magog, is also a Japhethite; cf. also Jub. viii, 25; ix, 8; Ant. I, vi, 1.

[2] For analysis see ch. 9, § 7.

[3] Already published *M.G.* i, 20; ii, 21. The full text confirms Sukenik's suggestion that the 'hero' is God. The various attributes derive from the O.T., see comm. The theory that the 'hero' is the Messiah (e.g. *Qumran* I, p. 129) is refuted by the beginning of the prayer. See comm. *ad loc.*

[4] 2 Macc. xii, 36–7. The connexion was pointed out by Dupont-Sommer, *Aperçus* p. 102, n. 5.

[5] For the readings cf. comm. on xii and xix.

assumed that part of the 'prayer for the appointed time of battle' was repeated once more before the decisive pursuit, again requesting God's intervention.

(2) *The Words of Encouragement*

According to xv, 5 ff., it is clear that prior to the final arraying of the formations, the chief priest recites the prayer while standing in front of the soldiers. It is only after the arraying that the 'priest destined for the appointed time of vengeance' speaks the words of encouragement, while walking in front of them. This fact is borne out also by two further passages:

(1) In the *Serekh* Series, vii, 8 ff.: 'When the battle formations are deployed over against the enemy, formation opposite formation, there shall go forth from the central interval into the space between the lines seven priests the sons of Aaron. . . . The one priest shall be walking along in front of all the men of the line so as to strengthen their hands in battle. In the hands of the six others there shall be the trumpets of calling,' etc. This passage establishes beyond doubt that the priest who encourages the warriors comes forth only after all formations are arrayed for battle.[1]

(2) In xvi, 2 ff., which follows immediately on the words of the priest who encourages the warriors, it is said that 'all this disposition they shall carry out that [day] in the place where they stand over against the camp of the Kittim. Afterwards the priests shall blow for them the trumpets of remembrance. They shall open the [battle] intervals, and the skirmishers shall go forth', etc. That is to say, as soon as the priest has finished speaking, the intervals are opened in the formations which stand deployed for battle, and the skirmishers go into action.[1]

This priest is called the one 'destined for the appointed time of vengeance'.[2] In the passage in col. vii quoted above, not only is he given no special name (the 'one priest', so as to distinguish him from the six other priests), but he is clothed exactly like the other six priests who carry the trumpets, and he goes forth with them.

The title of this priest corresponds to that of the 'priest anointed for battle', but in function he resembles the second priest of whom a memory has been preserved in Rabbinic tradition and amongst whose

---

[1] For the terms see ch. 7; for the priests and trumpets, ch. 5.

[2] Cf. the inscription on the trumpet, iii, 7, and comm. See comm. for ḥaruẓ = appointed and cf. *Tanḥuma* Beḥuqqothai i, 'God hath fixed (ḥaraẓ) the life-span of every man.'

duties was to 'make the words of the priest anointed for battle audible to the warriors'. The scroll stresses that the chief priest speaks standing still,[1] while the second priest—as the author notes in both passages—walks along while he exhorts. This priest's words of encouragement are given in full in section 23 (which is the first of the Kittim Series). The first passage of his address appears twice in the scroll (first in the 'prayer for the appointed time of battle' recited by the chief priest, which quotes Deuteronomy, see above) and several times in the O.T. The table on page 218 shows the textual relation of these citations.[2]

The words of the chief priest in the 'prayer for the appointed time of battle' correspond to those of the priest in Dt. xx (the trivial differences at times show the existence of a slightly different text), while the words of the 'priest destined for the appointed time of vengeance' are taken from other sources.[3]

The further words of encouragement are typical for the scroll and the writings of the sect. They emphasize—in addition to several verses from the O.T.—the main subject of the scroll: That the enemies—who are a 'wicked congregation' and whose deeds are in darkness—will be destroyed by the God of Israel with the aid of His angels. Their style resembles the exhortation of the chief priest after the defeat of the Sons of Light [4] (see below).

(3) *The Garments of the 'priest destined for the appointed time of vengeance'*

This priest and the six priests holding the trumpets are: 'Seven priests, of the sons of Aaron' (vii, 8–9);[5] all wear identical garments, described as 'garments for battle, and they shall not bring them into the sanctuary' (ib. 10–11). These are: 'of white byssus; a linen tunic and linen trousers, and girt with a linen girdle, twined byssus, blue, purple, and scarlet and a brocaded pattern, cunningly wrought, and turbaned head-dresses on their heads'. This description is very interesting, since: (*a*) we have no parallel to this detailed description;

---

[1] Note that in x, 2, and xv, 4, DSW has 'shall stand' for 'shall approach' of Dt. xx, 2, but in xvi, 11, 'shall approach . . . and shall stand . . .'

[2] The DSW text has 28 words where Dt. has 29, apart from 9 spelling variants and 10 textual variants.

[3] See also comm., and cf. the speech M. Soṭah viii, 1, which is a kind of Midrash on the Pent. source, quoting it phrase by phrase with interposed comments.

[4] Cf. in particular xv, 9–10; iv, 17.

[5] The name 'sons of Aaron' recurs frequently in the passages on priestly garments (e.g. Ex. xxviii, 40; xxxix, 27) and trumpets (Num. x, 8; cf. Ecclus. l. 13), which are the subjects dealt with here.

THE PRIESTS' SPEECHES BEFORE BATTLE—COMPARATIVE TABLE

2 Chr. xxxii, 7 sq.	Josh. x, 25	Dt. xxxi, 6	Priest destined for the Appointed Time of Vengeance (xv. 7–10)	Prayer for the Appointed Time of Battle (x, 3–5)	Textual Differences	Dt. xx
חזקו ואמצו	חזקו ואל תיראו אל תחתו	חזקו ואמצו	חזקו לבבכם ואל תיראו (+ חזק)	בהתקרבכם למלחמה היום	— התיצבו היום להתקרב למלחמה	אל ירך לבבכם [1] אל תיראו ואל תחפזו
				היום אל תיראו		אל תיראו ואל תערצו
				אל תיראו אתם קרבים היום למלחמה על איביכם		אתם קרבים היום למלחמה [3] על איביכם
אל תיראו ואל תחתו מפני מלך אשור ומפני כל ההמון אשר עמו	אל תיראו ואל תערצו מפניהם	אל תיראו ואל תערצו מפניהם	אל יראתם ואל תחתו (!) ואל יחפז לבבכם	אל תיראו ואל ירך לבבכם אל תיראו ואל תחפזו מפניהם	אל תיראו — אל תערצו אל תחפזו — אל	אל ירך לבבכם אל תיראו
כי עמנו רב מאשר עמו ... יהוה אלהינו לעזרנו ולהלחם מלחמתנו	כי ככה יעשה יהוה לכל אויביכם אשר אתם נלחמים אותם		ארור האיש אשר...	כי אלהיכם הולך עמכם	אלוהיכם — ה'	כי יהוה א' [4]
				להלחם אתם מאיביכם להושיע אתכם	הלהם עמכם	
					אבדכם — להושיע	
					אתכם — מאיביכם	

2 Sam. ii, 7:
תחזקנה ידיכם והיו לבני חיל (+ חזק)

2 Sam. xiii, 28:
חזקו והיו לבני חיל

(b) these garments are called 'garments for battle'; (c) this priest is dressed exactly like the other six priests.

(a) *Description of the Garments.*—This is based on several O.T. passages which the scroll combines with additions of its own:

Exodus xxxix, 27 ff.	Leviticus xvi, 3 ff.	Ezekiel xliv, 17 ff.	DSW vii, 9 ff.
'And they made the tunics of fine linen of woven work for Aaron and for his sons, and the mitre of fine linen, and the goodly head-tires of fine linen, and the linen breeches of fine twined linen, and blue, and purple, and scarlet, the work of the weaver in colours.'	'Herewith shall Aaron come into the holy place . . . he shall put on the holy linen tunic, and he shall have the linen breeches upon his flesh, and shall be girded with the linen girdle, and with the linen mitre shall he be attired; they are the holy garments.'	'And it shall be that when they enter in at the gates of the inner court, they shall be clothed with linen garments; and no wool shall come upon them, while they minister in the gates of the inner court, and within they shall have linen tires upon their heads, and shall have linen breeches upon their loins; they shall not gird themselves with any thing that causes sweat. And when they go forth into the outer court . . . to the people, they shall put off their garments wherein they minister, and lay them in the holy chambers, and they shall put on other garments that they sanctify not the people with their garments.'	'Dressed in garments of white byssus; a linen tunic and linen trousers, and girt with a linen girdle, twined byssus, blue, purple, and scarlet and a brocaded pattern, cunningly wrought, and turbaned head-dresses on their heads—garments for battle, and they shall not bring them into the sanctuary.'

Two interesting facts emerge from the comparison:

(i) Though the scroll bases itself on Exodus xxxix, it adds the word 'linen' to every single item (including the girdle), as in the description in Leviticus. (ii) The 'blue and purple' work, which according to Exodus is the 'work of the weaver', the scroll describes as a 'brocaded pattern, cunningly wrought'. That is how the Targums and the Rabbis always understood the description in Exodus,[1] but the author's emphasis on 'byssus', 'white', 'linen' suggests that he wished to rule out any doubt on this matter [2] and to indicate that for their tasks in battle (cf. below, §§ 2, 3) the priests should wear a different set of garments, though of the same type, from that in which they officiated in the Temple.

---

[1] Maimonides, *Code*, Hil. Kĕlē ha-Miqdash viii, summarizes the Tgs. and Rabb. discussion: 'The ordinary priest wears four garments: tunic, drawers, cap and girdle, all of white linen, woven of twice six threads, the girdle alone embroidered with wool. . . . The white garments are the six the High Priest wears on the Day of Atonement: tunic, drawers, girdle and turban, all white, woven of twice six threads, and entirely of linen. . . . Wherever the Law says *shesh* or *bad*, it means linen, which is also byssus.' Cf. also Rashi on Lv. xvi, 4: 'He does not serve within the Holiest of Holies in the eight garments in which he serves without, which are embroidered with gold—for an accuser cannot become an advocate—but he serves in the four garments of the ordinary priest, all made of linen.' Cf. also Galling p. 122; Barrois i, 469; A. S. Hershberg, *Ḥayyē ha-tarbuth bĕ-Yisra'el* etc., i, Warsaw 5684, p. 61 sq.

[2] Or perhaps this is connected with the Essenes' fondness for white garments (BJ II, viii, 3)?

I have not been able to discover why, against the Pentateuch, which defined the girdle as the 'work of the weaver',[1] the scroll writes 'brocaded pattern, cunningly wrought':[2] it may be due to the influence of the description of the *ephod*,[3]

(*b*) '*Garments for battle*'.—I know of no parallel for this expression in the sources.[4] Probably not a difference in their nature is intended, but only that this *set* of garments is reserved for battle and must not be brought into the sanctuary (cf. Ezek. xliv).

(*c*) *The Garments of the* '*priest destined for the appointed time of vengeance*' *and the Garments of the Priest* '*anointed for battle*'.—As we saw above, the sect did not identify the 'priest destined for the appointed time of vengeance' with the Rabbis' 'priest anointed for battle'. The tasks of the latter are here transferred to the 'chief priest'. This is confirmed by comparing the garments of the 'priest destined for the appointed time of vengeance' with the Rabbis' discussion of the garments of the 'priest anointed for battle'.[5]

(4) *The Exhortation After the Defeat of the Sons of Light*

The 'prayer for the appointed time of battle' and the words of encouragement were spoken at the beginning of the battle. Again three sections (25–27, xvi–xvii) are given over to a description of the relief of the defeated formation by the 'battle reserve'[6] and to words of encouragement spoken on that occasion.

In contrast to the words of encouragement spoken by the 'priest destined for the appointed time of vengeance', before the beginning of the first engagement, this time the speech is delivered by the chief priest himself (xvi, 11–12). This change of procedure was occasioned by the special circumstances, which required the full moral authority of the chief priest, as well as the contents of the speech, designed to explain the defeat.

This time, too (as at the 'prayer for the appointed time of battle'), the priest stands in front of the men of the relieving formation while they

---

[1] Apart from Ex. xxxix, 29 (see above), cf. also Ex. xxviii, 39.

[2] The same terms as used of the handle of the sword, v, 14; cf. ch. 6 § 6.

[3] Ex. xxviii, 6 (cf. also LXX); compare also Ecclus. xlv, 10–11; B.T. Yoma 72b and Maimonides, Hil. Kĕlē ha-Miqdash viii, 15: *ma'ăśeh roqem* means that the pattern is woven so as to appear on one side only, *ma'ăśeh ḥoshev* that the pattern appears on both sides of the material.

[4] Cf., however, Isa. lix, 17, and cf. p. 216, n. 2.

[5] In B.T. Yoma 72b: some say that the anointed priest officiates in eight garments like the High Priest others that he wears neither four nor eight garments; cf. also Maimonides, Hil. Kĕlē ha-Miqdash iv, 21.

[6] Cf. ch. 7, § 5 at end; also ch. 1.

are gathered around him, before being deployed in arrays.¹ His address, divided into two parts, is typical of the spirit of the sect.

In the first part (xvi, 13–xvii, 3) the priest explains that those who were slain, fell 'according to the mysteries of God', 'who examines and tries the heart of His people in justice and in righteousness'. Through the death of those who did not stand up to the test, God was sanctified in the eyes of the people, just as He was sanctified by the judgment on Nadab and Abihu.

The second part is devoted to words of encouragement, beginning like the earlier speech : ' But ye, be ye strong and fear them not' (xvii, 4 ff.) ; the Lord will annihilate Belial and the dominion of wickedness, for He has appointed this time for their destruction. At the head of the Sons of Light, the Lord's redeemed 'lot', He has placed the angel Michael, with whose help they will subdue Belial.² The time has come ' to raise among the angels the authority of Michael, and the dominion of Israel amongst all flesh ', and the Sons of Light will have light, joy, peace, and blessing.³

The priest ends with the words : ' Be ye strong in God's affliction until He shall lift up His hand,' etc. (xvii, 9). This prayer contains, in fact, the gist of the sect's doctrine on this subject.

The idea that the Period of Wickedness serves as a 'crucible' in which God tests His pious ones, is repeated in almost identical words in DSD, DST, and CDC.⁴ We find clear parallels to the leading ideas of this prayer in the O.T., e.g. the affair of Achan, and in 2 Maccabees xii, 39 ff. : ' Next day when the troops of Judas went—as it was high time they did—to pick up the corpses of the slain, in order to bring them home to lie with their kinsfolk in their fathers' sepulchres, they discovered under the shirts of every one of the dead men, amulets of the idols of Jamnia—a practice forbidden the Jews by law. All saw at once that this was why they had perished, and, blessing the (dealings) of the Lord, the just Judge who revealeth what is secret (cf. " according to God's mysteries " in DSW), all betook themselves to supplication, beseeching that this sin committed might be wholly blotted out ; and the noble-hearted Judas exhorted the people to keep themselves from sin, after what they had seen with their own eyes as the result of sin committed by those who had fallen.'

---

¹ xvii, 10, probably in order that the chief priest should not have to walk along the ranks, as did the first priest.

² Cf. especially ch. 9, § 5.

³ Similar i, 8–9, see comm. for comparison with the Book of Enoch.

⁴ Cf. e.g. DSD i, 17 sq. ; viii, 3 sq. ; DST v, 16 sq. ; CDC xx, 25 ; Yadin, JBL 74 (1955), 40 sq.

(5) *The Prayer after the Beginning of the Enemy's Defeat*

The first six 'lots' end without a final decision. In the seventh 'lot', 'when the great hand of God shall be raised,' after the Sons of Darkness begin to be defeated, the army of the Sons of Light is regrouped for the decisive general pursuit. This pursuit is described twice: (*a*) in the *Serekh* Series (ix, 3–7) we have the tactical description, which explains the organization of all the formations for the general pursuit; (*b*) in the Kittim Series (xviii, 1 ff.), the battle in the seventh 'lot' and the pursuit of the Kittim by all formations of the Sons of Light are described.[1]

At this stage the author states: 'When the sun hastens to set on that day, the chief priest and the priests and [levites] that are with him, and the ch[iefs of the formations and the men] of the Serekh shall stand up and bless in that place the God of Israel' (xviii, 5–6). Later in the prayer (xviii, 11) they say: 'Now the day is hastening for us [to] pursue their multitude.'

These passages prove, I think, that the general pursuit began at dusk, the six battles having taken up all the day, so that the Sons of Light were forced by nightfall to interrupt the pursuit.

The use of the words 'when the sun hastens to its setting' and 'now the day is hastening for us' clearly hints at the similar situation when Joshua pursued his enemies. Also the words 'and from that time there hath not happened the like of it' (xviii, 9) recall the miracle at Gibeon: 'And there was no day like that before or after it, that the Lord hearkened unto the voice of a man;—for the Lord fought for Israel' (Josh. x, 14).[2]

There is a further similarity between these two events in that the prayer was recited after the first defeat of the enemy, during the pursuit. I think that this helps to explain the contents of the prayer, which clearly recalls Joshua's pursuit and God's intervention and assistance. After mentioning that the Lord has many times opened the gates of deliverance for His people, the special request begins in xviii, 9.

The miracle which was performed (for Joshua or for them, i.e. the beginning of the enemy's defeat, cf. comm. to xviii, 9) is said to be a miraculous deed, the like of which has not occurred before, and they request that God may 'appear' a second time[3] for their assistance

---

[1] Cf. chapters 7 and 1.
[2] Cf. Ecclus xlvi, 4, also xlviii, 23.
[3] For the restoration see comm. ad loc. and i, 8. The verb 'shine forth' suggests that God's appearance in light is meant; cf. DST iv 6; iv, 23; ix, 26. The request to God to 'appear' at first sight supports Dupont-Sommer's view that in DSH xi, 7,

with wondrous deeds, since the day is hastening for them to pursue the Sons of Darkness. Perhaps this prayer also provides us with an idea of the nature of the battle between the Sons of Light and Darkness. The defeated Sons of Darkness try to save themselves with the help of the darkness. The result of the prayer and God's intervention were no doubt related in the missing parts of xviii and xix, and they cannot be restored with any certainty, though I would say that God's intervention on the side of the Sons of Light resembled the defeat of Sennacherib's army, i.e. when the Sons of Light rose in the morning to continue the pursuit they saw all the Kittim and the ' multitude of Asshur ' dead. For details cf. comm. xix, 9 ff.

If col. xix belonged to the length of parchment joined to the last complete sheet of the scroll, to which page xviii belongs,[1] this prayer ended with the hymn ' Arise, O mighty one ' as does the prayer for the appointed time of battle.

(6) *After the Defeat of the Sons of Darkness*

(a) *Close to the Enemy's Slain.*—In the *Serekh* Series, the scroll gives the contents of the prayers and thanksgivings which the Sons of Light recited after the enemy was defeated. These prayers are divided into several groups. They open, apparently, with the prayers to be recited immediately after the enemy's defeat and close to the place where his men fell. Section 21, xiv, 2, begins : ' After they have withdrawn from the battlefield and entered the camp.' Hence it seems that the group of prayers preceding this chapter (xii, 16–xiv, 1) was recited close to the enemy's dead. This assumption is confirmed by the contents of these prayers, which are made up of three subjects :

(1) The Sons of Light bless the God of Israel and curse Belial ;

(2) Prayer of general thanksgiving summarizing the doctrines of the sect ;

(3) The conclusion, of which only a few words remain.

(1) *The Blessing and the Curse.*—Unfortunately, the greater part of the beginning of section 17, xii, 16 ff., is worn away. Restoration is not easy,[2] but one can, I think, establish the general meaning from the remnants :

>line 16 : . . . the mighty men of war Jerusalem . . .
>line 17 : . . . above the heavens, O Lord . . .

the verb cannot refer to the Wicked Priest, which is the basis of his theory that the whole passage describes the capture of Jerusalem by Pompey (*Nouveaux Aperçus* p. 57 sq.). DST v, 32 ; vii, 3, however, clearly prove that in the sect's Hebrew the verb could also be used of ' appearances ' of the forces of evil.

[1] See ch. 1.
[2] See comm.

Since it seems unlikely that this passage should refer to the return to Jerusalem,¹ it appears to be dealing with the deployment of the warriors for the recitation of the blessings and curses and words of thanksgiving (which follow immediately afterwards), their faces turned in the direction of Jerusalem. The words 'the mighty men of war', 'Jerusalem', and 'above the heavens' are strongly reminiscent of Solomon's prayer at the consecration of the Temple (1 Kings viii, 44–45).²

The chief priest himself,³ in the presence of the priests, levites, and elders of the *Serekh*, conducts the ceremony of the blessing and the curse.

The author divided the blessing and the curse into two very short sections of three lines each, since he apparently did not want to have both in the same chapter. From the description here, it would appear that the blessing and the curse were recited together by the priests,

DSD	DSW
i, 18 ff. : 'And as they are entering into the covenant the priests and the levites shall bless the God of deliverances and all His deeds of faithfulness.'	xii, 1 ff. : '. . . and his brother priests and the levites and all the elders of the Serekh with him. They shall bless, from where they stand, the God of Israel and all His true deeds.'
i, 1 ff. : 'Then the priests shall bless all the men of God's Lot, who walk perfectly in all His ways.'	xiii, 1–2 : 'Blessed be all that serve Him in justice, that know Him in faith'
ii, 4 ff. : 'Then the levites shall curse all the men of Belial's Lot.'	xiii, 1–2 : 'And there they shall curse Belial and all the spirits of his Lot.'
'and shall respond and say : "Cursed be thou for all thy guilty, evil deeds . . . cursed be thou, without compassion, according to the darkness of thy deeds ; and damned be thou in the gloom of eternal fire."'	xiii, 4 : 'And cursed be Belial for the plan of hatred, and abhorred in his guilty authority. Accursed be all spirits of his Lot for their wicked plan and abhorred for all the works of their filthy uncleanness, for they are the Lot of darkness, but the Lot of God is destined for light [eternal].'

¹ The passage precedes the prayers after the enemy are slain (xiv) ; it can hardly still belong to the prayer of the appointed time of battle, as the words 'Rise O mighty man', etc., clearly end the prayers during the battle in xix, with line 9 beginning the prayers after the victory.

² Cf. also vs. 23, which influenced the later part of this prayer, cf. comm. here and col. xix.

³ The bottom part of xii is missing, but 'and his brother priests' xiii, 1, which recurs several times in connexion with the chief priest (also in O.T.), shows that he is meant. See also comm.

THE RITES OF THE CONGREGATION

levites, and elders of the *Serekh*, however, since the text of these chapters in general is based on Dt. xxvii [1] and the details of the ceremony resemble that in DSD (see above), the curse may have been pronounced by the levites alone.

The Sons of Light bless the 'God of Israel' and all that serve Him in justice and in faith in the Lot of God (the 'Lot of Light') and curse Belial and all 'spirits of his lot' (the 'Lot of Darkness').[2] The ceremony closely resembles the description in DSD, and thus represents one of the most important links between the two scrolls.

(2) *General Prayer of Thanks* (xiii, 7-16).—After a brief mention of God's covenant with Israel, the words of thanksgiving concentrate on the sect's doctrine. Israel is in the 'Lot of God', the 'Lot of Light'. The Lord, who created Belial, has defeated him with the aid of the Prince of Light whom He commanded to assist the Sons of Light.[3] In this war between the 'lots' of 'light' and 'darkness', the 'lot of light' was victorious because God Himself fought their battle and neither angel nor prince can stand up against Him.[4]

(3) This Section ends—like several others (e.g. the words of encouragement in section 27)—with the statement that Israel has been victorious in this battle because it was fought on the day the Lord appointed from of old for the destruction of the Sons of Darkness. This passage forms the link with the end of the prayer, which was in section 20, of which only fragments remain [5] and which opens with the words: '... for Thou hast appointed for us [an appointed time of vengeance ...]' (xiii, 17) and ends with the words of the prophets who foretold the destruction of God's enemies: ... 'like the fire of His wrath upon the idols of Egypt' (xiv, 1).[5]

(b) '*The Hymn of Return*'.—This was recited on their return from the slain to the camp close to the battlefield. The wording of this hymn is not supplied by the scroll (at least not in the columns in our possession). The author merely says: 'After they have withdrawn from the slain and entered the camp, they shall all together sing the hymn of return' (xiv, 2). 'Return' signifies the movement from the place of the actual fighting to the place where the warriors were drawn up at some distance from the enemy, or to the camp near the battlefield (iii, 10), as well as the return from the campaign, to Jerusalem, as in: 'And on the trumpets for the way of return from the battle

---

[1] Verse 14.
[2] For these, see ch. 9, § 3, and cf. comm.
[3] See in detail ch. 9, §§ 4-5.
[4] xiii, 14; cf. in detail ch. 9, §§ 4-5.
[5] For the restoration and the quotations see comm.

with the enemy to come back to the congregation to Jerusalem, they shall write: " Rejoicings of God in peaceful return." ' (iii, 10–11).[1]

(c) *The Prayer on the Day After the Victory.*—The description of this prayer of thanks, which was recited on the battlefield, is instructive: ' After they have withdrawn from the slain and entered the camp, they shall all together sing the hymn of return. In the morning they shall launder their clothes and bathe to remove the blood of the guilty cadavers and return to the place where they had stood, where they had arrayed the formation before the assault on the enemy. There they shall bless all together the God of Israel and exalt His name in joyful unison and shall solemnly declare . . . ' (xiv, 2–4).[2] As they washed their clothes and bathed to remove the blood of the corpses only in the morning, we learn that they returned to camp in their defiled garments and even sang the hymn of return before bathing.[3] After the first publication of the above passage, attention was drawn [4] to Num. xxxi, 21 ff.: ' And Eleazar the priest said unto the men of war that went to the battle . . . and ye shall wash your clothes on the seventh day, and ye shall be clean, and afterward ye may come into the camp '.[5]

The apparent contradiction between this and the scroll may, I think, be explained in that Eleazar referred to the final return to the camp of Israel after the war, while the scroll here deals with the return at evening-time to the camp by the battlefield.[6] It is of course possible that the last part of the scroll, which is missing, and which probably described the ceremonies after the final victory and the congregation's return to Jerusalem, contained detailed rites of purification similar to those in Numbers.

The definition in the prayer of the ' place where they had stood, where they had arrayed the formation before the assault on the enemy ', clearly establishes that it belongs to the group of prayers and thanksgivings to be recited after the victory on the battlefield, before the return to Jerusalem. In contrast to the preceding prayers, which were said directly upon the conclusion of the pursuit and the battle, in the

---

[1] For details see ch. 5, § 5 (1).
[2] This passage also helps to determine the stages of deployment: (1) the overnight encampment, (2) forming up of the formations, (3) the battlefield itself.
[3] Hence also the prayers near the enemy dead were said before the purification of clothes.
[4] Sukenik, *M.G.* i, 26 and 24.
[5] Kasher, *Talpiyoth* 4 (5710), 689, cites also Tos. Yad. ii, 20: ' The morning bathers said, we complain to you, O Pharisees, that ye pronounce the name of God from a body which has uncleanness upon it,' claiming that it refers to Essene customs.
[6] For ' camp ' see ch. 3, § 4.

place where the enemy had fallen, this one was recited in the place where the army had been drawn up before the beginning of the battles, i.e. at the same place where before the 'prayer for the appointed time of battle' and the words of encouragement before the battle had been performed.

In fact this prayer of thanksgiving resembles in its structure the 'prayer for the appointed time of battle' and the words of encouragement, except that it stresses the success of the prayer recited at the beginning of the battle and thanks the God of Israel, with whose help 'those that stumble' have brought about 'won[drous] deeds', and who has raised up by His judgment those 'whose heart had melted', hence the mouths of the dumb were opened 'to sing [His] mighty deeds'.[1] In this battle, victory was with the weak, for the Lord taught the 'weak hands' warfare and 'giveth to them whose knees totter strength to stand, and strength of loins to the shoulder of them that have been brought low'.

The members of the sect have fought so courageously because Belial did not succeed in beguiling them from their covenant with the Lord who guarded their soul from all 'the snares of his (Belial's) dominion'.[2] Similarities with the above two prayers appear throughout, except that now the salvation is stated as a past event.

Both prayers of thanksgiving end with praises to God for the wonderful deeds of creation (x, 11 ff.; xiv, 12 ff.).

Section 22, which ends (xv, 1-3) with a transition from the *Serekh* Series to the Battle Series, opens (xiv, 16) with the request 'rise up, O God of angels, and raise Thyself in [Thy power . . .]' (resembling 'arise O mighty one', xii, 9 ff.; xix, 2 ff.). This request may not belong any more to the prayer of thanksgiving, but represents possibly sentiments of the author himself, leading on to the description of the war with the Kittim. This view is supported by the ending of this chapter and the words: 'For it is a time of trouble for Israel,' which also form part of the words of the author in Section 22 (xv, 1).

Corresponding to the parts of the *Serekh* Series which deal with the prayers after victory, Section 31, in the Battle Series, also deals with actions after victory. Only the beginning of Section 31 is preserved, but from its close resemblance to the description of the final defeat in

---

[1] Almost literally repeated, though as a supplication, in the 'prayer for the appointed time of battle', xi, 9.

[2] Cf. M. Soṭah viii, 5, where R. Akiba takes the 'fearful and faint-hearted' literally (cf. ch. 4, p. 66, n. 3), while R. Jose the Galilean defines him as 'he that fears because of sins he has committed', cf. Tos. Soṭah vii, 22.

Section 28 (xviii)[1] and its connexion with the description in Section 21 (xiv, 2 ff.) enumerating the prayers for after the victory, it seems fairly certain that this chapter dealt with activities after the final victory.[2]

It may well be that this was followed by the 'hymn for the way of return' recited on the way back to Jerusalem, as may be seen from 1 Maccabees[3] and the inscription on the 'trumpets for the way of return': 'Rejoicings of God in peaceful return.'

(7) Summary Table

Purpose of Prayer or Thanksgiving	Tactical Phase	Officiant	Source
(a) 'Prayer for the appointed time of battle'	Close to the battlefield before the arraying of the formations	'Chief priest'	x–xii xv, 4–5
(b) Words of encouragement	After arraying the formations but before the battle	'The priest destined for the appointed time of vengeance'	xv, 6 xvi, 1 vii, 12
(c) Words of encouragement (after the defeat of the Sons of Light)	After the relief of the defeated formation by the 'battle reserve'	'Chief priest'	xvi, 11 xvii, 9
(d) Supplication for a miracle 'when the sun hastens to set'	After the beginning of the defeat of the Sons of Darkness in the seventh 'lot' (during the general pursuit)	'Chief priest'	xviii, 5 xix, 8?
(e) 1. God's blessing and Belial's curse	On the day of victory, close to the enemy's slain	'Chief priest'	xii, 16 xiv, 1
2. 'Beginning of the return'	On the day of victory on their return from the slain to camp, close to the battlefield	—	xiv, 2
3. General thanksgiving	The day after victory at the place of the initial deployment	'Chief priest'	xiv, 3–15 xix, 9–13

---

[1] Cf. xix, 10, and xviii, 2–3.

[2] Just as DSW distinguishes between the short thanksgiving near the enemy slain and the general thanksgiving on the following morning. See in particular 2 Macc. viii, 27 sq.

[3] Cf. 1 Macc. iv, 24; v, 53 sq.; also 2 Macc. x, 38.

Chapter 9

THE ANGELOLOGY OF THE SCROLL

§ 1. GENERAL REMARKS

DSW considerably extends our knowledge of Jewish angelology in general and that of the scrolls sect in particular, as the scroll uses every opportunity to explain the activities of the different angels and their names. This subject is of the utmost importance in the history of Judaism at that period, when every sect and group boasted of knowing the ultimate secrets of this doctrine. We must, therefore, briefly consider the views of the sect on this subject as expressed in DSW. This may, I think, assist in identifying the sect and in dating the scroll.

Though the various Biblical books devote considerable space to this subject, names of angels appear only in the book of Daniel and even then there are only two, Gabriel and Michael.[1]

Angelology, which developed speedily from Daniel onwards, emerges as a complete and complex doctrine in the Apocrypha and Pseudepigrapha. There the angels are divided into several classes, we find details of their names, their routine tasks, and particularly their role at the End of Days. Such doctrines appear, though to a lesser degree, in Rabbinic and early Christian literature and reach their climax in the Kabbalistic writings.

The importance of DSW in this matter derives from the fact that the above sources, though on the whole in agreement on principles, differ in some rather important details. It is enhanced by Josephus' statement (BJ, ii, viii, 7), that the Essenes swore to guard the secret of the angels' names. The details on this subject in DSW are of greater importance than the information gained from any of the scrolls published so far.[2] To a certain extent they also shed light on the more detailed descriptions found in some of the Apocrypha and Pseudepigrapha.

In the following investigation sources outside the scroll are adduced only when they assist in its comprehension or if the scroll puts their information in a new light.

---

[1] Dn. viii, 16; x, 21. Rabb. tradition claimed that the Jews brought knowledge of the angels' names back from the Babylonian exile (P.T. RSh. i, 2).

[2] Cf., however, now J. Strugnell, ' The Angelic Liturgy, etc.,' Suppl. VT viii (Congress Volume), p. 318 ff. This article should be referred to for all terms marked in the following paragraph with an asterisk.

INTRODUCTION

§ 2. Terminology

Like the other sources, from the Bible onwards, the scroll, too, uses several synonymous terms to denote angels in general. Though the influence of the O.T. is obvious, we witness interesting semantic developments.

1. *Elim.**—Frequently used as a synonym for angels :

' The congregation of *elim* and the assembly of men ' (i, 10).

' With the sound of a great tumult and the war-cry of *elim* and men ' (ib., i, 11).

' And to bring low some from among the *elim* ' (ib., xiv, 15).

' Rise up, rise up, O God of *elim* ' (ib., xiv, 16).

' Mighty *elim* shall gird themselves for battle ' (ib., xv, 14).

' So as to raise among the *elim* the authority of Michael ' (ib., xvii, 7). Also in DST :

' Behold Thou art the prince of *elim* and a king of honoured ones and the master of every spirit ' (DST, x, 8).

' Elim from the heavenly dwelling . . . ' (ib., xviii, line 3 from the left, on plate 52 in the *Oẓar*).

' Sons of *elim* . . . ' (ib., plate 53, frg. 2, line 3).

' . . .] *elim* to commune with the sons of heaven ' (ib., plate 53, frg, 2, line 10).

Similarly : ' And in the congregation of *elim* [and in the secret of holy] ones ' (' Dires de Moïse ', *Qumran* I, p. 95, col. iv, line 1).

The Biblical origin of this usage is clear; e.g. Ps. lxxxii, 1 (*el*); lxxxix, 7 (*elohim*), Dan. xi, 36, (*běnē elim*). However, the scroll differs from the Bible [1] in using *elim* (and *elim* only) exclusively for angels.

2. *Sons of heaven.**—In parallelism to *elim* we have in DST (plate 53, frg. 2, line 10) ' sons of heaven ', who also form a congregation, like the *elim*. Other occurrences :

' And to enter communion with the congregation of the sons of heaven ' (DST iii, 22).

' And He hath given them an inheritance in the lot of the holy ones ; and with the sons of heaven He hath united their assembly for a council of communion ' (DSD xi, 7-8).

Mighty Ones.*—Cf. comm. on xii, 7 ; xv, 14.

3. *Mal'akhim.*—This term is, of course, frequently used also in the scroll ; e.g. : ' And a host of angels are among those mustered with us ' (xii, 7).

---

[1] Cf. *Enc. Miqr.* i, 283, 302 sq. For Ugaritic parallels, see F. M. Cross Jr., JNES 12 (1953), 274 sq., particularly n. 1 ; Tur-Sinai, *Sefer Iyyov* 5714, p. 5.

4. *Holy Angels.*—e.g. : ' For the holy angels are with their hosts ' (vii, 6 ; and cf. below no. 8).

5. *Angels of Destruction.*—' The angels of destruction walk in the boundaries of darkness ' (xiii, 12). The form חבל as against חבלה (*ḥabbalah*) in Rabbinic literature is typical for the scrolls. I know only of two other occurrences : DSD, iv, 12 and CDC, ii, 6.

6. *Angels of the Presence* (*mal'akhē panim*).—DST vi, 13, cf. comm. xiii, 14. Also : ' Like an Angel of the Presence in the holy habitation ' (*Qumran I*, p. 126, iv, 25). ' And casts a lot with Angels of the Presence ' (ibid, 26).

7. ' *The angel Mastema* '.—See below § 3.

8. *Holy Ones* (*qĕdhoshim*).*—The scrolls frequently use ' holy ones ' as a synonym for angels. The expression appears in various combinations, e.g.' Realm of Holy Ones ' (xi, 8–9 ; DST, xi, 12), ' a Host of Holy Ones ' DST iii, 22 ; x, 34), ' a council (*sodh*) of Holy Ones ' (DST, iv, 25 ; frg. 63 ; 1QDM iv, 1). These phrases indicate the organization and tasks of the angels as advisers, messengers and fighters. Compare with the above combinations : ' So shall the heavens praise Thy wonders, O Lord, Thy faithfulness also in the assembly of the holy ones. For who in the skies can be compared unto the Lord, who among the sons of angels (*elim*, A.V. ' might ') can be likened unto the Lord, a God dreaded in the great council of the holy ones, and feared of all of them that are round about Him ? ' (Px. lxxxix, 6–9). See further the notes of Charles, *Apoc.*, II, p. 189 on Enoch, i, 9 for the use of this term in the Apocrypha and Pseudepigrapha.

9. *Spirits.**—In the Apocrypha and Pseudepigrapha and in the scrolls, the name ' spirit ' (*ruaḥ*) is frequently used as a synonym for angels, following passages like : ' The Lord, the God of the spirits ' (Num. xxvii, 16) ; ' Who makest spirits (A.V. ' winds ') Thy messengers, the flaming fire Thy ministers ' (Ps. civ, 4), cf. LXX.[1] A title of God, frequently found in the Apocrypha and Pseudepigrapha, is ' Lord of spirits '.[2] Typical phrases in the scrolls include : ' Master of every spirit ' (DST, x., 8) ; ' host of spirits ' (xii, 8 ; DST xiii, 8) ; ' spirits of the lot of Belial ' (xiii, 2, 4, 11 ; DSD. iii, 24) ; ' spirits of truth ' (|| ' angels of righteousness ') (xiii, 10 ; DSD., iii, 18 ; iv, 23) ; ' spirits of knowledge ' (|| ' congregation of sons of heaven ') (DST iii, 22–3) ; ' spirits of holiness ' (|| ' mighty ones ') (DST, viii, 10) ; ' spirits of wickedness '

---

[1] Cf. also Tg. ; 4 Ezra vi, 21, and Box's note in Charles, *Apocr.* ii, 595.

[2] 104 times in *Enoch* ; also 2 Macc. iii, 24 ; cf. Abel, *Livres Maccabées* p. 324.

(DST, pl. lv, frg. 5); 'spirits of evil' (*awlah*) (DSD, iii, 18; iv. 23; DST, pl. lv, frg. 5); 'spirits of sin' (*peshaʿ*) (*Qumran I*, no. 36, frg. 2). Among occurrences of *ruaḥ* = angel in other scrolls note especially 'before they became holy angels [   ], spirits of eternity in their dominions' (DST, i, 10–11).

10. *Prince* (*śar*).—As elsewhere, this term indicates the chief angels, e.g. 'prince of light' (xiii, 10), 'prince of the dominion of wickedness' (xvii, 5–6) and cf. below. The dominion of each of these princes is called 'authority' (*miśrah*), e.g. 'his guilty authority' (xiii, 4), 'the authority of Michael' (xvii, 6–7).

§ 3. BELIAL

God, the master of all spirits, both of light and darkness, of the holy spirits and of spirits of destruction, designates each one for a specific mission (Jubilees, ii, 2 ff.). At the head of the spirits of darkness, wickedness and destruction, the Lord placed Belial to carry out his specific task until He shall mete out justice to him with the assistance of the angels appointed for that task [1] ('And Thou wast the one who made Belial to corrupt', xiii, 10–11). Belial occurs thirty-three times in the Dead Sea Scrolls; twelve of those are in DSW, five in DSD, ten in DST, and six in CDC. This proves that the members of the sect were greatly interested in Belial, who in their view led all their enemies.[2] These passages enable us to recognize his characteristics and tasks as conceived by the sect:

Belial heads the forces of darkness and the enemies of the Sons of Light and is their military leader. In contrast to the 'lot of light', to which the Sons of Light belong, the Sons of Darkness and all the enemies of the Sons of Light belong to the 'Lot of Belial' (for details cf. below § 8). God created Belial 'to corrupt' and by 'his counsel to render wicked and guilty' (xiii, 11).

The period of our texts is the 'dominion of Belial': Thou 'hast bestowed Thy mercy upon the remnant [of Israel] in the dominion of Belial' (xiv, 9), 'And during all those years shall Belial be let loose upon Israel' (CDC, iv, 12–13; and cf. Asc. Is. ii, 8). During this period Belial reigns, spreading terror: 'Out of terror or fright or ordeal which may come under the dominion of Belial' (DSD, i, 17–18). The sect's laws were for the purpose of regulating their actions during

---

[1] Cf. Test. Levi iii, 3, and frequent in other Pseudepigrapha.

[2] 'The use of the name *Belial* as symbol of the ruler of the forces of evil is an important criterion of the literature of this whole trend, and of the sect in particular' (D. Flusser, *Yediʿoth* 17 (5713), 30).

the time of Belial's dominion : ' Thus they shall do year by year all the days of the dominion of Belial ' (DSD, ii, 19).

By encouraging the Sons of Light to observe His laws, God shields them in their struggle with Belial, who wants to seduce them ; Belial is powerless to harm those who observe the Law (cf. especially, xiv., 8–10). The curse (xiii, 4–6 ; DSD, ii, 4–5) also acts effectively against Belial and the spirits of his ' lot '. On the day ' appointed from of old ', the Lord with the assistance of His angels will destroy Israel's enemies, led by Belial. On that day, Belial himself and ' all the spirits of his Lot ' will come to an end, ' when the great hand of God shall be raised up against Belial and all the army of his dominion for eternal defeat ' (xviii, 1).

All this is in complete agreement with the statements about Belial (or *Beliar*) in the Apocrypha and Pseudepigrapha. Moses prays to the Lord : ' . . . and do not deliver them (Israel) into the hands of their enemies, the Gentiles . . . and let not the spirit of Beliar rule over them to accuse them before Thee, and to ensnare them from all the paths of righteousness, so that they may perish from before Thy face ' (Jub. i, 19–20). Belial is the angel of wickedness, the ruler of this world (Asc. Is. ii, 4) [1] and he is the head of the spirits of evil (ib. i, 8). Belial has no power over those who observe the Laws : ' For if fornication overcomes not your mind, neither can Belial overcome you ' (Test. Reuben, iv, 11). The Lord will redeem mankind from Belial and destroy all his spirits (Test. Zebulun, ix, 8) along with all Israel's enemies (Test. Dan, v, 10) ; Belial will be bound in fetters (Test. Levi, xviii, 12) and be cast into the fire (Test. Judah, xxv, 3).[2] The identity of attitude between DSW and the Apocrypha and Pseudepigrapha, particularly Jubilees and the Testaments, is thus obvious.[3]

Maśṭema.—In addition to Belial being labelled ' prince of the dominion of wickedness ' (xvii, 5–6), the word *maśṭemah* ' hatred ' is applied to him in various forms. ' And cursed be Belial for the plan of hatred ' (xiii, 4) ; ' and Thou wast the one who made Belial to corrupt, an angel of hatred ' (xiii, 11) ; ' in the dominion of Belial with all the mysteries of his hatred ' (xiv, 9) ; ' under the dominion of his (the angel of darkness) hatred ' (DSD, iii, 23).

These passages show that *maśṭemah* is not a proper name but, as in Hos. ix, 7 [4] must be taken as describing the characteristic actions of Belial. The forms ' angel of hatred ' and especially ' *the* angel of hatred ' (cf. ' the prince of hatred '), may explain how this word came to be

---

[1] Flusser, ibid.

[2] See Charles, *Apocr.* ii, Index s.v. Belial, Beliar.

[3] For the connexion in general, see ch. 1 ; ch. 2 ; ch. 8, §§ 2–3.

[4] See comm. on xiii, 4.

treated as a proper noun in the translations of Jubillees, *mal'akh ha mastemah* being taken as 'the angel Mastema'.[1]

The tasks of the '(prince) Mastema' in Jubilees are identical with those of Belial. The angel of evil spirits and destruction, he requests God not to destroy the evil spirits, since without them he cannot corrupt and lead astray (Jub. x, 8); the prince Mastema commands his spirits to cause men to transgress, to corrupt and to destroy (Jub. xi, 5); he sends ravens and other birds to devour the seed sown in the land (ib., xi, 11); he falsely accuses Abraham before God concerning the sacrifice of Isaac (ib., xvii, 16; xviii, 9); he attacks Moses during his return to Egypt from the Wilderness (ib., xlviii, 2) and tries to deliver him into the hands of the Egyptian sorcerers (ib., 9); the armies of Mastema slay the Egyptian firstborn (ib., xlix, 2); during Israel's exodus from Egypt, God imprisons the prince Mastema to prevent him from interfering (ib., xlviii, 15), but He later releases him so that he can assist Egypt in pursuing the children of Israel (ib., 16) and once more imprisons him to prevent him from denouncing Israel for taking vessels and garments from the Egyptians (ib., 18).

Hence we can conclude that the sect's name for this angel was Belial and that all the other names are simply titles describing his character and actions.[2]

§ 4. 'The God of Israel and the Angel of His truth'

At the head of Israel's enemies stands Belial, but God Himself will fight for the Sons of Light, the 'people of God' (i, 5), the 'Lot of God' (xiii, 5). Belial, mighty against his equals, the other angels, is powerless in this war with his Creator. This central theme, which is by no means confined to the writings of the sect, recurs frequently in the scroll. Thus, after noting that God created Belial, it continues: 'What angel or prince is like unto the help of [Thy face]' (xiii, 14).[3] This theme is expanded at length in Jub. xv, 31-2.[4] The Lord Himself cares for the

---

[1] See Rabin, *Zadokite Documents* p. 75; Charles, *Book of Jubilees* 1902, p. 80, n. 8; Lambert, NRTh 73 (1951), 960: 'le Mastêma apparait comme l'ange de la persécution.'

[2] Possibly *Belial* itself was etymologized as a description of his functions; cf. Flusser, op. cit. p. 30, n. 6; Habermann, *Sinai* 32 (5713), 157-8.

[3] In my view an allusion to Isa. lxiii, 9, understood more or less as in LXX; see comm. on xiii, 14.

[4] Cf. also En. xli, 9; already Ecclus. xvii, 14, to which Segal in his comm. quotes PRE xxiv, 'He appointed an angel over every nation, but Israel fell to His own share, hence " for the portion of the Lord is His people " (Dt. xxxii, 9)'; cf. LXX to Dt. xxxii, 9, and Oesterley, *Introduction to ... Apocrypha* p. 108; cf. also the 'Prayer of Mordecai and Esther', BHM v, 4; Grinz, *Sinai* 32 (5713), 21.

welfare of Israel when they observe the Law, and for victory over their enemies. In this He is assisted by an angel specially appointed for the purpose. Israel is not ' in the lot ' of this angel—in contrast to the Sons of Darkness who are ' in the lot ' of Belial,—but since this angel is specially appointed over the forces of good, light, truth, and justice, he is *eo ipso* at the head of the spirits who fight Belial and his spirits ; hence the Sons of Light i.e. Israel are connected with him.

§ 5. ' THE PRINCE OF LIGHT '

The identity and function of this angel must play an important part in our analysis of the sect's tenets and of their place in the thought of the period. In xiii, 10–11 we read : ' Thou didst appoint from of old the prince of light to assist us, [since all sons of justice are in his lot] and all spirits of truth in his dominion.' As against this : ' Thou wast the one who made Belial to corrupt, an angel of hatred, his [dominion] being in darkness and his counsel to render wicked and guilty '. The angel of light and the angel of darkness are similarly contrasted in DSD : ' In the hand of the prince of lights is the rule over all the sons of righteousness ; in the ways of light they walk. But in the hand of the angel of darkness is all the rule over the sons of perversion ; and in the ways of darkness they walk ' (iii, 20–22).

CDC notes that it was the ' prince of lights ' (plural !) who assisted Moses and Aaron against Belial and his helpers : ' For in ancient times Moses and Aaron arose by the hand of the Prince of Lights, and Belial raised Jannes and his brother by his evil device ' (v, 17–19).[1] Cf. also DSD, iii, 24 : ' But the God of Israel and His angel of truth have helped all the Sons of Light '.

The question of the identity of this angel has been much debated. Schechter thought ' prince of lights ' a corruption for the ' prince of the divine presence ', which he identified with the ' angel of the presence ' who dictated the Book of Jubilees to Moses (Jub. i, 27 ; ii, 1).[2] Ginzberg[3] proposed ' prince of watchers ' (*'irim* for *urim*). Charles,[4] though hesitantly identifying him with Uriel—who according to 1 Enoch was set over the luminaries (cf. also below)—was inclined to accept Schechter's suggestion. Brownlee [5] drew attention to 2 Cor. xi, 14, ' Satan himself is transformed into an angel of light '.

---

[1] Cf. B.T. Men. 85a ; Ex. Rabba ix ; Rabin, *Zadokite Documents* p. 21 ; Schechter, *Documents of Jewish Sectaries* i, p. lix.
[2] op. cit., note on v, 18.
[3] Cf. Rost ad loc., p. 14.
[4] Charles, *Apocr.* ii, 811.
[5] Brownlee, *Manual* p. 15, n. 33. It is curious that Aalen p. 169. n. 1, p. 180, still identifies the ' Prince of Lights ' with God himself.

The identification of the Prince of Light with Uriel seems at first glance reasonable for a sect whose members call themselves Sons of Light, except that Uriel does not appear among the four archangels in DSW ix, 15-16, and in his place is another angel called Sariel. We shall return to this ; here let us note only that the connexion of Uriel with light is not generally accepted in pseudepigraphal literature.

The key to the identity of the Prince of Light is now, to my mind, provided by DSW xvii, 6-8 : From that passage we learn that Michael was the prince sent to assist the Lot of God ' through eternal light to light up in joy the [house] of Israel '.[1] Michael's functions according to the sources outside the scrolls are :

He is the prince of Israel (Daniel, x, 21 ; xii, 1 ; Enoch, xx, 5 ; B. T. Yoma 77a, etc.).

He is ' set over the best part of mankind ' (Enoch, xx, 5).

He wreaks Israel's vengeance against her enemies at the end of days as God's principal assistant (Daniel, xii, 1 ; and cf. comm. to DSW i, 12 ; xxvii, 6).

He is at the head of the angels and holds the key to the kingdom of heaven (Syr. Baruch, xi-xv) and it is he who offers the sacrifices in the fourth heaven (*Zebul*) (B.T. Hag. 12b).

He reveals to Enoch the secrets of mercy and justice, the heavens, the stars and the luminaries.[2]

These tasks fit in very well with those of Michael, the Prince of Light, in DSW and in the other scrolls :

He is Israel's principal assistant against Belial (DSW xvi, 6-8 ; xiii, 10 ; CDC, v, 18-19).

He is the angel of justice and truth (DSW xiii, 10 ; DSD, iii, 20).

His office is above that of all other angels (DSW, xvii, 7), and he is the prince of light.[3]

This sect, which views light as the symbol of justice, truth, knowledge and everything good, when reading in Daniel that Michael is the ' great prince which standeth for Thy people ' at a ' time of trouble, such as never was since there was a nation even to that same time ' (Dn., xii, 1), were forced to the logical conclusion that Michael and the prince of light were one and the same, just as Belial is identical with the angel of darkness.

---

[1] For Michael's attributes, cf. comm. ad loc. and ad. i, 9.

[2] See Hartom's note *apud* Kahana, *Sefarim Ḥiẓonim* ii, 422 ; Hughes in Charles, *Apocr.* ii, 539 ; *Book of Adam and Eve* xxxviii, 1 ; xl, 1.

[3] See also Brownlee, *Manual* p. 51.

§ 6. THE WAR OF THE ANGELS

1. *The assistance given to Israel by the angels.*—' For the Lord is holy, and the king of glory is with us,—a people of saints. Mighty men and a host of angels are among those mustered with us, the mighty one of war is in our congregation, and the host of His spirits is with our steps ' (DSW, xii, 7–8).[1]

These wonderful verses succinctly express the sect's faith that Israel will overcome her enemies because God Himself and His angels fight in Israel's ranks. This concept, which is frequently expressed in the scrolls, is of course based on the numerous Biblical passages stating that God's angels fight with Israel against her enemies.[2] Also the Maccabees frequently turned to God requesting Him to send His angels to their aid.[3] The Pseudepigrapha and midrashic literature contain many descriptions of angels intervening in fights on Israel's side.[4]

2. *The four angels.*—The visible expression of the angels' participation as Israel's defenders in war we find in DSW ix, 14–16. The shields of the four ' towers ' are inscribed with the names of the four angels, one name being on the shields of each tower.[5] ' On all the shields of the towers they shall write, on the first " Michael ", [on the second " Gabriel ", on the third] " Sariel ", on the fourth " Raphael " '.

The four archangels together as guardians appear also in the Apocrypha and Pseudepigraphia and in Rabbinic literature. However, it is the names of the angels mentioned which are of special interest in the above description, more precisely the name Sariel in place of Uriel. The following table shows the order of names in the principal sources :[6]

---

[1] See comm. on i, 10–11 ; vii, 6 ; xii, 4–5 ; xv, 14 ; xviii, 2.

[2] By leading the people (Ex. xxiii, 20) ; driving out the Canaanites (ib. xxxiii, 2) ; destroying Sennacherib's camp (2 Kings xix, 35 ; 2 Chr. xxxii, 21) ; cf. also Ps. xxxi, 6 ; etc.

[3] In his prayer, Judas recalls the angel who destroyed Sennacherib (1 Macc. vii, 14) and asks him to be sent to destroy the Greeks (2 Macc. xv, 23) ; cf. ch. 8, § 5 (1). Angels appear to help him (2 Macc. x, 29) ; and he requests an angel's help at Beth Zur (2 Macc. xi, 6) ; cf. also 4 Macc. iv, 4.

[4] Very frequent. Cf. e.g. En. lvi, 5. Also Num. Rabba xvi : ' At the Red Sea I descended for your sake at the head of millions of myriads of myriads of angels and appointed for each of you two angels, one to help him in girding on his weapons, the other to place a crown upon his head ' ; B.T. Ḥag. 14b : ' The Shekinah is with us and the ministering angels accompany us,' close in wording to DSW xii, 7–8.

[5] See ch. 7, § 7 (2) ; comm. on ix, 14–16.

[6] Including some secondary sources representing various periods.

INTRODUCTION

Source	Names of Angels			
Enoch ix, 1 (Greek MS.)	Michael	Uriel [1]	Raphael [1]	Gabriel
Enoch xl, 9	Michael	Raphael	Gabriel	Phanuel
Enoch liv, 6	Michael	Gabriel	Raphael	Phanuel
Enoch lxxi, 8	Michael	Gabriel	Raphael	Phanuel
Enoch, lxxi, 8	Michael	Gabriel	Raphael	Phanuel
Book of Adam and Eve xl, 3 [2]	Michael	Gabriel	Uriel	Raphael
Num. Rabbah ii, 10	Michael	Gabriel	Uriel	Raphael
Pesiqta Rabbathi xlvi	Michael	Gabriel	Uriel	Raphael
Pirqe Rabbi Eliezer iv	Michael	Gabriel	Uriel	Raphael
Seder Gan Eden [3]	Michael	Gabriel	Raphael	Nuriel

The table shows the following facts:

(1) Michael, Gabriel, and Raphael are mentioned in all the versions;[4]

(2) In Enoch xl–lxxii the fourth angel is Phanuel and not Uriel;

(3) The Midrashim always have Uriel;

(4) Sariel is not mentioned amongst the four angels in any of these sources.[5]

On the other hand, the list of the seven principal angels and their functions in Enoch xx, according to the Greek text (G^g [1,2]) is of special interest:

(1) Uriel, (2) Raphael, (3) Raguel, (4) Michael, (5) Sariel,[6] (6) Gabriel, (7) Remiel.[7]

Sariel was at some time or in some circles reckoned equal in rank with the other angels in the list of the four; Phanuel, who is in other parts of Enoch the fourth angel—in place of Uriel—does not occur in this list.

Were it possible to give an exact date for the composition of the different parts of Enoch, this would thus help in dating DSW. The period when the 'Similitudes' (chs. xxxvii–lxxi) were written, in which not Uriel but Phanuel appears, is the most likely one. The identity of

---

[1] The Eth. MSS. mostly omit Raphael and have, with the exception of *tu*, Suriel for Uriel; one group has Suryāl and Uryāl (in some MSS. Suryān and Uryān); correct accordingly the note in Charles, *Apocr.* ii, 192. The angel which in x, 1, is called Uriel in G^g, appears as *Istrael* in G^g, as *Asreelyor*, etc., in Eth.

[2] Cf. Kahana, *Sefarim Ḥiẓonim* i, 16; Charles, *Apocr.* ii, 151.

[3] Version B, in BHM iii, 138.

[4] B.T. Yoma 37a, the angels who appeared to Abraham are named as Michael, Gabriel, and Raphael; Dt. Rabba xi Moses is buried by Michael, Gabriel, and Zagzag'el (?).

[5] See n. 1.

[6] Eth. *Sarāqā'ēl*.

[7] Cf. Charles ibid.

the fourth angel does not yet seem to have been fixed for Sariel to have appeared temporarily in this role.[1]

3. '*Uriel*' vs. '*Sariel*'.—It is instructive to compare the functions of Uriel and Sariel. There is no unanimity in our sources concerning Uriel's tasks.[2] He informs Noah of the approaching end (Enoch x); according to ch. xx (where he is listed with Sariel) he is set up 'over the world and over Tartarus'[3]; in ch. lxxv he is appointed over the luminaries; according to 4 Ezra x, 27, Uriel answers the questions of Ezra. According to some Midrashim Uriel stands to the left of the Throne of Glory, corresponding to the north, 'whence darkness goes forth to the world', and to Dan (the northernmost tribe) which 'is darkness', 'which darkens the world' (Num. Rabbah ii, 9; Pesiqta Rabbathi, xlvi). By deriving Uri-el from light (*or*) this explains his position over against darkness or north: 'For the Torah, Prophets and Hagiographa by which God atones [and gives light] for Israel as is written "though I sit in darkness, the Lord is a light unto me" (Micah, vii, 8)' (ib.).

Analysis of the sources proves that Uriel was the only archangel about whose duties opinions differed. On the one hand he was regarded as the angel appointed over hell-fire, over darkness[4] and the end of all flesh; on the other, as the angel set up over the luminaries. The double meaning of אור : *ur* 'fire', and *or* 'luminary', may have something to do with these differences of opinion.[4] The Midrashim just quoted belongs to a period which regarded Uriel as the angel of light, and their explanations justify the tradition according to which Uriel was placed to the left of the throne, corresponding to north and darkness.[4]

As shown above, the sect identified Michael, not Uriel as the prince of light. Hence the omission of Uriel from the list of the four angels is no accident.

---

[1] Cf. Charles, *Apocr.* ii, 170. Without entering into the question of the validity of his datings of the different parts of *Enoch*—some of which may need revision in the light of the DSS—we may note that he considers the 'Similitudes' to be the latest part and dates it in the end of the Hasmonean period, before Herod (cf. ch. 10).

[2] Cf. J. Guttmann, *Enc. 'Ivrith* ii, 259–60.

[3] The tasks of the angels mentioned in this chapter do not include one appointed over the luminaries.

[4] Cf. 'darkness of eternal fire', DSD ii, 8. Box, in Charles, *Apocr.* ii, 564: 'Later he became (mistakenly) associated with light (Heb. *ōr*) and was regarded as the enlightener.' See also Tur-Sinai, *Enc. Miqr.* i, 179 sq. s.v. *Urim we-Tummim*. Num. Rabba ii, 9, and *Midrash Konen*, BHM ii, 39: 'Uriel is in the north on His left, facing Dan, who is darkness. Why is he called Uriel? Corresponding to Torah (root ירה), Prophets and Hagiographa.'

As for Sariel, according to Enoch xx, 6 he is set over the ' spirits, who sin in the spirit ', but in later Kabbalistic sources a tradition is preserved which regards Sariel as the angel appointed over the winds of the south,[1] whence according to Enoch lxxvi, 8 went forth ' fragrant smells, and dew and rain and prosperity and health ',[2] as also in the Midrash : ' South—blessed dew and blessed rain go forth into the world ' (Num. Rabbah ii).

By writing the name of one angel on the shields of each of the four towers, the sect expressed the belief, also found in the Pseudepigrapha and Rabbinic literature, that the four angels personally lead the four units. Cf. : ' Four companies of Serving Angels give praise before God. The first company under Michael at His right, the second company under Gabriel at His left, the third company under Uriel before Him, the fourth company under Raphael behind Him and the divine presence in the middle ' (PRE iv).[3]

Unfortunately most of the part of the scroll (ix, 16) which gives the order of the towers according to the names of the angels is lost, which makes comparison with the above source difficult. I have provisionally restored : ' Michael and Gabriel on [the right side and Sariel and Raphael on the left side] '.[4]

§ 7. 'The Elect of the Holy People' and the angels

We must briefly discuss the sect's view on the position of the righteous and the angels. The problem of the belief of the sect in immortality of the soul has been extensively discussed in relation to the tenets attributed to the Essenes by Philo and Josephus. Without attempting a solution of this problem,[5] we ought to point out a number of descriptions in DSW and other scrolls, which show the 'elect of the holy people' together with the angels which stand before God, as well as parallels in

---

[1] Cf. M. Schwab, *Vocabulaire de l'Angélologie* etc., 1898, p. 260, and ib. 205 on Sariel ; *Hekhaloth Rabbathi*, BHM iii, 88 sq., 99 ; B.T. Ber. 51a ; Charles, *Apocr.* ii, 191, n. on *Sarial* ; in Ps.-Philo (Cohn, JQR 10 (1898), 305) *Seruihel* assists David against Goliath ; ib. p. 297 *Zeruel* assists Kenaz. See in particular Polotsky, ' Suriel der Trompeter,' *Muséon* 49 (1936), 231–43 (to which Prof. G. Sholem kindly drew my attention).

[2] En. lxxvii, 1 : ' the south, because the Most High will descend there ' (see Charles's note).

[3] Cf. the midrash works quoted in the table, and G. Friedländer, *Pirke R. Eliezer*, 1916, p. 22, in connexion with the recital of *Shema'* after retiring ; Cant. Rabba ad iii, 6 : ' like the *deghalim* up on high, such as Michael and his *deghel*, and Gabriel and his *deghel*.'

[4] For restoration and parallels see comm.

[5] Grinz, *Sinai* 32 (5713), 21 sq., compares the theology of the DSS, the Pseudepigrapha and Rabb. with what we know of Essene tenets.

the Apocrypha and Pseudepigrapha. Many passages in the scrolls show that the 'Sons of Light', 'the Righteous', 'the elect of the holy people' are in one and the same 'lot' as the angels, e.g. : 'And He has given to them an inheritance to the lot of the holy ones ; and with the sons of Heaven He has associated their assembly for a community council' (DSD, xi, 7-8) ; 'to be in a community with the sons of Thy truth and in a lot with Thine holy ones' (DST, xi, 11-12) ; 'so that they may stand amongst the host of holy ones and appear in communion with the congregation of the children of heaven, Thou hast allotted to man an everlasting portion amongst the spirits of wisdom to praise Thy name in communion' (DST, iii, 21-23) ; 'to all men of Thy council and in one lot with the angels of the divine presence'[1] (DST, vi, 13).

However, the most detailed description is in DSW, xii, 1-4. It establishes that the elect of the holy people are in heaven together with the angels before God and are grouped in 'thousands' and 'myriads' exactly like the angels.

Of special interest is the similarity with Enoch xliii : 'And I saw other lightnings and the stars of heaven, and I saw how He called them all by their *names* and they hearkened unto Him. And I saw how they are weighed in a righteous balance according to their proportions of light and the wind of their spaces and the day of their appearing, and how their revolution produces lightning and their revolution according to the *number* of the angels, and they keep faith with each other. And I asked the angel who went with me who showed me what was hidden : " What are these ? " And he said to me : " The Lord of Spirits hath showed Thee their parable : these are the *names* of the holy ones who dwell on the earth and believe in the name of the Lord of Spirits for ever and ever " '.[2]

This similarity appears also in ch. civ, addressing the righteous : 'I swear unto you, that in heaven the angels remember you for good before the glory of the Great One : and your names are written before the glory of the Great One . . . be hopeful, and cast not away your hope ; for ye shall have great joy as the angels of heaven . . . for ye shall become companions of the hosts of heaven'.[3]

This rounds off the picture of collaboration in this war : Not only will the angels fight side by side with the earthly 'holy people' (xii,

---

[1] Cf. § 2 (6).
[2] The word which Charles translates 'revolution' is probably a rendering of *těqufatham*, found in a very similar context DSD x, 3-4.
[3] Cf. DSW xii, 1-4.

7-8), but also the 'elect of the holy people', i.e. former earth-dwellers now in heaven, will fight side by side with the angels.[1]

§ 8. THE LOT OF LIGHT AND THE LOT OF DARKNESS

An analysis of the sect's views on this subject lies outside the scope of the present study,[2] for the scroll does not intend to explain the theory of light and darkness to the sect, which had on this subject[3] other writings. This determinist and dualist theory is defined especially in DSD, iii, 13-25[4] of which the author of DSW makes frequent use.[5] His purpose was to *apply* this doctrine to the war between the two opposing forces on the day appointed, or as DSD, iii, 18 has it, 'the appointed time of His visitation'. He is concerned with defining who were the Sons of Light and the Sons of Darkness in his own time.

The Sons of Light are the 'exiles of the Sons of Light' (i.e. the sect) who are composed of Levi, Judah, and Benjamin. At the time these dwell 'in the wilderness of the nations'. The Lord Himself will fight for the Lot of Light, the Lot of God, assisted by the 'angel of light', Michael.

The Sons of Darkness are the Kittim and the rest of Israel's traditional enemies, as well as the 'offenders against the covenant' from amongst Israel. To their aid comes Belial with all the 'spirits of his lot' and the 'angels of destruction' 'who walk in the boundaries of destruction and unto it shall be their desire altogether' (DSW, xiii, 12).

---

[1] Grinz, op. cit. p. 23, gives some Rabb. parallels.

[2] See Aalen, passim; Loewenstamm, *Enc. Miqr.* i, 168 sq.; cf. also p. 235, n. 5, and comm. on xii, 14.

[3] Cf. ch. 1, §§ 2, 6.

[4] Cf. Slav. Enoch xi, 65; cf. Charles, *Apocr.* ii, 499, for early Christian parallels. Cf. also Test. Asher i, 3 sq.; Test. Levi xiv, 4; xix, 1; Test. Joseph xx, 2;

Dream of Mordecai 7 (Charles, *Apocr.* i, 683), on the 'two lots'. For Christian use of 'Sons of Light' see Tournay, RB 56 (1949), 218, n. 9; Brownlee, *Manual* p. 8, n. 20. Cf. also S. Lieberman, *Hellenism in Jewish Palestine* 1950, pp. 12-13, who quotes Test. Job xliii, 6, where Elihu 'is a son of darkness, not of light'.

[5] Cf. §§ 3-5 and comm. on xiii, xiv (sections 19 and 21), xvii, 5.

Chapter 10

THE DATE OF THE SCROLL AND THE IDENTITY OF THE SECT

§ 1. GENERAL REMARKS

We must beware, at this stage, of trying to reach too definite conclusions about the date of the scroll and the identity of the sect to which its author belonged. This twofold problem, more than any other discussed in this Introduction, still requires systematic research, taking into account not only all material published so far, but that which has been discovered but not yet published.

Taking these limitations into consideration, this chapter merely intends to gather up a number of points discussed at length in the introduction and the commentary, which may help us in supplying, if not a complete, at least a partial answer to these problems.

In our endeavour to date the scroll we must distinguish between three distinct aspects:

(a) The date of composition;
(b) The date of the copy in our possession;
(c) The date when it was placed in the cave.

The third problem applies equally to all the scrolls or at least to those found in the same cave, e.g. the two Isaiah manuscripts, DSH, DSD, DST, etc.[1] The exact answer to this question is supplied by the excavations in the caves and in Khirbet Qumran. The results of excavations, and especially the numerous coins found at Khirbet Qumran, enable us to fix with some certainty the latest period in which the scrolls could have been hidden at 70 A.D.[2]

This date supplies part of the answer to the second problem, since the scroll cannot have been copied later than 70 A.D. A more exact dating is not yet possible. We must be content with assuming that the scroll was copied before the destruction of the Temple, probably[3] in the second half of the first century B.C. or in the first half of the first century A.D.[4]

---

[1] Cf. *Qumran* I, 46–7.
[2] RB 59 (1954), 206–236; 63 (1956), 533–577.
[3] Cf. Sukenik, *M.G.* i, 19.
[4] The Murabba'at documents clearly show the difference between both types of writing used at Qumran and that of the early second century.

The answer to the first problem, the time of composition, can be supplied, if at all, only by its contents.

§ 2. THE CONTENTS OF THE SCROLL AND THE TIME OF ITS COMPOSITION

In examining the contents of the scroll for the purpose of dating, we must concentrate on matter not supplied by the other scrolls. There are two important reasons for this :

(*a*) An examination of those matters which have a parallel in other scrolls is important for determining the relative dating. It is however liable to lead us into the same blind alley with regard to information on the historical interpretation of which scholars have so far been unable to agree.[1]

(*b*) The difference between DSW and the other scrolls is in the Battle *Serekh* Series,[2] which describes the military structure, weapons and methods of warfare. If we assume that these descriptions are based both on visual experience and on written sources,[3] they will provide an important means for dating the scroll's composition. This applies especially to details which have no connexion with the O.T. and point to military sources of the period of the scroll. These subjects and their connexion with the Hellenistic, Hasmonean and Roman methods of warfare are dealt with at length in the introduction.[4]

While examining these subjects, it must be remembered that it is precisely the small, relatively unimportant details, which are liable to shed light on the time of the composition, because in dealing with them the author had no tendentious aims, as he may have had in the descriptions of important and central matters. On the other hand, we would refer the reader to our reservations in ch. 7 § 1, concerning the use of military criteria for dating purposes.

The following table records some points, both military and other, which may have a bearing on the date :[5]

---

[1] For a resumé of dates proposed see Vermès, *Discovery in the Judean Desert* pp. 67–70 ; Rowley, ' The Covenanters of Damascus and the Dead Sea Scrolls,' *Bull. J. Rylands Library* 35 (1952–3), 111 sq. ; M. Burrows, *More Light on the Dead Sea Scrolls* 1958, p. 191 sq.

[2] Cf. ch. 1, § 3, section 4 onwards.

[3] For reasons see ch. 1, § 6.

[4] See tables in ch. 1, § 4, and list of contents of the Introduction.

[5] Explanations : col. 1 lists the subjects, discussion of which is found in references in col. 2. Sigla : + found in period in question ; − not found, or the opposite found ; (+), (−) denote doubt, with the probability towards positive or negative connexion. Absence of siglum in any case denotes negative rather than positive connexion.

DATE OF THE SCROLL AND IDENTITY OF THE SECT

Subject	References to Introduction and Commentary	Pre-Roman Hellenistic–Hasmonean			Roman	
		Whole period	2nd cent. B.C.	100–63 B.C.	Whole period	63 B.C.–1 A.D.	1–70 A.D.
Kittim sacrificing to their standards (Pesher Habakkuk vi, 3–5)	Ch. 3, § 10, and n. 5, p. 63	—			+		
'Kittim of Asshur' and 'Kittim in Egypt'	Ch. 2, § 3 (2); ch. 8, § 5 (sect. 15), comm. on i, 6; xi, 11–12; xix, sect. 31	+			+		
'King of the Kittim'	xv, 2; xix, 10	+			(+)	+ (44 B.C. ?)	+
Sariel in place of Uriel	Ch. 9, § 6 (2)						
Use of banner in battles	Ch. 3, § 10	(—)			+		
Use of trumpets for signalling	Ch. 5, § 10	(—)			+		
The oblong rectangular infantry shield and its measurements	Ch. 6, § 2	—			+	+	+
The round shield of the (heavy) cavalry	Ch. 6, § 2 (3)	+				+	—
Shin-guards for the (heavy) cavalry only	Ch. 6, § 3	—			+		
Shape and measurements of the sword	Ch. 6, § 6 (8)	—			+		
Method of girding on the sword	Ch. 6, § 6 (8)					+ (Caesar) (+) (Augustus)	
Absence of dagger	Ch. 6, n. 1, p. 129					+	
Measurements of spear	Ch. 6, § 11 (4)	(—)			(+)		
Absence of battle chariots	Ch. 7, § 6, n. 2, p. 179	—			+		
Absence of elephants	Ch. 7, § 6, n. 2, p. 179	—			+		
'Battle Intervals'	Ch. 7, § 2 (4)	—			+		
Distinction and use of 'skirmishing battalions' and 'front formations'	Ch. 7, § 4 (6)	—			+		
Structure and numbers of the front formation	Ch. 7, § 5 (10)	—				+ Caesar	
'The replacement for battle'	Ch. 7, § 5 (9)	—			+		
Number of 'frontal arrays'	Ch. 7, § 5 (9)	—			(+)		
Types of cavalry	Ch. 7, § 6 (5)	—			+		
The 'towers' and tactical formations	Ch. 7, § 7	(—)			(+)		

The table shows that in all items the indication is positive or partly positive for the Roman period, but for the pre-Roman period it is negative in at least twelve instances, and in a further four instances negative though not absolutely so. With regard to the Roman period we find that in seventeen instances the exact time within that period cannot be determined, in six cases the information points towards the second half of the first century B.C.; in two cases it is clearly against the first century A.D. With all due reserve, we may perhaps conclude that DSW was composed after the Roman conquest but before the end of Herod's reign.[1]

§ 3. THE SECT.

As with the problem of dating, scholars differ widely in their attempts to identify the sect of the scrolls with one of the sects known to us from other sources. In fact, the sect has been identified by various scholars with every single one of the numerous sects which existed toward the end and after the period of the Second Temple.[2] The reason is that the material we now possess on the tenets and constitution of the scrolls sect far exceeds our information on any sect in the period under discussion. Many scholars now accept the view, first suggested by E. L. Sukenik and developed by Dupont-Sommer, Brownlee, Grinz, De Vaux, and others[3] that the sect of the scrolls were Essenes. This is supported by two important facts: (*a*) The sect's place of habitation (Khirbet Qumran) agrees with that of the Essenes according to Pliny;[4] (*b*) the laws and customs of the sect, as set out especially in DSD, closely resemble in important points what Philo and Josephus tell us about the Essenes.[5] I have found no convincing proof for this in DSW, but it should be noted that no statement in our scroll contradicts anything we know about the Essenes and it seems to me that in some cases points can be better explained on the basis of Josephus' statements about this sect.

---

[1] In fact our evidence partly points to the period of Caesar and the early Augustan age. Hence I cannot follow M. H. Segal (in *Aspects* p. 138 ff.) who—though accepting my view that DSW shows Roman military influence—maintains that this reflects conditions of the Hasmonean period.

[2] See note 1, p. 277.

[3] Cf. Vermès p. 21, p. 57 sq.

[4] *Hist. Nat.* V, xvii; cf. Dupont-Sommer, *Aperçus* p. 105 sq.

[5] Cf. preceding note; Grinz, *Sinai* 32 (5713), 13 sq.; Burrows, *Oudt. St.* 8 (1950), 156-192.

Chapter 11

THE SCROLL

§ 1. GENERAL REMARKS

DSW is described in *M.G.* I, 18–21; II, 51; *Oẓar* 31–2, where there are also photographs of the scroll before and after unrolling. For a comparative table of the script, see above, fig. 20, *M.G.* II, 23. Before the complete publication of the text in *Oẓar*, E. L. Sukenik published the following portions: col. viii (which he called vii) in *M.G.* I, Pl. VIII; xii, 9–15 in transliteration only, in *M.G.* I, 20, and again, with corrections and commentary, ib. II, 51–2; the left half of col. xiv (which he called xii) ib. I Pl. IX, and transliteration of lines 2–5 ib. p. 24; the right half of col. xv (which he called xiii) ib.; notes on xiv–xv ib. p. 25–6. Two fragments in the possession of the Department of Antiquities of the Hashemite Kingdom of Jordan were published by J. T. Milik in *Qumran I*, Pl. XXXI, called by him frg. 33 (1) and 33 (2). The first, as Milik (ib. p. 135) saw, belongs to col. xviii; the second I have succeeded (in combination with frg. 8) in fitting into col. xix; cf. also ch. 1 n. 34. Both are reprinted, in an improved reading, in the appendix.

The following notes are not intended to exhaust the peculiarities of the script and the spelling (both of which require much further study), but deal briefly with some technical aspects: measurements, number of sheets and columns, number of lines per column, division into sections, scribal errors and corrections, and finally the spelling only where it is inconsistent.

§ 2. MEASUREMENTS

The scroll is made of leather, written on the hairy side. This, as Sukenik, *M.G.* I, 11, has pointed out, agrees with the regulations of P.T. Meg. i, 11, 71*d*. At present the scroll is *c.* 2 m. 90 cm. long (a little over 9 ft.), and it contains 19 columns, distributed over five sheets of skin:

Sheet 1	.	.	.	i–iv	4 columns
,, 2	.	.	.	v–x	6 ,,
,, 3	.	.	.	xi–xv	5 ,,
,, 4	.	.	.	xvi–xviii	3 ,,

Of the fifth sheet only one col. is partly preserved. Its exact position in the sheet cannot be established, but there are traces of one col.

following it ; cf. p. 13, n. 4. The first sheet begins with a blank portion of 40 cm. (16 in.) length, which was used to protect the outside of the scroll when rolled, see Sukenik, *M.G.* I, 18. The post-Talmudic *Massekheth Soférim* (ed. M. Higger, N.Y. 5697, ii, 10) prescribes : ' No sheet should have less than three columns or more than eight '.

Since all columns are eaten away at the bottom, the original height of the strip cannot be definitely established. The best-preserved columns are a little over 16 cm. (6¼ in.) high. The following table shows the number of lines in each col., including those of which mere traces have survived :

i	ii	iii	iv	v	vi	vii	viii	ix	x	xi	xii	xiii	xiv	xv	xvi	xvii	xviii	xix
17	16	17	17	17	16	17	18	18	18	18	17	17	18	15	15	17	14	13

If the suggested restoration of col. viii (see comm. ib. 18–20) proves correct, then the original cols. had about 20 lines ; so already Sukenik, *M.G.* I, 18. The margin at the top is on the average 30 mm. (1·2 in.), between columns 19 mm. (0·8 in.). This agrees with B. T. Men. 30*a*, *Mass. Sof.* ii, 4–5, see p. 116, n. 2.

All sections begin at the right margin. If the preceding section ends so as to leave at least half the line blank, no further spacing is made ; if the preceding line takes up more than half the column width, a whole line is left blank. Exceptions to this rule are sections 6 and 28. This is prescribed by Maimonides, *Code*, Hilkhoth Sefer Torah, viii, 1.

§ 3. THE WRITING

The elegant precise *ductus* of the Scroll resembles that of DSI*b*, DSH, and the first hand of DST, and differs sharply from that used in DSD and DSI*a*. The scribe consistently differentiates between medial and final forms of מנצפ״ך and between *resh* and *daleth* ; he often confuses *waw* and *yodh* but at times clearly distinguishes them (see, however, comm. xviii, 9).[1]

The letters are written *below* horizontal lines carefully ruled across a whole sheet at a time. Across these are ruled vertical lines to mark the right and left margins of each column. Sukenik, *M.G.* I, 11, quoted P.T. Meg. i, 11, 71*d* ; ' It is a *halakhah* given to Moses on Sinai that one should write on leather and with ink, and rule the lines with a reed '. Ib. he quoted, in connexion with the vertical lines, B.T. Men. 30*a* : ' If one has to write a word of five letters, let him not write two letters within the column and three outside it ', cf. also *Mass. Sof.* p. 379.

---

[1] On the script see now N. Avigad, ' The Palæography of the Dead Sea Scrolls, etc.', *Aspects*, pp. 71 ff. (The ' Herodian ' group).

THE SCROLL

Our scribe generally endeavours to remain within the column, and where he has to write across the line, he is careful not to write more than half the letters of the word beyond it (see, however, iv, 9; xi, 6; xii, 7; xvi, 9; xviii, 2, 9).

Almost everywhere the scribe has left between lines a space equal to the full height of a line (from the top of a *lamedh* to the lower ends of סוֹפ״ךְ), and between adjoining letters the width of a narrow letter, in keeping with *Mass. Sof.* ii, 2 : ' Between lines one must leave the width of a full line, between words the width of a full letter, between letters the breadth of a hair '.

§ 4. IRREGULARITIES AND CORRECTIONS

With all his care, the scribe was not able to avoid mistakes and irregularities, some of which were due to faults in the skin, and had to correct them. Some of these corrections may have been made by another scribe, and reflect not mistakes of the first scribe, but different texts. Because of the importance of this matter and the variety of methods of correction, we reproduce the mistakes and corrections on figs. 18–19, classified in seven groups.

Group A (fig. 18, 1–9) comprises ten passages where the scribe had to leave a blank between words or in the middle of a word because of a fault in the skin. The faults are discernible in almost all cases in the original.

No. 1 : In order to avoid dividing גדול (as he did in no. 6), the scribe wrote the whole word to the left of the fault. Same for no. 4.

No. 3 : It is not clear whether the blank between the two words is here due to a fault in the skin (invisible to me) or to some other cause. Interesting is the curved horizontal line to indicate that the words belong together.

No. 6 : After writing the first three letters, the scribe was forced to leave a blank, and thus divide the word נשמחה into two.

No. 8 : A clear case of a texture fault necessitating blanks in two lines.

No. 9 : Possibly due to a texture fault, cf. comm. ad loc.

Group B (fig. 18, 10–13) comprises cases where the scribe inadvertently omitted a word, and then placed it above the line, in no. 10 above the word following, in 11 and 12 between two words. In no. 13 there is a doubt, cf. comm. ad loc.

Group C (fig. 18, 14–22) are cases of the omission of one (nos. 14–16, 20, 22), or two (nos. 18, 19) letters. It is interesting that nos. 18–20 all concern the same word and in 18 and 19 the same letters within it.

The corrections in nos. 15, 18–20, were probably made by the original scribe; we cannot be sure about 14, 16, 21, and particularly about 22. For the method, cf. *Mass. Sof.* v, 2 : ' If one has written יהודה and omitted the *daleth*, one should " suspend " it above '.

Group D (fig. 19, 1-3) : the scribe started writing a word or letter, then noticed it was wrong, stopped in the middle or partly erased what he had written, and continued with the correct form.

No. 1 : The word בשלושים or בעשרים, corrected into בתשע. The last *'ayin* seems to have become effaced, or perhaps was never written, though there is room for it. The other two cases are of phonetic interest : in no. 2 the scribe began writing *śar* with a *samekh*, in no. 3 *qarqar* with a *kaph*.

Group E (fig. 19, 4-6) : the scribe or the corrector ' dotted ' the word or letters that were wrong. Note that in no. 4 the *waw* is dotted in the middle, the *kaph* and *beth* above and below. In no. 5 the dotting shows that only the *kaph* is to be ignored. Interesting is the method employed in no. 6, where part of the word as originally written is to be read with the superscribed letters. The correction is stylistic and the superscribed writing awkward ; it is likely that we have here a correction by another hand. For the system of ' dotting ', see Sukenik, *M.G.* I, 12, on the *puncta extraordinaria*.

Group F (fig. 19, 7-11), corrections by erasing. These seem all to have been made by the original scribe, except perhaps for no. 11. This was an accepted method, cf. B.T. Men. 30*b* : ' If one errs in a divine name, one must erase what one has written '.

No. 7 combines three methods of correction. The scribe wrote סרובים, erased the *kaph* and wrote *resh* above it ; and changed the *resh* into *daleth* by adding a thorn at its right. For this cf. *Mass. Sof.* v, 2 : ' If one has written יהודה instead of יהוה, one must turn the *daleth* into a *he*, and erase the last *he* '.

No. 8 : Stylistic correction, see comm.

No. 9 : The first word of על כול has been erased, and a *beth* written over the second, thus giving us *bĕkhol*. Note that the correct letter was not written upon the erasure, apparently for fear of smudging.

No. 10 is the most interesting ; it makes use of all possible methods at once. Having written ארבעים ••• חמשים and wanting to correct it into חמשים ••• ששים the scribe (*a*) erased the *aleph*, (*b*) altered *resh* into *ḥeth* by adding a left leg and a thorn at the right, (*c*) altered *beth* into *mem*, (*d*) erased *'ayin* and wrote a *shin* above it, (*e*) erased *ḥeth* and *mem* and wrote *shin* above them. The two superscript *shins* closely resemble those of the original scribe, and the correction is probably his own.

No. 11 : Possibly a correction by another hand. The superscript מוֹעֵד is in a more awkward script and does not resemble the form the word has ib., lines 5 and 6.

Group G (fig. 19, 12) : Correction affecting three words, and necessitated, apparently, by their having become obliterated or perhaps smudged in writing owing to a texture fault which absorbed the ink, and seems to have been made by another hand. It is effected by bracketing the faulty words (the left bracket is broken in the middle, because of the narrow space between the words) and drawing a short horizontal line above and below the group (somewhat like that in fig. 18, 3). The corrector clearly had no alteration of the text in mind, and wrote above the group exactly what had been written originally.

§ 5. The Spelling

The spelling closely resembles that known to us from DSI*a*, DSH, DSD, DST, etc.

(*a*) Plene writings :

כִּיא (=כִּי), מִיא (=מִי), הוּאָה (=הוּא), הִיאָה (=הִיא), רוֹאשׁ (=ראשׁ), הראישונ(ה) (=הראשונ(ה)), לוֹא (=לא), תואכלנה (=תאכלנה)

(*b*) Imperfects with an added *waw* (cf. Yalon, *Sinai* 26 (5710), 278) :

יחלוצו, יכתובו, יעמודו, ירדופו, יסרוכו, תערוצו

(*c*) Suffixes second person with added *he* : Almost invariably —כֹה (Yalon, ib. 272); —תֹה (Yalon, 274); —כמה; —תמה (cf. ונזכרתמה x, 7 ; cf. Yalon 276).

These matters belong, properly speaking, to an investigation comprising all the Scrolls. It should be noted, however, that the scribe, side by side with the above forms, also uses those employed in MT and DSI*b*. At times both forms of a word appear on the same column. A particularly interesting feature is that the hymn which appears in col. xii in the typical DSS spelling, is repeated in col. xix in the same hand, but with a less 'typical' spelling in many words (cf. comm. col. xii, where all variants are adduced). In col. x, 2–8 the Pentateuchal quotations introduce the features of DSS spelling rather inconsistently, especially with regard to feature (*c*), see comm. ad loc.

The following list exhibits irregularities with respect to feature (*a*) :

(1) הבנים vi, 11 ; הבינים vi, 8 a. fr., cf. ch. 7 n. 83–88.

(2) הגויים vii, 2 a. fr. ; (ה)גואים xvi, 1 ; xii, 13. גוים xix, 6, 10.

(3) ההואה xviii, 5 a. fr. ; ההוא xix, 9.

(4) יָדִי viii, 5, 7, 12 ; יָידִי xvii. 11.

(5) כְּמוֹהָה xviii, 9 ; כְּמוֹ i, 12.

(6) הַלּוֹהֵב v, 7, 10 (שַׁלְהוֹבֶת vi, 3) ; הַלַּהַב v, 10.

(7) הַלְוִיִּם ii, 2 a. fr. ; הַלְוִים xvi, 6.

(8) מֵאָדָה xii, 12 ; מוֹאָדָה xix, 5.

(9) מַרְדֻּף iii, 1, 9 ; vii, 12 ; מַרְדּוּף ix, 6.

(10) הַנָּשִׂיא iii, 15; v, 1 ; נְשִׂי iii, 14 ; iv. 1.

(11) עוּשָׁרוֹת ii, 16 ; iv, 4 ; עֲשָׁרוֹתָיו iv, 3.

(12) כּוֹהֵן הָרֹאשׁ ii, 1 ; xvi, 4 ; כּוֹהֵן הָרוֹאשׁ xvi, 11 ; xviii, 5 ; xix, 11.

(12a) רֹאשׁ of a lance, v, 11 ; רֹאוּשׁ of a sword, v, 12.

See further in the comm. concerning :

אֲבֹרְנַי, בַּדְנַי v, 6, 9 ; תִּשְׁבּוֹחַת iv, 8 ; יְעוּרְכוּה ii, 9 ; מִלְחַמְתָּה xvii, 1 ; פּוֹרָת ii, 12 ; and about כְּתִיִּים as against the כְּתִיאִים of DSH in ch. 2 § 3. (2).

§ 6. The Present Edition

The text printed here is based upon the transliteration in E. L. Sukenik's posthumous *Oẓar ha-Mĕgilloth ha-Gĕnuzoth*, except for some very minor changes. That transliteration, like those in the American *Dead Sea Scrolls of St. Mark's Monastery*, refrained from any restoration of missing or illegible matter. Great care has been taken in the text here to distinguish clearly between what can be read with certainty (printed in large letters), restorations based on context (small letters in brackets, even where the restoration exactly fits the gap), and restorations which to me seem certain (large letters in brackets). Letters extant in remnants, however small, are printed without brackets, but the degree of certainty with which they can be recognized is indicated by signs above them.

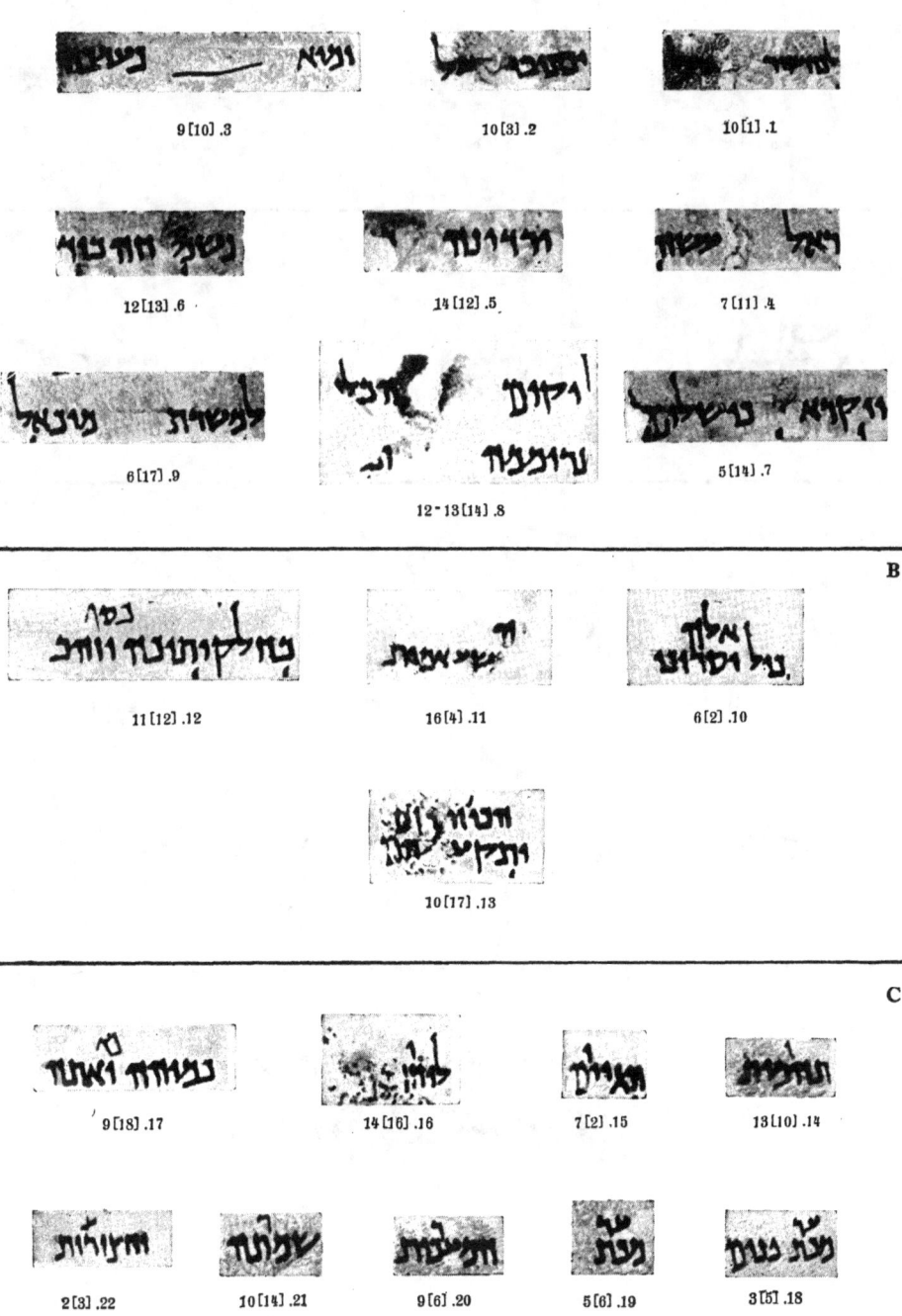

Fig. 18. Scribal errors in the scroll, groups A–C.

D

6[11].3   3[3].2   10[2].1

E

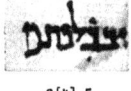
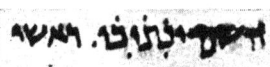

8[11].6   6[4].5   4[3].4

F

1[15].9   12[13].8   4[5].7

12[15].11   1[7].10

G

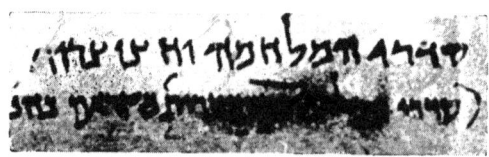

1[3].12

Fig. 19. Scribal errors in the scroll, groups D–G.

PART TWO

TEXT, TRANSLATION AND COMMENTARY

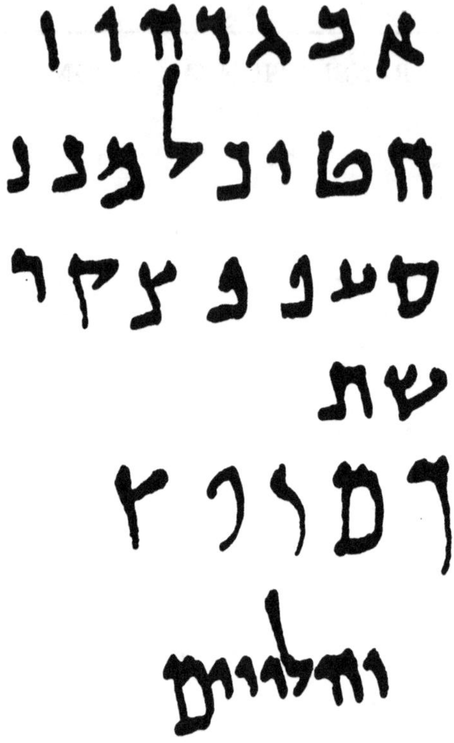

אבגדוהו
חטינלמנ
סעפצקר
שת

רמונצ

והלויים

Fig. 20. The alphabet of the scroll, and the word והלויים. *(The table is made up of photographs of individual letters.)*

CONVENTIONS

TEXT

הכוהנים	Words and letters clearly legible in the MS.
[הכוהנים]	Restored with certainty.
[הֹכֹוֹהֹנֹיֹםֹ]	Restored almost with certainty.
[הכוהנים]	Restored in accordance with the context.
הֹכֹוֹהֹנֹיֹםֹ	Partly visible, restored with certainty.
הֹכֹוֹהֹנֹיֹםֹ	Partly visible, but the restoration not certain.
-	Partly visible letter, no restoration possible.
/	Letter obliterated or erased in the MS.
לְהִלָּחֵם	Letter dotted in the MS.
[. . . .]	Gap equivalent to four letters.
[- - - -]	Gap equivalent to four average words.

TRANSLATION

|	Beginning of new line in the text.
[great]	Restored in the text.
shall be	Words without equivalent in the Hebrew.
(great)	Explanations, alternative translations (OR :), etc.

COMMENTARY

The following signs and conventions have been adopted :

= denotes that the words so glossed are a quotation.

¶ denotes that the words so glossed are an allusion to the O.T. passage specified.

cf. before a reference to Scripture implies linguistic similarity or connexion in subject-matter, without suggesting that the author of the scroll had that passage in mind.

... in a lemma means that the intervening words of the text are to be supplied.

— in a lemma means that the note refers only to the words quoted, though these are in the text separated by other words.

ch. refers to the chapters of the Introduction.

Roman numbers without further specification refer to columns of DSW.

Square brackets showing restorations have been omitted in the lemmas except where they seemed essential.

COLUMN I

SECTION 1

And th[is is the book of the disposition of] the war. The first engagement of the Sons of Light *shall be* to attack the lot of the Sons of Darkness, the army of Belial, the troop of Edom and Moab, and the sons of Ammon |
2. and the army [of the dwellers of] Philistia and the troops of the Kittim of Asshur, and in league with them the offenders against the covenant. The sons of Levi, the sons of Judah, and the sons of Benjamin, the exiles
3. of the wilderness, they shall fight against them | with [   ], yea, against all their troops, when the exiles of the Sons of Light return from the Wilderness of the Nations to encamp in the Wilderness of Jerusalem.

Column I

The blank column preceding this one shows it to have been the first in the scroll. The right-hand fragment has shrunk, and after fitting the two parts together at the level of line 11, the right-hand remnants of the preceding lines appear on the photograph somewhat lower than the corresponding lines.

and this ... the war. In this scroll, unlike some others, there is no indention at the beginning of a section. The restoration is based on DSD, v, 1; CDC, x, 4; xiv, 12, as well as DSW, xv, 5. Cf. ch. 1 §§ 1, 6.

the first. The word (lit. ' beginning ') has both the temporal sense and that of ' the most important ', cf. Ps. cxi, 10; Pr. i, 7; Ecclus. i, 12 (14). The enemies enumerated here are the principal ones, who must be eliminated even before the sect can deal with ' the Kittim in Egypt ' (line 4). Cf. ch. 2 §§ 1, 3. The choice of the word may have been influenced by ' the first (A.V. ' chief ') of the sons of Ammon ' in Dn. xi, 41, since the influence of that chapter is noticeable throughout this section.

engagement. Lit. ' putting forth the hand ', cf. Isa. xi, 14, to which this may be an allusion. The verbal phrase is used in the same meaning Dn. xi, 42; Est. ix, 2; DSW xvii, 13; CDC xii, 6; pPs 37 on vs. 14-15 (JBL 75 (1956) 95) line 3;

pHosea (quoted by Allegro, ibid. p. 93). In a non-military sense DSD x, 13; Qumran I, p. 111, ii, 20.

to attack. So used in Ju. x, 18 (A.V. ' begin '); Ezek. xx, 9; 22. Cf. P. P. Saydon, ' The Inceptive Imperfect in Hebrew and the Verb החל " to begin " ', Biblica 35 (1954) 43 sq.

the lot. Occurs in the sense of ' pre-ordained segment ' (of humanity, of time, of an event, of a collection of objects), 16 times in DSW, 18 in DSD, 5 in DST, 3 in CDC. Similar uses in O.T. occur Ju. i, 3; Isa. xvii, 14; Ps. cxxv, 3. For the sense see p. 79, n. 1; for the conception of two ' lots ' ch. 9, § 8 (see also Lv. xvi, 8).

Sons of Darkness. The concept is fully explained in DSD iii, 13-25; see ch. 9, § 8.

army of Belial. On Belial see ch. 9, § 3. The army includes both the human enemies immediately specified and the ' spirits of Darkness ' and ' angels of destruction '.

Edom, etc. The list is influenced by 2 Kings xxiv, 2 (where Pesh. reads ' Edom ' for MT ' Aram '); Isa. xi, 14; Dn. xi, 41-2; see ch. 2, § 3 and p. 22, n. 1. Cf. further Num. Rabba xiv: ' in the Messianic age God will permit Israel to destroy these three (Philistines, Moab, and Edom) ', quoting in support, *inter alia*, Isa. xi, 14.

2. army. Or restore ח[י]ל, with 2 Sam. xxiii, 13 (so also 1Q2 Sam). The meaning of this word (which some emend to חות)

I

[א]

1. חז[ה ספר סרך] המלחמה ראשית משלוח יד בני אור להחל בגורל
בני חושך בחיל בליעל בגדוד אדום ומואב ובני עמון

2. וחי[ל יושבי] פלשת ובגדודי כתיי אשור ועמהם בעזר מרשיעי ברית
בני לוי ובני יהודה ובני בנימין גולת המדבר ילחמו בם

3. ב] [- -] לכול גדודיהם בשוב גולת בני אור ממדבר העמים לחנות
במדבר ירושלים ואחר המלחמה יעלו משם

is doubtful, but seems to be 'clan' or 'camp'.

dwellers. Restored after Ex. xv, 14. One might restore *gĕliloth* 'regions' with Joel, iv, 4.

Kittim. On this name see ch. 2, § 3 (2).

troops of the Kittim of Asshur. Allusion to 'troops of the Chaldees', 2 Kings xxiv, 2. In DSH ii, 12 'Chaldees' is glossed 'Kittim'.

in league. Cf. Dn. xi, 34. For 'with them', cf. e.g. 2 Chr. xx, 1; Ps. lxxxiii, 9.

offenders, etc. ¶ Dn. xi, 32; see ch. 2, § 3 (3). Cf. CDC xx, 25 'and with them the offenders of Judah'. Theoretically one might connect: 'the offenders . . . of the sons of Levi, etc.', but this seems improbable.

sons of Levi. etc. On the composition of the sect, see p. 212, n. 3, and ch. 10; for the order of enumeration ch. 3, § 7. The order recurs in DSW and agrees with that current in the Testaments of the Twelve Patriarchs, against Ezra i, 5; ix, 1; 2 Chr. xi, 11–13. On the 'three tribes' see ch. 3, § 4.

exiles of the wilderness. See comm. line 3.

fight. On Levi as warrior see Gn. xxxiv, 25; xlix, 5; 1 Chr. ii, 26; Test. Simeon v, 5; Test. Levi v, 3. Cf. p. 46, n. 3.

3. when . . . return. Cf. Ps. xiv, 7; liii, 7; cxvi, 1 sq. For this dating of the war, see ch. 2, § 6.

Wilderness of the Nations. ¶ Ezek. xx, 35. Cf. 'they that return from the wilderness', pPs. 37, ii, 1; pIsa. 10 (cf. Yadin, IEJ 7 (1957), 67); *Midrash of Messianic Signs*, BHM II, 58, sign VIII. See ch. 3, § 1 and ch. 10. For the sect's (partial ?) emigration to the desert, see DSD viii, 12–14. It may have followed the emigration to 'Damascus' or 'the land of Damascus' mentioned in CDC; some recent writers, however, identify the two, taking 'Damascus' as referring to the Qumran region, cf. R. North, "The Damascus of Qumran Geography', PEQ 87 (1955) 34 sq.; F. M. Cross, *The Ancient Library of Qumran*. p. 59. DST iv, 8–9 and DSH xi, 4–6 (if we read אבית גלותו with Habermann, Yalon, Barthélemy, De Vaux, and others; cf. Flusser, *Yediʿoth*, 17 (5713), 28 sq.) would date the exile to Qumran in the days of the Teacher of Righteousness, but if we compare the language of Ps. Sol. xvii, 17–20, we may be led to think that DSH merely employed a figure of speech. For the role of the desert as such in the life of the sect, see ch. 3, § 1.

Wilderness of Jerusalem. The phrase does not occur in the O.T. or in Rabb. literature. Compare perhaps Isa. lii, 9, *horvoth Yerushalayim*, and cf. ib. lxiv, 9.

4. After the battle they shall go up thence | against [all the troops of] the Kittim in Egypt. In His appointed time He shall go forth with great wrath to fight against the kings of the north, and His anger *shall be such as*
5. to destroy utterly and to cut off the horn | [of Belial.
    That shall be] a time of deliverance for the People of God,
        an appointed time of dominion for all men of His lot,
        and eternal annihilation for all the lot of Belial.
6.   There shall be [great] panic | [amongst] the sons of Japheth,
    Asshur shall fall, and none shall help him,
    and the dominion of the Kittim shall depart,
  so that wickedness be subdued without a remnant,
7.   and none shall escape | of [all Sons of] Darkness. |

Section 2

8. [Knowledge and] justice shall shine unto all ends of the world, shining more and more until all the appointed times of Darkness are completed. At the appointed time of God, His lofty majesty shall shine

---

the battle. i.e. the battle against the Kittim of Asshur and their allies in the Wilderness of Jerusalem, the first phase of the War, cf. ch. 2, § 3.

go up . . . against. i.e. fight, not in the local sense, as the journey from Palestine to Egypt is invariably described as 'going down'. The restoration of 'against' is not certain.

4. all the troops. The restoration fits the gap precisely.

Kittim in Egypt. Not 'of', as 'Kittim of Asshur'. This shows that the Kittim had an army in Egypt, not that they dwelt there. The war against this part of the Kittim is the second phase, preparatory to the fight against the 'kings of the north', which is part of the 'war of separate divisions', cf. ch. 2, § 4.

in His appointed time . . . with great wrath. ⁋ Dn. xi, 40–44, though the influence is only in language, not in meaning. For *qeẓ* 'pre-ordained period or moment of history', cf. Sukenik, MG I, 22; B. J. Roberts, BJRL 34 (1952), 380 sq.

kings of the north. See ch. 2, § 5.

wrath . . . anger. A frequent combination in O.T. descriptions of divine vengeance, cf. Isa. xlii, 25; lxvi, 15; Dn. ix, 16; with 'great': Jer. xxi, 5; xxxvi, 7, etc. Cf. DSW iii, 9; iv, 1; DSD ii, 15; iv, 12.

to cut off the horn. In the O.T. only the verbs *gdʻ* and *shbr* are used with 'horn'.

5. of Belial. The gap is just right for this restoration.

time of deliverance. ⁋ Isa. xlix, 8, where 'time' = 'deliverance' (not according to Tg.). Cf. further Isa. xxxiii, 2; Jer. ii, 28; xi, 12; xiv, 8. The phrase contrasts with 'a time of mighty trouble', line 11–12.

People of God. This is also the inscription on the banner of the whole congregation (iii, 12). See ch. 3, § 3 and p. 44, n. 6.

an appointed time of dominion. See in detail Sukenik, MG I, 22. The word 'dominion' is from Dn. xi, 3, 5. For the concept, see comm. xvii, 7–8.

eternal annihilation. A frequent

TEXT, TRANSLATION, AND COMMENTARY 259

4. עָ[ל כול גדודי] הכתיים במצרים ובקצו יצא בחמה גדולה להלחם
במלכי הצפון ואפו להשמיד ולהכרית את קרן
5. [בליעל והי]אה עת ישועה לעם אל וקץ ממשל לכול אנשי גורלו
וכלת עולמים לכול גורל בליעל והיתה מהומה
6. ג[דולה ב]בני יפת ונפל אשור ואין עוזר לו וסרה ממשלת כתיים
להכני[ע] רשעה לאין שארית ופלטה לוא תהיה
7. לו[כול בנ]י חושך

[ב]

8. ד[עת וצ]דק יאירו לכול קצוות תבל הלוך ואור עד תום כול
מועדי חושך ובמועד אל יאיר רום גודלו לכול קצי

phrase in the DSS, e.g. DSW ix, 5–6; DSD ii, 15. In the O.T. ' eternal salvation ' Isa. xlv, 17 (with *'olamim*, as here), but *'olam* occurs in combination with other words for destruction, etc.

there shall be, etc. For the whole situation envisaged, cf. xviii, 1–3; xi, 11–12. For the connexion between Kittim, Asshur, and Japheth, see ch. 2, § 3 (2).

great panic. ¶ Dt. vii, 23; cf. also 1 Sam. v, 9; xiv, 20. Cf. ' panic of God ', iv, 7.

6. sons of Japheth. See ch. 2, § 3 (2).

and none, etc. ¶ Dn. xi, 45. Cf. also Lam. i, 7; Ps. lxxii, 12; Job xxix, 12; xxx, 13.

dominion of the Kittim. ¶ Dn. xi, 5; the same phrase is used DSH ii, 13–14. Cf. also ' dominion of wickedness ', DSW xvii, 5–6; ' dominion of wrongdoing ', DSD iv, 19. See further ch. 2, § 3 (2).

that wickedness be subdued. The reading ' subdue ' is certain: what looks like a *ẓadhe* on the photograph is only the left spur of the *he*. Similar phrases xvii, 5–6 and line 13 below.

and ... escape. The phrase from Ezra ix, 14; frequent in the DSS. See further comm. xviii, 2–3.

8. knowledge and justice. The two terms are combined *Qumran I*, p. 103, i, 6–7; DSW vii, 8; DSD iii, 1; x, 11–12; cf. ' they who know justice ', CDC i, 1. For the connexion between these two concepts and light, see Isa. lxii, 1; Ps. xxxvii, 6; etc., etc.; Wisd. v, 6; vii, 29; En. lviii, 4; Test. Benj. xi, 2. The planet *Ẓedeq*, i.e. Jupiter, ' gave light to Abraham ' (Gen Rabba xliii, 2). However, the traces of letters would also permit the restoration ז[יק וב]רק ' firebrand and lightning '; the two occur together DST i, 11; Ecclus. xliii, 15 (13). For the image cp. Ps. lxxvii, 19; xcvii, 4; 2 Baruch liii, 9; Mt. xxiv, 27.

shining more and more. ¶ Pr. iv, 18; cf. Gn. viii, 3.

appointed ... God. ¶ Ps. lxxiv, 8; also used iv, 7; xvii, 5–6; more freely i, 10; xiii, 14. For the following cp. Isa. ix, 1–2.

His lofty majesty. Cf. xiv, 17; ' lofty glory ', DSD x, 12; *Qumran I*, p. 127, v, 23. In Ps. cl, 2 *rov gudhlo*. See also Albright, *Studies in O.T. Prophecy*, p. 16 note kk.

shall shine. Cf. En. lviii, 5 sq., and see J. M. Grinz, *Sinai*, 16 (5713), 23.

9. unto all appointed times of | [eternity] for peace and blessing, glory and joy, and long life for all Sons of Light. On the day when the Kittim fall *there shall be* a mighty encounter and carnage before the God of |
10. Israel, for that is a day appointed by Him from of old for a battle of annihilation for the Sons of Darkness, on which there shall engage in a
11. great carnage the congregation of angels and the assembly of | men, the Sons of Light and the lot of Darkness, fighting *each* in communion through the might of God with the sound of a great tumult and the war
12. cry of angels and men for a day of doom. That *is* a time of | mighty trouble for the people to be redeemed by God. In all their troubles there was none like it, from its hastening until its completion for an eternal
13. redemption. On the day of their battle against the Kittim, | they shall go forth for a carnage in battle. *In* three lots shall the Sons of Light prove strong so as to smite the wicked, and *in* three the army of Belial
14. shall recover *so as to bring about* the withdrawal of the lot | [of Light. The] skirmishing battalions—their hearts shall be melted while the might of God strengthens [the heart of the Sons of Darkness,] but in

appointed times of eternity. Restored after DSD iv, 16.

9. for peace ... long life. A collection of promises for the 'end of days' in O.T.; similar xvii, 6-7 (see also xiii, 6 and comm.) DSD iv, 6-8; En. v, 7-9; x, 16 sq.; xi; xxv, 6; xxviii, 1, lv, lix; Jub. i, 29. Most of these terms are inscribed on the banners, cf. ch. 3, § 7. Most terms in Ps. xxi; cf. also Pr. iii, 2.

peace and blessing. The combination not in O.T., cf. however 2 Sam. viii, 10; M. Uktzin. iii, 12.

glory and joy. The combination does not occur in the O.T.

long life. Cf. p. 76, n. 5.

on the day, etc. Cf. Isa. xxx, 25, 'on the day of the great slaughter, when the towers fall.'

encounter. Cf. Zech. xiv, 3, also Job xxviii, 23; Ps. cxliv, 1. Cp. xiii, 14.

carnage. *naḥshīr*, like Syr. *naḥshīra* and *naḥshīrtānā* ('hunter', Gn. x, 9 Pesh.), Targumic *naḥshīrkān* ('hunter', Gn. xxv, 27 Onk.), comes from the Old Persian ancestor of Persian *nakhčīr* 'hunt, fight between wild beasts, fight between heroes, carnage'; see J. P. de Menasce, 'Iranien

naxčir', VT 6 (1956), 213 sq. The combination *qĕrāvā wĕ-naḥshīrūthā* occurs also in the Aramaic Test. Levi (on which now see *Qumran I*, p. 88, n. 1). Cf. 'day of bloodshed', En. xciv, 9; 'day of slaughter', DST xv, 9 (¶ Jer. xii, 3).

before the God of Israel. 'Before God', Gn. x, 9. 'God of Israel' frequent in DSS, cf. also comm. xiii, 1.

10. from of old. This characteristic expression of predeterminism recurs, e.g., xi, 11; xiii, 17; xv, 12; xvii, 5; xviii, 9; cf. also iii, 7; iv, 7; DSD iv, 18-20.

angels (*elim*). See ch. 9, § 2.

angels ... men. Cf. xv, 14; DST iii, 33-6; En. i, 9; liv; Test. Levi iii, 3; Test. Napht. viii, 4; Test. Joseph xix, 9 (acc. to Charles). Discussion ch. 9, § 6.

11. in communion (*yaḥad*). Cf. vii, 6; xii, 4. Perhaps also ¶ to Goliath's words, 1 Sam. xvii, 10.

might of God. Frequent in DSW; inscribed on a banner, iv, 12. Note that God's 'might' also assists the enemy in line 14.

tumult. 'Sound of tumult': Isa. xii, 3, etc.; cf. DST vi, 7. 'Great tumult': 2 Sam. xviii, 29.

9. עֹ[ולמים] לשלום וברכה כבוד ושמחה ואורך ימים לכול בני אור
וביום נפול בו כתיים קרב ונחשיר חזק לפני אל
10. ישראל כיא הואה יום יעוד לו מאז למלחמת כלה לבני חושך
בו יתקרבו לנחשיר   גדול עדת אלים וקהלת
11. אנשים בני אור וגורל חושך נלחמים יחד לגבורת אל בקול המון
גדול ותרועת אלים ואנשים ליום הווה והיאה עת
12. צרה ע[וֹזה] לעם פדות אל ובכול צרותמה לוא נהיתה כמוה
מחושה עד תומה לפדות עולמים וביום מלחמתם בכתיים
13. יצ[אוֹ לנ]חשיר במלחמה שלושה גורלות יחזקו בני אור לנגוף רשעה
ושלושה יתאזרו חיל בליעל למשוב גורל
14. [אור ודג]לי הבנים יהיו להמס לבב וגבורת אל מאמצת לנ[בב
בני חושך] ובגוֹרל השביעי יד אל הגדולה מכנעת

doom. The reading of הווה as the Tetragrammaton is precluded by the habit of the Scroll of avoiding it. (Other scrolls write it in Old Hebrew script). Nor is *howeh* ' happening ' probable. The Bibl. *hawwah* occurs 16 times in the published scrolls.

12. mighty trouble. Cp. xv, 1; ¶ Dn. xii, 1 (where also Michael, cf. xvii, 6). The same sentiment 1 Macc. ix, 27; Ass. Mosis viii, 1 (on Ass. Mos. and DSS see p. 199, n. 2); Mt. xxiv, 21; Rev. xvi, 18; BJ II, vi, 2; *Midr. of Messianic Signs*, BHM II, 61, seventh sign. The trouble here is not, as in DSH and CDC, restricted to the sect, but is that of all Israel: DSW does not discuss particular troubles of the sect.

to be redeemed. Cf. xi, 9; xiv, 5; xiv, 10; xv, 1; xviii, 10—influenced by verses like Ps. cxi, 9; cxxx, 7-8.

none like it. Cp. xviii, 9.

its hastening. In these lines, *w* and *y* are clearly distinguished. ¶ (with Qal for Hif'il) Isa. lx, 22 (cf. also Dt. xxxii, 35); also used DST vi, 29: ' then the sword of God shall hasten in (with ?) the appointed time of judgement '. Similar thought in Ecclus. xxvi, 7; fuller 2 Baruch i.

13. go forth. Cf., e.g., 1 Chr. xiv, 15. See comm. on iv, 9.

in three lots. i.e. ' pre-ordained occasions ': there are seven ' lots ' in all, of which six are engagements by the skirmishers only. As xvii, 16 proves, the two parties win alternately, the sixth being a victory of the Sons of Darkness. For the idea, cf. 2 Baruch i, 53–69; En. ii, 22; xlii; *Midr. Messianic Signs*, BHM, 58 sq.

prove strong ... recover. Both verbs denote in O.T. temporary recoveries, not victory, cf. 2 Sam. x, 11; Josh. xvii, 13; for *hith'azzar* Isa. viii, 9; 1 Sam. iv, 2. Cp. xv, 14; xvi, 9.

withdrawal. New word, also iii, 2, see comm. there. The sense here as in Ps. xliv, 10, ' thou makest us to turn back from the enemy '.

14. skirmishing battalions. On their role in battle see ch. 7, § 4–5; ib. § 7. For the spelling ib. § 4 (2).

melted. Cf. comm. on x, 5–6.

strengthens the heart. In O.T. only of hardening the heart of the wicked, e.g. Dt. ii, 20 (Sihon); 2 Chr. xxxvi, 13 (Zedekiah); cf. Dt. xv, 7. For the purpose of this encouragement, see xvi, 9.

15. the seventh lot the great hand of God shall subdue | [Belial and all] angels of his dominion, and for all men of [his lot *there shall be* eternal annihilation.] |

SECTION 3

16. [The glory of God with the congregation of the] holy ones shall shine forth in [eternal] alliance [   ] truth for the
17. annihilation of the Sons of Darkness [   ] | [   ] with the sound] of a great tumult [and war cry of angels
                    ] they will give hand in [   ]
last line   [and the chiefs of the tribes, twelve,]

COLUMN II

fathers of the congregation, fifty-two. The chiefs of the priests they shall dispose after the chief priest and his deputy, twelve chiefs to be serving |
2. in the daily burnt-offering before God. The chiefs of the courses, twenty-six, in their courses they shall serve. After them the chiefs of
3. the levites to serve continually, twelve, one to each | tribe. And the chiefs of their courses shall serve each man in his maʿamad. The chiefs of the tribes and fathers of the congregation after them, to stand

seventh lot. Described in xviii. The number seven plays a great role: seven skirmishing battalions, front formations, darts, sling-stones, nations of vanity (xi, 8), priests, levites.

the great hand of God. ¶ Ex. xiv, 31; also DSW xviii, 1; 'hand of God' xi, 1; xiii, 12-14; xviii, 3. God himself—as distinct from angels—interferes only in the seventh lot.

of [his lot . . . annihilation]. The length of the restoration results from the fact that the following paragraph begins at the next line, hence line 15 must have ended before or about the middle of the line. Parallels line 5 above; xviii, 1, etc.
16. For this section, see ch. 2 and ch. 8.
glory. Restored after xii, 6; CDC xx, 25.
shine forth. Cf. xvii, 5; DSD iii, 24,

and see Ps. xciv, 1. Discussion p. 222, n. 3.
[eternal]—truth. *c.* six words missing. The passage nearest in content, xiii, 15-16, also is damaged in just the decisive places.
17. with . . . tumult. Restored after i, 11. At beginning 2-3 words missing.
will give hand. Cf. perhaps Lam. v, 6 or Ezek. xvii, 18.
in. Restore perhaps בכלי מלחמתם 'will lay hands on their weapons', cf. xvi, 5-6; viii, 8. The reading *bĕ-khol* is excluded, as *kol* is always plene in DSW.
chiefs. etc. Restored after line 3.

Column II

fathers of the congregation. These also stand at the temple gates (line 3) and arrange for conscription (line 7); they have special trumpets for convening them

TEXT, TRANSLATION, AND COMMENTARY

15. [בליעל וכו]ל מלאכי ממשלתו ולכול אנשי [גורלו כלת עולמים]

[ג]

16. [וכבוד אל עם עֵדָתוֹ] קדושים יופיע בעזר [עולמים] - - - - [אמת לכלת
בני חושך - -

17. [- - - בקה]ל [הה]מֹון גדול ותר[ו]עָת אלים - - - - - -]ם יתנו יד בכל[-]
וראשי השבטים שנים עשר] ... (last line)

II

1. אבות העדה שנים וחמשים ואת ראשי הכוהנים יסרוכו אחר כוהן
הראש ומשנהו ראשים שנים עשר להיות משרתים

2. בתמיד לפני אל וראשי המשמרות ששה ועשרים במשמרותם ישרתו
ואחריהם ראשי הלויים לשרת תמיד שנים עשר אחד

3. לשבט וראשי משמרותם איש במעמדו ישרתו וראשי השבטים
ואבות העדה אחריהם להתיצב תמיד בשערי המקדש

(iii, 3–4; see ch. 5, § 4 (4). Num. xxxi, 26 proves that their full title is 'chiefs of the fathers of the c.', 'chiefs' being omitted because of the preceding 'chiefs of the tribes'; they are in fact so called in line 7 and in *Qumran I*, p. 109–11 (i, 16, 23, 25; ii, 16).

fifty-two. See ch. 8, § 3 (4).

chiefs of the priests. Cf. Neh. xii, 7.

dispose. The verb only here and line 6, but cp. v, 4; for the meaning cf. *Qumran I*, p. 110, i, 23 'to lead forth the whole congregation, each man in his *serekh*'. For *serekh*, see ch. 7, § 2(5).

chief priest. See ch. 8, § 6, for his duties ib. § 4.

deputy. See p. 207, n. 6.

twelve. See comm. on lines 3–4 and p. 207, n. 3.

2. in the daily burnt-offering. The Heb. word *tamidh* also means 'continually', and our passage distinguishes between chiefs of priests, of levites, of tribes, and of fathers of the congregation, who serve thus, and the chiefs of the courses etc., who serve at fixed intervals. See ch. 8, § 3 (2); on the courses ch. 8, § 3 (3), ch. 7, § 2 (3).

twenty-six. As against 24 in the O.T. see ch. 8, § 3 (4).

chiefs of the levites. Cf. Neh. xii, 24. See p. 207, n. 3.

3. ma'amad. On this see Danby. *The Mishnah*, p. 794; discussion ch. 7, § 2 (3), ch. 8, § 3 (3).

chiefs of the tribes. Cf. e.g. Dt. v, 20. In DSW usually 'princes of the t.', see iii, 3, 14, and ch. 3, § 5. Their number—twelve—appeared perhaps at the end of col. i.

to stand (*hithyaẓẓev*). Cf. Nu. xxiii, 3 (in connexion with the burnt-offering) a. fr.; also viii, 3; DST iii, 21; xi, 13; *Qumran I*, p. 110, i, 14, 16, 20, 21; ii, 8.

4. perpetually in the gates of the sanctuary. | The chiefs of their courses with their subordinates shall stand by on their festivals, on their new moons and on the sabbaths, and on all days of the year, from the age of fifty years
5. upwards. | These shall stand by at the burnt-offerings and the sacrifices, to set out the incense-offering of sweet savour for the pleasure of God, to atone for all His congregation, and to bring fat sacrifices before Him
6. perpetually on | the table of glory. All these they shall dispose at the time of the sabbatical year. In the remaining thirty-three years of the
7. war shall the men of renown | summoned to assembly and all the chiefs of the clans of the congregation choose *from time to time* for them warriors for all the lands of the gentiles. From all tribes of Israel they
8. shall mobilize | for them men of valour to go forth to serve according to the pre-ordained periods of the war year after year. But in the sabbatical
9. years they shall not mobilize *men* to go forth to serve ; for a sabbath | of rest that is for Israel. In the thirty-five years of service the war shall be
10. waged. For six years the whole congregation shall wage it together, | and the war of *separate* divisions *shall be waged* in the remaining twenty-nine. In the first year they shall fight against Aram Naharaim, in the second

gates of the sanctuary. Cf. Ezek. xliv, 1. The temple is in Jerusalem: iii, 11; vii, 4.
4. with their subordinates. ⁋ Nu. vii, 2 (note the interpretation implied in the word 'their', added to M.T.). Cf. also *Qumran* I, p. 109 i, 8–9; CDC xv, 5–6.
festivals . . . new moons . . . sabbaths. The order as in Ezek. xlv. 17—against 1 Chr. xxiii, 31; 2 Chr. ii, 3; viii, 13; xxxi, 3; Neh. x, 34; cf. Num. x, 10. It agrees with Jub. xlix, 1 (but not ii, 9); DSD x, 4–6; against CDC iii, 14–5; xii, 4. On the link of this order with the calendar, see ch. 8, § 3 (5).
fifty years. See ch. 4, § 4 (1–2). Of course only those above age are able to be present so as to represent the population of fighting age.
5. these. i.e. all those mentioned. This passage proves that the sect was not against animal sacrifices, provided these were offered by the Sons of Light, see ch. 8, § 2.
stand by. ⁋ Num. xxiii, 3, 6, 17. The combination 'burnt-offerings and sacrifices' is frequent in the O.T.
incense-offering. *miqtereth* = 'censer', Ezek. viii, 11; 2 Chr. xxvi, 19, but neither O.T. nor Rabb. for 'offering';

cf. also I. Brinktrine, *Biblica* 33 (1952), 90 ff. For the rite, cf. 1 Chr. vi, 34.
sweet savour (*niḥoaḥ*). So DSD ix, 5 (cf. p. 199, n. 4); iii, 11. In O.T. always *reaḥ niḥoaḥ*, as also in *Qumran* I, p. 123, iii, 1.
for the pleasure of God. Cf. Ez. xx, 41; Lev. i, 4; xxii, 17 sq. For the sect this refers to the effect of *their* sacrifices, and recurs frequently.
to atone, etc. Cf. Lev. xvi, 17 a. fr.; DSD iii, 11; viii, 6, 10; ix, 5.
to bring fat sacrifices. Also DSD x, 15; perhaps CDC i, 8; for the sense cf. Ecclus. xiv, 12 (11) ולאל ידך הדשן, LXX: προσφορὰς Κυρίῳ ἀξίως πρόσαγε. In Bibl. *yĕdashshĕneh*, Ps. xx, 4.
6. table. This word stands for 'altar' Ezek. xliv, 16 (cf. CDC iii, 21 sq.); xli, 22; Mal. i, 7 etc.; and see ch. 8, § 2. Cf. also *Qumran* I, p. 110, ii, 17–8. 'Table of glory' is probably formed after 'throne of glory', Jer. xvii, 12 etc.
dispose. Cf. line 1, Same sense as *serekh* in xvi, 2, also vii, 16; viii, 14.
time . . . year. ⁋ Dt. xxxi, 10. For the following, see ch. 2, § 2; 7.
remaining thirty-three years. After

TEXT, TRANSLATION, AND COMMENTARY

4. וראשי משמרותם עם פקודיהם יתיצבו למועדיהם לחודשיהם
ולשבתות ולכול ימי השנה מבן חמשים שנה ומעלה
5. אלה יתיצבו על העולות ועל הזבחים לערוך מקטרת ניחוח
לרצון אל לכפר בעד כול עדתו ולהדשן לפניו תמיד
6. בשולחן כבוד את כול יֺסרוכו במועד שנת השמטה ובשלוש
ושלושים שני המלחמה הנותרות יהיו אנשי השם
7. קרואי המועד וכול ראשי אבות העדה בחרים להם אנשי מלחמה
לכול ארצות הגוים מכול שבטי ישראל יחלוצו
8. להם אנשי חיל לצאת לצבא כפי תעודות המלחמה שנה בשנה
ובשני השמטים לוא יחלוצו לצאת לצבא כיא שבת
9. מנוח היאה לישראל בחמש ושלושים שני העבודה תערך המלחמה
שש שנים יעורכוה כול העדה יחד
10. ומלחמת המחלקות ב/תשע[ן] ועשרים הנותרות בשנה הראישונה
ילחמו בארם נהרים ובשנית בבני לוד בשלישית

deducting the six years of 'total' war and one sabbatical year. This shows that what precedes refers to a sabbatical year, and that this, and the rest from fighting during it, was indicated in the lost part of col. i.

of the war. i.e. as a whole: the years of fighting are called 'years of service' (line 9).

men of renown. This includes 'chiefs of tribes' and 'chiefs of fathers of the congregation'. The first are specified iii, 3-4; the latter Num. xvi, 2; i, 16-7; see ch. 3, § 5-6; ch. 4, § 5 (3); ch. 5, § 4(3). The group is mentioned in *Qumran I*, p. 109, i, 2, 8, 11. Cf. now Yadin, JBL 78 (1959), 238 ff.

7. choose, etc. The method of partial conscription is discussed ch. 4, § 5 (3).

mobilize. Read either *yaḥ(ă)lozu* (pausal form), Qal, as active form to the Niph'al Num. xxxi, 3; or *yaḥăliẓu* Hiph'il, with Sam. MSS and versions ibid. It seems as if the scribe wrote here *y*, but in line 8 *w*.

8. pre-ordained periods (*tĕʿudhoth*) **of the war.** Also *Qumran I*, p. 110 i, 26; cf. ' *tĕʿudhoth* of peace', ib. p. 138, frg. 36, 1. See ch. 4, § 5 (2).

sabbatical years. For the masc. pl., cf. Mishnah R. Sh. i, 1. On the cessation of fighting in these, see p. 20, n. 1.

sabbath of rest. *manoaḥ* also xix, 9; *shabbath menuḥatham* DSH xi, 8, cf. also M. Tamid, vii, 4.

9. years of service. i.e. of fighting, out of the total of 40 years; cf. Intr. ch. 2 § 2; 7.

six years. During which the fighting is against the main enemies (i, 1-4) within the Land of Israel as defined in Gen. xv, 18-21. See ch. 2, § 3 (Phase 2). This stage was probably dealt with in the lost part of col. i.

shall wage it. This use of the verb is frequent in BH. For the spelling, cf. H. Yalon, KS 28 (1951-2), 64 ff.

10. war of separate divisions. See. ch. 4, § 5.

twenty-nine. i.e. 33 years of 'partial' war minus 4 sabbaticals, or 35 fighting years minus 6 years 'total' war. On the following list—which partly agrees with Jub. against O.T.—see ch. 2, § 5, where also discussion of the peculiar forms of some names, only briefly indicated in the following.

11. against the sons of Lud, in the third | they shall fight against the remainder of the sons of Aram : Uz, Hul, Togar, and Masha, which are beyond the Euphrates, in the fourth and the fifth they shall fight against
12. the sons of Arpachshad, | in the sixth and the seventh they shall fight against all the sons of Asshur and Persia and the Kadmonite as far as the
13. Great Desert, in the eighth year they shall fight against the sons of | Elam, in the ninth year they shall fight against the sons of Ishmael and Keturah. In the ten years after these the war shall be divided against all the sons of
14. Ham | according to [their families in] their dwelling-places, and in the remaining ten years the war shall spread out against all [sons of Japheth] in their dwelling-places. |

Section 4

15. [The disposition of the trumpets of summoning and the trumpets] of the fanfare for all their service for [the summoning of the congregation and the summoning of the commanders and the chiefs of the clans] with their sub-
16. ordinates | [in myriads and thousands and hundreds and fifties] and tens.
Upon the [trumpets . . . .]

last line [and the trumpets of]

COLUMN III

the battle arrays, and the trumpets for summoning them when the battle intervals are opened for the advance of the skirmishers, the trumpets

11. Togar. O.T. 'Gether'. Cf. ch. 2, § 5 (3).
Masha. O.T. 'Mash' (Sam. 'Masha') and 'Meshekh'. Cf. ibid.
beyond the Euphrates. For the (aramaizing) spelling cf. Ant. I, i, 3 Φοράς and Arabic *Furāt*, Accadian *Purattu*. Cf. also *Genesis Apocryphon*, xxi, 17. For the phrase cf. ch. 2, § 5 (3) B.
12. sons of Asshur. The Semitic people (all this stage of the war is against sons of Shem), hence not the Japhethite 'Kittim of Asshur'.
Persia and the Kadmonite. Cf. ch. 2, § 5 (5).
13. shall be divided. In triple meaning: fought by 'divisions', divided amongst the

various Hamitic peoples, and 'spread out', as in ix, 6, cf. Gen. xiv, 15.
14. according to their families. Restored after Gen. x, 20.
in their dwelling-places. Restored after Num. xxxi, 10. Perhaps some influence of Ez. vi, 14; xxxvii, 23.
15. Beginning of the Serekh Series. Note that there are two lists of trumpets: A, names and functions, B, inscriptions. A third list, (C) in vii, 12. The reader is advised to consult ch. 5, §§ 3–5 before embarking on this section.
disposition. See comm. on iii, 12.
trumpets of summoning and trumpets of the fanfare. Two collective terms (for ceremonial and tactical trumpets) summarizing the following list.

TEXT, TRANSLATION, AND COMMENTARY 267

11. ילחמו בשאר בני ארם בעוץ וחול תוגר ומשא אשר בעבר פורת
ברביעית ובחמישית ילחמו בבני ארפכשד

12. בששית ובשביעית ילחמו בכול בני אשור ופרס והקדמוני עד
המדבר הגדול בשנה השמינית ילחמו בבני

13. עילם בתשיעית ילחמו בבני ישמעאל וקטורה ובעשר השנים אשר
אחריהם תחלק המלחמה על כול בני חם

14. לֹ[נִ]מִשְׁפְּחֹוֹתָם בְּמֹ[ו]שבותם ובעשר השנים הנותרות תחלק המלחמה
על כול [בני יפת] בְּמֹושבותיהם

[ד]

15. [סרך חצוצרות המקרא וחצוצר]וֹת התרועה לכול עבודתם ל[נ]מקרא
העדה ולמקרא השרים וראשי האבות] לפקודיהם

16. [לרבואות ואלפים ומאיות וחמשים] ועושרות על
חֹ[צֹוֹצֹרֹוֹת] [------

III

_{סדרי המלחמה וחצוצרות}

1. (סדרי המלחמה וחצוצרות) מקראם בהפתח שערי המלחמה
לצאת אנשי הבנים וחצוצרות תרועות החללים וחצוצרות

for all their service. i.e. both ceremonial and in battle; cf. 'service' = fighting, line 9. 'Service of the congregation', *Qumran* I, p. 109–110, i, 13, 16; ii, 1.

the chiefs ... subordinates. Restored after 1 Chr. xxiii, 24.

16. and tens. The list can be restored with certainty, as it recurs also in DSD, *Qumran* I, p. 110, and CDC, see ch. 3 §§ 6; 9. For the spelling, cf. comm. on iv, 4.

In the following lines were listed trumpets for calling the congregation, the commanders, the levies, the chiefs of the fathers of the congregation, the 'camps' and the expeditions, possibly with indication of their functions.

Column III

[the trumpets of] the battle arrays. i.e. the shoulder-to-shoulder alignment, to which the troops pass from the file alignment as soon as these trumpets sound, so as to advance in battle order. Both here and in list B these trumpets precede those for calling the skirmishers, as they are employed also for arraying the heavy infantry at the very first stage of the battle. See further ch. 3, § 5 (5)–(6); for *seder* ch. 7, § 1–2; for connexions see ch. 10.

battle intervals. The 'tactical intervals' within the formations through which the skirmishers advance; see ch. 3, §§ 2 (4)–5 (8).

skirmishers. See comm. on i, 14.

trumpets for the fanfare of the slain. In B 't. of the slain', in C included amongst 't. of the fanfare'. This fanfare gives the signal for the actual fighting, and lasts as long as the missiles are thrown. They are six in number, and produce a 'high intermittent note'; cf. ch. 5, §§ 5 (4), 6 (2).

2. for the fanfare of the slain, the trumpets of | the ambush, the trumpets of pursuit when the enemy is smitten, and the trumpets of withdrawal when the battle returns. Upon the trumpets for summoning the
3. congregation they shall write 'Those called by God'; | upon the trumpets for summoning the commanders they shall write 'Princes of God'; upon the trumpets of the formations they shall write 'Serekh of
4. God'; upon the trumpets of the men of | renown, the chiefs of the clans of the congregation, when they assemble at the house of convention, they shall write 'Convoked by God for a council of holiness'; upon
5. the trumpets of the camps | they shall write 'Peace of God in the encampments of His saints'; upon the trumpets for their expeditions they shall write 'God's mighty deeds to scatter the enemy and to put to
6. flight all opponents | of justice, and disgraceful retribution to the opponents of God'; upon the trumpets of the battle arrays they shall write 'Arrays of God's battalions for His wrathful vengeance upon all
7. Sons of Darkness'; | upon the trumpets for calling the skirmishers when the battle intervals open *for them* to go forth against the line of the enemy, they shall write 'Vengeful remembrance at the appointed

trumpets of the ambush. Only in A and B; in C included amongst 't. of the fanfare'. They give the signal for the ambush to sally forth. See ch. 5, § 5 (3) and for the ambush p. 196, n. 1.

2. trumpets of pursuit. (*mirdaf*, in ix, 6 *mirdof*), see ch. 5, § 5 (2) and ch. 7, § 7.

trumpets of withdrawal. Also in C; fuller in B: they serve both for withdrawal of units during battle into the main body and for the 'withdrawal' to Jerusalem after victory.

when the battle returns. Cf. 'and the battle drew near', 1 Kings, xx, 29.

List B

trumpets for summoning the congregation. See Nu. x, 2-4 and cf. ch. 5, § 4 (1), ch. 3, § 9, and p. 61, n. 7. As in A, the cult trumpets are enumerated first. For the system of inscriptions, see ch. 5, § 7.

called by God. Here *qĕru'e*, but iv, 10 and *Qumran I*, p. 110, ii, 2 *qĕri'e*, as Kethiv and Sam. in Num. i, 16, Qĕre and Sam. Num. xxvi, 9, pointing in Num. xvi. 2. 'God' in all inscriptions, cf. ch. 5, § 7. The phrase denotes, as in iv, 10, the whole congregation, 'the men who are called to the council of the community' (*Qumran I*, p. 110, i, 27).

3. the commanders. (see ch. 5, § 4 (2)). The inscription connects these trumpets with Num. x, 4. The commanders here are not military leaders, but heads of tribes and families, cf. ch. 3, § 6. In Num. all signals are given on the same trumpets, and differ only in tone and in the number used: the sect had different trumpets for each purpose, cf. ch. 5, § 3-4.

the formations. Also iii, 12; for the term see ch. 3, § 2 and p. 41, n. 2. Here the different units enumerated in ii, 16 are meant; this suggests that the sect, like some ancient versions, read in Num. x, 4 '*and* the chiefs of the thousands of Israel', cf. ch. 5, § 4 (3).

Serekh. The congregation in its military order. For this sense of *serekh* see ch. 7, § 2 (5).

3-4. men of renown . . . convention. The long explanation may be due to these being the only trumpets not mentioned in the O.T. For their purpose, see ch. 4, § 5 (3) and ch. 5, § 4 (4). Comparison with Job xxx, 23 suggests burial rites; it seems, however, more likely that we have here some communal assembly, for the

TEXT, TRANSLATION, AND COMMENTARY

2. הַמַאֲרָב וחצוצרות המרדף בהנגף אויב וחצורות המאסף בשוב
   המלחמה על חצוצרות מקרא העדה יכתובו קרואי אל
3. ועל חצוצרות מקרא ה/שרים יכתובו נשיאי אל ועל חצוצרות
   המסורות יכתובו סרך אל ועל חצוצרות אנשי
4. הַשֵׁם יִכְתּוֹבוּ ראשי אבות העדה בהאספם לבית מועד יכתובו
   תעודות אל לעצת קודש ועל חצוצרות המחנות
5. יכתובו שלום אל במחני קדושיו ועל חצוצרות מסעיהם יכתובו
   גבורות אל להפיץ אויב ולהניס כול משנאי
6. צדק ומשוב חסדים במשנאי אל ועל חצוצרות סדרי המלחמה
   יכתובו סדרי דגלי אל לנקמת אפו בכול בני חושך
7. ועל חצוצרות מקרא אנשי הבנים בהפתח שערי המלחמה לצאת
   למערכת האויב יכתובו זכרון נקם במועד

following reasons: (1) In such an equalitarian sect, even if there were special burial rites for ' men of renown ', we should expect details of rites for other ranks as well; (2) 'when they assemble' alludes to such passages as Neh. viii, 13, cf. also Dt. xxxiii, 5; it recurs, clearly not with reference to burial, cf. also *Qumran I*, p. 109, i, 1, 3, 'council of holiness' elsewhere denotes the sect or a part of it, cf. ch. 7, § 2 (5); DSD ii, 25; viii, 21; *Qumran I*, p. 110, ii, 9; DST vii, 10; CDC xx, 24; cf. also ' when they assemble as a community ', DSD v, 7. The occasion for using these trumpets is perhaps referred to in IQSa ii, 11–17 (on which see Yadin, JBL 78 (1959), 241, note 18).

4. convoked. The sense of *těʿudah* is still doubtful; cf. ch. 4, § 5 (3). In Ugaritic *tʿdt* means 'messenger', cf. C. H. Gordon, *Ugaritic Handbook*, Glossary no. 1466, and F. M. Cross, JNES 12 (1953), 274, n. 1, but this sense does not fit all DSS passages, see especially *Qumran I*, p. 110, i. 25.

5. peace of God. Recurs as inscription on the banner of the eighth grouping ' when they return from battle ' (iv, 14). It proves that this trumpet was not used in actual battle.

encampments of His saints. Cf. ' encampments of God ', iv, 9, and Dt. xxiii, 15; see also comm. on ix, 8, x, 10.

expeditions. Also in conjunction with ' encampments ' *Qumran I*, p. 110, ii, 15, derived from Num. x, 2, and ib. 5. See ch. 5, § 4 (5).

God's mighty deeds. Frequent phrase (cf. ad i, 11), recurs on the banner of the Fifty of Levi (iv, 4), on the trumpets of the slain (iii, 8), and on the first dart (vi, 2).

to scatter, etc. From Num. x, 35, cf. also Ps. lxi, 2. Another tradition uses this verse for the tribal banners, cf. ch. 5, § 7.

6. justice. Cf. comm. on i, 9. In a banner inscription, iv, 6.

disgraceful retribution. For *ḥesed* ' disgrace ', see esp. Ecclus. xli, 30 (22) where it glosses *ḥerpah*. Cf. *hashev ḥerpatham* Neh. iii, 36, also Ps. lxxix, 12; Hos. xii, 15; Dn. xi, 18. On the connexion with Num. x, 36 see p. 105, n. 2.

God's battalions. Recurs on the expedition banner of the fifth grouping = the Thousand, iv, 10. For *degel* as a basic military unit (never ' flag '), see ch. 3, § 6, p. 39, n. 1; p. 62, n. 2, and ch. 7, §§ 4, 5.

vengeance. Frequent in the inscriptions on trumpets and banners; see further, ch. 5, § 7.

7. vengeful remembrance at the appointed time of God. Combination of ' vengeance of God ' (iv, 12), ' appointed time of God ' (iv, 7), and ' appointed time of vengeance ' (xv, 6). Cf. further ch. 5, § 7.

8. time | of God'; upon the trumpets of the slain they shall write 'The hand of God's might in battle so as to strike down all sinful slain';
9. upon the trumpets of ambush they shall write | 'Mysteries of God for the perdition of wickedness'; upon the trumpets of pursuit they shall write 'God hath smitten all Sons of Darkness, His wrath shall not cease
10. until they are annihilated'; | when they disengage from battle to return to the line, they shall write upon the trumpets of withdrawal 'God hath gathered'; and upon the trumpets for the way of return |
11. from battle with the enemy so as to come unto the congregation to Jerusalem, they shall write 'Rejoicings of God in peaceful return'.

Section 5

12.   Disposition of the banners of the whole congregation according to their groupings.

13. Upon the great banner at the head of the whole people they shall write 'People of God' and the names 'Israel' and | 'Aaron' as well as the names of the twelve tribes of Israel according to their order of birth. Upon the banners of the chiefs of the 'camps' of three tribes |

---

8. hand of God's might. Cf. the inscriptions on the banner of the Hundred (iv, 2-3) and those on the darts (vi, 1-6). Cf. ch. 5, § 7. For 'hand of God', cf. i, 14.

sinful slain. Cf. vi, 3, 16, 'sinful flesh' iv, 3, 'sinful guilt' DST iv, 30, xi, 11.

9. mysteries. An allusion to the nature of the ambush. The Persian loan-word *raz* is frequent in the DSS, particularly in the combination *razē phele'* 'wondrous mysteries', cf. Sukenik, MG I, 24. 'Mysteries of God' is repeatedly used col. xvi of the reverses of the Sons of Light, also xvii, 17; DSD iii, 23; DSH vii, 8.

wickedness. As concrete term = 'the wicked', i, 6, 13; xi, 10; xiv, 7; xv, 9; xvii, 6. Cf. comm. on xiii, 11.

hath smitten (*nagaf*). Cf. *hinnagef* iii, 2; *maggefath* xviii, 1. The whole inscription resembles that of the battle arrays, line 6.

cease. Cf., e.g., Jer. xxiii, 20. The inscription defines the purpose of pursuit, cf. ch. 5, § 5 (2), § 7.

10. to return to the line. The addition is necessary as *milḥamah* means both 'battle' and 'war'; cf. 1 Sam. xiv, 20. For 'line' see ch. 7, § 5 (2).

withdrawal. Written with *waw* (elsewhere with *yod*), as in viii, 2; the scribe seems to have endeavoured to make a distinctive *waw*.

hath gathered. An allusion to the generic name of this and the next type of trumpet (line 2), cf. ch. 5, § 5 (1).

11. unto the congregation to Jerusalem, i.e. to the base, cf. comm. on i, 3, and ch. 5, § 5 (1).

rejoicings of God. The plural *giloth* does not occur in the O.T., cf. however, *gilath* Isa. xxxv, 2. Similar phrases occur on the banner inscriptions for the return, iv, 14, cf. ch. 5, § 7 at end.

12-16. Compare for these ch. 3, particularly §§ 1-2. There are four lists of banner inscriptions: A, basic inscriptions

TEXT, TRANSLATION, AND COMMENTARY 271

8. אל ועל חצוצרות החללים יכתובו יד גבורת אל במלחמה להפיל
כול חללי מעל ועל חצוצרות המארב יכתובו

9. רזי אל לשחת רשעה ועל חצוצרות המרדף יכתובו נגף אל כול
בני חושך לוא ישוב אפו עד כלותם

10. ובשובם מן המלחמה לבוא המערכה יכתובו על חצוצורת המשוב
אסף אל ועל חצוצרות דרך המשוב

11. ממלחמת האויב לבוא אל העדה ירושלים יכתובו גילות אל
במשוב שלום

[ה]

12. סרך אותות כול העדה למסורותם על האות הגדולה אשר בראש
כול העם יכתובו עם אל ואת שם ישראל

13. ואהרון ושמות שנים עשר ש[בטי ישרא]ל כתולדותם על אותות
ראשי המחנות אשר לשלושת השבטים

of the different units, in descending order; B, dto. for the levites; C, the changing inscriptions on the levites' banners; D, dto. for the rest of the congregation. These are followed by list E, the sizes of the banners.

12. disposition. For this word, see ch. 7, § 2 (5). It appears as opening of a paragraph in iv, 9; v, 3; ix, 10; DSD v, 1; vi, 8.

banners. In DSW *oth* always 'banner', *signum*, as also DSH vi, 4; Nu. ii, 2, cf. ch. 3, § 1, p. 39, n. 1; § 10, especially p. 62, n. 2.

the whole congregation. i.e. including the levites, so also at the head of list E (iv, 15), as against list D (iv, 9; v, 1). So also 'And this is the disposition for all armies of the congregation' (*Qumran I*, p. 109, i, 6).

their groupings. i.e. of the congregation. For the word, see comm. on iii, 3.

the great banner. Note that *oth* is here always fem., cf. comm. on iv, 9. This banner is 14 cubits long, cf. iv, 15, ch. 3, § 3.

people of God. Ibid., and p. 44, n. 6, for the connexion with the title of Simon Maccabee.

Israel and Aaron. So v, 1; CDC i, 7; DSD viii, 5–6; Ps. cxv, 9–10. The order 'Aaron and Israel' is more common in CDC and DSD; cf. also p. 212, n. 3 and ch. 10.

13–16. Inspection of the scroll suggests that some of the words were blurred as soon as written, owing to a fault of the skin. The letters are unusually crowded.

13. the twelve tribes of Israel. Certain restoration, cf. v, 2–3.

order of birth. According to Num. ii, cf. ch. 3, § 3.

camps of three tribes. These are the camps of Judah, Reuben, Ephraim, and Dan, as in Num. ii (cf. ch. 3, § 4), not 'Levi, Judah and Benjamin', as in i, 2. Each of these camps contained three tribes.

14. they shall write ' [of God ' and the names of the princes of three tribes. Upon] the banner of the tribe they shall write ' Ensign of God '
15. and the name of the prince of the tribe and the names of the princes | of its families. [Upon the banner of the family they shall write '   of God '] and the name of the prince of the myriad and the names of the
16. commanders of [his thousands. Upon the banner] | [of the thousand they shall write '   of God ' and the name of the commander of the thousand and the names of the commanders of] his hundreds. Upon the banner [of the hundred they shall write '   of God ' and the name
17. of] | [the commander of the hundred and the names of the commanders of his tens. Upon the banner of the fifty they shall write '   of
18. God ' and the name of the commander of the fifty and] | [the names of the commanders of his tens. Upon the banner of the ten they shall write '   of God ' and the name of the commander of ten and the names of the nine men in his charge.]

COLUMN IV

Upon the banner of Merari they shall write ' Heave-offering of God ' and the name of the prince of Merari and the names of the commanders of his thousands. Upon the banner of the thousand they shall
2. write ' Anger of God in wrath against | Belial and all the men of his lot without remnant ' and the name of the commander of the thousand and the names of the commanders of his hundreds. Upon the banner of the

---

14. princes of three tribes. According to Num. ii these were the chiefs of the four camps.

ensign of God. Cf. DST ii, 12 : ' Thou madest me an ensign for the righteous elect, a prophet of knowledge concerning wondrous mysteries '. *Nes*, which can also mean ' staff ', is here chosen because *matteh* ' staff, tribe ' could be misunderstood (Ex. iv, 20 ; xvii, 9) ; cf. ch. 3, § 5.

prince. Here and iv, 1 without *aleph*, but in iii, 15 the usual spelling. These princes are chiefs of tribes and families, cf. comm. on iii, 3 and ch. 3, § 5.

15. of the family. Or restore : ' of the myriad '. For the restoration cf. iv, 16 (list E) and iv, 10 (list D). The ' myriad ' is the military unit drawn from the family, cf. ch. 3, § 6. Cf. also *Qumran I*, p. 109, i, 9 : ' to enter the lot within the family unto a community in the holy congregation '.

the prince. Owing to blurring it cannot be checked whether the scribe attempted erasure of the superfluous definite article.

the myriad. Cf. iv, 16. For the spelling, current in Mishnaic texts, cf. Ezra ii, 64 ; Neh. vii, 66, 72.

commanders. Note that the officers of the myriad and upwards are called *naśi'*, from the thousand downwards *śar*.

16. his hundreds. The three words preserved of line 16, combined with iv, 1–5, enable us to restore lines 16–18 with absolute certainty. The spelling with extra *yod* also iv, 2 ; 2 Kings xi, 4, 9, 10 ; with *yod* also after the *mem* (cf. 2 K. xi, 15) in CDC xiii, 1, cf. Rabin's note ibid.

Column IV

1. upon the banner of Merari. End portion of list B. We may confidently

14. יכתובו ב̇ - - [אל ושמות נשיאי שלושת השבטים ע̇]ל̇ א̇ות השבט
יכתובו נס אל ואת שם נשי הש[בט ושמות נשיאי]
15. משפח̇[ותיו על אות המשפחה יכתובו - אל וא]ת̇ שם הנשיא הרבוא ואת
שמות שר[י אלפיו על אות]
16. [האלף יכתובו - אל ואת שם שר האלף ואת שמות שרי] מאיותיו ועל אות
[המאה יכתובו - אל ואת שם]
17. [שר המאה ואת שמות שרי עשרותיו ועל אות החמשים יכתובו - אל ואת שם שר
החמשים ואת]
18. [שמות שרי עשרותיו ועל אות העשרה יכתובו - אל ואת שם שר העשרה ואת שמות
תשעת אנשי תעודתו]

IV

1. ועל אות מררי יכתובו תרומת אל ואת שם נשי מררי ואת שמות
שרי אלפיו ועל אות הא[נל]ף̇ יכתובו אף אל בעברה על
2. בליעל ובכול אנשי גורלו לאין שארית ואת שם שר האלף ואת
שמות שרי מאיותיו ועל אות המאה יכתובו מאת

assume on the basis of iv, 6–8 that the last line of iii gave the basic inscriptions on the banners of Kohath and Gershon; since the scroll follows Num. in the fourfold division of the tribe of Levi, we may assume that there was also an inscription for the banner of the Sons of Aaron, which probably served as banner for the whole tribe of Levi; on all this see ch. 3, § 7. Our reconstruction of the content of the last lines of iii confirms the assumption that the columns of the scroll had only 20–22 lines each. Cf., however, J. Carmignac, NRTh 77 (1955), 738, n. 12, who assumes 29–32 lines to the column.

prince of Merari. Spelling as iii, 14. The title in fuller form Num. iii, 35, cf. ch. 3, § 7. Merari is a 'family' (Num. ibid.), hence subdivided, as the non-levite families or 'myriads', into thousands etc., i.e. the organization of the 'army of divine service' corresponded exactly to that of the 'army of battle', cf. ch. 3, § 1.

the banner of the thousand. It seems certain that the inscriptions here enumerated recurred on the banners of the subdivisions of the three families mentioned in the missing last lines of iii, as a full list of subdivisions of these families would have taken up some eight lines. Only the names of the commanders were different. Cf. also ch. 3, § 9.

anger of God. See ch. 3, § 8 (2) and p. 58, n. 2 for the connexion of the inscription with the name of the 'thousand'. These long inscriptions did not change according to the phases of the war, while the short texts on the family banners changed, cf. iv, 6. The structure of most of the long inscriptions is the same; they fall into three parts: God's wrath or its expression—definition of the enemy—an expression for complete destruction. Cf. also ch. 5, § 7.

274   TEXT, TRANSLATION, AND COMMENTARY

3. hundred they shall write ' Hundred | of God, a hand of battle against all unjust flesh ' and the name of the commander of the hundred and the names of the commanders of his tens. Upon the banner of the fifty
4. they shall write ' Ceased is | existence of the wicked [by] the might of God ' and the name of the commander of the fifty and the names of the commanders of his tens. Upon the banner of the ten they shall write
5. ' Rejoicings | of God upon the ten-stringed lyre ' and the name of the commander of the ten and the names of the nine men in his charge.

SECTION 6

6.   And when they go to battle they shall write upon their banners ' Truth of God ', ' Justice of God ', ' Glory of God ', ' Judgement of
7. God ', and after these the whole list of their names in full. | When they close in for battle they shall write upon their banners ' Right hand of God ', ' Appointed time of God ', ' Panic *sent* by God ', ' The slain
8. *by the hand* of God ', and after these their names in full. | When they return from battle they shall write upon their banners ' Exalt thou God ' (OR : ' God hath exalted '), ' Magnify thou God ' (OR : ' God hath magnified '), ' Praise of God ', ' Glory of God ', with all their names in full.|

2. **hundreds.** Cf. iii, 16.
hundred of God, hand. Reading *mĕ'ath*; we might also read *me-eth*, 'from God, a hand'. The double meaning is possibly intentional, cf. ch. 3, § 8 (2) and p. 58, n. 2. For ' hand of battle ' see p. 175, n. 5 ; cf. also comm. iii, 8.

3. **unjust flesh.** Cf. iii, 8; for ' flesh ' also ' guilty flesh ', xii, 11, and cf. xv, 13 ; xvii, 8 ; DST viii, 29.
tens. Here without the *waw* of line 4 and ii, 16. Note that the commander of fifty is here omitted.

4-5. **rejoicings etc.** The pl. form in *-oth* also xii, 12, and cf. *giloth*, iii, 11. See comm. xiv, 2. ¶ Ps. xxxiii, 1-2, cf. also Ps. xcii, 4 ; cxliv, 9 : the ' lyre of ten strings ' stands for the unit of ' ten ', cf. ch. 3, § 8 (2) and p. 58, n. 2 with special reference to the task of the levites as singers.

5. **nine men.** The commander was thus reckoned as one of the ten. The list completes the registration of the entire army on its standards ; cf. ch. 3, § 9.

The scribe did not leave a blank line between sections 5 and 6, although 5 ends close to the left-hand margin ; this may prove that he hesitated whether to begin a new section or to continue. On the nature of the following inscriptions cf. ch. 3, § 7, on parallels p. 58, n. 1.

6. **go to battle.** In list D, line 9 ' go forth to battle '. The two terms are proved to be identical by Ju. viii, 1 ; 1 Sam. xvii, 13 ; 2 Chr. xxv, 13, etc.

their banners. i.e. those of the four levite families. Any reference to banners of successive units (myriad, thousand, etc.) is excluded, as in that case at least five inscriptions would be needed.

truth of God, etc. These four inscriptions constitute a sort of declaration of war aims. For combinations of the four terms see Ps. xix, 10 ; Jer. iv, 2 ; DSD i, 5-6 ; viii, 2 ; xi, 13-4 ; DSW xi, 14 ; DST vii, 28 ; CDC xx, 30-1 ; cf. also comm. xiii, 1-3 ; xvii, 8. ' Truth of God ' also DSD xi, 4. ' Truth ' occurs *c.* 100 times in the Scrolls published to date. and frequently

TEXT, TRANSLATION, AND COMMENTARY 275

.3 אל יד מלחמה בכול בשר עול ואת שם שר המאה ואת שמות שרי
עשרותיו ועל אות החמשים יכתובו חדל

.4 מעמד רשעים [וב]גבורת אל ואת שם שר החמשים ואת שמות שרי
עשרותיו על אות העשרה יכתובו רנות

.5 אל בנבל עשו[ר] ואת שם שר העשרה ואת שמות תשעת אנשי
תעודתו

[ו]

.6 ובבלכתם למלחמה יכתובו על אותותם אמת אל צדק אל כבוד
אל משפט אל ואחריהם כול סרך פרוש שמותם

.7 ובגשתם למלחמה יכתובו על אותותם ימין אל מועד אל מהומת
אל חללי אל ואחריהם כול פרוש שמותם

.8 ובשובם מן המלחמה יכתובו על אותותם רומם אל גדל אל
תשבוחת אל כבוד אל עם כול פרוש שמותם

forms part of self-designations of the sect ('Community, council, house of truth', etc.); cf. M. Burrows, *Oudtest. St.* 8 (1950), 171.

glory of God. Here on the banner of Gershon, recurs on that of Merari at the stage of return (line 9). 'Glory' = might, cf. xii, 7, 9; Aalen, *Die Begriffe Licht und Finsternis*, p. 195, who however errs regarding the translation of xii, 14, see comm. ibid.

judgement. Cf. *Qumran I*, p. 110, i, 13.

list. On this word cf. ch. 7, § 2 (5); for the various formulas in the following lines p. 42, n. 1.

their names. Only the superscriptions change; the essential part of each banner, the list of names, remains of course the same.

7. close in. Cf. Ju. xx, 23; Jer. xlvi, 3; 1 Sam. xvii, 16; 2 Sam. x, 13 etc.

right hand of God. ¶ Hab. ii, 16; Ps. cxviii, 15; cf. comm. i, 14. This and the following three inscriptions are clear allusions to battle.

appointed time. Cf. comm. i, 10; xv, 6, 12.

panic. ¶ Zech. xiv, 13; cf. 1 Sam. v, 9 (= 'hand of God'); Isa. xxii, 5; see also comm. i, 5–6.

slain. This may refer to the slain amongst the Sons of Light (cf. xvi, 9), as the enemy dead are generally called 'sinful slain' or the like, cf. comm. iii, 8.

8. return. Cf. iii, 2, 10; iii, 11; xiv, 2. The inscriptions here express gratitude for the victory.

exalt. Nearest parallel 'exalt Thy mighty acts', xiv, 13. Cf. especially 'let the exaltations (*romĕmoth* of God be in their throats', Ps. cxlix, 6, of the Ḥasidim (note however, that *ḥasidim* never occurs in the DSS, a fact to which Dr. D. Flusser drew my attention); 'at Thine exaltation (*romĕmuth*) the nations are scattered', Isa. xxxiii, 3.

magnify. The orthographic habits of DSW (cf. i, 8) speak against reading *godel el* 'greatness of God', cf. Dt. xxxii, 3; 1 Chr. xxix, 11 (a chapter which inspired some further inscriptions, cf. lines 12–14).

Praise. Cf. Targumic Aramaic *tushbĕḥā*, Heb. *tishbaḥoth* pl. in Ecclus. li, 22 and in the liturgy (e.g. 'Yishtabbaḥ', Singer p. 36; 'Nishmath', ib. p. 125). Possibly ¶ Ps. cvi, 47 = 1 Chr. xvi, 35.

Glory. See line 6.

9.   Disposition of the banner of the congregation.
   When they go forth to battle, they shall write upon the first banner
'Congregation of God', upon the second banner 'Encampments of
10. God', upon the third | 'Tribes of God', upon the fourth 'Families
of God', upon the fifth 'Battalions of God', upon the sixth 'Assembly
11. of God', upon the seventh 'Those summoned | by God', upon the
eighth 'Hosts of God', and shall write their names in full according to
their whole order (OR : list).   When they close in for battle they shall
12. write upon their banners | 'Battle of God', 'Vengeance of God',
'Struggle of God', 'Retribution of God', 'Strength of God', 'Retaliation
of God', 'Might of God', 'Annihilation by God of all nations of
13. vanity', and shall write upon them all | their names in full.   When
they return from battle they shall write upon their banners 'Deliverance
of God', 'Victory of God', 'Help of God', 'Support of God', |
14. '[J]oy of God', 'Thanksgivings to God', 'Praise of God', 'Peace
of God'.

Section 7

15.   [Length of the Bann]ers.
   The banner of the whole congregation : length fourteen cubits.
16. The banner of th[ree tribes : length thir]teen cubits. | [The banner of a
tribe :] twelve cubits. The banner of a myriad : eleven [cubits. The
banner of a thousand : ten cubits. The banner of a hundre]d : nine

9. disposition. Here begins List D, the changing inscriptions on the banners of the non-levite units, beginning with the banner of the whole congregation, and ending with that of the 'ten'. Again, the scribe seems to have hesitated whether to begin a new section.
   go forth to battle. Cf. 1 Sam. xvii, 20; 2 Sam. v, 2, etc. The inscriptions of this phase are all terms used in the O.T. in connexion with the journeys of the Children of Israel.
   10. families. Corresponds to the ' myriads ', cf. iii, 15.
   battalions. This is the *locus probans* for the identification of the *degel* with the ' thousand '.
   assembly of God. Frequent phrase (Num. xv, 3, etc.), here in the military sense *qahal* has in Ez. xxxviii, 4, etc., also

in *Qumran I*, p. 110, i, 25, ii, 14. From the ' hundred ' onwards the inscriptions designate not the unit, but the army as a whole, perhaps because these units did not fight as separate entities.
   summoned by God. *Qĕru'im* as military term Ez. xxiii, 23; the verb in a military sense Ju. viii, 1. Cf. also ' these are the men summoned (*niqra'im*) to the council of the community' *Qumran I*, p. 110, i, 27. For the spelling, see iii, 2.
   11. hosts of God. Cf. Ex. xii, 41.
   12. The words ' upon the first banner ', etc., are to be supplied by the reader. The inscriptions are of warlike character, and several recur elsewhere : ' battle ' iii, 4; iii. 8; ' vengeance of God ' iii, 6, iii, 7; ' might of God ', iii, 5, iii, 8, iv, 4. Cf. *Yalqut Shim'oni*, Běshallaḥ 246 : ' But this does not apply to Him that Created the

9. סרך אותות העדה בצאתם למלחמה יכתבו על אות הראישונה
עדת אל על אות השנית מחני אל על השלישית
10. שבטי אל על הרביעית משפחות אל על החמישית דגלי אל על
הששית קהל אל על השביעית קריאי
11. אל על השמינית צבאות אל ופרוש שמותם יכתובו עם כול סרכם
ובגשתם למלחמה יכתובו על אותותם
12. מלחמת אל נקמת אל ריב אל גמול אל כוח אל שלומי אל גבורת
אל כלת אל בכול גוי הבל ואת כול פרוש
13. שמותם יכתובו עליהם ובשובם מן המלחמה יכתובו על אותותם
ישועות אל נצח אל עזר אל משענת אל
14. [ש]מחת אל הודות אל תהלת אל שלום אל

[ז]

15. [אורך הא[ו]ת[ו]ת אות כול העדה אורך ארבע עשרה אמה אות
של[ו]שת השבטים אורך שלוש ע[ש]רה אמה
16. [אות השבט] שתים עשרה אמה אות הרבוא עשתי עש[ר]ה אמה
אות האלף עשר אמות אות המא[ה תשע אמות

World by His Word; nay, His is strength, His is might, strategy (τάξις) and battle, for it is said, " For Battle belongs to God ".'
struggle. In strictly military sense Isa. iii, 13; xxxiv, 8; Jer. xxv, 31; Ps. xxxv, 1-2; lxxiv, 22; DST x, 33-4; and particularly *Qumran I*, p. 110, i, 13.
retribution. Cf. Isa. xxxv, 4 (for the influence of Isa. xxxv see comm. xiv, 5-7); Lam. iii, 64.
strength. Cf. 1 Chr. xxix, 12 (which influenced several inscriptions, cf. comm. xi, 1).
retaliation. Cf. Isa. xxxiv, 8.
all nations of vanity. So vi, 6; ix, 9; xi, 9; cf. also ' nations of wickedness ' xv, 2. ' Vanity ' said of gentiles: Jer. x, 15, a.o.

13. when they return. The inscriptions form a logical progression: victory—thanksgiving—peace. For these and the preceding inscriptions cf. David's prayer 1 Chr. xxix, 11-17, though some of the words are here used in a different sense.
victory. The use of this form in the sense of ' victory ' (not ' eternity ') may be connected with the MH use of the Qal verb for ' to conquer ', e.g. Pesiqta Rabbathi ix; cf. Ben-Yehudah s.v.
help. Cf. xvii, 6 and comm.; Dn. xi, 34; Ps. lxx, 6; cxxiv, 8; Ex. xviii, 4, etc.
support. Common BH word; for the phrase cf. 2 Sam. xxii, 19 (*mishʿan*); 2 Chr. xiv, 10 (verbal).

14. thanksgivings. The form occurs Neh. xii, 46; Ezra iii, 11; 1 Chr. xxv, 3; 2 Chr. vii, 3 (always with *tĕhillah*); Ecclus. xvii, 22 (27); xlvii, 11 (8); DSW xv, 5; DST xi, 4.
peace. Cf. i, 9 and comm.; also Sifre Num. vi, 14: ' Great is peace, for God is called by the name of peace '.

15. length. Supplied from the context (as only the length is given).
fourteen cubits. i.e. 6.41 m. For the method of reckoning the cubit see p. 116, n. 2.

16. three tribes ... thirteen. The gap corresponds exactly to the restoration; cf. iii, 13. The length is 5.95 m.

17. cubits. | [The banner of a fifty : eigh]t cubits. The banner of a ten : sev[en cubits. . . . .]

COLUMN V

and upon the [shield] of the Prince of the Whole Congregation they shall write his name [and] the names 'Israel', 'Levi', and 'Aaron', and the names of the twelve tribes of Israel according to their order of birth, |
2. and the names of the twelve commanders of their tribes. |

SECTION 8

3. Disposition for arraying the battle battalions when their establishment is at full, so as to form a front formation.

The formation shall be composed of *units of* a thousand men. *There*
4. *shall be* seven frontal arrays | to one formation, arrayed according to the disposition of placing one man behind another. All of them shall carry

17. **eight cubits.** This, 3.66 m., is the length of spear of the heavy cavalry and of the men of the ' towers ' (vi, 14 ; ix, 12).

s[even cubits]. i.e. 3.20 m. The preservations of the words ' banner of the ten ' provides the sure basis for all our reconstruction. The length is that of the spear of the heavy infantry, v, 7 ; cf. further ch. 6, § 11. Line 17 ended somewhat before the left margin, but may have been as long as line 8, i.e. not the end of a section. In the lost part may have been described the width of the banners, and the lengths of the levite banners. Cf. also p. 59, n. 2.

Column V

shield. The restoration is probable. On the other hand, נס, ' standard ', is impossible, being too short for the space (4 mm. ; *nes* in iii, 14 is 3 mm. long), also the first letter cannot be *nun*; מטה ' staff ' (cf. Num. xvii, 17 sq.) is too long (6½ mm. at least), and the last letter can hardly be a *he*. The word מגן (cf. line 6 middle) fits both in length and outline.

prince of the whole congregation. Also CDC vii, 18-21 (Num. xxiv, 17, there referred to the ' prince ', is quoted DSW xi, 6-7 without that reference); CDC v, 1-2 replaces the ' king ' of Dt. xvii, 17 by ' prince ', see Rabin ad CDC vii loc. cit. and p. 212, n. 3. ' Prince of the congregation ' *Qumran I*, p. 127, v, 20. It follows that the ' prince ' is the secular head of the congregation, as opposed to the chief priest, in contrast to the Hasmonean unification of the two offices in one person, and in conformity with the Pentateuch. On ' prince ' as Hasmonean title see p. 44, n. 6. Milik suggests identity of the ' prince ' with the ' anointed (Messiah) of Israel ', (*Qumran I*, p. 121-2, 128-9 ; RB 60 (1953), 290) ; less probable is the identification with the ' mighty man ' of DSW xii, 10 (*Qumran I*, p. 129), cf. comm. ad loc. and Yadin, JBL 78 (1959), 238 ff. The ' shield of the prince ' symbolizes his role as protector of the people, as does the ' shield of Saul ', 1 Sam. i, 21 ; this may also have something to do with the ' shield of David ', which appears late, but may well go back to early traditions. Mostly, though, ' shield ' is a term for God, e.g. Gn. xv, 1 ; yet from early times Ps. lxxxiv, 10 and xlvii, 10 were interpreted of earthly kings, cf. quotations in Ben-Jehudah s.v. *magen* ; Gen. Rabba xliv, 6 : ' I have not raised

17. [אוֹת הַחֲמִשִּׁים שְׁמוֹנָ]ה אמות אות העשרה שב[ע אמוֹת [???????]

V

1. ועל מ[ט]ה נשיא כול העדה יכתבו שמו [ו]שם ישראל ולוי ואהרון
ושמות שנים עשר שבטי ישראל כתול[ד]ותם
2. ושמות שנים עשר שרי שבטיהם

[ח]

3. סרך לסדר דגלי המלחמה בהמלא צבאם להשלים מב֗ת פנים על
אלף איש תאסר המערכה ושבעה סדרי
4. פנים למערכה האחת סדורים בסרך מעמד איש אחר איש וכולם
מחזיקים מגני נחושת מרוקה כמעשה

---

any shields of the righteous from the progeny of Noah, but I shall do so from yours'. The inscription closely corresponds to that of the banner of the tribal leaders, iii, 14, and the levite families, iv, 1.

Israel, Levi, and Aaron. Cf. comm. iii, 12–13; ch. 3, § 7 at end.

2. the twelve commanders. This corresponds to the banners of the tribal leaders, not to the banner of 'the whole people' (iii, 12–13). Note that the prince of all the congregation had no banner, nor was his name inscribed on the banner of the whole people; this may give expression to the precedence of the high priest. Cf. Yadin, in *Aspects of the Dead Sea Scrolls*, p. 48.

3. Disposition ... formation. A heading, indicating that the following deals with the heavy infantry, on which cf. ch. 7, § 5. This heading seems to have been taken over from a larger work; the author hurries on to his real theme, the description of their arms.

for arraying. Cf. ch. 7, § 2 (1).

battle battalions. i.e. excluding the skirmishing battalions, cf. ch. 7, § 5 (4).

establishment. For this meaning of ẓava, cf. Ex. Rabba xv: 'the meaning of "battalions" (dĕgalim) is the same as ẓĕva'oth'. See further ch. 7, § 5 (4), p. 167, nn. 2, 3.

form. Lit. 'complete' i.e. set out according to plan, cf. ch. 7, § 5 (4), First Phrase, and p. 167, n. 4.

front formation. See ch. 7, § 5 (1)–(2). The scribe made the same mistake in writing מכת for מערכת also in vi, 5, cf. also vi, 9, where only r is omitted. Cf. ch. 11, § 4, group C.

of units of. For this sense of ʿal cf. vii, 14. For the phraseology, see p. 167, n. 6.

seven frontal arrays. Besides consisting of units of one thousand, the formation—and each of its units—is drawn up in seven rows, called 'frontal' in opposition to the type of formation adopted by the skirmishing units, which operate between the 'fronts', cf. ch. 7, § 5 (2).

4. to one formation. There were seven, cf. ch. 7, § 5 (3).

one man behind another. i.e. the corresponding numbers of each array stand behind each other, while in viii, 6, for instance, the arrays are drawn up side by side, cf. ch. 7, § 4 (6).

all of them. The heavy infantry all bear identical weapons, unlike the skirmishers, where each unit is differently equipped, cf. ch. 7, § 4 (5), § 5 (6).

carry. On the verb, cf. p. 115, n. 5.

280 TEXT, TRANSLATION, AND COMMENTARY

5. shields of burnished copper, like | a face mirror. The shield shall be bordered with a rim of cable work and a pattern of running spiral,
6. work of an artificer, in gold, silver and copper welded together | and precious stones in ajour work, work of a smith, cunningly wrought. The length of the shield shall be two cubits and half, and its breadth one cubit
7. and a half. In their hands *they shall hold* a spear | and a sword. The length of the spear shall be seven cubits, of which the socket and the blade *take up* half a cubit. On the socket there shall be three rings engraved like a
8. rim | of cable work, of gold, silver and copper welded together like a pattern cunningly wrought, and running spiral, the pattern being on both
9. sides of the ring | all around, precious stones in ajour work, work of a smith, cunningly wrought, and ear of corn. The socket shall be fluted

burnished copper. The phrase 2 Chr. iv, 16 (in the parallel passage 1 Kings, vii, 45 *memorāṭ*), cf. also Lev. vi, 21; Jer. xlvi, 4; Mishnah Zeb. xi, 4.

like. Lit. 'like the work of', cf. Ex. xxviii, 15; 1 Kings, vii, 33, etc.

5. face mirror. Also line 11. On these metal mirrors, see Levi s.v. *mar'ah*; Krauss I, 67; Galling p. 493.

bordered. The word Ezek. xli, 7 (where it is a noun, and usually emended); the pl. *mĕsibbōth* Ex. xxviii, 11, etc.

rim. Cf. Ex. xxvi, 4; 1 Kings vii, 26; and see ch. 6, § 6 (2).

cable. Cf. 1 Kings, vii, 17; Dt. xxii, 12; B. T. Men. 39b. Tg. O. renders 'of wreathen work' Ex. xxviii, 14 by *ʿōvadh gĕdhīlū*. This is the guilloche so common in Hellenistic art; also on the Dura-Europos shield, cf. ch. 6, § 2 (1c) and p. 119, n. 1.

work. The word is spelled in DSW both with final *yod* and the more 'regular' final *he*; so also *mar'eh* vi, 12, and cf. Yalon's view quoted ibid. Cf. also Yadin, JBL 74 (1955), 40–43.

pattern. This use of *ẓurah*, common in MH, occurs also Ezek. xliii, 11; cf. also DSW vii, 10.

running spiral. For this see ch. 6, § 2 (1 c).

welded together. Also line 8. For *mzz* 'to melt, cast', cf. MH *mzmz*, 'to soften'.

6. precious stones. For their use on shields see ch. 6, § 2 (1c at end) and p. 119, n. 1. The word occurs Isa. liv, 12.

ajour work. In line 9 without *aleph*: either the *beth* was followed by *shewa*, and thus could attract an *aleph prostheticum*, or the *aleph* is the preposition *eb-* for *bĕ-*, as in אבית משכו in the Wadi Murabbaʿat letter, and possibly in DSH xi, 6, cf. comm. on DSW i, 2. The only possible cognate known to me is Arabic *badan* 'short sleeveless coat', which Saadiah uses to translate ḥoshen (cf. Dozy, *Vêtements*, p. 56 sq.; id., *Supplément* I, 58; H. F. Lutz, 'A Note Regarding the Garment called *badan* and its Etymology', JAOS 42, (1922), 206–7—I take this opportunity of thanking Mr. U. Ben-Ḥorin for drawing my attention to this). If the word meant such a garment in Hebrew, the connexion with *riqmah* may prove that it was usually brocaded, and thus could be compared with ajour work in metal. For *riqmah* cf. *avnē fukh we-riqmah* 1 Chr. xxix, 2, which LXX renders λίθους πολυτελεῖς καὶ ποικίλους; the latter word, besides 'wrought in various colours of woven or embroidered stuffs', may also mean 'cunningly wrought in bronze'. It might even be considered whether our author did not read אבדני for אבני in Chr. Also in Ju. v, 30; Ezek. xvi, 10, 13, etc., and in an old song B. T. AZ 24b, *r*. refers to embroidery in metal threads. DSW vii, 10 *r*. is called 'cunningly wrought', as other metal work.

TEXT, TRANSLATION, AND COMMENTARY   281

5. מראת פנים והמגן מוסב מעשי גדיל שפה וצורת מחברת מעשה
חושב זהב וכסף ונחושת ממוזזים
6. ואבני חפץ אבני ריקמה מעשה חרש מחשבת אורך המגן אמתים
וחצי ורוחבו אמה וחצי ובידם רמח
7. וכידן אורך הרמח שבע אמות מזה הסגר והלוהב חצי האמה
ובסגר שלושה צמדים מפותחים כמעשי
8. גדיל שפה בזהב וכסף ונחושת ממוזזים כמעשי צורת מחשבת
ומחברת הצ[נו]רה מזה ומזה לצמיד
9. סביב אבני חפץ בדני ריקמה מעשי חרש מחשבת ושבולת והסגר
מחורץ בין הצמידים כמעשי

work of a smith, cunningly wrought.
This phrase, which recurs here 4 times,
combines the BH 'work of a smith'
(English vv. 'engraver') Ex. xxviii, 11,
and 'devise ... skilful work' Ex. xxxv. 35
a.o. Cf. Driver, *Welt des Orients*, 1956, p.
254 sq.

the shield. Its size (115 cm. × 69 cm.)
is also that of the ark of testimony (Ex.
xxv, 10) and its cover (Ex. xxxvii, 6). A
cubit and a half occurs in the measurements
of the table (ib. 10), the boards of the
tabernacle (Ex. xxvi, 16; xxxv, 21) and
the molten sea of brass (1 Kings, vii, 31).
The agreement is hardly accidental, cf.
ch. 6, § 1, also § 2 (2).

7. the length of the spear. 3 m. 20 cm.,
as opposed to the spears of the men of the
'towers' (ix, 12) and the cavalry of the
Serekh (vi, 14), both of which were
8 cubits long; cf. ch. 6, § 11.

the socket. Cf. ch. 6, § 11 (3). The
nearest cognates known to me are BH
misgereth 'border', Ex. xxv, 25; 1 Kings
vii, 28, etc.; and MH *sugar* (Syr. *sūgārā*,
borrowed into Arabic as *sājūr*) 'collar of
an animal'. Concerning Ps. xxxv, 3 see
p. 137, n. 3.

the blade. Written in the DSS לוהב
(here and line 10), להוב (DST ii, 25)
as in Targumic (Na. iii, 3), and להב
(line 10) as in MT; cf. also שלהובת
for *shalheveth*, DSW vi, 3. The blade of a
spear (*ḥănith*) is *lahav* in Jb. xxxix, 23;
laheveth in 1 Sam. xvii, 7.

of which ... take up. Lit. 'of this
the socket and the blade half a cubit'.
It is possible to assume that *mizzeh*
means 'on this side of', thus excluding
the blade from the reckoning, and making
the whole spear 7½ cubits long. However,
the details which follow show that the
socket was itself fairly wide, and would
hardly have been ignored in measuring the
length, as the second interpretation implies.
Moreover, in ix, 12 the scroll gives the full
length of the spear.

rings. In BH 'rings' in general, here
clasps to hold the blade to the shaft; the
idea of clasping or linking is inherent in
the root *ṣmd*. Cf. ch. 6, § 11 (3).

engraved ... cunningly wrought.
Same combination of terms 2 Chr. ii, 13.
See fig. 7.

the pattern, etc. See ch. 6, § 11 (3),
and p. 138, n. 2.

on both sides of. The phrase Josh.
viii, 33.

9. ear of corn. See ch. 6, § 11 (2) and
figs. 4, 7 for this motif, which recurs on
the spear blade (line 10) and on the sword
(line 11). Cf. also comm. vi, 12.

fluted. MH root, cf. *ḥariẓ* 'ditch'
(M. Kil. v, 3), *ḥaruẓ* 'grooved' (B. T.
Shabb. 98*b*); cf. ch. 6, § 11 (3), comm.
on xv, 6; xvi, 9. The connexion with
columns suggests the pillars of Ex. xxvii,
10 with their 'fillets' (*ḥăshuqehen*), which
seem to have been something like the
'rings' here. Cf. also 1 Kings vii, 15-22.

10. between the rings like the working of | a column, cunningly wrought. The blade shall be of iron tempered in fire, work of a smith, cunningly wrought, and an ear of corn of pure gold in the midst of (OR : inlaid in)
11. the blade, *the blade being made* tapering towards | the point. The swords shall be of iron refined *and* purified in the furnace and tempered like a face mirror, work of a smith, cunningly wrought, with ear-of-corn
12. figures | of pure gold appliqué on it on both sides. The lips shall be straight up to the point, two on either side. The length of the sword
13. shall be a cubit | and a half and its breadth four fingers. The scabbard shall be four thumbs, and four hand-breadths up to the scabbard, the
14. scabbard being tied this way | and that way *with thongs of* five hand-breadths. The handle of the sword shall be bright horn, artificer's work, inlaid in ajour with gold and silver and precious stones.

Section 9

15. When the [priests and levites and all men of the Serekh] are on the spot, they shall array themselves into seven formations, one behind the
16. other, | and there shall be a space [between each front formation and the next . . . and] thirty cubits, where the skirmishers shall take up their

10. iron tempered in fire. Lit. ' white from fire '; for the term cf. Dn. xi, 35; xii, 10; M. AZ v. 12 (with *ur*, as here); B. T. Ḥul, 8*ab*. The process described is less elaborate than that for the steel of the sword (line 11): probably the metal was less hard, as is also suggested by the different method of attaching the ear-of-corn pattern, cf. ch. 6, § 6 (4), § 11 (2). It is also possible to read *me'ir* ' shining tempered iron '.
in the midst of the blade. Cf. Ex. xxxix, 3 a.o. Note the difference from the sword, where the pattern is appliqué.
tapering. Read *shafudh* part. pass., cf. Aram. *shappīdh* id., B. T. Bekh. 40a, from MH *shappudh*, Syr. *shappūdhā*, Ar. *saffūd* (cf. σποδός) ' spit ', hence lit. ' shaped like a spit '.
11. the point. Lit. ' head ', cf. ch. 6, § 11 (1).
swords. Cf. at length ch. 6, § 6 (1) p. 127, n. 4, and see fig. 4.
refined. Cf. Isa. xlix. 2 Possibly ' strong ', cf. Lieberman, *Greek in Jewish Palestine* (1942), p. 51. Cf. also comm. line 14.

purified. Cf. Ex. xxv, 11, etc.; Mal. iii, 3.
12. appliqué. The root *ḥbr* is frequently used for the joining of two objects after completion, e.g. Ex. xxvi, 3; xxviii, 7; M. Kel. xiv, 2, etc., cf. ch. 6 § 6 (4). For the use of this technique see p. 137, n. 1.
' **lips** '. (*samekh* for BH *śin*); see ch. 6, § 6 (2–3) and fig. 4.
point. For the spelling see comm. ii, 1.
a cubit and a half. i.e. 68.7 cm. The measurement apparently applies to the blade only, cf. ch. 6, § 6 (1). See also comm. line 6 for O.T. parallels.
13. four fingers. i.e. *c*. 6 cm. On the ' finger ', see p. 116, n. 2. The measure occurs once in the O.T., Jer. lii, 21, where also four, as also M. Men. xi, 4.
scabbard. Lit. ' belly ', cf. ch. 6, § 6 (5).
four thumbs. i.e. 7.6 cm., cf. p. 116, n. 2.
four hand-breadths. i.e. 30. 4 cm., cf. ibid. No ' four handbreadths ' occur in the O.T., hence this measurement is not based on some Biblical reminiscence (as e.g. the 1½ cubits). The handbreadth is frequent in the Mishnah.

TEXT, TRANSLATION, AND COMMENTARY 283

10. עמוד מחשבת והלוהב ברזל לבן מאיר מעשי חרש מחשבת ושבולת
זהב טהור בתוך הלהב ושפוד אל
11. הראש והכידנים ברזל ברור טהור בכור ומלובן כמראת פנים
מעשי חרש מנ[ח]שבת ומראי שבולת
12. זהב טהור חוברת בו לשני עבריו וספות ישר אל הראוש שתים
מזה ושתים מזה אורך הכידן אמה
13. וחצי ורחבו ארבע אצבעות והבטן ארבע גודלים וארבעה טפחים
עד הבטן והבטן מרוגלת הנה
14. והנה חמשה טפחים ויד הכידן קרן ברורה מעשה חושב צורת
ריקמה בזהב ובכסף ואבני חפץ

[ט]

15. ובעמוד ה[כוהנים והלויים וכול אנשי הסרך] יסדרו שבע המערכות
מערכה אחר מערכה
16. ור̇ו̇ח̇ [יהיה בין מערכת פנים למערכת פנים – וש]לושים באמה אשר
יעמודו שם אנ̇ש̇י̇

up to the scabbard. i.e. to the point where the scabbard is tied, cf. ch. 6, § 6 (5) and p. 127, n. 4, and see fig. 7.

tied. The *resh* is certain, cf. the *reshs* in the second and third words of this line as against the *daleth* in the seventh. For the word see ch. 6, § 6 (6) and p. 127, n. 2, for the method of attachment ib. (8) and figs. 3 and 4. It is of importance for determining the date.

14. five hand-breadths. i.e. 38 cm.
handle. The Biblical *niẓẓav*, Ju. iii, 22; cf. ch. 6, § 6 (7).
bright. I have not found any parallel to the use of this adjective with horn; presumably it denotes some special quality. Perhaps it means 'selected', cf. CDC x, 4 (Rabin).
horn. For the use of horn for sword handles, cf. ch. 6, § 6 (7).

15. when the priests, etc. This much-damaged passage described the troops as drawn up before regrouping for battle, in close formation, so as to facilitate the performance of the ceremonies. Cf. ch. 7, § 5 (7); ch. 8, § 5 (1), fig. 11. The restoration here follows xv, 4, and fits the gap precisely.

are on the spot. Lit. 'have stood up', perfective gerund, as in vii, 8. Other references to the same 'spot' xiv, 3; xvi, 2.
they shall array themselves. As opposed to the later stage, xv, 5–6, where the chief priest does the arraying, cf. ch. 8, § 5 (1).
seven formations. Cf. ix, 4; ch. 7, § 5 (3).
one behind the other. In depth for the review, as opposed to 'formation opposite formation', vii, 8; 1 Sam. xvii, 21. Cf. fig. 11.

16. a space. Cf. Gen. xxxii, 17; DSW vii, 6. The restoration follows vii, 6–7, and fits the gap.
thirty cubits. On the basis of the general system and the spaces needed, I tend to think that 'thirty' was not preceded by any units, cf. ch. 7, § 5 (7). Thirty cubits is the length of the curtains, Ex. xxvi, 8, and the circumference of the sea of molten brass, 1 Kings vii, 23; 2 Chr. iv, 2 (LXX: thirty-three). The diameter of the sea is 10 cubits: the depth of the formation—according to my calculation—is the same, which may not be entirely accidental.

17. position | [   ] to the men of the front formations
    [and the sk[irmishers   ]
last line [First two skirmishing battalions shall go forth, armed with slings and shields, and shall take up position between the lines, and shall throw]

COLUMN VI

seven times, and withdraw to their position. After these, three skirmishing battalions shall go forth and take up position between the lines.
2. The first battalion shall hurl into | the enemy line seven battle darts. On the blade of the *first* dart they shall write ' Flash of a lance to the
3. might of God ', on the second weapon they shall write | ' Sparks of blood to fell the slain by the anger of God ', on the third dart they shall write ' Glitter of a sword devouring the sinful slain by the judgement of
4. God '. | Each of these shall throw seven times and then return to their position. After these, two skirmishing battalions shall go forth and take
5. up position between the lines, | the first battalion being armed with lance and shield and the second with shield and sword

    To slay through the judgement of God

---

17. skirmishers. Cf. ch. 7, § 4 (2). Their battalions are at this stage drawn up separately in close order behind the front formation (fig. 11).

men of the front. The word ' front ' is the only one clearly legible. The extant remnants preceding it seem to me not to allow any other restoration.

to the men. Only *shin* is clearly identifiable. A possible restoration for the first half of line 17 is : ' [and the men of the cavalry shall also take up position on the right and the left] of the men of the front, etc. ' ; cf. vi, 7 ; viii, 4–5.

armed with slings and shields. The restoration is based on the following considerations : Our passage speaks of the order in which the skirmishers advance, not of the system of signals for this, which is dealt with in col. viii. There were seven skirmishing standards (ch. 7, § 4 (3)), the first of which were either two of sling-men, or one of sling-men and one of bowmen,

but there is little evidence for the latter alternative. For my reasons for putting these two units at the two extremities (fig. 8), see ch. 7, § 4 (5–6).

shall throw. Probably, as the rest, a shorter expression than in viii, 1.

Column VI

seven times. Cf. viii, 1–2. Every man throws seven stones, just as each dart-man throws seven darts.

their position. Cf. ch. 7, § 2 (3). This was, according to viii, 2–3, ' by the side of the first formation ', cf. ch. 7, § 4 (6) and fig. 8.

three skirmishing battalions. All armed with darts. These, after advancing, deploy in ' three arrays ' (viii, 7), i.e. one beside the others of ch. 7, § 4 (6), fig. 8b.

between the lines. Cf. ch. 7, § 5 (2).

the first battalion. Of the three now going out.

hurl. Cf. ch. 6, § 7.

TEXT, TRANSLATION, AND COMMENTARY 285

17. [הבינים — - - - - -] [וֹאַנ]שִׁי הפנים [וֹאֲנ]שִׁי֯ [- - -]

VI

1. שבע פעמים ושבו למעמדם ואחריהם יצאו שלושה דגלי בינים
   ועמדו בין המערכות הדגל הראישון ישליך [א]ל
2. מערכת האויב שבעה זרקות מלחמה ועל לוהב הזרק יכתובו
   ברקת חנית לגבורת אל ועל השלט השני יכתובו
3. זיקי דם להפיל חללים באף אל ועל הזרק השלישי יכתובו
   שלהובת חרב אוכלת חללי און במשפט אל
4. כול אלה יטילו שבע פעמים ושבו למעמדם ואחריהם יצאו שני
   דגלי בינים ועמדו בין שתי המערכות הדגל
5. הראישון מחזיק חנית ומגן והדגל השני מחזיקי מגן וכידן להפיל
   חללים במשפט אל ולהכניע מכֹ֗ת

2. **seven battle darts.** i.e. seven per soldier, not one per 'array', as there were no seven arrays, cf. ch. 6, § 7. On the 'dart' (*iaculum*, *c.* 1.17 m. long), see ibid.
   blade. For the spelling cf. v. 7.
   of the first dart. Of the first battalion. The darts of each battalion had a different device. Cf. ch. 6, §§ 9, 12; ch. 3, § 2; ch. 5, § 7. The detailed instructions suggest that such inscriptions were really customary and may one day come to light.
   flash of a lance. Cf. Hab. iii, 11; Nah. iii, 3 (in both *baraq*). Cf. also P. T. Yoma iii, 40 (Rabin).
   might of God. Cf. comm. iii, 8.
   the second weapon. i.e. that of the second battalion. For discussion of *shlṭ*, see ch. 6, § 8.

3. **sparks.** Cf. Pr. xxvi, 18; Isa. l, 11; CDC v, 13. Parallel with 'lightnings' in DST i, 12. See also p. 135, n. 2. For the rest of the device cf. iii, 8; iv, 1.
   the third dart. i.e. that of the third battalion. For the device cf. comm. v, 7; p. 135, n. 3; also Ezek. xxi, 3; Cant. viii, 6.
   a sword devouring. Cf. comm. xi, 11–12; ch. 6, § 6 (2–3).
   sinful slain. Cf. iii, 8; for the connexion of 'sword' and 'slain' see Num. xix, 16; Ezek. xxi, 19, etc.
   judgement of God. Also iv, 6.

4. **their position.** See ch. 7, § 4 (6).

5. **lance.** On this cf. ch. 6, § 10; for the shield ib. § 2 (2). This battalion is discussed ch. 7, § 4 (5).
   shield and sword. For close fighting, cf. ch. 6, § 2 (2), 6; ch. 7, § 4 (5).
   to slay, etc. A poetical passage pieced together from phrases occurring in the inscriptions on various objects. Possibly such inscriptions were also found on the weapons named here.
   to slay through the judgement of God. Combination of the devices on the second and third dart.

U

6.   and to vanquish the line | of the enemy by God's might,
to exact retribution for their wickedness
   upon all nations of vanity,
and the kingdom shall be of the God of Israel,
   and He shall do valiant deeds through the saints of His people.

Section 10

7. Seven arrays of horsemen shall also be posted at the right and at the left of the battle line. Their arrays shall take up position on either side,
8. seven hundred | horsemen being on one side and seven hundred on the other. Two hundred horsemen shall go forth with *each* thousand of the
9. formation of the skirmishers, and likewise | they shall take up position on all sides of the camp: in all four thousand six hundred, and one thousand four hundred cavalry attached to the men drawn up in the
10. formations, | fifty to each formation. Thus the horsemen *serving* with the cavalry of the men of the Serekh will be six thousand, *that is* five
11. hundred to a tribe. All the cavalry that go forth | to battle with the skirmishers shall be *on* male horses fleet of foot, tender of mouth, long

line. Same scribal error as in v, 3; cf. also vi. 9. For the formula cf. i, 14–15; vi, 2.

6. retribution . . . nations of vanity. Both together in iv, 12. Cf. Jer. li, 24, 56; Isa. lxvi, 6.

and the kingdom, etc. Enlarged quot. Ob. 21; also xii, 15; xix, 8.

God of Israel. Also xiii, 1; xvi, 1; xvii, 4–5 (?); xviii. 6. In O.T. only 'God, the God (*ĕlohē*) of Israel', Gn. xxxiii, 20.

valiant deeds. Cf. Ps. lx, 14; cviii, 14.

saints of His people. Also ix, 8; x, 8, 10; xii, 1, 7; xvi, 1. A similar sentence xvi, 1.

7. seven arrays of horsemen. Thus each 'array' had 100 men. For all questions affecting the cavalry see ch. 7, § 6; for the terminology employed, p. 144, n. 2.

at the right and the left. While the rest of the light cavalry stands 'on all sides of the camp' (line 9); cf. ch. 7, § 6 (2).

8. two hundred horsemen. Out of these 1,400. For the importance of this formulation for reconstructing the size of the battalion, cf. ch. 7, § 4 (3–4). The term 'formation' here denotes the combinations acting together in battle: (1) two battalions of sling-men (with 400 cavalry); (2) three battalions of darts-men (with 600 cavalry); (3) the lance-bearers and the swordsmen (with 400 cavalry); cf. ch. 7, § 4 (6).

9. they. i.e. further cavalry of the same type.

the camp. i.e. the entire army in battle order, cf. ch. 3, § 4. In fig. 8 these appear at the sides and only at the extremities of the rear, for reasons stated in ch. 7, § 6 (2).

6. אויב בגבורת אל לשלם גמול רעתם לכול גוי הבל והיתה לאל
ישראל המלוכה ובקדושי עמו יעשה חיל

[י]

7. ושבעה סדרי פרשים יעמודו גם המה לימין המערכה ולשמאולה
מזה ומזה יעמודו סדריהם שבע מאות
8. פרשים לעבר האחד ושבע מאות לעבר השני מאתים פרשים
יצאו עם אלף מערכת אנשי הבינים וכן
9. יעמודו לכול ע[ב]רֿי המחנה הכול שש מאות וארבעת אלפים
ואלף וארבע מאות רכב לאנשי סרך המעׄרכות
10. חמשים למערכהֿ [הא]חת ויהיו הפרשים על רכב אנשי הסרך
ששת אלפים חמש מאות לשבט כול הרכב היוצאים
11. למלחמה עם אנ[שי] הבנים סוסים זכרים קלי רגל ורכי פה
וארוכי רוח ומלאים בתבון ימיהם מלומדי מלחמה

in all. This leaves 3,200 for those 'on all sides of the camp'. For a full account, see ch. 7, § 6 (2).

cavalry. The rendering 'chariots' is out of question. These 1,400 (out of 4,600) make up the heavy cavalry; they are the 'horsemen of the Serekh' of line 13. For full discussion of the terms used, see ch. 7, § 6 (3); for comparison with Roman practice, ibid. (5). The different units, with numbers, are set out ibid. (4).

10. to each formation. Here this denotes the heavy infantry formation of 1,000 men; our passage proves there were 28 of these, and this conforms with the number 28,000 for the infantry in ix, 4–5; cf. ch. 7, § 5 (4).

men of the Serekh. This must mean here the entire 'congregation' or fighting force. The number is confirmed ix, 5. Cf. in detail ch. 7, § 2 (5).

five hundred to a tribe. Thus the cavalry, like all other troops, though drawn from the tribes, is not organized in tribal units; cf. ch. 4, §§ 4–5.

all the cavalry. As line 13 proves, the reference is to the 4,600 light cavalry, not merely to the 1,400 directly associated with the skirmishing units.

11. male horses. For discussion see ch. 7, § 6 (6), and p. 181, n. 2. Note the contrast in attitude with B. T. Pes. 103b: 'The horse loves lechery and battle, is proud, spurns sleep, eats much and passes out little, and some say it seeks to kill its master in battle'.

fleet of foot. Cf. 2 Sam. ii, 18; Isa. xxx, 16; Am. ii, 15.

tender of mouth. So that they easily obey the reins.

long of wind. We have here the literal meaning of the phrase which in O.T. and MH always means 'patient, forbearing'.

12. of wind, full in the measure of their years, trained for battle | and accustomed to hearing noises and to the sight of all spectacles. Their riders shall be men of valour for battle, trained in horsemanship, the
13. measure | of their age being from thirty to forty-five years. The horsemen
14. of the Serekh shall be from forty to fifty years old, and they | and their m[ounts shall be] g[arbed in cuir]asses, helmets and greaves, armed with
15. round shields and a spear eight cubits long, | [and the horsemen of the skirmishers shall hold a shield] and a bow and arrows and battle darts, all of them ready in their arr[ays for the day of vengeance, volunteers
16. for battle] | [to destroy the enemy in the battle of Go]d and to shed the blood of their guilty slain. These are the ho[rsemen according to their arrays. . . .   ]

SECTION 11

[   ]
last line [. . . The skirmishers shall be from thirty to forty-five years old,]

COLUMN VII

the men of the Serekh shall be from forty to fifty years old, the camp

measure. The noun occurs line 12; DSD v, 3, 7; vi, 4, 8, 9, 10, 22; viii, 4, 19; ix, 2, 7, 12, 18, 21; x, 5, 7, 9; DST xii, 5, 8, 9; DSH vii, 13. In BH only the verb *tikken*, Isa. xl, 12; Job xxviii, 25; Ecclus. xvi, 31 (27). Cf. also H. L. G[insberg] in Brownlee, *Manual* p. 36.

trained for battle. ¶ Cant. iii, 8; cf. also 1 Chr. v, 18; Isa. ii, 4; 2 Sam, ii. 22, 35.

12. and accustomed. Cf. Sukenik, *M. G.* I, 23, who compares CDC xiv, 9; Yalon, *KS* 26 (5702), 285.

noises. Cf. 'noise of war' Ex. xxxii, 17; Isa. xiii, 2-4; Jer. 1, 22; specially of the noise made by horsemen: Jer. iv, 29; viii, 16; xlvii, 3, etc. See also comm. i, 11, and cf. M. Sot. viii, 1; B. T. Sot. 42b.

the sight of all spectacles. The final *yodh* for *he* in *mar'eh* is a spelling common in the scrolls, cf. Yalon, *KS* 26 (5702), 286; Yadin, *JBL* 74 (1955), 40 sq. *Dimyonim* (cf. Ps. xvii, 12) is used here like its BH synonym *dĕmuyyoth* in MH.

their riders. i.e. the real cavalry, as opposed to the mounted infantry of the 'horsemen of the Serekh'.

men of valour for battle. ¶ Jer. xlviii, 14; cf. v.d. Ploeg, *Vivre et Penser* 1941, p. 121 sq.; Junge p. 43, 70, 71, 72, n. 2.

trained in horsemanship. Again in contrast to the horsemen of the heavy infantry.

13. their age. See ch. 4, § 4 (1).

the horsemen of the Serekh. The heavy cavalry, not to be confused with 'the horsemen with the cavalry of the men of the Serekh', line 10, cf. ibid.; ch. 7, § 6 (3).

from 40 to 50. The same age as the heavy infantry, vii, 1; cf. ch. 4, § 4 (1). lap by 5 years (40–45). In p. 181, n. 1, it is suggested that the part of the heavy cavalry which belonged to those five annual classes fought in conjunction with the skirmishing standards, whose ages also covered 30–45.

14. their mounts . . . greaves. The reconstruction hangs on reading the fourth

12. וּבְעוֹלִים לִשְׁמוֹעַ [קֹ]וֹלוֹת וּלְכוֹל מַרְאֵי דְמִיוֹנִים וְהָרוֹכְבִים עֲלֵיהֶם
    אַנְשֵׁי חַיִל לַמִּלְחָמָה מְלוּמְדֵי רֶכֶב וְתָכוּן
13. יְמֵיהֶם מִבֶּן שְׁלוֹשִׁים שָׁנָה עַד בֶּן חָמֵשׁ וְאַרְבָּעִים וּפָרָשֵׁי הַסֶּרֶךְ יִהְיוּ
    מִבֶּן אַרְבָּעִים שָׁנָה וְעַד בֶּן חֲמִשִּׁים וְהֵמָּה
14. זֹ[אֹת כֻּבָּם] לְ[בֻשִׁים שִׁרְיֹ]וֹנוֹת וּבָתֵּי רָאשִׁים וְשׁוֹקִיִם וּמַחֲזִיקִים בִּידָם
    מָגִנֵּי עֲגֻלָּה וְרֹמַח אָרוּךְ שְׁמֹנֶה [אַמּוֹת -]
15. [וּפָרָשֵׁי הַבֵּנַיִם יַחֲזִיקוּ מָגֵן] וְקֶשֶׁת וְחִצִּים וְזִרְקוֹת מִלְחָמָה וְכֻלָּם עֲתוּדִים
    בְּסִ[דְרֵיהֶם] לְיוֹם נָקָם אַנְשֵׁי נִדְבַת מִלְחָמָה]
16. [לְהַשְׁמִיד אוֹיֵב בְּמִלְחֶמֶת אֵ]ל וְלִשְׁפֹּךְ דָּם חַלְלֵי אַשְׁמָתָם אֵלֶּה הֵמָּה
    הָרֹ[וֹכְבִים לְסִדְרֵיהֶם]

[יא]

[. . .] וְאַנְשֵׁי הַבֵּנַיִם יִהְיוּ מִבֶּן שְׁלוֹשִׁים שָׁנָה עַד בֶּן חָמֵשׁ וְאַרְבָּעִים] (last line)

VII

1. וְאַנְשֵׁי הַסֶּרֶךְ יִהְיוּ מִבֶּן אַרְבָּעִים שָׁנָה וְעַד בֶּן חֲמִשִּׁים וְסוֹרְכֵי הַמַּחֲנוֹת
   יִהְיוּ מִבֶּן /חֲמִ/שִּׁים שָׁנָה וְעַד בֶּן //שִׁים וְהַשּׁוֹטְרִים

---

word *battē* (as Sukenik did), and not, e.g. וכתו, as allusion to Ju. xv, 8. The *beth* is, in my opinion, unmistakable (cf. the *kaph* in xviii, 2, second word from end). The ensuing restoration fits both traces and gaps, except for the first word, which I restore with some reserve. In line 10 *rekhev* both times might be translated as ' horses '; cf. p. 122, n. 3.

garbed in cuirasses. Cf. 1 Sam. xvii, 5, 38; Isa. lix, 17; Jer. xlvi, 4; 2 Chr. xxvi, 14; Ex. Rabba xv.

helmets and greaves. For the terms, oddly divergent from BH, see ch. 6, §§ 3–4.

round shields. Targumic expression, = *parma* or *clipeus*; cf. ch. 6, § 2 (3).

eight cubits. Tops of the letters still visible; cf. ix, 12; ch. 6, § 11 (4).

15. and the horsemen of the skirmishers. The restoration is based on two considerations: it is reasonable for the author to have gone on from the heavy to the light cavalry, and the weapons described would suit them perfectly; cf. ch. 7, § 6 (2).

arrays . . . for battle. The word ' arrays ' is fairly certain; the rest restored after vii, 5; cf. also x, 5 and comm. xv, 2.

16. to destroy . . . of God. Restored after ix, 5.

their guilty slain. Cf. iii, 8 and xiii, 4.

the horsemen. The *he* is certain, the *resh* less so.

the skirmishers. Restored after vi, 13; cf. ch. 4, § 4. Line 16 ends close to the left margin, and the space below it is rather large: hence presumably one line was left free and a new section started. Thus only two, at most three, lines seem to be lost at the end of col. vi.

Column VII

Serekh. Here = the front formations; cf. ch. 7, § 2 (5) and ch. 4, § 4. Their age is identical with that of the ' horsemen of the Serekh ', vi, 13.

camp prefects. See ch. 7, § 3 (1). They are above fighting age, cf. ch. 4, § 4 (2).

2. prefects shall be from fifty to sixty years old, the provosts, | too, shall be from forty to fifty years old.   All those that despoil the slain and collect
3. the booty and cleanse the land and guard the arms | and he who prepares the provisions, all these shall be from twenty-five to thirty years old. No young boy and no woman shall enter their encampments when they go
4. forth | from Jerusalem to go to battle, until their return. Any one halt or blind or lame, or a man in whose body is a permanent defect, or a man
5. affected by an impurity of | his flesh, all these shall not go forth to battle with them. All of them shall be volunteers for battle and sound in spirit
6. and flesh, and ready for the day of vengeance. Any | man who is not pure with regard to his sexual organs on the day of battle shall not join them in battle, for holy angels are in communion with their hosts. There
7. shall be a space | between all their camps and the place of the ' hand ', about two thousand cubits, and no unseemly evil thing shall be seen in the vicinity of their encampments.

50 to 60. Corrected from ' forty to fifty ' (by the scribe or by a later hand ?) by erasing the *aleph* and *ʿayin* of the first and *ḥeth* and *mem* of the second word, by altering in the first word *resh* into *ḥeth* and *beth* into *mem*, and finally by adding a *shin* above the line in each word. Cf. ch. 11, § 4 C (10).

provosts. On these see ch. 7, § 3 (2).

2. too. This word makes sense only with the first, erased, version of the age of the prefects. Apparently the scribe or redactor overlooked it, unless it be meant to refer back to the age of the heavy infantry.

that despoil the slain and collect the booty. Cf. ch. 7, § 3 (3).

and cleanse the land. i.e. bury the dead. Cf. Ezek. xxxix, 4-12 ; ch. 7, § 3 (4).

and guard the arms. Ibid. (5).

3. he who prepares the provisions. The singular is probably accidental, cf. ibid. (6).

from 25 to 30. i.e. under fighting age ; no one under 25 took part in war at all. Cf. ch. 4, § 4 (1). Cf. also *Qumran I*, p. 110, i, 12-15.

no young boy. Under 25. The word *zaʿṭuṭ* (also written זאטוט, זטוט) occurs in MH, and was written in an ancient copy of the Pent. instead of (or perhaps together with, as here ?) *naʿărē* in Ex. xxiv, 5 (P. T. Taan. iv, 2 ; cf. *Sifre*

Dt. xxxiii, 27 ; Segal, *JBL* 72 (1953), 41) ; it has been derived from Aram. *zūṭā* ' small ', cf. also Syr. *zṭūṭā*. The epithet, like ' small ' (1 Kings xi, 17 ; 2 Kings, ii, 23) or ' and tender ' (1 Chr. xxii, 5 ; xxix, 1, etc.) is to distinguish *naʿar* ' boy ' from its homonym *naʿar* ' warrior ', as in 1 Chr xii, 28, and cf. Yadin, JPOS 21 (1948), 114. For the reason for the prohibition see ch. 4, § 4 (1), § 3 (a). Similarly *Qumran I*, p. 110, i, 19 seq. forbids participation in battle to ' every young (? פותי) man '.

woman. Cf. ch. 4, § 2, § 3 (a). For the strict formulation, see ib. § 3.

when they go forth—until their return. See comm. iv, 9 seq.

4. permanent defect. In MH *mum qavuaʿ*, inclusive term for the defects enumerated before.   Cf. on the whole conception ch. 4, § 3 (b). Cf. also *Qumran I*, p. 110, ii, 4-10.

an impurity of his flesh. i.e. one of the impurities enumerated in Lev. xiii (where our compound term does not occur). These are forbidden within the camp (ib. 46). Cf. ch. 4, § 3 (b). The formulation, less severe than in the case of boys and women, suggests that they may have served away from the actual battlefield.

5. all of them. i.e. those who fight, cf. vi, 15 ; x. 5. ' Volunteers ' belongs to the

TEXT, TRANSLATION, AND COMMENTARY 291

2. יהיו גם הם מבן ארבעים שנה ועד בן חמשים וכול מפשיטי
החללים ושוללי השלל ומטהרי הארץ ושומרי הכלים
3. ועורך הצידה כולם מבן חמש ועשרים שנה ועד בן שלושים
וכול נער זעטוט ואשה לוא יבואו למחנותם בצאתם
4. מירושלים ללכת למלחמה עד שובם וכול פסח או עור או חגר
או איש אשר מום עולם בבשרו או איש מנוגע בטמאת
5. בשרו כול אלה לוא ילכו אתם למלחמה כולם יהיו אנשי נדבת
מלחמה ותמימי רוח ובשר ועתודים ליום נקם וכול
6. איש אשר לוא יהיה טהור ממקורו ביום המלחמה לוא ירד אתם
כיא מלאכי קודש עם צבאותם יחד ורוח יהיה
7. בין כול מחניהמה למקום היד כאלפים באמה וכול ערות דבר
רע לוא יראה סביבות כול מחניהם

characteristic vocabulary of the Scrolls: DSD v, 1, 6, 8; vi, 13; ix, 24 (see also i, 7, 11; v, 10, 21); DST xiv, 26; xv, 2. Cf. further v.d. Ploeg, *Le Manuel*, etc. p. 115, n. 2; Brownlee, *Manual*, p. 7, n. 4; p. 35, n. 7. The root *ndb* is used in connexion with war Ju. v, 2, 9; Ps. cx, 3; 2 Chr. xvii, 16; cf. also Cant. Rabba iv on Num. xxxi, 5: 'the twelve thousand were volunteers'. Cf. also Licht, *Hodayoth*, p. 39.

sound in spirit and flesh. Cf. Lev. i, 3 seq., etc.; 2 Sam. xxii, 26 'perfect warrior' (Ps. xviii, 26 'man of perfection', but LXX, Pesh. as 2 Sam.). Both as noun and adjective, *tamim* is frequent in the Scrolls.

ready for the day of vengeance. Cf. comm. vi, 15. ¶ Est. viii, 13 (Kethiv). Read perhaps עתוד for עתו in DSD ix, 23 and *Qumran I*, p. 110, i, 27; the word there may also be *ʿitti* (Lev. xvi, 21), explained P. T. Yoma vi, 3 as equivalent to *ʿattidh*, *mezumman* 'ready'. I thank Prof. S. Lieberman for drawing my attention to the P. T. passage.

6. who is not pure, etc. Cf. Dt. xxiii, 11 seq.; ch. 4, § 3 (c). Those who experienced a nocturnal emission must not partake in battle.

his sexual organs. Lit. 'his source'. This word is used in O.T. (Lev. xii, 7; Pr. v, 18) and MH (M. Nid. ii, 5, etc.) of the female genitalia, so also DST i, 22, and cf. Yadin, JBL 74 (1955), 40 seq.; of the male organ, PRE xxii. In view of the graphic similarity between מקרה [לילה] in Dt. xxiii, 11 (from which the preceding five words are taken) and מ[מקור] here, it should be considered whether we have not here a variant O.T. reading.

join them. Lit. 'go down', cf. 1 Sam. xxx, 24.

for holy angels . . . hosts. Based on Dt. xxiii, 15. The same expression *Qumran I*, p. 110, ii, 8–9. Cf. ch. 4, § 3, the comparative table. On angelic participation in battle, see comm. i, 10–11; xii, 7; ch. 9, § 6.

space. Cf. comm. v, 16.

the 'hand'. ¶ Dt. xxiii, 13. 'Hand' = 'sign', see viii, 5; and cf. ch. 4, § 3.

7. 2,000 cubits. Based on Josh. iii, 4. See ch. 4, § 3 for the connexion with the sabbath-limit.

no unseemly evil thing. Combined from Dt. xxiii, 10 and 15; also in x, 1. 'Shall be seen' corresponds to '(God) shall see' ib. 15.

Section 12

8. When the battle formations are deployed over against the enemy, formation opposite formation, there shall go forth from the middle
9. interval into the space between the lines seven | priests of the sons of Aaron, clad in garments of white byssus: a linen tunic and linen trousers,
10. and girt with a linen girdle of twined byssus, blue, | purple and scarlet, and a brocaded pattern, cunningly wrought, and turbaned headdresses upon their heads, *these being* garments for battle, and they shall not
11. bring them into the sanctuary. | The one priest shall be walking along in front of all the men of the line, to strengthen their hands in battle. In
12. the hands of the six *others* shall be | the trumpets of summoning, the trumpets of remembrance, the trumpets of the fanfare, the trumpets of
13. pursuit, and the trumpets of withdrawal. When the priests go forth | into the space between the lines, there shall go forth with them seven levites carrying seven ram's horns, and three provosts from among the levites
14. walking in front of | the priests and the levites. The priests shall blow the two trumpets of sum[moning when the battle intervals shall open] to
15. a width of fifty shields, | and fifty skirmishers shall come forth from the one interval [and fifty from the other interval, and there shall go forth with

---

8. when ... are deployed. Section 12 is the longest in the Scroll. The deployment alluded to here is that for battle, as opposed to the troops drawn up for being addressed before battle, v, 15.

formation opposite formation. Cf. 1 Sam. xvii, 21. On this order, see ch. 7, § 5 (8).

the middle interval. Cf. 'the middle (*tawekh*) gate', Jer. xxxix, 3, and ch. 7, n. 34. On the intervals see ib. § 2 (4). There were four of these, cf. ib. § 5 (8).

seven priests. Cf. Josh, vi, 4; Neh. xii, 41; 1 Chr. xv. 24; p. 107, nn. 1, 2; also below, line 13.

9. of the sons of Aaron. The addition alludes to the passages here used: Ex. xxviii, 40; xxxix, 27; Num. x, 8. Cf. p. 217, n. 5. For the deviations from the Biblical account, see ch. 8, § 5 (3).

10. brocaded pattern. etc. Cf. v, 6; p. 220, n. 3.

turbaned. Ex. xxxix, 28, cf. Ezek. xliv, 18, in both cases *pa'ărē*. Note the lack of *aleph*, hence probably also different vocalization. Since the word is borrowed from Egyptian *pyr*, we may have here a more genuine spelling than in MT (Rabin).

garments for battle. This refers to their use, not their shape or material, cf. ch. 8, § 5 (3b).

11. the one priest. He is called in xv. 6 'the priest destined for the appointed time of vengeance'; in contrast to the chief priest, he walks (also xv, 6) during his address, cf. ch. 8, § 5 (2), also ib. § 4, § 5 (1).

to strengthen their hands. Cf. Ezra vi, 22 (also here xv, 7). His address is given in full in xv, 7 seq.

the six others. Note that six priests blow trumpets, but seven levites blow the rams' horns, cf. p. 107, nn. 1, 2; p. 90, n. 1. The number of priests has no connexion with the different kinds of trumpet, cf. ch. 5, § 3 at end. Compare the list here with the two in ii, 15–iii, 11, and cf. ch. 5, ibid. for all details.

12. of summoning. Viz. the different units, mainly of skirmishers, cf. ch. 5, § 5 (7).

trumpets of remembrance. Also

TEXT, TRANSLATION, AND COMMENTARY

[יב]

8. ובסדר מערכות המלחמה לקראת אויב מערכה לקראת מערכה
   יצאו מן השער התיכון אל בין המערכות שבעה
9. כוהנים מבני אהרון לובשים בגדי שש לבן כתונת בד ומכנסי בד
   וחוגרים באבנט בד שש משזר תכלת
10. וארגמן ותולעת שני וצורת רקמה מעשה חושב ופרי מגבעות
    בראשיהם בגדי מלחמה ואל המקדש לוא
11. יביאום הכוהן האחד יהיה מהלך על פני כול אנשי המערכה לחזק
    ידיהם במלחמה וביד הששה יהיו
12. חצוצרות המקרא וחצוצרות הזכרון וחצוצרות התרועה
    וחצוצרות המרדף וחצוצרות המאסף ובצאת הכוהנים
13. אל בין המערכות יצאו עמהמה שבעה לויים ובידם שבעת
    שופרות היובל ושלושה שוטרים מן הלויים לפני
14. הכוהנים והלויים ותקעו הכוהנים בשתי חצוצרות המק[רא בהפתח
    שערי המ[לחמה על חמשים מגן
15. וחמשים אנשי בינים יצאו מן השער האחד [וחמשים מן השער השני
    ויצאו עמהמה ל[ויים שוטרים ועם

xvi, 3; xviii, 4; difficult to identify. Probably identical with the 'trumpets of battle arrays'.

trumpets of the fanfare. These include two classes of the other lists, see ch. 5, § 5 (4).

trumpets of pursuit. See ib. (2).

trumpets of withdrawal. Includes two classes of the other lists, see ib. (1).

13. seven levites, etc. In Josh. vi, 4 seven priests, see ch. 5, §§ 8-9, p. 107, nn. 1, 2. On the use of horns and trumpets in general, see ib. §§ 9-10.

provosts from among the levites. Cf. 1 Chr. xxiii, 4; 2 Chr. xxxiv, 13. These also sorted out the faint-hearted, cf. ch. 7, § 3 (2).

14. two trumpets of summoning. Cf. Num. x, 2. The sense, and the visible traces of a *qoph*, exclude the reading *ha-maʿăsaf*.

when the battle intervals shall open. Restored after iii, 7, cf. ib. line 1 and p. 96,

n. 2. These trumpets are blown after the opening of the intervals (cf. ch. 5, § 5 (5), ch. 7, § 5 (9)); the signal for the opening is given by the trumpets of remembrance, cf. xvi, 2-3 and ch. 5, § 5 (7).

fifty shields. i.e. 75 cubits, cf. p. 173, n. 1; comm. v, 3; ix, 13; ch. 6, § 2 (4) at end. On the method of opening, see ch. 7, § 5 (9).

15. fifty skirmishers. The skirmishers operate in units of fifty, cf. comm. iv, 3; ch. 7, § 4 (6). This corresponds to the strength of the *centuria* at certain periods, see ib. § 5 (9). Cf. possibly also Ex. xiii, 18; Josh. i, 14; iv, 12; Ju. vii, 11.

and fifty from the other interval. Restoration based on my reconstruction of the front line formation, ch. 7, § 5 (8) and fig. 8.

shall go forth. Or restore: shall take up position; in view of what follows, the former restoration is more probable.

16. them] levitical provosts. With | every formation they shall go forth according to all [this disposition. The priests shall blow the trumpets, and two] skirmishing [battalions shall go forth] from the intervals |
17. [and take up positi]on between the two lines, [carrying sling and shield . . . and the priests shall blow for them upon the trumpets of the[
18. batt[le array]s | [a level note   ]

COLUMN VIII

The trumpets shall keep blowing to direct the sling-men until they
2. have finished throwing seven | times. Then the priests shall blow on the [trumpets of withdrawal, and they shall come *to take up position* by the
3. side of the first formation | to fall in at their proper position. The priests
4. shall blow on the trumpets of summoning, and | three skirmishing battalions shall go forth from the intervals and take up position between
5. the lines, with cavalry on their flanks | on the right and on the left. The priests shall blow on their trumpets a level note, signals to array for
6. battle, | and the columns shall deploy into their proper arrays, each man

levitical provosts. Cf. line 13. Their task here seems to be the prevention of cowardice and flight, corresponding to the 'guards' (*zĕqifin*) armed with iron axes posted in front of and behind the fighters according to M. Soṭ. viii, 6; according to Maimonides (*Code*, Hilkhoth Melakhim vii, 3), these are posted behind each *ma'ărakhah*, as here.

16. every formation. Of the skirmishers, cf. vi, 8.

this disposition. Restored after viii, 14; cf. ch. 7, § 2 (5).

the priests . . . go forth. Restored after viii, 3-4, with the word 'calling' omitted for reasons of space, as these trumpets have been specified in line 14. Shorter version xvii 10. For 'two skirmishing formations' cf. ch. 7, § 4 (5).

the priests, etc. Here begins a detailed description of the advance of the skirmishing units, which was briefly sketched in vi, 1-6. The words following the gap recall viii, 3-4; cf. also vi, 4; but I have here omitted the word 'of calling' as the gap was not wide enough, and it is mentioned in line 14. For a shorter version see xvii, 10.

two skirmishing battalions. Cf. above and ch. 7, § 4 (5).

17. carrying sling and shield. Restored after vi, 4-5, and cf. 1 Sam. xvii, 40. The gap would seem to allow of the mention of one more weapon.

the priests . . . trumpets of the battle arrays. The word *ha-milḥamah* and the *yodh* preceding it are certain, so is the need for a statement parallel to that in viii, 5, which deals with the next group of skirmishers. As this is the first of a series, we may assume the description to have been fuller. The type of signal is here given at the end of the statement, as in viii, 13-14.

18. a level note. As col. viii opens with the concluding phases of the action of the sling-men, we may be sure that the rest of col. vii described their deployment. We cannot be sure that there was also a reference to a signal to advance (as in viii, 7), since the range of the slings is so much larger.

Column VIII

the trumpets. i.e. the 'trumpets of assault', cf. line 8 below.

TEXT, TRANSLATION, AND COMMENTARY 295

16. כול מערכה ומערכה יצאו בכול הס[ד]רך ה[ז]ה ותקעו הכוהנים בחצוצרות ויצאו שני דגלי ב[י]נים מן השערים
17. [ועמ]דו בין שתי המ[ער]כ[ו]ת ובן[י]דם קלע ומגן — ותקעו להם הכוהנים בחצוצרות סֹדרֹ[י] המל[חמה]
18. [קול מרודד . . .]

VIII

1. החצוצרות תהיינה מריעות לנצח אנשי הקלע עד כלותם להשליך שבע
2. פעמים ואחר יתקעו להם הכוהנים בחצוצרות המשוב ובאו ליד המערכה
3. הראישונה להתיצב על מעמדם ותקעו הכוהנים בחצוצרות המקרא ויצאו
4. שלושה דגלי בינים מן השערים ועמדו בין המערכות ולידם אנשי הרכב
5. מימין ומשמאול ותקעו הכוהנים בחצוצרות קול מרודד ידי סדר מלחמה
6. והראשים יהיו נפשטים לסדריהם איש למעמדו ובעומדם שלושה סדרים

to direct. Cf. viii, 9; ix, 2; xi, 2; xvi, 6; with *yĕdhē* xvi, 12; i.e. to give the rhythm so as to increase the efficiency of the action, see p. 99, n. 2, and comm. line 12 below. Another meaning in iv, 13. Dupont-Sommer's rendering *sans arrêt* (*Aperçus*, p. 100, reading *neẓaḥ*) is improbable both on contextual and on linguistic grounds. For the use here cf. Ezra, iii, 8–9; 1 Chr. xxiii, 4; 2 Chr. ii, 1, 17; xxxiv, 12–13.

sling-men. Cf. ch. 6, § 12; ch. 7, § 4 (5).

seven times. As in vi, 1, see comm. ibid.

2. by the side, etc. The sling-men return to a position by the side of the first row of the front formation, from where they can cover the withdrawal of the other skirmishing units, cf. ch. 7, § 4 (6).

4. three skirmishing battalions. These are the darts-men, described vi, 1–4.

cavalry. These are 'the cavalry that goes forth with the skirmishers', vi, 8.

5. the priests, etc. The following account of the action of the skirmishers concentrates mainly on the trumpet signals. Our scroll shows here much originality. See in detail ch. 5, § 6.

6. a level note. While all other signals are defined by pitch and type, this one is defined by one term only. See ch. 5, § 6 (2b).

signals. For this meaning of *yĕdhē*, see ch. 5, § 6 (1), also in the comparative table ib. (2).

to array for battle. Lit. 'of the array for b.'. This signal for the columns to fan out into arrays is given by the 'trumpets of the battle arrays'; cf. also xvi, 4 'fanfare for the array', and comm. vii, 12 'trumpets of remembrance'.

6. the columns shall deploy. i.e. pass from the column to the array order. Cf. ch. 7, § 2 (2).

296 TEXT, TRANSLATION, AND COMMENTARY

7. to his place. When they are drawn up in three arrays, | the priests shall blow for them a second fanfare, a low legato note, signals for advance,
8. until they approach | the enemy line and stretch their hands to *their*
9. weapons ; then the priests shall blow on the six trumpets | of assault a high-pitched intermittent note to direct the fighting, and the levites and
10. all the band of the horn-blowers shall blow | in unison a great battle
11. fanfare to melt the heart of the enemy. At the sound of the fanfare, | the battle darts shall go forth to fell the slain. The sound of the horns shall
12. cease, while on the trumpets | the priests shall keep on blowing a high-pitched intermittent note so as to direct, signals for fighting, until *the*
13. *skirmishers* have hurled into the line | of the enemy seven times. Then
14. the priests shall blow for them the trumpets of withdrawal, | a low note *alternately* level and legato. According to this disposition shall the
15. priests blow for the three battalions. When | the first *battalion* throws, [the priests and the levites and the whole band of horn-blowers] shall
16. blow a great fanfare | to direct the fighting [until they have thrown seven
17. times. Then there shall blow] for them the priests | on the trumpets [of withdrawal a low note *alternately* level and legato, and they shall come and

in three arrays. Each battalion forms one array, cf. ch. 7, § 4 (6).

7. a second fanfare. On the same trumpets. For the terms see Num. x and p. 87, n. 1.

low. Cf. ch. 5, § 6 (2c).

legato. i.e. rising and falling without breaking off. The root means ' to be adjoining ' in MH.

for advance. Apparently the same as ' to approach ', xvii, 11, i.e. moving forward *en masse* towards the range from which the darts are thrown, perhaps at the run. The root occurs 1 Sam. xx, 3 ; Isa. xxvii, 4, also (written with *samekh*) in MH. Cf. ch. 7, § 2 (2).

approach. Cf. xvii, 11.

8. stretch their hands. i.e. raise the arm so as to be ready for the throw, cf. p. 132, n. 2.

weapons. For this general term, see ch. 6, n. 4.

six trumpets. All six priests (cf. vii, 11) blow at once, see p. 90, n. 1.

9. high-pitched. Lit. ' sharp ', cf. Gen. Rabba xvi and ch. 5, § 6 (2a).

intermittent. Or ' staccato '—a rhythm particularly suitable for the moment of battle—cf. p. 103, n. 3, and P. T. Ber. ix, 13 ' if (the lightning) is *bĕ-ṭorĕdhin* one need only say the blessing once a day, if at intervals (*bĕ-mafsiqin*) one says a blessing each time ', hence *ṭrd* signifies ' recurrence in close succession ' (I thank Mr. I. Wartski for drawing my attention to this passage).

band of the horn-blowers. Also xvi 6–7. Cf. Josh. vi, 20 ; Ju. vii, 20 ; p. 107, n. 3.

10. in unison. Cf. Ex. xxiv, 3 ; 2 Chr. v, 13.

fanfare. Cf. ch. 5, § 8 and n. 64. ' Great fanfare ' Josh. vi, 20 ; 1 Sam. iv, 5 ; Ezra iii, 11, 13. ' Battle fanfare ' Jer, iv, 19 ; xlix. 2.

to melt the heart of the enemy. Cf. ' to melt (= disorganize) the enemy ', ix. 11–12. Not in O.T., but cf. Dt. i, 28 ; Isa. xix, 1. This is not a signal, but part of the battle tactics, cf. ch, 5, §§ 8–9.

at the sound of the fanfare. The trumpet signal starts both the fanfare and the action of the darts-men. For the use of *ʿim* cf. xvi, 7 ; xvii, 14 ; ch. 5, § 8.

11. shall go forth. i.e. shall be thrown ;

TEXT, TRANSLATION, AND COMMENTARY   297

7. ותקעו להם הכוהנים תרועה שנית קול נוח וסמוך ידי מפשע עד
   קורבם
8. למערכת האויב ונטו ידם בכלי המלחמה והכוהנים יריעו בשש
   חצוצרות
9. החללים קול חד טרוד לנצח מלחמה והלויים וכול עם השופרות
   יריעו
10. קול אחד תרועת מלחמה גדולה להמס לב אויב ועם קול התרועה
    יצאו
11. זרקות המלחמה להפיל חללים קול השופרות יחושו ובח[צוצ]רות
    יהיו
12. הכוהנים מריעים קול חד טרוד לנצח ידי מלחמה עד השליכם
    למערכת
13. האויב שבע פעמים ואחר יתקעו להם הכוהנים בחצוצרות המשוב
14. קול נוח מרודד סמוך כסרך הזה יתקעו ה[כו]הנים לשלושת
    הדגלים ועם
15. הטל הראישון יריעו ה[כוהנים והלויים וכול עם השופ]רות קול תרועה
16. גדולה לנצח מל[חמה ﬢﬥ השליכם שבע פעמים ואחר יתקעו] להם הכוהנים
17. בחצוצ[רות המשוב קול נוח מרודד סמוך ובאו והתיצ]בו על מעמדם
    במערכה

cf. ' his arrow shall go forth ' Zech. ix, 14 ; also ' shall my sword go forth ' Ezek. xxi, 9. For the accompaniment of action by fanfares, cf. lines 14–15; xvi, 7; xvii, 13–14.

shall cease. For discussion of the meaning see ch. 5, § 8, also comm. ix, 1.

12. **shall keep on blowing.** Cf. ix, 1–2; xvi, 8 ; xvii, 14–15.

to direct, signals for fighting. Cf. ' to direct the fighting ', line 9 ; the sound here also serves as a signal.

13. **seven times.** Cf. vi, 4 and comm.

14. **alternately level and legato.** Really two signals combined into one, one for reforming from arrays into columns, the other for withdrawing ; the ' low ' note signifies withdrawal as opposed to the high-pitched note for assault. Cf. ch. 5, § 6 (2c).

according to this disposition. i.e. in the same manner and with the same results for each battalion. Cf. vii, 16 and comm.

15. **the first battalion.** After describing the full ' disposition ' and its validity also for the next ' two battalions ' (cf. vi, 4), the author briefly returns to the action of the first battalion.

the priests. The restoration ' the levites ' is excluded by the absence of any traces of the top of a *lamedh*. The gap fits exactly.

a great fanfare. The connexion with the trumpet signal, etc., is here omitted for the sake of brevity.

16. **to direct, etc.** Restored after lines 12–13. The gap fits exactly.

17. **trumpets [of withdrawal].** These trumpets would be expected at this stage. The preserved words at the end of the line show that we deal here with this phase. The remainder of 17 restored after 13–14.

18. take up position] at their proper place in the formation, | [and the priests shall blow the trumpets of summoning, and two skirmishing battalions
19. shall go forth from the interval]s and shall take up position | [between the two lines within throwing range. The six priests shall blow a fanfare
20. on the trumpets of] assault, [and the levites] | [and the whole band of horn-blowers shall blow a battle fanfare very loudly. And as the sound goes forth,]

COLUMN IX

the skirmishers shall attack to fell among the slain, and all the band shall cease the fanfare, while the priests keep on blowing a fanfare upon
2. the trumpets | of the slain to direct the fighting, until the enemy are discomfited and turn their backs, while the priests sound the fanfare to
3. direct the fighting. | When they are discomfited before them, the priests shall blow the trumpets of summoning, and all the skirmishers shall go
4. forth against them from within | the front formations and take up position, six battalions as well as the battalion *already* engaged. The whole
5. army, seven formations, twenty-eight thousand | warriors, and the horsemen, six thousand *in number*, all these shall take up the pursuit so as to

in the formation. The word appears on the margin, a little below the line, and the last letter may be *he* or *taw*. In the latter case tr. 'in the front formation', supplying *panim* at the beginning of line 18.

18. and the priests, etc. For the restoration, cf. vi, 4; vi. 1; viii, 4; xvi, 3; xvi, 10; viii, 3–4.

and shall take up position. The reading is almost certain. For the shape of the ʿ*ayin*, cp. those in *mifsaʿ* line 7 and ʿ*adh* line 12.

19. between the two lines, etc. For the restoration, cf. vi, 4; xvi, 5–6.

of assault. Though the letters לליל appear at the left margin of line 18, only somewhat below the line, they form a correction to line 19, having been written over a destroyed part of the latter.

20. and the whole band, etc. For the restoration cf. xvi, 6–7. The whole text as restored is of course meant to represent the probable contents, not a guess at the actual wording, though it fits the space available. If the restoration is accepted, it would show that there were only 20 lines to each column.

Column IX

shall attack. Lit. 'they shall cause their hand to begin', also xvi, 7, without *yadh* xvii, 14; with *shalaḥ* xvii 13; cf. i, 1 and comm. The 'hand' is here to be taken literally, hence with the darts (viii, 10–11) the phrase is not used.

shall cease. Cf. ch. 5, § 8. In the meaning 'to cease' the verb occurs 1 Kings xxii, 3; Ps. xxviii, 1; Isa. lxii, 1; lxiv 11; in the meaning 'to be silent' Eccl. iii, 7; B. T. Ḥag. 13ab.

2. until the enemy are discomfited. The last two skirmishing units are equipped for close fighting and do not withdraw, but stay until their purpose is achieved; also vi, 1–6 stresses that their purpose is 'to vanquish the line of the enemy', not

TEXT, TRANSLATION, AND COMMENTARY 299

18. [ותקעו הכוהנים בחצוצרות המקרא ויצאו שני דגלי בינים מן הש֯עריֿ]ם֯ וע֯מדו֯[
[הח]ללים

19. [בין שתי המערכות כדי הטל וששת הכוהנים יריעו בחצוצרות והלויים]

20. [וכול עם השופרות יריעו תרועת מלחמה קול גדול ועם צאת הקול]

IX

1. יחלו ידם להפיל בחללים וכול העם יחשו מקול התרועה והכוהנים
יהיו מריעים בחצוצרות

2. החללים לנצח המלחמה עד הנגף האויב והסבו עורפם והכוהנים
מריעים לנצח מלחמה

3. ובהנגפם לפניהם ותקעו הכוהנים בחצוצרות המקרא ויצאו
אליהם כול אנשי הבינים מתוך

4. מערכות הפנים ועמדו ששה דגלים והדגל המתקרב כולם שבע
מערכות שמונה ועשרים אלף

5. אנשי מלחמה והרוכבים ששת אלפים כול אלה ירדופו להשמיד
אויב במלחמת אל לכלת

---

merely 'to slay'. See also comm. ii. 2 'trumpets of pursuit'.

turn their backs. In O.T. *sbb* is not used with *'oref*, but with *panim* (2 Chr. xxix, 6).

3. are discomfited. i.e. begin to flee.

trumpets of summoning. i.e. of calling the skirmishers. In xviii, 4 the whole army is called to the pursuit by the trumpets of remembrance, but here the various stages are telescoped. Cf. ch. 5, § 5 (7) and p. 98, n. 4.

all the skirmishers. Who have fought before this last unit.

from within the front formations. In fact each skirmishing battalion is tactically linked with a front formation, cf. ch. 7, §§ 4–5; now the skirmishers move up to keep contact with the fleeing enemy until the front formations have had time to regroup for pursuit, cf. comm. line 9 sq.

4. six battalions. *Locus probans* for the view that there were seven skirmishing units, cf. ch. 7, § 4 (3).

engaged. Lit. 'having approached'. The *hithpa'el* (i, 10; viii, 7; xvi, 11; xvii, 11) corresponds to BH *qal* (Dt. xx, 2–3, 10; 1 Kings xx, 29, etc.) in the technical military meaning 'to come to close quarters for battle' (cf. *qĕrav* 'battle'); cf. Yadin, *Ma'arakhoth* lx (Dec. 1949), 21.

seven formations, etc. An important passage for reconstructing the numerical structure of the army. The figure cannot refer to the skirmishers, of whom there were only 7,000, but must refer to them as well as to the 21,000 men of the front formations, just as the 6,000 horsemen represent the entire cavalry, light and heavy. Cf. ch. 7, § 4 (3)–(4); § 5 (4). For the horsemen see vi, 10; ch. 7, § 6.

5. all these. In the 'seventh lot' (xviii, 4), the decisive phase, all the army goes into action, except the priests (line 7–8).

6. destroy the enemy in the battle of God for an eternal | annihilation. The priests shall blow for them the trumpets of pursuit, and *the warriors* shall spread out against the whole enemy *force* for a pursuit of annihila-
7. tion, while the cavalry | roll back *the enemy* at the sides of the *field of battle* until *their* extermination. During the assault the priests shall
8. sound a fanfare from afar, and shall not come | into the midst of the slain so as to be defiled by their impure blood, for they are holy; they shall
9. not desecrate the oil of their priestly anointment with the blood | of the nations of vanity.

Section 13

10. Disposition for changing the array of the battle battalions, so as to form up in the shape of a rect[angle with t]owers, en-
11. veloping arms with towers, | an arc with towers, a flat *arc* with protruding columns, and wings [issuing] forth from
12. [both] sides of the line, to disorganize | the enemy. The shields of the *men of the* towers shall be three cubits long, and

to destroy ... annihilation. ¶ 2 Sam xxii, 38? Similar language in inscriptions on trumpets of pursuit (iii, 9) and banners in the attack phase (iv, 11-12), cf. also i, 5 and comm.

6. of pursuit. Spelled with *waw* only here, cf. comm. iii, 2.

spread out. Also xviii, 4, cf. ii, 13. BH, see Gn. xiv, 15.

a pursuit of annihilation. Since before *kalah* we invariably find nouns (e.g. *milḥamah* i, 10; *maggefah* xviii, 11; *kĕlimah* DSD iv, 13; *qin'ah* DST xii, 14), we must have here a noun not recorded in the O.T., probably *redef*, also in 'the pursuit of Asshur', xviii, 2.

7. roll back. Causative of *shuv* 'to withdraw', cf. i, 13; iii, 2, 10-11; iv, 8; cf. also Isa. xxviii, 6.

at the sides of. Literally, as in Num. xxxiv, 3; Ju. xi, 26 (differently Amos i, 8; Zech. xiii, 7; Ecclus. viii, 1; again differently DSD v, 2); the cavalry is stationed at the flanks, viii, 4-5; ix, 11-12; ch. 7, § 6 (2). A possible, though rather forced, interpretation would be 'respond to the signals (cf. viii, 12) of battle'; cf. however p. 175, n. 5; p. 99, n. 2; p. 99, n. 3; p. 100, n. 3.

extermination. Also xviii, 5; cf. 1 Sam. xv, 18; Josh, viii, 26; xi, 11; Num. xiv, 45; xxi, 3.

from afar. Cf. e.g. Ex. xx, 18.

and shall not come. Cf. 1 Macc. v, 67, where the priests are killed because they unadvisedly (ἀβουλεύτως) mingle in battle. See also Maimonides, *Code*, Hilkhoth Shemiṭṭah, xiii, 10-12.

8. to be defiled. Cf. Isa. lix, 3; Thr. iv, 14; Dn. i, 8; cf. Jub. xxi, 17. Impurity of the Lot of Belial: xiii, 5.

for they are holy. Cf. Lv. xxi, 1-6.

they shall not. The lacuna is not sufficient for *wĕ-lo'*.

desecrate. Hiph. Ezek. xxxix, 7; CDC xi, 15.

the oil. Cf. Ex. xxviii, 41; xl, 15. In Lv. xxi, 6 it is the name (*shem*) of God which they are forbidden to desecrate.

anointment. Read perhaps *mĕshuḥath*; M.T. *mishḥath* Lv. x, 7; xxi, 12.

9. nations of vanity. Cf. comm. iv, 12.

10. disposition. It seems that from this 'disposition', which dealt with various tactical regroupings (hence perhaps its position immediately after mentioning the regrouping for pursuit), our author only

6. עולמים ותקעו להמה הכוהנים בחצוצרות המרדוף ונחל[קו] על
כול האויב לרדף כלה והרכב
7. משיבים על ידי המלחמה עד התרם ובנפול החללים יהיו
הכו[הנ]ים מריעים מרחוק ולוא יבואו
8. אל תוך החללים להתגאל בדם טמאתם כיא קדושים המה ול[וא]
יחלו שמן משיחת כהונתם בדם
9. גוי הבל

[יג]

10. סרך לשנות סדר דגלי המלחמה לערוך המעמד על רב[ו]ע ארוך
ומ[גד]ל[ו]ת גלול כפים ומגדלות
11. וקשת ומגדלות ועל דרוך מעט וראשים יוצאים וכנפים [יוצאות]
מ[שנ]י עברי המערכה ול[ה]מיס
12. אויב ומגני המגדלות יהיו ארוכים שלוש אמות ורמחיהם א[ור]ך
שמונה אמות והמ[גד]לות

copied the heading and the part dealing with the 'towers'. On the various 'arrays' see ch. 7, § 7.

battle battalions. Also v, 3; i.e. all troops, not only the skirmishing units.

to form up. Lit. 'to array the standing', cf. ch. 7, § 2 (3) and comm. v, 4.

in the shape of. For this sense of *'al* see comm. v, 3; vii, 14.

rectangle. Only the *resh* is certain. The restoration is based on the Roman term *fronte longa quadro exercitu*, cf. ch. 7, § 7 (3). In this formation the formations of the second line moved forward into the gaps of the first, to form one long line in transition to various attack formations. It seems to be mentioned also xviii, 4.

towers. Restoration practically certain, as traces of *gimel*, *lamedh*, and *ṭeth* are visible, and the space fits exactly. See further comm. line 12.

enveloping arms. For the reading *gillul* see ch. 7, § 7 (4); cf. also ib. (9) on the use of this formation in the Battle of Cannae.

11. arc. The same shape, but with the convex side facing the enemy, cf. ch. 7, § 7 (5) and (9).

a flat arc. Lit. 'one tensioned a little', viz, an arc; cf. ch. 7, § 7 (6).

with protruding columns. As no towers are mentioned, it appears that 'a flat arc' and 'protruding columns' constitute one formation, not two separate ones. We have here the Roman *serra*, cf. ch. 7, § 7 (7).

wings. Probably not the formation called *alae*, but *alae* in the sense of units of cavalry, cf. ch. 7, § 7 (8) and (9).

issuing. The gap fits exactly, but the restoration is only suggested by the sense. On the language see comm. vi, 7–8; ix, 7.

from both. Almost certain restoration, as both the *yodh* and the ends of the *mem* are clearly visible.

to disorganize. Lit. 'melt'. Cf. viii, 10.

12. towers. These are equivalent to the Roman *testudo*, see ch. 7, § 7 (2).

three cubits. As compared with $2\frac{1}{2}$ cubits for the shields of the front formations, see ch. 6, § 2 (4).

x

13. their spears eight cubits long. The towers | shall protrude from the line by *the width of* a hundred shields, hundred *shields* being the front of the tower. Thus there shall be all round the tower in the three frontal
14. directions | three hundred shields. Each tower shall have two intervals, one on [the right and] one on the left. On all the shields of the *men*
15. of the towers | they shall write: on the first 'Mi[chae]l', [on the second
16. 'Gabriel', on the third] 'Sariel', on the fourth 'Raphael'; | 'Michael' and 'Gabriel' on [*the towers of* the right side, and 'Sariel' and 'Raphael' on *the towers of* the left side.]

SECTION 14

17. And [ ] for four [and] an
18. ambush they shall lay for [the Kittim] | [behind them]

COLUMN X

our camp, and to beware of every unseemly evil thing, and who told us that Thou art in our midst, O great and terrible God, to make spoil of

eight cubits. One cubit longer than those of the front formation, but equal to the spears of the heavy cavalry, cf. vi, 14; ch. 6, § 11.

13. a hundred shields. For the 'shield' as a unit of width, cf. vii, 14; ch. 7, § 7 (2).

the front. i.e. the side facing the enemy, as in 'front formations', cf. ch. 7, § 5 (9) seq.

thus, etc. As shown in the photograph, the gap would seem to allow for a longer word, but closer examination proves that the left-hand flap of col. ix must be raised a little, thus narrowing the gap; see in particular ורמחיהם in line 12. The gap thus fits the restoration exactly.

three frontal directions. As it protrudes beyond the line, each of the three sides of the 'tower', except its rear, is a 'front', being exposed to enemy fire.

14. three hundred shields. The shield-bearers only cover the outside of the 'tower' for protection for the troops advancing within it.

two intervals. Although the lower bar of the *nun* in *shnayim* is invisible, the reading cannot be in doubt; cf. *lifnehem* and *ha-panim* in lines 3 and 4. The reading *sarim* appears to me highly improbable.

on the right. For the fit of this restoration, cf. the remarks on 'thus, etc.', line 13.

on all the shields. i.e. on all shields of each tower the inscription is the same.

15. on the first. i.e. on the shields of the men of the first tower. For the language compare vi, 2–3 where 'the second weapon', 'the third dart' also means 'the darts of the second and third unit to throw'.

on the second Gabriel, on the third. The restoration is certain, and fits the gap precisely.

Sariel. The remains of the *śin* are clear enough to make the reading sure beyond all doubt, and to exclude 'Uriel'. On the importance of this reading, and on the meaning of the inscriptions, see ch. 9, § 6 and p. 270, n. 3.

16. the towers of the right side. The two towers right of centre bear for their

13. יוצאים מן המערכה מאה מגן ומאה פני המגדל כו[נה י]סבו המגדל
לשלושת רוחות הפנים
14. מגנים שלוש מאות ושערים שנים למג֯ד֯ל אח֯ד֯ ל[ימין וא]חד לשמאול
ועל כול מגני המגדלות
15. יכתובו על הראישון מי[כא]ל֯ [על השני גבריאל על השלישי] ש֯ריאל על
הרביעי רפאל
16. מיכאל וגבריאל ל[ימׄיׄן] שריאל ורפאל לשמאול]

[יד]

17. ו[...] לא֯ר֯ב֯ע֯ן֯ [--------] ו֯[אורב ישימו֯ן֯] ל֯[כתיי]ם֯
18. [מאחריהם?] [------------] [--] ל֯ [--]

X

1. מחנינו ולהשמר מכול ערוות דבר רע ואשר הגיד לנו כיא אתה
בקרבנו אל גדול ונורא לשול את כול

protection the names of the two more important angels. Cf. Midr. Tanḥuma, Mishpaṭim xix : 'Why are there a thousand angels on the left and ten thousand on the right? This is because the left side does not need the protection of so many angels, this being the side bearing the name of God written on the phylacteries, which are attached to the left arm'. As the next section is not separated by a blank line, line 16 is unlikely to have extended over more than half the page, so that our suggested restoration just fits.

17. and. Here begins the 'Ritual Serekh Series', mostly concerned with the 'Prayer for the Appointed Time of Battle'; cf. ch. 8, §§ 4, 5 (1). The following sections in the Scroll begin with 'and': 6 (iv, 6); 9 (v, 15); 10 (vi, 7); 12 (vii, 8); 21 (xiv, 2); 23 (xv, 4); 25 (xvi, 9); 26 (xvi, 13); 28 (xvii, 10). Perhaps the next word was 'there shall be'.

an ambush, etc. Cf. Josh. viii, 2; Ju. ix, 25; xx, 29. See further comm. iii,

2; p. 196, n. 1. The section, in linking the last phase of a tactical operation with the description of a prayer rite, resembles sections 21, 23, 25, and 28.

18. behind them. Restored after Josh. viii, 2.

Column X

and to beware. The lacuna as printed in *Oẓar* is too large; if reduced, our restoration will be seen to be certain.

every unseemly evil thing. Also vii, 7, see comm. ibid. In view of Dt. xxiii, 10, 15, supply perhaps at the end of col. ix the words כי קדוש יהיה : '[for let] our camp [be holy]'.

who told us. The subject is Moses. 'Told' implies theological instruction, as opposed to 'taught' etc., which imply legal ordinances. Cf. xi, 5, 8; Burrows, VT 2 (1952), 255 sq.; Rabinowitz, JBL 69 (1950), 45; CDC viii, 14.

Thou art ... before us. A combination of Dt. xxiii, 15 with Dt. vii, 21–2.

2. all | our enemies before us, and who has taught us from of old unto *all*
   our generations, saying :
       ' When ye are come nigh unto the battle, the priest shall stand up
3. and speak unto the people, | saying, Hear, O Israel, ye approach
   this day unto battle against your enemies : fear not and let not
4. your hearts faint, | do not tremble, neither be ye terrified because
   of them ; for your God goeth with you, to fight for you against your
5. enemies, to save | you '.
   And our provosts shall speak to all those prepared for battle, the willing-
6. hearted, to hold fast through the might of God, to turn back all | the
   faint-hearted, and to hold fast together, all mighty men of valour. And
   as to that which Thou hast s[poken] by the hand of Moses, saying :
7.   ' If there cometh a war | in your land against the enemy that
   oppresseth you, then ye shall blow an alarm with the trumpets, and
8. ye shall be remembered before your God, | and ye shall be saved from
   your enemies '—
   Who is like Thee, O God of Israel, in heaven and earth, that he can do
9. according to Thy great works | and Thy powerful might ; and who
            is like unto Thy people Israel, which Thou hast chosen for

2. and who has taught us. e.g. in Dt. v, 1.

from of old. Also xi, 6 ; cf. comm. i, 10.

unto all our generations. Also xiv, 9 ; adapted from the ' for your generations ' so often found in connexion with ordinances, e.g. Josh. xxii, 27, 28.

saying. Also line 6, to introduce direct quotation. The following is Dt. xx, 2-4, with a number of deviations from the MT, as shown below, see also ch. 8, § 5 (2) and p. 217, nn. 1, 2, 3. According to DSW these words are spoken by the chief priest, cf. ch. 8, § 5 (1).

DSW: בקרבכם למלחמה
MT: והיה כקרבכם אל המלחמה
DSW: ועמד הכוהן ודבר אל העם
MT: ונגש הכהן ודבר אל העם:
DSW: לאמור שמעה ישראל
MT: ואמר אלהם שמע ישראל
DSW: אתמה קרבים היום למלחמה
MT: אתם קרבים היום למלחמה
DSW: על אויביכמה אל תיראו
MT: על איביכם
DSW: ואל ירך לבבכמה
MT: אל ירך לבבכם אל תיראו

DSW: ואל תחפזו ואל תערוצו מפניהם
MT: ואל תחפזו ואל תערצו מפניהם:
DSW: כיא אלוהיכם הולך עמכם
MT: כי יהוה אלהיכם ההלך עמכם
DSW: להלחם לכם עם אויביכם
MT: להלחם לכם עם איביכם
DSW: להושיע אתכמה
MT: להושיע אתכם:

5. and our provosts. etc. The following is based on Dt. xx, 8, sq., but with omission of all that is said there about those who built a new house, planted a vineyard, or betrothed a wife. The difference is discussed ch. 4, § 2, where reasons are advanced for assuming it to be due to the existence of two distinct phases in the process of rejection, the ' social cases ' having been dismissed before leaving for the campaign. For the speech of the provosts see ch. 8, § 4 (2), (3) and p. 209, n. 6, p. 211, n. 2, for their tasks comm. vii, 13, 15 ; ch. 7, § 3 (2).

prepared for battle. Also vii, 5 (see comm.) ; xv, 2.

to hold fast. Cf. xvii, 4, 9 ; DSD v, 1,

TEXT, TRANSLATION, AND COMMENTARY 305

2. אויבינו לפ[נינו] וילמדנו מאז לדורותינו לאמור בקרבכם
למלחמה ועמד הכוהן ודבר אל העם

3. לאמור שמ[ע]ה ישראל אתמה קרבים היום למלחמה על
אויביכמה אל תיראו ואל ירך לבבכמה

4. ואל תח[נפזו] וא[ל] תערוצו מפניהם כיא אלוהיכם הולך עמכם
להלחם לכם עם אויביכם להושיע

5. אתכמה ו[נש]וטרינו ידברו לכול עתודי המלחמה נדיבי לב
להחזיק בגבורת אל ולשיב כול

6. מסי לבב ולחזיק יחד בכול גבורי חיל ואשר ד[ברת]ה ביד מושה
לאמור כיא תבוא מלחמה

7. בארצכמה על הצר הצורר אתכמה והריעות[מה] בחצוצרות
ונזכרתמה לפני אלוהיכם

8. ונושעתם מאויביכם מיא כמוכה אל ישראל בש[מי]ם ובארץ אשר
יעשה כמעשיכה הגדולים

9. וכגבורתבה החזקה ומיא   כעמכה ישראל אשר בחרתה
לכה מכול עמי הארצות

3; ix, 14-15; Jb. xxvii, 6; Pr. iii, 18;
iv, 13; 2 Chr. vii, 22.
   might of God. Cf. i, 11; iv. 12.
   to turn back. = להשיב; omission
of the Hiph'il prefix is frequent in the
Scrolls, as in MH. The verb takes up
wĕ-yashov Dt. xx, 8.
   6. the faint-hearted. Allusion to wĕ-lō
yimmas, etc., ibid.
   to hold fast. = להחזיק
   together. Double meaning: (1) military
term = fighting in a body, cf. comm. xiv,
6; 1 Sam. xi, 11; (2) one of the names of
the sect, cf. ch. 7, § 2 (5); comm. xiv, 4.
   mighty men of valour. In O.T. mainly
'military leaders' (p. 53, n. 1); so
perhaps here: the troops are to 'hold fast
together' with their leaders.
   Thou hast spoken. ¶ Num. x, 1.
   by the hand of. Cf. xi, 7-8; DST xvii,
12.
   if there cometh, etc. = Num. x, 9,
with variants, cf. also ch. 5, § 2. The
reading 'if there cometh' is also in the
Peshitta.

DSW:	כיא תבוא מלחמה בארצכמה
MT:	וכי תבאו מלחמה בארצכם
DSW:	על הצר הצורר אתכמה
MT:	על הצר הצרר אתכם
DSW:	והריעותמה בחצוצרות
MT:	והרעתם בחצצרות
DSW:	ונזכרתמה לפני אלוהיכם
MT:	ונזכרתם לפני יהוה אלהיכם
DSW:	ונושעתם מאויביכם
MT:	ונושעתם מאיביכם

   8. Who is like Thee. A prayer in poetical
style. Cf. Ps. xxxv, 10; lxxi, 19, etc.;
DST vii, 28 (quoting Ex. xv, 11); DSW
xiii, 13. The sentence is basically influenced
by Dt. iii, 24 (Ps. cxiii, 5-6), with additions
from Ps. xcii, 6 (lxxi, 19).

   9. Thy powerful might. Not in O.T.,
but may be adapted from the Dt. verse
quoted, which in LXX has the addition
τὴν ἰσχύν σου (Rabin). Another influence,
especially in the connexion with the
following sentence, is 2 Sam. vii, 22.

   and who   is. The scribe left a
space sufficient for one word, though there
is no fault in the skin; perhaps he did not
want to write the words relative to God
and those concerning Israel in one go. The
line was added later by the same hand,
perhaps, who corrected iii, 1. The first
words are ¶ 2 Sam. vii, 23.

   which Thou hast chosen. ¶ Dt. xiv,
2 (vii, 6).

10. Thyself from all the nations of the lands, | a people of *men* holy through the covenant, taught the statute*s*, enlightened in un[derstanding . . .],
11. hearing the glorious voice, seeing | the holy angels, open of ear and hearing (OR : understanding) deep things [   ] the expanse
12. of the skies, the host of luminaries, | the domain of spirits and the dominion of holy ones, treasures of gl[ory (?)   ] clouds. He
13. that created the earth and the boundaries of her divisions | into wilderness and plain-land, and all that springs from her, with the bu[rstings-forth of her waters], the compass of the seas, the reservoirs of the rivers and

nations of the lands. The phrase mainly Neh. and Chr.; cf. also DST iv, 26; Sukenik, MG II, 47.

10. a people of men holy through the covenant. Cf. Dt. xiv, 2 (a holy people); DSD iv, 22 (covenant); i, 7–9; Dn xi, 28, 30 (cf. xii, 7); viii, 24; comm. 1, 2.

taught the statutes. Lit. 'the statute'. Verb-form Cant. iii, 8; 1 Chr, xxv, 7; DSW vi, 12 and comm. Connexion with the Law : Dt. iv, 14; Ps. cxix, 12; Ezra vii, 10. Learning the statutes is one of the purposes of the sect, cf. DSD i, 12.

enlightened in understanding. Restored after such passages as Dn. ix, 22; xii, 10; xi, 33; cf. also 2 Chr. ii, 11; Ps. cxix, 99; Dt. iv, 6; CDC viii, 7–8; DSD iii, 13; iv, 3; xi, 18–19 (cf. line 11 below); DST ii, 16–17; xi, 28; *Qumran I*, p. 109, i, 7. After the estimated end of *binah* there is room for 2–3 more words. Towards the end, traces of an *aleph* are visible, perhaps we may guess at *emeth* or *pele*'.

hearing the glorious voice. ⁋ Dt. v, 21, cf. ib. iv, 12; perhaps reference to the Giving of the Law. 'Glorious voice' also DST frg. 12 line 5. The next phrase points, however, to Ezekiel (x, 5 etc.) or Daniel (viii, 16 ; x, 5–7); cf. also ' Thou wilt renew Thy covenant for them in a vision of glory', *Qumran I*, p. 154, line 6.

11. seeing the holy angels. The privilege of the elect, often alluded to in the Pseudepigrapha. Cf. also vii, 6.

open of ear. Cf. 1 Sam. ix, 15; Jb. xxxiii, 16, etc.; DST i, 20; frg. 5, line 10; frg. 18, line 4; CDC ii, 2–3; *Qumran I*, p. 102, 1, line 4.

deep things. Cf. Dn. ii, 22 (Jb. xii, 22; Ps. xcii, 6). For *shama'* = understand and *'ămuqqoth* = mysteries, cp. also Levy, *Neuhebr. & Chald. Wörterb.* s.v. The gap, wide enough for 2–3 words, must have contained some mention of God, whose creation is described in the following 5 lines in terms reminiscent of DST i; Ps. civ; Jb. xxxvi, xxxviii; Ecclus. xlii–xliii; Jub. ii (also Neh. ix), and classified under (1) the heavens and all that is in them, (2) the earth and all that is on it, (3) living creatures, (4) the early history of mankind, (5) the festivals. The rich and poetical language is distinguished by the frequency of nouns with *m-* prefixes.

the expanse of the skies. This must have been preceded by some word meaning 'Who did create' (perhaps one of the several used in DST i); near the end the foot of a *qoph* is visible, suggesting *raqia'*, the synonym of *shĕḥaqim*. The latter occurs in conjunction with *mifraś* in Jb. xxxvi, 28–9; cf. Tur-Sinai ad loc.; id., 'Raqia' und Sheḥaqim', *Studia Theologica* 1 (1948), 188–96; id., *Biblioth. Orient.* 8 (1951), 21. Cf. further Dt. xxxiii, 26; 2 Sam. xxii, 12; Zech. ii, 10; DST i, 8–9 (⁋ Ps. civ, 2). For *mifraś* cf. ' the *m.* of the whole sky ', *Mekhilta R. Ishmael*, ed.

TEXT, TRANSLATION, AND COMMENTARY 307

10. עם קדושי ברית ומלומדי חוק משכילי בי[נה - - -] ושומעי קול
נכבד ורואי

11. מלאכי קודש מגולי אוזן ושומעי עמוקות [- - -] מפרש שחקים
צבא מאורות

12. ומשא רוחות וממשלת קדושים אוצרות כב[וד? -] עבים הבורא
ארץ וחוקי מפלגיה

13. למדבר וארץ ערבה וכול צאצאיה עם פר[וֹ]צֵי מימ[י]ה חוג ימים
ומקוי נהרות ומבקע תהֻמות

Horovitz-Rabin (Frankfurt, 1931), p. 185 (I thank Prof. S. Lieberman for drawing my attention to this passage).
the host of luminaries. The combination is not found in the O.T., cf. however the ' host of the heavens ', Gn. ii, 1 ; Jer. viii, 2 ; Dn. viii, 10 ; with which cp. DST xii, 4–7 ; ib. i, 10–11.
12. domain of spirits. For ' spirits ' = angels, see ch. 9, § 2 (y). As in other passages quoted there, it may be used here in a double sense, implying also ' winds '. In the O.T. the root *nš* is frequent in connexion with wind ; here the parallelism suggests the meaning ' dominion '.
holy ones. i.e. angels, cf. ch. 9, § 2 (8) and DST i, 9–11 ' before they became angels of holiness . . . in their dominions '.
treasures of gl[ory]. Cf. DST i, 11–12 ' sparks and lightnings ' ‖ ' treasures of work cunningly wrought '. The treasures are storehouses containing rain, snow, and winds, cf. Dt. xxviii, 12 ; Jer, x, 13 ; Ps. xxxiii, 6 ; cxxxv, 7 ; Jb. xxxviii, 22 and Tur-Sinai's commentary ad loc. I restore ' glory ' with some hesitation, but it is parallel to ' blessing ' in xii, 11. Another possibility would be [כבוֹדִים] ' mighty treasures '. The first suggestion would allow the rest of the gap to be restored as [מפרשי] עבים ' expanses of clouds ', cf. Jb. xxxvi, 28–9. For ' clouds ' see ib.

xxviii, 8 and Tur-Sinai ad loc. Another possibility would be [וטל] עבים ' and the dew of clouds ', cf. below, xii, 8.
He that created the earth. Cf. DST i, 12, 17. This phrase proves that the gap in line 11 contained an apostrophe of God as creator of the heavens.
boundaries. For this meaning cf. Jer. xxxiii, 25 ; Jb. xxvi, 10 ; Pr. viii, 27–9, etc.
her divisions. In 2 Chr. xxxv, 12 *miflaggoth* in a different sense ; as here in DSD iv, 15, 17 ; DST viii, 19 (cf. ib. i, 16) ; cf. also Aram. *pillugh*, Tg. J., Num. x, 32.
13. wilderness and plain-land. The two are parallel in Jer. ii, 6 (' land of deserts ') ; cf. ibid. li, 43.
all that springs from her. Cf. Isa. xxxiv, 1 ; xlii, 5. Here probably the springs, as in xii, 8–9 ; DST xiii, 9 (cf. ib. i, 17).
burstings-forth. Restored after *pereẓ mayim* and *pĕraẓim* in 2 Sam. v, 20 ; 1 Chr. xiv, 11.
compass of the seas. Cf. Pr. viii, 27 ; Jb. xxvi, 10 (where Pesh., Tg. read *ḥugh* for MT *ḥagh* [Rabin]).
reservoirs of the rivers. Cf. Ex. vii, 19 and Jub. ii, 7. The word *miqwē* may also be sing., with *yodh* for *he*, as often in the Scrolls, cf. comm. vi, 12.

308   TEXT, TRANSLATION, AND COMMENTARY

14. rift of the depths, | the shaping of living beings and winged creatures, the forming of man and the is[sue of his ri]b, the confusion of tongue
15. and the separation of nations, the settling of families | and the allotment of countries, [   ] holy festivals,
16. seasons of years and epochs of | eternity [
          all Thy deeds.] These we have come to know from Thy
17. wisdom which [   ] | [
18. incline, pray, Thine ears] to our cry, for [it] | [is a time of trouble for Israel, the like of which there has not been   ] not in the days (?) of the [   ]

COLUMN XI

for Thine is the battle, and through the strength of Thine hand have their corpses been dashed to pieces, with no one to bury *them*. Also
2. Goliath the man of Gath, a mighty man of valour, | didst Thou deliver into the hand of Thy servant David, because he trusted in Thy great
3. name, and not in sword and lance, for Thine is the battle; and | he subdued the Philistines many times through Thy holy name. Also

rift of the depths. The noun not in O.T., but derived from phrases like Gn. vii, 11; Pr. iii, 20. The first *waw* in *těhomoth* was added subsequently.

14. the shaping of living beings. ⁋ Gn. i, 25.

winged creatures. Lit. ' sons of wing ', an expression not paralleled in the O.T. or the kindred languages (though in Tg. O. Dt. xiv, 13 *bath kanfā* translates *ra'ah* ' glede '). Cp. also ' sons of the eagle ' (Pr. xxx, 17) and ' sons of the dove ' (Lv. v, 11, etc.).

forming of man. Or: ' of Adam '. For *tavnith* cf. Dt. iv, 16, etc. The nearest parallel to our phrase appears in Is. xliv, 13. For the cognate *mivneh* in the Scrolls, see Yadin, JBL 74 (1955), 40–43.

issue of his rib. If restored as plural: the children of Adam; if restored as singular: Eve. The whole is a combination of Gn. i, 27 sq. with ii, 22.

confusion. Read *billah* (MH, see B. T. RSh. 13b; Ḥull. 83b), derived from *balal* Gn. xi, 9 to which it alludes.

separation. ⁋ *nifrĕdhu* Gn. x, 5. Cf. also comm. ii, 14.

15. allotment of countries. The phrase not in O.T., but the two words occur together Dt. xxxii, 8–9; Num. xxxvi, 2; Josh. xiii, 7, etc. Cf. also Driver, VT 2 (1952) 356. The gap which follows allows of *c*. 6 words. Perhaps it contained a reference to the creation of the luminaries.

holy festivals, etc. Thy hymn closes with the subject of the calendar, cf. ch. 8, § 3. For the language cf. Ecclus. xliii, 7 (6), 8 (7); DSD x, 1–10; DST xii, 1–9; see also comm. ii, 4.

16. these ... wisdom. Exact parallel to the conclusion of the hymn in DST i, 20; cf. comm. lines 10–11 above. The illegible word after ' which ' is certainly not *gillitha* ' Thou hast revealed ', as in DST l.c.

17. incline, etc. Restored after Ps. xxxiv, 16. These words form the transition to the prayer proper, and prove that the end of x and the whole of xi form one section.

TEXT, TRANSLATION, AND COMMENTARY

14. מעשי חיה ובני כנף תבנית אדם ותול[ד]ות צל[ם]עו בלת לשון
    ומפרד עמים מושב משפחות
15. ונחלת ארצות [- - - - -] מועדי קודש ותקופות שנים וקצי
16. עד [- - - - - - מעשי]ה אלה ידענו מבינתכה אשר - - -
17. [- - - - - - - הטה נא אוז]נכה אל שועתנו כיא [היאה]
18. [עת צרה לישראל אשר לוא היתה כמוה - - -]לאו בימי (ביתו?) הכו [...]

XI

1. כיא אם לכה המלחמה ובכוח ידכה רוטשו פגריהם לאין קובר ואת
   גולית הגתי איש גבור חיל
2. הסגרתה ביד דויד עבדכה כיא בטח בשמכה הגדול ולוא בחרב
   וחנית כיא לכה המלחמה ואת
3. פלשתיים הכנ[י]ע פעמים רבות בשם קודשכה וגם ביד מלכינו
   הושעתנו פעמים רבות

18. for it is, etc. Restored after i, 11-12, cf. comm. 1b. and xv, 1.

not in, etc. The restoration is uncertain. Perhaps there were borrowings from Ps. lxxxiii or similar Psalms.

Column XI

for thine is the battle. This phrase recurs frequently, and formed no doubt part of the 'prayer for the appointed time of battle'. Cf. especially 1 Sam. xvii, 47; also 1 Chr. v, 22; 2 Chr. xx, 15. See comm. xii, 9. The following prayer is discussed in ch. 8, § 5 (1).

Thine hand. Cf. i, 14; xv, 13; 1 Chr. xxix, 12 (a chapter which influenced the slogans on the banners, see comm. iv, 12 seq.); cf. also 'the strength of My hand', Isa. x. 13, quoted DST iv, 35.

corpses. It is not clear to which enemies this refers. The word occurs in 1 Sam. xvii, 46 in the Goliath episode—this, however, appears below—; 2 Kings xix, 35 in connexion with Sennacherib—who is also mentioned later—; and 2 Chr xx, 24 of the Ammonites and Moabites; cf. also Jer. xxv, 33.

dashed to pieces. In the O.T. only of the killing of children and women.

Goliath the man of Gath. Cf. 2 Sam. xxi, 19; 1 Chr. xx, 5.

a mighty man of valour. Goliath is only called 'a mighty man' (1 Sam. xvii, 51); the term here is used only of Boaz (Ruth, ii, 1); near parallels in 1 Kings xi, 28; 2 Kings v, 1, etc.

2. didst Thou deliver, etc. Cf. 1 Sam. xvii, 35-47.

David. For the importance of this reference to David, see p. 212, n. 3.

Thy great name. Frequent in O.T., cf. e.g. 1 Sam. xii, 22.

3. he subdued the Philistines. Cf. 2 Sam. viii, 1.

many times. Ps. cvi, 43.

Thy holy name. ibid., 47.

4. Thou didst deliver us many times by the hand of our kings | for Thy mercy's sake, not for our deeds, in that we have done wickedly, nor for our sinful actions. Thine is the battle, and from with Thee is the
5. might, | not ours. Neither our strength nor the power of our hand have done deeds of valour, but *it was* through Thy strength and the might of
6. Thy great valour (OR: army), as Thou hast told | us from of old, saying:
' There shall come forth a star out of Jacob, a sceptre shall rise out of Israel, and shall smite the corners of Moab and destroy all
7. sons of Sheth, | and he shall go down *to battle* from Jacob and shall cause to perish the remnant [out of] the city, and the enemy shall be a possession, and Israel shall do valiantly '.
8. By the hand of Thine anointed ones, | the seers of things ordained, Thou hast foretold us the e[pochs] of the wars of Thy hands, that Thou mayest be honoured upon our enemies, by felling the troops of Belial,
9. the seven | nations of vanity, by the hand of the poor ones that are to be redeemed by Thee [with powe]r and retribution, for wondrous might, and a heart that melteth *shall be* for a door of hope. Thou wilt do unto

Thou didst deliver us. Cf. ibid.
4. for Thy mercy[s sake. Cf. ' for the sake of Thy great name ', 1 Sam. xii, 22. For the theme, cf. Dn. ix, 18; Assumptio Mosis xii, 7.
our deeds . . . wickedly. Cf. Ezra ix, 13.
our sinful actions. Cf. Ezek. xx, 44; Ps. xiv, 1; DST iv, 34-5.
from with Thee is the might. Cf. Ps. lxxxix, 14; Job xii, 13; 1 Chr. xxix, 11-12.
5. not ours, etc. Cf. Dt. viii, 17-18.
as Thou hast told us, etc. Cf. comm. i, 10; x, 1, 2, 6.
6. there shall come. = Num. xxiv. 17-19. Vs. 17 is also quoted CDC vii, 19-21; 4Q Testimonia 12-13 (Allegro, JBL 75 (1956), 184). *Qumran I*, 121, 128. The insertion of this passage here obviously stresses the eschatological nature of the War described. The most important textual differences are the transposition of 18 and 19 (various transpositions have been proposed, none quite agreeing with that here) and the omission of 18b ' Seir also, even his enemies, shall be a possession ', long thought to be a later insertion, cf. BH³.
a sceptre shall rise. MT, CDC, 4Q Test. + ' and '.

and destroy. Supports MT against Samar. *wĕ-qodhqodh*. The scribe first began to write *wĕ-karkar*, but noticed this after writing the first *k*. CDC, 4Q Test. + *eth*.
Sheth. So 4Q Test.; MT and CDC without *yodh*.
7. the enemy. MT. ' Edom '; cf., however, ' his enemies ' in the omitted insertion 18b.
shall do. The Scroll evidently read *'aśah*, the perfect, not the participle *'ośeh* as in MT, as this would have been spelled with a *waw* in DS orthography. The space before the word is due to a fault in the skin.
by the hand of. Cf. Ezek. xxxviii, 17.
Thine anointed ones. i.e. prophets, cf. Ps. cv, 15; 1 Chr. xvi, 22.
8. seers. Cf. 2 Sam. xxiv, 11; Hab. i, 1; Lam. ii, 14. ' Seers ' is also the correct reading in CDC ii, 12 (last word), as I was able to convince myself by examining the MS through the courtesy of Dr. J. L. Teicher; there is thus no need for the theological speculations built on the reading הוזא. The opponents of the sect are called ' seers of error ' (DST iv, 20), ' seers of deceit ' (ib. 10). Cf. Yadin, IEJ 6 (1956), 158.

TEXT, TRANSLATION, AND COMMENTARY

4. בעבור רחמיכה ולוא במעשינו אשר הרעונו ועלילות פשעינו לכה
   המלחמה ומאתכה הגבורה

5. ולוא לנו ולוא בכוחנו ועצום ידינו עשה חיל כיא בכוחך ובעוז
   חילכה הגדול כא[שר] הגדתה

6. לנו מאז לאמור דרך כוכב מיעקוב קם שבט מישראל ומחץ פאתי
   מואב ו/קרקר כול בני שית

7. וירד מיעקוב והאביד שריד]מ[עיר והיה אויב ירשה וישראל
   עשה חיל וביד משיחיכה   כבד

8. חוזי תעודות הגדתה לנו ק]צי[מלחמות ידיכה להלחם באויבינו
   להפיל גדודי בליעל שבעת

9. גוי הבל ביד אביוני פדותכה]בכוֹ[חַ ובשלום לגבורת פלא ולב
   נמס לפתח תקוה ותעש להמה כפרעוה

things ordained. Cf. xiii, 8; xiv, 4; 13; DSD i, 9; iii, 10. The term for the opponents, תעות חוזי 'seers of going astray', may be a pun on the phrase used here. For the role of the prophets here, cf. DSH ii, 8–10 'all the words of His servants, the prophets, by whose hand (אשר ב]ידם[) He foretold all that would befall His people' (our passage confirms this restoration, as against that suggested by Talmon, VT 1 (1951), 33 sq.).

epochs of the wars. The restoration is certain, being based upon Dn. ix, 26; vs. 24 ib. is a parallel to the preceding clause, cf. ibid. xi, 40. For 'epoch' cf. comm. i, 5, and cf. DST xviii, 30; DSD iii, 15; DSH vii, 2, 7–8.

that Thou mayest be honoured. Cf. Ex. xiv, 4; xvii 18 (referring to Pharaoh, who is mentioned in line 9); Ezek. xxxix, 13 (Gog); DST ii, 23. The scribe wrote first להלחם and altered it by dotting the letters לחם and superscribing כבד.

9. the seven nations of vanity. Cf. Dt. vii, 1 ('seven nations') and DSW iv, 12 ('nations of vanity'). Here are meant the nations enumerated in i, 1–2.

the poor. Cf. xi, 13; xiii, 13–14; DSH xii, 3, 6, 10; DST ii, 31 ('Thou hast redeemed the soul of the poor man'); v, 16, 18, 22. As the last-named passage shows, the word *evyon* is synonymous in the sect's parlance with 'ani, ib. 13; 14; 21; with 'orphan', ib. 20; in DSW also with 'the low of spirit', line 10; 'them that are prostrate in the dust', line 13; 'them that stumble', xiv, 5; 'whose knees totter', ib. 6; 'that have been brought low', ib. 7; 'the poor in spirit', ibid.; 'whose way is undefiled', ibid., etc. etc. All these terms recur in similar senses in the O.T., e.g. 1 Sam. ii, 8 (cf. Ps. cxiii, 7); Isa. xxxii, 7; Jer. xx, 13; Ps ix, 19; xxxvii, 14; lxix, 34; lxxiv, 21–2; etc. Their use in DST and DSW—as well as in the other scrolls—is so natural, and in conformity with O.T. parlance, that it hardly justifies the theory of J. L. Teicher, who sees in our sect the Ebionites, cf. JJS 2 (1951), 67 sq. and later vols., also *Manchester Guardian* of 15. IX. 1953, where T. adduces 'the congregation of the poor' in pPs. 37.

that are to be redeemed by Thee. Cf. comm. i, 12 for parallels.

with power ... might. Cp. the inscriptions on the banners, iv, 12; also Hos. ix, 7.

wondrous might. Cf. xv, 13; CDC xiii, 8; DST ix, 27.

a heart that melteth. Cf. Na. ii, 11; also DSW xiv, 6.

a door of hope. ¶ Hos. ii, 17.

10. them as unto Pharaoh | and the captains of his chariots in the Red Sea. Thou wilt cause the low of spirit to burn like a torch of fire in a sheaf, devouring the wicked, which shall not (OR: Thou wilt not) return until |
11. the guilty are annihilated. From of old Thou hast announced to us the time appointed for the mighty deed of Thy hand against the Kittim, saying:
    'Then shall Asshur fall with the sword not of man, and the
12. sword, | not of men, shall devour him.'

SECTION 15

13. For into the hand of the poor ones Thou wilt deliver the [ene]mies *from* all lands, into the hands of them that are prostrate in the dust, so as to bring low all mighty men of the nations, to render the recompense |
14. of the wicked upon the head of [Thine enemies] and to bring forth the just judgement of Thy truth upon all sons of man and to make for]
15. Thyself an everlasting name through Thy [holy] people | [
    ] the wars, and to magnify and sanctify Thyself in the eyes of
16. the remnant of the nations, so that [they] may know [that] | [Thou art the God of Israel, as Thou hast spoken, when Thou] wilt perform judgements upon Gog and all his company that are assembled unto [him
17.] | [   ], for Thou wilt fight against them from the heavens [and wilt plead against them with pestilence and

unto Pharaoh. Allusion to Ex. xv, 4. For the use of *kĕ-*, cf. 'as unto Midian', Ps. lxxxiii, 10 (this Psalm influenced the Scroll much, cf. comm. i, 1–2). Cf. further ch. 8, § 5 (1).

10. low of spirit. Parallel to 'the poor'; in DST xviii, 15 'l. of s. and mourners'. Singular in Isa. lxvi, 2; cf. Pr. xv, 13; xvii, 22; xviii, 14.

like a torch of fire in a sheaf. = Zech. xii, 6. The picture of the fire burning the wicked is frequent in the O.T., e.g. Isa. ix, 16; cf. also DST vi, 18–19.

which shall not return, etc. Cf. iii, 9.

11. from of old . . . us. Restoration based on Isa. xliv, 8; cf. DSW i, 10. The passage, in a way typical for the sect, actualizes here the prophecies about Asshur.

11–12. then shall Asshur, etc. Isa. xxxi, 8; cf. also DSW i, 6. For the relation of 'Asshur' and the 'Kittim', see ch. 2, § 3 (2). Our passage proves that the phrase 'Kittim of Asshur' is intended to apply the prophecies about Sennacherib's destruction to the present enemies, cf. comm. col. xix.

13. for into the hand of the poor. Cf. line 9 above.

enemies. Restored as parallel to 'mighty men', and fits the size of the gap and remnants of letters. ¶ 1 Sam. xxvi, 8 (with *siggar*) 'delivered up', or Ps. xxxi, 9 'Thou hast not given me over (*hisgartani*) into the hand of the enemy', nay, the enemy has been given over into our hands.

all lands. Cf. ii, 7 and Ezek. xxxix, 27 (quoted immediately) 'out of their enemies' lands'.

that are prostrate in the dust. In O.T. only 'crawling things of the dust', Dt. xxxii, 24; 'that dwell in the dust', Isa.

10. וכשלישי מרכבותיו בים סו[ף] ונכאי רוח תבעיר כלפיד אש בעמיר
    אוכלת רשעה לוא תשוב עד
11. כלות אשמה ומאז השמי[ענתנו מ]וֹעד גבורת ידכה בכתיים לאמור
    ונפל אשור בחרב לוא איש וחרב
12. לוא אדם תואכלנו

[טו]

13. כיא ביד אביונים תסגיר [או]יבי כול הארצות וביד כורעי עפר
    להשפיל גבורי עמים להשיב גמול
14. רשעים בראש או[יביכה] ולהצדיק משפט אמתכה בכול בני איש
    ולעשות לכה שם עולם בעם
15. [קודשכה ----] המלחמות ולהתגדל ולהתקדש לעיני שאר הגוים
    לדעת[ו -]
16. [- ----] נַעֲשֹׂותכה שפטים בגוג ובכול קהלו הנק[ה]ל[ה]ים ע[ל]יו [-]
17. [------] כיא תלחם בם מן השמי[ם] ונשפטת אתם בדבר ובדם]

xxvi. 19, etc.; perhaps telescoped from 'all they that go down to the dust shall lie prostrate before Him', Ps. xxii, 30.

to bring low. Cf. xiv, 15.

mighty men of the nations. ¶ Ezek. xxxix, 18; cf. also xxxii, 21-2. 'Mighty men' of Israel's enemies: Jer. xlviii, 41; xlix, 22; li, 30; cf. xlvi, 5; Ob. 9. Cf. also xii, 6-7.

to render the recompense ... upon the head. For the language cf. Ob. 15; Joel iv, 4, 7. See also comm. iv, 12.

14. the recompense of the wicked. Also CDC vii, 9; xix, 6; slightly different DSD viii. 6-7. Perhaps adapted from Ps. xciv, 2, with 'the wicked' introduced from vs. 3.

Thine enemies. A possible restoration, based upon Isa. lxvi, 6.

to bring forth ... truth. Cf. comm. iv. 6.

sons of man. Cf. Ps. xlix, 3; lxii, 10; Thr. iii, 33.

to make ... an everlasting name. Cf. Isa. lxiii, 12; for the whole phrase Ezek. xxxix, 7.

15. the wars. A possible restoration is: 'to go forth before them like a man (or: a mighty man) of the wars', based on Isa. xlii, 13, and cf. 'mighty man of the war' below, xii, 8 and the parallelism 'mighty man'—'man of glory' ib. 9.

to magnify ... may know. ¶ Ezek. xxxviii, 23, with 'remnant of the nations' for MT 'many nations'.

that they may know. Read [ם]לדעת. For the rest of the restoration, cf. line 5; x, 6; xii, 7; xvi, 1; Ezek. xxxviii, 19.

16. judgements upon Gog. Cf. Ezek. xxxviii, 22.

all his company, etc. Cf. ib. 7.

17. for. The gap probably contained some allusions to Ezek. xxxviii, 19-21.

fight against them from the heavens. Cf. Ju. v, 20.

17-18. and wilt plead ... against them. Restored after Ezek. xxxviii, 22.

18. blood] | [and overflowing rain and hailstones; fire and brimstone thou wilt rain] upon them for a turmoil [   ]

COLUMN XII

For a multitude of holy ones Thou hast in the heavens and hosts of angels in Thy holy habitation [to praise Thy name]. The elect ones of
2. the holy nation | Thou didst place for Thyself in [a community; and the enumer]ation of the names of all their host is with Thee in Thy holy abode, and the n[umber of the ho]ly ones in the habitation of Thy
3. glory. | Mercy of blessing [for Thy thousands] and the covenant of peace Thou hast engraved for them with a stylus of life, so as to be king
4. [over them] in all appointed times of eternity | and to muster [the hosts of Thine el]ect by their thousands and their myriads together with Thy
5. holy ones [and the host] of Thine angels, for strength of hand | in battle [to subdue] them that have risen *against Thee on* earth by the strife of Thy judgements, but with the elect ones of heaven are [Thy] blessing[s].

18. turmoil. i.e. the word pointed *mehemehem* in Ezek. vii, 11, as *mĕhummah* 'panic' would in Scrolls orthography have a *waw*. Cf. however, Eccl. Rabba on xii, 12, where *mehemmah* of the text is interpreted as *mĕhummah*.

Column XII

for. The following provides the reason for God's participation, as described in the preceding lines. For parallels in Pseudepigrapha, see ch. 9, § 7; see ib. § 2 for 'holy ones' = angels (add Ecclus. xlii 24 (17)).

multitude. *Rov* has this meaning in DST iv, 32 (cf. *hămon* ib. 36); vi, 9; frg. 15, 7; xiv, 23; Isa. xxxvii, 24; Ps. xxxiii, 17; cvi, 7; Pr. xiv, 28. See also A. M. Habermann, *Sinai* 32 (5713), 146.

Thou hast. Reading uncertain: what appears to be the upright stroke of the *lamed* is inclined towards the right instead of the left. The word fits the context and the *lĕkhah* in line 2.

Thy holy habitation. Cf. Isa. lxiii, 15 (= heavens); B. T. Ḥag. 12b: '*zebul*, where there is (the heavenly) Jerusalem and Temple, and an altar, on which Michael the great prince offers a sacrifice'; see also Hughes, Introd. to 3 Baruch, in Charles, *Apocr. and Pseudep.* II, 530–1. Also in DST iii, 34.

to praise Thy name. Restored after Ps. cxlviii, 2; cf. Joel ii, 26; Ps. cxxxv, 1, etc.

the elect ones of the holy nation. Cf. comm. x, 9–10; Flusser, *Yediʿoth* 17 (5713), 34; ch. 9, § 7.

2. in a community. Restored after DSD xi, 7–8; DST iii, 21–3; cf. ch. 9, § 7.

the enumeration . . . Thy glory. Restored after Ps. cxlvii, 4; Isa. xl, 26. For the parallel in 1 Enoch, cf. ch. 9, § 7.

Thy holy abode. Frequent in O.T., e.g. Dt. xxvi, 15; cf. also 'in the abode of Thy glory' (DST frg. 9.7, Plate 55) = 'the habitation of Thy glory' here. 'The *maʿon* is where the companies of serving angels sing by night and are silent by day, out of respect for the children of Israel' (B. T. Ḥag, 12b). See also *Qumran I*, p. 126, iv, 25): 'like an angel of the Presence in the holy abode'.

the number of the holy ones. The left part of the *shin* is clearly visible. For the parallelism see Ps. cxlvii, 4, quoted above; for *minyan* Num. xxiii, 10; 1 Kings iii, 8; viii, 5; Ezra vi, 17.

3. for Thy thousands. Or: for thousands. Restored after Ex. xx, 6 ('thousands'),

TEXT, TRANSLATION, AND COMMENTARY 315

18. עֲלֵיהֶם לְמַהֲמָה [- - - - -] [וגשם שוטף ואבני אלגביש אש וגפרית תמטיר]
19. [- - - - - - - - -] ל [- - - - -]

XII

1. כיא רוב קדושים לכה בשמים וצבאות מלאכים בזבול קודשכה
להנלל שמ[כה ובחירי עם קודש
2. שמתה לכה בי[ח]ד ומ[ס]פר שמות כול צבאם אתכה במעון קודשכה
ומ[ענון קד[ו]שים בזבול כבודכה
3. וחסדי ברכה [לאלפיכה] וברית שלומכה חרתה למו בחרט חיים
למלוך ע[ליהם] בכול מועדי עולמים
4. ולפקוד צ[באות בח]יריכה לאלפיהם ולרבואותם יחד עם
קדושיכה [וצבא] מלאכיכה לרשות יד
5. במלחמה [להכריע] קמי ארץ בריב משפטיכה ועם בחירי שמים
בר[נ]ו[תיכה]

quoted CDC xx, 21-2; cf. Ex. xxxiv, 7; Dt. v, 10; Jer. xxxii, 18. There is not enough space for לאוהביכה, after Dt. vii, 9; Neh. i, 5; Dn. ix, 4, quoted CDC xix, 1; but there would be sufficient for ליראיכה, cf. Ps. ciii, 17-18.

the covenant of Thy peace. Cf. Isa. liv, 10; Ez. xxxiv, 25; xxxvii, 26 sq.

Thou hast engraved ... stylus. The image frequent in Jub. and Enoch; cf. also Nötscher, *Biblica* 34 (1953), 193-4. For engrave (*ḥrt*) see Ex. xxxii, 16; DSD x, 8, 11; for 'stylus' (*ḥrṭ*) Ex. xxxii, 4; Isa. viii, 1; cf. Tur-Sinai, JQR 39 (1948-9), 376, n. 5; id., *Hallashon Wehassefer* I, 388 sq. [In DST i, 24 we have the noun '*ḥrt* of remembrance': this may mean 'ink', as in MH (Aram. *ḥartā*), or be the verbal noun 'an engraving' (this occurs in Piyyuṭ)—Rabin.]

so as to be king. etc. Cf. Mic. iv, 7; DSW xii, 15; xix, 8.

appointed times of eternity. Also xiii, 8.

4. **to muster the hosts.** Cf. Isa. xiii, 4, and see comm. line 1.

myriads. Cf. comm. iii, 15.

and the host. Supplied after lines 7-8; cf. also comm. vii, 6.

strength. Cf. Arabic *rsw arsā*, 'be firm, steadfast'; Jew. Aram. *rĕshā* 'have power' (Rabin). The phrase is thus parallel to 'strength of Thy hand', xi, 1; 'might of Thy hand', ib. 11. For '*rĕshuth* of fear and terror', DSD x, 15, Yalon (*Kiriat Sefer* 28 (5712), 64) wants to read *memsheleth* 'dominion', but perhaps this, as well as '*brshwt* of the dominion of light' (Burrows: *brshyt — berēshith*) and '*b.* of the watches of darkness', ib. lines 1-2, should be read *bi-rshoth* 'when the ... become strong'. There is, in any case, no connexion with *horish* 'dispossess', Ex. xv, 9; Ps. xliv, 3, etc.

5. **to subdue.** Restored after 2 Sam. xxii, 40; but we might supply 'to destroy', after Ex. xv, 7, or 'to tread under' (לבוס), after Ps. xliv, 6.

on earth. Lit. 'of the earth', cf. 'wicked of the earth', Ps. lxxv, 9; ci, 8; cxix, 119; Ez. vii, 21.

the strife of Thy judgements. 'Strife' and 'He goes to judgement with' are parallel in Jer. xxv, 31 (quoted in telescoped form in CDC i, 2); both terms in inscriptions DSW iv, 6, 12; together *Qumran I*, p. 110, i, 13-14.

elect ones of heaven. Cf. comm. line 1; ch. 9, § 2.

Thy blessings. Uncertain restoration,

Section 16

6. And Thou, O God, [art terrible] in the glory of Thy majesty, and the congregation of Thy holy ones are amongst us for eternal alliance,
7. and we (OR : they) [shall render] scoffing unto kings, scorn | and derision unto mighty men, for the Lord is holy, and the King of Glory is with us, a people of saints ; Migh[ty men and] a host of angels are among those
8. mustered with us, | the Mighty One of War is in our congregation, and the host of His spirits is with our steps, and our horsemen are [like]
9. rain-clouds and like clouds of dew covering the earth, | and like a showery storm watering with judgement all that spring from her.
    Arise, O mighty one,
        take Thy captives, O man of glory,
10.   and take | Thy booty, *Thou* Who dost valiantly.
    Place Thy hand upon the neck of Thine enemies,
        and Thy foot upon the bodies of the slain.
    Crush the nations, Thine adversaries,

---

6. and Thou. Being the essential part of the prayer, this was given a section to itself. For the content, see ch. 8, § 5 (1). Same opening xiii, 7.
   terrible. Restored after Ps. lxxvi, 8, 13 ; cf. Dt. vii, 21 ; xxviii, 58 ; Ps. cxi, 9 ; Neh. ix, 32 ; also Zeph. ii, 11, in a prohecy concerning the nations mentioned in DSW. Other possible restorations are *niśśā* 'lofty' (Isa. lvii, 15 ; Book of Noah, frg. 13-14 in *Qumran I*, p. 85) ; or *niẓẓav* (Ps. lxxxii, 1) 'And Thou, O God, standest in the glory, etc.'.
   glory of Thy majesty. Cf. Ps. cxliv, 11 sq. For glory = might, see below.
   the congregation of Thy holy ones. Cf. comm. i, 10 ; vii, 6 ; ch. 9, § 2 (8), § 6 ; and comm. line 2 above.
   eternal alliance. Also xvii, 6. 'For 'alliance' cf. Ps. cxxi, 2 ; 2 Chr. xxxii, 8 ; for 'eternal salvation' Isa. xlv, 17. See also comm. i, 2.
   7. scorn and derision. Cf. Ps. xliv, 14 ; cf. 10. 'Derision' also DST ii, 9.
   kings . . . mighty men. Same parallelism CDC iii, 9-10 ; En. xxxviii, 5 (*nagast—'azīzān*) ; liii, 5 (*n.—khayālān*), etc.
   From here onwards the text runs parallel with xix, 1-8, henceforth 'B'.
   the Lord. Cf. Ps. xcix, 9 (and again in that Ps., which also influenced line 1, see comm.), and frequently ; *addirenu* 'our gallant one' B, cf. Ex. xv, 11 ; Ps. viii, 2 ; lxxvi, 5 ; xciii, 4.
   king of glory. Cf. Ps. xxiv, 7-10. 'Glory' in sense of 'might', cf. 'man of glory', line 9.
   a people of saints. Om. B. Cf. Num. xvi, 3 ; Dn. viii, 24. It is possible to read *'im* 'with the saints', but this is improbable.
   mighty men . . . with us. Om. B. Same parallelism Ps. ciii, 20-1 ; DST x, 33-4—in both passages 'mighty men of strength', but there is no room here for *koaḥ* ; see also xv, 14. For 'those mustered' see comm. ii, 4 ; for the whole sentence cf. B. T. Ḥag. 14b : 'and the Shekinah is with us and the serving angels accompany us'.

TEXT, TRANSLATION, AND COMMENTARY 317

[טז]

6. ואתה אל נ[ורא] בכבוד מלכותכה ועדת קדושיכה בתוכנו לעזר
עולמי[ם ונת]נו בוז למלכים לעג

7. וקלס לגבורים כיא קדוש אדוני ומלך הכבוד אתנו עם קדושים
גבו[רי]ם [ו]צבא מלאכים בפקודינו

8. וגבור המלח[מה] בעדתנו וצבא רוחיו עם צעדינו ופרשינ[ו כ]עננים
ובעבי טל לכסות ארץ

9. ובזרם רביבים להשקות משפט לכול צאצאיה קומה גבור שבה
שביכה איש כבוד ושול

10. שללך עושי חיל תן ידכה בעורף אויביכה ורגלכה על במותי
חלל מחץ גוים צריכה וחרבכה

8. The mighty one of war. i.e. God, cf. Ps. xxiv, 8; also Ex. xv, 3 (Sam., Pesh. Cf. Rabin, JThS 6 (1955), 177. Parallel to 'king of glory', line 7.

our congregation. Cf. iv. 9.

the host of His spirits. Also DST xiii, 8. Cf. ch. 9, § 2 (9).

our horsemen. The *nun* is quite clear, and we cannot read [ופרשיו] כעננים, following Job. xxvi, 9.

clouds of dew. Cf. Isa. xviii, 4. For the thought cf. Hos. xiv, 6; Mic. v, 6 (*ṭal . . . rĕvivim*—prophecy about Assyria!); Ezek. xxxviii, 16 ('to cover the land').

9. showery storm. 'Storm', cf. Isa. iv, 6; 'showers' also Qumran I, no. 34.3 (p. 136); cf. Dt. xxxii, 2; Mic. v, 6; Ps. lxxii, 6; cf. comm. x, 13.

arise . . . captives. Cf. Ju. v, 12. The parallel 'thy booty' here speaks against the reading *shovekha* 'thy captors' (with Syr., Arab.) in Judges. Cf. also Num. x, 35; comm. iii, 5-6. The form *qumah* (as against *qum* in Ju.) is typical for the style of Ps. There can be no reasonable doubt that the whole hymn is addressed to God, not to the Messiah (cf. Milik,

RB 40 (1953), 290 sq.; *Qumran I*, p. 129. Compare Isa. xlii, 13; Ps. xxiv, 8; Ecclus. xxxv. 19 (22-3); and numerous passages in Talmud and midrashim.

man of glory. 'Glory' and 'might' are synonymous, cf. Sukenik, *M.G.* II, p. 51; Yalon, *Sinai* 26 (5710), 267 sq.; they are parallel in DST x, 10.

10. take Thy booty. Cf. Ezek. xxix, 19.

Who dost. For the spelling cf. ad vi, 12; for the phrase vi, 6; Num. xxiv, 18; Ps. cxviii, 15-16, etc.

Thy hand upon the neck of Thine enemies. Cf. Gn. xlix, 8. איביך B.

Thy foot. וגלך B.

upon the bodies of the slain. Cf. 'thou shalt tread upon their bodies' (A.V. their high places), Dt. xxxiii, 29. על במותיך חלל occurs 2 Sam. i, 19 in quite a different sense. Cf. Sukenik and Yalon, *loc. cit.* On Egyptian victory stelae the king often grasps the enemies by the neck and treads upon their backs.

crush the nations, Thine adversaries. Cf. 'He devours the gentiles, his opponents . . . and *with* his arrows he crushes', Num. xxiv, 8. Cf. also Ecclus. xxxv, 19 (23).

Y

11.   and let Thy sword | devour the guilty flesh.
      Fill Thy land with glory
            and Thine inheritance with blessing :
         A multitude of cattle in Thy portions,
12.   silver and gold and precious | stones in Thy palaces.
      Zion, rejoice exceedingly,
            and shine forth in songs of joy, O Jerusalem,
            and be joyful, all ye cities of Judah.
13.   Open | [thy] gates forever,
            to let enter into thee the substance of the nations,
            and their kings shall serve thee.
      All they that afflicted thee shall bow down to thee,
14.   and the dust | [of thy feet they shall lick.
      O daughters] of my people, shout with a voice of joy,
            deck yourselves with ornaments of glory,
            and rule over the ki[ngdom of the Kittim]. |
15.   [And the kingdom shall be the Lord's,
            and I]srael for ruling eternally.

Section 17

16. [   ] them the mighty men of war Jerusalem [
17.   ] | [be Thou exalt]ed
   above the heavens, O Lord, [and let Thy glory be above all the
   earth   ]

11. and let ... flesh. From Dt. xxxii, 42, with the addition of guilty (lit. ' of guilt '), which is absent in B. To the whole cf. xi, 11-12.

fill ... glory. Cf. Num. xiv, 21 ; Ps. lxxii, 9.

blessing. Cf. 2 Sam. xxi, 3 ; Ps. xxviii, 9 ; and ' behold a blessing (A.V. ' present ') for you of the spoil of the enemies of the Lord ', 1 Sam. xxx, 26.

multitude of cattle. Cf. Jer. xlix, 32. For ' cattle ' || ' silver and gold ', cf. Gn. xiii, 2 ; see also Sukenik, l.c. ; comm. v, 14.

Thy portions. No plural in O.T., but frequently parallel to ' inheritance '.

12. Thy palaces. בהיכלותיך B.

Zion, etc. Cf. Zech. ii, 9 ; Isa. xiii, 6 ; xxxv, 10 ; Joel, ii, 23.

exceedingly. מואדה B, cf. comm. xix, 5. Same spelling DST frg. 10.9, Oẓar, plate 56 ; Qumran I, p. 93, ii, 9 ; DSIa passim ; cf. Sukenik, *M.G.* II, 52, 74.

shine forth in songs of joy, O Jerusalem. Om. B. Cf. ' shout, O daughter of J.', Zech. ix, 9 ; ' sing songs of joy together, O ruins of J.', Isa. lii, 9 ; Zeph. iii, 14 ; Zech. ii, 14. Cf. further iv, 4-5. For ' shine forth ', cf. comm. xviii, 9 ; the verb occurs DST iv, 6, 23 ; v, 32 ; vii, 3 ; ix, 26, 31 ; xi, 26 ; DSH xi, 7 ; CDC xx, 3, 25 ; Qumran I, p. 139, frg. 14.

and be joyful. The author took the verb as Hif'il, in spite of the occurrence of imv. *gilu, gil* in O.T. (Rabin).

all ye cities of Judah. For ' daughters of Judah ', Ps. xlviii, 12 ; xcvii, 8 (both times preceded by *taghelnah* 3rd. pl. f.),

TEXT, TRANSLATION, AND COMMENTARY

11. תואכל בשר אשמה מלא ארצכה כבוד ונחלתכה ברכה המון
מקנה בחלקותיכה וזהב ואבני
כספ

12. חפץ בהיכל[ו]ח[ת]יכה ציון שמחי מאדה והופיעי ברנות ירושלים
והגלנה כול ערי יהודה פתחי

13. שע[ריך] תמיד להביא אליך חיל גואים ומלכיהם ישרתוך
והשתחוו לך כול מעניך ועפר

14. [רגליך ילחכו בנות] עמי צרחנה בקול רנה עדינה עדי כבוד ורדינה
ב[מ]ל[כ]ות כתיאים]

15. [והיתה לאדוני המלוכה וי]שראל למלוך עולמים

[יז]

16. [- - - -] ··· [ל]ו[י]הם גבורי המלחמה ירושלים [- - -]
17. [- - - -] רו[ם] על השמים אדוני [ועל כל הארץ כבודכה - -]

here interpreted as 'daughter cities'. Cf. also Isa. lxv, 18.

13. open ... kings. = Isa. lx, 11, omitting 'day and night they shall not be shut' and the last word, 'in procession'. Cf. also Ps. Sol. xvii, 31. 'Gentiles': גוים B, cf. comm. xvi, 1.

and their kings shall serve thee. = Isa. lx, 10, reading yĕsharĕthukh for MT, DSIa, DSIb yĕsharĕthunekh.

all they ... bow down to thee. ¶ ib. 14.

14. and the dust, etc. Restored by Sukenik after Isa. xlix, 23; supported by the appearance of the *kaf* of *raghlekha* in B, xix, 6 at end.

daughters of my people. Cf. 'daughters of my city', Thr. iii, 51

shout. Cf. Zeph. i, 14 (Qal); Isa. xlii, 13 (Hiph.); also Isa. xlii, 11 DSIb for MT *yizwaḥu* on which cf. Orlinsky, JNES 11 (1952), 153 sq. In B הבענה 'utter', cf. Ps. cxix, 171.

deck yourselves with ornaments. Cf. Ezek. xxiii, 40; also ib. xvi, 11; hardly from *'wd* 'bear witness' (Aalen, *Licht und Finsternis*, p. 228).

over the kingdom of. Restored after xix, 7. The blank before this word is due to a fault in the leather.

15. and the kingdom shall be the

Lord's. Only 'kingdom' partly preserved in B; cf. also vi, 6; = Ps. xxii, 29 (+ and He is the ruler over the nations); Ob. 21.

16. This section contains the formulae of blessing, and section 18 that of cursing (separated from the blessings as a new section), which were probably pronounced immediately after the defeat of the enemy near the place where the slain lay; a fact stressed in the first words of section 21. For discussion, see ch. 8, § 5 (6), where also a comparison with the almost identical formulae in DSD. The letter *he* is suggested by the top part; the completion of the word will depend on the sense of the sentence as a whole. The most probable seems to me *me'alehem*. The whole seems to correspond to 1 Kings viii, 44-5, especially as that chapter also influenced what follows.

Jerusalem. The remains of the final *mem* exclude the reading *Yĕrushalaimah*. The end of the line may have contained the beginning of the prayer.

17. be Thou, etc. Restored after Ps. lvii, 6 (MT *rumah; ĕlohim;* cf. also xiv, 16). It fits the spirit of 2 Kings viii, especially vs. 23, see also p. 227, n. 2. The last word of col. xii was probably כוהן הרואש.

COLUMN XIII

and his brother [pr]iests and the levites and all the elders of the Serekh with him. They shall bless, from where they stand, the God of Israel

2. and all His true deeds, and they shall curse | Belial and all the spirits of his lot in the same place. And they shall solemnly declare :

Blessed be the God of Israel for all His holy plan and His true deeds.

3. Blessed be | all they that serve Him in justice, that know Him in faith.

SECTION 18

4. And cursed be Belial for the plan of hatred, and accursed in his guilty authority. Cursed be all spirits of his lot for their wicked plan, |
5. and accursed be they for all their works of filthy uncleanness ; for they
6. are the lot of darkness, but the lot of God is for light | eternal.

SECTION 19

7. But as for Thee, O God of our fathers, we bless Thy name for all eternity, being an [etern]al people. Thou madest a covenant with our

---

Column XIII

and his brother priests ... with him. Same formula xv, 4 ; xviii, 5–6. ' Brother priests ', cf. 1 Chr. xvi, 39 ; also Neh. iii, 1 ; Ezra iii, 2, to distinguish from ' all his brethren ', xv, 7 ; cf. ch. 8, § 3 (6).

elders of the Serekh. Only here : Serekh probably = the whole congregation as military unit, hence cf. Lv. iv, 15 ; see in detail ch. 7, § 2 (5). It is also possible that this term = *sorĕkhē ha-maḥănoth*, the ' camp prefects ' of vii, 1, who are the oldest amongst all the men in the field. They are mentioned next to the ' provosts ', thus cf. ' the elders of the people and the provosts ' Num. xi, 16, etc. ; cf. further ch. 7, § 3 (1)–(2). ' All the men of the serekh ', mentioned in the two passages quoted above, are missing here : perhaps they remained near the enemy slain while the priests etc. prayed at some distance, cf. ix, 7–8.

from where they stand. Cf. Neh. viii, 7 ; ix, 3 ; 2 Chr. xxxiv, 31 ; CDC xi, 1 ; DSW xiv, 3 ; xvi, 2. The term is equivalent to *maʿamad*, cf. ch. 7, § 2 (3).

true deeds. Also line 2 ; xiii, 9 ; xiv, 2 ; opposite ' false deeds ' DSH x, 12 ; cf. comm. iv, 6 ; ch. 8, § 5 (6).

shall curse. Same verb in lines 4, 5 ; cf. Num. xxiii, 7 ; Pr. xxiv, 24, etc. For the whole formula following, cf. Dt. xxvii, 12 ; Blank, HUCA 23 (1950–1), 73 sq.

2. Belial. See ch. 9, § 3.

spirits of his lot. See ib. § 2.

solemnly declare. Also vii, 15 ; xviii, 6 ; cf. Dt. xxvii, 14.

blessed be the God of Israel. Cf. 1 Sam. xxv, 32, etc. ; also cf. DSW xviii. 6.

plan. Of God : Jer. xlix, 20 ; Ps. xcii, 6 ; DST iv, 13 ; DSD iii, 16. Antonym in line 4.

3. that serve Him in justice. Cf. Ps. ciii, 21 ; comm. iv, 6.

that know Him. Cf. Ps. xxxvi, 11 ; Dn. xi, 32.

in faith. Cf. 2 Chr. xix, 9.

4. hatred. This *maśṭemah* is a quality peculiar to Belial, not a proper name, cf. also xiii, 11 ; xiv, 9 ; other occurrences ch.

TEXT, TRANSLATION, AND COMMENTARY

XIII

1. וְאֶחָיו הַ[כּוֹ]הֲנִים וְהַלְוִיִּים וְכוֹל זִקְנֵי הַסֶּרֶךְ עִמּוֹ וּבֵרְכוּ עַל עוֹמְדָם
   אֶת אֵל יִשְׂרָאֵל וְאֶת כּוֹל מַעֲשֵׂי אֲמִתּוֹ וְזָעֲמוּ
2. שָׁם אֶת בְּ[לִי]עַל וְאֶת כּוֹל רוּחֵי גוֹרָלוֹ וְעָנוּ וְאָמְרוּ בָּרוּךְ אֵל יִשְׂרָאֵל
   בְּכוֹל מַחֲשֶׁבֶת קוֹדְשׁוֹ וּמַעֲשֵׂי אֲמִתּוֹ וּבְ[רוּ]כִים
3. כוֹל מְשָׁרְתָיו בְּצֶדֶק יוֹדְעָיו בֶּאֱמוּנָה

[יח]

4. וְאָ[רוּ]ר בְּלִיַּעַל בְּמַחֲשֶׁבֶת מַשְׂטֵמָה וְזָעוּם הוּאָה בְּמִשְׂרַת אַשְׁמָתוֹ
   וַאֲרוּרִים כּוֹל רוּחֵי גוֹרָלוֹ בְּמַחֲשֶׁבֶת
5. רִשְׁעָם וְזָעוּמִים הֵמָּה בְּכוֹל עֲבוֹדַת נִדַּת טֻמְאָתָם
6. כִּיא הֵמָּה גּוֹרַל חוֹשֶׁךְ וְגוֹרַל אֵל לְאוֹר [עוֹלָמִ]ים

[יט]

7. וְאַ[תָּ]ה אֵל אֲבוֹתֵינוּ שִׁמְךָ נְבָרְכָה לְעוֹלָמִים וְאָנוּ עַם [עוֹ]לָם וּבְרִית
   [כָּ]רַתָּה לַאֲבוֹתֵינוּ וּתְקִימָהּ לְזַרְעָם

9, § 3. For B.'s 'plans' cf. DST iv, 12–14; vi, 21–2.

guilty. Cf. comm vi, 16; DSD ii, 5; DSW xiii, 15; xiv, 3; ch. 8, § 5 (6).

authority. In xvii, 7–8 ‖ *memshalah*: the *memshalah* of Belial occurs DSD i, 18, 24; ii, 19.

their wicked plan. Cf. DST vi, 21–2. The beginning of line 5 is smudged, and no traces of letters visible: as also nothing seems to be wanting, it is probable that the scribe left a blank, owing to some fault in the leather.

5. **filthy uncleanness.** From Lv. xviii, 19; in moral sense Ezra ix, 11 (both words separately); Ezek. xxxvi, 17 (*niddah*); DST xi, 11 (dto.); DSH viii, 12–13 (full phrase); see also comm. ix, 8. Cf. CDC ii, 1 and Rabin ad loc.

6. **eternal.** Restored after xv. 1; xvii, 6. Belial is in 'eternal dark fire', DSD ii, 8. See further comm. line 9; ch. 8, § 5 (6); ch. 9, § 8.

7. **but as for Thee.** For the restoration see xii, 6. The place of the following prayer in the battle liturgy is discussed ch. 8, § 5 (6); the doctrinal implications in ch. 9, §§ 3–5, 8.

God of our fathers. Cf. Ezra vii, 27, etc.

we bless. Cf. Ps. cxlv, 1; see also comm. iii, 2.

an eternal people. Cf. Isa. xliv, 7; Ezek xxvi, 20; cf. also 2 Sam. vii, 24; and line 9. In spite of the fact that the remains of the last letter of the second word suggest a *taw* rather than a final *mem*, this seems to be the only practicable reading; others, such as ‘*am zu ga'alta* (Ex. xv, 13); ‘*am naḥălathkha* (after Dt. iv, 20); ‘*am sĕghullah* (ib. xxvi, 18) ‘*am noladh* (Ps. xxii, 32); ‘*am ‘olamim* (cf. line 9) either do not fit the gap or have the *taw* in the wrong place.

Thou ... forefathers. Cf. 1 Kings viii, 21 (Solomon's prayer influenced the earlier part of this prayer); 2 Kings xvii, 15; for the *lĕ-* cf. Ps. lxxxix, 4, etc.

8. forefathers, and Thou wilt fulfil it unto their seed | for all appointed times of eternity. In all things ordained by Thy glory there has been remembrance of Thy [being] in our midst for the assistance of the remnant
9. and the survivors for the sake of Thy covenant | and to relate Thy true deeds and the judgements of Thy wonderful mighty acts. Thou, [O God], didst redeem us for Thyself as an eternal people, and into the lot
10. of light didst Thou cast us | for Thy truth. Thou didst appoint from of old the Prince of Light, to assist us, [since all sons of justice are in his lot] and all spirits of truth in his dominion. And Thou wast the one
11. who | made Belial to corrupt, an angel of hatred, his [dominion] being in darkness and his counsel to render wicked and guilty. All the spirits |
12. of his lot, the angels of destruction, walk in the boundaries of darkness, and unto it shall be their desire all together. But we, the lot of Thy
13. truth, rejoice in | Thy mighty hand, are glad in Thy salvation, and exalt in Thy he[lp] and Thy pe[ace]. Who is like unto Thee in strength,
14. O God of Israel, and yet | Thy mighty hand is with the poor. What angel or prince is like unto the help of [Thy face, for] from of old Thou hast

and Thou . . . their seed. Cf. Gn. xvii, 19; ib. ix, 9; CDC iii, 12–13.

8. for all appointed times of eternity. Cf. comm. xii, 3; see also 1QSb i, 1–3.

things ordained. Cf. comm. xi, 8; DSD iii, 16.

remembrance. Cf. Ps. cxi, 4; and the frequent MH *zekher* = allusion.

Thy being. Cf. Ju. xviii, 19.

in our midst. Cf. Num. xiv, 14; Dt. xxiii, 15, etc.

for the assistance. Cf. xii, 6.

the remnant and the survivors. 'Remnant' || 'to let survive' in Gn. xlv. 7; the noun = 'livelihood' in Ju. vi, 4; = 'survivors' Ezra ix, 8, 9; 2 Chr. xiv, 12; cf. DSW xiv, 4–5.

9. wonderful mighty acts. Also xi, 9; xv, 13.

didst redeem us. The restoration is almost certain. Cf. Dt. xxi, 8; 2 Sam. vii, 23; DSW i, 12.

didst Thou cast us. Cf. DSD iv, 26; DST iii, 22; vii, 34; CDC xx, 4; Ps. lxxviii, 55. See also ch. 9, § 8.

10. for Thy truth. Cf. 'the lot of Thy truth', line 12; comm. iv, 6.

from of old. Cf. xi, 6. The reference is probably to Dn. xii, 1; cf. comm. i, 12; ch. 9, § 5.

prince of light. i.e. Michael, cf. ch. 9, § 5. For *ma'or*, DSD iii, 20; CDC v, 18 have *orim* (? *urim*). For the whole idea, cf. xvii, 6, and comm. on 'spirits of truth'.

since . . . his lot. Restored after DSD iii, 20; cf. xvii, 8; comm. i, 8; iv, 6.

spirits of truth. Cf. 'the angel of His truth', DSD iii, 24; ch. 9, § 2 (9), § 4.

11. made Belial to corrupt. i.e. appointed him for that task. Cf. Isa. liv, 16; also 2 Sam. xxiv, 16; Ex. xii, 23; DSW iii, 9; DST frg. 4.6; frg. 45.3. Or: 'for hell' (Rabin).

angel of hatred. Also CDC xvi, 5; cf. above xiii, 4 and comm.

dominion. Cf. xv, 9–10; ch. 9, § 3.

darkness. The *waw* looks like *daleth* through being close to the right arm of the *shin*; the latter—contrary to what appears on the photograph—lies partly within the gap.

his counsel to render wicked. Both together in 2 Chr. xxii, 3. Hiphʿil of *rshʿ* = 'cause to be wicked', cf. DST frg. 6.3, 11; frg. 9. 9; comm. pl. 331 'convict of wickedness' in DSH ix, 11–12; x. 5.

TEXT, TRANSLATION, AND COMMENTARY 323

8. למוע[ד]י עולמים ובכול תעודות כבודכה היה זכר [הי]ות[]כה
בקרבנו לעזר שארית ומחיה לבריתכה
9. ולס[פר] מעשי אמתכה ומשפטי גבורות פלאכה את[]ה אל פ]דיתנו
לכה עם עולמים ובגורל אור הפלתנו
10. לאמתכה ושר מאור מאז פקדתה לעוזרנו וב[ג]ור[]לו כול בני
צד[ק] וכול רוחי אמת בממשלתו ואתה
11. עשיתה בליעל לשחת מלאך משטמה ובחוש[ך] מ[משל]תו ובעצתו
להרשיע ולהאשים וכול רוחי
12. גורלו מלאכי חבל בחוקי חושך יתהלכו ואליו [תשו]קתמה יחד
ואנו /גורל אמתכה נשמ חה ביד
13. גבורתכה ונשישה בישועתכה ונגילה בעז[]רתכה ובש[]לומכה מיא
כמוכה בכוח אל ישראל ועם
14. אביונים יד גבורתכה ומיא מלאך ושר כעזרת פנ[י]כה כי[]א מאז
יעדתה לכה יום קרב ר(ב)ב[······]ה

and (render) guilty. Hiph'il only once in O.T. (Ps. v, 11), with declarative force; here causative. For this activity of Belial cf. DST vi, 21–2; CDC iv, 15; DSW xiv, 9–10; ch. 9, § 3.

12. angels of destruction. Also DSD iv, 12; CDC ii, 6; Rabbinic *m. ḥabbalah*; cf. ch. 9, § 2 (5).

walk in the boundaries of darkness. Formed after 'walk in God's statutes', 1 Kings viii, 61; cf. also xv, 9–10. For *ḥoq* = boundary, see comm. x, 12; Job i, 7; ii, 2 and Tur-Sinai's comm. ad loc.

unto it shall be their desire. Also xv, 10; quot. Gn. iii, 16; iv, 7.

all together. Cf. Ps. xl. 15, etc.

the lot. A very faint *beth* is visible before this word: perhaps it was erased by the scribe; cf. the language in line 5.

rejoice. The gap in the middle of the word is due to a fault in the skin.

13. Thy mighty hand. Also line 14, lit. 'the hand of Thy might'. This and the following terms all appear on the banners and trumpets, cf. comm. iii, 12; iv, 12–14; xii, 12.

Thy help and Thy peace. The restoration exactly fits both the space and the traces.

who is like ... Israel. Cf. x, 8; DST vii, 28. For 'in strength' cf. Ex. xv, 6; comm. xi, 1.

14. the poor. Cf. comm. xi, 9.

Thy face. The first letter of this word can only be *pe*, not *ṭeth* (cf. *mishpĕṭē* line 9, *maśṭemah* line 11); the second letter can be *nun*: as so often, the impression gained from the photograph, that it ends before the gap, may be misleading, owing to the peeling of the surface near a break (cf. lines 9–11; *ha-milḥ[amah]* xii, 8). If our restoration is accepted, we have here Isa. lxiii, 9 as understood by LXX: Οὐ πρέσβυς (= *śar*: MT *ẓar*) οὐδὲ ἄγγελος, ἀλλ' (om. MT) αὐτός (= *panaw*) κύριος (om. mlt.) ἔσωσεν αὐτούς (Cf. Morgenstern, HUCA 23 (1950–1), 188 sq.). For the help of God's 'face', cf. Ex. xxxiii, 14, 15 (LXX both times αὐτός); Ps. xxvii, 9; lxxx, 17 (LXX literally). For the relation of the angels to Israel, see ch. 9, § 4; cf. also *Qumran I*, p. 126, iv, 23–4: '... in Thine own hand / the men of the council of God, and not by the hand of a *śar*.'

from of old, etc. Cf. i, 10; xv, 12; xvii, 5–6.

15. appointed for Thyself a day of encounter [   ] | [   ] to [he]lp *those of* the truth and to destroy *those of* guilt, to bring low darkness
16. and to lend might to light, and to [   ] | [in the community of God] for eternal existence, for annihilation of all Sons of Darkness and joy to all [Sons of Light]. |

Section 20

17. [f]or Thou wast the one who appointed us for an [appointed time of vengeance   ]

COLUMN XIV

'like the fire of His wrath upon the idols of Egypt'.

Section 21

2. After they have withdrawn from the slain towards the encampment, they shall all together sing the hymn of return. In the morning they
3. shall launder their garments, wash themselves | of the blood of the guilty cadavers, and return to the place where they had stood, where they had arrayed the line before the falling of the enemy's slain. In that place they
4. shall bless | all together the God of Israel and exalt His name in joyful unison, and shall solemnly declare :

Blessed be the God of Israel, Who preserveth mercy for His covenant

---

15. to help those of the truth. Cf. comm. i, 16. For the whole sentence, cf. xvii, 5–6 ; also xiii, 4.

to bring low. Cf. xiv, 15 ; xvii, 5.

to lend might. Cf. Dn. ix, 27 ; DST i, 35. Perhaps in the sense of 'to make great', cf. Qal in Ps. ciii, 11. For the whole thought cf. i, 8. The parallel of xvii, 5 suggests the restoration [ולהכניע] 'and to subdue'. After that we may expect to have appeared some words like '[and to place the Sons of Light in the community of G]od'.

16. in the community of God for eternal existence. Almost exact parallel (with ʿăẓath for maʿămad) in DSD ii, 22–3 ; hence this is more probable than restoring 'Israel' or 'Michael' after xvii, 7–8.

for annihilation...darkness. Cf. i, 16.

and joy to all sons of light. Cf. i, 9 ; xvii, 7. The latter passage might suggest

the restoration 'for the lot of' instead of 'to all', except that the gap fits *lĕkhol* precisely, while it would be *c*. ½ mm. too small for *lĕghoral*.

17. for Thou wast, etc. A close parallel to xviii, 9 ; cf. also i, 10 ; xiv, 14 ; xv, 12 ; ib. 6 ; except that here it is the appointing of the sect, not of the time, which is stressed. The remains near the gap do not clearly point to *waw*, but can hardly be of *shin*, *lamedh*, etc. For the language, cf. 2 Sam. xx, 5. This section, which closes the prayers pronounced near the slain, cf. ch. 8, § 5 (6a, 2), is the shortest in the work, as the page could hardly have contained more than 2–3 lines after 17.

Column XIV

like the fire of His wrath. ¶ Ezek. xxi, 36 ; 'fire' on Egypt also Ezek, xxx, 14 ; for 'God's wrath' cf. iv, 1. The sources quoted there suggest that the last

15. [ׄ׆׆׆׆] לׄ[עׄזׄ]וׄר באמת ולהשמיד באשמה להפיל חושך ולהגביר
 אור ולׄ[ׄ- ׄ- ׄ-]
16. [ׄ- ביחד אׄ]ל למעמד עולמים לכלות כול בני חושך ושמחה לׄ[כוׄ]לׄ
 [בני אור]

[כ]

17. [ׄ- ׄ- ׄ-] כׄ[י]א אתה יעדתנו למוׄעׄדׄ נקם [ׄ- ׄ- ׄ- ׄ- ׄ-]

XIV

1. כאש עברתו באלילי מצרים

[כא]

2. ואחר העלותם מעל החללים לבוא המחנה ירננו כולם את תהלת
 המשוב ובבוקר יכבסו בגדיהם ורחצו
3. מדם פגרי האשמה ושבו אל מקום עומדם אשר סדרו שם המערכה
 לפני נפול חללי האויב וברכו שם
4. כולם את אל ישראל ורוממו שמו ביחד שמחה וענו ואמרו ברוך
 אל ישראל השומר חסד לבריתו ותעודות

lines of col. xiii alluded similarly to divine judgements on other nations.

the idols of Egypt. Cf. Isa. xix, 1; also Ezek. xxx, 13.

2. withdrawn. Niph'al, cf. Jer. xxxvii, 11. For this section, cf. ch. 8, § 5 (6c). The left half of lines 2–14 was published with comm. by Sukenik in *M.G.* I, 26, with completion of some lines on p. 24.

towards the encampment. For the language cf. iii, 10, 11. The 'camp' is here the encampment by the battlefield, as distinct from the space where the army is drawn up before battle (cf. line 3) and the actual field of battle.

all together. Cf. line 4. Probably to include the priests, etc., as opposed to xiii, 1.

the hymn of return. We are not told anything about its contents: cf. also ch. 8, § 5 (6b). For 'hymn', cf. iv, 14; Ps. xl, 4; cxix, 171; cxlv, 1; Neh. xii, 46.

in the morning. After resting the night, cf. xix, 9.

they shall launder their garments. Thus the preceding prayers were spoken in a state of ritual impurity, cf. ch. 8, § 5 (6c).

3. the blood of the guilty cadavers. Cf. comm. ix, 8; vi, 16; xiii, 4.

the place where, etc. For the language cf. Ju. xx. 22. In the same space the admonitions of the 'priest destined for the appointed time of vengeance' were pronounced, cf. vii, 8; xiii, 1; xv, 5–6; cf. ch. 7, § 2 (1), § 5; ch. 8, § 5 (2).

4. in joyful unison. Similar (with *rinnah*) DST iii, 23; xi, 14; with *yaḥadh* as an adverb ib, xi 25–6; frg. 10.7; DSD x, 17 (on which cf. Yalon, *KS* 28 (5712), 64 sq.; cf. also Ps. xxxiv, 3–4 (*smḥ* and *yaḥdaw* together); Isa. lii, 8–9; also Ps. xxi, 7, etc.

blessed be the God of Israel. Cf. comm. xiii, 7.

Who preserveth mercy for His covenant. Allusion to Dt. vii, 9; cf. also Neh. i, 5; Dn. ix, 4; 2 Chr. vi, 14.

5. and times ordained | for salvation for the people to be redeemed by Him. He hath called them that stumble unto wondrous [mighty deeds], and an assembly of nations He hath gathered for annihilation without remnant
6. so as to raise up by judgement | them whose heart had melted, to open the mouth of the dumb ones to sing [God's] mighty deeds, and to teach weak [hands] warfare. He giveth them whose knees totter strength to
7. stand | and fortifying of loins to the shoulder of them that have been brought low. Through the poor in spirit [ ] there shall be gnaw]ed a hard heart, and through them that are upright in the way shall
8. all wicked nations come to an end, | and all their mighty men shall not be able to resist. But we, the remn[ant of Thy people, shall bless] Thy name, O God of mercies, Who hast kept the covenant with our fore-
9. fathers, and unto | all our generations Thou hast made passing great Thy mercies upon the rem[ains of the people of Israel] during the dominion of Belial. With all the mysteries of his hatred they have not

8	ולכול גבוריהם	5	ולגבו]ריהם[
9	הפלתה	6	אל החסדים
	חסדיכה לשאר		המפליא
	[ית עם ישראל]		חסדיך בנו
12	עם קודשכה	10	עמכה

times ordained. Cf. xi, 8; xiii, 8. Otherwise Yalon, loc. cit.; 't. o. for peace', *Qumran I*, no. 36, frg. 1 (p. 138).

5-16. Some of the lacunae in these lines have been restored with the help of a fragment of another copy of the War Scroll found in Cave IV (4QMa) and published by C.-H. Hunzinger, ZAW 69 (1957) 131–51. Hunzinger's restorations both of his 4Q fragment and of our scroll are not all adopted here. The following is a list of passages in the 4Q fragment (lines of the fragment) where our restoration differs from Hunzinger's:

line	our restoration	Hunzinger's restoration
4	[לנ]אלמים	[מ]תאלמים
6	נב]ורך	בר]וך שמך
7	[מפנינו]	[ממנו]
10	[יהיה כאין]	[תתן קלון]
11	[תמיד בכול]	[תפארתך בכול]

The two MSS differ in the following readings:

line	Hunzinger's frg. (= 4QM)	line	Our Scroll
3	ואין	5	אין
4	ילרנו	6	לרנן
4	בורכים	6	ברכים
4	חיזק	6	חזוק
4	ואימץ	7	ואמוץ
5	ל]עות	7	י]כור]סם

He hath called them that stumble. The space is due to a fault in the skin. Being parallel with 'gathered', 'called' has here the military sense of 'called up', as in Isa. xiii, 3 (also the rest of that chapter influenced our passage); cf. comm. v, 3. For 'stumble', cf. 1 Sam. ii, 4; *Qumran I*, p. 110, ii, 7. The whole passage resembles xi, 13 sq., and is influenced by Isa. xxxv.

unto wondrous mighty deeds. Restored after 4Q.

an assembly of nations. Cf. Jer. l, 9.

He hath gathered. Cf. Isa. xiii, 4; Mic. iv, 11; Hab. ii, 5; Zeph. iii, 8.

for annihilation without remnant. Cf. Ezra, ix, 14; CDC i, 5 *lĕ-khalah* as here (MT *'adh kalleh*); 'without remnant' also i, 6; CDC ii, 6–7; DSD iv, 14.

to raise up by judgement. Cf. perhaps Ps. x, 5; lxxxix, 17.

6. them whose heart had melted. Lit. 'a melted heart'; cf. xi, 9.

to open the mouth of the dumb. Based on Ezek. xxxiii, 22; cf. Isa. xxxv, 6; Ps. xxxix, 10.

TEXT, TRANSLATION, AND COMMENTARY 327

5. ישועה לעם פדותו ויקרא   בושלים ל[גבורות] פלא וקהל גויים
   אסף לכלה אין שארית ולהרים במשפט
6. לב נמס ולפתוח פה לנאלמים לרנן בגבור[ות] אל וידים] רפות
   ללמד מלחמה ונותן לנמוגי ברכים חזוק מעמד
7. ואמוץ מתנים לשכם מכים ובעניי רוח [- יכור]סם לבב קושי
   ובתמימי דרך יתמו כול גויי רשעה
8. ולכול גבוריהם אין מעמד ואנו שא[ר עמכה נברכה] שמכה אל
   החסדים השומר ברית לאבותינו ועם
9. כול דורותינו הפלתה חסדיכה לשאר[ית] עם ישראל] בממשלת
   בליעל ובכול רזי שטמתו לוא הדיחונ[ו]

to sing God's mighty deeds. Restored after 4Q. Cf. Ps. xxi, 14; cl 2.
to teach—warfare. Cf. 2 Sam. xxii, 35 = Ps. xviii, 35; cf. comm. vi, 11.
weak hands. Restored after Isa. xxxv, 3; Job iv, 4.
whose knees totter. The weakness of knees is a frequent image (Isa. xxxv, 3; Ezek. vii, 17; xxi, 12; Nah. ii, 11; Job iv, 4), but never with *mwg* Niph.; cf., however, Mekhilta *Beshallaḥ* on Ex. xv, 15 which equates *namogh* with *names*, and thus allows comparison with Ezek. xxi, 12
strength. Lit. 'strengthening', MH verbal noun Piʿel; also DSD x, 26; DST ii, 7–8.
to stand. Lit. 'of standing'; cf. DST iv, 36. On *maʿămad* as military term, see ch. 7, § 2 (3).
7. fortifying of loins. Cf. Nah. ii, 2: 'strengthen thy loins, fortify *thy* power'. The form as *ḥizzuq*, see above.
the poor in spirit. Based on Isa. lxvi, 2, also quoted xi, 10. Cf. also vii, 5; Pr. xvi, 19. Cf. Mt. v, 3. See Hunzinger op. cit., p. 143; Rabin JThS 6 (1955), 178.
there shall be gnawed. Restored according to the sense. The verb occurs once, Ps. lxxx, 14, but is frequent in MH (often spelled with *qoph*). 4QM has a different verb, see above.
a hard heart. Difficult construction, but cf. *qĕshē lev*, Ezek. iii, 7; *qĕshi* cstr., Dt. ix, 27. [Perhaps קושי = *qosheh*, cf. Arab. *qāsin* 'hard, cruel', Rabin]. Possibly ¶ Pr. xi, 20, where M.T. has עקשי; see next note.

that are upright in the way. Cf. Ps. cxix, 1; also DSD iv, 22; *Qumran I*, p. 110, i, 28; DST i, 36; cf. also *tĕmim derekh* 'the upright way', DSD viii, 18, 21; ix, 2, 5, 9; cf. comm. vii, 5. Opposition between the 'perverse in heart' and the 'upright in the way' also Pr. xi, 20.
come to an end. Play on the root *tmm*; for sense cf. Ps. civ, 35; also Dt. ix, 4–5; DSW xv, 9.
8. shall not be able to resist. For this sense of *maʿămadh* cf. iv, 3–4; xviii, 12; DST v, 29. The thought is developed in line 11.
the remnant of Thy people. Restored after Isa. xi, 11, 16—Isa. xi influenced DSW, cf. comm. i, 1–2.
shall bless Thy name. Restored after xiii, 7.
God of mercies. Not in O.T.
Who hast kept, etc. Cf. line 4.
9. hast made passing great Thy mercies. Cf. Ps. xvii, 7; see also below, xviii, 10. 4 QM 'O God of mercies Who hast made passing great Thy mercies towards us'.
the remains of the people of Israel. Restored after Jer. xxxi, 7—the chapter resembles our prayer.
during the dominion of Belial. Cf. DSD i, 17–18, 24; ii, 19; iii, 22; cf. ch. 9, § 3.
mysteries of his hatred. Cf. *masṭemah* xiii, 4, 13; 'mysteries of sin', DST v, 36; for the thought cf. Test. Dan. v, 6 (with reference to 'the book of Enoch the righteous').

328 TEXT, TRANSLATION, AND COMMENTARY

10. beguiled us away | from Thy covenant. His spirits of destruction Thou hast chided [away from us, and when there acted evilly the me]n of his dominion, Thou hast preserved the soul of those to be redeemed by
11. Thee. Thou hast raised up | the fallen through Thy power, but them that are high of stature Thou wilt hew down [and the haughty Thou wilt humble]. All their mighty men shall have no one to save *them*, their
12. swift ones shall have no place to which to flee, to their nobles | Thou wilt render contempt, and all their creatures of vanity [shall be as] nothing. But we, Thy holy people, through Thy true deeds shall praise Thy
13. name | and exalt Thy mighty acts for[ever in all turning-points] of epochs and appointed times of ordained things for eternity, as well as the coming-
14. in of daytime and night-time | and the going-forth of evening and morning, for Thy [glorious plan] is great and Thy mysterious secrets are in [Thy] high heavens, to [raise up] for Thyself of those belonging to the dust |
15. and to humble of those belonging to the angels.

Section 22

16.   Rise up, rise up, O God of angels
      and raise Thyself in power, [O King of Kings,
      To subdue the wicked so that there be no remnant,

beguiled. Cf. Dt. xiii, 14, where 'sons of Belial' is the subject.

10. of destruction. OR: the spirits of his share. Probably intentional *double entendre*, cf. xiii, 12. Less probably הבלו, 'his spirits of vanity'.

Thou hast chided. Cf. Zech. iii, 2; quoted DST frg. 4, 6, *Oẓar*, pl. 54.

away from us. This restoration is favoured by 4QM.

the men of his dominion. Restored after 4QM.

the soul of those to be redeemed by Thee. Based (?) on Job xxxiii, 28; for the construction cf. xi, 9.

11. raised up the fallen. Cf. Ps. cxlv, 14.

high ... humble. Restored after Isa. x, 33; cf. also lines 14–15.

their mighty men ... to flee. Enlarged from Jer. xlvi, 6; cf. Am. ii, 14. Possibly an allusion to the Kittim, who are called 'light and mighty ones' in DSH ii, 12–13.

nobles. Cf. Ps. cxlix, 8; in DST x, 8 = 'angels', cf. ch. 9, § 2.

12. Thou wilt render contempt. The *lamedh* seems superfluous; in O.T. only *hashev ḥerpah*, e.g. Ps. cxix, 22. Cf. however, DSH iv, 2 where the Kittim 'pour contempt (*bazu*) upon the nobles.'

their creatures of vanity. Lit. 'the creatures of their vanities'. In the O.T. *yěqum* (3 times), never construct, but in DSW also xv, 11. The space between the two words is due to a fault in the leather.

shall be as nothing. Though it would be attractive to restore, with Gn. vii, 23, *min ha-areẓ*, this is not possible. The vertical line is too much bent for a *ẓade*, nor is the *yodh* to the right of it similar to the thorn of a *ẓade*. I have restored after Isa. xli, 11.

but we. Cf. xiii, 7. The following section resembles x, 11 sq.

Thy holy people. Cf. Isa. lxiii, 18.

shall praise Thy name. Cf. Ps. cxlv, 2; DSW xiii, 7; DST xii, 8.

10. מבריתכה ורוחי [ח]ב[לי] גערתה מ[נ]מנו ובהתרשע אנ[ש]י ממשלתו
    שמתה נפש פדותכה ואתה הקימותה

11. נופלים בעוזכה ורמי קומה תגד[ע וגבוהים תשפיל ו]לכול גבוריהם
    אין מציל ולקליהם אין מנוס ולנכבדיהם

12. תשיב לבוז וכול יקום   הבלי[הם יהיה כא]ין ואנו עם קודשכה
    במעשי אמתך נהללה שמכה

13. וגבורותיכה נרוממה   תמ[י]ד בכול מולדי[ן] עתים ומועדי תעודות
    עולמים עם מ[בו]א יומם ולילה

14. ומוצאי ערב ובוקר כיא גדולה מ[ח]שבת כב[ו]דכה ורזי נפלאותיכה
    במרומי[כה ל]ה[רי]ם לכה מעפר

15. ולהשפיל מאלים

[כב]

16. רומה רומה אל אלים והנשא בעו[ז] מלך המלכים להכניע רשעה לאין
    שארית ופליטה לא תהיה]

---

13. exalt Thy mighty acts. The *bĕ*- also line 6; cf. Ps. cl, 2.

forever in all turning-points of epochs. Restored after DST xii, 7-8; the following is a summary of DST xii, 3-10; DSD x, 9-15, passages important for the sect's calendar, cf. ch. 8, § 3 (4). For ' forever ' cf. Ps. xxxiv, 2; xl, 17; lxx, 5. 4QM perhaps favours a restoration עתים ומועדי, see Hunzinger ibid.

appointed ... eternity. Cf. ' appointed times of eternity ', xii, 3; ' appointed times of ordained things ', DSD iii, 10; cf. also DST xii, 9.

14. Thy glorious plan. Restored after 4QM.

Thy mysterious secrets. Also (with *pele'*) CDC iii, 18; DSD ix, 18; xi, 5; DST ii, 13; iv, 27-8; vii, 27; xi, 10; xiii, 2; cf. also DSD xi, 3, 9; DST i, 10.

in Thy high heavens. Cf. Job xxv, 2.

to raise up. The restoration as in 4QM.

15. to humble ... angels. Cf. line 11;

xi, 13. The reference is apparently to the demotion of the ' prince of the dominion of wickedness ' and the raising of Michael, xvii, 5-7; cf. also ch. 9, § 2 (1), (10).

16. rise up, rise up. The whole sentence based on Ps. xxi, 14, where, however, *rumah* only once. For the double imperative S. Lieberman (PAAJR 20 (1951), 404, n. 68) compares *rumi rumi ha-shiṭṭah*, Gen. Rabba liv (ed. Theodor-Albeck, p. 581).

God of angels. Cf. Dn. xi, 36; see also Ex. xv, 11.

raise Thyself. Cf. Ps. xciv, 2; perhaps also Ps. vii, 7 (beginning with *qumah*).

in power, O King of Kings. Restored after 4QM.

to subdue ... to escape. Restored after i, 5-7, which there precedes a passage closely corresponding to line 17 here. Towards the end of the line a *shin* seems visible: perhaps the last word was *shĕ'erith* or *śaridh* ?

330   TEXT, TRANSLATION, AND COMMENTARY

17.   and that there be none to escape] | of all Sons of Darkness.
       Let the light of Thy majesty shi[ne for all epochs of eternity,
           for peace, blessing, glory, and joy for all Sons of Light.
18.   But the fire] | [of Thine anger shall burn unto Sheol,
           to consume [   ]

COLUMN XV

       For it is a time of trouble for Israe[l,
           a time pre-ordained] for battle with all the nations,
       And the lot of God is in eternal redemption, |
2.   but annihilation for all nations of wickedness.
       And all those [prepared] for battle shall go and encamp over against
3. the king of the Kittim and all the army | of Belial that are gathered unto him for a day [of vengeance] through the Sword-of-God.

SECTION 23

4. The chief priest and his brother [priests] and the levites shall stand up and all the men of the Serekh with him, and he shall read in their
5. hearing | the prayer for the appointed time of batt[le, as is written in the boo]k Serekh 'Itto, including all the texts of their thanksgivings.

17. of all. The size of the gap excludes the restoration *lĕ-goral*.

the light ... sons of light. Restored after i, 8–9; cf. also *Qumran I*, p. 126, iv, 27–8.

18. the fire ... unto Sheol. Restored after Dt. xxxii, 22; cf. also Jer. xv, 14. Since the last lines of this section show that it is a transition from the 'Serekh Series' to the 'Kittim Series', it appears that the preceding passage is not part of the battle ritual, but a private prayer of the author; cf. ch. 1, § 3 ad loc.; ch. 8, § 5 (6c) at end.

Column XV

for it ... Israel. Abbreviated version of i, 11–12, see there. In the *Oẓar*, pl. 30, the two halves have been set too wide apart. The gap in line 1, for instance, should be 11 mm. instead of 30 mm.

a time pre-ordained for battle. Cf. *Qumran I*, p. 110, i, 26; DSW ii, 8. In DSW elsewhere *moʿedh ha-m.*, xv, 5 12, or verbal forms, i, 10; xiii, 14; *tĕʿudhah* (in the apocalyptic sense) and *moʿedh* are thus near-synonyms.

with all the nations. The scribe first wrote 'al' against' (Isa. xiv, 26; Jer, x, 25; etc.), and then corrected so as to agree with Ex. xxxiv, 10.

the lot of God. Cf. i, 5, to which the whole sentence closely corresponds.

eternal redemption. Also i, 12; xviii, 10; cf. 'eternal light', xiii, 5.

2. nations of wickedness. Cf. 'wickedness' in the same sense, i, 13; 'nations of vanity', vi, 6.

prepared. Restored after vii, 5; cf. vi, 15. With these words the Kittim Series proper begins.

encamp over against. This is the first phase, followed by 'standing over against', xvi, 2 (i.e. drawn up at some distance from the enemy) and then by 'standing near', xvi, 5, just before making contact; cf. viii, 7–8; comm. lines 4–5 below. For the phrase, cf. 1 Kings xx, 27, 29; Yadin, *Maʿarakhoth* 60 (December 1949), 27.

TEXT, TRANSLATION, AND COMMENTARY 331

.17 לכו[ל ב]ני חושך ואור גודלכה יא[ני]ר לכול קצי עולמים לשלום וברכה
כבוד ושמחה לכול בני אור ואש[

.18 [אפכה עד ש]א[ו]ל תוקד לשרו[נך ---------]

XV

.1 כיא היאה עת צרה לישר[אל תע[ו]דת מלחמה // ב[ו]ל הגוים וגורל
אל בפדות עולמים

.2 וכלה לכול גוי רשעה וכול ע[ו]תו[דו]י המלחמה ילכו וחנו נגד מלך
כתיים ונגד כול חיל

.3 בליעל הנועדים עמו ליום [נקם] בחרבאל

[כג]

.4 ועמד כוהן הראש ואחיו הכ[והנים] והלויים וכול אנשי הסרך עמו
וקרא באוזניהם

.5 את תפלת מועד המלח[מה ככתוב בס]פר סרך עתו עם כול דברי
הודותם וסדר שם

king of the Kittim. Only here and possibly in the Pesher to Ps. lxviii, *Qumran I*, p. 82, according to Milik's restoration. In DSH iv, 5, 10 and pNahum line 3 'rulers of the K.' (cf. ch. 2, § 3 (2)), which Dupont-Sommer (*Aperçus*, p. 41, n. 9) considers evidence for the identification with the Romans. Note, however, that from 44 B.C. onwards Caesar was to all intents and purposes a king, cf. *Oxford Classical Dictionary*, p. 153, § 3. For the possible connexion of our phrase with 2 Chr. xxxii, 21, see comm. xix.

3. army of Belial. Also, i, 1.

are gathered. Frequent of Israel's enemies, e.g. Josh. xi, 5; Ps. xlviii, 5. The Kittim thus head the enemy forces.

day of vengeance. Restored after vii, 5; perhaps restore 'day of doom', with i, 11.

sword-of-God. Also written in one word in xix, 11; in two words in DST vi, 29: 'and then the s. of G. will hasten' (cf. comm. i, 12); cf. 's. of YHWH' in the O.T., and see also 2 Macc. xv, 15–16. On the connexion of this event with prophecies, see comm. xi, 11–12; xvi, 1.

4. the chief priest. Cf. comm. xiii, 1; ch. 8, § 4.

and his brother priests and the levites. So xiii, 1. This highly probable restoration proves that the gap in the photograph is too large, cf. comm. line 1.

all men of the Serekh. In xiii, 1 'all elders, etc.': at this phase the entire army takes part, cf. comm. v, 15.

5. the prayer, etc. See ch. 8, § 5 (1).

the appointed time of battle. So line 12, see comm. there; also cf. line 1.

as is written in the book. The restoration exactly fits; no other seems possible, cf. ch. 4, § 2 (c); 'as is written' also in line 6: the space does not permit *ki-mĕdhuqdaq*, as in CDC xvi, 3. The prayer is set out in full in section 14 and onwards.

Serekh 'ittō. Cf. comm. vii, 5; i.e. 'the order of His (proper) time', or 'the order of occasions' (cf. Lv. xvi, 21). Also in Rabbinic usage a prayer-book is called *sedher* or *siddur*. See further ch. 1, § 6.

their thanksgivings. For the form, see comm. iv, 14; for the concept, ch. 8, § 5 (1). All these prayers are said at the encampment near the enemy, but before the ranks are drawn up.

6. In that very place he shall array | all the formations, as writ[ten in the Book of the Wa]r. Then the priest destined for the appointed time of
7. vengeance by the agreement | of all his brethren shall walk along and strengthen [their hands for the battl]e, and he shall solemnly declare :
8.   Be ye strong and courageous and be men of valour, | fear not, nor be ye dismayed [and let not your hearts faint], do not tremble, neither
9. be ye terrified because of them, be not | turned back nor [flee from them]. For they are a wicked congregation : in darkness are all their
10. deeds, | and unto it is their desire. [They have made lies] their refuge, their might is like unto smoke that vanisheth away, and all their
11. assembled | multitude [is as chaff that passeth away, and it shall become] a desolation, and shall not be found. All their creatures of
12. evil intention shall quickly wither away | [like a flow]er in ha[rvest time. But ye be courageous and] be strong for the battle of God, for this day
13. is an appointed time of battle | [unto Go]d against all the [nations, and strife of judgem]ent against all flesh. The God of Israel is raising His

6. all the formations. Both the front formations and the skirmishers. The process is described v, 15 ; vii, 8.

as written. Cf. Josh. viii, 31, etc.; CDC xix, 1 ; in CDC vii, 19 ; DSD viii, 14 *ka'ăsher kathuv*.

the book (?) of the war. It is impossible to say whether the missing word was *sefer*—in which case a military handbook of some kind may have been meant—or *serekh*. In the latter case, the reference may actually be to the first part of our scroll, see ch. 1, § 6.

the priest. On this functionary, see ch. 8, § 4 (3), § 5 (3); comm. vii, 11.

destined. Also xvi, 9 ; an apocalyptic term, cf. Dn. ix, 26 ; 27 ; xi, 36, etc.; Tur-Sinai's commentary on Job xiv, 5 ; RB 58 (1951), 179 sq.

appointed time of vengeance. Also vii, 5 ; cf. iii, 7–8.

7. shall walk along. Cf. vii, 11 ; in contrast to the chief priest, who delivers his oration standing.

strengthen their hands for the battle. Restored after vii, 11 ; cf. also xvi, 11–12.

shall solemnly declare. Cf. xiii, 2.

The following differs—intentionally—from the text of the words of the 'chief priest' in Dt. xx, quoted x, 3–4, and bears the influence of Josh. x; Dt. xxxi, 2 Chr. xxxii ; 2 Sam. ii, 7 ; xiii, 28. For detailed comparison, see ch. 8 § 5 (2).

8. fear not, nor be ye dismayed. From Josh. x, 25.

and let not your hearts faint. From Dt. xx, 3 ; cf. DSW x, 3.

9. be not turned back. Cf. Ps. ix, 4 ; xliv, 11 ; lvi, 10.

flee. Cf. M. Sot. viii, 6 ; but perhaps restore *tissoghu* ' shrink back ', cf. Isa. l, 5.

for they are. A similar turn of phrase in xvii, 4, the address of the chief priest after victory, which the following resembles as well as the thanksgiving prayer in xiii, 7 onwards.

a wicked congregation. Cf. ' a congregation of violent men ', Ps. lxxxvi, 14, and ' wicked nations ', DSW xv, 2.

in darkness are all their deeds. Cf. ' they walk in the boundaries of darkness ', xiii, 12.

10. and unto it is their desire. Cf. ibid. (+ ' all together '); also cf. xvii, 4.

TEXT, TRANSLATION, AND COMMENTARY

6. אֵת כול המערכות ככת[וב בספר המ]ל[חמ]ה והתהלך הכוהן החרוץ למועד נקם על פי

7. כול אחיו וחזק את [ידיהם במ]ל[חמ]ה וענה ואמר חזקו ואמצו והיו לבני חיל

8. אל תיראו ואל תח[ו]תו ואל ירך לבבכ[ם ואל] תחפזו ואל תערוצו מפניהם ואל

9. תשובו אחור ואל [תנוסו מפניהם] כיא המה עדת רשעה ובחושך כול מעשיהם

10. ואליו תשוק[תמה בכוב ישימו] מחסיהם וגבורתם כעשן נמלח וכול קהל

11. [ה]מונם [כמוץ עובר והיה לש]ממה לוא ימצא וכול יקום הוותם מהר ימלו

12. [בצי]ץ בק[ו]צי[ר ואתם אמצו ו]התחזקו למלחמת אל כיא /// מועד מלחמה היום הזה

13. [לא]ל על כול ה[גו]יים וריב מש[פ]ט על כול בשר אל ישראל מרים ידו ב[גבור]ת פלאו

---

they have made lies their refuge. Restored after Isa. xxviii, 15.

like unto smoke, etc. Cf. Isa. li, 6; *Livre des Mysteres* i, 6 (*Qumran I*, p. 103); see also DSW xvii, 4; comm. i, 8.

11. multitude. This word and the beginnings of lines 11-15 appear on fragment no. 1, Oẓar Plate 47, lower half.

as chaff that passes away. The phrase (cf. Isa. xxix, 5) fits the sense, but the restoration is far from certain. Cf. also comm. xviii, 1, 3.

shall not be found. Cf. Dn. xi, 19; DST, iv, 20.

creatures. Cf. xiv, 12.

of evil intention. This BH word (e.g. Pr. x, 3) occurs frequently in the Scrolls.

12. quickly ... time. Compounded of Ps. xxxvii, 2 (MT *mĕherah*); Job xiv, 2; xviii, 16.

but ye ... strong. Cf. xvii, 4; 1 Sam. iv, 9; 2 Sam. x, 12.

the battle of God. = the inscription on the banner of the congregation when going to battle, iv, 12; cf. comm. i, 11.

an appointed time of battle. Also line 5; cf. xvii, 5; also i, 10; xiii, 14; xvii, 9. The scribe wrote at first 'days of battle'; the word 'days' was erased and corrected, apparently by a second hand.

13. nations. The extant letter seems to be either *ḥeth* or *he*.

strife of judgement. Cf. xii, 5. The last letter could be *ṭeth* or *beth*, but my choice was decided by the fact that the letter before it could not possibly be the *resh* of *ḥerev*. The sentence seems in any case to be borrowed from Isa. lxvi, 16.

His hand. Cf. i, 14; xviii, 1.

14. hand in His wondrous [might] | against all the spirits of wick[edness. The battalions of the mi]ghty angels are girding themselves for battle,
15. [and] the array[s of the sa]ints | [are pre]paring themselves for a day of
16. |vengeance   ] | the God of I[srae]l
17. [   ] | to remove Bel[ial
18.   ] | in his perdition (OR : hell) [   ]

COLUMN XVI

until every source [of uncleanness] is come to an end. [For] the God of Israel has called a sword upon all the nations, and through the saints of His people He will do mightily.

SECTION 24

2. All this disposition they shall carry out on that [day] in the place where they stand over against the camp of the Kittim. Afterwards the
3. priests shall blow for them the trumpets | of remembrance. They shall open the [battle] intervals, and the skirmishers shall go forth and take up position in columns between the lines. The priests shall blow
4. for them | a fanfare *for the* array, and the column[s shall keep fanning out] at the sound of the trumpets until each man has fallen in at his proper
5. position. Then the priests shall blow for them | another fanfare, [signals for engag]ing. When they stand near the line of the Kittim within

in His wondrous might. Cf. xi, 9.
14. against all the spirits of wickedness. Cf. ch. 9, § 2 (9). For ' against ', cf. xviii, 1 ; for ' wickedness ' (*rish'ah* rather than *resha'*) cf. xv, 2.
battalions. Restored after ' battalions of God ', iii, 6 ; cf. Cant. Rabba vi, on vi, 10 : ' like the battalions of heaven, such as Michael and his battalion, or Gabriel and his battalion ' ; cf. ch. 9, § 6 (1).
the mighty angels. Lit. ' the mighty ones of the angels '. The angels are called ' mighty ones ' in xii, 7 ; DST iii, 35–6 ; v, 21 ; viii, 11–12 ; x, 33–4. The participation of the angels is alluded to in i, 10, 11 ; cf. ch. 9, § 2.
are girding themselves. Also i, 13 ; xvi, 9. The Hithp. without ' strength '. etc. only Isa. viii, 9 ; Pi'el with ' might for battle ' in Ps. xviii, 40.

arrays. The reading is uncertain. Cf. vi, 7, 16.
15. preparing themselves. Cf. Job xv, 28. Parallel to ' gird themselves ' ; the word might also be *mĕ'uttadhim*. Cf. Test. Levi iii, 3.
16. God of Israel. The reading is obtained by fitting in fragment 9, as shown in *Oẓar*, p. 47, and restoring after xvi, 1 and xvii, 4–5.
17. to remove Belial. Cf. xviii, 10, ' to remove the dominion of the enemy '. The letter after *beth* might, however, be a *qoph*.
18. perdition. It is not clear whether we have here BH *avdan, ovdan* ' perdition ' (Est. viii, 6 ; ix, 5) or *avaddon*, ἀβάδδων, ' hell ', on which cf. Charles in Hastings *Dictionary of the Bible*, I, 3.

14. על כול רוחי רש[ע]ה דגלי ג[ב]ורי אלים מתאזרים למלחמ[נ]ה
ו[סדר]י קד[ושים
15. [מתע]תדים ליום [נקם - -]ל[נ - -]ל[נ - -]ל[נ ···]
16. אל י[שרא]ל [- - - - - - - -]
17. להסיר בל[י]ע'ל [- - - - - - - -]
18. באבדונו ח[נ - - - - - - -]

XVI

1. עד תום כול מקור [טומאה בו]א] אל ישראל קרא חרב על כול
הגואים ובקדושי עמו יעשה גבורה

[כד]

2. את כול הסרך הזה יעשו [ביום ה]הואה על עומדם נגד מחני כתיים
ואחר יתקעו להמה הכוהנים בחצוצרות
3. הזכרון ופתחו שערי המ[לחמה וי]צאו אנשי הבינים ועמדו ראשים
בין המערכות ותקעו להם הכוהנים
4. תרועה סדר והראשי[ם יהיו נפשטי]ם לקול החצוצרות עד התיצבם
איש על מעמדו ותקעו להם
5. הכוהנים תרועה שני[ת ידי התק]רב ובעומדם ליד מערכת כתיים
כדי הטל ירימו איש ידו בכלי

Column XVI

until—is come to an end. Also i, 8.
source of uncleanness. Or restore 'corrupted spring', Pr. xxv. 26; and cf. comm. vii, 6. The *resh* looks like a *daleth*.
has called a sword. Cf. Jer. xxv, 29, etc.; see also xv, 3 above.
nations. Same spelling xii, 13.
and through the saints, etc. So vi, 6, but with *gĕvurah* for *ḥayil*.
2. in the place, etc. After having been drawn up according to vii, 8. See also comm. xv, 2.
afterwards. After the completion of the speech.
trumpets of remembrance. Cf. comm. vii, 12; ch. 5, § 5 (7).
3. battle intervals. Certain restoration, cf. comm. iii, 1.
4. a fanfare for the array. Cf. v, 8.
fanning out. Restored after viii, 6.
5. signals for engaging. Restored after xvii, 11. This is the 'signal to advance' of viii, 7.
stand near the line of the Kittim. Cf. comm. xv, 2.
within throwing range. So xvii, 12; cf. comm. viii, 15. This use of *kĕdhē* is Talmudic.

6. throwing range, they shall each man raise his hand with his | weapon. Then the six [priests shall blow on the tr]umpets of assault a high-pitched intermittent note to direct the fighting, and the levites and the whole
7. band | of horn-blowers shall sound [a battle fanfare], a great noise. As soon as the sound goes forth, *the skirmishers* shall attack to fell the slain
8. of the Kittim, and all | the people shall cease from the sound of the fanfare, [while the priests] keep on blowing a fanfare on the trumpets of assault and the battle is waged victoriously against the Kittim.

Section 25

9. When [Belial] girds himself for assistance to the Sons of Darkness, and the slain among the skirmishers begin to fall, according to God's
10. mysteries and to test thereby all those destined for battle, | the priests shall blow the trumpets of summoning for another formation to go forth as a battle reserve, and they shall take up position between the
11. lines, | while to those engaged in battle *the priests* shall blow *a signal* to withdraw. Then the chief priest shall come forward and stand in front
12. of the formation, and shall strengthen | their heart through [the might of God and] their hands for His battle.

they shall ... weapon. So xvii, 12; cf. also viii, 8.
6. the six ... trumpets. Restored after vii, 11–12; viii, 8–9, where 'six' is attached to the trumpets.
high-pitched ... fighting. So viii, 9.
7. a battle fanfare. Restored after viii, 10 and parallels, see comm. ib. The wording differs somewhat.
as the sound goes forth. Cf. xvii, 14 and comm.; and viii, 10 (without 'goes forth').
attack. Cf. comm. ix, 1.
8. shall cease. In ix, 1 with *min*; viii, 11 intransitive; xvii, 14 *yan(n)iḥu* in the same sense. Cf. ch. 5, § 8.
the priests. Restored after ix, 1.
is waged victoriously. We are here in the thick of the battle, while in other passages the signal marks the beginning of battle only, cf. comm. viii, 1, 9 (see also iv, 13). Here the description immediately passes on to the second 'lot', in which the Kittim get the upper hand, cf. ch. 1, § 3.

9. Belial. The restoration is practically certain; the size of the gap suggests that the word was written rather cramped, like the two following.
girds himself. Cf. xiv, 15. The word implies a gain of strength, cf. comm. i, 13.
for assistance to the sons of darkness. In the first six engagements, Belial helps them as Michael helps the Sons of Light, but God intervenes in the seventh (xviii, 1). Here we begin the account of the second engagement (as shown by xvii, 16, 'and in the third lot'), in which the enemies recover; this is followed by a speech of encouragement delivered by the Chief Priest (cf. discussion in ch. 8, § 5 (4)). As in section 18, the speech starts a new section, for obvious reasons.
the skirmishers. In the first six engagements only the skirmishers fight, cf. comm. i, 14.
according to God's mysteries. For reasons unfathomable to the human mind. For the phrase, cf. iii, 9; xvi, 14; xvii, 17;

TEXT, TRANSLATION, AND COMMENTARY

6. מלחמתו וששת [הכוהנים יריעו בח]צוצרות החללים קול חד
טרוד לנצח מלחמה והלוים וכול עם
7. השופרות יריעו[תרועו]ת [מלחמה] קול גדול ועם צאת הקול
יחלו ידם להפיל בחללי כתיים וכול
8. העם ישבו קול התרועה [והכוהני]ם יהיו מריעים בחצוצרות
החללים והמלחמה מתנצחת בכתיים

[כה]

9. ובהתאזר [בליעל] לעזרת בני חושך וחללי הבינים יחלו לנפול
ברזי אל ולבחון בם כול חרוצי המלחמה
10. והכ[ו]הנים יתק[ו]עו בח[צו]צרות המקרא לצאת מערכה אחרת
חליפה למלחמה ועמדו בין המערכות
11. ולמתקרבי[ו]ם למ[ל]חמה יתקעו לשוב וגש כוהן הרואש ועמד לפני
המערכה וחזק את
12. לבבם ב[גבורת אל ואת] ידיהם במלחמתו

DSD iii, 23; (xi, 19; DST xii, 20); DSH vii, 8.

to test. On this purpose of the battle, cf. xvi, 13; xvii, 1; p. 221, n. 4.

destined. The word recurs in the title of the priest 'destined for the day of vengeance'. Here it probably also has the two other connotations: 'whose term of life is determined' (cf. Job xiv, 5), i.e. who are to die; and 'who are tested like gold (ḥaruẓ)', cf. DST v, 16; see also p. 221, n. 4.

10. shall blow the trumpets. Reading and restoration seem certain.

formation. Presumably of skirmishers, cf. comm. vi, 8.

reserve. Cf. Job xiv, 14 (see above s.v. 'destined'; cf. however Tur-Sinai ad loc.); MH ḥilluf, M. Ber. iii, 1. For the military meaning and its significance for the date of the Scroll, see ch. 7, § 5 (9).

11. those engaged. Reading and restoration certain; for the language cf. ix, 4; viii, 7–8; xvii, 11. It is in keeping with the best military practice to throw in the reserve *before* ordering those in the field to retreat, cf. ch. 7, § 5 (9).

the chief priest. At this juncture his full moral authority is required, cf. ch. 8, § 5 (4). In contrast to the 'priest destined for the day of vengeance', the chief priest stands still and the troops gather round him: xvii, 10 shows that the units were only drawn up after his speech.

shall come forward. Based on Dt. xx, 2; but in x, 2 he 'stands up', see comm.

strengthen their heart. Cf. Josh. xi, 20; the 'priest destined, etc.' strengthens 'their hands', vii, 11—see however line 12.

12. the might, etc. Restored to suit the context, cf. xv, 12; xiv, 6; vii, 12.

Section 26

13. And he shall solemnly declare :
[God inquires in justice, and] the heart of His people He tests with judgement (OR : legitimately). Not [without cause] have your slain
14. [fallen]. For ye have understood from of old | the mysteries of God
15. [   ] to unique ones | according to their deserts [   ]

COLUMN XVII

and He shall render their retribution like the burning [of wood (?), and they shall be] those tested in the crucible. He shall sharpen His weapons, and they shall not become blunt until [there come to an end
2. all nations] | of wickedness. But ye, remember ye the judgement [of Nadab and Abi]hu, the sons of Aaron, through whose judgement God
3. hallowed Himself in the sight [of all the people ; but Eleazar] | and Ithamar He preserved for Himself for a covenant [of the appointed times of et]ernity.

Section 27

4. But ye, be ye strong and fear them not, [for] their *destiny* is for chaos and their desire is for the void, and their support is as if it had not

---

13. shall solemnly declare. Cf. xv, 7.

God ... judgement. The last word is fairly certain : the second letter could well be *mem*, the third just possibly a *shin* (note the thorn bending to the left), the third shows the hump typical for *ṭeth*. The distance between the *lamedh* and *beth* of 'heart' requires an intervening letter. The rest is restored after 1 Chr. xxix, 18 ; ib. 17 ; Jer. xvii, 10 ; ib. xi, 20. For the 'testing' cf. xvii, 1. This section contains the justification of the defeat.

without cause. Restored after Ezek. xiv, 23.

your slain. One could also read מ[עלליכם] 'your doings'. It seems to me that my reading fits better with the sense of the passage ; moreover the remains of the letter recall the *ḥeths* of *haḥalalim* and *hamilḥamah* in line 6.

ye have understood. Cf. x, 11.

from of old. Cf. xi. 6. The whole sentence is composed of terms typical for this literature.

14. mysteries of God. As a subject of study : DSD ix, 18 ; DST ii, 12 ; xii, 13, etc. The 'mysteries' in this case are the ensuing references to events and prophecies ; cf. xvii, 2.

to unique ones. Or 'individuals' (sense in MH).

15. deserts. The reading is certain. The idea, ' God gives to everyone according to his deserts ', is confirmed by the beginning of col. xvii. Since two lines are left blank in this column, we may assume that three lines are missing at the end.

Column XVII

their retribution. Read *shillumam*, MH for BH *shillumim* pl., cf. Isa. xxxiv, 8–10, which seems to be the source of our phrase. See also xiv, 18 and Isa. lx, 17.

like the burning of wood. Or read בעץ ' by means of the ... '. The restoration, somewhat doubtful, is based on

TEXT, TRANSLATION, AND COMMENTARY

[כו]

13. וענה ואמר [חוקר אל בצדק ו]ה[לוב]ב עמו יבחן במשפט ולוא [חנם
נפלו] חלליכם כיא מאז שמעתם
14. ברזי אלן - - - - - - - -] הם ליחדיו[ם]
15. בגמולו[ם - - - - - - - - -] לו [-]

XVII

1. ושם שלומם בדלק [עצים? וה]ן בחוני מצרף ושנן כלי מלחמתה
ולוא יכהו עד [כלות כול גויי]
2. רשע ואתמה זכורו משפט [נדב ואבי]הוא בני אהרון אשר התקדש
אל במשפטם לעיני [כול העם ואלעזר]
3. ואיתמר החזיק לו לברית [מועדי ע]ולמים

[כז]

4. ואתם התחזקו ואל תיראום [כיא] המה לתהו ולבהו תשוקתם
ומשענתם כלוא ה[יתה] לוא [ידעו כיא מאל]

Ezek. xxiv, 9–11; the first letter in the gap could easily be an 'ayin.

tested in the crucible. Cf. 'purified by the crucible', DST frg. 18, 4, Oẓar, pl. 57. 'Crucible', which occurs once in the O.T. (Pr. xvii, 3), is frequent in the DSS as a symbol for the testing of the Sons of Light in the 'epoch of Belial', cf. p. 221, n. 4; Yadin, JBL 74 (1955), 40 sq.

His weapons. i.e. the Sons of Light, who will fight His war. The spelling -*h* for the suff. 3rd sg. msc. is unique in DSW.

become blunt. This idea is in BH (esp. Piel in Eccl. x, 10), Jew. Aram., and Syr. expressed by *qhy*, while *khy* (Acc., Aram., BH) means 'to be weak' (Brockelmann, *Lexicon Syriacum*, 2nd ed., col. 650a, thinks the two roots cognate—Rabin). The choice here may be influenced by Isa. xlii, 4.

come to an end. etc. Restored after xv, 2.

2. remember, etc. The choice of Nadab and Abihu (Lev. x, 1–6; cf. Dt. iii, 4) as example is intended to prove that God deals justice even to the most select; possibly also the punishment by fire suggested the analogy.

hallowed Himself. Quotation from Lev. x, 3, where MT has Niphʿal; the use of Hithp. here is MH, cf. also xi, 15. In commenting on Num. xx, 13, Rashi 'translates' *yiqqadhesh* by *yithqaddesh*.

of all the people. Restored after Lev. ib.

3. Eleazar and Ithamar. Cf. Num. iii, 4. On these two, see *Enc. Miqr.* i, 131–4.

the appointed times of eternity. Restored after xii, 3, which adds 'all', for which there is no room here. For the thought cf. *Qumran I*, p. 124, iii, 22–3.

4. be ye strong. So xv, 12. This portion of the chief priest's speech closely resembles in structure that of the 'priest destined for the day of vengeance', xv, 7 onwards. Like it, it is divided into (1) an admonition to be strong, (2) proof that the enemies are an evil lot, (3) promise of victory on this day, (4) the assertion that Israel will rule the world. In contrast to xv, and in conformity with col. xiii, it devotes much space to the assistance which will be given by the archangel Michael.

for . . . void. Cf. xv, 9–10. The gap is a little too large for *kī*, but closer inspection of the photograph suggests that there was a fault in the skin, and the scribe left an

340   TEXT, TRANSLATION, AND COMMENTARY

5. [existed]. They do not [know that from the God] | of Israel is all that is and that will be, and He [will annihilate Belia]l in all future times of eternity. Today is His appointed time to subdue and to humble the
6. prince of the dominion | of wickedness. He will send eternal assistance to the lot to be redeemed by Him through the might of an angel : He
7. hath magnified the authority of Michael through eternal light | to light up in joy [the house of I]srael, peace and blessing for the lot of God, so as to raise amongst the angels the authority of Michael and the dominion |
8. of Israel amongst all flesh. And justice shall rejoice up on high, and all sons of His truth shall be glad in eternal knowledge. But ye, sons of His
9. covenant, | be ye strong in God's crucible, until He shall lift up His hand and shall complete His testings *through* His mysteries with regard to your existence.

SECTION 28

10. And after these words the priests shall blow for them *a signal* to array the battalions of the formation. The columns shall fan out at the

empty space. For the meaning given here to *tohu* and *bohu*, cf. esp. 1 Sam. xii, 21 ; Isa. xxxiv, 11 ; DST v, 32.

their support. Cf. comm. iv, 13.

as if it has not existed. ¶ Ob. 16 ; cf. CDC ii, 20.

they do not know. Same expression and idea in ' Livre des Mystères ' i, 3-4 (*Qumran I*, p. 103) ; cf. comm. i, 8.

that from ... will be. The nearest parallel is DSD iii, 15 sq. (where ' God of knowledge ') ; cf. also ib. xi, 11 ; CDC ii, 9-10 ; Ass. Mosis xii, 4-6 and Charles's comm. ; see also DST xv, 9 ; DSW i, 10. The much-debated question whether *nihyeh* refers to the past or the future, seems to be decided in favour of the future by the above quotations ; cf. also Ecclus. xlviii, 25, where the future sense is unmistakable and the Greek has ἐσόμενα. It is a typical eschatological term.

5. He will annihilate. Almost certain : both the gap and the traces of letters fit.

today is His appointed time. Cf. xv. 12 ; also iv, 7 and comm.

to subdue. Cf. i, 14. **and to humble.** Cf. xiii, 15 ; xiv, 15.

the prince of the dominion of wickedness. i.e. Belial ; cf. xv, 2 for ' wickedness ' as applied to the heathen ; xiii, 4 ; xiv 9 for Belial's ' dominion ' ; ch. 9, § 3.

6. the lot to be redeemed by Him. For the restoration and parallels, cf. xv, 1.

an angel. Cf. xiii, 10 ; DSD iii, 24 ; DSW xii, 6 ; Dn. x, 13 ; ch. 9, § 5.

magnified. In Isa. xlii, 21 ∥ *highdil*.

the authority of Michael. Between the two words is a gap (because of a fault in the leather?). Based on Dn. xii, 1 ; on which see also comm. i, 12. On. M., see ch. 9, § 5.

eternal light. Also xiii, 5-6.

7. to light up ... lot of God. Cf. ' shall shine ... for all sons of light ', i, 9 ; perhaps also DST xviii, 29 sq.

ישראל בכול הווה ונהיה ונ[יכל]ה [בליע]ל בכול נהיי עולמים היום .5
מועדו להכניע ולהשפיל שר ממשלת
רשעה וישלח עזר עולמים לגורל פ[ד]ותו בגבורת מלאך האדיר .6
למשרת מיכאל באור עולמים
להאיר בשמחה ב[י]ת י[שראל שלום וברכה לגורל אל להרים .7
באלים משרת מיכאל וממשלת
ישראל בכול בשר ושמח צדק ב[מ]רומים וכול בני אמתו יגילו .8
בדעת עולמים ואתם בני בריתו
התחזקו במצרף אל עד יניף ידו ו[מ]לא מצרפיו רזיו למעמדכם .9

[כח]
הכוה[נ]ים

ואחר הדברים האלה יתקעו להם לסדר דגלי המערכה והראשים .10
נפשטים לקול החצוצרות

house. The word exactly fits.

to raise, etc. In contrast to Belial's being brought low (line 5); cf. xiv, 15.

8. and the dominion of Israel. Cf. ch. 9, § 5.

all flesh. Also xv, 13.

justice. i.e. the God of Justice (xviii, 8), cf. Ps. lxxxv, 12; Isa. xlv, 8; for 'justice' cf. i, 8; iv, 6; DSD iii, 20; x, 11–12.

sons of His truth. Or: 'His sons of truth'. Cf. 'the sons of Thy truth', DST vii, 30. 'Sons of t.' DSD iv, 5–6, etc.

knowledge. Cf. comm. i, 8; see also En. lxxxi.

sons of His covenant. Or: 'His sons of the covenant'. Cf. 'sons of the covenant' = Jews, M. BQ i, 2 etc. For 'covenant' cf. comm. i, 2.

9. be ye strong. Cf. line 4.

lift up His hand. Allusion to Zech. ii, 13; cf. below, xviii, 1.

His mysteries. Cf. xvi, 9.

your existence. Cf. 'my existence is from Thee', DST ii, 21. The word (different from the military use, for which cf. ch. 7, § 2 (3)) seems to designate the place allotted to man in the Divine Plan, also iv, 4 (?), xiii, 16 (Rabin).

10. and after these words. Exactly as Ezra vii, 1, the only O.T. passage beginning 'and after'. Very abbreviated account of the third 'lot', even shorter than xvi, 2–8; based on the detailed description in section 12, vii, 14 sq. Contrary to his usual practice, the scribe did not leave a blank line although the preceding section ended with a line more than half filled. The only other place where he did this is sect. 6, iv, 6.

the priests shall blow for them. The way the word 'priests' is written suggests the sequence יתקעו הכוהנים להם; but since everywhere else in the Scroll the order is as given here, we must assume that the scribe not only forgot the word at first, but also added it out of place.

the battalions of the formation. i.e. the relief formation of skirmishers, cf. comm. xvi, 10, which during the speech was drawn up in columns.

11. sound of the trumpets, | until each man has fallen in at his proper position. Then the priests shall blow another fanfare on the trumpets,
12. signals for engaging. When | the skir[mishers] have reached *a position* [near the li]ne of the Kitt[im] within throwing range, they shall each man raise his hand with his weapon. Then the priests shall blow a
13. fanfare on the trumpets | of the slain [while the levites and the whole] band of horn-blowers sound a battle fanfare. The skirmishers shall
14. attack the army | of the Kittim, [and as soon as there goes forth the sound of the fanf]are, they shall begin to fell their slain. Then all the people
15. shall still the sound of the fanfare, while the priests | keep on sounding the fanfare [on the trumpets of the slain, and the battle [is waged victoriously] against the K[ittim, and the troops of Belia]l are dis-
16. comfited before them. | Thus in the th[ird] lot [the Sons of Light shall prove stronger, but in the fourth the Sons of Darkness shall gird themselves *with strength*, and the skirmishers shall begin] to fall slain |
17. [through] the mysteries of God, and [   ]

COLUMN XVIII

[and in the seventh lot], when the great hand of God shall be raised up against Belial and against all the army of his dominion for eternal
2. discomfiture | [with the noise of a great multitude] and the shouting of the holy ones in pursuit of Asshur, then shall the sons of Japheth

---

11. until, etc. Restored after xvi, 4.

signals for engaging. = 'signals to advance', viii, 7. The spelling with two *yodhs* is unique.

12. reached ... the line. The restoration is almost certain. For *lĕyadh* see xvi, 5.

13. the levites and the whole. Restored after xvi, 6; quite certain.

a battle fanfare. Very much abbreviated as compared with xvi, 7.

attack. Cf. i, 1; in xvi, 7 with *hll* Hiph.

14. as soon ... fanfare. The restoration (cf. xvi, 7) is almost certain, and fits both the available space and the traces of letters.

shall still. No other reading seems possible. This passage is important, because the clear sense of the verb here employed throws light on the parallel expressions, cf. comm. viii, 11; p. 108, n. 4.

15. on the trumpets of the slain. Restored after xvi, 8, and fits the gap.

is waged victoriously. Restored after xvi, 8, and fits the gap and the traces. In the third 'lot', as the phrase shows, the Sons of Light gain the upper hand.

and the troops of Belial. Restored after xi, 8.

16. Thus in the third lot. It is clear that these words sum up the preceding description (and hence 'and' cannot indicate sequence), because (*a*) three 'lots' have so far been described (sections 24, 25, 28), and (*b*) each party wins alternately, and the Sons of Light win the seventh 'lot', so that they must also have won the third. See at length ch. 1, § 3.

to fall slain. This proves that a new 'lot', the fourth, has been mentioned in the lost part of the line.

11. עד התיצ[ובם אי]ש על מעמדו ו[ת]קעו הכוהנים בחצוצרות
תרועה שנית יידי התקרב ובהגיע
12. אנשי [הבינים ליד מע]רכת כתי[ים] כדי הטל ירימו איש ידו בכלי
מלחמתו והכוהנים יריעו בחצוצרות
13. החללי[ם] [והלויים וכ]ל עם השופרות יריעו תרועת מלחמה
ואנשי הבינים ישלחו ידם בחיל
14. הכתיים [ועם צאת קו]ל [התר]ועה יחלו להפיל בחלליהם וכול
העם יניח[ו] קול התרועה והכוהנים
15. יהיו מריעים [בחצוצרות החללים] וה̇מ̇[חמ]ה מ̇[תנצח]ת בכ[ו]תיים
וגדודי בליע[ל] [נ]גפים לפניהם
16. ובגורל הש̇ל̇[יש]י̇ יחזקו בני אור וברביעי יתאזרו בני חושך ואנשי הבינים
יחלו ל[נפ]ו̇ל חללים
17. [בר]ז̇י̇ אל ו[- - - - - - - - -]

XVIII

1. [ובגורל השביעי]֯ בהנשא יד אל הגדולה על בליעל ועל כול ח̇[י]ל
ממשלתו במגפת עולמים
2. [בקול המון גדול] ות̇רועת קדושים ברדף אשור ונפלו בני יפת לאין
קום וכתיים יכתו לאין

17. through the mysteries of God. Restoration almost certain, cf. xvi, 9. There were three more lines at least to the end of the column; these contained the brief description of lots four, five, and six.

Column XVIII

Most of this column (except for the beginnings of lines 5–8, 10–11) has come away from the rest of the scroll, and a piece covering parts of the right-hand portions of lines 7–10 was subsequently recovered amongst the rubbish in Cave I and published by Milik (who brilliantly divined its right place on the basis of the text as published in *Megilloth Genuzoth* I, plate V) in *Qumran I* as no. 33, 1, see ib. p. 135. The text as shown in *Oẓar* pl. 33 makes the gap between the two parts of the scroll a few millimetres too small.

and in the seventh lot. The restoration is based upon i, 14: the trace at the utmost right does not form part of *běhinnaśe'*.

shall be raised up. Cf. i, 14; line 3 below; in O.T. only active, Isa. xlix, 22; Ps. x, 12.

army. Restored after i, 1; xv, 2 (where the word takes up exactly the space needed here); neither גורל nor קהל is graphically possible. The whole passage which follows closely resembles i, 5–7; 14–17.

eternal discomfiture. In i, 5 'eternal annihilation'; see also line 11 below.

2. with the noise . . . holy ones. Restored after i, 11 ('angels'—'holy ones' ib. 16).

pursuit. See ix, 6.

Japheth—Kittim. Cf. Japheth—Asshur—Kittim, i, 5–7; and see ch. 2, § 3 (2); xi, 11–12. Note the pun: *Japheth-naphělu* (cf. Isa. xxiv, 20); *Kittim-yukkattu* (cf. Jer. xlvi, 5).

3. fall never to rise again, and the Kittim shall be smashed without | [remnant and survivor, and there shall be] an upraising of the hand of the God of Israel against the whole multitude of Belial. At that time the
4. priests shall sound a fanfare | [on the six trumpet]s of remembrance, and all battle formations shall follow their call and spread out against the
5. entire army of the Kittim | to destroy them utterly. [And] when the sun hastens to set on that day, the chief priest and the priests and the [levites]
6. that are | with him, and the chiefs [of the formation and the men] of the Serekh shall stand up and at that place bless the God of Israel, and shall solemnly declare :
7.   Blessed be Thy name, O God [of angel]s, for | Thou hast done great things for Thy people wondrously, and hast kept Thy covenant with us from of old. Thou hast many a time opened for us the gates of deliver-
8. ances | for the sake of Thy covenant—[for] we were poor—according to Thy goodness towards us. Thou, O God of justice, hast done *it* for the sake of Thy name.

Section 29

9.   [   ] Thou hast done marvellous work among us, even a marvellous work [and] a wonder, and from of old there hath not happened the like of it, for Thou hast foreknown it to be our appointed time.

3. without remnant and survivor. Restored after Ezra ix, 14, also qu. CDC ii, 6-7.

an upraising of the hand. Cf. Ps. cxli, 2.

multitude. Cf. xv, 11 ; also ' multitude of Gog ', Ezek. xxxix, 11.

at that time. i.e. when the enemy lines begin to weaken. For the regrouping which now follows, cf. at length ix, 3 onwards ; ch. 7, § 7 ; ib. § 5.

4. the six trumpets of remembrance. Abbreviated expression, as in xvi, 2-3.

shall follow their call. Lit. ' shall gather unto them ', but of course the literal meaning, as if they assembled around the priests, is out of question here. For the Roman parallel, see p. 98, n. 4. In addition to the skirmishers, who carried on the fighting till now, ' all battle formations ', the heavy infantry, rally at this stage, cf. comm. ix, 4.

5. spread out. Cf. comm. ix, 6.

army. Restored after xvi, 2. The gap is just sufficient.

5. to destroy them utterly. In ix, 7 the grammatical construction differs. After this word the scribe left a space, perhaps to indicate the change of subject.

hastens. Allusion to Josh. x, 13 (also qu. below, xviii, 11) ; for the connexion with that event, see ch. 1, § 3 (28-9) ; ch. 8, § 5 (5).

6. chiefs of the formation and the men of the Serekh. Restored after xiii, 1 ; fits the space and the context.

7. blessed be Thy name. A conflation of the formulas ' blessed be the God of Israel ' (xiii, 2) and ' we bless Thy name ' (ib. 7). This prayer, which extends over two sections, is a request to repeat the miracle at Gibeon, so that the rout of the enemy can be completed.

God of angels. Restored after xiv, 16. The remaining traces strongly suggest a *mem*, more so in the original photograph than in the reproduction of the *Oẓar* ; and

TEXT, TRANSLATION, AND COMMENTARY

3. [שארית ופליטה והית]ה משאת יד אל ישראל על כול המון בליעל
בעת ההיאה יריעו הכוהנים

4. [בשש חצוצר]ות הזכרון ונאספו אליהם כול מערכות המלחמה
ונחלקו על כול מ[חני הכת]יים

5. להחרימם [ו]באוץ השמש לבוא ביום ההואה יעמוד כוהן הרואש
והכוהנים וה[לוי]ם אשר

6. אתו ורא[שי המערכות וזקני] הסרך וברכו שם את אל ישראל וענו
ואמרו ברוך שמכה אל [אלי]ם כיא

7. הגדלתה עם עמ[כה] להפליא ובריתכה שמרתה לנו מאז ושערי
ישועות פתחתה לנו פעמ[י]ם רבות

8. למען ב[ריתכה [כי]א ענינו כטובכה בנו ואתה אל ה[צ]דק עשיתה
למען שמכה

[כט]

9. [- - ה]פלתה עמנו הפלא [ו]פלא ומאז לוא נהיתה כמוהה וָאתה
ידעתה למועדנו והיום הופיע

---

in any case there is not enough space for 'Israel'.

Thou ... wondrously. Cf. 1 Sam. xii, 24; Joel ii, 26; Isa. xxviii, 29. The letters ה עמך עם are on the fragment published by Milik (cf. above), printed in the appendix as frg. 33 (1).

and hast kept ... of old. Again conflated from xiii, 7 and xiv, 4, cf. comm. ib.

many a time. Also xi, 3.

opened. In the photograph, *Oẓar*, pl. 33, the *ḥeth* and the *taw* have become partly superimposed, owing to a tear in the scroll.

gates of deliverances. Cf. 'deliverances of God', iv, 13. 'Gates' and 'deliverance' (sg.) occur together Ps. cxviii, 19–21; Isa. xxviii, 1–2; but here possibly we have an actual allusion to Isa. lx, 18, since vs. 20 ib., 'Thy sun shall no more go down', contains the subject of our prayer. Isa. lx influenced our Scroll, cf. comm. xii, 13.

8. for the sake ... to us. The letters ריתכה [ ] א ענינו כטו are on frg. 33 (1). Cf. xi, 9 sq.; xiv, 4 sq.

God of justice. Cf. Ps. iv, 2. See also above, xvii, 8.

for the sake of. Not certain. Cf., however, Jer. xiv, 7 a. fr.

9. Thou hast done ... a wonder. The first three words on frg. 33 (1). Adapted from Isa. xxix, 14. For the spelling הפלתה cf. GK § 23f. At the beginning of the line may have been some words like ובגבורת ידכה 'and by the power of Thine hand'.

there hath not happened the like of it. Also i, 12 (spelled כמוה). Possibly an allusion to Josh. x, 14.

for Thou. The scribe originally wrote 'and Thou'; then he (or another scribe) placed *kaph* and *aleph* over the *waw*, thus making it into *ky*': a more tangible proof for the absolute identity of *waw* and *yodh* in the Scrolls script could hardly be imagined. It cannot be entirely disregarded, however, that we may have here a symbol of unknown meaning.

hast foreknown. It is hardly likely that we have here a mere error for יעדתה, for which cf. xiii, 17 (see also xvii, 5).

10. Today appear Thou | to us [in light-of-perfection and shew] us the hand of Thy mercies towards us in eternal redemption, so as to remove the dominion of the enemy, to be no more, and the hand of Thy might, |
11. and in [Thy battle against all] our enemies for a discomfiture of annihilation. But now the day is hastening for us [to] pursue their multitude, for
12. Thou | [and] the heart of mighty men Thou hast broken so that they cannot withstand. Thine is the might, and in
13. Thy hand is the battle, and there is no one | [to save them   ] Thy times and appointed times according to Thy pleasure, and retribution [   ] Thou wilt render unto Thine enemies], and Thou wilt cut off from [   ]

COLUMN XIX
[SECTION 30]

to mighty men, for our Gallant One is holy, and the King of Glory is with us. The ho[st] of His spirits is with our steps, and our horsemen
2. are like rain-clouds] | [and like clouds of de]w covering the earth, and like a showery storm watering with judgement [all that spring from her.]
    Arise, O mighty one,
3.   take Thy captives], | [O man of glory,
    and take] Thy booty, *Thou* Who dost valiantly.
    Place Thy hand in the neck of Thine enemies,
    and Thy foot [upon the bodies of the slain.

appear. Imperative, form as in Ps. xciv, 1 (cf. GK § 53m). On the meaning of the verb, see p. 222, n. 3.

10. in light-of-perfection. This word is here restored after DST iv, 5, 23; in both passages it appears with forms of *hofiaʿ*. To the various suggestions concerning its etymology and meaning, I would like to add a reference to the names of the sun in En. lxxviii, 1: *ūryārēs* (*ōryārēs*, *aryarěʾēs*, *ēryōrēs*) and *tōmās* (*tōmāsěs*). Though these are no doubt corrupted, it is remarkable that *or-tom* combines the initial elements of both. This suggests that we have here a name for the 'perfect light', the light made at the Creation and then hidden, which according to the Midrash (Gen. Rabba iii, 6) will appear in the Messianic age. Note also the closeness of the two elements in i, 8 above. On the possible connexion with Urim and Thummim (proposed by Sukenik, *M.G.* II, 10) see now Yadin, *IEJ* 9 (1959), xxx.

and show us the hand of Thy mercies. As far as preserved, this is on frg. 33 (1) (which ends here); restored after Ps. lxxxv, 8: 'show us, O Lord(!), Thy mercy'.

eternal redemption. So xv, 1.

to remove. Cf. xv, 17, where the object is 'Belial'. A further effort is needed to complete the destruction of the enemy.

dominion. The restoration is quite certain.

to be no more. No O.T. parallel.

11. and in Thy battle. For this restoration, cf. the parallelism of *gěvurah* and *milḥamah* in line 12, and of *m.* and 'the strength of Thine hand' in xi, 1.

is hastening for us. Cf. comm. lines 3, 6. For the language cf. Josh. xvii, 15.

12. Thou hast broken. BH *miggen* in Gen. xiv, 20 is translated by all versions (except the Vulgate) as 'delivered, handed over', and is so understood by modern

TEXT, TRANSLATION, AND COMMENTARY   347

10. לנ[ו באורתום והרא]תנו יד חסדיכה עמנו בפדות עולמים להסיר
ממ[ש]לת אויב לאין עוד ויד גב[ו]רתכה
11. ובמ[ל]חמתכה בכו[ל] אויבינו למגפת כלה ועתה היום אץ לנו
[ל]רדוף המונם כיא אתה
12. [- - -]לב גבורים מגנתה לאין מעמד לכה הגב[ור]ה ובידכה
המלחמה ואין
13. [מציל - - עתו]תיכה ומועדים לרצונכה וגמו[ל] - תשיב לאויב]יכה
ותבצור ממחר[- -]
14. [- - - - -] ל [- - - - -]

XIX

[ל]

1. [ל]בורים כיא קדוש אדירנו ומלך הכבוד אתנו וצ[בא רוחיו עם
צעדינו ופרשינו כענים
2. וכעבי ט[ל ל]ב[ס]ות ארץ וכזרם רביבים להשקות משפט לכ[ול
צאצאיה קומה גבור שבה שביכה
3. איש כבוד וש[וב]ל שללכה עושי חיל תן ידכה בעורף אויביך ורג[ל]ך
על במותי חלל מחץ

scholars. It probably means 'to give at one's request', cf. Ugaritic *mgn* 'to beseech' (Rabin). However, the fact that in Lam. Rabba iii (on iii, 65) *mĕghinnath lev* is explained by one school (also represented by the late Targum Lamentations) as 'brokenness of heart', suggests that an interpretation of *mgn* as 'to break' was also current at the time (I thank Mr. I. Wartski for drawing my attention to the Midrash passage). The phrase here is based on Lam. iii, 65, and also agrees with the midrash in reading *mĕghinath* (MH verbal noun) for the MT's *mĕghinnath*.

so that they cannot withstand. Cf. xiv, 8.

13. no one to save them. Restored after xiv, 11; Mic. v, 7, etc.

Thy times. Before this restore perhaps 'and Thou didst make', cf. comm. xiv, 13.

wilt render. It is impossible to restore תשלם, which would have left the top of the *lamedh* showing.

Thou wilt cut off. This suggests some adaptation of Ps. lxxvi, 13: 'He shall cut off the spirit of princes, terrible to the kings of the earth'. The last word may perhaps be restored as ממחרפיכה 'from them that blaspheme Thee', and taken as an allusion to Rabshakeh, Isa. xxxvii, 4; cf. below, xix, 9 sq. If col. xix was originally attached after xviii, then the lost lines of xviii contained a text resembling xii, 6 onwards.

Section 30

Col. xix is separate from the rest if the scroll. It forms part of a separate sheet of skin, as the left side of col. xviii, with its marks of sewing, was the end of a sheet, and there is no way of saying how much came originally between that seam and col. xix. This col. can be completed a little by means of a fragment (no. 2) which fits its top right hand corner, a second (no. 8) at the left of lines 9–11, and a third, which fits the ends of lines 6–10 and was published by Milik in *Qumran I* as no. 33 (2), plate XXXI. This fragment clearly shows at the left traces of another

348   TEXT, TRANSLATION, AND COMMENTARY

4.   Crush] | [the nations, Thine adversaries],
           and let Thy sword devour flesh.
       Fill Thy land with glory
           and Thine inheritance with blessing :
       A mu[ltitude of cattle in Thy portions], |
5.   [silver and gold and precious stones in] Thy palaces.
       Zion, rejoice exceedingly,
           and be joyful, all ye cities of Ju[dah.
6.   Open thy gates] | [forever,
           to let enter into thee] the substance of the nations,
           and their kings shall serve thee.
       [All that afflicted thee] shall bow down to thee,
7.   and the dust of thy feet] | [they shall lick.
       O daughters of my peo]ple, utter with a voice of joy,
           deck yourselves with ornaments of glory,
8.   and rule [over the kingdom] | [of the Kittim.
       And the kingdom shall be the Lord's],
           and Israel for eternal sovereignty.

[SECTION 31]

9. [And all] that night [shall be to them] for rest until the morning. In
10. the morning they shall come to the place of the line | [mighty
    me]n of the Kittim, the multitude of Asshur, and the army of all the
    nations that were assembled unto them—[and behold, they are all] slain |
11. [for] they have fallen there by the sword-of-God. And there
    shall come forward in that place the ch[ief] priest [and] his [deputy],

column, so that xix was not the end of our work.

Lines 1-8 contain the same text as xii, 6-15, with some variants, which in the comm. on xii have been listed under the siglum *B*. The interesting feature is that in spelling the text of xix is closer to that of the MT than the text in xii, which is pretty much the spelling normal for the scrolls. On the problem why the text appears here a second time, see ch. 1, § 3 and ch. 8, § 5 (1).

Section 31

The text consists of the lower half of the piece called here col. xix (Oẓar, pl. 34), frg. 8 (Ib. Pl. 47), and frg. 33 (2) (cf.

above). The restoration is based on the theory that our Scroll applies to the Kittim the words of Isa. xxxi, 8, quoted above, xi, 11-12 ; cf. ch. 2, § 3 (2) and p. 25. n. 4. The word 'sword-of-God' (line 11) also occurs in xv, 13, and if we accept the restoration suggested there, relating it to the 'day of vengeance', the purpose of the prayer and the following story becomes clear: The Sons of Light are forced to stop the pursuit because the sun 'hastens to set'. They return to camp for the night, and in the morning find the Kittim dead. ' In the morning ' clearly alludes to 2 Kings xix, 35 ; Isa. xxxvii, 36, while ' the mighty men of the Kittim ' (line 10) seems to be derived from the version of 2 Chr. xxxii,

TEXT, TRANSLATION, AND COMMENTARY 349

4. גואים צריכ]ה וחרבך תואכל בשר מלא ארצכה כבוד ונחלתכה
ברכה ה[מ]ון מקנה בחלקותיכה

5. כסף וזהב ואבני חפץ ב[היכ]לותיך ציון שמחי מואדה והגלנה כול
ער]י יהו[ד]ה פתחי שעריך

6. תמיד להביא אליך] חיל גוים ומלכיהם ישרתו[נ]ך וישתחוו לך [כול
מעניך ועפר רגליך

7. ילחכו בנות ע[מ]י הבענה בקול רנה עדינה עדי כבוד ור[ד]ינה
במלכות

8. [כתיאים והיתה לאדוני המ[ל]וכה וישראל למלכות [ע]ו[למים

[לא]

9. [והיה להמה כול ה[ל]י[ל]ה ההוא למנוח עד הבוקר ובבוקר יבואו
עד מקום המערכה

10. [— ג]ב[ו]רי כתיים והמון אשור וחיל כול הגוים הנקהלים את[ו]ם והנה
כול[ם] חללים

11. [— כיא] נפלו שם בחרבאל ונגש שם כוהן הרו[א]ש ומש[נ]הו [ואחיו
הכוהנים והלויים וכול זקני

21, whence apparently comes also the 'king of the Kittim' in xv, 2. The 'angel of the Lord' is alluded to in xiii, 10 and xvii, 6, cf. comm. ib.

9. that night. Note the spelling, unusual for the Scrolls.

for rest. Cf. comm. ii, 8–9. After the prayer at sunset, fighting stops till the morning.

they shall come to. The letters ר יבואו עד מ are on frg. 8, which admirably fits both the outline of the main fragment and the remnants of letters, such as the *resh* of *ba-boqer*. The black spot at the top of frg. 8 is not part of any letter (there is none it would fit), but a stain due to decomposition, such as can be seen on col. xvi (*Oẓar*, Pl. 31) on either side of the central gap.

place of the line, On frg. 33 (2).

10. mighty men. Restoration almost certain. The first letter visible is *resh*, not *daleth*, hence *gĕdhudhē* is excluded. Possibly allusion to 2 Chr. xxxii, 21, see

above. The 'mighty men' of the enemy: xii, 7; xiv, 8, 11; xix, 12.

multitude. Cf. xviii, 3.

Kittim—Asshur—army of all the nations. Cf. comm. i, 2; xviii, 2; xv, 1–3.

that were assembled unto them. The letters את הנקהלים are on frg. 8, the *he* being partly on the main piece, partly on the frg. Cf. xv, 3; xi, 16.

slain. The letters ם חללים are on frg. 33 (2).

11. they have fallen. For the *nun*, cf. that in *wĕ-niggash* in the same line. Possibly an allusion to Isa. xxxi, 8, 'and Asshur hath fallen'.

come forward in that place. Cf. comm. xiii, 1; xvi, 11.

and his deputy. The letters נהו are on frg. 8. It is possible that a similar formula appeared at the end of col. xii; for the formula see comm. ii, 1. In the Serekh series, xiv, 3–4, we only find 'and they shall bless all together', but there both the enemy and the Sons of Light are carefully enumerated.

12. [and his brother priests, and the levites and all the elders] | [of the Serekh, and the mighty men] of war, and all chiefs of the formations and [their] subordinates, [and they shall bless the God of Israel. Then they shall
13. return to the place] | [where they had stood before] the slain of the Kitt[im fell, and they shall prai]se in that place the God [of Israel   ]

  and his brother ... Serekh. Restored after xiii, 1; fits the gap.
  12. mighty men. Restored after xii, 16, where these also appear in connexion with the final prayers; but it might also be 'those prepared for battle' (*'attudhē ha-m.*, xv, 2).
  chiefs of the formations. Occur only here. The term helps in defining the military sense of 'formation', see ch, 7, § 5 (1).

  their subordinates. i.e. all the army; cf. comm. ii, 4, 15.
  and they shall bless the God of Israel. Restored after xiii, 1; xiv, 3-4. There is not enough room for 'and they shall curse Belial' (as in xiii, 1); the description is much shorter than in the Serekh sections; [and Belial is already dead (Rabin)].

12. הסרך וגבורי ה[מ]לחמה וכול ראשי [ה]מערכות ופקוד[יהם וברכו
את אל ישראל ושבו אל מקום
13. [עומדם לפני נפו]ל [ח]ללי כתיאים וה[ללו שם [א]ת אל [ישראל
[- - - -

then they shall return ... stood before. The restoration, after xiv, 3, fits in precisely with the extant traces of *lamedhs*. This, of course, is the place 'where they had arrayed the line' (ib.) before the battle started.

13. and they shall praise, etc. The restoration is quite certain in view of the traces of letters and intervening spaces. Parallel to xiv, 3–4, and may have continued as there. The remainder of the Scroll presumably described the return to Jerusalem and the ensuing ceremonies, cf. ch. 1, § 3 end.

THE FRAGMENTS
Ozar, Pl. 47.

fgt. 1.
.1 [ה]מונם [כמוץ עובר והיה לש]ממה לוא ימצא   (= xv 11)
.2 [בצי]ץ בק[ציר ואתם אמצו ו]התחזקו   (= xv 12)
.3 [לא]ל על כול ח[ניל בליעל ומש]פֿטֿ   (= xv 13)
.4 [על] כול רוחי רש[עה - וג]בורי   (= xv 14)
.5 [מתע]תֿדים ליום [נקם   (= xv 15)
.6 [- - - - - - - -] ל[-]   (= xv 16)

fgt. 2.
.1 [לג]בורים כיא קדוש אדירנו   (= xix 1)
.2 [וכעבי ט]ל ל[כ]סות   (= xix 2)

fgt. 3.
.1 - - -
.2 [....] ים מכול ומ[   ]

fgt. 4.
.1 - -
.2 [   ] בררתי [   ]

fgt. 5.
.1 [   ] יֿא [- -] [   ]
.2 [   ] וק [   ] [   ]

fgt. 6.
.1 [   ] לֿהֿ - - [   ]
.2 [   ] לוֿ [   ]

fgt. 7.
.1 [   ] הו [   ]

fgt. 8.
.1 [   ]ר יבואו עֿדֿ מֿ[   ]   (= xix 9)
.2 [נקהלים אתֿ]   (= xix 10)
.3 [   ]נֿהֿוֿ[   ]   (= xix 11)

fgt. 9.
.1 אל י[שרא]ל   (= xv 16)
.2 להסיר ב[   ]   (= xv 17)
.3 באבדונו ח[   ]   (= xv 18)

fgt. 10.
.1 [   ] וֿת בֿ [   ]

fgt. 33(1)

(7 xviii =)	]ה֯ ע֯ם֯ ע֯מ֯כ֯[ ]	.1
(8 xviii =)	]ריתכה [כי]א עניינו כטו[ ]	.2
(9 xviii =)	]פ֯לתה עמנו הפלא [ ]	.3
(10 xviii =)	]תנו יד חסדיכה [ ]	.4

fgt. 33(2)

(6 xix =)	[ך֯]	.1
(7 xix =)	]ינה במלכות]	.2
(9 xix =)	]ק֯ו֯ם המערכה]	.3
(10 xix =)	]ם֯ חללים]	.4

INDEX I

AUTHORS

Aalen, S., 47, 149, 205, 235, 242, 275, 319
Abel, F. M., 24, 44, 107, 108, 111, 117, 176, 231
Albright, W. F., 28, 51, 259
Allegro, J. M., 23, 256, 310
Andrews, H. T., 119
Avigad, N., 29, 32, 248
Avi-Yonah, M., 22, 30, 58, 76, 116, 142, 144, 152, 175, 196, 208

Barrois, A. G., 50, 116, 219
Barthélemy, O., 44, 150, 205, 206, 257
Bea, A., 62
Ben-Hayyim, Z., 41
Ben-Horin, U., 280
Bennet, 45
Ben Sira, 109
Ben-Yehuda, A., 62, 103, 123, 124, 134, 168, 277, 278
Bertinoro, O., 168
Blank, Sh. H., 320
Bonnet, H., 139
Box, C. F., 231, 239
Brand, J., 179, 203
Brinktrine, I., 264
Brockelmann, C., 134, 339
Brown, F. E., 116, 117, 118
Brownlee, W. H. 41, 58, 61, 205, 206, 207, 235, 236, 242, 246, 288, 290
Buber, S., 140
Büchler, A., 56, 107, 204, 207
Burrows, M., 25, 41, 244, 246, 275, 303, 315

Caesar, 113, 117, 176, 178, 189
Carmignac, J., 25, 273
Cassius, Dio, 189
Cassuto, M. D., 29, 52
Cato, 185
Charles, R. H., 24, 25, 28, 32, 42, 45, 69, 119, 123, 149, 205, 207, 231, 233, 234, 235, 236, 238, 239, 240, 241, 242, 260, 314, 334, 340
Cheesman, G. L., 161
Cincius, 193
Cohn, L., 46, 140, 240
Couissin, P., 116, 117, 119, 121, 123, 129, 133, 138, 139
Conquest, 123
Cross, F. M., 230, 257, 269

Danby, H., 168, 263
Daremberg-Saglio, 101, 150
Delbrück, H., 152, 169, 170, 172, 194

Delcor, M., 62, 200, 201
Dio Cassius, 189
Domaszewski, A. von, 116, 176
Dozy, R., 133, 134, 280
Driver, G. R., 103, 108, 134, 281, 308
Dupont-Sommer, A., 24, 58, 60, 63, 95, 104, 107, 144, 147, 179, 200, 201, 205, 206, 215, 222, 246, 295, 331

Epstein, J. N., 205

Farmer, H. B., 90
Faulkner, R. D., 62
Finesinger, S. B., 107
Finkelstein, L., 34
Flusser, D., 25, 44, 201, 232, 233, 234, 257, 275, 314
Friedlander, G., 240
Frontinus, 196

Galili, E., Lt.-Col., 179
Galling, K. v., 62, 109, 116, 137, 191, 219, 280
Gelb, A. J., 29
Gellius, 184, 185, 186, 189, 191, 193
Gemser, B., 30
Ginsberg, H. L., 24, 46, 288
Ginzberg, L., 211, 235
Goldmann, M., 28, 29
Gordon, C. H., 269
Gottstein, M., 208
Grinz, J. M., 25, 79, 200, 201, 205, 234, 240, 242, 246, 259
Guttmann, J., 51, 52, 239

Habermann, A. M., 46, 234, 257, 314
Hartom, A. S., 236
Heidelberger, 176
Hermann, A., 31
Hershberg, A. S., 219
Hershman, 211
Higger, M., 248
Hirschberg, H. Z., 15, 33
Holmes, T. R., 123, 189
Horovitz, S. 104
Horovitz-Rabin, 307
Hughes, 314
Hunzinger, C. H., 326, 327, 329

Jaubert, A., 205
Josephus Flavius, 17, 24, 25, 30, 31, 59, 79, 110, 111, 117, 133, 174, 176, 200, 201, 240, 246
Junge, E., 53, 80, 83, 84, 152, 288

Kahana, A., 28, 29, 236, 238
Kasher, M. M., 16, 47, 101, 102, 103, 104, 226
Kimchi, 131, 167
Krauss, S., 77, 115, 116, 117, 122, 124, 190, 280
Kromayer, I., 169, 172
Kromayer, I., Veith G., 62, 63, 64, 98, 100, 111, 112, 113, 116, 117, 121, 123, 129, 133, 138, 139, 144, 147, 149, 152, 155, 160, 161, 162, 170, 172, 173, 174, 175, 178, 181, 182, 185, 186, 187, 189, 194
Kutscher, Y., 131

Lambert, G., 179, 234
Lane, E. W., 133
Lauterbach, J. Z., 167
Levy, J., 105, 121, 124, 306
Licht, J., 291
Liddell-Scott, 149
Lieberman, S., 125, 126, 192, 242, 282, 291, 307, 329
Livius, 133, 194
Lods, A., 50
Lowenstamm, S. A., 28, 31, 242
Luther, B., 50
Lutz, H. F., 280

Maimonides, 35, 69, 103, 209, 211, 219, 220, 248, 294, 300
Maisler, B., 28, 30, 31, 33
Malamat, A., 68
Marcus, R., 150
Marquardt, J., 63, 64, 112, 116, 133, 138, 139, 140, 161, 162, 170, 172, 175, 178, 179, 181, 182, 185, 186, 187, 189, 190, 191, 193
Mayer, L. A., 122, 125, 137
Meek, T. J., 125
Meissner, B., 62
de Menasce, J. P., 260
Meyer, E., 50
Migne, J. B., 79
Mignon, M., 188
Milik, J. T., 205, 247, 317, 331, 343, 345, 347
Morgenstern, J., 205, 323
Mowinckel, S., 199

Nahmanides, 104
Neriyah, M. Z., 20
Nischer, E. v., 113, 185
Nonius, 190
North, R., 20, 258
Noth, M., 45, 48
Nötscher, F., 315

O'Callaghan, R. T., 28, 30, 131
Oesterley, W. O. E., 234

Oppenheim, A. L., 127
Orlinsky, H. M., 319

Parker, H. M., 161
Pauly-Wissowa, 31, 150
Petrie, F. L., 51
Philo, 200, 201, 240, 246
Plinius, 246
Polotsky, H. J., 240
Polybius, 116, 117, 139, 161, 170, 174, 175, 186, 191, 194, 195
Poznański, S., 205
Pseudo-Hieronymus, 79
Pseudo-Philo, 46, 140
Ptolemy, 31

Rabin, C., 42, 60, 71, 74, 79, 198, 234, 235, 272, 278, 283, 285, 292, 305, 307, 315, 317, 318, 321, 322, 327, 339, 341, 347, 350
Rabinowitz, I., 303
Roberts, B. J., 258
Rashi, 71, 72, 131, 134, 167, 219, 339
Ratzhavi, J., 93
Rolfe, J. C., 188
Rost, L., 74
Rostovtzeff, M. I., 64
Rowley, H. H., 62, 244

Saadiah, 280
Sallust, 121
Saydon, P. P., 256
Schechter, S., 74, 235
Schwab, M., 240
Schwarzlose, F. W., 133
Segal, M. H., 150, 234, 246, 290
Sellers, O. R., 139
Scholem, G., 240
Sieg, E., 31
Siegling, W., 31
Spaulding, Brig. Gen. O. C., 173, 176, 181, 194
Stauffer, E., 179
Strabo, 31
Stoffel, 176
Strugnell, J., 229
Sukenik, E. L., 3, 93, 99, 102, 103, 104, 144, 147, 149, 208, 215, 226, 243, 246, 247, 248, 250, 252, 258, 270, 288, 306, 317, 318, 319, 325, 343, 346

Talmon, S., 205, 206, 311
Teicher, J. L., 214, 310, 311
Thackeray, H. St. J., 31, 112
Thomas, D. W., 167
Tournay, R. J., 24, 99, 103, 107, 144, 147, 242
(Torczyner) Tur-Sinai, N. H., 49, 52, 62, 64, 130, 134, 143, 206, 230, 239, 306, 307, 315, 321, 332, 337
Trogus Pompeius, 31

INDEX OF SCRIPTURAL PASSAGES 357

Van der Ploeg, J., 48, 51, 61, 207, 288, 290
De Vaux, R., 46, 205, 246, 257
Vegetius, 112, 113, 173, 178, 185, 186, 190, 191, 196
Veith, G., 100, 172, 176, 181
Vermès, G., 244, 246
Vriezen, Th. C., 15
Wartski, I., 296, 347
Wavell, Field Marshal, 68
Weiss, M., 15
Wieder, N., 37, 38, 63, 64
Wolf Umhau, C., 44, 50

Xenophon, 188

Yadin, Y., 29, 32, 33, 38, 62, 72, 80, 83, 84, 91, 139, 188, 200, 212, 221, 258, 265, 269, 280, 288, 290, 291, 298, 299, 308, 310, 330, 339, 346
Yalon, H., 99, 100, 102, 103, 257, 265, 280, 288, 315, 317, 325, 326
Yeivin, S., 83, 84

Zeitlin, S., 25, 104, 211
Zimmern, H., 121

INDEX II
REFERENCES TO ANCIENT LITERATURE
(i) Old Testament

GENESIS
i. 25 [308], 27 [308]
ii. 1 [307], 22 [308]
iii. 16 [323], 25 [135]
iv. 7 [323]
vi. 3 [126]
vii. 11 [307], 23 [328]
viii. 3 [259]
ix. 9 [322]
x. [26, 27], 2–3 [215], 4 [23], 5 [308], 9 [260], 10 [11], 20 [266]
xi. 9 [308]
xiii. [31], 2 [318]
xiv. 2 [144], 7 [322], 15 [266, 300], 20 [346]
xv. [35], 1 [278], 9 [32], 18 [27, 32, 65], 18–21 [34, 265], 19 [32]
xvii. 19 [322]
xxiv. 10 [28], 38 [52]
xxv. [27], 2–7 [32], 6 [33], 12–18 [32]
xxix. 21 [167]
xxxi. 7–8 [47]
xxxii. 17 [283]
xxxiii. 20 [286]
xxxiv. 25 [257]
xlvi. 11 [54]
xlix. 5 [257], 8 [317], 11 [167]

EXODUS
iv. 20 [48, 272]
v. 6 [152], 19 [152]
vi. [52], 16 [54]
vii. 3 [316], 6 [323], 7 [315], 9 [315], 13 [321], 19 [307]
ix. 29 [191]
xi. 23 [155]

xii. 23 [322], 41 [276]
xiii. 8 [293]
xiv. 4 [311], 24 [63], 31 [262]
xv. 4 [312], 11 [305, 316, 329], 14 [257]
xvii. 9 [82, 272], 15 [49], 18 [311]
xviii. 4 [277], 21 [59], 25 [59]
xix. 13 [107]
xx. 6 [314], 18 [300], 25 [130]
xxi. 20 [134]
xxiii. 2 [237], 15 [325], 20 [237]
xxiv. 3 [296], 5 [290]
xxv. 11 [282], 23 [119], 25 [281]
xxvi. 3 [282], 4 [280], 8 [283], 16 [281]
xxvii. 10 [281]
xxviii. 6 [220], 7 [282], 9–10 [44], 11 [280], 12 [45], 15 [279], 21 [45], 32 [125], 39 [220], 40 [217, 292], 41 [300]
xxxii. 4 [315], 16 [315], 17 [288], 26 [47]
xxxiii. 14 [323]
xxxiv. 7 [315], 10 [330]
xxxv. 10 [281], 21 [281], 35 [281]
xxxvi. 11–13 [118, 138]
xxxvii. 6 [281], 10 [281], 14 [123]
xxxix. 3 [137, 282], 4 [137], 27 [217, 219, 292], 29 [220]
xl. 45 [300]

LEVITICUS
i. 3 [291], 4 [264]
iv. 15 [320]
v. 11 [308]
vi. 21 [279]
x. 1–6 [339], 3 [339], 6 [44], 7 [300], 21 [331]
xii. [290], 7 [291]
xiii. 46 [73]

358 INDEX OF SCRIPTURAL PASSAGES

LEVITICUS—*continued*
xv. 8 [71]
xvi. 3 [219], 4 [219], 8 [256], 17 [264], 21 [291, 331]
xviii. 19 [321], 22 [71], 23 [71]
xx. 13 [71], 15 [71]
xxi. 1–6 [300], 12 [300], 17–20 [72]
xxii. 17 [264]
xxv. 4 [20]
xxvii. 3 [78]

NUMBERS
i. 2–3 [71], 3 [77], 15 [53], 16 [268], 18 [44], 47 [44], 50 [44], 52 [40, 47, 52, 100, 167]
ii. [48, 54, 271, 272], 2 [39, 53, 62, 100, 271], 3 [167], 17 [100], 34 [52, 53]
iii. [54, 55], 4 [339], 5 [273], 8 [154], 17 [54], 27 [153], 32 [56], 35 [54], 50 [153], 51 [153], 53 [153]
iv. [54], 2 [78], 22 [54], 23 [78], 29 [54], 30 [78], 35 [78], 39 [78], 47 [78]
vii. 2 [48, 204, 264], 18 [48]
viii. 24 [78], 25 [39, 78], 26 [78]
x. [90, 110], 1 [305], 1–10 [87], 2 [92, 269, 293], 2–3 [90], 2–4 [268], 3 [92], 4 [44, 51, 53, 91, 92, 268], 5 [92, 269], 7 [91, 95, 104], 8 [217, 292], 9 [95, 106, 212, 305], 10 [264], 25 [93], 35 [105, 269, 317], 36 [269]
xi. 16 [320], 29 [44], 30 [92]
xiv. 14 [322], 21 [318], 29 [77], 45 [300]
xv. 3 [276]
xvi. 2 [265, 268], 3 [216]
xvii. 6 [44], 7 [278], 17 [39], 18 [39, 45, 56], 25 [39]
xviii. 6 [54], 8 [54], 24 [54]
xix. 16 [285]
xx. 13 [339]
xxi. 3 [300], 8 [49]
xxiii. 3 [263, 264], 6 [264], 7 [320], 10 [314], 17 [264]
xxiv. 8 [317], 17 [17, 278], 17–19 [310], 18 [317], 24 [23, 25]
xxvi. [52], 2 [77], 4 [77], 9 [268], 26 [57]
xxvii. 16 [231], 17 [44]
xxviii. 2 [203]
xxxi. [153, 154], 3 [100, 265], 3–5 [41], 6 [87], 14 [59], 16 [44], 21 [39, 226]
xxxiv. 3 [300], 18 [48], 25 [48]
xxxv. 4 [74], 5 [168], 10 [266], 26 [263], 48 [59], 52 [59]
xxxvi. 2 [308]

DEUTERONOMY
i. 15 [59, 151, 154], 28 [296], 41 [115]
ii. 20 [261]

iii. 4 [339], 24 [305]
iv. 6 [306], 12 [306], 14 [306], 16 [308], 20 [321]
v. 1 [304], 10 [315], 20 [263], 21 [306]
vii. 1 [311], 6 [305], 9 [315, 325], 21 [303, 316], 22 [303], 23 [259]
viii. 17 [310], 18 [310]
ix. 4 [327], 5 [327], 7 [327]
x. 2 [337], 3 [332], 4 [332]
xi. 23 [34], 24 [35]
xii. 20 [34]
xiii. 4 [328]
xiv. 2 [305, 306]
xv. 7 [261]
xvi. 18 [152]
xvii. 7 [277]
xx. [72, 218, 332], 2 [209, 217, 299, 337], 2–4 [212, 304], 2–9 [66], 3 [299, 332] 5 [151, 152, 212], 8 [67, 304, 305], 10 [299]
xxi. 8 [322]
xxii. 12 [280]
xxiii. 3 [275], 10 [291, 303], 10–15 [47, 212], 11 [29], 11–12 [73], 13 [73, 291], 14 [74], 15 [212, 269, 291, 303, 322]
xxiv. 5 [66, 69, 83]
xxvi. 15 [314]
xxvii. 4 [225], 12 [320]
xxviii. 12 [307], 58 [316]
xxx. 5 [34]
xxxi. 2 [332], 6 [218], 10 [264]
xxxii. 2 [317], 8 [308], 9 [234, 308], 22 [330], 24 [312], 35 [261], 42 [318]
xxxiii. 5 [269], 26 [306], 29 [317]

JOSHUA
i. 10 [152], 11 [155], 14 [293]
iii. 2 [152], 4 [74, 291]
iv. 12 [293]
vi. [154], 4 [107, 292, 293], 5 [107], 9 [107], 19 [153], 20 [107, 296], 21 [153]
vii. [52], 3 [175], 4 [175], 14 [52], 21 [153]
viii. 2 [303], 3 [81], 18 [129], 19 [94, 100], 26 [300], 29 [129], 31 [332], 33 [152, 281]
x. [13, 332], 13 [344], 14 [222, 345], 25 [218, 332]
xi. 5 [331], 6 [182], 9 [179, 182], 11 [300], 20 [337]
xiii. 7 [308]
xvii. 13 [261], 15 [346]
xxi. 1–8 [54], 4–7 [55], 10 [54], 20 [54], 27 [54]
xxii. 14 [53], 16–17 [44], 27 [304], 28 [304], 30 [53]
xxiii. 2 [152]
xxiv. 14 [30], 15 [30]

INDEX OF SCRIPTURAL PASSAGES 359

JUDGES
i. 3 [256]
iii. 2 [128], 16 [125], 22 [283]
v. [80], 8 [115], 11 [44], 12 [317], 20 [313], 30 [280]
vi. 4 [322], 15 [53]
vii. 2 [293], 3–6 [68], 8 [155], 16 [145], 18 [58], 19 [47], 20 [58, 296]
viii. 1 [80, 274, 276]
ix. 25 [303], 43 [145]
x. 18 [256]
xi. 6 [300], 35 [94]
xv. 2 [291], 8 [288], 9 [291], 11 [175]
xviii. 9 [52], 11 [115], 19 [322]
xx. [51, 81, 94], 2 [44], 8–10 [51], 10 [155], 22 [325], 23 [275], 29 [303]

I SAMUEL
i. 21 [278]
ii. 4 [326], 8 [311], 24 [44]
iv. 2 [163, 261], 5 [296], 9 [333], 12 [163], 16 [164]
v. 9 [259, 275]
vi. 7 [164]
viii. 12 [59]
ix. 21 [52]
x. 19 [53], 21 [52]
xi. 11 [145, 305], 15 [306]
xii. 21 [340], 22 [309, 310], 24 [345]
xiii. 2 [82, 175], 3 [109], 17 [145]
xiv. 20 [259, 270]
xv. 18 [300]
xvii. 1 [47], 2 [163], 4 [156], 5 [289], 6 [45, 131], 7 [131, 281], 8 [163, 164], 10 [163, 260], 13 [274], 16 [122, 275], 17 [53, 155], 18 [53], 20 [154, 163, 276], 21 [163, 283, 292], 22 [154, 163], 23 [156], 26 [163], 35 [144], 35–47 [309], 36 [163], 38 [289], 40 [140, 294], 45 [131], 46 [309], 47 [309], 51 [131, 309]
xviii. 11 [135]
xix. 2 [59]
xx. 3 [296]
xxi. 10 [131]
xxiii. 3 [163], 23 [53], 27 [145]
xxiv. 3 [81, 175]
xxv. 13 [154], 32 [320]
xxvi. 2 [82, 175], 8 [312]
xxvii. 8 [175]
xxxi. 8 [153], 9 [153]

II SAMUEL
i. 12 [44], 19 [317], 27 [115]
ii. 7 [218, 332], 18 [287], 22 [288], 25 [168], 35 [288]
v. 2 [276], 20 [307]

vii. 22 [305], 23 [305, 322], 24 [321]
viii. 1 [309], 4 [164], 7 [137], 10 [260], 12 [22]
x. 4 [82], 9 [164], 11 [261], 12 [333], 13 [275], 16 [30]
xi. 15 [164]
xiii. 28 [218, 332]
xiv. 13 [44]
xv. 10 [109], 27 [208]
xvii. 1 [82]
xviii. 1 [59], 4 [59, 134], 10 [109], 12 [22], 18 [100], 29 [260]
xx. 1 [109], 5 [324], 8 [127], 22 [109]
xxi. 3 [318], 16 [130], 19 [309]
xxii. 12 [306], 19 [277], 26 [291], 35 [327], 38 [299], 40 [315]
xxiii. 7 [134], 10 [134], 13 [256], 21 [134]
xxiv. 11 [310], 16 [322]

I KINGS
i. 39 [109]
iii. 8 [314]
iv. 7 [86]
v. 4 [30], 18 [36], 27 [86], 28 [82, 86]
vii. 15–22 [281], 17 [280], 23 [283], 26 [280], 28 [281], 31 [281], 33 [279], 41 [191], 45 [279]
viii. 5 [314], 21 [321], 23 [224], 44 [225, 319], 45 [30, 225], 61 [323]
xi. 17 [290], 28 [390]
xiv. 27–28 [117]
xviii. 44 [167]
xx. 14 [167], 27 [330], 29 [268, 299, 330]
xxii. 3 [298]

II KINGS
ii. 23 [290]
iii. 25 [139]
v. 1 [309]
viii. 23 [319]
xi. 4 [272], 9 [272], 10 [120, 133, 272], 15 [272]
xii. 11 [207]
xiv. 8 [164]
xvii. 15 [321]
xix. 35 [237, 309, 348]
xxiii. 4 [207], 7 [123]
xxiv. 2 [22, 23, 256, 257]
xxv. 4 [148], 18 [207]

ISAIAH
ii. 4 [288]
iii. 13 [277], 20 [123]
iv. 6 [317]
viii. 1 [315], 9 [261, 334]
ix. 1 [259], 2 [259], 3 [134], 16 [312], 22 [259]
x. 5 [134], 6 [153], 13 [309], 15 [130], 33 [328]

INDEX OF SCRIPTURAL PASSAGES

ISAIAH—continued
xi. 2 [167], 11 [25, 33, 327], 14 [22, 35, 256], 16 [327]
xii. 3 [260], 6 [318]
xiii. 2 [100, 288], 3 [288, 326], 4 [288, 315, 326]
xiv. 26 [330]
xvii. 3 [29], 14 [256]
xviii. 3 [109], 4 [317]
xix. 1 [296, 325]
xxii. 5 [275], 19 [146]
xxiii. 1 [24], 12 [24, 25], 13 [25]
xxiv. 20 [343]
xxv. 6 [326]
xxvi. 19 [312–13]
xxvii. 4 [296]
xxviii. 1–2 [345], 6 [300], 15 [333], 29 [345]
xxix. 5 [333], 14 [345]
xxx. 16 [287], 25 [260]
xxxi. 8 [312, 348, 349]
xxxii. 7 [311]
xxxiii. 2 [258], 3 [275], 12 [25], 13 [25]
xxxiv. 1 [307], 8 [277], 8–10 [338], 11 [34]
xxxv. [326], 2 [270], 3 [327], 4 [277], 10 [318]
xxxvi. 8 [179], 9 [179]
xxxvii. 4 [347], 24 [314], 36 [348]
xxxviii. 12 [167]
xl. 12 [288], 26 [314]
xli. 11 [328]
xlii. 5 [307], 11 [319], 13 [317, 319], 25 [258]
xliv. 7 [321], 8 [312], 13 [308], 26 [167]
xlv. 8 [341], 17 [258, 316]
xlix. 2 [282], 8 [258], 23 [319]
l. 11 [285]
li. 6 [333]
lii. 8 [325], 9 [325], 13 [319]
liv. 10 [315], 12 [280], 16 [322]
lvii. 15 [316]
lix. 3 [300], 17 [220, 289], 22 [343]
lx. 10 [319], 11 [319], 18 [345]
lxii. 1 [259, 298], 9 [257, 313, 318], 13 [313]
lxiii. 9 [234], 12 [313], 15 [314], 18 [328]
lxiv. 9 [257], 11 [298]
lxv. 18 [319]
lxvi. 2 [312, 327], 5 [100], 6 [313], 15 [258], 16 [333]

JEREMIAH
i. 22 [288]
ii. 6 [307], 28 [258]
iv. 2 [274], 5 [109, 167], 19 [296], 21 [109], 29 [288]
v. 8 [182]

vi. 1 [109], 17 [109], 23 [115, 130]
viii. 2 [307], 16 [288]
x. 13 [307], 15 [277], 25 [330]
xi. 12 [258], 20 [338]
xii. 3 [260]
xiv. 7 [345], 8 [258]
xv. 14 [330]
xvii. 10 [338], 12 [264]
xx. 13 [311]
xxi. 5 [258]
xxiii. 20 [106, 270]
xxv. 29 [335], 31 [277, 315], 33 [309]
xxxi. 7 [327]
xxxii. 18 [315]
xxxiii. 25 [307]
xxxiv. 4 [148]
xxxvi. 7 [258]
xxxvii. 11 [325]
xxxix. 3 [292]
xliv. 4 [289]
xlvi. 3 [155, 275], 4 [123, 163, 167, 279], 5 [343], 6 [328], 9 [120]
xlvii. 3 [288]
xlviii. 14 [288]
xlix. 2 [296], 20 [320], 32 [318]
l. 9 [326], 4 [124, 130]
li. 11 [134], 43 [307]
lii. 7 [148], 21 [282], 24 [207]

EZEKIEL
iii. 7 [327]
vi. 14 [266]
vii. 17 [327], 21 [315]
viii. 11 [264]
x. 2 [132, 135], 5 [306]
xiv. 23 [338]
xvi. 10 [280], 11 [319], 13 [280], 33 [126]
xvii. 18 [262]
xx. 9 [256], 22 [256], 35 [257], 41 [264], 44 [310]
xxi. 3 [285], 9 [296], 12 [327], 19 [285], 21 [165], 36 [324]
xxiii. 20 [182], 23 [276], 40 [319]
xxiv. 9–11 [339]
xxvi. 20 [321]
xxvii. 6 [27, 25], 11 [134]
xxix. 19 [317]
xxx. 14 [324, 325]
xxxii. 21 [313], 22 [313]
xxxiii. 3 [109]. 22 [326]
xxxiv. 25 [315]
xxxvi. 17 [321]
xxxvii. 23 [266], 26 [315]
xxxviii. [33], 4 [120, 276], 7 [313], 12–13 [153], 16 [317], 17 [310], 19 [313], 20 [313], 21 [313], 22 [313], 23 [313]
xxxix. [33], 4–12 [290], 7 [300, 313], 9 [37], 11 [344], 12 [134], 13 [311], 14 [154], 18 [313], 27 [312]

INDEX OF SCRIPTURAL PASSAGES

EZEKIEL—continued
xl. 17 [264]
xli. 7 [280]
xliii. 11 [280]
xliv. 1 [263], 16 [264], 17 [219], 18 [292]
xlviii. 31 [45]

HOSEA
ii. 17 [311]
v. 8 [87]
vi. 9 [168]
vii. 1 [145]
ix. 7 [233, 311]
xii. 15 [269]
xiv. 6 [317]

JOEL
ii. 20 [32], 23 [318], 26 [314, 345]
iv. 4 [257], 7 [313]

AMOS
i. 8 [300]
ii. 14 [328], 15 [27]

OBADIAH
i. 9 [313], 15 [313], 16 [340], 21 [319]

MICAH
iv. 7 [315], 11 [326]
v. 6 [317], 7 [347]
vi. 9 [134]
vii. 8 [239]

NAHUM
ii. 2 [311, 327], 11 [327]
iii. 3 [285]

HABAKKUK
i. 1 [310], 6 [23]
ii. 5 [326], 16 [275], 17 [72]
iii. 2 [285]

ZEPHANIAH
i. 14 [319]
ii. 11 [316]
iii. 8 [326], 14 [318]

ZECHARIAH
ii. 10 [306], 13 [341], 14 [318]
iii. 2 [328]
iv. 3 [211], 12 [137]
ix. 9 [318], 14 [297]
xii. 6 [312]
xiii. 7 [300]
xiv. 3 [260], 13 [275]

MALACHI
i. 7 [264]
iii. 3 [282]

PSALMS
iv. 2 [345]
v. 11 [323]
vii. 7 [329]
viii. 2 [316]
ix. 4 [332]
x. 5 [326], 12 [343]
xiv. 1 [310], 7 [257]
xvii. 7 [327], 12 [288]
xviii. 26 [291], 35 [327], 40 [334]
xix. 3 [146], 10 [274]
xx. 4 [264]
xxi. [260], 7 [325], 14 [327, 329]
xxii. 20 [313], 29 [319], 32 [321]
xxiii. 9 [323]
xxiv. 7–10 [316], 8 [317]
xxvii. 3 [47], 9 [32]
xxviii. 1 [298], 9 [318]
xxxi. 6 [237], 9 [312]
xxxii. 1 [230]
xxxiii. 1 [274], 2 [274], 6 [307], 17 [314]
xxxiv. 2 [329], 3 [325], 4 [325], 16 [308]
xxxv. 1 [277], 2 [277], 3 [137, 281], 10 [305]
xxxvi. 11 [320]
xxxvii. 2 [333], 6 [259], 14 [311]
xxxix. 10 [326]
xl. 4 [325], 15 [323], 17 [329]
xliv. 3 [315], 6 [315], 10 [261, 316], 11 [332], 14 [316]
xlvi. 10 [121]
xlvii. 10 [278]
xlviii. 5 [331], 12 [318]
xlix. 3 [313]
liii. 7 [257]
lvi. 10 [332]
lvii. 6 [319]
lx. 19 [311]
lxi. 2 [269]
lxii. 10 [313]
lxix. 34 [311]
lxx. 5 [329], 6 [277]
lxxi. 19 [305]
lxxii. 6 [317], 9 [318], 12 [259]
lxxiv. 21 [311], 22 [277, 311]
lxxv. 9 [315]
lxxvi. 5 [316], 8 [316], 13 [316]
lxxvii. 12 [105, 259]
lxxviii. [322]
lxxix. 12 [269]
lxxx. 14 [327], 17 [323]
lxxxii. 1 [44]
lxxxiii. 7–9 [22], 9 [257], 10 [312]
lxxxiv. 10 [278]
lxxxv. 8 [346], 12 [341]
lxxxvi. 13 [347], 14 [332]
lxxxix. 4 [321], 6–9 [231], 7 [230], 14 [310], 17 [326]
xcii. 4 [274], 6 [305, 306, 320]

PSALMS—continued
xciii. 4 [316]
xciv. 1 [262], 2 [313], 3 [329]
xcvii. 8 [318]
xcviii. 6 [109]
xcix. 9 [316]
ci. 8 [315]
ciii. 11 [324], 18 [315], 20–21 [316], 11 [324], 17–18 [315]
civ. [306], 2 [306], 4 [231], 35 [327]
cv. 9–10 [271], 15 [310]
cvi. 7 [314], 43 [309], 47 [275, 309]
cx. 3 [291]
cxi. 4 [322], 9 [261, 316], 10 [256]
cxiii. 5–6 [305], 7 [311]
cxvi. 1 [257]
cxviii. 15 [275, 317], 16 [317], 19–21 [345]
cxix. 1 [327], 12 [306], 22 [328], 99 [306], 119 [315], 171 [318, 325]
cxxi. 2 [316]
cxxiv. 8 [277]
cxxv. 3 [256]
cxxx. 7–8 [261]
cxxxii. 1 [316]
cxxxiii. [309]
cxxxv. 1 [314], 7 [307]
cxli. 2 [344]
cxliv. 1 [260], 9 [274], 11 [316]
cxlv. 1 [321, 325], 2 [328], 14 [328]
cxlvii. 4 [314]
cxlviii. 2 [314]
cxlix. 6 [3, 125, 275], 7 [3], 8 [328]
cl. 2 [259, 329]

PROVERBS
i. 7 [256]
iii. 2 [260], 18 [305], 20 [307]
iv. 13 [305], 18 [259]
v. 5 [125], 18 [291]
vi. 7 [151]
viii. 27–29 [307]
ix. 2 [155]
x. 3 [333]
xi. 20 [327]
xiv. 28 [314]
xv. 13 [312]
xvi. 19 [327]
xvii. 3 [339], 22 [312]
xviii. 14 [312]
xix. 13 [103]
xxiv. 24 [320]
xxv. 26 [335]
xxvi. 18 [285]
xxx. 17 [308]

JOB
i. 7 [323], 17 [145]

ii. 2 [323]
iv. 4 [327]
vii. 1 [167]
x. 22 [143]
xii. 13 [310], 22 [306]
xiv. 2 [332], 5 [332, 337], 14 [337]
xv. 28 [334]
xviii. 16 [333]
xxv. 2 [329]
xxvi. 9 [317], 10 [307]
xxvii. 6 [305]
xxviii. 8 [307], 23 [260], 25 [288]
xxix. 12 [259], 20 [130]
xxx. 13 [259], 23 [268]
xxxiii. 16 [306], 28 [328]
xxxvi. 28–29 [309]
xxxviii. [306], 22 [307]
xxxix. 20 [130], 23 [281]
xl. 17 [72]
xli. 18 [130], 21 [130]

CANTICLES
ii. 4 [62], 6 [62]
iii. 8 [306]
iv. 4 [137]
v. 14 [191], 15 [191]
viii. 6 [135, 285], 10 [188]

RUTH
ii. 1 [309]

LAMENTATIONS
i. 7 [259]
ii. 14 [310]
iii. 8 [288], 33 [313], 44 [108], 51 [319], 64 [277], 65 [347]
iv. 14 [300]
v. 6 [262]

ECCLESIASTES
iii. 7 [298]

ESTHER
i. 6 [191]
viii. 6 [334], 13 [291]
ix. 2 [256], 5 [334]

DANIEL
i. 8 [300]
ii. 22 [306]
viii. 10 [307], 16 [229, 306], 24 [306, 316]
ix. 4 [315, 325], 16 [258], 18 [310], 22 [306], 26 [311, 332], 27 [324, 332], 32 [320]
x. 5–7 [306], 13 [340], 21 [229, 236]
xii. 3 [258], 5 [258, 259], 18 [105, 269], 19 [333], 28 [306], 30 [24, 306], 32

INDEX OF SCRIPTURAL PASSAGES

[26, 257], 33 [306], 34 [257, 277], 35 [282], 36 [236, 329, 332], 41 [22, 256], 42 [256], 45 [259]
xii. 1 [236, 261, 322, 240], 7 [306], 10 [282, 306]
xvii. 6 [261]

EZRA
i. 5 [257]
ii. 64 [272]
iii. 2 [320]. 8 [78, 295], 9 [295], 11 [277, 296], 13 [296]
vi. 17 [314], 22 [292]
vii. 1 [341], 2–5 [207], 10 [306], 27 [321]
viii. 24 [204], 31 [94], 36 [30]
ix. 1 [257], 4 [344], 8–9 [322], 11 [321], 13 [310], 14 [259, 326]

NEHEMIAH
i. 5 [315, 325]
ii. 7 [30]
iii. 1 [320], 36 [269]
iv. 2 [168], 10–11 [115], 12 [109, 167], 16 [115]
vii. 36 [105], 66 [272], 72 [272]
viii. 7 [320], 11 [108], 13 [92, 269]
ix. [306], 3 [320], 32 [316]
x. 34 [264]
xii. 7 [263], 24 [263], 41 [107, 292], 46 [277, 325]

I CHRONICLES
i. [27]
ii. [52], 26 [257]
iv. [52]
v. [52], 18 [120, 288], 22 [309], 23–26 [53], 24 [53], 27 [54]
vi. 34 [267], 42 [54]
vii. [52, 53], 4 [53], 7 [53], 11 [53], 12 [53], 40 [53]
viii. [52]
ix. [154]
x. 8 [153], 9 [153]
xii. [85], 8 [155], 28 [290], 30 [175], 35 [120, 135], 38 [144]
xiii. 12–14 [109]
xiv. 11 [307], 15 [261]
xv. 5–7 [54], 24 [107, 292]
xvi. 22 [310], 35 [275], 39 [320]

xviii. 3 [100], 7 [134], 11 [22]
xix. 10 [82]
xx. 5 [309]
xxi. 5 [84], 16 [132], 27 [126]
xxii. 5 [290]
xxiii. 4 [152, 293, 295], 6 [54], 24 [78, 267], 27 [78], 31 [264]
xxiv. 1–8 [204], 7 [207]
xxv. 3 [277], 7 [306], 8 [207], 9–31 [204], 10 [204]
xxvi. 26 [59], 29 [152]
xxvii. [33, 79, 82, 85, 86], 1 [59], 1–5 [83], 23 [77], 34 [84]
xxix. [154], 1 [290], 6 [59], 10 [164], 11 [275, 310], 11–17 [277], 12 [277, 309, 310], 17 [338], 18 [338]
xxxiv. 35 [155]

II CHRONICLES
i. 2 [59]
ii. 1 [295], 2 [264], 11 [306], 13 [281], 17 [295]
iv. 2 [283], 16 [279]
v. 13 [296]
vi. 14 [325]
vii. 3 [277], 22 [305]
viii. 13 [264]
xi. 1 [144], 11–13 [257]
xiii. 3 [163, 167], 9 [120], 12–14 [87], 13 [94]
xiv. 10 [277], 11 [207], 12 [322]
xvii. 14 [53], 16 [291]
xix. 9 [320], 11 [207]
xx. 1 [257], 6 [212], 15 [212, 309], 24 [309]
xxii. 3 [322]
xxiii. 9 [133, 135]
xxiv. 6 [207], 14 [289]
xxv. 5 [53, 59, 77, 82], 13 [274]
xxvi. 14 [115], 19 [264], 20 [207]
xxix. 6 [299], 12 [54]
xxx. 10 [207]
xxxi. 3 [264], 10 [208]
xxxii. [332], 7 [218], 8 [316], 21 [237, 331, 348, 349]
xxxiv. 12 [295], 13 [152, 293, 295]
xxxv. 12 [307]
xxxvi. 13 [261]

(ii) *New Testament*

MATTHEW
v. 3 [327]
xxiv. 21 [261], 27 [259]

II CORINTHIANS
xi. 14 [235]

REVELATION
xvi. 18 [261]

(iii) *Apocrypha and Pseudepigrapha*

I MACCABEES
iii. 12 [196], 46 [70], 55 [59], 56 [68], 57 [70]
iv. 8 [213], 9 [214], 13 [111], 17–18 [154], 24 [222], 30 [214], 40 [111]
v. 3 [22], 6 [22], 33 [145], 42 [152], 53 [228], 67 [300]
vi. 49 [20], 53 [20]
vii. 14 [237], 40 [213], 41 [214], 45 [111]
viii. 5 [24]
ix. 12 [111], 27 [261], 38 [196]
xiv. 27–28 [44]

II MACCABEES
ii. 8 [214], 15 [214]
iii. 24 [231]
iv. 13 [58]
viii. 23 [58], 27 [228]
x. 29 [237], 38 [228]
xii. 15 [213, 214], 36–37 [215], 39 [221]
xiii. 15 [58]
xv. 15–16 [331], 22 [213], 23 [237], 25 [111], 26 [111]
xvi. 6 [237]

III MACCABEES
ii. 1–20 [214]
vi. 1–15 [214]

ECCLESIASTICUS
viii. 1 [300]
x. 10 [339]
xiv. 11 [264], 12 [264]
xvi. 31 (27), [288]
xvii. 14 [234], 22 (27) [277]
xxvi. 7 [261]
xxxv. 18 [108], 19 (22–23) [317], 20 [108]
xli. 22 [269], 30 [269]
xlii. [306], 24 (17) [314]
xliii. [306], 7 (6) [308], 8 (7) [308], 13 [259], 15 [259]
xlv. 10–11 [220]
xlvi. 4 [222], 4 (2) [130]
xlvii. 11 (8) [277]
xlviii. 23 [222], 25 [340]
l. 12 [256], 13 [217], 14 [256], 19 (14) [144]
li. 22 [275]

WISDOM OF SOLOMON
v. 6 [259]
vii. 29 [259]

DREAM OF MORDECAI
[242]

BOOK OF JUBILEES
i. 19–20 [233], 27 [235], 29 [260]
ii. [306], 2 [232], 7 [307], 9 [264]
iii. 7 [75]
v. 18 [235]
vi. 23 [205], 29 [205]
viii. [27], 9 [33], 16 [32], 21 [32], 25 [215]
ix. [27], 2 [32], 4 [31], 5 [29], 6 [29], 8 [215]
x. 8 [234], 11 [234]
xi. 5 [234]
xii. 27 [205, 206]
xiii. 1 [25]
xiv. 18 [34]
xv. 31–32 [234]
xvii. 16 [234]
xviii. 9 [234]
xx. 12–13 [32]
xxi. 7 [300]
xxiv. 28–29 [24]
xxv. 16 [206]
xxviii. 8 [24]
xxxii. 18–19 [33]
xxxiv. [16], 1–8 [33]
xxxvii. [16, 33], 6 [22, 24], 10 [24], 14 [24], 15 [24, 131]
xxxviii. [16, 33], 16 [46]
xlviii. 2 [234], 9 [234], 15 [234], 16 [234], 18 [234]
xlix. 1 [264], 2 [234], 5 [199]
l. 3 [20], 11 [199], 12–13 [20]

LETTER OF ARISTEAS
57 [119], 58–59 [138]

BOOK OF ADAM AND EVE
xxxviii. 1 [236]
xl. 1 [236], 3 [238]

ASCENSION OF ISAIAH
i. 8 [233]
ii. 4 [233], 8 [232]

BOOK OF ENOCH
i. [260, 314], 9 [231, 260]
ii. 22 [261]
v. 7–9 [260]
vi. 5 [32]
GREEK
ix. 1 [238]
x. [239], 16 [260]
xi. [260]
SLAVIC 63 [240]
xx. [238, 239], 5 [234], 6 [240]

APOCRYPHA AND PSEUDEPIGRAPHA

BOOK OF ENOCH—*continued*
xxv. 6 [260]
xxviii. 1 [260]
xxxviii. 5 [316]
xl. 9 [238]
xli. 9 [234]
xlii. [261]
xliii. [241]
liii. 5 [316]
liv. [260], 6 [238]
lv. [260]
lvi. 5 [237]
lviii. 4 [259], 5 [259]
lix. [260]
lx. 7–8 [72]
lxxi. 8 [238]
lxxiv. 12 [205]
lxxv. 1 [206], 2 [205]
lxxvi. 8 [240]
lxxvii. 1 [240]
lxxviii. 1 [346]
lxxxi. [341]
lxxxii. 4 [206], 5 [205], 9–15 [47]
xciv. 9 [260]

TESTAMENTS OF THE PATRIARCHS
Reuben
iv. 11 [233]
Simeon
v. 2 [257]
vi. 3 [24, 33], 4 [33]
Levi
i. [149]
iii. 3 [232, 260, 334]
v. 3 [257]
ix. 2–7 [54]
xiv. 4 [242]
xviii. 12 [233]
xix. 1 [242]
Aramaic Test. of Levi
[260]
Judah
iii. 1 [123]
iii–vii. [16, 33]
ix. [16, 33]

xxv. 3 [233]
Zebulun
ix. 8 [233]
Dan
v. [3], 6 [327], 8 [14], 10 [233]
Naphtali
viii. 4 [260]
Asher
i. 3 [242]
Joseph
xix. 9 [260]
xx. 2 [242]
Benjamin
xi. 2 [259]

TESTAMENT OF JOB
xliii. 6 [242]

ASCENSION OF MOSES
iv. 8 [199]
v. 4 [199]
viii. 1 [261]
xii. 4–6 [340], 7 [310]

IV EZRA
v. 88 [149]
vi. 21 [231], 49 [72]
x. 27 [239]

PSALMS OF SOLOMON
xvii. 17–20 [257], 31 [319]

IV MACCABEES
iv. 4 [237]

II BARUCH
i. [261], 53–69 [261]
liii. 9 [259]

III BARUCH
[314]

SYRIAC BARUCH
xi–xv. [236]

(iv) *Dead Sea Scrolls*

BOOK OF NOAH
frg. 13–14 [316]

DAMASCUS COVENANT
(*Zadokite Fragments*)
i. 1 [259], 2 [315], 5 [326], 7 [271], 8 [264]

ii. 1 [321], 2–3 [306], 6 [231, 323, 326, 340], 7 [326, 340], 9 [42, 340], 10 [340], 12 [310], 13 [42], 20 [340]
iii. 1 [272], 9–10 [316], 12–13 [322], 14–15 [264], 18 [329], 21 [264]
iii. 20–iv., 2 [198]
iv. 3 [208], 5–6 [42], 8 [42], 12–13 [232], 15 [323]

DAMASCUS COVENANT—*continued*
v. 1–2 [278], 13 [285], 17 [235], 18 [235, 236, 322], 19 [235, 236]
vi. 11–14 [198], 17–19 [206]
vii. 6 [47, 67, 152], 6a [148], 7 [67], 9 [313], 12–13 [212], 18–21 [278], 19 [332], 19–21 [310], 20 [44]
viii. 3 [212], 7–8 [306], 11 [25], 14 [303]
x. [74, 75], 4 [44, 148, 256, 283], 5 [55, 78], 6 [76], 7–8 [76], 21 [71]
xi. [74, 75], 1 [320], 5–6 [74], 15 [300], 17–21 [199], 21–22 [95], 21–23 [91]
xii. 1 [71], 4 [264], 6 [256], 8–11 [67], 19 [148], 22 [47, 60], 23 [60]
xiii. 1–2 [60], 2–6 [55], 4 [47], 7 [47], 8 [311], 13 [47], 20 [47]
xiv. 3 [47], 3–7 [55, 60], 8 [47], 9 [47, 288], 12 [256], 17–18 [42]
xv. 5–6 [264]
xvi. 2 [42, 206], 3 [331], 5 [322]
xix. 1 [315, 332], 2–3 [47, 67], 6 [313], 23 [25]
xx. 3 [318], 4 [322], 5 [257], 15 [37], 21–22 [315], 24 [269], 25–27 [26], 25 [221, 262, 318], 30 [274], 31 [274]
xli. 22 [264]

DIRES DE MOISE
Qumran I
p. 95 iv. 1 [230]

DISCIPLINE SCROLL
i. 1 [224], 5 [274], 6 [274], 7 [290], 7–9 [306], 8 [150], 9 [310], 10 [150], 11 [290], 12 [306], 13–15 [206], 16 [149], 17 [221, 232, 327], 18 [224, 232, 321, 327], 21 [55], 24 [321, 327]
ii. 1 [55], 4 [55, 224, 233], 5 [233, 321], 8 [239, 321], 10 [310], 11 [264], 13 [306], 15 [258, 310], 16 [320], 19–21 [55, 61], 19–24 [206], 19 [233, 321, 327], 20–22 [149], 21 [150], 22 [204, 324], 23 [270, 324], 25 [269]
iii. 1 [259], 4–11 [199], 13–25 [242, 256], 15 [340], 16 [322], 18 [231, 232, 242], 20–22 [235], 20 [236, 241, 322], 22 [327], 23 [233, 337], 24 [231, 235, 262, 322, 340]
iv. 3 [306], 5 [341], 6–8 [260], 6 [259, 322, 341], 12 [231, 258, 323], 13 [300], 15 [307], 17 [307], 18–20 [260], 19 [259], 22 [306, 327], 23 [231, 232]
v. 1 [148, 150, 256, 271, 290, 304], 2 [300], 3 [288, 305], 6 [290], 7 [269, 288], 8 [290], 10 [290], 20 [44], 21 [290], 23 [60, 148, 149]

vi. 2–3 [77], 4 [200, 288], 5 [200], 8 [271, 288], 9–24 [207, 288], 10 [288], 13 [290], 22 [148, 149, 288]
vii. 13 [75], 22 [150]
viii. 2 [274], 3 [221], 4 [288], 5 [271], 6 [271, 313], 7 [313], 12–14 [257], 14 [332], 18 [327], 19 [288], 21 [269, 327]
ix. 2 [288, 327], 3 [199], 5 [264, 327], 7 [288], 9 [327], 12 [288], 18 [288, 329, 338], 21 [288], 23 [291], 24 [290]
x. 1–10 [308], 3 [241], 4 [41, 241, 264], 5 [264, 288], 6 [167, 264], 7 [167, 288], 8 [315], 9 [288], 10 [329], 11 [259, 315, 341], 12 [259, 341], 13 [256], 15 [264, 315, 329], 17 [325], 26 [327]
xi. 3 [329], 4 [274], 5 [329], 7–8 [230, 241, 314], 9 [329], 11 [340], 13 [274], 14 [274, 305], 15 [305], 18–19 [306], 19 [327]

GENESIS APOCRYPHON
xxi. 7 [266]

HABAKKUK PESHER
ii. 8–10 [311], 12 [25, 328], 13 [259, 328], 14 [259]
iv. 2 [328], 5 [331]
vi. 3–5 [63, 64], 4 [271], 11 [206]
viii. 2 [310], 7 [310], 8 [270, 310, 337], 12 [321], 13 [288, 331]
ix. 7 [222], 11–12 [322]
x. 5 [322], 12 [320]
xi. 4–6 [257], 6 [280], 7 [318], 8 [265]
xii. 3 [311], 4–5 [72], 6 [311], 10 [311]

ISAIAH
(*Version A*)
lx. 10 [319]
(*Version B*)
xlii. 11 [319]
lx. 10 [319]

NAHUM PESHER
line 3 [331]
frg. B, line 6 [23]
frg. C, line 5 [23]

OZAR HA-MEGILLOTH HA-GENUZOTH
p. 47, frg. 1 [333]
— frg. 9 [334]
frg. 33 [348]
plate 30 [330]

OZAR—*continued*
plate 31 [349]
plate 33 [343, 345]
plate 34, fig. 8 [346]

PSALMS PESHER
xxxvii. [311]
xxxvii., frg. 1, line 8 [37]
xxxvii. ii, 1 [257]
xxxvii. vs. 14-15, line 3 [256]
lxviii. Qumran I, p. 82 [331]

QUMRAN I
pp. 46-47 [243]
p. 82 [3, 22, 206, 331]
p. 88 [260]
p. 93. ii, 9 [318]
p. 94 [20]
p. 95. iv, 1 [230]
p. 102. i, 4 [306]
p. 103 [333, 340], i, 6-7 [259]
p. 109. i, 1-3 [269]
—— —— 2 [265]
—— —— 6 [271]
—— —— 7 [306]
—— —— 8 [265]
—— —— 8-9 [264]
—— —— 9 [272]
—— —— 11 [265]
—— —— 13 [267]
pp. 109-111. i, 16, 23, 25 [263], ii, 16 [263]
p. 110 [267]
—— i. 2 [265], 8 [265], 11 [265], 12-15 [290], 13 [275, 277, 315], 14 [263, 315], 16 [263, 267], 19 [290], 20 [263], 21 [263], 22 [55], 23 [55, 263], 25 [269, 276], 26 [265, 276, 330], 27 [268, 276, 291], 28 [327]
—— ii. 1 [267], 2 [268], 4-10 [290], 7 [326], 8 [263, 291], 9 [269, 291], 15 [47, 269], 17-18 [264], 19-22 [72]
p. 111
—— ii. 7 [200]
pp. 121-122 [278]
pp. 121-128 [310]
p. 123. iii, 1 [264]
p. 124. iii, 22 [339], 23 [339]
p. 126. iv, 23-24 [323], 25 [231, 314], 27-28 [330]
p. 127. v, 20 [278], 23 [259]
p. 128. v, 27 [213]
pp. 128-129 [278]
p. 129. [215, 317]
p. 135. no. 33 [343]
p. 136. no. 34.3 [317]
p. 138. frg. 36.1 [265]
p. 139. frg. 14 [318]
no. 36, frg. 2 [232]

Plates
ii. 20 [256]
xxv-xxix. [17]
xxxi. [247]
xxxi. 33.2 [13, 347]

SAMUEL
i, 1-3 [322]
ii, 11-17 [269]
xxiii. 13 [256]

THANKSGIVING HYMNS
i. [306], 8 [306], 9 [306, 307], 10 [232, 307, 329], 11 [232, 259, 307], 12 [285, 307], 16 [307], 17 [307], 20 [306, 308], 22 [291], 24 [315], 35 [324], 36 [327]
ii. 3 [329], 7-8 [327], 9 [316], 12 [272, 338], 16-17 [306], 21 [341], 23 [311]
iii. 4 [314], 21-23 [314], 21 [146, 241, 263], 22 [146, 230, 231, 241, 322], 23 [231, 241, 325], 33-36 [260], 33 [334], 36 [334]
iv. 5 [346], 6 [222, 318], 8-9 [257], 12-14 [321], 13 [320], 14 [326], 20 [310, 333], 23 [222, 318, 346], 25 [231], 26 [306], 27 [329], 28 [329], 30 [270], 32 [314], 34 [310], 35 [309, 310], 36 [327]
v. 15 [126], 16 [221, 337], 21 [334], 29 [327], 32 [222, 318, 340], 36 [327]
vi. 7 [260], 9 [314], 13 [231, 241], 18-19 [312], 21-22 [321, 323], 29 [261, 331]
vii. 3 [222, 318], 10 [269], 27 [329], 28 [274, 323], 30 [341], 34 [322]
viii. 10 [231], 11-12 [334], 19 [307], 29 [274]
ix. 13 [146], 26 [222, 318], 27 [311], 31 [318]
x. 8 [230, 231, 328], 10 [317], 33 [277, 316, 334], 34 [231, 277, 316, 334]
xi. 4 [277], 10 [329], 11 [241, 270, 321], 12 [231], 13 [263], 14 [325], 25 [325], 26 [318, 325], 28 [306]
xii. 1-9 [308], 3-10 [329], 4-7 [307], 5 [288], 7 [329], 8 [288, 329], 9 [288], 13 [338], 14 [300], 20 [337]
xiii. 2 [329], 8 [231, 317], 9 [307], 14 [231]
xiv. 23 [314], 26 [290]
xv. 2 [290], 9 [260, 340]
xvii. 12 [305], 28 [305]
xviii. 15 [312], 29 [341], 30 [311]
Ozar Ha-Megilloth Ha-Genuzoth
plate 52, frg. 18, 3 [230]
plate 53, frg. 2, 3 [230]
—— frg. 2, 10 [230]
plate 54, frg. 4, 6 [328]
plate 55, frg. 5 [232]
—— frg. 9, 7 [314]
—— 9, 9 [322]

JOSEPHUS

THANKSGIVING HYMNS—*continued*
plate 56, frg. 10, 9 [318]
plate 57, frg. 18, 4 [339]
frg. 4, 6 [322]
frg. 5, 10 [306]
frg. 6, 3 [322]
frg. 6, 4 [322]

frg. 10, 7 [325]
frg. 12, 5 [306]
frg. 15, 7 [314]
frg. 18, 4 [306]
frg. 45, 3 [322]
frg. 63 [231]

(v) *Josephus*

ANTIQUITIES
I. i. 3 [266]
iv–vi. [27]
vi. [33], 1 [24, 215], 4 [29, 30, 31, 32]
III. iv. 1 [59]
vi. 6 [119]
vii. 5 [45, 111]
viii. 3 [111]
xii. 10 [110]
IV. iv. 2 [45]
VI. [33]
ix. 1 [156]
VII. xiii. 1 [52]
xiv. 7 [204], 8 [79]
XII. vi. 2 [20]
viii. 3 [59]
XIII. viii. 1 [20]
XIV. xvi. 1 [176]
XVIII. i. 5 [176, 201], 8 [200]
XX. ii. 2–3 [31]

BELLUM JUDAICUM
I. Prooem. 2 [30]
ii. 4 [20]
xvii. 9 [176]
II. vi. 2 [261]
vii. 10 [72]
viii. [150], 3 [219], 5 [200], 7 [229], 9 [74], 10 [79], 13–14 [150]
xvi. 4 [5, 27, 30]
xix. 5 [189]
xx. 7 [59, 112]
III. ii. 3 [196]
iv. 2 [162]
v. 4 [111, 112], 5 [121, 133], 13 [150]
vi. 2 [150, 174, 181]
vii. 2 [63], 27 [112, 175, 189]
V. ix. 4 [214]
VI. vi. 1 [63]

CONTRA APIONEM
ii. 29 [154]

(vi) *Rabbinic Literature*

MISHNAH
Berakhoth
iii, 1 [337]
Kil'ayim
v, 3 [138, 281]
Shabbath
v, 3 [127]
vi, 2 [122, 124]
xvi, 5 [190]
'Erubin
iv, 3 [74]
v, 7 [74]
Sheqalim
v, [204]
Yoma
ii, 5 [207]
Sukkah
v, 5 [205], 7 [205], 8 [205]
Rosh Ha-Shanah
i, 1 [265]
iv, 6 [167]
Ta'anith
ii, 1 [214]
iv, 1 [204], 2 [203]

Ḥagigah
i, 1 [71]
Soṭah
v, 3 [74]
viii, [217], 1 [209, 213, 217, 288], 2 [163], 2–4 [66], 4 [66, 69], 5 [66, 168, 227], 6 [68, 294, 332], 7 [65, 68]
Baba Qamma
i, 2 [341]
Sanhedrin
i, 6 [35]
ii, 4 [35]
'Eduyoth
iii, 5 [124]
Horayoth
xiii 1 [204]
'Abodah Zarah
v, 12 [282]
Aboth
v, 21 [77]
Zebaḥim
xi, 4 [279]
xii, 1 [72]

RABBINIC LITERATURE

MISHNAH—*continued*
Menaḥoth
iii, 6 [144]
xi, 4 [281]
Bekhoroth
ii, 2 [72]
Tamid
i, [204]
ii, 4 [144]
iii, 5 [144]
v, 1 [205]
vii, 4 [58, 265]
Middoth
iii, 5 [144]
Kelim
iv, 3 [125]
xi, 8 [122, 131]
xiii, 1 [128]
xiv, 2 [144, 282]
xvi, 5 [126]
xx, 5 [190]
xxiv, 1 [117]
xxix, 6 [128]
Niddah
ii, 5 [291]
'Uḳtzin
iii, 12 [260]

TOSEPHTA
Berakhoth
i, 1 [171]
Shabbath
iv (v), 3 [127]
Sukkah
iv, [20]
Ta'anith
ii, 2 [204]
iv, [204], 2 [204], 3 [203]
Soṭah
vii, 18 [69, 163], 22 [68, 227], 23 [66, 255]
Sanhedrin
xiv, 6 [125]
'Abodah Zarah
ii, 3 [182]
Makhshirin
i, 8 [103]
Yadayim
ii, 20 [226]

PALESTINIAN TALMUD
Berakhoth
ix, 13 [296]
Shebi'ith
vi, 1 [35]

Ḥallah
ii, 1 [35]
Yoma
iii, 40 [285]
vi, 3 [291]
Rosh Ha-Shanah
[110]
i, 2 [229]
Ta'anith
iv, 2 [203, 204, 290]
Megillah
i, 11 [115], 11, 71d [247], 72d [248]
Soṭah
viii, 3 [63, 190], 9 [66], 23a [66], end [65]
Qiddushin
i, 8, 61d [34, 35]

BABYLONIAN TALMUD
Berakhoth
32b [199], 55a [200]
Shabbath
36a [110], 65a [123], 98b [281]
Pesaḥim
103b [287], 113b [182]
Yoma
24b [144], 37a [238], 71b [209], 72b [220], 77a [236]
Rosh Ha-Shana
13b [308], 34a [104]
Ta'anith
27ab [204]
Megillah
17b [37]
Moed Qaṭan
25b [16]
Ḥagigah
12b [314, 236], 13a, b [298], 14b [237, 316]
Nazir
47b [209]
Soṭah
42a, b [69], a [209], b [288], 43a [110, 209], 44b [35, 68], 48b [179]
Sanhedrin
68b [191], 99a [37], 108a [126]
'Abodah Zarah
24b [280]
Horayoth
13a [209]
Menaḥoth
28 [110], 30a [248, 250], 39b [280], 85a [235]

BABYLONIAN TALMUD—*continued*
Ḥullin
8a, b [282], 83b [308], 106a [148]
Bekhoroth
40a [282]
Niddah
67b [148]
Soferim
ii, 2 [249], 4–5 [248]
v, 2 [250]

MIDRASHIM—*Halakhic*
Mekhilta Beshallaḥ
[237]
Mekhilta R. Ishmael
[307]
Sifre
  NUMBERS
  vi, 14 [277]
  BEHA'ALOTHEKA
  lxxv [110]
  DEUTERONOMY
  xxxiii, 27 [29]
  li, [35]
  lxxv, [34]
  cxcii, [70]
  SHOFEṬIM
  [72]
Sifre Zuṭa
[104]

MIDRASH RABBA
Genesis
ii, [102], 3 [24]
iii, 6 [346]
vii, 4 [72]
xvi, [296], 4 [25]
xliii, 2 [259]
xliv, [34], 6 [278]
liv, [34, 329]
xciii, 7 [134]
Exodus
viii, [149]
ix, [235]
xv, [279, 289]
xxiii, [182]
Leviticus
xxix, 4 [113]
xxx, [168]
Numbers
ii, [240], 2 [62, 168], 5 [168], 6 [49], 9 [74, 239], 10 [238]
iii, [204], 12 [55]
iv, 7 [55], 11 [54, 78]
xiv, [256]
xv, [62]
xvi, [237]

Deuteronomy
xi, [238]
Canticles
i, 9 [182]
iii, 6 [240]
iv, [291], 4 [188]
v, 14 [191],
vi, [334]
20a, [41]
Lamentations
iii, (on iii, 65), [347]
Ecclesiastes
xii, 12 [314]

MIDRASH TEHILLIM
(PSALMS)
iv, 17 [37], 20 [62, 63]

TANḤUMA
Exodus
  MISHPATIM
  xix, [303]
Leviticus
  BEḤUQQOTHAI
  i, [216]
Numbers
  BAMIDBAR
  ix, [74]
  MAṬṬOTH
  ii, [106]
  iv, [41, 150]
  BEHA'ALOTHĔKA
  x, [110]

PIRQEI R. ELIEZER
iv, [238, 240]
xxii, [291]
xxiv, [234]

MIDRASH SAMUEL
xxi, [140]

MIDRASH SHOḤAR ṬOB,
  See Midrash Tehillim

YALKUṬ SHIM'ONI
Genesis: Wayyishlaḥ
33 [123, 146, 167]
Exodus: Beshallaḥ
246 [276]

PESIQTA RABBATHI
iv, 1 [37]
viii, [211]
xlvi, [238, 239]

ANCIENT VERSIONS

MIDRASH OF MESSIANIC SIGNS
ii 58
viii, [257, 261]

MIDRASH HEKHALOTH RABBATHI
ii, 88, 99 [240]

MIDRASH SEDER GAN EDEN
iii, 138 [238]

MIDRASH PRAYER OF MORDECAI AND ESTHER
v, 4 [234]

MIDRASH KONEN
ii, 39 [239]

MIDRASH GOLIATH
iv, 140 [132]

MIDRASH WAYYISSA'U
iii, 1 [131, 167], 4 [167]

(vii) Versions and Translations

SAMARITAN
Genesis
x. 23 [31]
xlix. 10 [62]

Exodus
v. 3 [317]

Numbers
i. 52 [101]

SEPTUAGINT
Genesis
x. 23 [31]

Exodus
xviii. 6 [220]
xxxiii. 14 [323], 15 [323]

Numbers
iv. 2, 23, 30, 35, 39, 47 [78]
x. 3 [92], 6 [87]
xxxi. 5 [41]

Deuteronomy
iii. 24 [305]
xxxii. 9 [234]

Joshua
iii. 4 [74]

I Samuel
xvii. 6 [122, 131]

II Samuel
viii. 7 [134]

Isaiah
lxiii. 9 [234, 323]

Jeremiah
li. 11 [134]

Ezekiel
xxvii. 11 [134]

Psalms
xviii. 26 [291]
xxvii. 9 [323]
xlvi. 10 [121]
lxxx. 17 [323]
civ. 4 [231]

Job
x. 22 [143]

Canticles
iv. 4 [134]

Daniel
xi. 30 [24]

I Chronicles
xxix. 2 [280]

II Chronicles
iv. 2 [283]

TARGUM ONKELOS
Genesis
xxv. 27 [260]

Exodus
xxviii. 14 [280]

Numbers
xxiv. 24 [23, 25]
xxxi. 5 [41]

Deuteronomy
xiv. 13 [308]

TARGUM JONATHAN
Exodus
xxviii. 28 [168]

Numbers
ii. 3 [42]
x. 32 [307]
xxiv. 24 [24]

ANCIENT VERSIONS

TARGUM
Isaiah
xxxiii. 4 [133]
xlix. 8 [258]
Nahum
iii. 3 [281]
Psalms
xlvi. 10 [121]
civ. 4 [231]
cxci. 4 [121]
Job
xxvi. 10 [307]
Lamentations
[347]

PESHITTA
Genesis
x. 9 [260]
Exodus
xv. 3 [317]
Judges
v. 12 [317]
II Kings
xxiv. 2 [22, 256]
Psalms
xlvi. 10 [121], 26 [291]
Job
xxvi. 10 [307]

VULGATE
Numbers
xxxi. 5 [41]
Joshua
iii. 4 [74]
Ezekiel
xxvii. 6 [24]
Psalms
xlvi. 10 [121]

Daniel
xi. 30 [24]

ARABIC
Judges
v. 12 [317]

A.V.
Exodus
xxv. 23 [119]
Numbers
xvii. 2–3 [39], 10 [39]
xxiv. 24 [23]
xxvii. 16 [231]
xxxi. 5 [41]
Deuteronomy
xxxiii. 29 [317]
Joshua
vi. 9 [93]
Judges
ix. 43 [145]
x. 18 [256]
I Samuel
xi. 11 [145]
xiii. 17 [145]
xxx. 26 [318]
II Samuel
xviii. 4 [134]
Jeremiah
xli. 11 [134]
Zechariah
iv. 12 [137]
Psalms
lxxxix. 6–9 [231], 16 [113]
Job
i. 17 [145]
Daniel
xi. 41 [256]

INDEX III
FOREIGN WORDS AND PHRASES
(i) *Greek*

ἀσπίς, 116
ἐθνάρχης, 44
ενασαραμελ, 44
θυρεός, 116, 121
κερατίνη, 110

κνημῖδες, 122, 123
μοῖρα, 79
οὐκ, 201
παράταξις, 164
παρεμβολή, 47, 164

INDEX OF WORDS

πυργηδόν, 188
πύργος, 188
προμαχόμενος, 116
σάλπιγξ, 110 111, 112, 113
σάρισα, 138

Σαραμελ, 44
σύνθημα, 58
τάγμα, 62, 150
τάξις, 149, 150, 168, 277
Φοράς, 266

(ii) Hebrew

אבדן: באבדונו, 334
אדון: אדון הרוחות, 231
אורתם: [באורתום], 346
אוצר: אוצרות כב[וד] עבים, 307
אור: יאירו 259
אות, 38, 49
אותות כול העדה, 271
אז: מאז, 260
איש: אנשי שם, 268
אל: אלים, 230
אמץ: מאמצת לבב, 261
אסף: 93
האספם, 268, 269
המאסף, 93
אסר: תאסר, 165, 166, 167
ארב: מארב, 94
ארך רוח: וארוכי רוח, 287
בדן: אבדני ריקמה, 280
בחר: בחורים, 81, 82
בטן: והבטן, 126, 282
בינים: אנשי בינים, 156
דגלי בינים, 156
בית הראש, 123, 124
בית מועד: לבית מועד, 268, 269
בתי שוקים: 122, 123
בליעל, 232
בן: בני חשך, 242
בני שמים, 230
בעל: ובעולים, 288
בקע: מבקע, 307
גבור: גבורי חיל, 305
גדיל: גדיל שפה, 118, 280
גולה: גולת המדבר, 257
גורל, 207
בגורל, 256
גילה: גילות, 270, 274
גלל: גלול כפים, 190, 191
גנן: מגיני עגלה, 121

דגל: 39, 49, 52, 62, 149, 156, 157,
161, 166, 167, 168, 240, 276, 279
דגלי אל, 49, 269
דגלי בינים, 156
דגלי מלחמה, 163, 301
דמה: דמיונים, 288
דרך: דרוך מעט, 191, 301
הבל: גוי הבל, 286
היה: ליום הווה, 261
הווה ונהיה, 340
המם: למהמה, 314
זיק: זיקי דם, 285
זעטוט: וכול נער זעטוט, 290
זרק: זרקות, 132
חבל: חבלו, 328
מלאכי חבל, 231
חבר: מחברת, 118
חד: קול חד, 103
קול חד וטרוד, 101, 102, 103, 104, 296
חוש: מחושה, 261
חזק: להחזיק, 305
מחזיקים, 115
חלל: להחל, 256
יחלו ידם, 298
חלף: חליפה למלחמה, 175, 337
חלץ: יחלוצו, 265
חלק: תחלק, 266
חנית, 135
חסד: חסדים 269
חרץ: חרוצי המלחמה, 337
החרוץ למועד נקם, 209, 332
מחורץ, 138, 281
חשב: מחשבת, 280, 281
חשה: יחשו, 107, 108, 298
[טקס, 168]
טרוד: קול...טרוד, 101, 102, 103,
104, 296
יד: 40, 291

INDEX OF WORDS

נחשיר: ונחשיר חזק, 260
נטה: ונטו ידם, 296
נס: 62, 272
נס אל, 48, 49, 272
נשיא, 48, 272
סבב: מוסב, 280
סגר: הסגר, 137, 281
סדר: 142, 143, 144, 164
נפשטים לסדריהם, 144
" דגלי הבינים, 143
" מלחמה, 142
" פנים, 142
" פרשים, 143
וסדרו שבע המערכות, 143
סמוך: קול...סמוך, 101, 102, 103, 104, 296, 297
ספה: ספות, 125
סרך: 5, 7, 144, 148, 149, 150, 151, 164, 176, 177, 268, 271, 289, 320
אנשי סרך המערכות, 179, 180
יסרוכו, 148
עבודה: לכל עבודתם, 266
עגל: מגיני עגלה, 121
עדה: 42
עדת אל, 44
עם: 44
עם אל, 44
עם ועמהם בעזר, 257
עמד: מעמד, 146, 206, 207, 263, 324
על עומדם, 320
בית מעמד, 207
למעמדכם, 341
עמוד: עמוד מחשבת, 138
ערך: מערכה, 143, 144, 149, 161, 164, 167, 176, 177, 180
מערכות הפנים, 163–5, 180
סרך המערכות, 179
עורך הצידה, 155
עת: עת ישועה, 258
עתד: ועתודים, 291
פנים: 164, 165
מלאכי פנים, 231
מערכת הפנים, 164
בעזרת פניך, 323
תרש: מחרש, 47
פרוש שמותם, 42, 275

ידי: 99, 100, 102, 295
ידע: ידעתה למועדנו, 245
יחד: נלחמים יחד, 261
יפע: להופיע, 222
יצב: להתיצב, 263
כבוד: כבוד אל, 275
כדי: כדי הטל, 335
כהה: יכהו, 339
כהן: כהן הראש, 207, 208
כידון: 124, 125, 129–131
כלה: וכלת עולמים, 258
לכלת עולמים, 299
כלי: כלי המלחמה, 115
כנף: וכנפים...מ[שנ]י עברי המערכה, 192
כף: גלול כפים, 190
כרסם: [יכור]סם, 327
למד: ומלומדי חוק, 306
מלומדי מלחמה, 288
מארב, 94
מגדל: המגדלות, 301
מגן: מגנתה, 346, 347
מדבר: ממדבר העמים, 257
מהמה: למהמה, 314
מועד: ידעתה למועדנו, 345
לבית מועד, 268, 269
מזז: ממוזזים, 118, 280
מחנה: 47
ראשי המחנות, 47
מטה, 134
מלאך: מלאכי הפנים, 231
מסורה: מסורות, 41, 148
מעשה: כמעשה, 279
מעשה חרש מחשבת, 280
מעשי חרש מחשבת, 280
מצרף: בחוני מצרף, 339
מראה: מראת פנים, 280
מראי דמיונים, 188
משמרות, 204
משטמה: מלאך המשטמה, 233
משרה: משרת מיכאל, 232
נדב: נדבת מלחמה, 290, 291
נדן, 126
נוח: קול נוח, 102, 103
קול נוח מרודד וסמוך, 101, 104, 297
קול נוח וסמוך, 101, 102, 103, 104, 296

INDEX OF WORDS

רנה: רנות, 274
רשה: רשות יד, 315
רשע: להרשיע, 322
מרשיעי ברית, 257
שבולת: מראה שבולת זהב, 118, 136, 137
שבט, 134
שוב: המשוב, 93, 112, 225
למשוב, 261
משיבים, 300
שוקים: בתי שוקים, 122, 123
שלח: משלוח יד, 256
שלט: השלט השני, 133, 134, 285
שלם: להשלים, 163, 167
שמע: שומעי עמוקות, 306
שנן: ושנן כלי מלחמתה, 339
שען: משענת אל, 277
שער: שערי המלחמה, 146, 147
שפה: גדיל שפה, 118, 280
שפוד: שפוד אל הרואש, 136, 282
שר: 232, 272
שר המאור, 235, 322
תכן: בתכון ימיהם, 288
תמיד: בתמיד, 263
תמם: תמימי רוח ובשר, 291
תעודה: תעודות אל, 269
תעודות מלחמה, 330
תעודות המלחמה, 265
תקיעה, 88, 95
תרועה, 87, 88, 95, 103

פרש: מפרש שחקים, 306, 307
פשט: נפשטים, 14, 145
פשע: מפשע, 100, 112, 145, 146, 296
צאצא: צאצאיה, 307
צבא: בהמלא צבאם, 167, 279
צמיד: צמידים, 138, 281
צרף: מצרף, 339
קדוש: קדושים, 231
קום: קמי ארץ, 315
קטר: מקטרת, 264
קץ: ובקצו, 258
קרב: המתקרב, 100, 299
קשת, 191, 301
ראה: מראי דמיונים, 288
ראש: והראשים, 144, 145
אל הרואש, 136
ראשית: 256
רגל: ומרוגלת, 127, 283
רדד: קול ... מרודד, 99, 101, 102, 103, 104, 294, 235, 297
רדף: המרדף, 94, 268
רוח: וארוכי רוח, 287
רוחות, 231
רומח, 135
רז: רזי אל, 270, 338
רטש: רוטשו, 309
ריב: ריב אל, 277
רך: ורכי פה, 287
רכב: הפרשים על רכב, 179
מרכבות, 179

(iii) *Latin*

Accensi velati, 152
acies, 161, 164, 165, 167, 177
—— *duplex*, 171
—— *triplex*, 161, 171
—— *simplex*, 171, 175
aciem constituere, 167
agmen, 164
ala, 184, 187, 192, 193, 301
auxilium, 161, 162, 181
bucina, 110, 112, 113
caput porcinum, 186
centuria(e), 175, 293
cettin, 24
certamen, 164
clipeus, 121, 289

cohors, 161
—— *caetrata*, 120
—— *equitata*, 182
—— *milliaria*, 162
—— *peditata*, 182
—— *scutata*, 120
concursus, 146
confertus, ordo, 172
contarius, 162
cornu, 112
cuneus, 164, 186, 191
custos armorum, 155
depugnatio obliqua, 185
forfex, 184, 186, 191
frons, 184, 185

frons prima, 161
—— *longa*, 185, 190, 301
funditores, 139, 162
gladius, 127, 129
globus, 184, 186, 190
hasta, 133, 139
—— *velitaris*, 133, 139
iaculum, 133, 139, 285
intervallum, 148
iuniores, 76
laxatus, 172
manipulus, 100, 113, 161, 175
orbis, 184, 186
ordo, 143, 149
v. confertus, laxatus
parma, 121, 289
—— *equestris*, 121
pilum, 138, 139
prima acies, 161

proelium, 164
pugna, 164
quadratus exercitus, 185, 190, 301
sagittarius, 162
scutum, 116, 117, 170
scutatus, 162
seniores, 76
serra, 184, 186, 192, 301
signum, signa, 23, 62, 63, 64, 98, 100, 271
—— *conferre*, 98
—— *inferre*, 100
—— *referre*, 100
subsidium, 184, 186
testudo, 187, 188, 189, 301
tuba, 110, 112
—— *cornea*, 110
turris, 184, 187, 188, 189
vagina, 126
velites, 133, 161

IV GENERAL INDEX

Aaron, Sons of, 12, 39, 44, 45, 49, 55, 56, 60, 72, 88, 137, 140, 208, 212, 216, 217, 235, 271, 273, 279, 292
Abihu, 12, 221, 339
Abijah, 94, 109
Abraham, 27, 28, 31, 140, 214, 233, 259, 339
Accadian, 44, 121, 137, 266
Achan, 153, 221
Adiabene, 31
'advance', 145-6
advance guard, 93
age, *see* conscription
Agrippas, 5, 27
Ahiram, inscription of, 47
Ai, 81, 94, 100, 129
Alexander the Great, 24, 139, 173, 174
Alexander Jannaeus, 116, 117
altar, *see* table
Alluf, 52
Amalek, 24, 33, 35
'*Am*, *see* Index of Hebrew Terms
Amana, 31
ambush, 94, 141, 196, 303, *see* trumpet
Ammon(ites), 7, 21, 22, 24, 25, 30, 34, 35, 36, 82, 213, 214, 256, 309
angels, archangels, 5, 8, 10, 12, 15, 70, 183, 215, 217, 229-42, 303, 306, 316, 329, 334, 343, 344, *see also* Michael, Raphael, *etc.*; Holy Ones; spirits; Elim; pseudepigrapha
—— in the Bible, 229, 230, 231
—— four, 183, 236, 237, 238

angels, of destruction, 15, 231, 242, 256, 323
—— of *Maśtema*, 233-4, 320, 322
—— of the presence, 231, 235, 241
—— of truth, 234-5, 236, 322
Angelology, 14, 229-42
Antigonus, 176
Antiochus, 23
Antiochus IV, 179
Antiquities of the Jews, Book of, 27, 28, *see* index of references
Antonius, 181
Apocrypha, 16, 24, 33, 45, 205, 229, 231, 233, 237, 241, *see* pseudepigrapha
Arabs, 27, 33, 35
Aram, 22, 24, 28, 30
—— Naharaim, 27, 28, 29, 30, 36
—— Sons of, 27, 28, 29, 30, 31, 35, 36
Aramaic, influence of, 134
Aramus, 29
Arameans, 29, 30, 82
Arârâ, land of, 29
Ararat, Land of, 29
arc, the (formation), 184, 187, 191, 194, 196, 197
—— the flat (formation), 184, 191-2, 194, 196, 197, 301
Arch of Titus, 110
Ariovistus, 178
Armenia, 31
armour, 9, 123
—— cavalry, 176
—— heavy, 122

armour, front formation, 9, 122, 123, 176
—— horse, 122
—— skirmishers, 9, 122, 176
arms, see weapons
—— enveloping, see enveloping arms
—— guardians of, 75, 115, 151, 154-5, 290
army and warfare
—— Alexander the Great, see below, Hellenistic
—— American, 153
—— British Territorial, 40
—— of David, 83, 84, 86
—— Diadochi, see below, Hellenistic
—— German (ancient), 178
—— Greek, see below, Hellenistic
—— Hasmonean, 17, 59, 62, 63, 111, 116, 159, 244, 246
—— Hellenistic (Diadochi, Greek, Macedonian), 62, 64, 111, 116, 117, 123, 129, 138, 141, 142, 148, 149, 161, 163, 169, 170, 173, 174, 178, 179, 182, 244, 245
—— Israel(ite), 62, 64, 79, 175
—— —— First Temple, 17, 84, 86, 94, 155, 156, 163
—— —— Second Temple, 17, 63, 64, 77, 83, 86, 111, 141, 155, 175, 176, 179
—— Israeli Defence Force, 77, 86, 111, 159, 175
—— Jewish, 208
—— Josephus (In time of), 17, 59, 112, 121, 181, 182
—— Judas Maccabeus, 111, 159, 175
—— Judges, Period of, 156
—— Macedonian, see above, Hellenistic
—— organization and tactics, 5, 16, 75, 141-97, 244
—— regulations, laws of, 4, 5, 6, 67, 216, see Bible ; Battle (Serekh) Series
—— Roman see Roman
—— Swiss, 40
—— tactics, see above organization
Arpakhshad, Sons of, 27, 28, 29, 31, 36
arrays, 142-4, 160, 164, 165, see trumpets
—— battle, 142
—— cavalry, 143
—— frontal, 142-3, 163, 164, 165, 245, 279
—— skirmishing battalions, 143
Asaph, Song of, 213
Asher, 46, 52
Ashkelon, 196
Asia, 35
Asia Minor, 29, 31

Asshur, Assyria(n), 22, 23, 25, 26, 27, 28, 29, 30, 31, 32, 34, 36, 223, 258, 266, 300, 312, 343, 349, see Kittim
—— Sons of, 27
Asreelyor, angel, 238
Asshurbanipal, 30
Atonement, see Day
Augustus, 117, 129, 182, 245, 246
Babylon, 32
Bactria(ns), 31
Balaam, Song of, 23
banner(s), 16, 38-64, 105
—— Aaron, Sons of, 55, 56, 273
—— armies, 61-64
—— —— Greek, 111
—— —— Roman, 111
—— battalion(s), 49-53, 57
—— Bible, 39, 62, 63, 105
—— camp, 46, 57, 105
—— chiefs of, 46, 49
—— [heads of] three-tribe, 43, 45, 46-8
—— congregation (entire), 9, 40, 42-6, 57, 58, 105, 106, 148, 245, 258, 269, 276, 279, 333
—— cult of, 63, 245
—— family, 49-53, 57
—— fifty (unit), 43, 57, 269, 277
—— Gershon(ites), 54, 55, 56, 57, 273, 275
—— Greek, see above, army
—— grouping(s), 41, 42, 48, 49, 58, 61, 269
—— hundred (unit), 43, 57, 106, 270
—— inscriptions, 9, 39, 40-61, 104, 105, 106, 134, 258, 260, 269, 270, 271, 273, 274, 275, 276, 277, 299, 309, 311, 323
—— —— battle phases, 9, 41, 42, 43, 55, 56, 58, 59
—— —— desert camps, 39, 47, 105
—— —— thanksgiving and prayer, 41
—— Kohathites, 54, 55, 56, 57, 273
—— Levi, tribe of, 39, 55, 56, 269, 273, 274, 278, 279
—— Levite families, 9, 40, 45, 53-7, 58, 59, 60, 106, 271
—— measurements, 9, 40, 43, 44, 48, 57-8, 59, 277, 278
—— Merari, 54, 55, 56, 57, 272, 273, 275
—— myriad (unit), 43, 49-53, 57
—— Priests, 45, 55, 60
—— Roman, see Roman
—— Sect, 60, 61, 64
—— —— function of, 64
—— Skirmishers, 284
—— ten (unit), 9, 41, 43, 57, 58, 59, 278
—— thousand (unit), 41, 43, 49-53, 55, 57, 105, 157, 269, 273

GENERAL INDEX

banner(s), tribe, 43, 48–9, 57
—— —— leaders of, 279
—— —— Princes of, 49
Barak, 80, 213
Basan, 30
battalion(s), 41, 49–53, 132, 156, 166, 168, 279, see skirmishers ; sword ; javelin ; sling ; dart
—— battle, 163, 166, 168, 183, 279, 301
—— of God, 166, 269, 334
Battē Shoqayim, see index of Hebrew terms
battle, appointed time of, 330, 331, 333, see Day
—— course of, 193–6
—— darts, see darts
—— forms, 197
—— intervals, see intervals
—— orders, 183–7, 245
—— regrouping, see regrouping
—— reserves, replacements, 11, 174–5, 245, 337
—— Serekh Series, 6, 8–10, 11, 12, 14, 16, 17, 141, 210, 212, 227, 244
Behemoth, 72
Benjamin, Sons of, 4, 7, 19, 33, 46, 52, 81, see camp
—— war against, 51, 155
Belial, 4, 6, 7, 8, 10, 11, 12, 14, 19, 33, 36, 61, 221, 223, 224, 225, 231, 232–4, 235, 236, 242, 256, 300, 320, 322, 323, 327, 328, 331, 334, 336, 339, 342, 346, 350
Beth Ezbaʿoth, see finger-stall
Beth Horon, 213
Beth Rosh, see index of Hebrew terms
Bethsur(a), 20, 213, 237
Beth yadh, see hand-guard
Bethzacharias, 117
'beyond the river', see Euphrates
Bible, see index of references
—— angels, see angels
—— army, laws of, see below, warfare
—— banners, see banners
—— congregation, organization of, 38, 39, 45, 46, 51, 53
—— conscription and exemption, 65, 66, 67, 69, 73
—— eschatological sections, 8, 14, 16, 33
—— horns, 109–10
—— *Kidhon* (sword), 129–31
—— prayers, influence on, 13
—— trumpets, 109–10
—— quotations from, 14, 16, 17, 25, 212, 215, 217, 251, 304, 305, 310
—— trumpets, 87–88, 90, 91, 94, 105, 109–10, 268
—— variations (textual), 16, 17, 25, 74, 212, 217, 218, 268, 291, 304, 305, 310

Bible, warfare, army, laws of, 4, 5, 6, 16, 20, 66, 68, 69, 72, 78 212, 216
blemish, see disabled
blessing and curse, 15, 215, 223–5, 228, 319, 320
Boaz, 309
Booty, collectors of, 75, 151, 153–4, 290
Bow(s), 124, 130, 140, 161, 182
—— light cavalry, 140
—— skirmishers, 140, 158, 159, 284
boy(s), young, 70, 71, 77, 290
breastplate, *Hoshen*, 45, 47, 49
builder of a house, see conscription (exemption from)
Caesar, Julius, 117, 121, 123, 173, 174, 175, 176, 178, 181, 182, 245, 246, 331, see index of authors
calendar, see sect
camp(s), 42, 46, 178, 286, 325
—— Benjamin, 271
—— chiefs of, 46, 47
—— Dan, 46, 47, 82, 105, 271
—— Ephraim, 46, 47, 271
—— Judah, 46, 105, 271
—— Levi, 271
—— overseer of all, 76
—— prefects, 47, 75, 79, 151–2, 289, 292, 296, 320
—— purity of, 5, 9, 66, 70–5, 77, 212, 290
—— Reuben, 46, 47, 271
—— three-tribe, 45, 271, see banner
Canaan, 24, 25, 33, 35, 39
Cannae, battle of, 186, 191, 193, 194–5, 196, 301
Cappadocians, 24, 33
Capua, battle of, 133
Caracalla, 113
Carthage, 35
Caspin, 213
cavalry, 9, 66, 75, 115, 133, 135, 141, 142, 150, 156, 157, 158, 159, 161, 166, 176–82, 190, 192, 193, 195, 196, 245, 284, 286, 287, 288, 289, 295, 299, 300, 301, 317, see also armour ; dart ; front formation shield ; skirmishers ; spear
—— age, 75, 76, 158, 176, 177, 178, 179, 180, 181
—— heavy, 75, 76, 115, 116, 120, 121, 135, 136, 150, 156, 176, 178, 179–80, 181, 193, 287, 289, 299, see Serekh (cavalry)
—— light, 131, 133, 135, 156, 177–9, 196, 287, 299
—— structure and number, 9, 166, 177, 178, 179, 180, 181, 286, 287, 299
—— terminology, 179, 180–1
—— weapons, 179

C.D.C., *see* Damascus Covenant
censorship, 25
census, *see* muster(ings)
centuriae, *see* index of Latin terms
ceremonies, *see* sect
Chaldaea(ns), Chaldees, 23, 25, 29, 31, 257
chariots, 179, 245
Chetim(a), Chetimos, 24
chiefs, *see specific subject*
Christian literature, 229, *see* index of references
clan(s), 51, 52, 53
—— chiefs of, 20, 35, 80, 81, 204, *see* trumpet
cleansers of the land, 75, 151, 154
Coelesyria, 30
cohort, *see* Roman
'columns', 144–5, 160
—— protruding, 184, 192–3, 197, 301
commanders, chiefs, 61, 62, 144, 272, 273, 279, *see specific subject*
congregation, *see* banner
—— chiefs of, 40, 42, 202, 263, 262, 203, 204, *see* trumpet
—— fathers of, 48, 263, 265, *see* trumpet
—— of God, 44
—— judges of, 76
—— organization of, 16, 38–61, 81, 202, 203, 204, 206, 262, 267, 278, 279
—— Prince of all, the, 42, 44, *see* shield
—— Princes of, 48, 53
—— rites of, 198–228
—— war of, *see* war
conquest, *see* Joshua ; Jericho
Conscription, 51, 262, *see* Bible
—— age of, 9, 75–9, 80, 151, 152, 157, 158, 168, 176, 177, 181, 204, 290, *see* service troops ; skirmishers ; front formations
—— exemption from, 9, 66–73, 152
—— laws of, 65–86
—— Biblical, *see* Bible
—— system of, 51, 52, 79–86, 265
—— period of judges, 51, 53, 68, 80
—— planter of vineyards, builder of house, 66, 67, 68, 304
covenant, offenders of, 7, 19, 21, 26, 241
covenant of pieces, 27, 34
courses, 204–6
—— chiefs of, 202, 204, 206, 263
—— Israelite, 202, 203, 207
—— Levite, 202, 203, 204, 206, 207, 263
—— number, 202, 203, 204, 205, 206, 263
—— priestly, 202, 203, 204–6, 207
cuirasse, 122, 124, 289
curse, *see* blessing
Cush, 34

Cyprus, 24
Dagger, 129, 245
Dagon, siege of, 201
Damascus, 30, 35, 257
—— Land of, 257
Damascus Covenant, 15, 60, 67, 76, 198, 199, 200, 201, 206, 221, 225, 232, 235, 257, 261, 267, *see* index of references, p. 365
Dan, 33, 46, 52, 239, *see* camp
Daniel, Book of, 14, 229, *see* index of references
dart(s), 93, 105, 107, 108, 124, 131–3, 135, 140, 154, 158, 162, 165, 182, 262, 284, 285, 295, 296, 302
—— battalions, 132, 145, 159, 173, 177, 286
—— blade, 131, 132, 285
—— inscriptions, 104, 106, 131, 132, 134–5, 269, 270, 285
—— light cavalry, 131, 133, 135
—— material, 132
—— measurements, 133, 285
—— number, 131, 132, 133, 135, 284
—— Roman, *see* Roman
—— skirmishers, 131, 135, 284
David, 53, 81, 84, 131, 132, 133, 134, 140, 154, 160, 204, 213, 214, 240, 277, 278
—— army of, *see* army
—— House of, 35, 212, 309
Day
—— appointed, 4, 6, 8, 15, 225, 242, 333
—— of Atonement, 206, 219
—— of God, 15
—— of Remembrance, 205, 206
—— of Vengeance, 70, 291, 331, 348
Dead Sea Scrolls, 243, *see* DSW ; pseudepigrapha ; sect
Deborah, 80
Deghel, *see* index of Hebrew terms
Demetrius, king of Greece, 23
'deployment', 144–5, 160, 166, 226, 295
despoilers of the slain, 75, 151, 153–4, 290
Deuteronomy, Book of, 16, 17, 209, 217, 218, *see* index of references
Diadochi, 161, 163, 173, 174, *see* army
disabled, blemished, the, 70, 71, 72, 290
Discipline Scroll, 15, 60, 200, 206, 221, 225, 232, 235, 246, 267, *see* index of references
'disposition', 6, 146, 148–50, 164, 165, 183, 279, 300
divisions, 60, 79–86, 177
—— war of, *see* war
DSD, *see* Discipline Scroll
DSH, *see* Habakkuk Pesher
DSI, *see* Isaiah

GENERAL INDEX

DST, *see* Thanksgiving Hymns
DSW, Scroll
—— comparison with DSS, 3, 60, 208, 221, 244, 248, 251, 311
—— —— pseudepigrapha, *see* pseudepigrapha
—— contents, 7–13, 244
—— date of composition, 3, 15, 17, 32, 59, 141, 154, 179, 208, 243–6, 337
—— date of copy, 243
—— date when stored away, 243
—— description of, 247
—— emendations in, 144, 249–51, 279, 289, 311, 333, 345
—— measurements of, 247–8
—— orthography, 156, 251–2, 310, 314, 348, 349
—— purpose, 4–7, 15
—— sources of, 14–17, 26, 27, 29, 101, 103, 114, 115, 141, 183, 202, 213, 214, 217, 244, 330
—— terminology, *see* index of Hebrew terms
—— version B, 316, 317, 318, 319, 321, 348
—— writing, 248–9
Dura Europus, shield of, *see* shield
Dyrrhachium, battle of, 176, 181
'Ear of corn' pattern, 118, 138, 281, 282
Eber, 23, 25
Ebionites, 311, *see also* poor
Ecclesiasticus, 100, *see* index of references
Edom, 7, 19, 21, 22, 24, 25, 34, 35, 36, 256
Egypt, 23, 25, 31, 34, 325, *see* Kittim
—— River of, 27, 34
Egyptians, 27
Ehud, 125
Elam, 27, 28, 31, 32, 34, 36
Elasa, battle of, 111
Eldad Ha-Dani, 82, 157, 205
Eleazar (Son of Aaron), 56, 226, 339
Eleazar, prayer of, 214
Elect of the Holy People, 215, 240–2
Elef, 52
Elephantine Papyri, 62
elephants, 179, 245
Elihu, 242
Elijah, 214
Elim (angels), 230, 260, 291
Emmaus, 68, 70, 154, 213
encouragement, *see* word
end of days, 15, 38, 229, 260, *see also* Messiah ; Messianic Period
Enoch, Book of, 3, 47, 206, 221, 238, 239, 327, *see* index of references
—— Ethiopic, 238
—— Greek, 238
—— Similitudes, 238, 239

ensign of God, 48, 51
'enveloping arms', 184, 190–1, 193, 194, 195, 196, 197, 301
ephod, 220
—— shoulder pieces, 44, 45
Ephraim, 34, 45, 46, 52, *see* camp
Esau, Sons of, 22, 24
Essenes, 72, 74, 75, 79, 150, 176, 200, 201, 219, 226, 229, 240, 246
Euphrates, 25, 27, 29, 30, 31
—— beyond the, 28, 29, 30, 36, 266
—— 'Beyond the River', 30
exiles, *see* Sons of Light ; wilderness
exemption, laws of, *see* conscription
Exodus, Book of, 219, *see* index of references
Ezekiel, Book of, 37, 198, 215, 219, *see* index of references
Ezra, Book of, 109, *see* index of references
faint-hearted, the, 66, 67, 68, 69, 70, 152, 209, 212, 227, 284, 289, 293, 305
family, the, 40, 42, 49–53, 56, 273, *see* banner
fanfare, *see* trumpet
festivals, *see* sect
fifty, unit of, 51, 54, 56, 59–61, *see* banner,
—— commander of, 57
finger-stall, 123
'flat arc', *see* arc
formation(s), 9, 11, 41, 42, 50, 93, 98, 144, 148, 149, 163, 164, 166, 167, 168, 177, 178, 216, 268, 279, 283, 292, 293, 299, 332, 344, 350, *see* armour ; infantry ; skirmishers
—— chief(s) of, 163, 222, 344, 350
—— reserve, 11, 174–5
—— structure, 9
forming for battle, terminology, 142–50
front formation(s), 9, 75, 76, 98, 122, 123, 132, 135, 149, 150, 158, 159, 160, 161, 162–76, 179, 180, 181, 182, 190, 245, 279, 295, 299, 332
—— age, 168–9, 177, 289
—— chief(s), 63
—— disposition of, 177
—— forming up of, 167, 169–72
—— numbers and structure, 157, 165–8, 171, 172, 173, 175, 245, 262, 283, 299
—— weapons, 169
Gabriel (angel), 187, 229, 237, 238, 240, 302, 334
Gad, 46, 52, 82
Gĕdil, *see* index of Hebrew terms
Genesis, Book of, 28, *see* index of references
Gershon(ites), *see* banner

GENERAL INDEX 381

Gether, 31, 266
Gibeah, 51
Gibeon, miracle of, 222, 344
Gideon, 53, 68, 70, 107, 109, 213
Gog, 37, 215, 311, 313, 344
Goliath, 121, 122, 129, 131, 156, 212, 213, 240, 260, 309
'Goral', see lot; index of Hebrew terms
Gorgias, 111, 175, 213, 215
greaves, 122-3, 182, 288, 289
Greece, 23
Greeks, 25, 29, 31, 237, see army; banner; trumpet; shield; sword
grouping(s), 41, 42, 51, 56, 57, 61, 150, see banner
guilloche, 118, 280
Habakkuk Pesher, 22, 23, 26, 179, 243, 248, 251, 257, 261, see index of references
Hadadezer, 30, 134
Hagi, Book of, 17
Ham, Sons of, 26, 27, 33, 36, 37, 266
Hamath, 34
'hand,' the, 73, 74, 291
hand-guard, the, 123
Hannibal, 186, 191, 194, 195, 196
Haran, 25
Hasmonean Period, 154, 208, see army; Maccabees
Hasidim, 275
Ḥāzōzĕrah, see trumpet; Septuagint; Vulgate
head-guard, 124
helmet, 122, 123-4, 289
Herod, 176, 245, 246
Ḥesed, see index of Hebrew terms
Hittites, 24
Holy Ones (angels), 231, 314, 343
Homer, 188
homosexuality, 71
Horites, 22, 24
horn(s), 9, 95, 102, 103, 107-10, 111, 212, 258, 292, 296, see Shofar
—— Bible, 109-10
—— ram's, 107, 110
—— religious use of, 110
horses, stallions, 9, 71, 75, 122, 130, 176, 179, 180, 182, 287
horsemen, see cavalry; Serekh
Hosea Pesher, 256
Ḥoshen, see breastplate
household, 53
Hul, 27, 29, 31, 36
hundred (unit), 51, 54, 56, 59-61, 273, see banner
—— commander, 57
Hyrcanus, 20
Hymn of Return, see Prayer

impure, the, 70, 71, 73, 291
India, 32
infantry, 75, 120, 141, 156, 180, 196, see shield; spear
—— age, 75
—— formation, 192
—— heavy, 75, 76, 156, 162, 195, 279, 287, 288, 280, 344, see Serekh, men of
—— mounted, 121, 182, 288
—— number, 168, 173, 177, 179, 196, 287
inscriptions, see specific subject
intervals, battle, 89, 97, 98, 121, 146-8, 159, 160, 171, 172, 174, 180, 187, 188, 216, 245, 292, 293, 302, 335
Isaiah, Book of, 14, 17, 25, 215, see index of references
—— DSIa, 248, 251
—— DSIb, 248, 251
—— Manuscripts, 243
—— Pesher, 22, 23, see index of references
Ishmael, Sons of, 27, 28, 32, 33, 36
Israel
—— dominion and victory, 12, 215, 221, 225, 258, 339
—— election of, 214, 235, 305
—— Land of, 35, 37, 65, see also Palestine
—— tribes of, 4, 20, 44, 45, 46, 50, 51, 67
—— worthies of, 15
Israelites (organization), 77, 198, see course
Istrael (angel), 238
Isaac, 24, 140
Issachar, 46, 47, 52
Ithamar, 339
Jabin, 213
Jacob, 24, 140
—— Sons of, 45, 46
Jahaziel, 212
Japheth, Sons of, 22, 23, 26, 27, 33, 36, 37, 215, 259, 266, 343
Jasher, Book of, 46
Javan (Yāwān), 23, 25
javelin, 134
—— battalions, 159
—— inscriptions, 58, 100
Jehoshaphat, 207, 212
Jeremiah, 130
Jericho, conquest of, 87, 107, 108, 109, 110, 213, 214
Jeroboam, 94, 109
Jerusalem, 13, 20, 23, 25, 71, 89, 92, 106, 147, 203, 204, 215, 223, 224, 225, 226, 227, 268, 270, 351, see wilderness
Jethro, 59
Joab, 82, 84, 127, 164

cc

Job, 30
—— Book of, 30, *see* index of references
Jonah, 213
Jonathan (Son of Saul), 213, 214
Jonathan Maccabeus, 175
Joseph, 45
Josephus, *see* army ; index of authors, index of references
Joshua, 13, 17, 94, 100, 107, 153, 213, 214, 221
—— Book of, 13, 42, 51, *see* index of references
—— conquest of, 37
Joshua b. Galgola, 46
Josiah, 84
Jotapata, siege of, 112
Jubilees, Book of, 3, 22, 27, 28, 30, 31, 32, 205, 206, 233, 234, 235, 265, *see* index of references
Judah, Sons of, 4, 7, 19, 33, 34, 46, 47, 52, 212, 243, 257, 271, *see* camp
Judas Maccabaeus, 58, 59, 68, 69, 70, 111, 154, 213, 214, 221, 237
Judges, 76, 78
—— Book of, 42, 51, *see* index of references
justice and knowledge, 15, 259, 341
Kabbala, 229, 240
Kadmonite(s), 27, 28, 32, 34, 35, 36, 266
Karnaim, 30
Kenaz, Kenizzite, 34, 55, 240
Kenite, 34, 35
Keturah, Sons of, 27, 28, 32, 36
Kidhon, *see* sword ; index of Hebrew terms
Kings, Book of, 109, *see* index of references
Kings of the North, 7, 19, 258
Kittim, 4, 6, 7, 8, 10, 11, 12, 13, 19, 22, 23, 24, 25, 26, 33, 63, 64, 65, 99, 108, 147, 215, 216, 222, 223, 227, 242, 245, 259, 312, 328, 335, 336, 343, 348, 349
—— of Asshur, 7, 19, 21, 22–6, 36, 245, 257, 258, 266, 312
—— identity of, 22–6
—— in Egypt, 7, 19, 23, 26, 36, 245, 256, 258
—— King of, 22, 23, 24, 210, 245, 331, 349
—— series, 7, 10–11, 13, 14, 166, 209, 217, 222, 330
Kohath(ites), 78, *see* banner
Lachish, 140
lance, the, 119, 120, 124, 129, 130, 131, 132, 135, 138, 159, 161, 285, 286, *see* Roman
land, *see* cleansers
Latin, *see* Roman

law(s)
—— observance of, 233, 235
—— of Moses, 4, 6
—— of Torah, 5, 6, 16
—— of warfare, *see* army
Lebanon, 31
legion, *see* Roman
Letter of Aristeas, 138, *see* index of references
Levi(tes), families, Sons of, 4, 7, 9, 12, 19, 33, 38, 39, 41, 42, 44, 45, 46, 53–7, 60, 61, 77, 78, 107, 108, 109, 110, 146, 148, 150, 152, 160, 198, 199, 202, 203, 204, 206, 207, 210, 212, 222, 224, 225, 242, 257, 262, 271, 274, 279, 292, 293, 331, 342
—— chiefs, 202, 206, 263
—— cities, 74
—— courses, *see* courses
—— princes, 56
—— provosts, 152, 294
Leviticus, Book of, 109, 219, *see* index of references
lot, 207, 256
—— of darkness, 7, 15, 19, 36, 242
—— of light, 15, 225, 232, 242
—— of Sons of Darkness, 7, 19, 225
Lud, Sons of, 27, 28, 29, 30, 31, 36
Lydians, Ludians, Ludas, 29
Ma'ămad, 202-4, 206-7, 263, *see* index of Hebrew terms
—— number of, 203
—— chiefs, 204
Ma'ărakh, *see* index of Hebrew terms
Ma'ărav, *see* index of Hebrew terms
Ma'asaf, *see* index of Hebrew terms
Maccabees, 22, 237, *see* army ; Jonathan ; Judas ; Simeon
—— Books of, 17, 24, 62, 110, 213, *see* index of references
Macedonia, 24
Maggafayim, 221 *see* greaves
Maghen, *see* shield
Magog, 37, 215
Mahbereth, *see* index of Hebrew terms
Manasseh, 45, 46, 52, 53
Marius, 139
marriage, *see* sect
Mash(a), 27, 29, 31, 36, 266
Mastema, *see* angels
Megiddo, 191
men of renown, 20, 80, 81, 265, 268, *see* trumpet
Merari, 273, *see* banner
Mĕruddadh, *see* index of Hebrew terms
Mĕruggeleth, *see* index of Hebrew terms
Mesopotamia, 28

Messiah, 33, 34, 37, 60, 212, 215, 278, 317
Messianic Age, Period, 34, 37, 201, 256, 346, see also end of days
Michael, angel, 12, 15, 187, 221, 229, 230, 232, 236, 237, 238, 239, 240, 242, 261, 314, 322, 324, 334, 336, 339
Midian, 41, 94, 105, 106, 109, 153, 188
Midrash, 33, 49, 46, see index of references
—— Samuel, 140
—— Wayyissa'u, 33
miracles, 12, 13, 214, 222, 228, 344
Mishnah, 203, 204, 208
—— Kelim, 114
—— Shabbath, 122
Miẓḥoth, 122, see greaves
Mizpah, 70
Moab(ites), 7, 19, 21, 22, 24, 25, 34, 35, 36, 256, 309
mobilization, see conscription
mosaic floors, 118
Moses, 39, 48, 105, 106, 109, 110, 140, 204, 233, 234, 235, 303, see law
myriad (unit), 49–53, 272, 273, 276
music, military, 102
muster(ings), census, 11, 51, 52, 53, 60, 61, 77, 84
mysteries, 11, 221, 270, 329, 336, 342, 343
Nabataeans, 35
Nadab, 12, 221, 339
Naharaim, see Aram
Nahor, city of, 28
Nahum, Pesher, 22, 23, 25, see index of references
Naphtali, 46, 52, 82
Nĕdhan, see index of Hebrew terms
Nehemiah, 109
—— Book of, 109, see index of references
Nēs, see index of Hebrew terms
new moon(s), 202, 264
New Testament, see index of references
Nicanor, 111, 213
Nineveh, 25, 32
Niẓẓav, see sword-hand
Noah, 27
nocturnal emission, 73, 291
north, see Kings
Numbers, Book of, 16, 17, 38, 39, 42, 45, 109, 110, see index of references
Nuriel, (angel), 238
Obadiah of Bertinoro, 122
omen, 49
Onkelos, see Targum
organization, see congregation ; sect
Oth, see index of Hebrew terms

Oreb, 213
Palestine, 25, 28, 30, 32, 35
—— boundaries of, 22, 26, 34
Paran, 32
Pathros, 34
patriarchs, 30, 140
Pentateuch, see Bible ; sect
People of God, 44
Perseus, king of Macedonia, 24
Persia, 27, 28, 32, 36, 266
Persian Gulf, 32
Pesharim (scrolls), 22, 26
phalanx, 62, 64, 129, 138, 139, 142, 148, 149, 159, 151, 163, 170, 173, 174, 175, 182
Phanuel (angel), 238
Pharsalus, battle of, 174, 175, 181
Philistia, Philistines, Pelesheth, 7, 19, 21, 22, 24, 25, 34, 36, 213, 214, 256, 309
Phineas, 53, 94, 106, 208
planter of vineyards, see conscription
Pompeius, 5, 63, 117, 161, 223
poor, the, 311, 312, 323
'position,' 146, 203, 206, 207
prayer(s), 6, 7, 10, 12, 13, 16, 17, 41, 111, 201, 208–28, 277, 303, 305, 309, 321, 324, 325, 327, 330, 331, 344, 349, 350
—— appointed time, day of battle, 11, 13, 17, 66, 69, 70, 97, 152, 208, 210–16, 217, 220, 223, 227, 228, 303, 309
—— hymn of return, 225–6, 228, 325
—— thanksgiving, 13, 17, 41, 208–28, 331, 332
prefect(s), see camp
priest(s), 9, 12, 17, 23, 38, 60, 61, 77, 78, 93, 109, 110, 113, 146, 148, 150, 152, 170, 198, 199, 201, 202, 203, 206, 207, 208, 210, 216, 217, 222, 224, 262, 283, 292, 300, 320, 325, 331, 336, 344, see banner ; course ; trumpet
—— anointed for battle, 209, 216, 217, 220
—— appointed for battle, 208, 209, 211, 216, 217, 218, 2220
—— appointed (destined) for time of vengeance, 11, 152, 210, 211, 216, 217, 220, 228, 292, 325, 332, 337
—— chief, 12, 204, 206, 207–8, 209, 210, 211, 212, 215, 216, 217, 220, 221, 222, 224, 228, 263, 283, 292, 304, 319, 331, 332, 336, 337, 339
—— deputy, 207, 209, 262
—— garments, 9, 137, 216, 217–20, 292
—— head of the many, 76
—— high, 11, 12, 44, 208, 209, 219, 22
—— purity of, 300
—— wicked, 223
prince (*śar*), 232

prince(s), *see specific subject*
Prince of Light, 235–7, 322
prophets, 6, 14, 203, 204, 214, 225, 310, 311
provisions, preparers of, 51, 75, 151, 155
provosts, 75, 79, 151, 152–3, 289, 293, 294, 304, 320
Psalms, Book of, 25, *see* index of references
pseudepigrapha, 14, 24, 45, 76, 205, 229, 231, 233, 237, 240, 241, 306, *see* index of references
pseudepigrapha and apocrypha
—— angelology, *see* angelology
—— eschatological sections, 8, 33
—— relation to DSW, 3, 4, 8, 14, 233
—— wars, 16, 33
Ptolemy, 116
Purath, 29
purification, rites, rules of, 114, 226
purification, rites, rules of, 114, 226, *see* camp
quartermaster, 152–3
quiver(s), 134
Qumran caves, 3
—— exile, 257
—— Khirbet, 17, 67, 243, 246
—— sect, 3, 150, 201
Rabshakeh, 347
Raguel (angel), 238
Raphael (angel), 237, 238, 240
rearguard, 93
rectangle, 109, 184, 189, 190, 194, 196, 197, 301
regrouping for battle, 183–97
Rehoboam, 117
Remiel (angel), 238
reserves, *see* battle
Reuben, 46, 49, 52, *see* camp
Ribbua', *see* rectangle
rites, *see* congregation
Ritual Serekh series, 6, 10, 11, 13, 14, 17, 209, 303
Roman(s), 5, 23, 24, 25, 110, 331
—— army, 17, 50, 59, 76, 100, 101, 111, 112, 120, 123, 124, 133, 140, 142, 148, 150, 155, 161, 162, 164, 169, 170, 174, 175–6, 178, 181–2, 184, 185, 186, 187, 188, 189, 191, 192, 193, 194, 196, 244, 245, 344
—— banners, 61, 62, 63, 64
—— cavalry, 116, 133, 181–2
—— centuriae, *see* index of Latin terms
—— cohort(s), 50, 63, 161, 162, 174, 175, 192, *see also* index of Latin terms
—— dart, 133
—— lance, 137

Roman(s), Latin terms, 115, *see* index of Latin terms
—— legion(ary), 50, 113, 116, 117, 133, 138, 139, 148, 155, 170, 174, 175, 176, 181, 194
—— shield, 116, 117, 119, 121, 133, 189
—— spear, 136, 138, 139
—— soldiers, 129 fig.
—— sword, 112, 113, 128, 129
—— tactics, warfare, 64, 133, 142, 148, 165, 173, 175
—— trumpets, 111, 112, 113
Sabbath, 202, 264
—— boundary, limit, 74, 291
—— bodily functions on, 74, 75
—— service, 198, 199
—— warfare, 5
Sabbatical years, 26, 35, 36, 37, 198, 264, 265
—— Temple service, 8, 18, 20, 76, 90, 198
—— warfare, 8, 19, 20, 21, 36, 37
sacrifices, *see* sect
Sagaris, 137
saints, 316
Samuel, 204
—— Book of, 17, 154, *see* index of references
sanctuary, *see* temple
Sanir, 31
Sārāqā'ēl, 238
Sariel (angel), 187, 236, 237, 238, 239–40, 245, 302
Sarissa, 138, 139, 174, 179
Saul, 81, 82, 278
Scipio, 179, 194, 195
scroll, *see* DSW
Scythians, 31
seasons, four, 47
sect, DSS
—— angelology, *see* angelology
—— banners, *see* banners
—— calendar, 15, 199, 205, 206, 308, 329
—— ceremonies, 55, 60, 200, 206, 224, 225, 226, 283, 331
—— commandments, observance of, 72, 201, 233, 235, 306
—— festivals, 17, 202, 206, 264, 308
—— identity of, 75, 150, 200, 243–6, 311
—— marriage, attitude towards, 67, 72, *see also* women
—— meals, 200
—— mustering, census, 60, 61
—— names of, 149, 150 305
—— organization 59–61, 207, *see also* congregation
—— prayers, 201, *see* prayers; Serekh-'itto

sect, Sabbath, *see* Sabbath
—— sacrifices, attitude towards, 198–202, 203, 204, 264
Sedher, *see* index of Hebrew terms
Sefer Ha-Yashar, 33
Seleucids, 179
Sennacherib, 25, 213, 214, 223, 237, 309, 312
Septuagint, 24, 41
—— ' Camp,' 47
—— ' *Degel*,' 62
—— ' *Shofar*,' 110
—— ' *Ḥăzozĕrah*,' 110, 111
—— ' *Ma'ărakhah*,' 164
see also index of Greek terms
Serekh, *see* index of Hebrew terms
—— cavalry, horsemen of, 76, 120, 148, 176, 177, 178, 179, 180, 181, 193, 287, 288, 289, *see also* cavalry (heavy)
—— chiefs of, 12
—— formations, 178, 179, 180
—— elders of, 12, 148, 150, 177, 224, 225, 320, 344
—— 'Itto, Book of, 11, 16, 17, 210, 211, 331
—— Series, 6, 8, 10, 16, 98, 141, 156, 157, 162, 209, 210, 212, 216, 222, 223, 227, 267, 330, 349, 350, *see also* battle ; ritual
Seruihel, 240
service units, troops, 75, 76, 115, 150–5, *see specific units*
—— age, 75
seven, symbolic number, 157, 165, 174, 262
Sha'ar, *see* intervals
Shalmaites, 35
Shechem, 25
Sheleṭ, *see* index of Hebrew terms
Shem, Sons of, 22, 26, 27, 28, 29, 32, 36, 37, 266
Shema' (prayer), 240
Sheth, 310
shield(s), 9, 115–22, 123, 124, 135, 158, 159, 162, 173, 174, 182, 278, 284, 285, 293, 294
—— cavalry, 115, 116, 120, 121, 245
—— dartmen, 115
—— Dura Europos, 116, 117, 118, 119, 122, 137, 280
—— front formations, 9, 115–19, 120 fig., 124, 170, 187, 294, 301, 337
—— Greek, Hellenistic, 116, 117, 170
—— infantry, 121, 122, 145
—— inscriptions, 10, 40, 183, 187, 237, 240, 302
—— Maccabean, Hasmonean, 116, 117
—— material, 117

shield(s), measurements and shape, 114, 115–17, 118, 120, 121, 122, 169, 170, 187, 245, 281, 293, 301
—— number, 187, 293, 303
—— ornamentation, 114, 118–19
—— Prince of Congregation, 40, 45, 278
—— Roman, *see* Roman
—— shape, *see above*, measurements
—— skirmishers, 115, 119–20
—— slingmen, 115
—— Spanish auxiliaries, 117
—— towers, 10, 121–22, 183, 187, 188, 190, 237, 240, 301
Shinar, Shinear, 32, 34
shin-guard, 122, 123, 124, 245, *see also* greaves
Shobach, 213, 214
Shofar, 103, 110, 113, *see* horns
Shoṭĕrim, *see* provosts
signal(ling), *see* trumpet
Simeon (tribe), 46, 52
Simeon Maccabeus, 44
Simeon (Priest), 214
Similitudes, *see* Enoch
Sisera, 213
skirmishers, 75, 76, 92, 93, 96, 98, 116, 135, 147, 150, 156–62, 163, 165, 165, 169, 170, 176, 180, 216, 261, 279, 284, 289, 293, 299, 332, 336, 344, *see* armour ; banner ; dart ; sling ; spear ; sword ; trumpet
—— age, 75, 158
—— battalions, 9, 10, 75, 92, 96, 98, 124, 132, 133, 135, 142, 144, 149, 152, 156, 157, 158, 159, 160, 161, 162, 163, 165, 166, 171, 172, 173, 174, 177, 180, 181, 182, 183, 185, 190, 196, 245, 261, 284, 294, 295, 298, 299, 300
—— cavalry, 75, 157, 158, 159, 176, 177
—— number, 157, 166, 168, 172, 177, 262, 263, 295, 299
—— weapons, 158, 159, 177
slain, *see* despoilers ; trumpets
sling(s), 93, 95, 124, 139–40, 154, 158, 160, 161, 162, 284, 294
—— Assyrian reliefs, 140
—— battalions, 159, 173, 177, 185, 286
—— inscriptions, 140
—— men, 95, 115, 139, 140, 284, 294, 295
—— number, 140, 262, 284, 286
—— skirmishing units, 135, 139
Soherah, 121
Solomon, 84, 191, 214, 224, 321
Sorĕkhē Ha-Maḥanoth, *see* camp prefects
Sons of Light, exiles of, 4, 7, 33, 257
soul, immortality of, 240

Spain, 35
Spanish auxiliaries, *see* shield
Spasinou Charax, 31
spear(s), 9, 124, 131, 135–9, 162, 174
—— blade, 118, 125, 136, 137, 138, 139, 281, 282
—— clasp, socket, 118, 137–8, 281
—— front formations, 9, 124, 135, 136, 138, 169, 302
—— heavy cavalry, 135, 136, 138, 139, 281, 302
—— heavy infantry, 139, 245, 278
—— material and ornamentation, 114, 125, 126, 136–7, 138, 282
—— measurements and shape, 135–6, 138, 139, 169, 187, 245, 277, 278, 281, 289, 302
—— Roman, *see* Roman
—— skirmishers, 139
—— socket, *see above* clasp
—— towers, 135, 136, 138, 187, 278, 281, 302
spirits (angels), 231–2, 237, 240, 241, 256, 307, 317, 322
—— lord of, 231, 241
standards, *see* banners
supplies, *see* provisions ; quartermaster
sword(s), 9, 120, 124–31, 135, 158, 162, 174, 220, 282, 283, 285
—— battalions, 135, 139
—— ' belly ' of, 126
—— blade of, 118, 124, 126, 136, 137, 282
—— Canaanite, 125
—— front formations, 9, 124, 169
—— Greek, 129
—— ' hand ' of, 128, 283
—— lips of, 125, 136, 282
—— material and ornamentation, 114, 124, 125–6, 135, 137, 281, 283
—— measurements and shape, 124–5, 126, 127, 128, 129, 136, 169, 245, 281
—— ' mouth(s) ' of, 125
—— men, 286
—— point, 125, 126, 282, 283
—— Roman, *see* Roman
—— scabbard, 126–7, 128, 282, 283
—— skirmishers, 124, 135
Syria(ns), 29, 30
Tabernacle, 118
table, 119, 200, 264
tactics, *see* army
Targum Jonathan, 47, 105, *see* index of references
Targum Onkelos, 23, 25, 41, *see* index of references
Temple, sanctuary, 13, 110, 111, 199, 201, 262, 263
—— first, 179, 191, 207

Temple, second, 5, 110, 122, 124, 179, 203, 204
—— service, 21, 81, 198, 199, 202–8, 246, *see* Sabbatical years
ten (unit), 42, 51, 54, 56, 59–61, 274, *see* banner
—— commander, 57, 59
Tĕqiʿah, 88, 95
Tĕruʿah, 87, 88, 95, 103
Testaments of the Twelve Patriarchs, 3, 33, 149, 233, 257, *see* index of references
—— Aramaic version, 149
Thanksgiving Hymns, DST, 15, 26, 206, 221, 230, 232, 243, 248, 251
thanksgivings, *see* prayer
thousand (unit), 41, 49–53, 54, 56, 59–61, 166, 168, 276, *see* banner
—— chiefs, commanders, 48, 53, 54, 57, 268
Tigris, 29, 31, 32
Togar, 27, 29, 31, 36, 266
Torah, *see* Bible ; laws
tower(s), 147, 164, 184, 187–90, 196, 197, 240, 245, 300, 301, 302, *see* shield ; spear
—— intervals, 187, 188
—— measurements and shape, 187, 188, 190
—— men of, 135, 136, 187
—— number of, 172, 187, 190
Trachonitis, 30
tribe(s), 40, 42, 56, 79, 80
—— chief(s), 27, 81, 202, 203, 263, 265, 272
—— of Israel, *see* Israel
—— Prince(s), 39, 46, 48, 49, 53, 263
—— twelve, 204, 206
trumpet(s), 8, 40, 61, 81, 87–113, 139, 245, 266, 295
—— ambush, 89, 93, 94, 106, 196, 267, 270
—— assault, 94, 101, 106, 107, 108, 294
—— arrays, 89, 95, 96, 97, 98, 99, 101, 104, 105, 106, 142, 143, 148, 267, 293, 294, 295
—— battle, 92–9
—— Bible, 109–10
—— calling, 90, 93, 96, 97, 98, 99, 216, 267, *see below*, summoning
—— camps, 89, 92, 267
—— ceremonial, 61, 90–2, 105
—— chiefs, *see below*, men of renown
—— commanders, 61, 89, 91, 267, 268
—— congregation, 61, 88, 89, 90, 91, 267, 268
—— —— fathers of, 262, 267
—— expeditions, journeys, 87, 89, 92, 105, 267

GENERAL INDEX 387

trumpet(s), fanfare, 89, 94, 95, 212, 266, 267, 293, 296, 337, 342
—— formations, 61, 89, 91, 268
—— Greek, 111
—— infantry, 267
—— inscriptions, 48, 58, 89, 91, 93, 96, 104–6, 134, 228, 266, 268, 269, 299, 323
—— men of renown, 83, 89, 91, 92, 268
—— names, 88, 89, 93, 266
—— number, 88, 95, 267, 293, 296, 336, 344
—— Priests, 9, 87, 90, 94, 95, 96, 97, 98, 99, 102, 107, 108, 143, 144, 146, 147, 160, 166, 216, 217, 267, 292, 294, 296, 297, 336
—— Princes, 48, 88
—— pursuit, 89, 93, 94, 105, 106, 196, 268, 293, 299,
—— religious use of, 113
—— remembrance, 89, 90, 93, 95, 97, 99, 147, 160, 166, 216, 292, 293, 299, 335, 344
—— Roman, *see* Roman
—— signal(ling), 9, 16, 61, 87, 90, 93, 94, 95, 96, 97, 98, 99–104, 107, 108, 112, 113, 143, 148, 160, 174, 293, 296, 297, 300, 335, 336, 342
—— —— laws of, 66, 87
—— —— names, 101
—— skirmishers, 89, 93, 95, 96, 97, 98, 99, 106, 267, 292
—— slain, 89, 94, 95, 108, 109, 169, 196, 267, 269, 342
—— summoning, 89, 90, 95, 96, 97, 144, 147, 174, 266, 267, 292, 293, 299, *see above*, calling
—— task, 89
—— tones, 98, 101–4, 146, 267
—— types, 89, 90
—— war cry, 88, 90, 106, 107, 111
—— way of return, 89, 92, 93, 101, 106, 225, 228
—— withdrawal, 88, 89, 92, 93, 268, 293, 297
truth, 15, 274, 313
Turks, 35
Ugaritic, 131, 230, 269, 347
Uriah, 164
Uriel (angel), 235, 236, 237, 238, 239–40, 245, 302
Uz, 27, 29, 30, 36
Uzziel, King, 82
variants, *see* Bible
vessels, holy, 114
Vulgate, 23, 24
—— '*Degel*,' 62

Vulgate '*Ḥazōzĕrah*,' 110
—— '*Shofar*,' 110
—— '*Maʿărakhah*' 164
see index of references
war, *see* Sabbath ; Sabbatical years
—— Book of, 11, 16, 332
—— eschatological nature of, 310, *see* Bible ; pseudepigrapha
—— Messianic, 37
—— of congregation (entire), 4, 6, 8, 19, 20, 21, 35, 36, 37, 65, 66, 67, 198
—— of divisions (separate), 4, 6, 19, 20, 21, 22, 27, 33, 35, 36, 37, 65, 80, 82, 258
—— of duty, commandment, 35, 65, 67–9, 70, 71, 72
—— of free choice, 35, 65, 69, 70
—— phases of, 7, 8, 19, 21, 26, 36, 37, 257
—— plan of, 18–37, 39
—— Series, section, 6, 7–8, 10, 13, 14, 16
—— years of, 4, 6, 7, 8, 19, 20–1, 26, 27, 33, 35, 36, 37, 80, 82, 108, 264, 265
warfare, laws of, *see* army
—— tactics of, *see* army
weapon, the, 133–4
weapons, arms, 16, 114–40, 158, 279, *see specific weapon* ; skirmishers ; front formations
wickedness, period of, 198, 199, 221
wilderness
—— exiles of, 7, 15, 19, 33, 37
—— great, 27, 32, 36
—— Israelite sojourn in, 37, 38, 52
—— of Jerusalem, 4, 7, 15, 19, 33, 257
—— of Nations, 4, 7, 19, 33, 257
'wings,' 31, 184, 189, 192–3, 194, 196, 197
women, 67, 68, 70, 71, 72, 290
words of encouragement, 208, 210, 211, 212, 213, 216–7, 218, 220, 221, 225, 227, 228, 336
Zadok, Sons of, 198, 208
Zadokite documents, *see* Damascus convenant
Zagzagʿel, 238
Zalmunna, 213
Zama, Battle of, 179, 193, 195
Zebah, 213
Zebulun, 46, 47, 52
Zeeb, 213
Zeruel (angel), 240
Ziklag, 154
Zinnah, 115, 121, *see* shield
Zion, 215
Zkr, Inscription of, 47

www.ingramcontent.com/pod-product-compliance
Lightning Source LLC
Chambersburg PA
CBHW071142300426
44113CB00009B/1049